# Your Companion
## Even more help for studying!

bedfordstmartins.com/henretta

**FREE** **Online Study Guide —**
**Improve your understanding!**

Get immediate feedback on your
progress with

- Quizzes
- Key terms review
- Map and visual activities
- Timeline activities
- Note-taking outlines

**FREE** **History Research and Writing Help**

Refine your research skills, evaluate sources,
and organize your findings with

- *Make History* maps, documents, images, and Web sites
- History Research and Reference Sources
- More Sources and How to Format a History Paper
- Build a Bibliography
- Tips on Avoiding Plagiarism

Calgary

Regina

Vancouver

Seattle
★ Olympia
WASHINGTON                Spokane                                    Great
                                                                    Falls          Missouri R.          NORTH DAKO
Portland                  Columbia R.                                                                   Bismarck
★ Salem                                            Helena ★    MONTANA
                                                                         Billings    Yellowstone R.     SOUTH DAKO
OREGON                              IDAHO                                                               ★ Pierre
                                    Boise ★
                                              Snake R.                              WYOMING             NEBRASK
                                                        Great
                                                        Salt Lake                            Cheyenne   North Platte R.
        Reno       NEVADA                          Salt ★                                     ★
Sacramento ★   ★ Carson City                       Lake                                           South Platte R.
San Francisco   Oakland                            City        UTAH          Green R.          ★ Denver
San Jose        San Joaquin R.                                                               COLORADO        KAN
                                                                       Colorado R.            ● Colorado
        Fresno       SIERRA NEVADA                                                               Springs     Arkansas R.
                                                                                                            OKLAH
        CALIFORNIA        Las Vegas
                                                                                    M           ★ Santa Fe
                                                                                    O                       ● Amarillo
                          Los Angeles                           ARIZONA             U    Albuquerque ●
PACIFIC                                                                              N
OCEAN                                                                               T    NEW MEXICO
                          San Diego ●                       ★ Phoenix               A                        TEXAS
125°W          120°W      Tijuana ●                                                 I
                          Mexicali ●                            Tucson ●            N                        Colorado R.
                                                                                    S
                                                                Nogáles ●      Ciudad    El Paso ●
                                                                               Juárez             Pecos R.
                                                                Hermosillo ●                                 S
                                                                                                            Anto
                                                            Chihuahua ●               Rio Grande            Nueces R.
                                                                                                            Piedras
                                                                                                            Negras
                                                                                                            Nuevo
                                                            M E X I C O                                     Laredo
                                                                                                            Monter
                                                                Culiacán ●        Torreón ●   Saltillo ●
                                                                                                            ● Monter
                          La Paz ●                          Durango ●
                  Cabo San Lucas ●                                                           Zacatecas ●
                                                            Mazatlán ●
                                                                                             San Luis Potos

45°N

40°N

35°N

**PACIFIC OCEAN**
125°W    120°W

---

**Inset — Hawaii:**

125°W          120°W      22°N
Honolulu ★
*PACIFIC OCEAN*
**HAWAII**
20°N
0   50   100 miles
0   50   100 kilometers
160°W          155°W

---

**Inset — Alaska:**

170°W          115°W
**ARCTIC OCEAN**
RUSSIA        Arctic
              Circle    70°N    BROOKS RANGE
              **ALASKA**              Yukon River
                                              **CANADA**
60°N
              ALASKA RANGE
                   ● Anchorage
*Bering*
*Sea*          *Gulf of Alaska*    ★ Juneau
              0       250      500 miles
ALEUTIAN       0       250      500 kilometers
ISLANDS
160°W   150°W   140°W   130°W   110°W
              25°N
              30°N

ARCTIC OCEAN

NORWAY
SWEDEN
FINLAND
ESTONIA
LATVIA
LITHUANIA
DEN.
NETH.
GER. POLAND
LUX.
CZ. REP.
AUS. SLK.
SLN. HUNG.
CR. B.H. SER.
ITALY
MONT. MAC.
KOS.
ALB.
MALTA
GREECE
TUNISIA

RUSSIAN FEDERATION

BELARUS
UKRAINE
MOLDOVA
ROMANIA
BULGARIA
GEORGIA
ARMENIA
TURKEY
AZERBAIJAN
CYPRUS
ISRAEL
SYRIA
LEBANON
IRAQ

KAZAKHSTAN
UZBEKISTAN
KYRGYZSTAN
TURKMENISTAN
TAJIKISTAN

MONGOLIA

N. KOREA
S. KOREA
JAPAN

PACIFIC OCEAN

LIBYA
EGYPT
JORDAN
KUWAIT
SAUDI ARABIA
QATAR
UNITED ARAB
EMIRATES
IRAN
BAHRAIN
OMAN
AFGHANISTAN
PAKISTAN

CHINA

BHUTAN
NEPAL
BANGLADESH
INDIA
MYANMAR
(BURMA)
TAIWAN

Mariana Is.
(U.S.)

Guam
(U.S.)

MARSHALL
IS.

NIGER
CHAD
SUDAN
ERITREA
YEMEN
DJIBOUTI

LAOS
VIETNAM
THAILAND
CAMBODIA

PHILIPPINES

NIGERIA
BENIN
TOGO
CENTRAL
AFRICAN REP.
CAMEROON
EQ. GUINEA
ETHIOPIA
SOMALIA
MALDIVES
SRI
LANKA

BRUNEI
PALAU

FEDERATED STATES
OF MICRONESIA

GABON
CONGO
RWANDA
UGANDA
KENYA
SINGAPORE
MALAYSIA

NAURU
KIRIBATI

SÃO TOMÉ
& PRÍNCIPE
DEM. REP. OF
THE CONGO
BURUNDI
TANZANIA
COMOROS
SEYCHELLES

INDONESIA

PAPUA
NEW
GUINEA

SOLOMON
IS.

TUVALU

ANGOLA
ZAMBIA
MALAWI
MADAGASCAR

INDIAN OCEAN

EAST TIMOR

VANUATU
FIJI

NAMIBIA
ZIMBABWE
BOTSWANA
MAURITIUS

AUSTRALIA

New Caledonia
(Fr.)

SOUTH
AFRICA
MOZAMBIQUE
SWAZILAND
LESOTHO

Tasmania
(Aust.)

NEW
ZEALAND

**ABBREVIATIONS**

| ALB. | ALBANIA |
| AUS. | AUSTRIA |
| BEL. | BELGIUM |
| B.H. | BOSNIA AND HERZEGOVINA |
| CR. | CROATIA |
| CZ. REP. | CZECH REPUBLIC |
| DEN. | DENMARK |
| GER. | GERMANY |
| HUNG. | HUNGARY |
| KOS. | KOSOVO |
| LUX. | LUXEMBOURG |
| MAC. | MACEDONIA |
| MONT. | MONTENEGRO |
| NETH. | NETHERLANDS |
| SER. | SERBIA |
| SLK. | SLOVAKIA |
| SLN. | SLOVENIA |
| SWITZ. | SWITZERLAND |

ANTARCTICA

20°E   40°E   60°E   80°E   100°E   120°E   140°E   160°E

# America's History

## Volume 1: To 1877

SEVENTH EDITION

# AMERICA'S HISTORY

## Volume 1: To 1877

**James A. Henretta**
University of Maryland

**Rebecca Edwards**
Vassar College

**Robert O. Self**
Brown University

**BEDFORD / ST. MARTIN'S**
Boston • New York

*For Bedford/St.Martin's*
*Publisher for History:* Mary Dougherty
*Executive Editor for History:* William J. Lombardo
*Director of Development for History:* Jane Knetzger
*Developmental Editor:* Danielle Slevens
*Senior Production Editor:* Deborah Baker
*Production Supervisor:* Andrew Ensor
*Executive Marketing Manager:* Jenna Bookin Barry
*Editorial Assistant:* Robin Soule
*Production Assistant:* David Ayers
*Copyeditor:* Janet Renard
*Indexer:* Ed Prucha, EdIndex
*Photo Researcher:* Pembroke Herbert and Sandi Rygiel/Picture Research Consultants & Archives
*Permissions Manager:* Kalina Ingham Hintz
*Senior Art Director:* Anna Palchik
*Cover Designer:* Marine Miller
*Cover Photo: Shoshone Indians.* Yale Collection of Western Americana, Beinecke Rare Book and Manuscript Library
*Cartography:* Mapping Specialists Limited
*Composition:* NK Graphics
*Printing and Binding:* RR Donnelley and Sons

*President:* Joan E. Feinberg
*Editorial Director:* Denise B. Wydra
*Director of Marketing:* Karen R. Soeltz
*Director of Production:* Susan W. Brown
*Associate Director, Editorial Production:* Elise S. Kaiser
*Managing Editor:* Elizabeth M. Schaaf

Library of Congress Control Number: 2010928991

Copyright © 2011, 2008, 2004, 2000 by Bedford/St. Martin's

All rights reserved. No part of this book may be reproduced, stored in a retrieval system, or transmitted in any form or by any means, electronic, mechanical, photocopying, recording, or otherwise, except as may be expressly permitted by the applicable copyright statutes or in writing by the Publisher.

Manufactured in the United States of America.
6 5 4 3 2 1
f e d c b

*For information, write:* Bedford/St. Martin's, 75 Arlington Street, Boston, MA 02116 (617-399-4000)
ISBN: 978-0-312-38789-1   (combined edition)
ISBN: 978-0-312-38791-4   (Vol. 1)
ISBN: 978-0-312-38792-1   (Vol. 2)
ISBN: 978-0-312-38793-8   (high school edition)

### Acknowledgments

*Acknowledgments and copyrights can be found at the back of the book on pages C-1–C-2, which constitute an extension of the copyright page. It is a violation of the law to reproduce these selections by any means whatsoever without the written permission of the copyright holder.*

# Preface for Instructors

How do we teach our students to think like historians? How do we give them a basic understanding of key events and facts, while also helping them engage the past, not as a rote list of names and dates, but as the fascinating, conflicted prelude to their lives today? In the seventh edition of *America's History*, we aim to help instructors meet those challenges. *America's History* has long been known for its breadth, balance, and ability to explain to students not just what happened, but *why*. The latest edition both preserves and substantially builds upon those strengths.

The extensive changes in this edition begin with the author team. All three of us—James Henretta, who has guided the book from the start, and new authors Rebecca Edwards and Robert Self—have spent our careers working to integrate top-down narratives of politics and economic affairs with bottom-up narratives of lived experience. Using the findings of the new social history and details of the experiences of ordinary people, James Henretta has in his work offered new ways of looking at the lives of early Americans, both free and enslaved. Rebecca Edwards has used insights from women's and gender history to reinterpret nineteenth-century electoral politics. Robert Self has explored the relationship between urban and suburban politics, social movements, and the state. In *America's History*, we bring those perspectives to bear on the full sweep of America's past. Our goal is to help students achieve a richer understanding of politics, diplomacy, war, economics, intellectual and cultural life, and gender, class, and race relations, by exploring how developments in all these areas were interconnected.

The core of a textbook is its narrative, and we have endeavored to make ours clear, accessible, and lively. In it, we focus not only on the marvelous diversity of peoples who came to call themselves Americans, but also on the institutions that have forged a common national identity. Without losing our central focus on U.S. history, we call attention to connections with the histories of Canada, Latin America, Europe, Africa, and Asia. Many of today's students were born outside the United States; those who were not may one day live or do business abroad (and they may, as we write, be conversing over the Internet with people on other conti-

nents). Meanwhile, we confront political problems of global scope, ranging from financial crises and oil spills to terrorist attacks. As it has since its inception, *America's History* helps students understand the world in which we live, by drawing links between events in the United States and those elsewhere.

## New Parts and New Scholarship

One of the greatest strengths of *America's History* is its part structure, which helps students identify the key forces and major developments that shaped each era. A four-page Part Opener begins each part, using analysis, striking images, and a detailed timeline to orient students to the major themes of each era and the ways in which those themes were manifest in society, culture, politics, and the economy. By organizing U.S. history into seven distinct periods, rather than just thirty-one successive chapters, we encourage students to trace changes and continuities over time and grasp connections between political, economic, social, and cultural events.

While retaining a seven-part framework, the latest edition significantly reshapes it, offering instructors a bold reconceptualization of U.S. history that reflects the latest, most exciting scholarship in the field. Throughout the book, we have given increased attention to political culture and political economy, using this analysis to help students understand how society, culture, politics, and the economy informed one another. A sharpened continental perspective, in this edition, is based on expanded coverage of Native American history, environmental history, and the trans-Mississippi West. Religion receives new attention throughout the text, particularly in the late nineteenth and twentieth centuries. Enhanced coverage of gender, ethnicity, and race includes greater emphasis on gay and lesbian history, Asian and Latino immigration, and the Civil Rights Movement, the last of which now receives a complete chapter of its own.

**Part 1, "The Creation of American Society,"** focuses on the period 1450–1763. This part explores the impact of men and women of European origin on Native American cultures, and the creation of new kinds of social, political, economic, and cultural life in the English mainland colonies. **Part 2, "The New Republic"**—spanning the years 1763–1820—explores the evolving values and institutions of the colonial social order and the fundamental changes Americans made in their economic, religious, and cultural practices. **Part 3, "Overlapping Revolutions,"** now focuses on the period 1820–1860 and the political, economic, and social and cultural revolutions that shaped it: the creation of a democratic polity, the shift from a predominantly agricultural to a booming industrial economy, and the advent of the Second Great Awakening, as well as a host of social reforms and a complex intellectual culture.

Three fields of scholarship contribute many of the additions to Parts 1–3. New research on Native Americans informs and deepens our treatment of Bacon's Rebellion in Virginia in the 1670s, the interaction between Lewis and Clark and the Mandans of the Upper Missouri River Valley in the 1800s, and the character of the buffalo-hunting peoples of the Great Plains between 1820 and 1870. New findings in African American history likewise enhance our discussion of the transition to slavery in Virginia, the repercussions of the Haitian Revolution, and many other aspects of the black experience. Finally, using new scholarship on the building of early modern empires, we have sharpened our analysis of Britain's purposeful pursuit of trade and imperial power in the period between 1650 and 1750.

**Part 4, "Creating and Preserving a Continental Nation"**—now covering the period from 1844 to 1877—traces the rise of America's continental empire. It places the shattering events of the Civil War in the context of other wars that textbooks too often underemphasize: the Mexican American War, and the final conquest of North America's native peoples. Part 4 treats these as three interrelated conflicts, showing how all of them contributed to confirmation of the nation's modern borders and to the consolidation of federal authority. This analysis helps students situate North-South sectionalism and the Civil War in broad contexts, and to compare the end of slavery and the emergence of the modern American nation with similar projects in other countries. Part 4 also provides expanded coverage of the California Gold Rush and development of the Pacific coast; Native American history during and after the Civil War; and Reconstruction as it was experienced by ordinary southerners, both black and white.

The reorganization of Part 4 also offers instructors expanded options as they decide where to draw the dividing line between the first and second halves of the U.S. survey. The entirety of Part 4—including not only the chapter on Reconstruction (Chapter 15) but also a substantially revised chapter on post–Civil War diplomacy, economic development, and the trans-Mississippi West (Chapter 16)—is included in Volume 1 of *America's History*. First-half instructors can thus either choose the Civil War or Reconstruction as the end point for their classes, or they can include Chapter 16 and invite students to explore additional long-term consequences of Union victory, with special attention to the West. As Volume 2 begins with Chapter 15, those teaching the second half of the survey can, likewise, choose the chapter and context in which they wish to begin their course.

**Part 5, "Bold Experiments in an Era of Industrialization,"** now covers the years between 1877 and 1929 as a single, unified era. In doing so, it offers a streamlined and innovative treatment of the decades when the United States became a global industrial power. Reflecting recent scholarship, we locate the origins of modern America in the post-Reconstruction years, rather than after 1900. Revising older views of progressivism as primarily an elite and middle-class, urban phenomenon, we also emphasize the significant roles played by rural and working-class Americans in demanding stronger government to combat the ills of industrialization. This approach allows students to receive a more inclusive and coherent picture of state-building from the era of Reconstruction to the New Deal.

Part 5 also gives more attention to such topics as the rise of high school and college education and women's political activism in the post–Civil War decades. All students will enjoy new material on the emergence of college and professional sports. In keeping with the urgent economic issues that confront the United States today, such as the "Great Recession" that began in 2008, a reorganized chapter on the 1920s connects the "boom" of that decade more clearly to the "bust" of the Great Depression that followed. And the United States' military and diplomatic involvement in World War I, formerly covered in a distinct chapter, is now folded into broader treatment of America's rise to global diplomatic power. The result is a clearer, more compelling analysis of the ways in which Americans both contributed to and critiqued imperialism, extending through the catastrophic legacies of the Great War. As a happy side effect of Part 5's new integrated narrative, a chapter has also been trimmed from this section, enabling instructors to move ahead briskly and devote more attention to later events.

**Part 6, "The Modern State and the Age of Liberalism,"** has been reconceptualized to include the period between the beginning of the Great Depression in 1929 and the economic turmoil that began in 1973. This broader canvas places the New Deal, World War II, and the 1960s into a single interpretation of the growth, flowering, and retreat of political liberalism. Students can view the depression-era welfare state and the rights-based politics of the 1960s as part of a continuum in twentieth-century American politics. Taking the narrative into the early 1970s brings the women's movement, the later antiwar movement, and the Chicano and Native American movements into this structure, rather than arbitrarily breaking apart those histories at 1968.

In Part 6, we have devoted an entire chapter to the civil rights movement, which covers the full period between World War II and the early 1970s—what many historians have called the "long Civil Rights Movement." We have also expanded our coverage of women, gay and lesbian communities, suburbanization, and the rise of the Sunbelt. Finally, a major theme of Part 6 remains the emergence of the United States as a major force in global geopolitics during and after World War II. A largely reluctant international power outside of the Western Hemisphere before 1941, the United States came to project its military power and economic might into the far corners of the globe during and after the Second World War. We have retained the traditional focus on the Cold War at home and abroad, while revising themes and topics to reflect new scholarly interpretations. Our aim is for students to see the close connections between developments at home and abroad in this turbulent era.

**In Part 7, "Global Capitalism and the End of the American Century,"** we have sought a delicate balance between the historian's scholarly distance and the immediacy of recent events. For instance, we treat globalization as a unique force reshaping American society and its economy, but we stress that global economic networks have always been intimately linked to national history. Students will find that our approach to the recent past helps them connect developments in their own lives with deeper, more long-term historical patterns. American involvement in the Middle East, the nation's increasing racial and ethnic diversity, and the role of digital technology, to name just three examples, have each been contextualized in terms of developments across much of the twentieth century.

Part 7 includes a new emphasis on how ordinary Americans experienced and tried to make sense of the sexual revolution, economic malaise, and changing family structure in the 1970s. This includes treatment of religious fundamentalism and the extraordinary growth of evangelical churches in recent decades. Of special interest in Part 7 is our enhanced treatment of domestic political events in the era after 1973, a year of profound domestic and international shifts. Drawing from recent work in gender and sexuality studies, the history of race, women's history, and political economy, we offer a synthetic treatment of the complex movement known as the New Right. And while it is still too early to offer definitive historical interpretations of the election of Barack Obama to the presidency and the passage of major health-care legislation, we encourage students to assess the significance of these events with the knowledge they've gained from Part 7 as a whole.

# Primary-Source Features and Study Aids

To offer further entry points into this appealing narrative, each chapter provides aids to student comprehension and study. An opening **chapter outline** and **thematic introduction** orient readers to the central themes of each chapter. At the end of each chapter, we use a **timeline** to remind students of important events and reiterate the themes in an **analytic summary**. We append **focus questions** to the major subsections of each chapter and close with a set of **review questions** for the chapter as a whole. Where students are likely to stumble over a key concept, we boldface it in the text wherever it is first mentioned and provide a **glossary** that defines each term. Brief end-of-chapter essays entitled **"For Further Exploration"** direct students to resources for additional reading. To assist instructors and advanced students, a **full bibliography** is available online at **bedfordstmartins.com/henretta**.

*America's History* has long emphasized primary sources. In addition to weaving lively quotations throughout the narrative, we offer students substantial excerpts from historical documents—letters, diaries, autobiographies, public testimony, and even poems and novels. These documents allow students to experience the past through the words and perspectives of those who lived it and, equally important, to gain skill in interpreting historical evidence. Each chapter contains three primary-source features. **Comparing American Voices**, a two-page feature in each chapter, helps students learn to think critically by comparing texts written from two or more perspectives. **Reading American Pictures** helps students learn to interpret paintings, cartoons, and other visual images from the past.

**Voices from Abroad** uses commentary from foreign observers—and occasionally from Americans who traveled overseas—to situate U.S. history in its global context. Many instructors rely on these rich and varied features to introduce beginning students to primary-source analysis.

For the Seventh Edition we have revised one-third of the primary-source features, choosing topics that will engage students' interest and sharpen their understanding of the past. "Comparing American Voices," for example, now includes selections that contrast the beliefs and outlooks of advocates of evangelical religion and Enlightenment rationalism; documents from the Reconstruction-era debate over Mormon plural marriage; and a debate between Phyllis Schlafly and her feminist opponents. In "Voices from Abroad," we have incorporated more non-European documents for a truly global perspective. In the Sixth Edition, no Asian perspectives appeared in this feature before Chapter 25; now students can read the demand of merchant Norman Assing (Yuan Sheng) for equal treatment of Chinese migrants in California in 1852 (Chapter 13); a Chinese official's poetic protest over the treatment of his countrymen during the era of Exclusion (Chapter 17); and a Japanese Buddhist's 1893 assessment of Christian missions in his country (Chapter 18). African voices also receive their due. In Chapter 27, students can read an Ethiopian journalist's account of American race relations. In keeping with the growing economic strength of East Asia in the twentieth century, we have included the perspectives of a Japanese commentator on the American economy in Chapter 30.

As in past editions, an outstanding **visual program** engages students' attention. The Seventh Edition features over 450 paintings, cartoons, illustrations, photographs, and charts, most of them in full color and many new to this edition. We also provide informative captions that set the illustrations in context. Keenly aware that students lack geographic literacy, we have included dozens of **maps** and cross-referenced them in the narrative text; map captions help students interpret what they see.

Taken together, these documents, maps, and illustrations provide instructors with a trove of teaching materials, so that *America's History* offers not only a compelling narrative, but also—right in the text—the ancillary materials that instructors need to bring the past alive. We also believe this edition will appeal to your students. Whatever their backgrounds, interests, and concerns may be, *America's History* will help students link the complex events of U.S. history to their experiences today, in ways that increase their understanding

of the world around them and provoke critical engagement with the American past.

# Acknowledgments

We are grateful to the following scholars and teachers who reported on their experiences with the Sixth Edition or reviewed chapters of this Seventh Edition. Their comments often challenged us to rethink or justify our interpretations and always provided a check on accuracy down to the smallest detail.

Paul C. Anderson, Clemson University
Alexis Antracoli, Saint Francis University
Charles Pete Banner-Haley, Colgate University
Heather Barry, St. Joseph's College
Ken Bridges, South Arkansas Community College
Jennifer Brooks, Auburn University
Jared S. Burkholder, Grace College
Laurie Chin, California State University–Long Beach
Stephen Cresswell, West Virginia Wesleyan College
Paul Doucette, Frederica Academy
Elisa Guernsey, Monroe Community College
Dixie Haggard, Valdosta State University
Michael Harkins, William Rainey Harper College
Andrew Johns, Brigham Young University
David Johnson, University of South Florida
Jon Timothy Kelly, West Valley College
Jeff Kleiman, University of Wisconsin–Marshfield
Rebecca Kosary, Texas Lutheran University
Derek Maxfield, Capital Community College
Ryan McMillen, Santa Monica College
Michelle Morgan, University of Wisconsin–Whitewater
Scott Newman, Loyola University Chicago
Robert Owens, Wichita State University
Ronnie Peacock, Community College of Aurora
Donald Rogers, Central Connecticut State University
Mary Ellen Rowe, University of Central Missouri
Matthew Schaffer, Florence-Darlington Technical College
Lois Scozzari, Holyoke Community College
Aaron Shapiro, Auburn University
David Sicilia, University of Maryland, College Park
John Simpson, Pierce College
E. Timothy Smith, Barry University
Nikki Taylor, University of Cincinnati
Jennifer Terry, American River College
Ruth Terry, Johnson County Community College and Lee's Summit Community Christian School

David Thompson, Illinois Central College
Russell Tremayne, College of Southern Idaho
Jere Vincent, Great Bay Community College
Cheryl Waite, Community College of Aurora
Eddie Weller, San Jacinto College
Jennifer Williams, Firelands College

As the authors of *America's History*, we know better than anyone else how much this book is the work of other hands and minds. We are grateful to departing author David Brody, who extended a welcoming hand and wise guidance to his successors. We are indebted to Mary Dougherty, William J. Lombardo, and Jane Knetzger, who oversaw this edition, and Danielle Slevens, who asked the right questions, suggested a multitude of improvements, and expertly guided the manuscript to completion. As usual, Joan E. Feinberg generously provided the resources we needed to produce an outstanding volume. Deborah Baker did a masterful job consulting with the authors and implementing a bold and powerful new design. Karen Melton Soeltz and Jenna Bookin Barry in the marketing department understood how to communicate our vision to teachers; they and the members of the college and high school sales force did wonderful work in helping this edition reach the classroom. We also thank the rest of our editorial and production team for their dedicated efforts: Robin Soule; Janet Renard, who copyedited the manuscript; Pembroke Herbert and Sandi Rygiel at Picture Research Consultants and Archives; and Kalina Ingham Hintz and Diane Kraut. Finally, we want to express our appreciation for the invaluable assistance of Rebecca Henretta, who redesigned many of the charts and graphs; Michelle Cantos and Mark Seidl, for invaluable research aid; and Linglan Edwards and Hiraku Shimoda, for assistance with translations. Many thanks to all of you for your contributions to this new edition of *America's History*.

James A. Henretta
Rebecca Edwards
Robert O. Self

# Versions and Supplements

*America's History* is supported by loads of resources—study tools for students, instructor materials, and many options for packaging the book with documents readers, trade books, atlases, and other guides—for free or at a substantial discount. Descriptions follow, but for more information, visit this book's catalog site at **bedfordstmartins.com/henretta/catalog** or contact your local Bedford/St. Martin's sales representative.

## Available Versions of This Book

To accommodate different course lengths and course budgets, this title is available in several different formats. The three-hole punched loose-leaf Budget Books versions and the e-books are available at a substantial discount.

Combined Volume (Chapters 1–31)—available in hardcover, loose-leaf, and e-book formats
Volume 1: To 1877 (Chapters 1–16)—available in paperback, loose-leaf, and e-book formats
Volume 2: Since 1865 (Chapters 15–31)—available in paperback, loose-leaf, and e-book formats

With our innovative e-books your students get the content you want in a convenient format—for about half the cost of a print book. **Bedford/St. Martin's e-Books** have been optimized for reading and studying online. **CourseSmart e-Books** can be downloaded or used online, whichever is more convenient for your students.

## Companion Site at bedfordstmartins.com/henretta

Our new companion sites gather free and premium resources, giving students a way to extend their Bedford book, online. These book-specific sites provide one destination to practice, read, write, and study—and to find and access quizzes and activities, study aids, and history research and writing help.

**FREE** **Online Study Guide.** Available at the companion site, this popular resource provides students with self-review quizzes and activities for each chapter, in-cluding a multiple-choice self-test that focuses on important concepts; an identification quiz that helps students remember key people, places, and events; a flashcard activity that tests students' knowledge of key terms; and map activities to strengthen students' geography skills. Instructors can monitor students' progress through an online Quiz Gradebook or receive e-mail updates.

**FREE** **History Research and Writing Help.** Also available on the companion site, this resource includes the textbook authors' **Suggested References** organized by chapter; **History Research and Reference Sources**, with links to history-related databases, indexes, and journals; **More Sources and How to Format a History Paper**, with clear advice on how to integrate primary and secondary sources into research papers and how to cite and format sources correctly; **Build a Bibliography**, a simple Web-based tool that generates bibliographies in four commonly used documentation styles; and **Tips on Avoiding Plagiarism**, an online tutorial that reviews the consequences of plagiarism and features exercises to help students practice integrating sources and recognize acceptable summaries.

## Instructor Resources

Bedford/St. Martin's has developed a wide range of teaching resources for this book and for this course. They range from lecture and presentation materials to assessment tools and course management options. Most can be downloaded or ordered at **bedfordstmartins .com/henretta/catalog**.

*HistoryClass for America's History*. *HistoryClass*, a Bedford/St. Martin's Online Course Space, puts the online resources available with this textbook in one convenient place—an interactive e-book and primary sources reader; maps, images, documents, and links; chapter review quizzes; interactive multimedia exercises; and research and writing help. Get into *HistoryClass* and get all our premium content and tools in one completely customizable course space; then assign, rearrange, and mix our resources with yours. For more information visit **yourhistoryclass.com**.

**Bedford/St. Martin's Course Cartridges.** Whether you use Blackboard, WebCT, Desire2Learn, Angel, Sakai, or Moodle, we have free content and support available for you to plug our content into your course management system. Registered instructors can download cartridges with no hassle, no strings attached. Content includes our most popular free resources and book-specific content for *America's History*. Visit **bedfordstmartins .com/cms** to get a demo, find your version, or download your cartridge.

**Instructor's Resource Manual.** The instructor's manual offers both experienced and first-time instructors tools for presenting textbook material in engaging ways. It includes chapter review material, teaching strategies, and a guide to chapter-specific supplements available for the text.

**Guide to Changing Editions.** Designed to facilitate an instructor's transition from the previous edition of *America's History* to the Seventh Edition, this guide presents an overview of major changes as well as changes in each chapter.

**Computerized Test Bank.** The test bank includes a mix of fresh, carefully crafted multiple-choice, fill-in-the-blank, short-answer, and essay questions for each chapter. The questions appear in Microsoft Word format and in easy-to-use test bank software that allows instructors to easily add, edit, re-sequence, and print questions and answers. Instructors can also export questions into a variety of formats, including WebCT and Blackboard.

**PowerPoint Maps, Images, Lecture Outlines, and i>clicker Content.** Look good and save time with *The Bedford Lecture Kit*. These presentation materials are downloadable individually from the Media and Supplements tab at **bedfordstmartins.com/henretta/ catalog**, and they are available on *The Bedford Lecture Kit Instructor's Resource* CD-ROM. They include ready-made and fully customizable PowerPoint multimedia presentations built around lecture outlines that are embedded with maps, figures, and selected images from the textbook and are supplemented by more detailed instructor notes on key points. Also available are maps and selected images in JPEG and PowerPoint format; content for i>clicker, a classroom response system, in

Microsoft Word and PowerPoint formats; and outline maps in PDF format for quizzing or handouts. All files are suitable for copying onto transparency acetates.

*Make History* **— Free Documents, Maps, Images, and Web Sites.** *Make History* combines the best Web resources with hundreds of maps and images, to make it simple to find the source material you need. Browse the collection of thousands of resources by course or by topic, date, and type. Each item has been carefully chosen and helpfully annotated to make it easy to find exactly what you need. Available at **bedfordstmartins .com/makehistory**.

**NEW** *America in Motion: Videoclips for U.S. History*. Set history in motion with *America in Motion*, an instructor DVD containing dozens of digital movie files of events in twentieth-century American history. From the wreckage of the battleship *Maine*, to FDR's Fireside Chats, to Oliver North testifying before Congress, *America in Motion* engages your students with dynamic scenes from key events and challenges them to think critically. All files are classroom-ready, edited for brevity, and easily integrated with PowerPoint or other presentation software for electronic lectures or assignments. An accompanying guide provides each clip's historical context, ideas for use, and suggested questions.

**Videos and Multimedia.** A wide assortment of videos and multimedia CD-ROMs on various topics in U.S. history is available to qualified adopters through your Bedford/St. Martin's sales representative.

## Packaging Opportunities

Save your students money and package your favorite text with more! For information on free packages and discounts up to 50%, visit **bedfordstmartins.com/ henretta/catalog** or contact your local Bedford/St. Martin's sales representative.

**e-Book.** The e-book for this title can be packaged with the print text at no additional cost.

***Documents for America's History***. Edited by Melvin Yazawa, University of New Mexico (Volume 1), and Kevin Fernlund, University of Missouri, St. Louis (Volume 2), this primary-source reader offers a chorus of voices from the past to enrich the study of U.S. history. Both celebrated figures and ordinary people, from Frederick Douglass to mill workers, demonstrate the diversity of America's history while putting a human face on historical experience. Brief introductions set each document in context, while questions for analysis help link the individual source to larger historical themes. Available free when packaged with the text.

*E-Documents for America's History.* The documents reader is also available as an e-book. When packaged with the print or electronic version of the textbook, it is available for free.

*Rand McNally Atlas of American History.* This collection of more than eighty full-color maps illustrates key events and eras from early exploration, settlement, expansion, and immigration to U.S. involvement in wars abroad and on U.S. soil. Introductory pages for each section include brief overviews, timelines, graphs, and photographs to establish a historical context. Available for $3.00 when packaged with the text.

*Maps in Context: A Workbook for American History.* Written by historical cartography expert Gerald A. Danzer (University of Illinois at Chicago), this skill-building workbook helps students comprehend essential connections between geographic literacy and historical understanding. Organized to correspond to the typical U.S. history survey course, *Maps in Context* presents a wealth of map-centered projects and convenient pop quizzes to give students hands-on experience working with maps. Available free when packaged with the text.

*The Bedford Glossary for U.S. History.* This handy supplement for the survey course gives students historically contextualized definitions for hundreds of terms — from *abolitionism* to *zoot suit* — that students will encounter in lectures, reading, and exams. Available free when packaged with the text.

*U.S. History Matters: A Student Guide to U.S. History Online.* This resource, written by Kelly Schrum, Alan Gevinson, and the late Roy Rosenzweig (all of George Mason University), provides an illustrated and annotated guide to 250 of the most useful Web sites for student research in U.S. history as well as advice on evaluating and using Internet sources. This essential guide is based on the acclaimed "History Matters" Web site developed by the American Social History Project and the Center for History and New Media. Available free when packaged with the text.

**The Bedford Series in History and Culture.** The more than one hundred titles in this highly praised series combine first-rate scholarship, historical narrative, and important primary documents for undergraduate courses. Each book is brief, inexpensive, and focused on a specific topic or period. For a complete list of titles, visit **bedfordstmartins.com/bshc**. Package discounts are available.

**Trade Books.** Titles published by sister companies Hill & Wang; Farrar, Straus and Giroux; Henry Holt and Company; St. Martin's Press; Picador; and Palgrave Macmillan are available at a 50% discount when packaged with Bedford/St. Martin's textbooks. For more information, visit **bedfordstmartins.com/ tradeup**.

*Going to the Source: The Bedford Reader in American History.* Developed by Victoria Bissell Brown and Timothy J. Shannon, this reader's strong pedagogical framework helps students learn how to ask fruitful questions in order to evaluate documents effectively and develop critical reading skills. This reader's wide variety of chapter topics complements the survey course and its rich diversity of sources — from personal letters to political cartoons — provoking students' interest as it teaches them the skills they need to successfully interrogate historical sources. Package discounts are available.

*America Firsthand.* With its distinctive focus on ordinary people, this primary documents reader, by Robert D. Marcus, David Burner, and Anthony Marcus, offers a remarkable range of perspectives on America's history from those who lived it. Popular "Points of View" sections expose students to different perspectives on a specific event or topic, and "Visual Portfolios" features invite analysis of the visual record. Package discounts are available.

*A Pocket Guide to Writing in History.* This portable and affordable reference tool by Mary Lynn Rampolla provides reading, writing, and research advice useful to students in all history courses. Concise yet comprehensive advice on approaching typical history assignments, developing critical reading skills, writing effective history papers, conducting research, using and documenting sources, and avoiding plagiarism — enhanced with practical tips and examples throughout — have made this slim reference a best-seller. Package discounts are available.

*A Student's Guide to History*. This complete guide to success in any history course provides the practical help students need to be successful in any history course. In addition to introducing students to the nature of the discipline, author Jules Benjamin teaches a wide range of skills from preparing for exams to approaching common writing assignments, and explains the research and documentation process with plentiful examples. Package discounts are available.

# Brief Contents

# Contents

**PART 1** The Creation of American Society, 1450–1763    *3*

## CHAPTER 1
### The New Global World, 1450–1620    *7*

## CHAPTER 2
### The Invasion and Settlement of North America, 1550–1700    *41*

**PART 3  Overlapping Revolutions, 1820–1860**  *269*

**CHAPTER 10**

**A Democratic Revolution, 1820–1844**  303

**CHAPTER 11**

**Religion and Reform, 1820–1860**  331

# Maps

# Figures and Tables

# Special Features

# America's History

## Volume 1: To 1877

# PART

# 1

# THE CREATION OF AMERICAN SOCIETY, 1450-1763

Historians know that societies are the creation of decades, even centuries, of human endeavor and experience. Historians also know that the first Americans were hunters and gatherers who migrated to the Western Hemisphere from Asia. Over many generations, these migrants—the Native Americans—came to live in a wide variety of environments and cultures. In much of North America, they developed kinship-based societies that relied on farming and hunting. But in the lower Mississippi River Valley around A.D. 900, Native Americans fashioned a hierarchical social order similar to those of the impressive civilizations of the Aztecs, Mayas, and Incas.

In Part 1, we describe how Europeans, with their steel weapons, attractive trade goods, and diseases, shredded the fabric of many Native American cultures. These settlers—the Spanish in Mesoamerica and South America, the French in Canada, and the English along the Atlantic coast of North America—gradually came to dominate the native peoples.

Our story focuses on the Europeans who settled in the English mainland colonies, expecting to transplant their traditional societies, cultures, and religious beliefs into the soil of the New World. But things did not work out exactly as planned. In learning to live in the new land, English, German, and Scots-Irish settlers created societies that differed from those of their homelands in their economic life, social character, political systems, religions, and cultures. Here, in brief, is the story of that transformation as we explain it in Part 1.

## ECONOMY

. . . the settlers in North America created a bustling economy

### From Subsistence to Staple Crops to Diversification

Britain's American colonies were a great economic success, as part of an expanding commercial empire. Traditional Europe consisted of poor, overcrowded, and unequal societies that periodically suffered devastating famines. But with few people and bountiful resources, the settlers in North America created a bustling economy in what British and German migrants called "the best poor man's country." Communities of independent farm families produced crops to be sold in Europe and the West Indies, the sugar islands that were the driving force of the Atlantic economy.

## SOCIETY

. . . some European settlements became places of oppressive captivity for Africans

### Changing Class, Racial, and Ethnic Conflicts

Simultaneously, some European settlements became places of oppressive captivity for Africans, with profound consequences for America's social development. As the supply of white indentured servants from Europe dwindled after 1680, planters in the Chesapeake region imported enslaved Africans to work in their tobacco fields. Spurred by profits in the sugar trade, British slave traders also procured hundreds of thousands of African slaves and transported them to West Indian sugar plantations. Slowly and with great effort, these slaves and their descendants created a variety of African American cultures within the European-dominated societies in which they labored.

## GOVERNMENT

**...white settlers ... devised an increasingly free and competitive political system**

## From Imperial Control to Local Autonomy

The first English migrants transplanted authoritarian institutions to America and, beginning around 1650, the home government intervened frequently in their affairs. But after the Glorious Revolution of 1688, white settlers in the English mainland colonies devised an increasingly free and competitive political system. Thereafter, local governments and representative assemblies became more powerful and created a tradition of self-rule that would spark demands for political autonomy after the Great War for Empire ended in 1763.

## RELIGION

**American Protestant Christianity became ... tolerant, democratic, and optimistic**

## From Established Churches to Pluralism

The American experience profoundly changed religious institutions and values. Many migrants fled Europe because of government persecution and conflicts among rival Christian churches. For the most part, they practiced their religions in America without interference. Religion became more prominent in colonial life after the evangelical revivals of the 1740s, and the churches less dogmatic. Americans increasingly rejected the harshest tenets of Calvinism (a strict version of Protestantism), and a significant minority of educated colonists embraced the rational outlook of the European Enlightenment. As a result, American Protestant Christianity became increasingly tolerant, democratic, and optimistic.

## CULTURE

**This new American society was pluralistic**

## The Creation of American Identities

Life in America changed traditional family and community life. The first English settlers lived in families ruled by dominant fathers, in communities controlled by men of high status. However, by 1750, many American fathers no longer strictly managed their children's lives and, because of widespread property ownership, many men and some women enjoyed greater personal independence. This new American society was pluralistic, being composed of migrants from many European ethnic groups—English, Scots, Scots-Irish, Dutch, and Germans—as well as enslaved Africans and generally subordinated Native American peoples. Distinct regional cultures developed in New England, the Middle Atlantic colonies, the Chesapeake, and the Carolinas. Consequently, an overarching American identity based on the English language, English legal and political institutions, and shared experiences emerged very slowly.

The multifaceted story of the colonial experience is both depressing and uplifting. European acquisitiveness and diseases destroyed many Native American peoples, and European planters held tens of thousands of Africans in bondage. However, white migrants enjoyed unprecedented opportunities for economic security, political freedom, and spiritual fulfillment. This contradictory experience—of native decline, black bondage, and white opportunity—would continue far into the American future.

# THE CREATION OF AMERICAN SOCIETY, 1450–1763

| | ECONOMY | SOCIETY | GOVERNMENT | RELIGION | CULTURE |
|---|---|---|---|---|---|
| **1450** | • Native American subsistence economy<br>• Europeans fish off North American coast | • Sporadic warfare among Indian peoples<br>• Spanish conquest of Mexico and Peru (1519–1535) | • Rise of monarchical nation-states in Europe<br>• English monarchs adopt mercantilist policies | • Protestant Reformation (1517) sparks century of religious warfare<br>• Henry VIII creates Church of England | • Diverse Native American cultures in eastern woodlands |
| **1600** | • First staple export crops: furs and tobacco<br>• Subsistence farms in New England | • First set of English-Indian wars<br>• African servitude begins in Virginia (1619) | • James I claims divine right to rule England<br>• Virginia House of Burgesses (1619) | • Persecuted English Puritans and Catholics migrate to America | • Puritans embed Calvinism, education, and freehold ideal in New England |
| **1640** | • South Atlantic System on sugar islands<br>• Mercantilist regulation: first Navigation Act (1651) | • White indentured servitude shapes Chesapeake society<br>• Indians retreat inland; Africans lose rights (1670s) | • English Puritan Revolution<br>• Stuart restoration (1660)<br>• Bacon's Rebellion in Virginia (1675) | • Established churches set up in Puritan New England and Anglican Virginia<br>• Dissenters settle in Rhode Island | • Aristocratic aspirations in Chesapeake region |
| **1680** | • Tobacco trade stagnates<br>• Rice cultivation in South Carolina<br>• Britain dominates slave trade | • Indian wars and slavery grow in the Carolinas<br>• Major influx of Africans creates "slave societies" | • Central control: dominion of New England<br>• Revolutions in England and colonies (1688–1689) | • Rise of tolerance among colonial Protestants<br>• Wars with Catholic France in Europe and America | • Quaker influence in Pennsylvania<br>• Africans create new African American languages and cultures |
| **1720** | • Mature yeoman farm economy in northern colonies<br>• 1740s: imports from Britain increase | • Large-scale Scots-Irish and German migration<br>• Inequality grows among whites in rural and urban areas | • Salutary Neglect allows rise of the colonial assemblies<br>• British state supports commercial expansion in Atlantic and India | • German and Scots-Irish Pietists in Middle Atlantic colonies<br>• Great Awakening revives religion and splits churches | • Expansion of colleges, news-papers, and magazines<br>• Franklin and the American Enlightenment |
| **1760** | • End of British military aid sparks postwar recession | • Uprisings by tenants and backcountry farmers | • Britain vanquishes France in Great War for Empire (1757–1763) | • Rise of evangelical Baptists in Virginia | • First signs of a distinct American identity within the Atlantic world |

# The New Global World, 1450–1620

**"Before the French** came among us," an elder of the Natchez people of Mississippi complained, "we were men . . . and we walked with boldness every road, but now we walk like slaves, which we shall soon be, since the French already treat us . . . as they do their black slaves." Before the 1490s, the Natchez and other Native American peoples knew nothing of the light-skinned inhabitants of Europe and the dark-complexioned peoples of Africa. But when Christopher Columbus, a European searching for a sea route to Asia, encountered the peoples of the Western Hemisphere in 1492, the destinies of four continents quickly became intertwined. In 1502, when Nicolás de Ovando replaced Columbus as governor of Hispaniola, his fleet of thirty ships carried both Spanish adventurers and enslaved Africans, initiating the centuries-long process that would produce a diaspora of Africans and Europeans and the creation of tri-racial societies in the Americas.

These new societies were based on exploitation, not equality. As early as 1494 Columbus, frustrated by his inability to govern the native peoples of Hispaniola, decided to "subjugate by force of arms." To terrorize the natives he unleashed 200 troops, twenty on horseback, and (according to Bartolomé de las Casas) "the other most terrible and frightful weapon for the Indians, after the horses and this was twenty greyhound catch-dogs, whom after being set loose . . . in one hour each tore 100 Indians to pieces." Two centuries later, the Natchez suffered a similar fate. Helped by Indian allies, the French savagely killed hundreds of Natchez and sold the survivors into slavery in the West Indies, where tens of thousands of forced migrants from Africa already toiled on European-run sugar plantations. In the centuries following Columbus's first voyage, many native peoples came under the domination of Europeans — Spanish, Portuguese, French, English, and Dutch — who seized their lands and often worked them with enslaved Africans.

How did this happen? What made Native Americans vulnerable to conquest by European adventurers? What led to the transatlantic trade in African slaves? And how did Europeans become leaders in world trade and create an economically integrated Atlantic world? In the answers to these questions lie the origins of the United States.

**Astronomers at Istanbul (Constantinople), 1581**

As the heirs of Byzantine civilization, Arab and Turkish scholars transmitted ancient Greek and Roman texts and learning to Europeans during the Middle Ages and the Renaissance. Their works, and practical classical inventions such as the globe and the astrolabe shown in this painting, provided much of the geographical and astronomical knowledge used by European explorers between 1450 and 1600, the great Age of Discovery. ©University Library, Istanbul, Turkey/The Bridgeman Art Library.

# The Native American Experience

When the Europeans arrived, about 7 million Native Americans resided in what is now the United States and Canada. These northern peoples mostly lived in hunter-gatherer or agricultural communities governed by kin ties. However, most native people—about 40 million, scholars estimate—lived in Mesoamerica (present-day Mexico and Guatemala) and along the western coast of South America (present-day Peru). The Mayas and Aztecs in Mesoamerica and the Incas in Peru fashioned societies ruled by warrior-kings and priests, and created civilizations whose art, religion, and economy were as complex as those of Europe and the Mediterranean world.

## The First Americans

Every people has a creation story. In the Mayan version, the god of lightning, K'awiil, hurled a bolt that split a great mountain and revealed two life-giving plants: maize and cacao. The Kiowa entered the world from a hollow log. For Judeo-Christians, God created Adam and Eve. But the first Iroquois fell from the sky; Algonquians descended from ash trees.

**Inca Cup**

This painted wooden *q'iru* (drinking cup) shows how the Incas, who ruled a great sixteenth-century empire in present-day Peru (see Map 1.5), made use of history. Around A.D. 1000, the Tiwanaku people ruled an empire in the highlands of Peru. A central motif of their culture was a sacred staircase symbolizing heavens, earth, and the underworld. By placing that Tiwanaku motif on the central band of this cup and adding a symbol of their own—the man with the staff, shield, and headdress—the Incas grounded their claim of royal authority in the prestige of the Tiwanaku. Courtesy, National Museum of American Indian, Smithsonian Institution.

According to modern scientists, migrants from Asia crossed a 100-mile-wide land bridge connecting Siberia and Alaska during the last Ice Age and thus became the first Americans. An oral history of the Tuscarora Indians, who settled in present-day North Carolina, tells of a famine in the old world and a journey over ice toward where "the sun rises," bringing their ancestors to a lush forest with abundant food and game. But the most compelling evidence is a genetic marker on the male Y chromosome, shared by Asians and Native Americans. This migratory stream from Asia lasted from about fifteen thousand to nine thousand years ago. Then the glaciers melted, and the rising ocean waters submerged the land bridge and created the Bering Strait (Map 1.1). Around eight thousand years ago, a second movement of peoples, traveling by water across the narrow strait, brought the ancestors of the Navajos and the Apaches to North America. The forebears of the Aleut and Inuit peoples, the "Eskimos," came in a third migration around five thousand years ago. Then, for three hundred generations, the peoples of the Western Hemisphere were largely cut off from the rest of the world.

During this long era, hunting and gathering became the economic basis for a remarkably variegated and complex tribal world. Everywhere, the first Americans proved highly adaptive and inventive. In the most favorable spots, such as the Pacific Northwest and along the California coast, Native Americans lived in permanent villages, sometimes of a thousand or more inhabitants. On the Great Plains, after hunting mastodons and other Paleolithic mammals to extinction, they adopted new weapons—the *atlatl* (a spear thrower) and later the bow and arrow—for bringing down swifter prey. Against the bison, these horseless hunters organized drives that were marvels of intricate planning. In the eastern woodlands, Algonquians engaged in controlled burning, creating parklike forests that, in the eyes of the first Europeans, were "very beautiful and commodious." Simple kin-based groupings evolved into complex tribal structures, cemented by rituals, founding myths, and distinctive crafts.

By about 6000 B.C., some Native American peoples in present-day Mexico and Peru were raising domesticated crops. They gradually bred maize into a nutritious plant that had a higher yield per acre than did wheat, barley, or rye, the staple cereals of Europe. They learned to plant beans and squash with the maize, a mix of crops that provided a diet rich in amino acids and kept the soil fertile. The resulting agricultural surplus encouraged population growth and eventually laid the economic foundation for wealthy, urban societies in Mexico, Peru, and the Mississippi River Valley (Map 1.2).

Using a global projection, the cartographer has placed North America in the center of the map, but parts of four other continents appear.

Evidence indicates that peoples came from Asia to the Americas during the Ice Age, when the sea level was much lower than today and a large land bridge-labeled Beringia on the map-connected the continents.

As scholars learn more about the advances and retreats of the ice sheets, the camping sites of the migrating peoples, and changes in vegetation zones, a more complete picture of the peopling of the Americas will emerge.

Current scholarship holds that the migrating peoples initially traveled on a narrow strip of ice-free land along the Pacific coast. As the area between the Cordilleran and Laurentide ice sheets lost its cover of ice, probably between 14,000 and 12,000 B.C., migrants may also have used the inland routes from present-day Alaska to the American interior.

Many groups, accustomed to living at the ocean's edge, probably continued along this route, pushing ever southward into South America.

25,000–12,000 B.C. Land bridge open

**Migration Routes into America, c. 16,000–10,000 B.C.**

- Ice sheets, c. 16,000 B.C.
- Ice sheets, c. 12,000 B.C.

Vegetation zones:
- Tundra
- Conifer forest
- Deciduous forest
- Prairie
- Desert
- → Migration route

(after Tanner)

0    500    1,000 miles
0    500   1,000 kilometers

## MAP 1.1

### The Ice Age and the Settling of the Americas

Some sixteen thousand years ago, a sheet of ice covered much of Europe and North America. The ice lowered the level of the world's oceans, which created a broad bridge of land between Siberia and Alaska. Using that land bridge, hunting peoples from Asia migrated to North America as they pursued woolly mammoths and other large game animals and sought ice-free habitats. By 10,000 B.C., the descendants of these migrant peoples had moved south to present-day Florida and central Mexico. In time, they would settle as far south as the tip of South America and as far east as the Atlantic coast of North America.

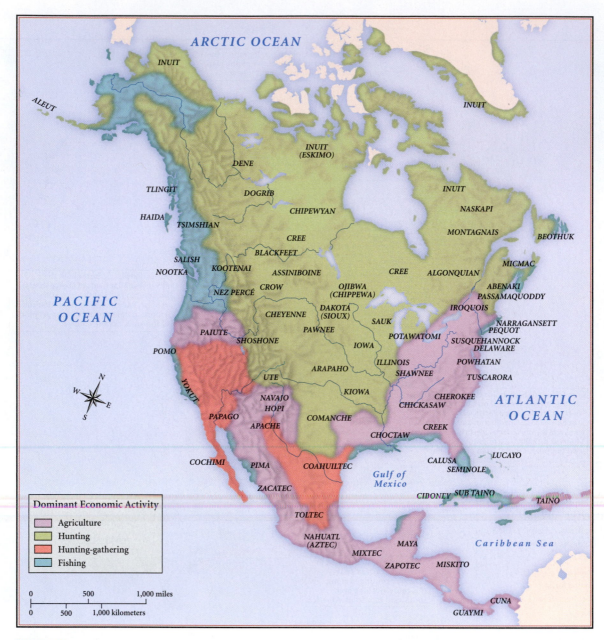

**MAP 1.2**

**Native American Peoples, 1492**

Having learned to live in many environments, Native Americans populated the entire Western Hemisphere. They created cultures that ranged from centralized agriculture-based societies (the Mayas and Aztecs), to societies that combined farming and hunting (the Iroquois and Algonquians), to seminomadic tribes of hunter-gatherers (the Micmacs and Ottowas). The great diversity of Native American peoples — in language, tribal identity, and ways of life — and the long-standing rivalries among neighboring peoples usually prevented them from uniting to resist the European invaders.

## The Mayas and the Aztecs

The flowering of Mesoamerican civilization began around 700 B.C. among the Olmec people, who lived along the Gulf of Mexico. Subsequently, the Mayas of the Yucatán Peninsula of Mexico and the neighboring rain forests of Guatemala built large urban centers that relied on elaborate systems of irrigation. By A.D. 300, more than 20,000 people were living in the Mayan city of Tikal [*TEE-kall*]. Most were farmers, whose labor built the city's huge stone temples. An elite class claiming descent from the gods ruled Mayan society and lived

Temple ubi sacrificant,
Capita sacrificatorum,
Templum,
Domus ad,

**Understanding the Cosmos of the Aztecs**

Using Aztec sources, German geographers drew this map of Tenochtitlán in 1524. Recent scholarship suggests that the Aztecs viewed their city as a cosmic linchpin, where the human world brushed up against the divine. In the center of the city stand two elevated temples that represent Coatepec, the Serpent Mountain and the mythic birthplace of the Aztecs' tribal god Huitzilopochtli. Priests sacrificed thousands of men and women here, a ritual the Aztecs believed transformed the temples into the Sacred Mountain and sustained the cosmos. Bildarchiv Preussischer Kulturbesitz/Art Resource, NY.

in splendor on goods and taxes extracted from peasant families. Drawing on the religious and artistic traditions of the Olmecs, Mayan artisans decorated temples and palaces with depictions of jaguars and warrior-gods. Mayan astronomers accurately predicted eclipses of the sun and the moon, and scholars developed hieroglyphic writing to record royal lineages and wars. Aside from boosting the authority of the ruling class of warriors and priests, these intellectual skills provided the Mayans with a sense of history and a complex, prosperous culture.

But between A.D. 800 and 900, Mayan civilization went into decline. Evidence suggests that a two-century-long drought led overtaxed peasants to desert the temple cities and retreat to the countryside. Consequently, when the Spanish invaders arrived in the 1520s, there were few strong Mayan city-states to resist them.

A second Mesoamerican civilization developed among the peoples who lived in the fertile valleys in the highlands of Mexico. A major center was the city of Teotihuacán [*tay-o-tee-wa-KAHN*]. At its zenith, about A.D. 500, Teotihuacán had more than one hundred temples, including the magnificent Pyramid of the Sun; some four thousand apartment buildings; and a population of at least 100,000. By 800, the city was in decline, the victim of long-term drought and recurrent invasions by seminomadic warrior peoples. Some of these invaders, such as the Toltecs and the Aztecs, established even more extensive empires.

The Aztecs settled on an island in Lake Texcoco, not far from the great pyramid. There, in 1325, they built a new city, Tenochtitlán [*teh-noch-teet-LAN*]— Mexico City today — that was designed to reflect their understanding of the divine cosmos. The Aztecs mastered the complex irrigation systems of the long-resident peoples and established a hierarchical social order. Priests and warrior-nobles ruled over free Aztec commoners who farmed communal land. The nobles also used huge numbers of non-Aztec Indians to labor as slaves or serfs on their private estates.

An aggressive people, the Aztecs soon subjugated most of central Mexico. Their rulers demanded both economic and human tribute from subject peoples, and their priests brutally sacrificed thousands of men and women; they believed that these ritual murders sustained the cosmos, ensuring fertile fields and the daily return of the sun.

Aztec merchants forged trading routes that crisscrossed the empire, importing furs, gold, textiles, food, and obsidian from as far north as the Rio Grande and as far south as present-day Panama. By 1500, Tenochtitlán was a magnificent metropolis with more than 200,000 inhabitants—far more populous than most European cities. Its splendor and wealth dazzled Spanish soldiers. "These great towns and pyramids and buildings arising from the water, all made of stone, seemed like an enchanted vision," marveled one Spaniard. The Aztecs' strong political institutions and military power posed a formidable challenge to the Spanish intruders.

## The Indians of the North

North of the Rio Grande, as the practice of agriculture spread, so did the urban, trade-oriented Mesoamerican way of life. But apart from a few exceptions—such as the Hopewell, Pueblo, and Mississippian peoples—northern Indian societies were far less populous, wealthy, and culturally complex than those of the Aztecs and the Mayas. Consequently, when Europeans intruded into North America after 1500, there were neither powerful Indian empires to confront them nor densely settled and rich societies for them to exploit.

**The Hopewell Culture** | Indeed, by 1500 the great periods of northern Indian economic and cultural creativity lay mostly in the past. Around A.D. 100, the vigorous Hopewell people of present-day Ohio had domesticated plants, organized themselves into large villages, and set up a trading network that stretched from present-day Louisiana to Wisconsin (see Reading American Pictures, "Maize for Blankets: Indian Trading Networks on the Great Plains," p. 13). They imported obsidian from the Yellowstone region of the Rocky Mountains, copper from the Great Lakes, and pottery and marine shells from the Gulf of Mexico. The Hopewells built large burial mounds in extensive earthworks that still survive, and skilled artisans fashioned striking ornaments that were buried with the dead. For unknown reasons, the Hopewells' elaborate trading network collapsed around 400.

**The Peoples of the Southwest** | Another complex culture—densely settled, with highly developed crafts and governing institutions—appeared among the Pueblo peoples of southwestern North America: the Hohokams, Mogollons, and Anasazis. By A.D. 600, the Hohokam [ho-HO-kam] people in the high country of present-day Arizona and New Mexico were using irrigation to grow two crops a year, fashioning fine pottery with red-on-buff designs, and worshipping their gods on platform mounds; by 1000, they had built elaborate multistory, multiroom stone or mud-brick structures called **pueblos** and had adopted the Mayan ritual of drinking chocolate on sacred occasions. To the east, in the Mimbres Valley of present-day New Mexico, the Mogollon [mog-ga-YON] people developed a distinctive black-on-white pottery. And by A.D. 900, the Anasazi people had become master architects. They built residential-ceremonial villages in steep cliffs, a pueblo in Chaco Canyon that housed 1,000 people, and 400 miles of straight roads. But as soil exhaustion and extended droughts disrupted maize production, the Pueblo peoples' expansive urban culture gradually declined after 1150 and they abandoned Chaco Canyon and other large pueblos. Their descendants—including the Acomas, Zunis, and Hopis—built smaller village societies that were better suited to the dry and unpredictable climate of the Southwest.

**Mississippian Civilization** | The Mississippi River Valley was home to the last large-scale northern Indian culture. Beginning about A.D. 800, the Mississippian peoples planted new strains of maize imported from Mesoamerica—the northern flint variety—and produced an agricultural surplus. They built small, fortified temple cities with a robust religious culture. By 1150, the largest city, Cahokia [ka-HO-kee-ah], near present-day St. Louis, boasted a population of 15,000 to 20,000 and more than one hundred temple mounds. As in the Mayan city-states in Mesoamerica, the tribute paid by peasant farmers supported a privileged class of nobles and priests who claimed descent from the sun god, patronized artisans, and waged war against neighboring chiefdoms. But none of the Mississippian peoples had the military or civil skills of the Toltecs or the Aztecs, and so there were no great Indian empires in the Mississippi Valley.

# Maize for Blankets: Indian Trading Networks on the Great Plains

In most Native American societies, there were no merchants, storekeepers, or traders. Yet many Indian peoples exchanged goods with their neighbors and often acquired wares produced in distant lands. They also acquired captives taken in raids, mostly women and children, who were put to work as household slaves or integrated into the host society though marriage or adoption. This 1973 painting by Tom Lovell offers a historical reconstruction of the commerce in goods at the fortified Towa pueblo of Cicúye (in what today is Pecos, New Mexico). The pueblo, which stands on a high mountain pass between the Rio Grande Valley and the Great Plains, looms in the background to the left.

**Tom Lovell, *Trading at the Pecos Pueblo*.** Courtesy of Abell-Hanger Foundation and of the Permian Basin Petroleum Museum, Library and Hall of Fame of Midland, Texas, where the painting is on permanent display.

## ANALYZING THE EVIDENCE

- Why did the location of the Towa pueblo at Pecos make it a major trading post? One clue comes from a Spanish explorer who visited the pueblo in 1541 with Francisco Vásquez de Coronado's expedition. He reported that Indians from the Great Plains exchanged "*cueros de Cíbola* [bison hides] and deer skins" for the "maize and blankets" produced by the Pueblo peoples. Do you see any other pueblo products in this painting?

- What do the clothing, material goods, and lodgings of the two peoples—the Towas and the Apaches—tell us about their respective ways of life?

- How have the Apaches transported their goods to the pueblo? Based on what you have read in the text, can you explain why no horses appear in this painting, which is set in A.D. 1500?

- Look closely at what the men and women are doing. What does the painting suggest about gender roles among native peoples of the region?

**The Great Serpent Mound**

Scholars long believed that this mound was the work of the Adena peoples (500 B.C.–A.D. 200) because of its proximity to an Adena burial site in present-day southern Ohio. Recent research places the mound at a much later date (A.D. 950–1200) and, because of the serpent imagery, ties it to the culture of Mississippian peoples. The head of the serpent is aligned with the sunset of the summer solstice (June 20 or 21 in the Northern Hemisphere), an event of great religious significance to a sun-worshipping culture. © Richard Cooke/Corbis.

As the climate cooled after 1300, crop yields declined, undermining the economic basis of urban life. By 1350, Mississippian civilization was in rapid decline. Tuberculosis and other urban diseases took the lives of many Indians, and relatively dense populations overburdened the environment, depleting nearby forests and herds of deer. Still, Mississippian institutions and practices endured for centuries. When Spanish conquistador Hernán de Soto invaded the region in the 1539, he found the Calusa, Apalachee [*ap-a-LAH-chee*], Timucua [*TEE-moo-KOO-wa*], and other Mississippian peoples living in permanent settlements under the command of powerful chiefs (see Voices from Abroad, "De Soto's March of Destruction," p. 16). "If you desire to see me, come where I am," a chief told de Soto. "Neither for you, nor for any man, will I set back one foot." A century and a half later, French traders and priests reported that the Natchez people were rigidly divided

among hereditary chiefs, nobles and honored people, and a bottom class of peasants. "Their chiefs possess all authority and distribute their favors and presents at will," a Frenchman noted. Influenced by Mesoamerican rituals, the Natchez marked the death of a chief by sacrificing his wives and burying their remains in a ceremonial mound.

**Eastern Woodland Peoples** Most native peoples east of the Mississippi lived in self-governing tribes made up of **clans**, groups of families that traced their lineage to a real or legendary common ancestor. These kin-based societies looked inward; the names they called themselves—Innu, Lenape, and dozens of others—mean "human beings" or "real people"; all others were aliens. Clan elders and village chiefs conducted ceremonies, resolved personal feuds, set war policy, and enforced customs such as a ban

**Timucua Raid, 1560s**

In 1564, French Protestants founded Fort Caroline, near present-day Jacksonville, Florida. Soon, the Spanish governor of Florida wiped it out and executed hundreds of those he called "Lutheran heretics." The artist Jacque Le Moyne de Morgues was among the few survivors. His watercolors inspired a series of beautiful engravings by Theodor de Bry. Here, Timucua warriors attack a neighboring people, shooting burning arrows into a fortified village and seizing those who flee. Library of Congress.

on marriage between members of the same clan. But they lacked the spiritual authority and coercive institutions of Mesoamerican priests and elites, and relied on kin ties to govern. "When you command, all the French obey and go to war," the Chippewa chief Chigabe [*chi-GAH-bee*] told the governor of Canada, the Comte de Frontenac, "[but] I shall not be heeded and obeyed by my nation [except by] those immediately allied to me."

The culture of these lineage-based societies discouraged accumulation; individual ownership of goods and land was virtually unknown. "[They] possess hardly anything except in common," noted a French missionary among the Iroquois. Strong customs dictated that members would share food and other scarce goods, fostering an ethic of reciprocity rather than one of self-interest. "You are covetous, and neither generous nor kind," the Micmac Indians of Nova Scotia told acquisitive French fur traders. "As for us, if we have a morsel of bread, we share it with our neighbor."

In other respects, the cultures of the native peoples of eastern North America were diverse. Like the Natchez, the Creeks, Choctaws, and Chickasaws who lived in present-day Alabama and Mississippi had once been organized in powerful chiefdoms. However, the European epidemic diseases carried by members of de Soto's expedition killed thousands of Indians in the 1540s and destroyed their traditional institutions. The survivors intermarried and settled in smaller, less disciplined agricultural communities.

In these Muskogean-speaking societies—and among the Algonquian-speaking and Iroquoian peoples to the north and east—the men hunted and fished while the women, using flint hoes, raised corn, squash, and beans. Because of the importance of farming, a **matrilineal** system of kinship and inheritance developed among some eastern Indian peoples, such as the Five Nations of the Iroquois, who resided in present-day New York State. In these matrilineal societies, fathers stood outside the main lines of descent and authority. Women passed use-rights to cultivated fields to their daughters, and mothers and their brothers took principal responsibility for child rearing. Emotional intimacy between spouses was muted: "My wife is not my friend," explained a Delaware man. "[T]hat is, she is not related to me, . . . she is only my wife." Religious rituals centered on the agricultural cycle. For example, the Iroquois celebrated green corn and strawberry festivals. Although eastern woodland peoples enjoyed an adequate diet, they had a sparse, uncertain material life and their populations grew slowly.

It was these relatively small and weak lineage-based societies that confronted the English, Dutch, and French adventurers in eastern North America around 1600. Lacking numbers, valuable manufactured goods, and gold, they could provide the invaders with only furs from the forests and the land on which they lived.

- What were the main characteristics of the Indian civilizations of Mesoamerica?

- How were eastern woodland Indian societies organized and governed?

All the nations and people I had hitherto passed through resembled
own in their manners, customs and lang

# Hernán de Soto
## De Soto's March of Destruction

From 1539 to 1542, Hernán de Soto and an army of 600 Spaniards roamed through northern Florida and the southeastern part of the present-day United States. They killed, raped, and enslaved hundreds of Indians from many different peoples, and inadvertently introduced smallpox, measles, and other viruses that took the lives of tens of thousands more. All to no avail: The Spanish found no gold, de Soto died of a fever in 1542, and only a few hundred of his soldiers survived the ordeal. One was Rodrigo Rangel, de Soto's private secretary, whose diary provided the material for this account, composed in 1546 by royal historian Gonzalo Fernandez de Oviedo.

On Sunday, the tenth of October [1540], the Governor [de Soto] entered in the town of Tascalua, which was called Athahachi, a new town; and the cacique [the Calusa chieftain] was on a balcony that was made on a mound to one side of the plaza, about his head a certain headdress like an almaizar [turban] worn like a Moor, which gave him an appearance of authority, and a pelote or blanket of feathers down to his feet, very authoritative, seated upon some high cushions, and many principals of his Indians with him. He was of as tall a stature as that Antonico of the guard of the Emperor our lord, and of very good proportions, a very well built and noble man; he had a young son as tall as he, but he was more slender. Always in front of this cacique was a very graceful Indian on foot, with a sunshade, on a pole, which was like a round and very large fly-flap. . . . And although the Governor entered in the plaza and dismounted and went up to him, he did not rise but rather was quiet and composed, as if he were a king, and with much gravity. The Governor sat with him a bit, and after a little while he [de Soto] rose and said that they should go to eat and took him with him, and Indians came to dance; and they danced very well in the way of the peasants of Spain, in such a manner that it was a pleasure to see.

At night he [the chieftain] wished to go [from our camp], but the adelantado [de Soto] told him that he had to sleep there; and he understood it and showed that he scoffed at such a decision, being lord, to give him so suddenly a restraint or impediment to his liberty. . . . The next day the Governor [de Soto] asked for tamemes [carriers] and one hundred Indian women, and the cacique gave them four hundred tamemes and said that he would give them the rest of the tamemes and the women in Mabila, the province of a principal vassal of his, and the Governor was content that the rest of his unjust demand would be satisfied in Mabila. . . .

On Saturday, the sixteenth of October, they departed from there and went to a forest, where one of the two Christians that the Governor had sent to Mabila came; and he said that there was a great gathering of armed people in Mabila. . . . On Monday, the eighteenth of October, the day of St. Luke, the Governor arrived at Mabila. . . . The Indians then did an areito, which is their kind of ball with dancing and singing.

While watching this, some soldiers saw them [the Indians] placing bundles of bows and arrows secretively in some palm leaves, and other Christians saw that the huts were filled high and low with concealed people. The Governor was warned, and he placed his helmet on his head and commanded that all should mount their horses. . . . And all the Spaniards fought like men of great spirit, and twenty-two of them died, and they wounded another one hundred and forty-eight [Spaniards] with six hundred and eighty-eight arrow wounds, and they killed seven horses and wounded twenty-nine others. The women and even boys of four years struggled against the Christians, and many Indians hanged themselves in order not to fall into their hands. . . .

The battle having taken place in the manner stated above, they rested there until Sunday, the fourteenth of November, treating the wounded and the horses, and they burned a great part of the land. From the time that this Governor and his armies entered in the land of Florida up to the time that they left from there, all the dead were one hundred and two Christians, and not all, to my way of thinking, in true penitence.

Source: "Account of the Northern Conquest and Discovery of Hernando de Soto by Rodrigo Rangel," trans. John E. Worth, in *The De Soto Chronicles: The Expedition of Hernando de Soto to North America in 1539–1543*, 2 vols., eds., Lawrence A. Clayton, Vernon James Knight Jr., and Edward C. Moore (Tuscaloosa: University of Alabama Press, 1993), 1:288–294.

### ANALYZING THE EVIDENCE

- What were the causes of this particular battle?
- What do the results of the battle suggest about the relative strength of the Spaniards and the Indians?
- What is the stance of the author toward these events? How can you tell?

# Tradition-Bound Europe

In 1450, no one would have predicted that Europeans would become overlords of the Western Hemisphere. A thousand years after the fall of the Roman Empire, Europe remained a mosaic of small and relatively weak kingdoms with populations that relied on subsistence agriculture. Moreover, around 1350, a deadly plague that was introduced from the subcontinent of India—the Black Death—had killed one-third of Europe's population. The future looked as difficult and dark as the past.

## European Peasant Society

In 1450, most Europeans were **peasants** who lived in small, compact agricultural villages surrounded by open fields. Because the fields were divided into narrow strips cultivated by different families, cooperative farming was a necessity. The community decided which crops to grow, and every family followed the community's dictates. On manorial lands, tillage rights came in exchange for weekly labor on the lord's estate, an arrangement that turned peasants into serfs. Gradually, obligatory manorial services gave way to paying rent; or, as in France, customary tillage rights became, for practical purposes, land ownership. Once freed from their obligation to labor for their farming rights, serfs had fresh incentives to work. The peasants' output, once inferior to the corn culture of Native Americans, produced surpluses and created a local market economy.

**The Peasantry**  For European peasants, as for Native Americans, the rhythm of life followed the seasons. The agricultural year began in late March, when the ground thawed and dried and the villagers began the exhausting work of plowing and then planting wheat, rye, and oats. During the busy spring months, the men sheared the thick winter wool of their sheep, which the women washed and spun into yarn. In June, peasants cut the first crop of hay and stored it as winter fodder for their livestock. During the summer, life was more relaxed, and families repaired their houses and barns. Fall brought the strenuous harvest, followed by solemn feasts of thanksgiving and riotous bouts of merrymaking. As winter approached, peasants slaughtered excess livestock and salted or smoked the meat. During the cold months, they threshed grain and wove textiles, visited friends and relatives, and celebrated the winter solstice or the birth of Christ. Just before the farming cycle began again in the spring, they held carnivals, celebrating with drink and dance the end of the long winter night. Even births and deaths followed the seasons: For reasons not yet fully understood, more successful conceptions took place in early summer than at any other time of the year. And many rural people died either in January and February, victims of viral diseases, or in August and September in epidemics of fly-borne dysentery (Figure 1.1).

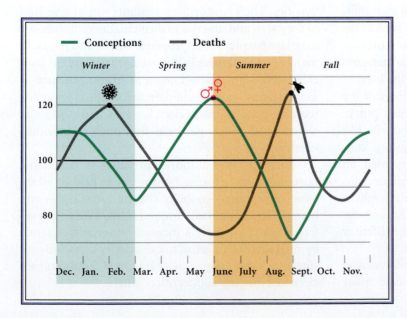

**FIGURE 1.1**

**The Yearly Rhythm of Rural Life and Death**

The annual cycle of nature profoundly affected life in the traditional agricultural world. The death rate soared by 20 percent in February (from viruses) and September (from fly-borne dysentery). Summer was the healthiest season, with the fewest deaths and the most successful conceptions (as measured by births nine months later). A value of 100 indicates an equal number of deaths and conceptions.

**The Peasant's Fate** | For most peasants, survival meant constant labor, breaking the soil with primitive wooden plows and harvesting hay and grain with small hand sickles. In the absence of today's high-quality seeds, chemical fertilizers, and pesticides, output was pitifully small—less than one-twelfth of present-day yields. The margin of existence was small, and poverty corroded family relationships. Malnourished mothers fed their babies sparingly, calling them "greedy and gluttonous," and many newborn girls were "helped to die" so that their brothers would have enough to eat. Half of all peasant children died before the age of twenty-one, victims of malnourishment and disease. "I have seen the latest epoch of misery," a French doctor reported as famine struck. "The inhabitants . . . lie down in a meadow to eat grass, and share the food of wild beasts." Often destitute, usually exploited by landlords and nobles, many peasants drew on strong religious beliefs, "counting blessings" and accepting their harsh existence. Others, however, hoped for a better life for themselves and their children. It was the peasants of Spain, Germany, and Britain who would supply the majority of white migrants to the Western Hemisphere.

## Hierarchy and Authority

In traditional hierarchical societies—Mesoamerican or European—authority came from above. In Europe, kings and princes owned vast tracts of land, forcibly conscripted men for military service, and lived in splendor off the peasantry's labor. Yet monarchs were far from supreme: Local nobles also owned large estates and controlled hundreds of peasant families. Collectively, these nobles challenged royal authority with both their military power and their legislative institutions, such as the French *parlements* and the English House of Lords.

Just as kings and nobles ruled society, so men governed families. Rich or poor, the man was the head of the house, his power justified by the teachings of the Christian church. As one English clergyman put it: "The woman is a weak creature not embued with like strength and constancy of mind"; law and custom "subjected her to the power of man." Once married, an Englishwoman assumed her husband's surname, submitted to his orders, and surrendered the legal right to all her property. Her sole protection: When he died, she received a **dower**, usually the use during her lifetime of one-third of the family's land and goods.

Men also controlled the lives of their children, who usually worked for their father into their middle or late

**Artisan Family**

Work was slow and output limited in the preindustrial world, and survival required the efforts of all family members. Here a fifteenth-century French woodworker planes a panel of wood while his wife twists flax fibers into linen yarn for the family's clothes. Their young son cleans up wood shavings to use later to start fires.   Giraudon/Art Resource, New York.

twenties. Then landowning peasants would give land to their sons and dowries to their daughters and choose marriage partners of appropriate wealth and status. In many regions, fathers bestowed all their land on their eldest son—a practice known as **primogeniture**—forcing many younger children to join the ranks of the roaming poor. In this society, few men and even fewer women had much personal freedom or individual identity.

Hierarchy and authority prevailed in traditional European society because of the power held by established institutions—nobility, church, and village—and because, in a violent and unpredictable world, they offered ordinary people a measure of security. Carried by migrants to America, these security-conscious institutions would shape the character of family and society well into the eighteenth century.

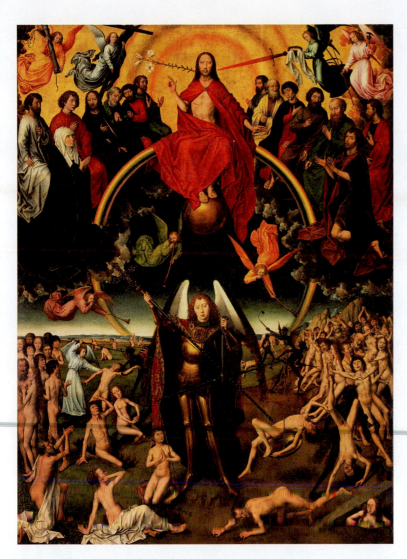

***The Last Judgment***, 1467–1471

Death—and their fate in the afterlife—loomed large in the minds of fifteenth-century Christians, and artists depicted their hopes and fears in vividly rendered scenes. In this painting by the German-Flemish artist Hans Memling (c. 1433–1494), Christ and his apostles sit in judgment as the world ends and the dead rise from their graves. The archangel Michael weighs the souls of the dead in a balance to determine their final fate; either eternal life with God in heaven or everlasting punishment in hell.   Erich Lessing / Art Resource, NY.

## The Power of Religion

For centuries, the Roman Catholic Church was the great unifying institution in Western Europe. The pope in Rome headed a vast hierarchy of cardinals, bishops, and priests. Catholic theologians preserved Latin, the great language of classical scholarship, and Christian dogma provided a common understanding of God and human history. Every village had a church, and holy shrines served as points of contact with the sacred world.

Christian doctrine penetrated deeply into the everyday lives of peasants. Originally, most Europeans were **pagans** who, like the Indians of North America, were animists; that is, they believed that the natural world—the sun, wind, stones, animals—was animated by spiritual forces that had to be heeded. However,

Christian priests taught that spiritual power came from outside nature, from a supernatural God who had sent his divine son, Jesus Christ, into the world to save humanity from its sins. The Christian Church devised a religious calendar that transformed animist festivals into holy days. The winter solstice, which for pagans marked the return of the sun, became the feast of Christmas, to celebrate the birth of Christ. Christianized peasants no longer made ritual offerings to nature in hopes of averting famine and plague; instead, they offered prayers to Christ.

The Church also taught that Satan, a lesser and wicked supernatural being, was constantly challenging God by tempting people to sin. If a devout Christian fell mysteriously ill, the cause might be an evil spell cast by a witch in league with Satan. Prophets who spread

**MAP 1.3**

**The Eurasian Trade System and European Maritime Ventures, c. 1500**

For centuries, the Mediterranean Sea was the meeting point for the commerce of Europe, North Africa, and Asia — via the Silk Road from China and the Spice Route from India. Beginning in the 1490s, Portuguese, Spanish, and Dutch rulers and merchants subsidized Christian maritime explorers who discovered new trade routes around Africa and new sources of wealth in the Americas. These initiatives undermined the commercial primacy of the Arab Muslim–dominated Mediterranean.

heresies—doctrines that were inconsistent with the teachings of the Church—were seen as the tools of Satan. Suppressing false doctrines became an obligation of Christian rulers. So did combating Islam, a religion that, like Christianity, proclaimed a single god. Following the death in A.D. 632 of the prophet Muhammad, the founder of Islam, the newly converted Arab peoples of North Africa used force and fervor to spread the Muslim faith into sub-Saharan Africa, India, and Indonesia, as well as deep into Spain and the Balkan regions of Europe. Between 1096 and 1291, Christian armies undertook a series of Crusades to reverse the Muslim advance into Europe and win back the holy lands where Christ had lived.

The crusaders had some military successes, but their most profound impact was on European society. Religious warfare intensified Europe's Christian identity and prompted the persecution of Jews and their expulsion from many European countries. The Crusades also broadened the horizons of Western European merchants, who became aware of the trade routes that stretched from Constantinople to China along the Silk Road and from the Mediterranean Sea through the Persian Gulf to the Indian Ocean (Map 1.3).

- **Compare and contrast the main features of the traditional agricultural society of Europe with those of Mesoamerica and the eastern woodlands of North America.**

# Europeans Create a Global World, 1450–1600

Whatever the hopes of European merchants, they faced formidable odds. Arabs controlled trade in the Mediterranean region, Africa, and the Near East. Moreover, China—a vast empire of 75 million people—seemed about to seize control of world commerce. Between 1405 and 1433, Ming emperors dispatched seven mammoth maritime expeditions to the Indian Ocean. Commanded by Admiral Zheng He, fleets of 300 ships and 28,000 men subdued pirates in the South China Sea, set up a major port at Malacca on the Malaysian peninsula, and exchanged silk and porcelain for spices and jewels in India and East Africa. Then, abruptly, China-centered bureaucrats at the imperial court halted these voyages to Southwest Asia. Two generations later, explorer Vasco da Gama's puny fleet of four ships and 170 men would seize the trade of the vast Indian Ocean for Portugal.

## The Renaissance Changes Europe, 1300–1500

The Crusades exposed educated Europeans to Arab learning and Eastern luxuries. Arab merchants had access to spices from India and silks, magnetic compasses, water-powered mills, and mechanical clocks from China. Arab scholars carried on the legacy of Byzantine civilization, which had preserved the great achievements of the Greeks and Romans in medicine, philosophy, mathematics, astronomy, and geography. Stimulated by this knowledge, first Italy and then the countries of northern Europe experienced a rebirth of cultural life, scientific progress, and economic energy.

**Innovations in Economics, Art, and Politics** | The Renaissance had its greatest impact on the upper classes. Merchants from the Italian city-states of Genoa, Florence, Pisa, and especially Venice dispatched ships to Alexandria, Beirut, and other eastern Mediterranean ports, where they purchased goods from China, India, Persia, and Arabia to be sold throughout Europe. This enormously profitable commerce created wealthy merchants, bankers, and textile manufacturers who expanded trade, lent vast sums of money, and spurred technological innovation in silk and wool production. Italian moneyed elites ruled their city-states as **republics**, with no prince or king. They celebrated **civic humanism**, an **ideology** that praised public virtue and service to the state and in time profoundly influenced European and American conceptions of government.

Perhaps no other age in European history has produced such a flowering of artistic genius. Michelangelo, Andrea Palladio, and Filippo Brunelleschi designed and built great architectural masterpieces. Leonardo da Vinci, Jacopo Bellini, and Raphael produced magnificent religious paintings, setting styles and standards that have endured into the modern era. This creative energy inspired Renaissance rulers as well: In *The Prince* (1513), Niccolò Machiavelli summed up a century of monarchical experience in accumulating political power. The kings of Western Europe had created royal law courts and bureaucracies to reduce the power of the landed nobility and had forged alliances with merchants and urban artisans. Monarchs allowed merchants to trade throughout their realms, granted privileges to the artisan organizations called **guilds**, and safeguarded commercial transactions in royal law courts, thereby encouraging domestic manufacturing and foreign trade. In return, kings and princes extracted taxes from towns and loans from merchants to support their armies and officials.

**Maritime Exploration** | Around 1400, the Portuguese monarchy propelled Europe into overseas expansion, initially by confronting Muslim states in North Africa. As a young soldier of the Crusading Order of Christ, Prince Henry of Portugal (1394–1460) learned of Arab merchants' rich trade in gold and slaves across the Sahara. Seeking a maritime route to the source of this trade in West Africa, Henry drew on the work of Renaissance thinkers and Arab and Italian geographers. In 1420, he founded a center for oceanic navigation in southern Portugal. He urged his captains to find a way around Cape Bojador in North Africa, a region of fierce winds and treacherous currents, and to explore the "Sea of Darkness" to the south. Eventually, Henry's mariners designed a better-handling vessel, the caravel, rigged with a lateen (triangular) sail that enabled the ship to tack into the wind. This innovation allowed them to sail far into the Atlantic, where they discovered and colonized the Madeira and Azore islands. From there, they sailed in 1435 to sub-Saharan Sierra Leone, where they exchanged salt, wine, and fish for African ivory and gold. By the 1440s, the Portuguese were trading in humans as well, the first Europeans to engage in the long-established African trade in slaves. Henry's mission of enhancing Portugal's wealth through trade with West Africa had succeeded.

## West African Society and Slavery

Vast and diverse, West Africa stretches from present-day Senegal to the Democratic Republic of Congo. In the 1400s, tropical rain forests covered much of the coast, but a series of great rivers — the Senegal, Gambia, Volta, Niger, and Congo — provided relatively easy access to the woodlands and savannas of the interior, where most people lived. There were few coastal cities because there was little seaborne trade (Map 1.4).

**West African Life** | West Africa was in general a hard place to live, with a thin soil and daunting diseases. Most West Africans lived in small villages and farmed modest plots. Normally, the men cleared the land and the women planted and harvested the crops. Tsetse flies, carriers of sleeping sickness to humans and disease deadly to cattle, wiped out livestock in wooded and low-lying areas, leaving people with a diet deficient in protein and milk. To secure meat, forest dwellers exchanged palm oil and kola nuts (which contained a highly valued stimulant), for the livestock, leather goods, and cotton textiles that savanna dwellers produced. Merchants collected valuable salt, which was gathered along the coast and mined in great de-posits in the Sahara, and traded it for iron, gold, and manufactures along the Niger and other rivers.

West Africans lived in diverse ethnic groups and spoke four basic languages, each with many dialects. Among West Atlantic–speakers, the Fulani and Wolof peoples were most numerous. Mande-speakers in the upper Niger region included the Malinke and Bambara peoples; the Yorubas and the Ibos of southern Nigeria spoke varieties of the Kwa language. Finally, the Mossis and other Voltaic-speakers inhabited the area along the upper Volta River. Most West Africans lived in societies similar to those of the Mayans and Aztecs: socially stratified states ruled by kings and princes. Some lived in city-states that produced high-quality metal, leather, textiles, and pottery. Other West African societies were stateless, organized by household and lineage, much like those of the eastern woodland Indians in North America.

Spiritual beliefs varied greatly. Some West Africans who lived immediately south of the Sahara — the Fulanis in Senegal, Mande-speakers in Mali, and Hausas in northern Nigeria — learned about Islam from Arab merchants and imams, knew the Koran, and worshipped only a single God. But most West Africans acknowledged the presence of multiple gods, as well as spirits that lived in the earth, animals, and plants. Many people believed that their kings had divine attributes and could contact the spirit world. They treated their ancestors with great respect, believing that the dead resided in a nearby spiritual realm and interceded in their lives. Most West African peoples had secret societies, such as the Poro for men and the Sande for women, which united people from different lineages and clans. These societies educated their members in sexual practices and conducted tribal rituals that celebrated male virility and female fecundity. "Without children you are naked," said a Yoruba proverb. Happy was the man with a big household, many wives, many children, and many relatives — and, in a not very different vein, many slaves.

**Portuguese Trade** | European traders initially had a positive impact on West Africa by introducing new plants and animals and expanding African trade networks. Portuguese merchants brought coconuts from East Africa; oranges and lemons from the Mediterranean; pigs from Western Europe; and, after 1492, maize, manioc, and tomatoes from the Americas. From small, fortified trading posts on the coast, merchants shipped metal products and manufactures to inland regions and took gold, ivory, and pepper in return. To handle the inland trade, the Portuguese relied on Africans, since Portuguese ships could travel no

## MAP 1.4

### West Africa and the Mediterranean in the Fifteenth Century

Trade routes across the Sahara had long connected West Africa with the Mediterranean region. Gold, ivory, and slaves moved north and east; fine textiles, spices, and the Muslim faith traveled south. Beginning in the 1430s, the Portuguese opened up maritime trade with the coastal regions of West Africa, which were home to many peoples and dozens of large and small states. Over the next century, the transatlantic movement of gold and slaves would surpass that across the Sahara.

more than 150 miles up the slow-flowing Gambia and lesser distances on the other rivers. Moreover, yellow fever, malaria, and dysentery quickly struck down Europeans who spent time in the interior of West Africa, often killing as many as half of them each year.

From West Africa, Portuguese adventurers looked for an ocean route to Asia. In 1488, Bartholomeu Dias rounded the Cape of Good Hope, the southern tip of Africa. Ten years later, Vasco da Gama reached East Af-

rica and India; his ships were mistaken for those of Chinese traders, the last pale-skinned men to arrive by sea. Although da Gama's inferior goods—tin basins, coarse cloth, honey, and coral beads—were snubbed by the Arab and Indian merchants along India's Malabar Coast, he managed to acquire a highly profitable cargo of cinnamon and pepper. To acquire more spices and Indian textiles, da Gama returned to India in 1502 with twenty-one fighting vessels, which outmaneuvered

**Vasco da Gama**

Appearances can be deceiving. Pictured here as a humble courtier, Vasco da Gama was in fact an ambitious, unscrupulous, and often cruel adventurer. During his second voyage to India in 1502, da Gama plundered the ships of Arab merchants, brutally slaughtered many of the ships' crews, and destroyed the fleets of local Indian princes. His depredations secured an extraordinarily valuable cargo of silks and spices that he took back to Portugal in 1503 and which eventually prompted his elevation into the nobility, as the Count of Vidigueira.    The Pierpoint Morgan Library/Art Resource, NY.

and outgunned the Arab fleets. That expedition netted 1,700 tons of spices, as much as flowed through Venice in an entire year. Soon the Portuguese government set up fortified trading posts for its merchants at key points around the Indian Ocean, in Indonesia, and along the coast of China. In a transition that sparked the momentous growth of European wealth and power, the Portuguese and then the Dutch replaced the Arabs as the leaders in Asian commerce.

**The Slave Trade** | Portuguese traders likewise ousted Arab merchants as the prime purveyors of African slaves. Coerced labor—slavery, serfdom, or indentured servitude—was the norm in most premodern societies, and in Africa, slavery was wide-

spread. Some Africans were held in bondage as security for debts; others were sold into servitude by their kin, in exchange for food in times of famine; many others were war captives. As a major form of property, slaves were also a key commodity of exchange, sold as agricultural laborers, concubines, or military recruits. Sometimes the descendants of slaves were freed, and became low-status members of society, but others endured hereditary bondage. Sonni Ali (r. 1464–1492), the ruler of the powerful upper Niger Islamic kingdom of Songhay, personally owned twelve "tribes" of hereditary agricultural slaves, many of them seized in raids against stateless peoples.

Slaves were also central to the international trade network as payment for the prestige goods African rulers coveted from the Mediterranean region. When the renowned Tunisian adventurer Ibn Battuta crossed the Sahara from the Kingdom of Mali around 1350, he traveled with a caravan of 600 female slaves, destined for domestic service or concubinage in North Africa, Egypt, and the Ottoman Empire. The first Portuguese in Senegambia found that the Wolof king, with his horse-mounted warrior aristocracy, "supports himself by raids which result in many slaves. . . . He employs these slaves in cultivating the land allotted to him; but he also sells many to the [Arab] merchants in return for horses and other goods."

To exploit this trade in slaves, Portuguese merchants established forts at small ports—first at Elmina in 1482 and later at Gorée, Mpinda, and Loango—where they bought gold and slaves from African princes and warlords. Initially, they carried a few thousand Africans each year to work on sugar plantations on São Tomé (off the coast of Gabon), and the Cape Verde, Azore, and Madeira islands; they also sold slaves in Lisbon, which soon had an African population of 9,000. After 1550, the maritime slave trade—a forced diaspora of African peoples—expanded enormously as Europeans set up sugar plantations in Brazil and the West Indies.

## Europeans Explore America

As Portuguese traders sailed south and east, the Spanish monarchs Ferdinand II of Aragon and Isabel I of Castile financed an explorer who looked to the west. As Renaissance rulers, Ferdinand (r. 1474–1516) and Isabel (r. 1474–1504) saw national unity and foreign commerce as the keys to power and prosperity. Married in an arranged match to combine their Christian kingdoms, the young rulers completed the centuries-long *reconquista* by capturing Granada, the last Islamic territory in Western Europe, in 1492. Using Catholicism to build a sense of

**The Arab Saharan Slave Trade**
Long before the Atlantic slave trade began around 1500, Arab merchants had been driving Africans across the Sahara to the Mediterranean region, where they sold them as domestic servants and concubines. Between 1000 and 1900, some 9 million enslaved Africans endured the walk across the desert from Timbuktu to Marrakesh or from Bilma to Tripoli. They usually traveled shackled together in large coffles, like that pictured in this engraving of unknown date.
© Bettmann/Corbis.

"Spanishness," they launched the brutal Inquisition against suspected Christian heretics and expelled or forcibly converted thousands of Jews and Muslims.

**Columbus and America** | Simultaneously, Ferdinand and Isabel sought trade and empire by subsidizing the voyages of Christopher Columbus, an ambitious and daring mariner from Genoa. Misinterpreting the findings of Italian geographers, Columbus believed that the Atlantic Ocean, long feared by Arab merchants as a 10,000-mile-wide "green sea of darkness," was a much narrower channel of water separating Europe from Asia. After cajoling and lobbying for six years, Columbus persuaded Genoese investors in Seville; influential courtiers; and, finally, Ferdinand and Isabel to accept his dubious theories and finance a western voyage to Asia.

Columbus set sail in three small ships in August 1492. Six weeks later, after a perilous voyage of 3,000 miles, he disembarked on an island in the present-day Bahamas. Believing that he had reached Asia—"the Indies," in fifteenth-century parlance—Columbus called the native inhabitants Indians and the islands the West Indies. He was surprised by the crude living conditions but expected the native peoples "easily [to] be made Christians." He claimed the islands for Spain and for Christendom by naming them after the Spanish royal family and Catholic holy days. Columbus then explored the neighboring Caribbean islands and demanded tribute from the local Taino [*TIE-no*], Arawak [*air-a-WAK*], and Carib peoples. Buoyed by stories of rivers of gold lying "to the west," Columbus left 40 men on the island of Hispaniola (present-day Haiti and the Dominican Republic) and returned triumphantly to Spain.

Although Columbus brought back no gold, the Spanish monarchs supported three more of his voyages. Columbus colonized the West Indies with more than 1,000 Spanish settlers—all men—and hundreds of domestic animals. But he failed to find either golden treasures or great kingdoms, and his death in 1506 went virtually unnoticed.

A German geographer soon labeled the newly found continents "America" in honor of a Florentine explorer, Amerigo Vespucci. Vespucci, who had explored the coast of present-day South America around 1500, denied that the region was part of Asia. He called it a *nuevo mundo*, a "new world." The Spanish crown called the two continents *Las Indias* ("the Indies") and wanted to make them a new Spanish world.

## The Spanish Conquest

Spanish adventurers ruled the Caribbean with an iron hand. After subduing the Arawaks and Tainos on Hispaniola, the Spanish probed the mainland for gold and slaves. In 1513, Juan Ponce de León explored the coast of Florida and gave that peninsula its name. In the same year, Vasco Núñez de Balboa crossed the Isthmus of Darién (Panama) and became the first European to see the Pacific Ocean. Rumors of rich Indian kingdoms encouraged other Spaniards, including hardened veterans of the *reconquista*, to invade the mainland. The Spanish monarchs offered successful conquistadors noble titles, vast estates, and Indian laborers.

**The Map Behind Columbus's Voyage**

In 1489, Henricus Martellus, a German cartographer living in Florence, produced this huge (4 feet by 6 feet) view of the known world, probably working from a map devised by Christopher Columbus's brother, Bartholomew. The map uses the spatial projection of the ancient Greek philosopher Claudius Ptolemy (A.D. 90–168) and incorporates information from Marco Polo's explorations in Asia and Bartolomeu Dias's recent voyage around the tip of Africa. Most important, it greatly exaggerates the width of Eurasia, thereby suggesting that Asia lies only 5,000 miles west of Europe (rather than the actual distance of 15,000 miles). Using Martellus's map, Columbus persuaded the Spanish monarchs to support his westward voyage. Bildarchiv Preussischer Kulturbesitz/Art Resource, NY.

**The Fall of the Aztecs**

Hernán Cortés (1485–1547) conquered the Aztec empire and destroyed its civilization. Cortés came from a family of minor gentry; seeking military adventure and material gain, he sailed to Santo Domingo, the capital of Hispaniola, in 1506. Ambitious and charismatic, he distinguished himself in battle, putting down a revolt and helping to conquer Cuba. These exploits and his marriage to a well-connected Spanish woman won Cortés an extensive Cuban estate and a series of administrative appointments.

Eager to increase his fortune, Cortés jumped at a chance in 1519 to lead an expedition to the mainland. He landed with 600 men near the Mayan settlement of Potonchan, which he quickly overpowered. Then Cortés got lucky. The defeated Mayans presented him with slave women to serve as servants and concubines. Among them was Malinali, a young woman of noble birth and, a Spanish soldier noted, "of pleasing appearance and sharp-witted and outward-going." Malinali spoke Nahuatl, the Aztecs' language. Cortés took her as his mistress and interpreter, and soon she became his guide. When the Spanish leader learned from Malinali the extent of the Aztec empire, his goal became power rather than plunder. He would depose its king, Moctezuma [mok-tah-ZOO-mah], and take over his realm.

Of Malinali's motives for helping Cortés, there is no record. Like his Spanish followers, she may have

**Premonition of Disaster**

This watercolor comes from a history of the Aztec people written in 1570 by Fray Diego Durán, a Spanish Dominican monk. It records the moment when Moctezuma heard of the arrival of white-skinned strangers and also saw a comet plunging to the earth. According to Aztec belief, the fall of a comet was an omen of a disaster that mere mortals were helpless to prevent. This belief helps to explain Moctezuma's failure to mount an aggressive attack against the Spanish intruders. Library of Congress.

been dazzled by his powerful personality. Or perhaps she calculated that Cortés was her best hope for escaping slavery and reclaiming her noble status. Whatever her reasons, Malinali's loyalty was complete. As the Spanish marched on the Aztec capital of Tenochtitlán, she warned Cortés of a surprise attack in the city of Cholula and negotiated his way into the Aztec capital. "Without her," concluded Bernal Díaz del Castillo, the Spanish chronicler of the conquest, Cortés would "have been unable to surmount many difficulties."

Awed by the Spanish invaders, Moctezuma received Cortés with great ceremony (see Comparing American Voices, "The Spanish Conquest of Mexico," pp. 28–29). However, Cortés soon held the emperor captive, and when Moctezuma's supporters tried to expel the invaders, they faced superior European military technology. The sight of the Spaniards in full metal armor, with guns that shook the heavens and inflicted devastating wounds, made a deep impression on the Aztecs, who knew how to purify gold but not how to produce iron tools or weapons. Moreover, the Aztecs had no wheeled carts or cavalry, and their warriors, fighting on foot with flint- or obsidian-tipped spears and arrows, were no match for Spanish horsemen wielding steel swords and aided by vicious attack dogs. Although suffering great losses, Cortés and his men fought their way out of the Aztec capital.

Winning a battle was one thing; conquering an empire was another. Had Moctezuma ruled a united empire, he could have overwhelmed the 600 Spanish invaders. But many Indian peoples hated the Aztecs, and Cortés deftly exploited their anger. With the help of Malinali, he formed military alliances with the Tlaxcaltecs and other subject groups whose wealth had been seized by Aztec nobles and whose people had been sacrificed to the Aztec sun god. Moctezuma's empire collapsed, the victim of a vast Indian rebellion instigated by the wily Cortés.

**The Impact of Diseases** The Spanish also had a silent ally: disease. Having been separated from Eurasia for thousands of years, the inhabitants of the Americas had no immunities to common European diseases. After the Spanish exodus, a massive smallpox epidemic ravaged Tenochtitlán, "striking everywhere in the city," according to an Aztec source, and killing Moctezuma's brother and thousands more. "They could not move, they could not stir. . . . Covered, mantled with pustules, very many people died of them." Subsequent outbreaks of smallpox, influenza, and measles killed hundreds of thousands of Indians and sapped the survivors' morale. Exploiting this demographic weakness, Cortés quickly extended Spanish rule over the Aztec empire. His lieutenants then moved against the Mayan city-states of the Yucatán Peninsula, eventually conquering them as well.

In 1524, Francisco Pizarro set out to accomplish the same feat in Peru. There the rich and powerful

# The Spanish Conquest of Mexico

How could a Spanish force of 600 men take control of an empire of 20 million people? That the Spanish had steel swords and armor and some guns, horses and attack dogs certainly gave them a military advantage. Still, concerted attack by the armies of the Aztecs and their allies would have overwhelmed the invaders before they reached the Mexican capital of Tenochtitlán. Why was there no such attack? One reason was that Cortés's force was bolstered by a sizable army of Tlaxcaltecs, from the independent coastal kingdom of Tlaxcala. The combined forces had shown their might by massacring thousands of residents of the city of Cholula, an Aztec ally. Also, some influential Aztecs, including Moctezuma, thought that Cortés might be an emissary of their god Quetzalcoatl.

These documents, which describe Cortés's initial entry, come from the memoir of a participant and an oral history. Consider them first as *sources*: How trustworthy are they? Are they biased in any way? Then think about their *contents*: Do their accounts agree? Do they identify key events? Do they explain why the Spaniards reached the city unmolested?

## Bernal Díaz del Castillo

### Cortés and Moctezuma Meet

Bernal Díaz was an unlikely chronicler of great events. Born poor, he went to America as a common soldier in 1514 and served under conquistadors in Panama and Cuba. In 1519, he joined Cortés's expedition, fought in many battles, and as a reward received an estate in present-day Guatemala. In his old age, Díaz wrote *The True History of the Conquest of New Spain*, a compelling memoir written from the perspective of a common soldier. In fresh and straightforward prose, it depicts the conquest as a divinely blessed event that saved the non-Aztec peoples of Mexico from a barbarous regime.

The Great Moctezuma had sent these great Caciques in advance to receive us, and when they came before Cortés they bade us welcome in their language, and as a sign of peace, they touched their hands against the ground. . . .

When we arrived near to [Tenochtitlán], . . . the Great Moctezuma got down from his litter, and those great Caciques supported him with their arms beneath a marvelously rich canopy of green coloured feathers with much gold and silver embroidery . . . which was wonderful to look at. The Great Moctezuma was richly attired according to his usage, and he was shod with sandals, the soles were of gold and the upper part adorned with precious stones. . . .

Many other Lords walked before the Great Moctezuma, sweeping the ground where he would tread and spreading cloths on it, so that he should not tread on the earth. Not one of these chieftains dared even to think of looking him in the face, but kept their eyes lowered with great reverence. . . .

When Cortés was told that the Great Moctezuma was approaching, and he saw him coming, he dismounted from his horse, and when he was near Moctezuma, they simultaneously paid great reverence to one another. Moctezuma bade him welcome and our Cortés replied through Doña Marina [Malinali, also called Malinche, Cortés's Indian mistress and interpreter] wishing him very good health. . . . And then Cortés brought out a necklace which he had ready at hand, made of glass stones, . . . which have within them many patterns of diverse colours, these were strung on a cord of gold and with musk so that it should have a sweet scent, and he placed it round the neck of the Great Moctezuma. . . . Then Cortés through the mouth of Doña Marina told him that now his heart rejoiced having seen such a great Prince, and that he took it as a great honour that he had come in person to meet him. . . .

Thus space was made for us to enter the streets of Mexico, without being so much crowded. But who could now count the multitude of men and women and boys who were in the streets and in canoes on the canals, who had come out to see us. It was indeed wonderful. . . . Coming to think it over it seems to be a great mercy that our Lord Jesus Christ was pleased to give us grace and courage to dare to enter into such a city; and for the many times He has saved me from danger of death . . . I give Him sincere thanks. . . .

They took us to lodge in some large houses, where there were apartments for all of us, for they had belonged to the father of the Great Moctezuma, who was named Axayaca. . . .

Cortés thanked Moctezuma through our interpreters, and Moctezuma replied, "Malinche, you and your brethren are in your own house, rest awhile," and then he went to his palaces, which were not far away, and we divided our lodgings by companies, and placed the artillery pointing in a convenient direction, and the order which we had to keep was clearly explained to us, and that we were to be much on the alert, both the cavalry and all of us soldiers. A sumptuous dinner was provided for us according to their use and custom, and we ate it at once. So this was our lucky and daring entry into the great city of Tenochtitlan Mexico on the 8th day of November the year of our Saviour Jesus Christ, 1519.

Source: Bernal Díaz del Castillo, *The True History of the Conquest of New Spain*, trans. A. P. Maudslay (1632; London: Routledge, 1928), pp. 272–275.

## Friar Bernardino de Sahagún

## Aztec Elders Describe the Behavior of Moctezuma

During the 1550s, Friar Bernardino de Sahagún published *General History of the Things of New Spain*. According to Sahagún, the authors of the *History* were Aztec elders who lived through the Conquest. They told their stories to Sahagún in a repetitive style, according to the conventions of Aztec oral histories, and he translated them into Spanish.

Moctezuma enjoyed no sleep, no food, no one spoke to him. Whatsoever he did, it was as if he were in torment. Ofttimes it was as if he sighed, became weak, felt weak. . . . Wherefore he said, "What will now befall us? Who indeed stands [in charge]? Alas, until now, I. In great torment is my heart; as if it were washed in chili water it indeed burns." And when he had so heard what the messengers reported, he was terrified, he was astounded. . . . Especially did it cause him to faint away when he heard how the gun, at [the Spaniards'] command, discharged: how it resounded as if it thundered when it went off. It indeed bereft one of strength; it shut off one's ears. And when it discharged, something like a round pebble came forth from within. Fire went showering forth; sparks went blazing forth. And its smoke smelled very foul; it had a fetid odor which verily wounded the head. And when [the shot] struck a mountain, it was as if it were destroyed, dissolved . . . as if someone blew it away.

All iron was their war array. In iron they clothed themselves. With iron they covered their heads. Iron were their swords. Iron were their crossbows. Iron were their shields. Iron were their lances. And those which bore them upon their backs, their deer [horses], were as tall as roof terraces.

And their bodies were everywhere covered; only their faces appeared. They were very white; they had chalky faces; they had yellow hair, though the hair of some was black. . . . And when Moctezuma so heard, he was much terrified. It was as if he fainted away. His heart saddened; his heart failed him. . . . [but] he made himself resolute; he put forth great effort; he quieted, he controlled his heart; he submitted himself entirely to whatsoever he was to see, at which he was to marvel. . . . [He then greeted Cortés, as described above.]

And when [the Spaniards] were well settled, they thereupon inquired of Moctezuma as to all the city's treasure . . . the devices, the shields. Much did they importune him; with great zeal they sought gold. . . . Thereupon were brought forth all the brilliant things; the shields, the golden discs, the devils' necklaces, the golden nose crescents, the golden leg bands, the golden arm bands, the golden forehead bands.

Source: Friar Bernardino de Sahagún, *Florentine Codex: General History of the Things of New Spain*, trans. Arthur J. O. Anderson and Charles E. Dibble (Santa Fe, NM, and Salt Lake City: The School of American Research and University of Utah Press, 1975), book 12: pp. 17–20, 26.

## ANALYZING THE EVIDENCE

- Díaz's account is a memoir, written in retrospect. What effect does that have on the structure and tone of the account? How is the Aztec selection different in those respects?

- Why does Moctezuma pay "great reverence" to Cortés? Why does Cortés return the honor? What is the strategy of each leader?

- What is Díaz's explanation for the easy entry of the Spanish into the city? What explanation is suggested by the elders' account?

Inca empire stretched 2,000 miles along the Pacific coast of South America. To govern this far-flung empire (and avert local famines), the Inca rulers had laid 24,000 miles of roads and built dozens of administrative centers, filled with finely crafted stone buildings. An Inca king, claiming divine status, ruled the empire through a bureaucracy of nobles. By the time Pizarro and his small force of 168 men and 67 horses finally reached Peru in 1532, half of the Inca population had already died from European diseases spread by Indian traders. Weakened militarily and divided between rival claimants to the throne, the Inca nobility was easy prey. Pizarro killed Atahualpa, the last Inca emperor, and seized his enormous wealth. Although Inca resistance continued for a generation (and the dream of an "Inca Return" persisted until a failed rebellion in 1781), Spain was now the master of the wealthiest and most populous regions of the Western Hemisphere (Map 1.5).

The Spanish invasion changed life forever in the Americas. Disease and warfare wiped out virtually all of the Indians of Hispaniola — at least 300,000 people. In Peru, the population of 9 million in 1530 plummeted to fewer than 500,000 a century later. Mesoamerica suffered the greatest losses: In one of the great demographic disasters in world history, its population of 30 million Native Americans in 1500 had dwindled to just 3 million in 1650.

**The Legacy of the Conquest**  Once the conquistadors had triumphed, the Spanish monarchs quickly transferred Iberian institutions — municipal councils, the legal code, the Catholic Church — to America, creating a bureaucratic empire. From its headquarters in Madrid, the Council of the Indies issued laws and decrees to viceroys, governors, judges, and other Spanish officials. But the conquistadors and their descendants remained powerful because they held many

**MAP 1.5**

**The Spanish Conquest of the Great Indian Civilizations**

The Spanish first invaded the islands of the Caribbean, largely wiping out the native peoples. Rumors of a gold-rich civilization led to Cortés's invasion of the Aztec empire in 1519. By 1535, other Spanish conquistadors had conquered the Mayan temple cities and the Inca empire in Peru, completing one of the great conquests in world history.

positions in the colonial bureaucracy and owned **en-comiendas**, royal grants giving them legal control over land and Native American workers. They ruthlessly exploited their laborers, forcing them to raise crops and cattle for local consumption and for export to Europe. The Spanish invasion permanently altered the natural as well as the human environment: Eurasian and African livestock (horses, cattle, sheep, and goats), grain crops (wheat, barley, and rice), and diseases (smallpox, measles, chickenpox, influenza, malaria, and yellow fever) now became part of life in the Americas.

The Spanish conquest changed the ecology of Europe, Africa, and Asia as well. In a process that historians call the **Columbian Exchange**, the food products of the Western Hemisphere—especially maize, potatoes, manioc, sweet potatoes, and tomatoes—significantly increased agricultural yields and population growth in other continents (Map 1.6). Maize and potatoes, for example, reached China around 1700; in the following century, the Chinese population tripled from 100 million to 300 million. Vast amounts of silver poured across the Pacific Ocean to China, where it was minted into money. In exchange, Spain received valuable Chinese silks, spices, and ceramics. In Europe, the gold that had formerly honored Aztec and Inca gods now flowed into the countinghouses of Spain and gilded the Catholic churches of Europe. A less welcome transfer was the virulent strain of syphilis Columbus's sailors took back with them. The American wealth that flowed around the globe between 1540 and 1640 made Spain the richest and most powerful nation in Europe. Indeed, Spanish rulers now claimed a "lordship of all the world."

Meanwhile, the once magnificent civilizations of Mexico and Peru lay in ruins. "Of all these wonders"—

**MAP 1.6**

**The Columbian Exchange**

As European traders and adventurers traversed the world between 1430 and 1600, they began what historians call the Columbian Exchange, a vast intercontinental movement of the plants, animals, and diseases that changed the course of historical development. The nutritious, high-yielding American crops of corn and potatoes enriched the diets of Europeans, Africans, and Asians. However, the Eurasian and African diseases of smallpox, diphtheria, malaria, and yellow fever nearly wiped out the native inhabitants of the Western Hemisphere and virtually ensured that they would lose control of their lands.

the great city of Tenochtitlán, the bountiful irrigated fields, the rich orchards, the overflowing markets — "all is overthrown and lost, nothing left standing," recalled Bernal Díaz, who had been a young soldier in Cortés's army. So, too, with native religion and culture: Cortés built a grand cathedral with the stones from Moctezuma's palace, while Spanish priests suppressed traditional religious ceremonies and gave Catholic identities to Indian gods. As early as 1531, an Indian convert reported a vision of a dark-skinned Virgin Mary, later known as the Virgin of Guadalupe, a Christian version of the "corn mother" who traditionally protected the maize crop.

A new society took shape on the lands emptied by disease and exploitation. Between 1500 and 1650, at least 350,000 Spaniards migrated to Mesoamerica and western South America. More than 75 percent were men — poor, unmarried, and unskilled refugees from Andalusia and later a broader mix of Castilians — and many took Indian women as wives or mistresses. Consequently, a substantial mixed-race population, called **mestizos**, quickly appeared, along with an elaborate **caste system** based on racial ancestry (and, within that, on skin color) that endured for centuries. Around 1800, the Spanish colonies stretched from the tip of South America to the northern border of present-day California. They contained about 16 million people (6 million more than in Spain itself): a privileged caste of 3.2 million, the Españols, who claimed pure Spanish descent; 5.5 million mestizos, people of mixed Indian and Spanish genetic and cultural heritage; 1.0 million enslaved Africans; and 6.5 million Indians, who often lived in mountainous regions. The harsh collision among the peoples of three old worlds — European, African, and Native American — had created a new Atlantic world.

- Why and how did Portugal and Spain pursue overseas commerce and conquest?

- Compare and contrast the Portuguese impact in Africa with the Spanish impact in America.

# The Rise of Protestant England, 1500–1620

On the basis of Columbus's discovery, Pope Alexander VI (r. 1492–1503) issued an edict declaring Spain's absolute dominion over the New World: Any intruder "even imperial and royal, . . . will incur the wrath of Almighty God." Soon, however, Roman Catholicism ceased to be a unifying force in European society. During the 1520s, religious doctrines preached by Martin Luther and other reformers divided Europe between Catholic and Protestant states and plunged the continent into a century of religious warfare. During these conflicts, France replaced Spain as the most powerful Catholic state and, along with the Protestant states of Holland and England, colonized North America in defiance of the papal edict.

## The Protestant Movement

Over the centuries, the Catholic Church had become a large and wealthy institution. Renaissance popes and cardinals used the Church's wealth to patronize the arts and enrich themselves. Pope Leo X (r. 1513–1521) received half a million ducats a year (about $20 million in 2009 dollars) by selling religious offices. Corruption at the top encouraged ordinary priests to seek economic or sexual favors. An English reformer denounced the clergy as a "gang of scoundrels" who should be "rid of their vices or stripped of their authority," but he was ignored. Other critics, such as Jan Hus of Bohemia, were executed as heretics.

**Martin Luther's Attack on Church Doctrine** | In 1517, Martin Luther, a German monk and professor at the university in Wittenberg, took up the cause of reform. His *Ninety-five Theses* condemned the Church for many practices, including the sale of **indulgences**, certificates that allegedly pardoned sinners from punishment in the afterlife. Outraged by Luther's charges, the pope dismissed him from the Church, and the Holy Roman Emperor, King Charles I of Spain (r. 1516–1556), threatened to imprison him. However, the princes of northern Germany, who were resisting the emperor's authority, protected Luther from arrest and allowed his protest movement to survive. To restore Catholic control and imperial authority, Charles I dispatched armies to Germany, setting off a generation of warfare. Eventually, the Peace of Augsburg (1555) divided Germany into Lutheran states in the north and Catholic principalities in the south.

Luther took issue with Roman Catholic doctrine in three major respects. First, he argued that humans were innately depraved and could not secure salvation through good deeds or the purchase of indulgences; instead, they could be saved only by grace, which came as a free gift from God. Second, Luther downplayed the role of the clergy as mediators between God and believers: "Our baptism consecrates us all without exception and makes us all priests." Third, he said that Christians must look to the Bible—not to the Church—as the ultimate authority in matters of faith. So that every literate German could read the Bible, previously available only in Latin, Luther translated it into German.

**The Doctrines of John Calvin**  Meanwhile, in Geneva, Switzerland, French theologian John Calvin established a rigorous Protestant regime. Even more than Luther, Calvin stressed human weakness and God's omnipotence. His *Institutes of the Christian Religion* (1536) depicted God as an absolute sovereign who governed the "wills of men so as to move precisely to that end directed by him." Calvin preached the doctrine of **predestination**, the idea that God chooses certain people for salvation before they are born and condemns the rest to eternal damnation. In Geneva, he set up a model Christian community, eliminating bishops and placing spiritual authority in ministers chosen by their congregations. Ministers and pious laymen ruled the city, prohibiting frivolity and luxury. "We know," wrote Calvin, "that man is of so perverse and crooked a nature, that everyone would scratch out his neighbor's eyes if there were no bridle to hold them in." Calvin's authoritarian doctrine won converts all over Europe, becoming the theology of the Huguenots in France, the Reformed Dutch Church, and the Presbyterians and Puritans in Scotland and England (Map 1.7).

**English Protestantism**  The English King Henry VIII (r. 1509–1547) had initially opposed Protestantism. However, when the pope refused to annul his marriage to the Spanish princess Catherine of Aragon in 1534, Henry broke with Rome and placed himself at the head of the new Church of England, which promptly granted an annulment. Although Henry's new church maintained most Catholic doctrines and practices, Protestant teachings continued to spread. Faced with popular pressure for reform, Henry's daughter and successor, Queen Elizabeth I

**MAP 1.7**

**Religious Diversity in Europe, 1600**

By 1600, Europe was permanently divided among rival Christian churches. Catholicism remained dominant in the south; Lutheran princes and monarchs ruled northern Europe; and Calvinism had strongholds in Switzerland, Holland, and Scotland. By persecuting radical Christian sects, the legally established churches—both Protestant and Catholic—encouraged the migration of sect members to America.

**A Dutch Merchant Family**

This 1563 painting of Antwerp wine merchant Pierre de Moucheron and his family by artist Cornelius de Zeeuw captures both the prosperity of the Dutch merchant class and the severe Calvinist ethos of sixteenth-century Holland. It also illustrates the character of the traditional patriarchal family, in which status reflected a rigid hierarchy of gender and age.   Rijksmuseum, Amsterdam.

(r. 1558–1603), approved a Protestant confession of faith that reflected both the Lutheran doctrine of salvation by grace and the Calvinist belief in predestination. To satisfy traditionalists, Elizabeth retained the Catholic ritual of Holy Communion as well as the hierarchy of bishops and archbishops.

Elizabeth's compromises angered radical Protestants, who condemned bishops as "proude, pontificall and tyrannous" as well as "anti-Christian and devilish and contrary to the Scriptures." These reformers took inspiration from the Presbyterian system pioneered in Calvin's Geneva and developed by John Knox for the Church of Scotland. In Scotland, congregations elected presbyters (lay elders) who helped ministers and sat in the synods (councils) that decided Church doctrine. By 1600, five hundred Church of England clergy were demanding the ouster of bishops and the creation of a republican-like presbyterian form of church government.

Other radical English Protestants called themselves "unspotted lambs of the Lord." These extraordinarily devout Calvinists wanted to "purify" the church of all Catholic teachings and magical or idolatrous practices, such as burning incense and praying to dead saints. Labeled Puritans, they sought inspiration from carefully argued sermons and placed emphasis on the "conversion experience," the felt infusion of God's grace. To ensure that all men and women had direct access to God's commands in the Bible, Puritans promoted literacy and Bible study. Finally, most Puritans believed that authority over clerical appointments and religious doctrine rested in the local congregation. Eventually, thousands of Puritans and Presbyterian migrants would carry their radical Protestant doctrines to North America.

## The Dutch and English Challenge Spain

Luther's challenge to Catholicism in 1517 came shortly before Cortés conquered the Aztec empire, and the two events became linked. Gold and silver from Mexico and Peru made Spain the wealthiest nation in Europe and King Philip II (r. 1556–1598) its most powerful ruler. In addition to Spanish America, Philip presided over wealthy states in Italy; the commercial and manufacturing provinces of the Spanish Netherlands (present-day Holland and Belgium); and, after 1580, Portugal and all its possessions in America, Africa, and the East Indies. "If the Romans were able to rule the world simply by ruling the Mediterranean," boasted a Spanish priest, "what of the man who rules the Atlantic and Pacific oceans, since they surround the world?"

An ardent Catholic, Philip tried to root out Islam in North Africa and Protestantism in England and the Netherlands. He failed to do either. A massive Spanish fleet defeated a Turkish armada at Lepanto in the east-

**Elizabeth I (r. 1558–1603)**

Dressed in richly decorated clothes that symbolize her power, Queen Elizabeth I celebrates the destruction of the Spanish Armada (pictured in the background) and proclaims her nation's imperial ambitions. The queen's hand rests on a globe, asserting England's claims in the Western Hemisphere.   © The Gallery Collection/Corbis.

ern Mediterranean in 1571, freeing 15,000 Christian galley slaves, but Muslims continued to rule all of North Africa. Moreover, the Spanish Netherlands remained a hotbed of Calvinism. These Dutch- and Flemish-speaking provinces had grown wealthy from textile manufacturing and trade with Portuguese outposts in Africa and Asia. To protect their Calvinist faith and political liberties, they revolted against Spanish rule in 1566. After fifteen years of war, the seven northern provinces declared their independence, becoming the Dutch Republic (or Holland) in 1581.

Elizabeth I of England aided the Dutch cause by dispatching 6,000 troops to Holland. She also supported military expeditions that imposed English rule over Gaelic-speaking Catholic Ireland. Calling the Irish "wild savages" who were "more barbarous and more brutish in their customs . . . than in any other part of the world," English soldiers brutally massacred thousands, prefiguring the treatment of Indians in North America. To meet Elizabeth's challenge to Catholicism, Philip sent a Spanish Armada — 130 ships and 30,000 men — against England in 1588. Philip intended to restore the Roman Church in England and then to wipe out Calvinism in Holland. But he failed utterly: A fierce storm and English ships destroyed the Spanish fleet.

Philip continued to spend his American gold and silver on religious wars, an ill-advised policy that diverted workers and resources from Spain's fledgling industries. The gold was like a "shewer of Raine," complained one critic, that left "no benefite behind." Oppressed by high taxes on agriculture and fearful of

military service, more than 200,000 residents of Castile, once the most prosperous region of Spain, migrated to America. By the time of Philip's death in 1598, Spain was in serious economic decline.

As mighty Spain faltered, tiny Holland prospered. Dutch warships sacked Spain's Caribbean ports and in 1628 captured the entire Spanish bullion fleet. This booty financed the capture of Portuguese trading posts in the Indian Ocean and its valuable sugar colony in Brazil. Amsterdam emerged as the financial capital of northern Europe, and the Dutch East India Company became the dominant trader from West Africa to Indonesia, China, and Japan. Dutch merchants also created the West India Company (1621), which invested in Brazilian sugar and established the fur-trading colony of New Netherland along the Hudson River.

Like Holland, England grew significantly during the sixteenth century, its economy stimulated, as colonial advocate Richard Hakluyt noted, by a "wounderful increase of our people." As England's population soared from 3 million in 1500 to 5 million in 1630, its monarchs supported the expansion of commerce and manufacturing. English merchants had long supplied European weavers with high-quality wool; around 1500, they created their own **outwork** textile industry. Merchants bought wool from the owners of great estates and sent it "out" to landless peasants in small cottages to spin and weave into cloth. The government aided textile entrepreneurs by setting low wage rates, and helped merchants by giving them monopolies in foreign markets. Queen Elizabeth granted exclusive licenses to the

Levant Company (to trade tin for silk and spices in Turkey) in 1581, the Guinea Company (to exchange manufactures for slaves in Africa) in 1588, and the East India Company (to import cotton cloth and spices from India) in 1600.

This system of state-assisted manufacturing and trade became known as **mercantilism**. By encouraging textile production, Elizabeth reduced imports and increased exports. The resulting favorable balance of trade caused gold and silver to flow into England and stimulated further economic expansion. Increased trade with Turkey and India also boosted import duties, which swelled the royal treasury and the monarch's power. By 1600, Elizabeth's mercantile policies had laid the foundations for overseas colonization. Now the English, as well as the Dutch, had the merchant fleets and wealth needed to challenge Spain's control of the Western Hemisphere.

## The Social Causes of English Expansion

England sent people as well as merchant fleets and manufactures to America. Rapid population growth after 1550 provided a large body of potential settlers, and economic hardship put them in motion. Their troubles stemmed in part from the massive influx of American gold and silver, which doubled the money supply of Europe and sparked a major inflation—an upheaval known today as the **Price Revolution** (Figure 1.2)

**The Decline of the Nobility** England's landed nobility was the first casualty of the Price Revolution. Aristocrats customarily rented out their estates on long leases for fixed rents, which provided a secure income and plenty of leisure. As one English nobleman put it, "We eat and drink and rise up to play and this is to live like a gentleman." Then inflation struck. In less than two generations, the price of goods tripled while the nobility's income from rents barely increased. As the purchasing power of the aristocracy fell, that of the gentry and the yeomen rose. The **gentry**, nonnoble landholders with substantial estates, kept pace with inflation by renting land on short leases at higher rates. **Yeomen**, described by a European traveler as "middle people of a condition between gentlemen and peasants," owned small farms that they worked with family labor. As wheat prices tripled, yeomen used the profits to build larger houses and provide their children with land.

Economics influenced politics. As nobles lost wealth, the House of Lords, their branch of Parliament, lost power. Simultaneously, members of the rising gentry entered the House of Commons, the political voice of the propertied classes, and demanded greater authority over taxation and other policies. In this way, the Price Revolution enhanced the influence of representative institutions in which rich commoners and property-owning yeomen had a voice. And it encouraged the spread of republican principles that

**FIGURE 1.2**

**Price Inflation and Living Standards in Europe**

American gold and silver poured into Europe after 1520, and the metals were minted into money. People then used that money to bid up the price of grain, which was in short supply. As the number of Europeans rose from 68 million in 1500 to 120 million in 1700, the scarcity of food and other goods caused a century-long decline in living standards. Along with the enhanced supply of money, scarcity of goods also created the great Price Inflation, which altered the relations among social classes. (See Figure 1.1 for another example of an indexed figure.)

changed the course of English—and American—political history.

**The Dispossession of the Peasantry** | The Price Revolution likewise transformed the lives of peasants, who made up three-fourths of the English population (Figure 1.3). As Spanish gold and silver spurred the expansion of the textile industry, profit-minded landlords and wool merchants persuaded Parliament to pass **enclosure acts**. These laws allowed owners to kick peasants off their lands, fence in their fields, and put sheep to graze there. Dispossessed peasant families lived on the brink of poverty, spinning and weaving wool or working as agricultural wage laborers. Wealthy men had "taken farms into their hands," an observer noted with disgust in 1600, "whereby the peasantry of England is decayed and become servants to gentlemen."

These social changes were magnified by the coldest decades of "the Little Ice Age," an era of low global temperatures (c. 1350–c. 1850). Throughout Europe between 1620 and 1660, crop yields fell and grain prices soared, bringing famine and social unrest. "Thieves and rogues do swarm the highways," warned one justice of the peace. Beset by an onslaught of "necessitous people, the fuel of dangerous insurrections," the Virginia Company persuaded thousands of poor young men and women to migrate to America. By signing contracts known as **indentures**, the migrants sold their labor (and freedom) for four or five years. In return, they received passage across the Atlantic and a promise of land at the end of their service. Dispossessed peasants and weavers threatened by a recession in the English cloth trade were likewise ready to try their luck elsewhere. Thousands of yeomen families were also on the move, looking for affordable land on which to settle

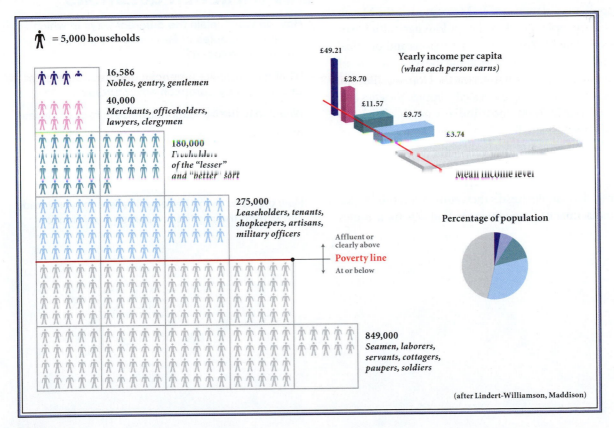

**FIGURE 1.3**

**The Hierarchy of English Society, 1688**

The graphic on the left was created from a famous table devised by Gregory King, a seventeenth-century statistician. According to King, the majority of English families (some 849,000) lived below the poverty line and were "Decreasing the Wealth of the Kingdom." In fact, the labor of the poor produced much of the wealth owned by the 511,586 families on the higher rungs of the social scale. Historians continue to revise King's data and have arranged them to show the wealth of individuals in each of King's social groups, as shown in the two graphs to the right.

their children. By 1640, more than 100,000 English and Scots had migrated to Ulster in Ireland, and 50,000 more had moved to North America and the Caribbean Islands. As Puritans looked for religious freedom and peasants for economic security, they formed a powerful migratory movement.

- How did Protestant religious doctrine differ from that of Roman Catholicism?

- What was the impact of the Columbian Exchange in food, people, diseases, and gold on the Americas, Europe, and Africa?

- What factors prompted the large-scale migration from England to America?

## SUMMARY

In this chapter, we have seen that the first human inhabitants of the Western Hemisphere were hunter-gatherers from Asia. Their descendants would form many cultures and speak many languages. In Mesoamerica, the Mayan and Aztec peoples developed populous agricultural societies and highly sophisticated religious and political systems; so, too, did the Incas along the western coast of South America. In North America, the Hopewell, Pueblo, and Mississippian peoples created complex societies and cultures; but in 1500, most Indians north of the Rio Grande lived in small self-governing communities of foragers, hunters, and horticulturalists.

We have also traced the maritime expansion that brought Europeans to the Americas. The Spanish crown, eager to share in Portugal's mercantile success in Africa and India, financed expeditions to find new trade routes to Asia. When Christopher Columbus revealed the "new world" of the Western Hemisphere to Europeans in 1492, Spanish adventurers undertook to conquer it. By 1535, conquistadors had destroyed the civilizations of Mesoamerica and Peru and inadvertently introduced diseases that would kill millions of Native Americans. Through the Columbian Exchange in crops, animals, plants, and diseases, there was a significant alteration in the ecology of much of the world.

Population growth, religious warfare, and American gold and silver transformed European society in the sixteenth century. As religious warfare sapped Spain's strength, the rise of strong governments in Holland, France, and England, along with a class of increasingly powerful merchants, enhanced the economies of those countries and whetted their peoples' appetites for overseas expansion.

## CHAPTER REVIEW QUESTIONS

- How do you explain the different ways in which the Indian peoples of Mesoamerica and North America developed?

- What made Native American peoples vulnerable to conquest by European adventurers?

- What led to the transatlantic trade in African slaves?

- What was mercantilism? How did this doctrine shape the policies of European monarchs to promote domestic manufacturing and foreign trade?

- How did Europeans become leaders in world trade and extend their influence across the Atlantic?

## FOR FURTHER EXPLORATION

Kenneth Pomeranz, *The Great Divergence: China, Europe, and the Making of the Modern World Economy* (2000), examines the impact of the Americas on world history. Brian M. Fagan, *The Great Journey: The Peopling of Ancient America* (1987), and Alvin M. Josephy Jr., ed., *America in 1492: The World of the Indian Peoples Before the Arrival of Columbus* (1991), are reliable and vividly written studies. Visit "1492: An Ongoing Voyage" (**www.loc.gov/exhibits/1492/intro.html**) for images and analysis of the native cultures of the Western Hemisphere.

For the European background of colonization, consult George Huppert's highly readable study, *After the Black Death*, 2nd ed. (1998); see also the engaging biography by William D. Phillips Jr. and Carla Rahn Phillips, *The Worlds of Christopher Columbus* (1992). A fine comparative study is J. H. Elliott, *Empires of the Atlantic World: Britain and Spain in America, 1492–1830* (2006). Giles Milton, *Nathaniel's Nutmeg* (1999), tells the rousing tale of European competition for the spice trade and, subsequently, the New World.

Geoffrey Parker, *The World Crisis, 1635–1665* (2010), sets the context for events in England, which are directly addressed in Andrew McRae, *God Speed the Plough* (2002), and Alison Games, *The Web of Empire: English Cosmopolitans in an Age of Expansion, 1560–1660* (2008). The "Martin Luther" Web site (**www.luther.de/en**) offers biographies and striking images of the era of the Protestant Reformation.

### TEST YOUR KNOWLEDGE

To assess your command of the material in this chapter, see the Online Study Guide at **bedfordstmartins.com/henretta**.

For Web sites, images, and documents related to topics and places in this chapter, visit **bedfordstmartins.com/makehistory**.

## TIMELINE

| | |
|---|---|
| 13,000–3000 B.C. | Asian migrants reach North America |
| 3000 B.C. | Horticulture begins in Mesoamerica |
| A.D. 100–400 | Flourishing of Hopewell culture |
| 300 | Rise of Mayan civilization |
| 500 | Zenith of Teotihuacán civilization |
| 600 | Pueblo cultures emerge |
| 632–1100 | Arab people adopt Islam and spread its influence |
| 800–1350 | Development of Mississippian culture |
| 1096–1291 | Crusades link Europe with Arab learning |
| 1300–1450 | Italian Renaissance |
| 1325 | Aztecs establish capital at Tenochtitlán |
| 1430 on | Portugal trades along West and Central African coasts |
| 1492 | Christopher Columbus makes first voyage to America |
| 1498 | Portugal's Vasco da Gama reaches India |
| 1513 | Juan Ponce de León explores Florida |
| 1517 | Martin Luther sparks Protestant Reformation |
| 1519–1521 | Hernán Cortés conquers Aztec empire |
| 1520–1650 | Price Revolution in Europe |
| 1532–1535 | Francisco Pizarro vanquishes Incas |
| 1534 | Henry VIII establishes Church of England |
| 1536 | John Calvin publishes *Institutes of the Christian Religion* |
| 1550–1630 | English crown supports mercantilism Parliament passes enclosure acts |
| 1556–1598 | Reign of Philip II, king of Spain |
| 1558–1603 | Reign of Elizabeth I, queen of England |
| 1560–1620 | Growth of English Puritan movement |
| 1588 | Storms and English ships destroy Spanish Armada |

The manner of their attire and
painting them selues when
they goe to their generall
huntings or at theire
Solemne feasts.

## CHAPTER 2

# The Invasion and Settlement of North America, 1550–1700

**Establishing colonies** in North America was not for the faint of heart. First came a long voyage over stormy, dangerous waters, where shipwrecks, spoiled food, and disease claimed many lives. Of 300 migrants to New France in 1663, seventy died en route. On arrival, the settlers had to build shelters, quickly plant crops, and survive an often dangerous climate. Two French Huguenots who migrated to Carolina in the 1670s protested they had "never before seen so miserable a country, nor an atmosphere so unhealthy. Fevers prevail all the year, from which those who are attacked seldom recover." Many other migrants faced hostile Indian peoples. "We neither fear them nor trust them but rely on our musketeers," declared Francis Higginson, a Puritan settler in the Massachusetts Bay Colony. Still, despite great risks and uncertain rewards, thousands of English, French, and Spanish migrants crossed the Atlantic, driven from their homelands by wars, epidemics, and poverty. To escape the life that English political philosopher Thomas Hobbes famously described in 1650 as "solitary, poor, nasty, brutish, and short," Europeans looked to America. There, an early explorer assured them, "every man may be master of his own labour and land . . . and by industry grow rich."

For Native Americans, however, the intrusion of thousands of Europeans ended the world as they had long known it. Whether they came as settlers, fur traders, or missionaries, the Christian peoples and their African slaves brought new diseases and beliefs that threatened the Indians' lives and cultures. "Our fathers had plenty of deer and skins, . . . and our coves were full of fish and fowl," Narragansett chief Miantonomi recalled in 1642 of his peoples' lands (in what is now Connecticut and Rhode Island), "but these English having gotten our land . . . their cows and horses eat the grass, and their hogs spoil our clam banks, and we shall all be starved." Indeed, hogs brought to North America by the new arrivals and left to forage for their own food became a dynamic vehicle of English expansion, destroying traditional food sources such as corn fields as well as clam beds, and disrupting Indian communities. Miantonomi went to Long Island seeking other tribes to join together

**A Carolina Indian, 1585**

The artist John White was one of the English settlers in Sir Walter Raleigh's colony on Roanoke Island. Fortunately, he returned to England before the colony met its mysterious fate (see p. 50), as his watercolors provide a rich visual record of Native American life. As White explains, the Secotan and Pomeiooc warriors appeared this way—carrying their bow and quiver full of arrows, and painted and dressed in deerskin and feathers, as well as beaded ornaments—"when they goe to their generall huntings, or at theire Solemne Feasts." © Trustees of the British Museum/Art Resource, NY.

in a united resistance: "We [are] all Indians [and must] say brother to one another, . . . otherwise we shall all be gone shortly." The chief's fate—murdered in 1643 at the behest of officials of the Massachusetts Bay Colony—and his plea foretold the course of North American history: The European invaders would advance, enslaved Africans would endure, and Indian peoples would decline.

# Rival Imperial Models: Spain, France, and Holland

In Mesoamerica and South America, the Spanish had seized the Indians' lands, converted many Indians to Catholicism, and forced them to mine gold and farm large estates. In the sparsely populated eastern regions of North America, by contrast, the newly arrived French and Dutch merchants created fur-trading colonies, and the native peoples retained their lands and political autonomy (Figure 2.1). Whatever the Europeans' colonial goals, Indian peoples diminished in numbers and those who remained soon sought to expel the invaders.

## New Spain: Colonization and Conversion

In their ceaseless quest for gold, Spanish explorers penetrated deep into the present-day United States. In the 1540s, Francisco Vásquez de Coronado searched in vain for the legendary seven golden cities of Cíbola; what he discovered was the Grand Canyon, the Pueblo peoples of the Southwest, and the grasslands of Kansas. Meanwhile, Hernán de Soto and a force of 600 Spaniards were cutting a bloody swath across what is now northern Florida and Alabama, battling the Apalachee and the Coosa peoples but finding no gold (Map 2.1).

By the 1560s, Spanish officials had given up the search for gold and now began to focus on defending their empire. Roving English "sea dogs" were plundering Spanish treasure ships, and French Protestants were settling Florida. Following King Philip II's order to cast out the Frenchmen "by the best means," Spanish troops massacred 300 members of the "evil Lutheran sect" near the St. Johns River. To safeguard the route of its treasure fleet, Spain established a fort at St. Augustine in 1565, making it the first permanent European settlement in the future United States. However, raids by the Calusas and Timucuas wiped out a dozen other Spanish military outposts in Florida, and Algonquians destroyed Jesuit religious missions further north along the Atlantic coast, including one near the Chesapeake Bay.

**FIGURE 2.1**

**Chronology of European Colonies in the Americas**

**MAP 2.1**

**New Spain Looks North, 1513–1610**

The search for gold drew Spanish explorers first to the Florida peninsula and then deep into the present-day United States. When the wide-ranging expeditions of Hernán de Soto and Francisco Vásquez de Coronado failed to find gold or flourishing Indian civilizations, authorities in New Spain limited settlements in the northern territories to St. Augustine in Florida (to protect the treasure fleet) and Santa Fe in the upper Rio Grande Valley.

**Franciscan Missions and Indian Revolts**

These military setbacks and the urgings of Franciscan friars prompted Spanish leaders to adopt a new policy of Christianizing the Indian peoples. The Comprehensive Orders for New Discoveries (1573) placed the task of pacification primarily in the hands of missionaries, not conquistadors. Over the next century, Franciscan friars set up missions among the Apalachees in Florida and the Pueblo peoples in the lands the Spanish named Nuevo México. The friars often learned Indian languages, but they also systematically attacked the natives' culture. And their methods were anything but peaceful. Protected by Spanish soldiers, missionaries whipped Indians who continued to practice **polygamy**, smashed the Indians' religious idols, and punished those who worshipped traditional gods. On one occasion, forty-seven "sorcerers" in Nuevo México were sold into slavery.

Religious conversion, cultural assimilation, and forced labor went hand in hand. The Franciscans encouraged the Indians to talk, cook, and dress like Spaniards. They ignored laws that protected the native peoples and allowed privileged Spanish landowners (*encomenderos*) to extract goods and forced labor. The missions themselves depended on Indian workers to grow crops and carry them to market.

Native Americans initially tolerated the Franciscans because they feared military reprisals and hoped to learn the friars' spiritual secrets. But when Christian prayers failed to protect their communities from European diseases, droughts, and raids by nomadic Apaches and Pawnees, many Pueblos returned to their ancestral gods. As an Indian explained, the people of the Zuni pueblo of Hawikuh refused to become "wet-heads" (as they called baptized Christians) "because with the water of baptism they would have to die." In 1598, the tense relations between Indians and Spaniards exploded into open warfare. An expedition of 500 Spanish soldiers and settlers led by Juan de Oñate seized corn and clothing from the Pueblo peoples and murdered or raped those who resisted. When Indians of the Acoma pueblo retaliated by killing 11 soldiers, the Spanish troops destroyed the pueblo and murdered 800 men, women, and children. Now faced with bitterly hostile native peoples, most settlers left New Mexico. In 1610, the Spanish returned, founded the town of Santa Fe, and reestablished the missions and forced-labor system. Over the next two generations, European diseases, forced tribute, and raids by nomadic Indians from the Great Plains reduced the Pueblos' population from 60,000 to just 17,000.

**Popé and the Uprising of 1680**    In 1680, in a carefully coordinated rebellion, the Indian shaman Popé and his followers killed more than 400 Spaniards and forced 1,500 colonists (along with 500 Pueblo and Apache slaves) to flee 300 miles to El Paso. At Popé's behest, the Pueblo peoples burned "the seeds which the Spaniards sowed" and planted "only maize and beans, which were the crops of their ancestors." Repudiating Christianity, they desecrated churches and rebuilt the sacred kivas, the round stone structures in which they had long worshipped. Like many later Native American rebels, Popé marched forward while looking backward, seeking to restore the traditional way of life.

It was not to be. A decade later, Spain reasserted control over most of the Pueblo peoples. The oppressed natives rebelled again in 1696 and were again subdued. Exhausted by a generation of warfare, the Pueblos agreed to a compromise that reduced the amount of forced labor. In return, they spoke Spanish, accepted a patrilineal kinship system, and helped defend Nuevo México against nomadic Apaches and Comanches. Some Pueblo women married Spaniards, and their offspring formed a bicultural mestizo population. But most Pueblos continued to practice the old ways, worshipping the Corn Mother as well as Jesus. As a Franciscan friar admitted, "They are still drawn more by their idolatry and infidelity than by the Christian doctrine." Spain had maintained its northern empire, but had done so without assimilating the Indian peoples.

Spain experienced similar disappointment in Florida. In the early 1700s, English raiders from Carolina destroyed most of the Franciscan missions and killed or enslaved most Catholic converts. These setbacks persuaded imperial officials not to settle the distant northern province of California. Santa Fe and St. Augustine stood alone as the northern outposts of Spain's American empire.

**Madonna on Buffalo Hide, c. 1675**

Even as the shaman Popé was successfully urging the Pueblo peoples to rebel against Spanish rule and revive traditional religious rituals, some Indians were embracing Christianity. A native artist painted the image of Christ's mother on tanned bison hide, and, in a sign of religious syncretism, gave the Virgin Mary the facial features of a Pueblo woman.    Elisabeth Waldo-Denzel Art Collection.

## New France: Fur Traders and Missionaries

Far to the northeast, the French were confronting the 250,000 native peoples of eastern Canada — Cree-speaking Montagnais; Algonquian-speaking Micmacs, Ottawas, and Ojibwas; and Iroquois-speaking Hurons. In the 1530s, Jacques Cartier had claimed the lands bordering the Gulf of St. Lawrence for France.

The first permanent settlement came in 1608, when Samuel de Champlain founded the fur-trading post of Quebec. But the colony languished until 1662, when King Louis XIV (r. 1643–1714) turned New France into a royal colony and subsidized the migration of indentured servants. French servants labored under contract for three years, received a salary, and could eventually lease a farm—far more generous terms than those for indentured servants in the English colonies.

Nonetheless, few people moved to New France, a cold and forbidding country "at the end of the world," as one migrant put it. Also, state policies discouraged migration. More intent on expanding France's boundaries in Europe than on encouraging overseas settlements, Louis XIV drafted tens of thousands of men into military service. The Catholic monarch also barred Huguenots (French Calvinist Protestants) from migrating to New France, fearing they might win converts and take control of the colony. Moreover, the French legal system gave peasants strong rights to their village lands, whereas migrants to New France faced an oppressive, aristocracy- and church-dominated feudal system. In the village of Saint Ours in Quebec's fertile Richelieu Valley, for example, peasants paid 45 percent of their wheat crop to nobles and the Catholic Church. By 1698, only 15,200 Europeans lived in New France, compared to 100,000 in England's North American colonies.

Lacking settlers to farm the land, New France developed as a vast enterprise for acquiring furs. Furs—mink, otter, and beaver—were in great demand in Europe to make felt hats and fur garments. To secure plush beaver pelts from the Hurons, who controlled trade north of the Great Lakes, Champlain provided them with manufactures. Selling pelts, an Indian told a French priest, "makes kettles, hatchets, swords, knives, bread." It also made guns, which Champlain sold to the Hurons to fight the expansionist-minded Five Nations of New York (see Voices from Abroad, "Samuel de Champlain: Going to War with the Hurons," p. 46). Searching for more furs, explorer Jacques Marquette reached the Mississippi River in present-day Wisconsin in 1673 and floated south on the river as far as Arkansas. Then, in 1681, Robert de La Salle traveled down the majestic river to the Gulf of Mexico, trading as he went. As a French priest noted with disgust, La Salle and his associates hoped "to buy all the Furs and Skins of the remotest Savages, who, as they thought, did not know their Value; and so enrich themselves in one single voyage." To honor Louis XIV, La Salle named the region Louisiana; by 1718, French merchants had founded the port of New Orleans where the Mississippi empties into the Gulf of Mexico.

**The Rise of the Iroquois**   Despite their small numbers, the French settlers had a disastrous impact. Unwittingly introducing European diseases, they triggered epidemics that killed from 25 to 90 percent of many Indian peoples. Moreover, by bartering guns for furs, the French (and Dutch) sparked a series of deadly wars. The Five Nations of the Iroquois were the prime aggressors. From their strategic location in central New York, the Iroquois obtained guns and goods from Dutch merchants at Albany and attacked other Indian peoples. Iroquois warriors moved east along the Mohawk River as far as New England and south along the Delaware and Susquehanna rivers as far as the Carolinas. They traveled north via Lake Champlain and the Richelieu River to Quebec. And they journeyed west via the Great Lakes to exploit the rich fur-bearing lands of the upper Mississippi River Valley.

The rise of the Iroquois was breathtakingly rapid. In 1600, the Iroquois numbered about 30,000 and lived in large towns of 500 to 2,000 inhabitants. Over the next two decades, they organized themselves into a confederation of five nations: Senecas, Cayugas, Onondagas, Oneidas, and Mohawks. Partly in response to a virulent smallpox epidemic in 1633, which cut their number by one-third, the Iroquois waged a series of devastating wars against the Hurons (1649), Neutrals (1651), Eries (1657), and Susquehannocks (1660)—all Iroquoian-speaking peoples. They razed villages and killed most of the men, cooking and eating their flesh to gain access to their spiritual powers. They took thousands of women and children captive and ritually adopted them into Iroquois lineages. The conquered Hurons simply ceased to exist as a distinct people; survivors trekked westward with displaced Algonquian peoples and formed a new tribe, the Wyandots.

**The Jesuit Missions**   Between 1625 and 1763, hundreds of French priests lived among the Huron, Iroquois, and other Great Lakes peoples. Most were members of the Society of Jesus (or Jesuits), a Catholic religious order founded to combat the Protestant Reformation. The Jesuits—unlike the Spanish Franciscan monks—came to understand and respect the Indians' values. One priest noted the Hurons' belief that "our souls have desires which are inborn and concealed, yet are made known by means of dreams." Many Indian peoples initially welcomed the French "Black Robes" as powerful spiritual beings with magical secrets, including the ability to forge iron. But when prayers to the Christian god did not protect them from disease, the Indians grew skeptical. A Peoria

## Samuel de Champlain
## Going to War with the Hurons

Samuel de Champlain is best known as the founder of Quebec, but he was primarily a soldier and an adventurer. After fighting in the religious wars within France, Champlain joined the Company of New France and set out to create an empire in North America. In 1603, he traveled down the St. Lawrence River as far as Quebec. He then lived for several years in the company's failing settlement in Maine and returned to Quebec in 1608. To ensure French access to the western fur trade, Champlain joined the Hurons in a raid against the Iroquois in 1609, which he later described in a book of his American adventures.

Pursuing our route, I met some two or three hundred savages, who were encamped in huts near a little island called St. Eloi. . . . We made a reconnaissance, and found that they were tribes of savages called Ochasteguins I [Hurons] and Algonquins, on their way to Quebec to assist us in exploring the territory of the Iroquois, with whom they are in deadly hostility. . . . [We joined with them and] went to the mouth of the River of the Iroquois [the Richelieu River, where it joins the St. Lawrence River], where we stayed two days, refreshing ourselves with good venison, birds, and fish, which the savages gave us.

In all their encampments, they have their Pilotois, or Ostemoy, a class of persons who play the part of soothsayers, in whom these people have faith. One of these builds a cabin, surrounds it with small pieces of wood and covers it with his robe: after it is built, he places himself inside, so as not to be seen at all, when he seizes and shakes one of the posts of his cabin, muttering some words between his teeth, by which he says he invokes the devil, who appears to him in the form of a stone, and tells them whether they will meet their enemies and kill many of them. . . . They frequently told me that the shaking of the cabin, which I saw, proceeded from the devil, who made it move, and not the man inside, although I could see the contrary. . . . They told me also that I should see fire come out from the top, which I did not see at all.

Now, as we began to approach within two or three days' journey of the abode of our enemies, we advanced only at night. . . . By day, they withdraw into the interior of the woods, where they rest, without straying off, neither making any noise, even for the sake of cooking, so as not to be noticed in case their enemies should by accident pass by. They make no fire, except in smoking, which amounts to almost nothing. They eat baked Indian meal, which they soak in water, when it becomes a kind of porridge. . . .

In order to ascertain what was to be the result of their undertaking, they often asked me if I had had a dream, and seen their enemies, to which I replied in the negative. . . . [Then one night] while sleeping, I dreamed that I saw our enemies, the Iroquois, drowning near a mountain, within sight. When I expressed a wish to help them, our allies, the savages, told me we must let them all die. . . . This, upon being related [to our allies], gave them so much confidence that they did not doubt any longer that good was to happen to them. . . .

[After our victory over the Iroquois] they took one of the prisoners, to whom they made a harangue, enumerating the cruelties which he and his men had already practiced toward them without any mercy, and that, in like manner, he ought to make up his mind to receive as much. They commanded him to sing, if he had courage, which he did; but it was a very sad song.

Meanwhile, our men kindled a fire; and, when it was well burning, they each took a brand, and burned this poor creature gradually, so as to make him suffer greater torment. Sometimes they stopped, and threw water on his back. Then they tore out his nails, and applied fire to the extremities of his fingers and private member. Afterwards, they flayed the top of his head, and had a kind of gum poured all hot upon it.

Source: Samuel de Champlain, *Voyages of Samuel de Champlain, 1604–1618,* ed. W. L. Grant (New York: Charles Scribner's Sons, 1907), 79–86.

### ANALYZING THE EVIDENCE

- **How do you account for the differences between the Hurons' and Champlain's perceptions of the soothsayer's hut? What do the differences suggest about their respective views of the world?**

- **Having read this passage, what would you say was the role of dreams in Huron culture?**

- **At the beginning of this passage, Champlain refers to the Indians as savages. Would the torture he describes help to explain that characterization? How might a modern anthropologist, sensitive to differences among cultures, explain the Indians' custom of torturing war captives?**

chief charged that a priest's "fables are good only in his own country; we have our own [beliefs], which do not make us die as his do." When a drought struck, Indians blamed the missionaries. "If you cannot make rain, they speak of nothing less than making away with you," lamented one Jesuit.

Whatever the limits of their powers, the French Jesuits did not exploit Indian labor. Moreover, they tried to keep brandy, which wreaked havoc among the natives, from becoming a bargaining chip in the French fur trade. And the Jesuits won converts by adapting Christian beliefs to the Indians' needs. In the 1690s, for example, the Jesuits introduced the cult of the Virgin Mary to the young women of the Illinois people. Its emphasis on chastity reinforced the existing Illinois belief that unmarried women were "masters of their own body."

Despite the Jesuits' efforts, however, the French fur trade brought cultural devastation. Epidemics killed tens of thousands of Indians, and pelt-hungry Iroquois warriors murdered thousands more. Nor did the Iroquois escape unscathed. Although they forged an alliance—the so-called Covenant Chain—with the English in New York in the 1670s, the French and their Algonquian allies invaded Iroquois lands in the 1690s, burned villages and cornfields, and killed many warriors. "Everywhere there was peril and everywhere mourning," recalled an oral Iroquois legend.

## New Netherland: Commerce

By every measure—wealth, trade, art, scholarship, naval prowess—the Dutch Republic was a powerhouse of seventeenth-century Europe. No small nation ever cast a bigger shadow. By 1600, Amsterdam had become the financial and commercial hub of northern Europe. Strategically located near the Baltic Sea and the mouth of the great Rhine River, the city boasted an enterprising class of merchants and entrepreneurs. Dutch financiers dominated the European banking, insurance, and textile industries; Dutch merchants owned more ships and employed more sailors than did the combined fleets of England, France, and Spain. Indeed, the Dutch managed much of the world's commerce. During their struggle for independence from Spain and Portugal (ruled by Spanish monarchs, 1580–1640), the Dutch seized Portuguese forts in Africa and Indonesia and sugar plantations in Brazil. These conquests gave the Dutch control of the Atlantic trade in slaves and sugar and the Indian Ocean commerce in East Indian spices and Chinese silks and ceramics (Map 2.2).

In 1609, Dutch merchants dispatched the English mariner Henry Hudson to locate a navigable route to the riches of the East Indies. What he found as he probed the rivers of northeast America was a fur bonanza. Following Hudson's exploration of the river that now bears his name, the merchants built Fort Orange (Albany) in 1614 to trade for furs with the Munsee and Iroquois Indians. Then, in 1621, the Dutch government chartered the West India Company, which founded the colony of New Netherland, set up New Amsterdam (on Manhattan Island) as its capital, and brought in farmers and artisans to make the enterprise self-sustaining. The new colony did not thrive. The population of the Dutch Republic was too small to support much emigration—just 1.5 million people, compared to 5 million in Britain and 20 million in France—and its migrants sought riches in Southeast Asia rather than fur-trading profits in America. To protect its colony from rival European nations, the West India Company granted huge estates along the Hudson River to wealthy Dutchmen who promised to populate them. But by 1664, New Netherland had only 5,000 residents, and fewer than half of them were Dutch.

Like New France, New Netherland flourished as a fur-trading enterprise. Trade with the powerful Iroquois, though rocky at first, rose by 1635 to 16,300 pelts, a tidy business at 8 guilders a pelt in Amsterdam. Dutch settlers had less respect for their Algonquian-speaking neighbors. They seized prime farming land from the Algonquian peoples and took over their trading network, which exchanged corn and wampum from Long Island for furs from Maine. In response, in 1643 the Algonquians launched attacks that nearly destroyed the colony. "Almost every place is abandoned," a settler lamented, "whilst the Indians daily threaten to overwhelm us." To defeat the Algonquians, the Dutch waged vicious warfare—maiming, burning, and killing hundreds of men, women, and children—and formed an alliance with the Mohawks, who were no less brutal. The grim progression of Euro-Indian relations—an uneasy welcome, followed by rising tensions and war—afflicted even the Dutch, who had few designs on Indian lands or on their "unregenerate" souls and were only looking to do business.

After the crippling Indian war, the West India Company ignored New Netherland, and expanded its profitable trade in African slaves and Brazilian sugar. In New Amsterdam, Governor Peter Stuyvesant ruled in an authoritarian fashion. He rejected the demands of English Puritans on Long Island for a representative system of government and alienated the colony's diverse

**MAP 2.2**

**The Eurasian Trade System and European Spheres of Influence, 1650**

Between 1550 and 1650, Spanish, Portuguese, and Dutch merchants took control of the maritime trade routes between Europe, and India, Indonesia, and China. They also created two new trading connections. The South Atlantic System carried slaves, sugar, and manufactured goods between Europe, Africa, and the valuable plantation settlements in Brazil and the Caribbean Islands. And a trans-Pacific trade carried Spanish American silver to China in exchange for silks, ceramics, and other manufactures. (To trace long-term changes in trade and empires, see Map 1.3 on p. 20 and Map 5.1 on p. 143.)

**New Amsterdam, c. 1640**

As the wooden palisade suggests, New Amsterdam was a fortlike trading post at the edge of a vast land populated by alien Indian peoples feared by the Dutch. The city was also a pale miniature imitation of Amsterdam, with its many canals. The first settlers built their houses in the Dutch style, with gable ends facing the street (note the two middle houses), and excavated a canal across lower Manhattan Island (New York City's Canal Street today).   Library of Congress.

Dutch, English, and Swedish residents. Consequently, the residents of New Netherland offered little resistance when England invaded the colony in 1664.

The Duke of York, the overlord of the new English colony of New York, initially ruled with a mild hand, allowing the Dutch residents to retain their property, legal system, and religious institutions. However, after the Dutch briefly recaptured the colony in 1673, the duke's governor, Edmund Andros, shut down the Dutch courts, imposed English law, and demanded an oath of allegiance. Thereafter, Dutch residents largely avoided the English courts and resisted cultural assimilation: They spoke Dutch, married among themselves, and worshipped at the Dutch Reformed Church. Once dominant over the Algonquians, the Dutch had themselves become a subject people. As an English resident noted in 1699, New York "seemed rather like a conquered Foreign Province held by the terror of a Garrison, than an English colony."

- What were the colonial goals of the Spanish, French, and Dutch? How successful were they in achieving those goals?
- What happened to the Five Nations of the Iroquois between 1600 and 1700? Were the Iroquois better off at the beginning of the period or at the end? Why?

# The English Arrive in the Chesapeake

Unlike the Dutch and the French, the English founded colonies in North America that attracted thousands of settlers. But that was not the plan of the London investors who financed an expedition to Virginia in 1607. They expected to establish a trading outpost, like those recently set up in India, Sierra Leone, and Morocco, to buy gold or other valuable goods from the native peoples. Not finding such goods, the adventurers gradually created a tobacco-growing economy based on the labor of indentured English servants and enslaved Africans.

## Settling the Tobacco Colonies

The first English ventures in North America were private enterprises, organized by minor nobles, merchants, and religious dissidents. Although the English monarch and ministry approved these ventures, they did not control them. Consequently, the English settlements, unlike the state-supervised Spanish and French colonies, enjoyed considerable autonomy and developed in markedly different ways.

The private ventures organized by the nobles were abject failures. In the 1580s, Sir Humphrey Gilbert's settlement in Newfoundland collapsed for lack of financing, and Sir Ferdinando Gorges's colony along the coast of Maine floundered in the harsh climate. Sir Walter Raleigh's three expeditions to North Carolina likewise ended in disaster when 117 settlers on Roanoke Island vanished without a trace. (Roanoke is still known as the "lost colony.")

**The Jamestown Settlement**  Merchants then took charge of English expansion. In 1606, King James I (r. 1603–1625) granted to the Virginia Company of London all the lands stretching from present-day North Carolina to southern New York. To honor the memory of Elizabeth I, the never-married "Virgin Queen," the company's directors named

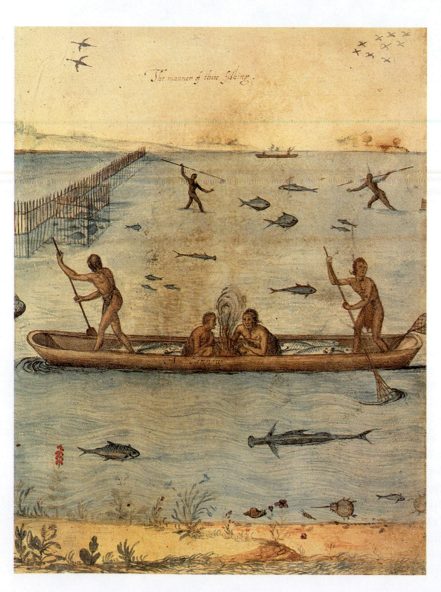

### Carolina Indians Fishing, 1585

Though maize was a mainstay of the Indian diet, native peoples along the Atlantic coast also harvested protein-rich fish, crabs, and oysters. In this watercolor by the English adventurer John White, Indians gather fish (in their "cannow," or dugout canoe) in the shallow waters of the Albemarle Sound, off present-day North Carolina. On the left, note the weir used both to catch fish and to store them live for later consumption.
© Trustees of the British Museum/Art Resource, NY.

the region Virginia (Map 2.3). For the Virginia Company, trade with the native population was the primary goal. So in 1607, it dispatched a group of male traders—no women, farmers, or ministers—who were employees of the company. They were to procure their own food and to ship gold, exotic crops, and Indian goods to England. Some traders were young gentlemen with personal ties to the company's shareholders: a bunch of "unruly Sparks, packed off by their Friends to escape worse Destinies at home." Others were cynical men looking for a quick profit: All they wanted, one of them said, was to "dig gold, refine gold, load gold."

But there was no gold, and the traders fared poorly in their new environment. Arriving in Virginia after an exhausting four-month voyage, they settled on a swampy peninsula, which they named Jamestown to honor the king. There the adventurers lacked access to fresh water, refused to plant crops, and quickly died off; only 38 of the 120 men were alive nine months later. Death rates remained high: By 1611, the Virginia Company had dispatched 1,200 settlers to Jamestown, but fewer than half remained alive. "Our men were destroyed with cruell diseases, as Swellings, Fluxes, Burning Fevers, and by warres," reported one of the settlement's leaders, "but for the most part they died of meere famine."

Powhatan, the paramount chief of the thirty tribal chiefdoms between the James and Potomac rivers, treated the English traders as potential allies and a source of valuable goods. The Powhatan chief spared the life of Captain John Smith, who had been taken captive by his brother Opechancanough, and provided the hungry English adventurers with corn. In return, he demanded that the English offer him tribute of "hatchets . . . bells, beads, and copper" as well as "two great guns" and become a dependent community within his chiefdom of Tsenacommacah. Subsequently, Powhatan arranged a marriage between his daughter Pocahontas and John Rolfe, an English colonist. But these tactics failed. Rolfe had imported tobacco seed from the West Indies and produced a crop of "pleasant, sweet, and strong Tobacco," which fetched a high price in England and spurred the migration of thousands of English settlers. Now Powhatan accused the English of coming "not to trade but to invade my people and possess my country."

To foster the flow of migrants, the Virginia Company allowed individual settlers to own land, granting 100 acres to every freeman and more to those who imported servants. The company also issued a "great Charter" that created a system of representative government: The House of Burgesses, first convened in 1619, could make laws and levy taxes, although the governor and the company council in England could veto its acts. By

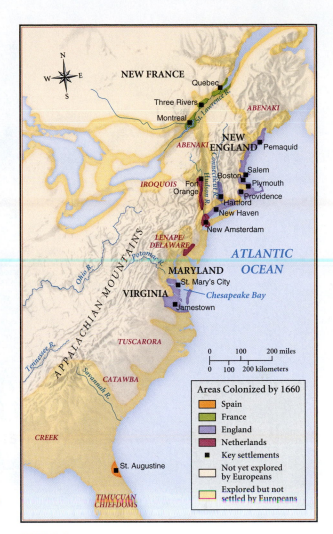

**MAP 2.3**

**Eastern North America, 1650**

By 1650, four European nations had permanent settlements along the eastern coast of North America, but only England had substantial numbers of settlers, some 25,000 in New England and another 15,000 in the Chesapeake region. Europeans also had a small presence in the interior, as French and Dutch fur traders carried European goods—and diseases—to distant tribes.

1622, land ownership, self-government, and a judicial system based on "the lawes of the realme of England" had attracted some 4,500 new recruits. To encourage a transition to a settler colony, the Virginia Company recruited dozens of "Maides young and uncorrupt to make wifes to the Inhabitants."

**The Indian War of 1622**  The influx of land-hungry migrants and conversion-minded ministers into Virginia sparked an all-out conflict with the Indian peoples. The struggle began with an assault led by Opechancanough [*O-pee-chan-KA-no*],

C. Smith taketh the King of Pamaunkee prisoner   1608

**John Smith and Opechancanough**

The powerful Indian warrior Opechancanough towers over English explorer John Smith in this engraving showing the two men in confrontation over English access to Indian food supplies in 1607. Never having seen an Indian, the engraver apparently relied on John White's watercolor of a Carolina Indian (see p. 40) in depicting the future chief of the Powhatan confederacy. The note at the bottom of the engraving is doubly mistaken, as it was Opechancanough (not Powhatan) who took Smith captive.   Library of Congress.

Powhatan's younger brother and successor. In 1607, Opechancanough had attacked some of the first English invaders, killing many of them and capturing Captain John Smith. Subsequently, the Indian chief "stood aloof" from the English settlers and "would not be drawn to any Treaty." In particular, he resisted English proposals to place Indian children in schools to be "brought upp in Christianytie." Upon becoming the main chief in 1621, Opechancanough told the leader of the Potomacks: "Before the end of two moons, there should not be an Englishman in all their Countries."

Opechancanough almost succeeded. In 1622, he coordinated a surprise attack by twelve Indian chiefdoms that killed 347 English settlers, nearly one-third of the white population. The English fought back by seizing the fields and food of those they now called "naked, tanned, deformed Savages," and declared "a perpetual war without peace or truce" that lasted for a decade. They sold captured warriors into slavery, "destroy[ing] them who sought to destroy us" and taking control of "their cultivated places."

Shocked by the Indian uprising, James I revoked the Virginia Company's charter and, in 1624, made Virginia a royal colony. Now the king and his ministers appointed the governor and a small advisory council, retaining the House of Burgesses but stipulating that the king's Privy Council (a committee of political advisers), must ratify all legislation. The king also decreed the legal establishment of the Church of England in the colony, which meant that residents had to pay taxes to support its clergy. These institutions—an appointed governor, an elected assembly, a formal legal system, and an established Anglican church—became the model for royal colonies throughout English America.

**Lord Baltimore Settles Catholics in Maryland**    A second tobacco-growing colony, with a very different set of institutions, developed in neighboring Maryland. King Charles I (r. 1625–1649), James's successor, was secretly sympathetic toward Catholicism. So in 1632, he granted the lands bordering the vast Chesapeake Bay to Catholic

Why was Fort West located here and what was its major function?

Note the location of the Indian villages. How do you explain their position in relation to the English settlements?

Use the scale of miles to estimate the distance between Jamestown and the outlying settlements (or Hundreds). What does this suggest about the nature of early Virginia society?

Note the lack of roads and the dependence of the settlements on river transportation. Why was river transport particularly important for the tobacco trade?

- ● English settlement
- ⚓ English fort
- ▲ Indian village
- ▨ Fresh-salt transition zone

## MAP 2.4

### River Plantations in Virginia, c. 1640

The first migrants settled in widely dispersed plantations along the James River, a settlement pattern promoted by the tobacco economy. From their riverfront plantations wealthy planter-merchants could easily load heavy hogsheads of tobacco onto oceangoing ships, and offload supplies that they then sold to smallholding planters. Consequently, few substantial towns or trading centers developed in the Chesapeake region.

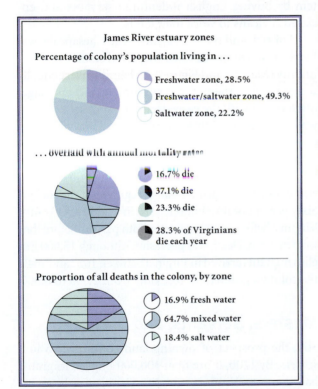

James River estuary zones

Percentage of colony's population living in . . .

- ◗ Freshwater zone, 28.5%
- ◗ Freshwater/saltwater zone, 49.3%
- ◖ Saltwater zone, 22.2%

. . . overlaid with annual mortality rates

- ◗ 16.7% die
- ◗ 37.1% die
- ◖ 23.3% die
- ▬ 28.3% of Virginians die each year

Proportion of all deaths in the colony, by zone

- ◗ 16.9% fresh water
- ◗ 64.7% mixed water
- ◖ 18.4% salt water

## FIGURE 2.2

### Environment and Death in Virginia, 1618–1624

Virginia was a deadly place for the English during the settlement's first decades. About 28 percent of the residents died each year; the colony grew only because of a constant stream of migrants. Most settlers lived along the James River estuary and, as Map 2.4 and this figure show, their location along the river determined their chances of survival. Those who lived in the zone with a mix of freshwater and saltwater had the highest death rates by far. The inflow of salt water during the dry summer months (when the river's freshwater volume decreased) trapped human and animal waste from upriver. That fecal matter contaminated the water and its fish, oysters, and crabs, leading to epidemics of typhoid and dysentery (which residents called "the bloody flux"). Source: Adapted from Carville V. Earle, "Environment, Disease, and Mortality in Early Virginia," in *The Chesapeake in the Seventeenth Century*, ed. Thad W. Tate and David L. Ammerman (New York: W.W. Norton, 1979), table 3.

aristocrat Cecilius Calvert, who carried the title Lord Baltimore. As the territorial lord (or proprietor) of Maryland, Baltimore could sell, lease, or give away the land as he pleased. He also had the authority to appoint public officials and to found churches.

Lord Baltimore wanted Maryland to become a refuge for Catholics, who were subject to persecution in England. In 1634, twenty gentlemen, mostly Catho-lics, and 200 artisans and laborers, mostly Protestants, established St. Mary's City at the point where the Po-tomac River flows into Chesapeake Bay. To minimize religious confrontations, the proprietor instructed the governor (his brother, Leonard Calvert) to allow "no scandall nor offence to be given to any of the Protes-tants" and to "cause All Acts of Romane Catholicque Religion to be done as privately as may be."

**Early Virginia House**

Many early English adventurers to the Chesapeake hoped to amass wealth quickly and return home just as quickly. Some, including Captain John Smith, hailed from Lincolnshire, and they built "mud and stud" houses similar to peasant dwellings in their home county. Much like this reconstruction at James Fort, these structures consisted of a frame of slender timbers covered with a mud and straw mix and a thatched roof. Housing remained a low priority for two generations, until the passage of time nurtured a "settler mentality" and—as evidenced by the construction by elite Virginians of brick houses—a commitment to life in the American "wilderness." Structure at Jamestown Settlement history museum re-created by archaeologists at Historic Jamestowne; photo courtesy Jamestown Settlement.

Maryland's population grew quickly because the Calverts imported many artisans and offered ample lands to wealthy migrants. But political conflict threatened the colony's stability. Disputing Baltimore's lordly powers, settlers demanded that he govern in accordance with the "Advice, Assent, and Approbation" of the freemen. They elected a representative assembly and insisted on the right to initiate legislation, which Baltimore grudgingly granted. Anti-Catholic agitation by Protestants also threatened the Calverts' religious goals. To protect his coreligionists, who remained a minority, Lord Baltimore persuaded the assembly to enact the Toleration Act (1649), which granted all Christians the right to follow their beliefs and hold church services.

In Maryland, as in Virginia, tobacco quickly became the main crop. Indians had long used tobacco as a medicine and a stimulant, and the English came to crave the nicotine it contained. By the 1620s, they were smoking, chewing, and snorting tobacco with abandon. James I initially condemned the plant as a "vile Weed" whose "black stinking fumes" were "baleful to the nose, harmful to the brain, and dangerous to the lungs." But the king's attitude changed as taxes on imported tobacco bolstered the royal treasury.

European demand for tobacco set off a forty-year economic boom in the Chesapeake region. "All our riches for the present do consist in tobacco," a planter remarked in 1630. Exports rose from 3 million pounds in 1640 to 10 million pounds in 1660. Initially, most plantations were small **freeholds**, owned and farmed by families or male partners. But after 1650, wealthy migrants from gentry or noble families established large estates along the coastal rivers. Coming primarily from southern England, where tenants and wage laborers farmed large manors, they copied that hierarchical system by buying English indentured servants and enslaved Africans to work their lands.

For rich and poor alike, life in the Chesapeake was harsh. The scarcity of towns deprived settlers of community (Map 2.4 and Figure 2.2). Families were equally scarce because there were few women, and marriages often ended with the early death of a spouse. Pregnant women were especially vulnerable to malaria, which was spread by the mosquitoes that flourished in the warm climate. Many mothers died after bearing a first or second child, so orphaned children (along with unmarried young men) formed a large segment of the society. Sixty percent of the children born in Middlesex County, Virginia, before 1680 lost one or both parents before they were thirteen. Death was pervasive. Although 15,000 English migrants arrived in Virginia between 1622 and 1640, the colony's population rose only from 2,000 to 8,000.

## Masters, Servants, and Slaves

Still, the prospect of owning land continued to lure settlers. By 1700, more than 100,000 English migrants had come to Virginia and Maryland, mostly as indentured servants. Shipping registers from the English port of Bristol reveal the backgrounds of 5,000 embarking servants. Three-quarters were young men, many of them displaced by the enclosure of their village lands (see Chapter 1). They came to Bristol searching for work; once there, merchants persuaded them to sign contracts to labor in America. The indenture contracts bound the men—and the quarter who were women—to work for a master for four or five years, after which they would be free to marry and work for themselves.

**Indentured Servitude** For merchants, servants were valuable cargo: Their contracts fetched high prices from Chesapeake (and West Indian) planters (Figure 2.3). For the plantation owners, indentured servants were an incredible bargain. During the tobacco boom, a male servant could produce five times his purchase price in a single year. To maximize their gains, most masters ruthlessly exploited servants, forcing them to work long hours, beating them without cause, and withholding permission to marry. If servants ran away or became pregnant, masters went to court to increase the term of their service. Female servants were especially vulnerable to abuse. A Virginia law of 1692 stated that "dissolute masters have gotten their maids with child; and yet claim the benefit of their service." Planters got rid of uncooperative servants by selling their contracts. In Virginia, an Englishman remarked in disgust that "servants were sold up and down like horses."

Most indentured servants in the Chesapeake colonies did not escape poverty. Half the men died before completing the term of their contract, and another quarter remained landless. Only one-quarter achieved their quest for property and respectability. Female servants generally fared better. Men had grown "very sensible of the Misfortune of Wanting Wives," so many propertied planters married female servants. Thus, by migrating to the Chesapeake, a few — very fortunate — men and women escaped a life of landless poverty.

**African Laborers** The first African workers in North America faced even worse prospects than indentured servants did. In 1619, John Rolfe noted that "a Dutch man of warre . . . sold us twenty Negars"—slaves originally shipped by the Portuguese from the port of Luanda in Angola. For a generation, the number of Africans remained small. About 400 Africans lived in the Chesapeake colonies in 1649, just 2 percent of the population. By 1670, that figure had reached 5 percent and, significantly, the growing numbers of Africans labored primarily for powerful men: members of the Virginia council and wealthy officers of county governments. Although most of these early African workers served their English masters for life, they were not legally enslaved. English **common law** did not acknowledge **chattel slavery**, the ownership of a human being as property. Also, some of these Africans came from the Kingdom of Kongo, where Portuguese missionaries had converted the king and some of his subjects to Christianity. Knowing the customs of Europeans, a few of these workers found ways to escape their bondage. Once free, some ambitious Africans even purchased slaves, bought the labor contracts of English servants, or married Englishwomen.

Social mobility for Africans ended in the 1660s with the collapse of the tobacco boom and the increasing political power of the gentry. Tobacco had once sold for 30 pence a pound; now it fetched less than one-tenth of that. The "low price of Tobacco requires it should bee made as cheap as possible," declared Virginia planter-politician Nicholas Spencer, and "blacks can make it cheaper than whites." As they imported more African workers, the English-born political elite grew more race-conscious. Increasingly, Spencer and other leading legislators distinguished English from African residents by color (white-black) rather than by religion (Christian-pagan). By 1671, the Virginia House of Burgesses had forbidden Africans to own guns or

**FIGURE 2.3**

**Chesapeake Whites: Workers, Dependents, and Indentured Servants, 1640–1700**

The Chesapeake's white population grew tenfold in the years after 1640, and changed significantly in character. As more women migrated to Virginia and Maryland and bore children, the percentage of the population who worked in the fields daily fell dramatically, from 75 percent to 46 percent. The proportion of indentured servants in the labor force likewise declined, from 30 percent to 10 percent.   Source: Adapted from Carville V. Earle, "Environment, Disease, and Mortality in Early Virginia," in *The Chesapeake in the Seventeenth Century*, ed. Thad W. Tate and David L. Ammerman (New York: W. W. Norton, 1979), table 3.

join the militia. It also barred them—"tho baptized and enjoying their own Freedom"—from owning English servants. Being black was increasingly a mark of inferior legal status, and slavery was fast becoming a permanent and hereditary condition. As an English clergyman observed, "These two words, Negro and Slave had by custom grown Homogeneous and convertible."

## Bacon's Rebellion

As the tobacco boom went bust, long-standing social conflicts flared into political turmoil. Falling tobacco prices signaled an imbalanced market; exports doubled between 1670 and 1700, outstripping European demand. But the falling prices also reflected Parliament's passage of Acts of Trade and Navigation in 1651, 1660, and 1663. The Navigation Acts allowed only English or colonial-owned ships to enter American ports, thereby excluding Dutch merchants, who paid the highest prices for tobacco, sold the best goods, and provided the cheapest shipping services. The legislation also required colonists to ship tobacco, sugar, and other "enumerated articles" only to England, where monarchs continually raised import duties, stifling market demand. By the 1670s, tobacco planters were getting just a penny a pound for their crop; one Virginian grumbled that the planters had become mere "beneficial Slaves" to England's merchants and monarch.

**The Seeds of Social Revolt**   Despite the low prices, Virginians continued to plant tobacco because there was no other cash crop. To preserve soil fertility without costly manuring, yeomen adopted a long-fallow system (rotating fields over a twenty-year cycle) and pocketed just enough income to scrape by. Worse off were newly freed indentured servants, who could not earn enough to buy tools and seed or to pay the fees required to exercise their right to 50 acres of land. Many ex-servants had to sell their labor again, either signing new indentures or becoming wage workers or tenant farmers.

Consequently, after 1670, a planter-merchant elite dominated the Chesapeake colonies. By securing grants from royal governors, they owned nearly half of all settled land in Virginia. Like the English gentry, the planter-merchants leased these large estates to the ever-more-numerous group of former servants. Other well-to-do planters became commercial middlemen and moneylenders, setting up stores that sold imported goods and charging commissions for shipping tobacco grown by smallholding farmers. In Maryland, well-connected Catholic planters were equally powerful; by

1720, one of those planters, Charles Carroll, owned 47,000 acres of land, which was farmed by scores of tenants, indentured servants, and slaves.

William Berkeley, governor of Virginia between 1642 and 1652 and again after 1660, set the stage for conflict. A corrupt man with equally corrupt allies, Berkeley bestowed large land grants on members of his council. The councilors promptly exempted these lands from taxation and appointed friends as local justices of the peace and county judges. To win support in the House of Burgesses, Berkeley bought off legislators with land grants and lucrative appointments as sheriffs and tax collectors. But social unrest erupted when the Burgesses took the vote away from landless freemen, who by now constituted half the adult white men. Property-holding yeomen retained their voting rights, but were angered by falling tobacco prices, political corruption, and "grievous taxations" that threatened the "utter ruin of us the poor commonalty." Berkeley and his gentry allies were living on borrowed time.

**Indians and Frontiersmen**   As the aggressive planter-entrepreneurs of Virginia confronted a multitude of free, young, and landless laborers, armed political conflict broke out during the 1670s. This struggle would leave a complex legacy: a decrease in class conflict among whites, violent campaigns against neighboring Indians, and increasing racial divisions because of massive imports of enslaved Africans.

An Indian conflict ignited the flame of social rebellion. In 1607, when the English intruded, 30,000 Native Americans resided in Virginia; by 1675, the native population had dwindled to only 3,500. By then, Europeans numbered some 38,000 and Africans another 2,500. Most Indians lived on treaty-guaranteed territory along the frontier, where poor freeholders and landless former servants now wanted to settle. They demanded that the natives be expelled or exterminated. Opposition to expansion came from wealthy river-valley planters, who wanted a ready supply of tenant farmers and wage laborers, and from Governor Berkeley and the planter-merchants, who traded with the Occaneechee Indians for beaver pelts and deerskins.

Fighting broke out late in 1675, when a vigilante band of Virginia militiamen murdered 30 Indians. Defying Berkeley's orders, a larger force of 1,000 militiamen then surrounded a fortified Susquehannock village and killed five chiefs who came out to negotiate. The Iroquoian-speaking Susquehannocks, recent migrants to the Chesapeake region from Pennsylvania, retaliated by attacking outlying plantations and killing 300 whites. In response, Berkeley proposed a defensive military strategy: a series of frontier forts to deter Indian intrusions. The settlers dismissed this scheme as a militarily useless plot by planter-merchants to impose high taxes and take "all our tobacco into their own hands."

**Nathaniel Bacon, Rebel Leader** | Nathaniel Bacon, a young, well-connected migrant from England, emerged as the leader of the rebels. Bacon held a position on the governor's council, but as the owner of a frontier estate, he differed with Berkeley on Indian policy. When the governor refused to grant him a military commission, Bacon mobilized his neighbors and attacked any Indians he could find. Condemning the frontiersmen as "rebels and mutineers," Berkeley expelled Bacon from the council and had him arrested. But Bacon's army forced the governor to release their leader and to hold legislative elections. The newly elected House of Burgesses enacted far-reaching political reforms that not only curbed the powers of the governor and council but also restored voting rights to landless freemen.

These much-needed reforms came too late. Bacon remained bitter toward Berkeley, and poor farmers and servants resented years of exploitation by wealthy planters, arrogant justices of the peace, and "wicked & pernicious Counsellors." As one yeoman rebel complained, "A poor man who has only his labour to maintain himself and his family pays as much [in taxes] as a man who has 20,000 acres." Backed by 400 armed men, Bacon issued a "Manifesto and Declaration of the People" that demanded the death or removal of the Indians and an end to the rule of wealthy "parasites." "All the power and sway is got into the hands of the rich," Bacon proclaimed as his army burned Jamestown to the ground and plundered the plantations of Berkeley's allies. When Bacon died suddenly of dysentery in October 1676, the governor took revenge, dispersing the rebel army, seizing the estates of well-to-do rebels, and hanging 23 men.

Bacon's Rebellion was a pivotal event in the history of the Chesapeake colonies. Thereafter, landed planters retained their dominance by curbing corruption and appointing ambitious yeomen to public office. They appeased yeomen and tenants by cutting taxes and expelling the Susquehannocks, Piscataways, and other Indian peoples from the region. Most important, planters forestalled another rebellion by poor whites by cutting the use of indentured servants and instead importing thousands of African laborers; the Burgesses explicitly legalized chattel slavery in 1705. Those fateful decisions

**Nathaniel Bacon**

Condemned as a rebel and a traitor in his own time, Nathaniel Bacon emerged in the late nineteenth century as a Southern hero, a harbinger of the Confederate rebels of 1860–1865. The Association for the Preservation of Virginia Antiquities, founded in 1888, commissioned this stained-glass window depicting Bacon in dual guises of a well-dressed gentleman and a rebel in body armor. Installing Bacon's portrait in a window of the Powder Magazine in Williamsburg (built by Governor Alexander Spotswood in 1715) explained a leading member of the association, would connect "present Virginia with her great and noble past" and commemorate those who shed their "blood for Virginia and the South." The Association for the Preservation of Virginia Antiquities.

committed subsequent generations of Americans to a social system based on racial exploitation.

- **What were the various systems of bound labor that took hold in the Chesapeake colonies? What accounts for their appearance?**

- **Compare the Indian uprising in Virginia in 1622 with Bacon's Rebellion in 1675. What were the consequences of each for Virginia's development?**

# Puritan New England

As people scrambled for wealth in the Chesapeake, Puritans created colonies in New England that had strong spiritual goals. Between 1620 and 1640, thousands of Puritans fled to America seeking land and religious freedom. By distributing land broadly, they built a society of independent farm families. And by establishing a "holy commonwealth," Puritans tried to preserve a "pure" Christian faith. Their "errand into the wilderness" gave a moral dimension to American history that survives today.

## The Puritan Migration

New England differed from other European colonies. Unruly male adventurers founded New Spain and Jamestown, and male traders dominated life in New France and New Netherland. By contrast, the leaders of the Plymouth and Massachusetts Bay colonies were pious Protestants, and the settlers included women and children as well as men (Map 2.5).

**The Pilgrims** The Pilgrims were religious separatists—Puritans who had left the Church of England. When King James I threatened to drive Puritans "out of the land, or else do worse," some Puritans chose to live among Dutch Calvinists in Holland. Subsequently, 35 of these exiles resolved to maintain their English identity by moving to America. Led by William Bradford and joined by 67 migrants from England, the Pilgrims sailed to America in 1620 aboard the *Mayflower* and settled in Plymouth, near Cape Cod in southeastern Massachusetts. Because they lacked a royal charter, their leader explained, we "combine[d] ourselves together into a civill body politick." This Mayflower Compact used the Puritans' self-governing religious congregation as the model for their political structure.

The first winter in Plymouth tested the Pilgrims. Of the 102 migrants who arrived in November, only half survived until spring. Thereafter Plymouth became a healthy and thriving community, as the cold climate inhibited the spread of mosquito-borne disease, and the Pilgrims' religious discipline encouraged a strong work ethic. Moreover, a smallpox epidemic in 1618 had killed most of the local Wampanoag people, so the migrants faced few external threats. The Pilgrims built solid houses and planted ample crops, and their numbers grew rapidly. By 1640, there were 3,000 settlers in Plymouth. To ensure political stability, they issued a written legal code that provided for representative self-government, broad political rights, property ownership, and religious freedom of conscience.

Meanwhile, England plunged deeper into religious turmoil. When King Charles I repudiated certain Protestant doctrines, including the role of grace in salvation, English Puritans, now powerful in Parliament, accused the king of "popery"—of holding Catholic beliefs. In 1629, Charles dissolved Parliament, claimed the authority to rule by "divine right," and raised money through royal edicts and the sale of monopolies. When Archbishop William Laud, whom Charles chose to head the Church of England, dismissed hundreds of dissident ministers, thousands of Puritan families fled to America.

**John Winthrop and Massachusetts Bay** The Puritan exodus began in 1630 with the departure of 900 migrants led by John Winthrop, a well-educated country squire who became the first governor of the Massachusetts Bay Colony. Calling England morally corrupt and "overburdened with people," Winthrop sought land for his children and a place in Christian history for his people. "We must consider that we shall be as a City upon a Hill," Winthrop told the migrants. "The eyes of all people are upon us." Like the Pilgrims, the Puritans envisioned a reformed Christian society with "authority in magistrates, liberty in people, purity in the church," as minister John Cotton put it. By creating a genuinely "New" England, they hoped to inspire religious reform throughout Christendom.

Winthrop and his associates governed the Massachusetts Bay Colony from the town of Boston. They transformed their **joint-stock corporation**, the General Court of shareholders, into a representative political system with a governor, council, and assembly. To ensure rule by the godly, the Puritans limited the right to vote and hold office to men who were church members. Rejecting the Plymouth Colony's policy of religious tolerance, the Massachusetts Bay Colony established Puritanism as the state-supported religion, barred other faiths from conducting services, and used the Bible as a legal guide. "Where there is no Law," they said, magistrates should rule "as near the law of God as they can." Over the next decade, about 10,000 Puritans migrated to the colony, along with 10,000 others fleeing hard times in England.

The New England Puritans sought to emulate the simplicity of the first Christians. Seeing bishops as "traitours unto God," they placed power in the congregation of members—hence the name *Congregationalist* for their churches. Inspired by John Calvin,

**MAP 2.5**

**The Puritan Migration to America, 1620–1640**

Forty-five thousand Puritans left England for America and the West Indies between 1620 and 1640, but they created religion-based colonies only in New England — at Plymouth, Massachusetts Bay, and Connecticut. Migrants from the three major centers of Puritanism in England — Yorkshire, East Anglia, and the West Country — commonly settled among those from their own region. Often they named American communities after their English towns of origin and tried to live as they had in Old England. For example, settlers from Rowley in Yorkshire transplanted their customary system of open-field agriculture to Rowley in Massachusetts Bay.

many Puritans embraced predestination, the doctrine that God chose (before their birth) only a few men and women for salvation. Church members often lived in great anxiety, worried that God had not placed them among these "elect." Some hoped for a conversion experience, the intense sensation of receiving God's grace and being "born again." Other Puritans relied on "prep-aration," the confidence in salvation that came from spiritual guidance by their ministers. Still others believed that they were God's chosen people, the new Israelites, and would be saved if they obeyed his laws (see Reading American Pictures, "Ideology and Architecture: Catholic Churches and Protestant Meetinghouses," p. 60).

## Ideology and Architecture: Catholic Churches and Protestant Meetinghouses

The Christian worship that Europeans brought to the Americas took distinct architectural forms, as these images attest. The photograph to the left shows the altar of the Spanish Catholic church at Mission San Xavier del Bac, in present-day Tucson, Arizona. The church was built between 1783 and 1797, mostly by Indian workers under the direction of Franciscan monks. The photograph to the right depicts the pulpit and pews of the Congregational Meeting House in Sandown, New Hampshire, constructed in 1773 and 1774 by house carpenters hired by Puritan migrants from Massachusetts.

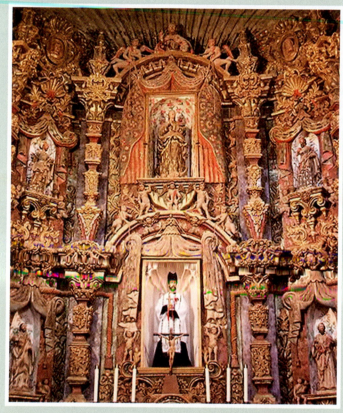

**Altar of the Spanish Catholic Mission San Xavier del Bac.** Geremia.

**Pulpit of the Congregational Meeting House, Sandown, New Hampshire.** Image copyright William Owens www.wwowens.com.

### ANALYZING THE EVIDENCE

- How would you describe the look or the feel of each house of worship? What is the central visual focus of each image? Why is that important?

- The great English Puritan poet John Milton argued that Catholics made God "earthy and fleshy because they could not make themselves heavenly and spiritual." Are there any features of the altar of the Mission San Xavier del Bac that give credence to Milton's claim?

- Puritans were sometimes called "people of the Word" because of their reliance on the Bible and their attention to carefully argued sermons. How does the interior design of the New Hampshire meetinghouse express their religious outlook?

- The purpose of the Mission San Xavier del Bac was to convert the Tohono O'odham (Papago) Indians to Catholicism. Would the altar aid that effort? If so, how? Protestant clergy in New England likewise sought to convert native peoples to their religion. Given Puritan practices and doctrines, how might they approach that task and what role, if any, would the meetinghouse play?

**Roger Williams and Rhode Island** To maintain God's favor, the Massachusetts Bay magistrates purged their society of religious dissidents. One target was Roger Williams, the Puritan minister in Salem, a coastal town north of Boston. Williams opposed the decision to establish Congregationalism as the official religion and praised the Pilgrims' separation of church and state. He advocated toleration, arguing that political magistrates had authority over only the "bodies, goods, and outward estates of men," not their spiritual lives. Williams also questioned the Puritans' seizure of Indian lands. The magistrates banished him from the colony in 1636.

Williams and his followers settled 50 miles south of Boston, founding the town of Providence on land purchased from the Narragansett Indians. Other religious dissidents settled nearby at Portsmouth and Newport. In 1644, these settlers obtained a corporate charter from Parliament for a new colony—Rhode Island—with full authority to rule themselves. In Rhode Island, as in Plymouth, there was no legally established church, and individuals could worship God as they pleased.

**Anne Hutchinson** The Massachusetts Bay magistrates saw a second threat to their authority in Anne Hutchinson. The wife of a merchant and mother of seven, Hutchinson held weekly prayer meetings for women and accused various Boston clergymen of placing undue emphasis on good behavior. Like Martin Luther, Hutchinson denied that salvation could be earned through good deeds: There was no "covenant of works"; God bestowed salvation only through the "covenant of grace." Hutchinson likewise declared that God "revealed" divine truth directly to individual believers, a controversial doctrine that the Puritan magistrates denounced as heretical.

The magistrates also resented Hutchinson because of her sex. Like other Christians, Puritans believed that both men and women could be saved. But gender equality stopped there. Women were inferior to men in earthly affairs, said leading Puritan divines, who told married women: "Thy desires shall bee subject to thy husband, and he shall rule over thee." Puritan women could not be ministers or lay preachers, nor could they vote in church affairs. As Pilgrim minister John Robinson put it, women "are debarred by their sex from ordinary prophesying, and from any other dealing in the church wherein they take authority over the man." In 1637, the magistrates accused Hutchinson of teaching that inward grace freed an individual from the rules of the church and found her guilty of holding heretical views.

Banished, she followed Roger Williams into exile in Rhode Island.

Such coercive policies and a quest for better farming land prompted some Puritans to move to the Connecticut River Valley. In 1636, pastor Thomas Hooker and his congregation established the town of Hartford, and other Puritans settled along the river at Wethersfield and Windsor. In 1660, they secured a charter from King Charles II (r. 1660–1685) for the self-governing colony of Connecticut. Like Massachusetts Bay, Connecticut had a legally established church and an elected governor and assembly; however, it granted voting rights to most property-owning men, not just to church members as in the original Puritan colony.

**The Puritan Revolution in England** Meanwhile, a religious civil war had engulfed England. Archbishop Laud had imposed the Church of England prayer book on Presbyterian Scotland in 1637; five years later, a rebel Scottish army invaded England. Thousands of English Puritans (and hundreds of American Puritans) joined the Scots, demanding religious reform and parliamentary power. After years of civil war, parliamentary forces led by Oliver Cromwell emerged victorious. In 1649, Parliament executed King Charles I, proclaimed a republican commonwealth, and banished bishops and elaborate rituals from the Church of England.

The Puritan triumph in England was short-lived. Popular support for the Commonwealth ebbed after Cromwell took dictatorial control in 1653. Following his death in 1658, moderate Protestants and a resurgent aristocracy restored the monarchy and the hierarchy of bishops. For many Puritans, Charles II's accession to the throne in 1660 represented the coming of Antichrist, the false prophesying "beast" described in the biblical Book of Revelation.

For the Puritans in America, the restoration of the monarchy began a new phase of their "errand into the wilderness." They had come to New England to preserve the "pure" Christian church, expecting to return to Europe in triumph. When the failure of the English Revolution dashed that sacred mission, ministers exhorted congregations to create a godly republican society in America. The Puritan colonies now stood as outposts of Calvinism and the Atlantic republican tradition.

## Puritanism and Witchcraft

Like Native Americans, Puritans believed that the physical world was full of supernatural forces. Devout Christians saw signs of God's (or Satan's) power in blazing

**The Reverend Increase Mather, 1688**

Increase Mather (the father of Cotton Mather) was an influential Massachusetts minister; the president of Harvard College (1692–1701); and, as the portrait suggests, a prolific author (of 125 sermons and books). Jan van der Spriett executed this painting in London, where Mather persuaded King William to approve the Massachusetts Charter of 1692 and thereby preserved Puritan power in the colony. In *Cases of Conscience Concerning Evil Spirits* (1693), Mather criticized the use of "spectral evidence" in the Salem witchcraft trials but, to uphold the colony's fragile new government, defended the verdict of the judges and execution of the alleged witches.   Bridgeman Art Library Ltd.

The PROTESTANT
**ALMANACK,**
For the Year 1700.

The Creation of the World ——————— 5706
The Incarnation of Jesus Christ —————— 1700
*England* received the Christian Faith ———— 1510
*Martin Luther* wrote against the Pope ———— 184
Our first Deliverance from Popery by K. *Edward* VI.—152
Our second deliverance from Popery by Q. *Elizabeth*—141
The horrid design of the Gun-Powder Plot——— 95
The Burning of the City of *London* —————— 34
Our Third Deliverance from Popery, by K.*Will.* & Q.*Mary* 12

Being the
**BISSEXTILE or LEAP-YEAR.**
WHEREIN
The Bloody Aspects, Fatal Oppositions, Diabolical Conjunctions, and Pernicious Revolutions of the Papacy against the Lord and his Anointed, are described.

With the Change of the Moon, some probable Conjectures of the Weather, the Eclipses, the Moons place in the Zodiack, and an account of some principal Martyrs in each Month.

Calculated according to Art, for the Meridian of *Babylon*, where the Pope is elevated a hundred and fifty degrees above all Right and Religion; above Kings, Canons, Councils, Conscience, and every thing therein called God. 2 *Theff.* 2. And may without sensible Errour, indifferently serve the whole Papacy.

By *Philoprotes*, a well-willer to the Mathematicks.

*London,* Printed by *John Richardson* for the Company of STATIONERS. 1700.

**The Protestant Almanack, 1700**

The conflict between Protestants and Catholics took many forms. To reinforce the religious identity of English Protestants, a writer using the pseudonym "Philopretes" published this almanac that charted not only the passage of the seasons (and the influence of the pagan signs of the "Zodiack") but also the "Pernicious Revolutions of the Papacy against the Lord and his Anointed."   By permission of the Syndics of Cambridge University Library.

stars, birth defects, and other unusual events. Noting after a storm that the houses of many ministers "had been smitten with Lightning," Cotton Mather, a prominent Puritan theologian, wondered "what the meaning of God should be in it."

Belief in "forces" and "spirits" stemmed in part from Christian teachings—the Catholic belief in miracles, for example, and the Protestant faith in grace. It also reflected pagan influence. Samuel Sewall, a well-educated Puritan merchant and judge, fended off evil spirits by driving a metal pin into his new house. And thousands of farmers—Puritan saints as well as non–church members—followed pagan astrological charts printed in almanacs to determine the best times to plant crops, marry off their children, and take other important actions.

Zealous Puritan ministers and laypeople attacked these practices as "superstition" and condemned "cunning" individuals who claimed powers as healers or prophets. Indeed, many believed such conjurers were Satan's "wizards" or "witches." People in the town of Andover "were much addicted to sorcery," claimed one observer, and "there were forty men in it that could raise

the Devil as well as any astrologer." Between 1647 and 1662, civil authorities in New England hanged 14 people for witchcraft, most of them older women accused of being "double-tongued" or of having "an unruly spirit."

The most dramatic episode of witch-hunting occurred in Salem in 1692. Several girls who had experienced strange seizures accused neighbors of bewitching them. When judges at the accused witches' trials allowed the use of "spectral" evidence—visions of evil beings and marks seen only by the girls—the accusations spun out of control. Eventually, Massachusetts Bay authorities tried 175 people for witchcraft and executed 19 of them. The causes of this mass hysteria were complex and are still debated. Some historians point to group rivalries: Many accusers were the daughters or servants of poor farmers, whereas many of the alleged witches were wealthier church members or their friends. Because 18 of those put to death were women, other historians see the episode as part of a broader Puritan effort to subordinate women. Still others focus on political instability in Massachusetts Bay in the early 1690s and on fears raised by recent Indian attacks in nearby Maine, which had killed the parents of some of the young accusers. It is likely that all of these causes played some role in the executions.

Whatever the cause, the Salem episode marked a major turning point. Shaken by the number of deaths, government officials now discouraged legal prosecutions for witchcraft. Moreover, many influential people embraced the outlook of the European Enlightenment, a major intellectual movement that began around 1675 and promoted a rational, scientific view of the world. Increasingly, educated men and women explained strange happenings and sudden deaths by reference to "natural causes," not witchcraft. Unlike Cotton Mather (1663–1728), who believed that lightning was a supernatural sign, Benjamin Franklin (1706–1790) and other well-read men of his generation would investigate it as a natural phenomenon.

## A Yeoman Society, 1630–1700

In building their communities, New England Puritans consciously rejected the feudal practices of English society. Many Puritans came from middling families in East Anglia, a region of pasture lands and few manors, and had no desire to live as tenants of wealthy aristocrats or submit to oppressive taxation by a distant government. They had "escaped out of the pollutions of the world," the settlers of Watertown in Massachu-

**An Affluent Puritan Woman of the 1670s**

This well-known painting of Elizabeth Clarke Freake and her daughter, Mary (the youngest of her eight children), is perhaps the finest portrait we have of a seventeenth-century American. The unknown artist gives most attention to the finery of Mrs. Freake's silk dress, with its elaborate lace collar and its red underskirt embroidered with gold and silver. The painting testifies to the prosperity of Boston's Puritan merchants and their embrace of a cosmopolitan outlook. As minister Samuel Torrey complained at the time, "a spirit of worldliness, a spirit of sensuality" had asserted itself among the younger generation of Puritans.   Worcester Art Museum.

setts Bay declared, and vowed to live "close togither" in self-governing communities. Accordingly, the General Courts of Massachusetts Bay and Connecticut bestowed land on groups of settlers, or **proprietors**, who then distributed it among the male heads of families.

Widespread ownership of land did not mean equality of wealth or status. "God had Ordained different degrees and orders of men," proclaimed Boston merchant John Saffin, "some to be Masters and Commanders, others to be Subjects, and to be commanded." Town proprietors normally awarded the largest plots to men of high social status who often became selectmen and justices of the peace. However, all families received some land, and most adult men had a vote in the **town meeting**, the main institution of local government (Map 2.6).

**Andover, 1650–1692**
Nucleated to dispersed in fifty years

**New houses**
- ● By 1650
- ● By 1692
- ▲ Meeting House

0    2    4 miles

(after Vaughn)

The key to the right indicates that a central purpose of this map is to show the geographic distribution of nucleated and dispersed villages. Why are there so many nucleated towns in the Connecticut River Valley and so many dispersed settlements in eastern Massachusetts?

0    10    20 miles
0    10    20 kilometers

**Village types**
- ● Nucleated
- ◉ Initially nucleated, dispersed by 1700
- ○ Dispersed
- ▬ Continuous English settlements by 1700
- — Roads
- — Field boundaries

The map of Andover shows how an originally nucleated settlement changed over time into a dispersed town. New farms tended to be located farther and farther from the meeting house and town center, represented by a triangle on the town plan.

*ATLANTIC OCEAN*

Hampton
Haverhill
Ipswich
Andover
Manchester
Greenfield    Northfield
Deerfield    Sunderland
Hatfield
Salem
M A S S A C H U S E T T S
Newton
Hadley
Sudbury
Worcester
Dedham
Westfield
Oxford
Medfield
Plymouth
Woodstock
Windsor    Hartford
C O N N E C T I C U T
RHODE ISLAND
Farmington    Wethersfield
Barnstable
Waterbury
Wethersfield in 1640 is an example of a nucleated village, with house lots clustered around the meeting house and fields arranged in geometric patterns in the surrounding countryside.
Wallingford
Newtown    Guilford
Derby

BERKSHIRE MOUNTAINS
Connecticut River
Housatonic River

*Long Island*

The field boundaries in Wethersfield indicate that the land is flat in the Connecticut River Valley. In contrast, the pattern of roads and paths in Andover suggests a hilly topography. These uplands gave the Merrimack River a strong current and many rapids, which were later harnessed for industrial development. (See Map 9.1 on page 277.)

(after Wood)

0    0.5    1 mile

**Wethersfield, 1640**

Meeting House

(after Andrews)

## MAP 2.6

## Settlement Patterns in New England Towns, 1630–1700

Initially, most Puritan towns were compact: Regardless of the local topography—hills or plains—families lived close to one another in village centers and traveled daily to work in the surrounding fields. This 1640 map of Wethersfield, Connecticut, a town situated on the broad plains of the Connecticut River Valley, shows this pattern clearly. The first settlers in Andover, Massachusetts, also chose to live in the village center. However, the rugged topography of eastern Massachusetts encouraged the townspeople to disperse. By 1692 (as the varied location of new houses shows), many Andover residents were living on farms distant from the village center.

In this society of independent households and self-governing communities, ordinary farmers had much more political power than Chesapeake yeomen and European peasants did. Although Nathaniel Fish was one of the poorest men in the town of Barnstable—he owned just a two-room cottage, 8 acres of land, an ox, and a cow—he was a voting member of the town meeting. Each year, Fish and other Barnstable farmers levied taxes; enacted ordinances governing fencing, road building, and the use of common fields; and chose the selectmen who managed town affairs. The farmers also selected the town's representatives to the General Court, which gradually displaced the governor as the center of political authority. For Fish and thousands of other ordinary settlers, New England had proved to be a new world of opportunity.

- Why did the Puritans of Massachusetts Bay create an established church and persecute dissenters when they had fled England to escape those things?

- What was the social and political structure of the New England colonies? Why did they develop in that fashion?

# The Eastern Indians' New World

Native Americans also lived in a new world, but for them, it was a bleak and dangerous place. In New England, an observer reported, so many Indians were stricken in a smallpox epidemic that they were "not able to help one another, no not to make a fire nor fetch a little water to drink, nor any to bury the dead." Those Indians who survived lacked the numbers to retain their ancestral lands. However, some Indian peoples, most prominently the Iroquois, used European weapons to resist the intruders and dominate other tribes. Other native peoples retreated into the mountains or moved westward to preserve their traditional cultures.

## Puritans and Pequots

As the Puritans embarked for New England, they pondered the morality of acquiring Native American lands. "By what right or warrant can we enter into the land of the Savages?" they asked themselves. Responding to such concerns, John Winthrop detected God's hand in a recent smallpox epidemic: "If God were not pleased with our inheriting these parts," he asked, "why doth he still make roome for us by diminishing them as we increase?" Citing the Book of Genesis, the Massachusetts Bay magistrates argued that the Indians had not "subdued" their land and therefore had no "just right" to it. Decades later, political philosopher John Locke would offer the same justification.

Believing they were God's chosen people, the Puritans often treated Native Americans with a brutality equal to that of the Spanish conquistadors and Nathaniel Bacon's frontiersmen. When Pequot warriors resisted English encroachment onto their Connecticut River Valley lands in 1636, a Puritan militia attacked a Pequot village and massacred some 500 men, women, and children. "God laughed at the Enemies of his People," one soldier boasted, "filling the Place with Dead Bodies."

English Puritans saw the Indians as "savages" who were culturally, though not racially, inferior. To their minds, Europeans and Native Americans were genetically the same; sin, not race, accounted for their degeneracy. "Probably the devil" delivered these "miserable savages" to America, Cotton Mather suggested, "in hopes that the gospel of the Lord Jesus Christ would never come here." To convert Indians to Christianity, Puritan minister John Eliot translated the Bible into Algonquian. Only a few Native Americans became full members of Puritan congregations, because of the rigorous admission standards. However, Eliot and other ministers turned fourteen Indian villages, such as Natick (Massachusetts) and Maanexit (Connecticut), into **praying towns**. Like the Franciscan missions in New Mexico, these towns were intended as intensely Christian communities. By 1670, more than 1,000 Indians lived in these settlements, losing their independence and traditional culture but, by infusing their churches with traditional spiritual beliefs, creating new native forms of Christianity.

## Metacom's War of 1675–1676

By the 1670s, Europeans in New England outnumbered Indians by three to one. The English population had multiplied to 55,000, while native peoples had diminished—from an estimated 120,000 in 1570 to 70,000 in 1620, to barely 16,000. To the Wampanoag leader Metacom (also known as King Philip) the prospects for coexistence looked dim. When his people copied English ways by raising hogs and selling pork in Boston, Puritan officials accused them of selling at "an under rate" and restricted their trade. When Indians killed wandering hogs that devastated their cornfields,

**Metacom (King Philip), Chief of the Wampanoags**
The Indian War of 1675–1676 left an indelible mark on the history of New England. This painting from the 1850s, done on semitransparent cloth and lit from behind for effect, was used by traveling performers to tell the story of King Philip's War. Notice that Metacom is pictured not as a savage but as a dignified man. No longer in danger of Indian attack, nineteenth-century whites in New England adopted a romanticized version of their region's often brutal history. © Shelburne Museum, Shelburne Vermont.

authorities prosecuted them for violating English property rights (see Comparing American Voices, "The Causes of the War of 1675–1676," pp. 68–69).

Like Opechancanough in Virginia and Popé in New Mexico, Metacom concluded that the Europeans had to be expelled. In 1675, the Wampanoags' leader forged a military alliance with the Narragansetts and Nipmucks and attacked white settlements throughout New England. Almost every day, settler William Harris fearfully reported, he heard new reports of the Indians' "burneing houses, takeing cattell, killing men & women & Children: & carrying others captive." Bitter fighting continued into 1676, as the Indians exploited

their strategic control of large tracts of territory and most of the rivers. It ended only when the Indian warriors ran short of gunpowder and the Massachusetts Bay government hired Mohegan and Mohawk warriors, who killed Metacom.

Metacom's War of 1675–1676 (which English settlers also called King Philip's War) was a deadly affair. Indians destroyed one-fifth of the English towns in Massachusetts and Rhode Island and killed 1,000 settlers, nearly 5 percent of the adult population. The Puritan experiment hung in the balance. Had "the Indeans not been divided," remarked one settler, "they might have forced us [to evacuate] to Som Islands: & there to have planted a little Corne, & fished for our liveings." But the natives' losses—from famine and disease, death in battle, and sale into slavery—were much larger: About 4,500 Indians died, one-quarter of an already-diminished population. Many of the surviving Wampanoag, Narragansett, and Nipmuck peoples migrated into the backcountry, where they intermarried with Algonquian tribes allied to the French. Over the next century, these displaced Indian peoples would take their revenge, joining with French Catholics to attack their Puritan enemies.

## The Destructive Impact of the Fur Trade

As English towns filled the river valleys along the Atlantic coast, the Indians in the great forested areas beyond the Appalachian Mountains remained independent. Yet the distant Indian peoples—the Iroquois, Ottawas, Crees, Illinois, and many others—felt the European presence through the fur trade. As they bargained for woolen blankets, iron cookware, knives, and guns, Indians avoided the French at Montreal, who demanded two beaver skins for a woolen blanket. Instead, they dealt with the Dutch and English merchants at Albany, who asked for only one pelt and could be played off against one another. "They are marvailous subtle in their bargains to save a penny," an English trader complained. "They will beate all markets and try all places . . . to save six pence." Still, because the Indians did not know the value of their pelts in Europe, they rarely secured the highest possible price.

Nor could they stop European diseases, guns, and rum from sapping the vitality of their society. In South Carolina, a smallpox epidemic killed nearly half of the Catawbas, and "strong spirits" took a toll among the survivors: "Many of our people has Lately Died by

**The Hurons' Feast of the Dead**

Hurons buried their dead in temporary raised tombs so they could easily care for their spirits. When they moved their villages in search of fertile soil and better hunting, the Hurons held a Feast of the Dead and reburied the bones of their own deceased and often bones from other villages in a common pit lined with beaver robes. This solemn ceremony united living as well as dead clan members, strengthening the bonds of the Huron Confederacy. It also was believed to release the spirits of the dead, allowing them to travel to the land where the first Huron, Aataentsic, fell from the sky, "made earth and man," and lived with her son and assistant, Iouskeha.   Library of Congress.

the Effects of that Strong Drink," a Catawba lamented. Most native societies also lost their economic independence. As they exchanged furs for European-made iron utensils and woolen blankets, Indians neglected their traditional artisan skills, making fewer flint hoes, clay pots, and skin garments. "Every necessity of life we must have from the white people," a Cherokee chief complained. Religious autonomy vanished as well. When French missionaries won converts among the Hurons, Iroquois, and Illinois, they divided Indian communities into hostile religious factions.

Likewise, constant warfare for furs altered the dynamics of tribal politics by shifting power from cautious elders to headstrong young warriors. The sachems (chiefs), a group of young Seneca warriors said scornfully, "were a parcell of Old People who say much but who Mean or Act very little." The status of Indian women changed in especially complex ways. Traditionally, eastern woodland women had a voice in political councils because they were the chief providers of food and handcrafted goods. As a French Jesuit noted of the Iroquois, "The women are always the first to deliberate. . . . They hold their councils apart and . . . advise the chiefs . . . so that the latter may deliberate on them in their turn." The disruption of farming by warfare and the influx of European goods undermined women's economic power. Yet, paradoxically, among victorious warring tribes such as the Iroquois, the influence of women probably increased in other respects, because they managed the cultural assimilation of hundreds of captives.

There is no doubt that the sheer extent of the fur industry—the slaughter of hundreds of thousands of beaver, deer, otter, and other animals—profoundly altered the environment. As early as the 1630s, a French Jesuit worried that the Montagnais people, who lived north of the St. Lawrence, were killing so many beaver that they would "exterminate the species in this Region, as has happened among the Hurons." As the animal populations died off, streams ran faster (there were fewer beaver dams) and the underbrush grew denser (there were fewer deer to trim the vegetation). The native environment, as well as its animals and peoples, were now part of a new American world of relentless exploitation and little civility.

- **Compare the causes of the uprisings led by Popé in New Mexico and Metacom in New England. Which rebellion was more successful? Why?**

- **What were the major social and environmental changes that made America a new world for Indians?**

Thus I have given you, I think, the Substance of the Arguments ... both sides of that great and important Quest...

# The Causes of the War of 1675–1676

The causes of — and responsibility for — every American war are much debated, and the war of 1675–1676 between Puritans and Native Americans is no exception. The English settlers called it King Philip's War, suggesting that the Wampanoag chief Metacom (King Philip) instigated it. Was that the case? We have no firsthand Indian accounts of its origins, but three English accounts offer different versions of events. Given the variation among the accounts and their fragmentary character, how can historians reconstruct what "really happened"? Moreover, should the story be told from the Indian or the English point of view?

## John Easton

### A Relacion of the Indyan Warre

John Easton was the deputy governor of Rhode Island and a Quaker. Like many Quakers, Easton was a pacifist and tried to prevent the war. He wrote this "Relacion" shortly after the conflict ended.

In [January 1675], an Indian was found dead; and by a coroner inquest of Plymouth Colony judged murdered. . . . The dead Indian was called Sassamon, and a Christian that could read and write. . . .

The report came that . . . three Indians had confessed and accused Philip [of employing them to kill Sassamon, and that consequently] . . . the English would hang Philip. So the Indians were afraid, and reported that . . . Philip [believed that the English] . . . might kill him to have his land. . . . So Philip kept his men in arms.

Plymouth governor [Josiah Winslow] required him to disband his men, and informed him his jealousy [his worry about land seizure] was false. Philip answered he would do no harm, and thanked the Governor for his information. The three Indians were hung [on June 8, 1675]. . . . And it was reported [that] Sassamon, before his death had informed [the English] of the Indian plot, and that if the Indians knew it they would kill him, and that the heathen might destroy the English for their wickedness as God had permitted the heathen to destroy the Israelites of old.

So the English were afraid and Philip was afraid and both increased in arms; but for forty years' time reports and jealousies of war had been very frequent that we did not think that now a war was breaking forth. But about a week before it did we had cause to think it would; then to endeavor to prevent it, we sent a man to Philip. . . .

He called his council and agreed to come to us; [Philip] came himself, unarmed, and about forty of his men, armed. Then five of us went over [to speak to the Indians]. Three were magistrates. We sat very friendly together [June 14–18]. We told him our business was to endeavor that they might not . . . do wrong. They said that was well; they had done no wrong; the English wronged them. We said we knew the English said that the Indians wronged them, and the Indians said the English wronged them, but our desire was the quarrel might rightly be decided in the best way, and not as dogs decide their quarrels.

The Indians owned that fighting was the worst way; then they propounded how right might take place; we said by arbitration. They said all English agreed against them; and so by arbitration they had had much wrong, many square miles of land so taken from them, for the English would have English arbitrators. . . .

Another grievance [of the Indians]: the English cattle and horses still increased [and that] . . . they could not keep their corn from being spoiled [by the English livestock]. . . .

So we departed without any discourtesies; and suddenly [c. June 25] had [a] letter from [the] Plymouth governor, [that] they intended in arms to [subjugate] Philip . . . and in a week's time after we had been with the Indians the war thus begun.

Source: John Easton, "A Relacion of the Indyan Warre, by Mr. Easton, of Roade Isld., 1675," in *Narratives of the Indian Wars, 1675–1699*, ed. Charles H. Lincoln (New York: Charles Scribner's Sons, 1913), 7–17.

## Edward Randolph

### Short Narrative of My Proceedings

Edward Randolph, an English customs official in Boston, denounced the independent policies of the Puritan colonies and tried to subject them to English control. His "Short Narrative," written in 1675, was a report to his superiors in London.

Various are the reports and conjectures of the causes of the present Indian war. Some impute it to an impudent zeal in the magistrates of Boston to Christianize those heathen before they were civilized and enjoining them the strict observation of their laws, which, to a people so rude and licentious, hath proved even intolerable. . . . While the magistrates, for their profit, put the laws severely in execution against the Indians, the people, on the other side, for lucre and gain, entice and provoke the Indians . . . to drunkenness, to which those people are so generally addicted that they will strip themselves to their skin to have their fill of rum and brandy. . . .

Some believe there have been vagrant and jesuitical [French] priests, who have made it their business, for some years past, to go from Sachem to Sachem [chief to chief], to exasperate the Indians against the English and to bring them into a confederacy, and that they were promised supplies from France and other parts to extirpate the English nation out of the continent of America. . . . Others impute the cause to some injuries offered to the Sachem Philip; for he being possessed of a tract of land called Mount Hope . . . some English had a mind to dispossess him thereof, who never wanting one pretence or other to attain their end, complained of injuries done by Philip and his Indians to their stock and cattle, whereupon Philip was often summoned before the magistrate, sometimes imprisoned, and never released but upon parting with a considerable part of his land.

But the government of the Massachusetts . . . do declare [that because of the sins of the people] . . . God hath given the heathen commission to rise against them. . . . For men wearing long hair and periwigs made of women's hair; for women    cutting, curling and laying out the hair. . . . For profaneness in the people not frequenting their [church] meetings.

Source: Albert B. Hart, ed., *American History Told by Contemporaries* (New York: Macmillan, 1897), 1: 458–460.

## Benjamin Church
## Entertaining Passages

Captain Benjamin Church fought in the war and helped end it by capturing Metacom's wife and son and leading the expedition that killed the Indian chieftain. Forty years later, in 1716, Church's son Thomas wrote an account of the war based on his father's notes and recollections.

While Mr. Church was diligently settling his new farm . . . Behold! The rumor of a war between the English and the natives gave a check to his projects. . . . Philip, according to his promise to his people, permitted them to march out of the neck [of the Mount Hope peninsula, where they lived]. . . . They plundered the nearest houses that the inhabitants had deserted [on the rumor of a war], but as yet offered no violence to the people, at least none were

killed. . . . However, the alarm was given by their numbers, and hostile equipage, and by the prey they made of what they could find in the forsaken houses.

An express came the same day to the governor [c. June 25], who immediately gave orders to the captains of the towns to march the greatest part of their companies [of militia], and to rendezvous at Taunton. . . .

The enemy, who began their hostilities with plundering and destroying cattle, did not long content themselves with that game. They thirsted for English blood, and they soon broached it; killing two men in the way not far from Mr. Miles's garrison. And soon after, eight more at Mattapoisett, upon whose bodies they exercised more than brutish barbarities. . . .

These provocations drew out the resentment of some of Capt. Prentice's troop, who desired they might have liberty to go out and seek the enemy in their own quarters [c. June 26].

Source: Benjamin Church, *Entertaining Passages Relating to Philip's War Which Began in the Month of June, 1675*, ed. Thomas Church (Boston: B. Green, 1716).

## ANALYZING THE EVIDENCE

- What event or set of events led to the war?
- Where do the documents agree and disagree about the causes of the war? Given what you know from the discussion in the text, how might the war have been prevented?
- According to Randolph, what did the magistrates of Massachusetts Bay believe to be a major cause of the war? Could historians verify or disprove their explanation? How? What additional sources of evidence might be useful?
- Who was the prime instigator of the war? Which documents provide the most compelling evidence for your conclusion? Why?

## SUMMARY

We have seen that Spain created a permanent settlement in North America in 1565 and that England, France, and the Dutch Republic did likewise between 1607 and 1614. All of these European incursions inadvertently spread devastating diseases among the native residents and reduced some Indians to subject peoples. But there were important differences among the groups of settlers. The French and the Dutch established fur-trading colonies, while the Spanish and the English created settler colonies. Spanish settlers frequently intermarried with the Indians, but the English did not. Alone among the colonizers, the Dutch did not seek to convert the Indians to Christianity.

We also saw major differences between England's Chesapeake colonies, in which bound laborers raised tobacco for export to Europe, and those in New England, where pious Puritan yeomen lived in self-governing farming communities. Still, both regions boasted representative political institutions. Both experienced Indian wars in the first decades of settlement (1622 in Virginia and 1636 in New England) and again in 1675–1676. Indeed, the simultaneous eruption of Bacon's Rebellion and Metacom's War suggests that the histories of the two English regions had begun to converge.

## CHAPTER REVIEW QUESTIONS

- Outline the goals of the directors of the Virginia Company and the leaders of the Massachusetts Bay Company. Where did they succeed? In what ways did they fall short?

- Why were there no major witchcraft scares in the Chesapeake colonies and no uprising like Bacon's Rebellion in New England? Consider the possible social, economic, and religious causes of both phenomena.

## FOR FURTHER EXPLORATION

A fine narrative of Spanish activities north of the Rio Grande is David Weber's *The Spanish Frontier in North America* (1992). Alison Games, *Migration and the Origins of the English Atlantic World* (2001), sets English settlement in context. In *American Slavery, American Freedom* (1975), Edmund Morgan offers a compelling portrait of white servitude and black slavery in early Virginia. Colin Calloway, *New Worlds for All: Indians, Europeans, and the Remaking of Early America* (1997), is a broad overview, while John Demos, *The Unredeemed Captive* (1994), relates the gripping tale of Eunice Williams, a captured Puritan girl who lived her life among the Mohawks. Three recent books are Francis J. Bremer, *John Winthrop: America's Forgotten Founding Father* (2003); James D. Rice, *Nature & History in the Potomac Country* (2009); and Virginia DeJohn Anderson, *Creatures of Empire: How Domestic Animals Transformed Early America* (2004).

Two fine Web sites focus on the Pilgrims at Plymouth: "Caleb Johnson's Mayflower History" (**www.mayflowerhistory.com**) and "The Plymouth Colony Archive Project" (**www.histarch.uiuc.edu/plymouth/index.html**). For insight into early New England life, see the excellent eight-part PBS series *Colonial House* and its Web site (**www.pbs.org/wnet/colonialhouse**). Extensive materials on the Salem witchcraft trials can be viewed at **etext.virginia .edu/salem/witchcraft**.

## TEST YOUR KNOWLEDGE

To assess your command of the material in this chapter, see the Online Study Guide at **bedfordstmartins.com/henretta**.

For Web sites, images, and documents related to topics and places in this chapter, visit **bedfordstmartins.com/makehistory**.

## TIMELINE

| | |
|---|---|
| **1539–1543** | Coronado and de Soto lead gold-seeking expeditions |
| **1565** | Spain establishes fort at St. Augustine |
| **1598** | Acomas rebel in New Mexico |
| **1603–1625** | Reign of James I, king of England |
| **1607** | English traders settle Jamestown (Virginia) |
| **1608** | Samuel de Champlain founds Quebec |
| **1613** | Dutch set up fur-trading post on Manhattan Island |
| **1619** | First Africans arrive in Chesapeake region<br>House of Burgesses convenes in Virginia |
| **1620** | Pilgrims found Plymouth Colony |
| **1620–1660** | Chesapeake colonies enjoy tobacco boom |
| **1621** | Dutch West India Company chartered |
| **1622** | Opechancanough's uprising |
| **1624** | Virginia becomes royal colony |
| **1625–1649** | Reign of Charles I, king of England |
| **1630** | Puritans found Massachusetts Bay Colony |
| **1634** | Settlers arrive in Maryland |
| **1636** | Puritan-Pequot War<br>Roger Williams founds Providence |
| **1637** | Anne Hutchinson banished from Massachusetts Bay |
| **1640s** | Iroquois initiate wars over fur trade |
| **1642–1659** | Puritan Revolution in England |
| **1651** | First Navigation Act |
| **1660** | Restoration of English monarchy<br>Tobacco prices fall and remain low |
| **1664** | English conquer New Netherland |
| **1675** | Bacon's Rebellion in Virginia |
| **1675–1676** | Metacom's War in New England |
| **1680** | Popé's rebellion in New Mexico |
| **1692** | Salem witchcraft trials |
| **1705** | Virginia enacts law defining slavery |

# Creating a British Empire in America, 1660–1750

**When Charles II** came to the throne in 1660, England was a second-class commercial power, its merchants picking up the crumbs left by the worldwide maritime empire of the Dutch. "What we want is more of the trade the Dutch now have," declared the Duke of Albemarle, a trusted minister of the king and a proprietor of Carolina. To get it, the English government embarked on a century-long quest for trade and empire in America and Asia. It passed the Navigation Acts, which prohibited "Ships of any Foreign Nation whatsoever to come to, Trade in, or Traffice with any of the English Plantations in America." Then, the English went to war to destroy Holland's maritime dominance. By the 1720s, Great Britain (the recently unified kingdoms of England and Scotland) had seized control of the transatlantic trade in American sugar, and the Royal African Company—and subsequently Liverpool merchants—had taken over the Atlantic slave trade. The emerging British Empire, boasted the ardent imperialist Malachy Postlethwayt, "was a magnificent superstructure of American commerce and naval power on an African foundation."

That was only the half of it. Great Britain's commerce now spanned the world: Its merchants exported woolen and iron manufactures to Europe, America, and Africa. From its trading posts in India, the British East India Company sent home cotton, indigo, and tea—15 percent of all British imports in 1720—and company ships carried silver to China to exchange for tea, ceramics, and silks. To protect the empire's valuable sugar colonies and trade routes and to force entry into the commerce of other empires, British ministers repeatedly waged war, first against the Dutch and then against the French. Boasted one English pamphleteer: "We are, of any nation, the best situated for trade, . . . capable of giving maritime laws to the world."

That dictum included Britain's North American and West Indian colonies, which were becoming increasingly valuable parts of the empire. By 1685 Charles II was earning £100,000 a year on excise taxes on tobacco from Virginia and even more from duties on sugar from the Caribbean. So when imperial official Edward Randolph reported that "there is no notice taken of the act of navigation," the home government decided to impose its political will on the American settlements.

**Power and Race in the Chesapeake**

**In this 1670 painting by Gerard Soest, proprietor Lord Baltimore holds a map of Maryland, the colony he owned, and which would soon belong to his grandson Cecil Calvert, shown in the painting as already grasping his magnificent inheritance. The presence of a young African servant foretells the importance of slave labor in the post-1700 economy of the Chesapeake colonies.** Enoch Pratt Free Library of Baltimore.

# The Politics of Empire, 1660–1713

Before 1660, England governed its New England and Chesapeake colonies haphazardly. Taking advantage of that laxness and the English civil war, local "big men" (Puritan magistrates and tobacco planters) ran their societies as they wished. Following the restoration of the monarchy in 1660, royal bureaucrats tried to impose order on the unruly settlements and, enlisting the aid of Indian allies, warred with rival European powers.

## Imperial Expansion and Aristocratic Power

Charles II (r. 1660–1685) expanded English power in Asia and America. In 1662, he married the Portuguese princess Catherine of Braganza, whose dowry included the islands of Bombay (present-day Mumbai). The following year, Charles initiated new outposts in America by authorizing eight loyal noblemen to settle Carolina, an area that had long been claimed by Spain and populated by thousands of Indians. Subsequently, he awarded the just-conquered Dutch colony of New Netherland to his brother James, the Duke of York (who renamed the colony New York). In a great land grab, England had ousted the Dutch from North America and intruded into Spain's northern empire.

**The Carolinas** Like Lord Baltimore's Maryland, the new settlements—the Restoration Colonies, as historians call them—were proprietorships: The Duke of York and his fellow aristocrats in Carolina owned all the land and could rule their colonies as they wished, provided that their laws conformed broadly to those of England (Table 3.1). Indeed, in New York, James II refused to allow an elective assembly and ruled by decree. The Carolina proprietors envisioned a traditional European society; the Fundamental Constitutions of Carolina (1669) legally established the Church of England and prescribed a **manorial system**, with a mass of serfs governed by a handful of powerful nobles.

The manorial system proved a fantasy. The first North Carolina settlers were a mixture of poor families and runaway servants from Virginia and English Quakers, an equality-minded Protestant sect (also known as the Society of Friends). Quakers "think there is no difference between a Gentleman and a labourer," complained an Anglican clergyman. Refusing to work on large manors, the settlers raised corn, hogs, and tobacco on modest family farms. Inspired by Bacon's Rebellion in Virginia, the residents of Albemarle County staged an uprising in 1677 against taxes on tobacco and rebelled again in 1708, this time against taxes to support the Anglican Church. The residents were "stubborn and disobedient," a wealthy Anglican landowner charged; nonetheless, and by resisting a series of governors, they

---

**TABLE 3.1**

**English Colonies Established in North America, 1660–1750**

| Colony | Date | Original Colony Type | Religion | Status in 1775 | Chief Export/ Economic Activity |
|---|---|---|---|---|---|
| Carolina | 1663 | Proprietary | Church of England | Royal | |
| North | 1691 | | | | Farming, naval stores |
| South | 1691 | | | | Rice, indigo |
| New Jersey | 1664 | Proprietary | Church of England | Royal | Wheat |
| New York | 1664 | Proprietary | Church of England | Royal | Wheat |
| Pennsylvania | 1681 | Proprietary | Quaker | Proprietary | Wheat |
| Georgia | 1732 | Trustees | Church of England | Royal | Rice |
| New Hampshire (separated from Massachusetts) | 1741 | Royal | Congregationalist | Royal | Mixed farming, lumber, naval stores |
| Nova Scotia | 1749 | Royal | Church of England | Royal | Fishing, mixed farming, naval stores |

forced the proprietors to abandon their dreams of a feudal society.

In South Carolina, the colonists also went their own way. The leading white settlers there were migrants from the overcrowded sugar-producing island of Barbados, and wanted to re-create that island's hierarchical slave society. They used enslaved workers—both Africans and Native Americans—to raise cattle and food crops for export to the West Indies. Carolina merchants opened a lucrative trade in deerskins with neighboring Indian peoples. In exchange for rum and guns, the Carolinians' Indian trading partners also provided slaves—captives from other Native American peoples. By 1708, white Carolinians were working their coastal plantations with 1,400 Indian and 2,900 African slaves, and brutal Indian warfare continued in the backcountry. South Car-

olina would remain a violent frontier settlement until the 1720s.

**William Penn and Pennsylvania** | In dramatic contrast to the Carolinians, the 15,000 migrants who settled in Pennsylvania in the late seventeenth century pursued a pacifistic policy toward Native Americans and quickly became prosperous. In 1681, Charles II bestowed Pennsylvania (which included present-day Delaware) on William Penn as payment for a large debt owed to Penn's father. The younger Penn, though born to wealth—he owned substantial estates in Ireland and England, and lived lavishly—joined the Quakers, who condemned extravagance. Penn designed Pennsylvania as a refuge for his fellow Quakers, who were persecuted in England because they refused to

**William Penn's Treaty with the Indians, 1683**

Benjamin West executed this famous picture of William Penn's meeting with the Lenni-Lenapes, who called themselves the Common People. A Quaker pacifist, Penn refused to seize Indian lands by force and negotiated their purchase. But his son, Thomas Penn, probably had a political purpose when he commissioned the painting in 1771. By evoking a peaceful past, West's work reinforced the Penn family's proprietary claims, which were under strong attack by the Pennsylvania assembly. Courtesy of the Pennsylvania Academy of Fine Arts, Philadelphia (Gift of Mrs. Sarah Harrison; the Joseph Harrison Jr. Collection).

serve in the military or pay taxes to support the Church of England. Penn himself had spent more than two years in jail in England for preaching his beliefs.

Like the Puritans, the Quakers sought to restore Christianity to its early simple spirituality. But they rejected the Puritans' pessimistic Calvinist doctrines, which restricted salvation to a small elect. The Quakers followed the teachings of two English visionaries, George Fox and Margaret Fell, who argued that God had imbued all men—and women—with an "inner light" of grace or understanding. Reflecting the sect's emphasis on gender equality, 350 Quaker women would serve as ministers in the colonies.

Penn's Frame of Government (1681) applied the Quakers' radical beliefs to politics. It ensured religious freedom by prohibiting a legally established church, and it promoted political equality by allowing all property-owning men to vote and hold office. Cheered by these provisions, thousands of Quakers—mostly yeoman families from the northwest Midland region of England—flocked to Pennsylvania. Initially, they settled along the Delaware River near the city of Philadelphia, which Penn himself laid out in a grid with wide main streets and many parks. To attract European Protestants, Penn published pamphlets in Germany promising cheap land and religious toleration. In 1683, migrants from Saxony founded Germantown (just outside Philadelphia), and thousands of other Germans soon followed. Ethnic diversity, pacifism, and freedom of conscience made Pennsylvania the most open and democratic of the Restoration Colonies.

## From Mercantilism to Imperial Dominion

As Charles II distributed his American lands, his ministers devised policies to keep their trade—and that of other colonies—in English hands. Since the 1560s, the English crown had pursued mercantilist policies, using government subsidies and charters to stimulate English manufacturing and foreign trade. Now it extended these mercantilist strategies to the American settlements through the Navigation Acts (Table 3.2).

**The Navigation Acts** | English ministers wanted the colonies to produce agricultural goods and raw materials for English merchants to carry to England. Certain products would then be exported immediately to Europe in return for gold or goods; other imports would be manufactured into finished products and then exported. The Navigation Act of 1651 attempted to keep colonial trade in English hands by excluding Dutch and French vessels from American ports; the act also required that goods be carried only on ships owned by English or colonial merchants. New parliamentary acts in 1660 and 1663 strengthened the ban on foreign traders, requiring colonists to export sugar and tobacco only to England, and mandating that colonists import European goods only through England. To pay the customs officials who enforced these mercantilist laws, the Revenue Act of 1673 imposed a "plantation duty" on American exports of sugar and tobacco.

| TABLE 3.2 | | |
|---|---|---|
| **Navigation Acts, 1651–1751** | | |
| | **Purpose** | **Compliance** |
| Act of 1651 | Cut Dutch trade | Mostly ignored |
| Act of 1660 | Ban foreign shipping; enumerate goods that go only to England | *Partially obeyed* |
| Act of 1663 | Allow European imports only through England | *Partially obeyed* |
| Staple Act (1673) | Ensure enumerated goods go only to England | Mostly obeyed |
| Act of 1696 | Prevent frauds; create vice-admiralty courts | Mostly obeyed |
| Woolen Act (1699) | Prevent export or intercolonial sale of textiles | *Partially obeyed* |
| Hat Act (1732) | Prevent export or intercolonial sale of hats | *Partially obeyed* |
| Molasses Act (1733) | Cut American imports of molasses from French West Indies | **Extensively violated** |
| Iron Act (1750) | Prevent manufacture of finished iron products | **Extensively violated** |
| Currency Act (1751) | End use of paper currency as legal tender in New England | Mostly obeyed |

The English government backed these policies with military force. In three commercial wars between 1652 and 1674, the English navy drove the Dutch from New Netherland and contested Holland's control of the Atlantic slave trade by attacking Dutch forts and ships along the West African coast. Meanwhile, English merchants expanded their fleets, which increased in capacity from 150,000 tons in 1640 to 340,000 tons in 1690.

Many colonists ignored the mercantilist laws and, until the wars of the 1690s, continued to trade with Dutch merchants. They also imported sugar and molasses from the French West Indies. The Massachusetts Bay assembly boldly declared: "The laws of England are bounded within the seas [surrounding it] and do not reach America." Outraged by this insolence, customs official Edward Randolph called for troops to "reduce Massachusetts to obedience." Instead, the Lords of Trade—the administrative body charged with colonial affairs—opted for a punitive legal strategy. In 1679, it denied the claim of Massachusetts Bay to New Hampshire and eventually established a separate royal colony there. Then, in 1684, the Lords of Trade persuaded an English court to annul the Massachusetts Bay charter by charging the Puritan government with violating the Navigation Acts and virtually outlawing the Church of England.

### The Dominion of New England

The Puritans' troubles had only begun, thanks to the accession of King James II (r. 1685–1688), an aggressive and inflexible ruler. During the reign of Oliver Cromwell, James had grown up in exile in France, and he admired its authoritarian king, Louis XIV. Believing that monarchs had a "divine right" to rule, James instructed the Lords of Trade to impose strict royal control on the American colonies. In 1686, the Lords revoked the corporate charters of Connecticut and Rhode Island and merged them with the Massachusetts Bay and Plymouth colonies to form a new royal province, the Dominion of New England. As governor of the Dominion, James II appointed Sir Edmund Andros, a hard-edged former military officer. Two years later, James II added New York and New Jersey to the Dominion, creating a vast colony that stretched from Maine to Pennsylvania (Map 3.1).

The Dominion extended to America the authoritarian model of colonial rule that the English government had imposed on Catholic Ireland. James II ordered Governor Andros to abolish the existing legislative assemblies. In Massachusetts, Andros immediately banned town meetings, angering villagers who prized local self-rule; and advocated public worship in the Church of England, offending Puritan Congregationalists. Even worse,

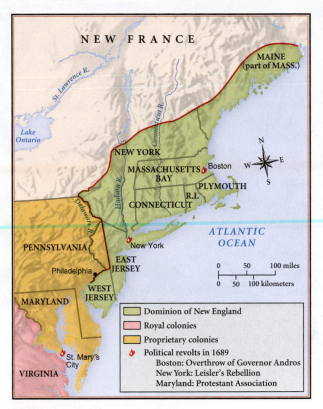

**MAP 3.1**

### The Dominion of New England, 1686–1689

In the Dominion, James II created a vast royal colony that stretched nearly 500 miles along the Atlantic coast. During the Glorious Revolution in England, politicians and ministers in Boston and New York City led revolts that ousted Dominion officials and repudiated their authority. King William and Queen Mary replaced the Dominion with governments that balanced the power held by imperial authorities and local political institutions.

from the colonists' perspective, the governor challenged all land titles granted under the original Massachusetts Bay charter. Andros offered to provide new deeds, but only if the colonists would agree to pay an annual fee.

## The Glorious Revolution in England and America

Fortunately for the colonists, James II angered English political leaders as much as Andros alienated American settlers. The king revoked the charters of English towns, rejected the advice of Parliament, and aroused popular opposition by openly practicing Roman Catholicism. Then, in 1688, James's Spanish Catholic wife gave birth to a son, raising the prospect of a Catholic heir to the throne. To forestall that outcome, Protestant bishops and parliamentary leaders in the **Whig** Party led

**The Leviathan Absolutist State**

This detail from the title-page engraving of Thomas Hobbes's *Leviathan* (1651) conveys Hobbes's belief that peace and security required submission to a powerful sovereign. In this image, a giant king looms over his domain, his staff and sword symbolizing his civil and religious powers. He is the head of a body made up of the multitudes of his faceless and voiceless subjects, as they carry out his commands. What Hobbes celebrated, a majority of English politicians and people rejected. Fearing the claims of absolute power by Stuart kings, they revolted twice, executing Charles I in 1642 and deposing James II in 1688.    Library of Congress.

a quick and bloodless coup known as the Glorious Revolution. Backed by the populace and the military, the bishops and Whigs forced James into exile and in 1689 enthroned Mary, his Protestant daughter by his first wife, and her Dutch Protestant husband, William of Orange. Whig politicians forced King William and Queen Mary to accept the Declaration of Rights, creating a constitutional monarchy that enhanced the powers of the House of Commons at the expense of the crown. The Whigs wanted political power — especially the power to levy taxes — to reside in the hands of the gentry, merchants, and other substantial property owners.

To justify their coup, the members of Parliament relied on political philosopher John Locke. In his *Two Treatises on Government* (1690), Locke rejected the divine-right monarchy celebrated by James II, arguing that the legitimacy of government rests on the consent of the governed and that individuals have inalienable natural rights to life, liberty, and property. Locke's celebration of individual rights and representative government had a lasting influence in America, where many political leaders wanted to expand the powers of the colonial assemblies.

**Rebellions in America** | The Glorious Revolution sparked rebellions by Protestant colonists in Massachusetts, Maryland, and New York. When news of the coup reached Boston in April 1689, Puritan leaders and 2,000 militiamen seized Governor Andros,

accused him of Catholic sympathies, and shipped him back to England. Heeding American complaints of authoritarian rule, the new monarchs broke up the Dominion of New England. However, they refused to restore the old Puritan-dominated government of Massachusetts Bay, instead creating in 1692 a new royal colony (which included Plymouth and Maine). The new charter empowered the king to appoint the governor and customs officials, gave the vote to all male property owners (not just Puritan church members), and eliminated Puritan restrictions on the Church of England.

The uprising in Maryland had economic as well as religious causes. Since 1660, falling prices had hurt tobacco-growing smallholders, tenant farmers, and former indentured servants. These poorer farmers were overwhelmingly Protestant, and they resented the rising taxes and fees imposed by wealthy proprietary officials, who were mostly Catholic. When Parliament ousted James II, a Protestant association mustered 700 men and forcibly removed the Catholic governor. The Lords of Trade supported this Protestant initiative: They suspended Lord Baltimore's proprietorship, imposed royal government, and made the Church of England the legal religion in the colony. This arrangement lasted until 1715, when Benedict Calvert, the fourth Lord Baltimore, converted to the Anglican faith and the king restored the proprietorship to the Calvert family.

In New York, Jacob Leisler led the rebellion against the Dominion of New England. Leisler, once a German

**A Prosperous Dutch Farmstead**

Dutch farmers in the Hudson River Valley prospered because of their easy access to markets downstream at New York, and their exploitation of black slaves (three of whom can be seen in this painting), which they owned in far greater numbers than did their English neighbors. To record his good fortune, Martin Van Bergen of Leeds, New York, had this mural painted over his mantelpiece.   New-York State Historical Association.

soldier for the Dutch West India Company, had become a merchant and married into a prominent Dutch family in New York. He was a militant Calvinist, rigid and hot-tempered; but he quickly emerged as a leader of the Dutch Protestant artisans in New York City, who welcomed the succession of Queen Mary and her Dutch husband. Led by Leisler, the Dutch militia ousted Lieutenant Governor Nicholson, an Andros appointee and an alleged Catholic sympathizer.

Initially, all classes and ethnic groups rallied behind Leisler, who headed a temporary government. However, Leisler's denunciations of political rivals as "popish dogs" and "Roages, Rascalls, and Devills" soon alienated many English-speaking New Yorkers. When Leisler imprisoned 40 of his political opponents, imposed new taxes, and championed the artisans' cause, the prominent Dutch merchants who had traditionally controlled the city's government also condemned his rule. In 1691, the merchants found an ally in Colonel Henry Sloughter, the newly appointed governor, who had Leisler indicted for treason. Convicted by an English jury, Leisler was hanged and then decapitated, an act of ethnic vengeance that corrupted New York politics for a generation.

The Glorious Revolution of 1688–1689 began a new, nonauthoritarian political era in both England and America. In England, William and Mary ruled as constitutional monarchs and promoted an empire based on commerce. Because the new Protestant monarchs wanted American support for a war against Catholic France, they accepted the overthrow of the Dominion of New England and allowed the restoration of self-government in Massachusetts and New York. Parliament created a Board of Trade in 1696 to supervise the American settlements, but it had limited success. Settlers and proprietors resisted the board's attempt to install royal governments, as did many English political leaders, who feared an increase in monarchical power. The result was another period of lax political administration. The home government imposed only a few laws and taxes on the North American settlements, allowed rule by local elites, and encouraged English merchants to develop them as sources of trade.

## Imperial Wars and Native Peoples

In a world of commercial competition, Britain's success depended on both mercantile skills and military power. Between 1689 and 1815, Britain fought a series of increasingly intense wars with France (Table 3.3). To win wars in Western Europe, the Caribbean, and far-flung oceans, British leaders created a powerful central state that spent three-quarters of its revenue on military and naval expenses. As the conflicts spread to the North American mainland, they drew in Native American peoples, who tried to turn the fighting to their own advantage.

The first significant battles in North America occurred during the War of the Spanish Succession

**TABLE 3.3**

**English Wars, 1650–1750**

| War | Date | Purpose | Result |
|---|---|---|---|
| Anglo-Dutch | 1652–1654 | Control markets and African slave trade | Stalemate |
| Anglo-Dutch | 1664 | Markets; conquest | England takes New Amsterdam |
| Anglo-Dutch | 1673 | Commercial markets | England makes maritime gains |
| King William's | 1689–1697 | Maintain European balance of power | Stalemate in North America |
| Queen Anne's | 1702–1713 | Maintain European balance of power | British acquire Hudson Bay and Nova Scotia |
| Jenkins's Ear | 1739–1741 | Expand markets in Spanish America | English merchants expand influence |
| King George's | 1740–1748 | Maintain European balance of power | Capture and return of Louisbourg |

(1702–1713), which pitted Britain against France and Spain. English settlers in the Carolinas armed the Creeks, whose 15,000 members farmed the fertile lands along the present-day border of Georgia and Alabama. A joint English-Creek expedition attacked Spanish Florida, burning the town of St. Augustine but failing to capture the nearby fort. To protect Havana in nearby Cuba, the Spanish reinforced St. Augustine and unsuccessfully attacked Charleston, South Carolina.

**Indian Goals** The Creeks had their own agenda: To become the dominant tribe in the region, they needed to vanquish their longtime enemies, the pro-French Choctaws to the west and the Spanish-allied Apalachees to the south. Beginning in 1704, a force of Creek and Yamasee warriors destroyed the remaining Franciscan missions in northern Florida, attacked the Spanish settlement at Pensacola, and captured a thousand Apalachees, whom they sold to South Carolinian slave traders for sale in the West Indies. Simultaneously, a Carolina-supported Creek expedition attacked the Iroquois-speaking Tuscarora people of North Carolina, killing hundreds, executing 160 male captives, and sending 400 women and children into slavery. The surviving Tuscaroras joined the Iroquois in New York (who now became the Six Nations of the Iroquois). The Carolinians, having used the Creeks to kill Spaniards, now died at the hands of their former allies. When English traders demanded payment for trade debts in 1715, the Creeks and Yamasees revolted. They killed 400 colonists before being overwhelmed by the Carolinians and their new Indian allies, the Cherokees.

Native Americans also joined in the warfare between French Catholics in Canada and English Protestants in New England. With French aid, Catholic Mohawk and Abenaki warriors took revenge on their Puritan enemies. They destroyed English settlements in Maine and, in 1704, attacked the western Massachusetts town of Deerfield, where they killed 48 residents and carried 112 into captivity. In response, New England militia attacked French settlements and, in 1710, joined with British naval forces to seize Port Royal in French Acadia (Nova Scotia). However, a major British–New England expedition against the French stronghold at Quebec, inspired in part by the visit of four Indian "kings" to London, failed miserably.

The New York frontier remained quiet. French and English merchants did not want to disrupt the lucrative fur trade, and the Earl of Bellomont, governor of New York, counseled caution: A "general defection of the Indians," he warned in 1700, would "drive us quite out of this Continent." However, the Iroquois, tired of war, had adopted a policy of "aggressive neutrality." In 1701, they concluded a peace treaty with France and its Indian allies and renewed the Covenant Chain, a quasi-alliance with the English government in New York and various Indian peoples who were their dependents (see Chapter 2). For the next half century, the Iroquois exploited their strategic location by trading with both the English and the French colonies but refusing to fight for either. Their strategy, according to their Delaware ally Teedyuscung, was "to defend our land against both."

Stalemated militarily in America, Britain won major territorial and commercial concessions through its

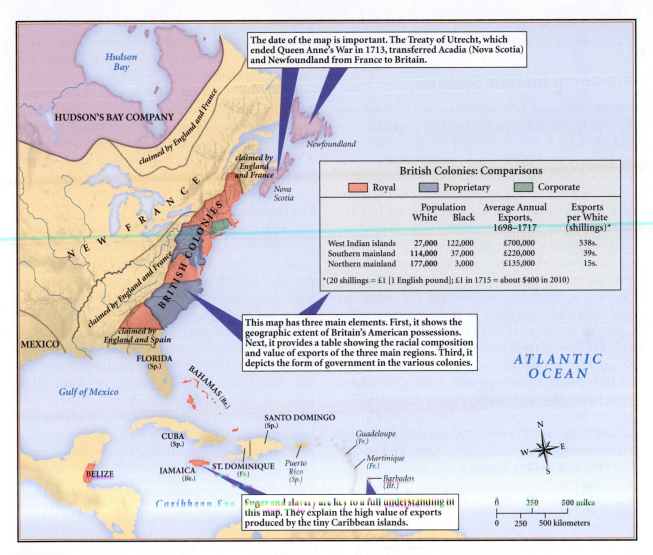

The date of the map is important. The Treaty of Utrecht, which ended Queen Anne's War in 1713, transferred Acadia (Nova Scotia) and Newfoundland from France to Britain.

| British Colonies: Comparisons | | | |
|---|---|---|---|
| ■ Royal | ■ Proprietary | ■ Corporate | |

| | Population White | Black | Average Annual Exports, 1698–1717 | Exports per White (shillings)* |
|---|---|---|---|---|
| West Indian islands | 27,000 | 122,000 | £700,000 | 538s. |
| Southern mainland | 114,000 | 37,000 | £220,000 | 39s. |
| Northern mainland | 177,000 | 3,000 | £135,000 | 15s. |

*(20 shillings = £1 [1 English pound]; £1 in 1715 = about $400 in 2010)

This map has three main elements. First, it shows the geographic extent of Britain's American possessions. Next, it provides a table showing the racial composition and value of exports of the three main regions. Third, it depicts the form of government in the various colonies.

Sugar and slavery are key to a full understanding of this map. They explain the high value of exports produced by the tiny Caribbean islands.

**MAP 3.2**

**Britain's American Empire, 1713**

Many of Britain's possessions in the West Indies were tiny islands, mere dots on the Caribbean Sea. However, in 1713, these small pieces of land were by far the most valuable parts of the empire. Their sugar crops brought wealth to English merchants, commerce to the northern colonies, and a brutal life and early death to the hundreds of thousands of African slaves working on the plantations.

victories in Europe. In the Treaty of Utrecht (1713), Britain obtained Newfoundland, Acadia, and the Hudson Bay region of northern Canada from France, as well as access through Albany to the western Indian trade. From Spain, Britain acquired the strategic fortress of Gibraltar at the entrance to the Mediterranean and a thirty-year contract to supply slaves to Spanish America. These gains advanced Britain's quest for commercial supremacy and brought peace to eastern North America for a generation (Map 3.2).

● **What was the role of the colonies in the British mercantilist system?**

● **Explain the causes and the results of the Glorious Revolution in England and America.**

# The Imperial Slave Economy

Britain's focus on America reflected the growth of a new agricultural and commercial order—the South Atlantic System—that produced sugar, tobacco, rice, and other subtropical products for an international market. At its center stood plantation societies ruled by

European planter-merchants and worked by hundreds of thousands of enslaved Africans (Figure 3.1).

## The South Atlantic System

The South Atlantic System had its center in Brazil and the West Indies, and sugar was its primary product. Before 1500, there were few sweet foods in Europe — mostly honey and fruits — so when European planters developed vast sugarcane plantations in America, they found a ready market for their crop. (The craving for the potent new sweet food was so intense that, by 1900, sugar accounted for an astonishing 20 percent of the calories consumed by the world's people.)

European merchants, investors, and planters garnered the profits of the South Atlantic System. Following mercantilist principles, they provided the plantations with tools and equipment to grow and process the sugarcane and ships to carry it to Europe. But it was the Atlantic slave trade that made the system run. Between 1520 and 1650, Portuguese traders carried about 820,000 Africans across the Atlantic — about 4,000 slaves a year before 1600 and 10,000 annually thereafter. Over the next half century, the Dutch dominated the Atlantic slave trade; then, between 1700 and 1800, the British transported about 2.5 million of the total of 6.1 million Africans carried to the Americas.

**England and the West Indies**  England was a latecomer to the plantation economy. In the 1620s, the English colonized some small West Indian islands — St. Christopher, Nevis, Montserrat, and especially Barbados, which had an extensive amount of arable land. Most early settlers were small-scale English farmers (and their indentured servants) who exported tobacco and livestock hides and created a thriving colony. In 1650 there were more English residents in the West Indies (some 44,000) than in the Chesapeake (20,000) and New England (23,000) colonies combined.

Sugar transformed Barbados and the other islands into slave-based plantation societies. To provide raw sugar for refineries in Amsterdam, Dutch merchants provided English planters with money to buy land, sugar-processing equipment, and slaves. By 1680, an elite group of 175 planters — described by one antislavery writer of the time as "inhumane and barbarous" — dominated Barbados's economy; they owned more than half of the island, thousands of indentured servants, and half of the more than 50,000 slaves on the island. In 1692, exploited Irish servants and island-born African slaves staged a major uprising, which was brutally suppressed. The "leading principle" in a slave society, declared one West Indian planter, was to instill "fear" among workers and a commitment to "absolute

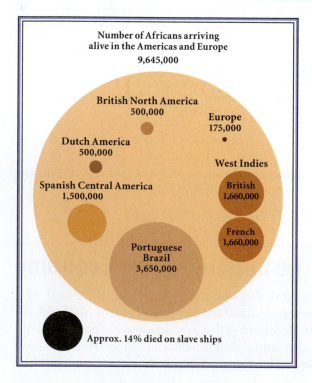

**FIGURE 3.1**

**The Transit of Africans to the Americas**

Though approximately 11 million enslaved Africans boarded ships to the Americas, about 1.5 million (14 percent) of them died en route. Two-thirds of the survivors ended up in Brazil (3.65 million) and the West Indies (3.32 million), where they worked primarily on sugar plantations. Only 0.5 million landed in the present-day United States.

**A Sugar Mill in the French West Indies, 1655**
Making sugar required both hard labor and considerable expertise. Field slaves labored strenuously in the hot tropical sun to cut the sugarcane and carry or cart it to an oxen- or wind-powered mill, where it was pressed to yield the juice. Then skilled slave artisans took over. They carefully heated the juice and, at the proper moment, added ingredients that granulated the sugar and separated it from the molasses, which was later distilled into rum.   The Granger Collection, New York.

coercive" force among masters. As social inequality and racial conflict increased, hundreds of English farmers fled to South Carolina and the large island of Jamaica, which England had seized from Spain in 1655. But the days of Caribbean smallholders were numbered. English sugar merchants soon invested heavily in Jamaica; by 1750, it had seven hundred large sugar plantations—worked by more than 105,000 slaves—and had become the wealthiest British colony.

Sugar was a rich man's crop because it could be produced most efficiently on large plantations. Scores of slaves planted and cut the sugarcane, which was then processed by expensive equipment—crushing mills, boiling houses, distilling apparatus—into raw sugar, molasses, and rum. The affluent planter-merchants who controlled the sugar industry drew annual profits of more than 10 percent on their investment. As Scottish economist Adam Smith noted in his famous treatise *The Wealth of Nations* (1776), sugar was the most profitable crop grown in America or Europe.

**The Impact on Britain** The South Atlantic System brought wealth to the entire British—and European—economy, and helped Europeans achieve world economic leadership. Most British West Indian plantations belonged to absentee owners who lived in England, where they spent their profits and formed a powerful "sugar lobby." The Navigation

Acts kept the British sugar trade in the hands of British merchants, who exported it to foreign markets. By 1750, reshipments of American sugar and tobacco to Europe accounted for half of British exports. Enormous profits also flowed into Britain from the slave trade. The value of the guns, iron, rum, and cloth that were used to buy slaves was only about one-tenth (in the 1680s) to one-third (by the 1780s) of the value of the crops those slaves produced in America. This substantial differential allowed the Royal African Company and other English traders to sell slaves in the West Indies for three to five times what they paid for them in Africa.

These massive profits drove the slave trade. At its height in the 1790s, Britain annually exported three hundred thousand guns to Africa, and a British ship carrying 300 to 350 slaves left an African port every other day. This commerce stimulated the entire British economy. English and Scottish shipyards built hundreds of vessels, and thousands of people worked in trade-related industries: building port facilities and warehouses, refining sugar and tobacco, distilling rum from molasses, and manufacturing textiles and iron products for the growing markets in Africa and America. More than one thousand British merchant ships were plying the Atlantic by 1750, providing a supply of experienced sailors and laying the foundation for the supremacy of the Royal Navy.

## Africa, Africans, and the Slave Trade

As the South Atlantic System enhanced European prosperity, it imposed enormous costs on West and Central Africa. Between 1550 and 1870, the Atlantic slave trade uprooted eleven million Africans, draining lands south of the Sahara of people and wealth and changing African society (Map 3.3). By directing commerce away from the savannas and the Islamic world on the other side of the Sahara, the Atlantic slave trade changed the economic and religious dynamics of the African interior. It also fostered militaristic, centralized states in the coastal areas.

**Africans and the Slave Trade** | Warfare and slaving had been part of African life for centuries, driven by conflicts among numerous states and ethnic groups. But the South Atlantic System made slaving a favorite tactic of ambitious kings and plundering warlords. "Whenever the King of Barsally wants Goods or Brandy," an observer noted, "the King goes and ransacks some of his enemies' towns, seizing the people and selling them." Supplying slaves became a way of life in the West African state of Dahomey, where the royal house monopolized the sale of slaves and used European guns to create a military despotism. Dahomey's army, which included a contingent of 5,000 women, raided the interior for captives; between 1680 and 1730, Dahomey annually exported 20,000 slaves exported from the ports of Allada and Whydah. The Asante kings likewise used slaving to conquer states along the Gold Coast as well as Muslim kingdoms in the savanna. By the 1720s, they had created a prosperous empire of 3 to 5 million people. Yet participation in Atlantic trade remained a choice for Africans, not a necessity. The powerful kingdom of Benin, famous for its cast bronzes and carved ivory, prohibited for decades the export of all slaves, male and female. Other Africans expiated their guilt for selling neighbors into slavery by building hidden shrines, often in the household granary.

The trade in humans produced untold misery. Hundreds of thousands of young Africans died, and millions more endured a brutal life in the Americas. In Africa itself, class divisions hardened as people of noble birth enslaved and sold those of lesser status. Gender relations shifted as well. Two-thirds of the slaves sent across the Atlantic were men, because European planters paid more for men and "stout men boys" and because Africans sold enslaved women locally and across the Sahara as agricultural workers, house servants, and concubines. The resulting sexual imbalance prompted African men to take several wives, changing the meaning of marriage. Finally, the expansion of the Atlantic trade increased the extent of slavery in Africa. Sultan Mawlay Ismail of Morocco (r. 1672–1727) owned 150,000 black slaves, obtained by trade in Timbuktu and in wars he waged in Senegal. In Africa, as in the Americas, slavery eroded the dignity of human life.

**The Middle Passage** | Africans sold into the South Atlantic System suffered the bleakest fate. Torn from their villages, they were marched in chains to coastal ports, their first passage in slavery. Then, they endured the perilous **Middle Passage** to the New World in hideously overcrowded ships. The captives had little to eat or drink, and some died from dehydration. The feces, urine, and vomit below-decks prompted outbreaks of dysentery, which took more lives. "I was so overcome by the heat, stench, and foul air that I nearly fainted," reported a European doctor. Some slaves jumped overboard, choosing to drown rather than endure more suffering (see Voices from Abroad, "Olaudah Equiano: The Brutal 'Middle Passage,'" p. 88). Others staged violent shipboard revolts. Slave uprisings occurred on two thousand voyages, roughly one of every ten Atlantic passages. Nearly 100,000 slaves died in these

**MAP 3.3**

**Africa and the Atlantic Slave Trade, 1700–1810**

The tropical rain forest of West Africa was home to scores of peoples and dozens of kingdoms. With the rise of the slave trade, some of these kingdoms became aggressive slavers. Dahomey's army, for example, seized tens of thousands of captives in wars with neighboring peoples and sold them to European traders. About 14 percent of the captives died during the grueling Middle Passage, the transatlantic voyage between Africa and the Americas. Most of the survivors labored on sugar plantations in Brazil and the British and French West Indies (see Table 3.4).

insurrections, and nearly 1.5 million others—about 14 percent of those who were transported—died of disease or illness on the month-long journey.

For those who survived the Atlantic crossing, things only got worse as they passed into endless slavery. Life on the sugar plantations of northwestern Brazil and the West Indies was one of relentless exploitation. Slaves worked ten hours a day under the hot semitropical sun; slept in flimsy huts; and lived on a starchy diet of corn, yams, and dried fish. They were subjected to brutal discipline: "The fear of punishment is the principle [we use] . . . to keep them in awe and order," one planter

**Cape Coast Castle, Ghana (on the Gold Coast)**
The guns that once protected this British slave-trading fort from naval attacks by rival European nations and pirate ships still point out to sea. Behind the fort lay a substantial town, home to African slave traders, merchants, and the mixed-race families of African women and British soldiers, sailors, and slave traders. Between 1660 and 1800, tens of thousands of enslaved Africans stayed briefly in the dungeons of Cape Coast Castle before being shipped primarily to Britain's sugar colonies in the West Indies.   Werner Foreman/Art Resource, NY.

declared. With sugar prices high and the cost of slaves low, many planters simply worked their slaves to death and then bought more: Between 1708 and 1735, British planters on Barbados imported about 85,000 Africans; however, in that same time the island's black population increased by only 4,000 (from 42,000 to 46,000). The constant influx of new slaves kept the population thoroughly "African" in its languages, religions, and culture. "Here," wrote a Jamaican observer, "each different nation of Africa meet and dance after the manner of their own country . . . [and] retain most of their native customs."

## Slavery in the Chesapeake and South Carolina

West Indian–type slavery came to Virginia and Maryland following Bacon's Rebellion as elite planter-politicians led a "tobacco revolution." They took advantage of the expansion of the British slave trade (following the end of the Royal African Company's monopoly in 1698) and bought more Africans, putting these slaves to work on ever-larger plantations. By 1720, Africans made up 20 percent of the Chesapeake population; by 1740, nearly 40 percent. Slavery had become a core institution, no longer just one of several forms of unfree labor. Moreover, slavery was now defined in racial terms. Virginia legislators prohibited sexual intercourse between English and Africans and defined virtually all resident Africans as slaves: "All ser-

vants imported or brought into this country by sea or land who were not Christians in their native country shall be accounted and be slaves."

Still, slaves in Virginia and Maryland had much better conditions than those in the West Indies, and lived relatively long lives. Unlike sugar and rice, which were "killer crops" that demanded strenuous labor in a subtropical climate, tobacco cultivation required steady, careful, physically undemanding labor in a more temperate environment. Workers planted young tobacco seedlings in spring, hoed and weeded the crop in summer, and in fall picked and hung the leaves to cure over the winter. Also, diseases did not spread as easily in the Chesapeake, because plantation quarters were less crowded and more dispersed than those in the West Indies. Finally, because tobacco profits were lower than those from sugar, planters treated their slaves less harshly than West Indian planters did.

Many tobacco planters increased their workforce by buying female slaves and encouraging them to have children. In 1720, women made up more than one-third of the Africans in Maryland and the black population had begun to increase naturally. "Be kind and indulgent to the breeding wenches," one slave owner told his overseer, "[and do not] force them when with child upon any service or hardship that will be injurious to them." By midcentury, more than three-quarters of the enslaved workers in the Chesapeake were American-born.

Slaves in South Carolina labored under much more oppressive conditions. The colony grew slowly

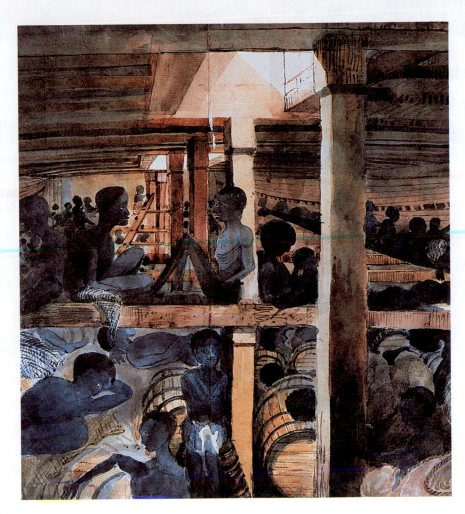

**Two Views of the Middle Passage**

An 1846 watercolor (on the right) shows the cargo hold of a slave ship en route to Brazil, which imported large numbers of African slaves until the 1860s. Painted by a ship's officer, the work minimizes the brutality of the Middle Passage—none of the slaves are in chains—and captures the Africans' humanity and dignity. A layout of the hold (on the left) captures the reality of the slave trade, in which the human cargo was packed in with no more respect than that given to hogsheads of sugar and tobacco.    Private Collection/© Michael Graham-Stewart/The Bridgeman Art Library. / © National Maritime Museum, London.

until 1700, when planters began to plant and export rice to southern Europe, where it was in great demand. To expand production, planters imported thousands of Africans—some of them from rice-growing societies. By 1705, Africans formed a majority of the total population, rising to 80 percent in rice-growing areas (Figure 3.2).

Most rice plantations lay in inland swamps, and the work of cultivation was dangerous and exhausting. Slaves planted, weeded, and harvested the rice in ankle-deep mud. Pools of stagnant water bred mosquitoes, which transmitted diseases that claimed hundreds of African lives. Other slaves, forced to move tons of dirt to build irrigation works, died from exhaustion. "The labour required [for growing rice] is only fit for slaves,"

a Scottish traveler remarked, "and I think the hardest work I have seen them engaged in." In South Carolina, as in the West Indies and Brazil, there were many slave deaths and few births, and the arrival of new slaves continually "re-Africanized" the black population.

## An African American Community Emerges

Slaves came from many peoples in West Africa and the Central African regions of Kongo and Angola (Table 3.4). White planters welcomed ethnic diversity to deter slave revolts. "The safety of the Plantations," declared a widely read English pamphlet, "depends upon having Negroes from all parts of Guiny, who do not understand each

All the nations and people I had hitherto passed through resembled
own in their manners, customs and lang

# Olaudah Equiano
## The Brutal "Middle Passage"

Olaudah Equiano claimed to have been born in Igboland (present-day southern Nigeria). But Vincent Carretta of the University of Maryland has recently discovered strong evidence that Equiano was born in South Carolina and lived on an American plantation as a boy. He suggests that Equiano drew on conversations with African-born slaves to create a fictitious history of an idyllic childhood in West Africa, his kidnapping at the age of eleven, and a traumatic passage across the Atlantic. After being purchased by an English sea captain, Equiano bought his freedom in 1766. In London, he became an antislavery activist, and in 1789 published the memoir from which the following selections are drawn.

My father, besides many slaves, had a numerous family of which seven lived to grow up, including myself and a sister who was the only daughter. . . . I was trained up from my earliest years in the art of war, my daily exercise was shooting and throwing javelins, and my mother adorned me with emblems after the manner of our greatest warriors. One day, when all our people were gone out to their works as usual and only I and my dear sister were left to mind the house, two men and a woman got over our walls, and in a moment seized us both, and without giving us time to cry out or make resistance they stopped our mouths and ran off with us into the nearest wood. . . .

At length, after many days' travelling, during which I had often changed masters, I got into the hands of a chieftain in a very pleasant country. This man had two wives and some children, and they all used me extremely well and did all they could to comfort me, particularly the first wife, who was something like my mother. Although I was a great many days' journey from my father's house, yet these people spoke exactly the same language with us. This first master of mine, as I may call him, was a [blacksmith], and my principal employment was working his bellows.

I was again sold and carried through a number of places till . . . at the end of six or seven months after I had been kidnapped I arrived at the sea coast.

The first object which saluted my eyes when I arrived on the coast was the sea, and a slave ship which was then riding at anchor and waiting for its cargo. I now saw myself deprived of all chance of returning to my native country . . . ; and I even wished for my former slavery in preference to my present situation, which was filled with horrors of every kind. . . . I was soon put down under the decks, and there I received such a salutation in my nostrils as I had never experienced in my life; so that with the loathsomeness of the stench and crying together, I became so sick and low that I was not able to eat, nor had I the least desire to taste any thing. I now wished for the last friend, death, to relieve me; but soon, to my grief, two of the white men offered me eatables, and on my refusing to eat, one of them held me fast by the hands and laid me across I think the windlass, and tied my feet while the other flogged me severely. I had never experienced anything of this kind before, and although, not being used to the water, I naturally feared that element the first time I saw it, yet nevertheless could I have got over the nettings, I would have jumped over the side, but I could not. . . . One day, when we had a smooth sea and moderate wind, two of my wearied countrymen who were chained together (I was near them at the time), preferring death to such a life of misery, somehow made it through the nettings and jumped into the sea. . . .

At last we came in sight of the island of Barbados; the white people got some old slaves from the land to pacify us. They told us we were not to be eaten but to work, and were soon to go on land where we should see many of our country people. This report eased us much; and sure enough soon after we were landed there came to us Africans of all languages.

Source: *The Interesting Narrative of the Life of Olaudah Equiano, or Gustavus Vassa, the African, Written by Himself* (London, 1789), 15, 22–23, 28–29.

## ANALYZING THE EVIDENCE

- In what ways is Equiano's evocation of slavery in Africa consistent with the analysis in this text?
- What evidence does Equiano offer in his description of the Middle Passage that explains the average slave mortality rate of about 14 percent during the Atlantic crossing?
- Assuming that Carretta is correct, and Equiano was not born in Africa, why do you think he composed this fictitious narrative of his childhood instead of describing the facts of his own life in slavery?

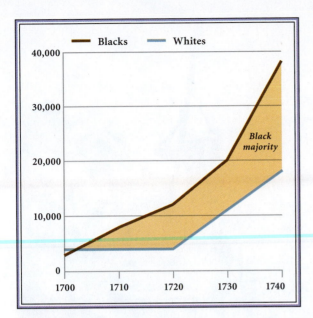

**FIGURE 3.2**

**A Black Majority Emerges in South Carolina, 1700–1740**

Between disease and the toll taken by the Indian wars, South Carolina's white population hardly grew at all between 1690 and 1720. But white planters imported thousands of enslaved Africans to grow rice, an extremely profitable plantation crop. As early as 1705, the colony had a black majority, which allowed the development among slaves of a strong Afrocentric language and culture.

other's languages and Customs and cannot agree to Rebel." By accident or design, most plantations drew laborers of many languages, including Kwa, Mande, and Kikongo. Among Africans imported after 1730 into the upper James River region of Virginia, 41 percent came from ethnic groups in present-day Nigeria, and another 25 percent from West-Central Africa. The rest hailed from the Windward and Gold coasts, Senegambia, and Sierra Leone. In South Carolina, plantation owners preferred laborers from the Gold Coast and Gambia, who had a reputation as hardworking farmers. But as African sources of slaves shifted southward after 1730, more than 30 percent of the colony's workers later came from Kongo and Angola.

Initially, the slaves did not think of themselves as Africans or blacks but as members of a specific family, clan, or people—Wolof, Hausa, Ibo, Yoruba, Teke, Ngola—and they sought out those who shared their language and customs. In the upper James River region, Ibo men and women arrived in equal numbers, married each other, and maintained their Ibo culture.

**Building Community**  Over time, slaves made friendships and married across ethnic lines, in the process creating new common languages. Thus, the Gullah dialect of the South Carolina lowlands combined words from English and a variety of African languages in an African grammatical

**TABLE 3.4**

**African Slaves Imported into North America by Region of Departure and Ethnicity, 1700–1775**

| Region of Departure | Ethnicity | Number | Percentage of Imported Slaves |
|---|---|---|---|
| Senegambia | Mandinka, Fulbe, Serer, Jola, Wolof, Bambara | 47,300 | 17 |
| Sierra Leone | Vai, Mende, Kpelle, Kru | 33,400 | 12 |
| Gold Coast | Ashanti, Fanti | 19,500 | 7 |
| Bight of Benin, Bight of Biafra | Ibo, Ibibio | 47,300 | 17 |
| West Central Africa | Kongo, Tio, Matamba | 44,600 | 16 |
| Southeast Africa | Unknown | 2,800 | 1 |
| Other or unknown | | 83,500 | 30 |
| **Total** | | **278,400** | **100** |

NOTE: The numbers are extrapolated from known voyages involving 195,000 Africans. The ethnic origins of the slaves are tentative because peoples from different regions often left from the same port and because the regions of departure of 83,500 Africans (30 percent) are not known.
SOURCE: Aaron S. Fogleman, "From Slaves, Convicts, and Servants to Free Passengers: The Transformation of Immigration in the Era of the American Revolution," *Journal of American History* 85 (June 1998), table A.4.

**Hulling Rice in West Africa and Georgia**

Cultural practices often extend over time and space. The eighteenth-century engraving on the left shows West African women using huge wooden mortars and pestles to strip the tough outer hull from rice kernels. In the photo on the right, taken a century and a half later, African American women in Georgia use similar tools to prepare rice for their families.   Library of Congress. / Georgia Division of Archives and History, Office of Secretary of State.

structure. "They have a language peculiar to themselves," a missionary reported, "a wild confused medley of Negro and corrupt English." In the Chesapeake region, where there were more American-born slaves, most people of African descent gradually lost their native tongues. In the 1760s, a European visitor reported with surprise that in Virginia "all the blacks spoke very good English."

A common language — Gullah or English or French (in Louisiana and the French West Indies) — was one key to the emergence of an African American community. Nearly equal numbers of men and women — which encouraged marriage, stable families, and continuity between generations — was another. In South Carolina, the high death rate among slaves undermined ties of family and kinship; but after 1725, Chesapeake-area blacks created strong nuclear families and extended kin relations. On one of Charles Carroll's estates in Maryland, 98 of the 128 slaves were members of two extended families. These African American kin groups passed on family names, traditions, and knowledge to the next generation, and thus a distinct culture gradually de-

veloped. As one observer suggested, blacks had created a separate world, "a Nation within a Nation."

As the slaves forged a new identity, they carried on certain African practices but let others go. Many Africans arrived in America with ritual scars that white planters called "country markings"; these signs of ethnic identity fell into disuse on culturally diverse plantations. But the slaves' African heritage took some tangible forms, including hairstyles, motifs used in wood carvings and pottery, the large wooden mortars and pestles used to hull rice, and the design of houses, in which rooms were arranged from front to back in a distinctive "I" pattern, not side by side as was common in English dwellings.

African values also persisted (see Reading American Pictures, "Jumping the Broomstick: An African Marriage Ceremony," p. 91). Some slaves passed down Muslim beliefs, and many more told their children of the spiritual powers of conjurers, known as *obeah* or *ifa*, who knew the ways of the African gods. Enslaved Yorubas consulted Orunmila, the god of fate, and other Africans (a Jamaican planter noted) relied on *obeah*

## Jumping the Broomstick: An African Marriage Ceremony

Enslaved Africans carried their customs to the Americas, where they created a variety of new cultures that combined the traditions of many African and European peoples. How can we better understand this cultural synthesis? Slaves left few written records; but we do have visual evidence, such as this painting of a dance on a South Carolina plantation—probably a wedding ceremony—by an unknown artist.

*The Old Plantation*, c. 1800. Abby Aldrich Rockefeller Folk Art Museum, Williamsburg, VA.

### ANALYZING THE EVIDENCE

- The painting depicts a scene on a South Carolina plantation. What clues can you see in the image suggesting that the location is a rice plantation in the low country of that colony?

- Does the evidence in the picture suggest that these people are recent arrivals from Africa? What artifacts might be African in origin? What have you learned from the text about the conditions on rice plantations that would account for a steady stream of African-born slaves?

- African peoples from different ethnic groups mingled on large plantations. Do you see any evidence in the painting that suggests different ethnic identities? Look carefully at the clothes of the two dancers—perhaps the bride and groom—at the left-center of the painting; what might indicate that they come from different African peoples?

- Around 1860, a Virginia slave recounted the story of her parents' marriage: "Ant Lucky read sumpin from de Bible, an' den she put de broomstick down an' dey locked dey arms together an' jumped over it. Den dey was married." In the scene depicted in this painting from around 1800, the man in the red breeches is holding a long stick, similar to a broomstick. If this is a wedding, is there any evidence of Christianity in the ceremony as there was in the marriage described above?

- Look closely at the men's and women's clothes. Do they reveal signs of European cultural influence?

"to revenge injuries and insults, discover and punish thieves and adulterers; [and] to predict the future."

## Resistance and Accommodation

There were drastic limits on creativity among African Americans. Most slaves were denied opportunities to gain an education, accumulate material possessions, or create associations. Slaves who challenged these boundaries did so at their peril. Planters whipped slaves who refused to work; some turned to greater cruelties. Declaring the chronic runaway Ballazore an "incorrigeble rogue," a Virginia planter ordered all his toes cut off: "Nothing less than dismembering will reclaim him," the planter reasoned. Thomas Jefferson, who witnessed such punishments on his father's Virginia plantation, noted that each generation of whites was "nursed, educated, and daily exercised in tyranny," and concluded that the relationship "between master and slave is a perpetual exercise of the most unremitting despotism on the one part, and degrading submission on the other." A fellow Virginian, planter George Mason, agreed: "Every Master is born a petty tyrant."

The extent of white violence often depended on the size and density of the slave population. As Virginia planter William Byrd II complained of his slaves in 1736, "Numbers make them insolent." In the northern colonies, where slaves were few, white violence was sporadic. But plantation owners and overseers in the sugar- and rice-growing areas, where Africans outnumbered Europeans eight to one, routinely whipped assertive slaves. They also prohibited their workers from leaving the plantation without special passes and called on their poor white neighbors to patrol the countryside at night, a duty that (authorities regularly reported) was "almost totally neglected."

Slaves dealt with their plight in several ways. Some newly arrived Africans fled to the frontier, establishing traditional villages or marrying into Indian tribes. American-born blacks who were fluent in English fled to towns, and tried to pass as free. Those who remained enslaved bargained continually with their masters over the terms of their bondage. Some blacks bartered extra work for better food and clothes; others seized a small privilege and dared the master to revoke it. In this way, Sundays gradually became a day of rest—asserted as a right, rather than granted as a privilege. When bargaining failed, slaves protested silently by working slowly or stealing. Others, provoked beyond endurance, killed their owners or overseers. In the 1760s, in Amherst County, Virginia, a slave killed four whites; in Elizabeth City County, eight slaves strangled their master in bed.

A few blacks even plotted rebellion, despite white superiority in guns and, in many regions, numbers.

**The Stono Rebellion** | Predictably, South Carolina witnessed the largest slave uprising: the Stono Rebellion of 1739. The Catholic governor of the Spanish colony of Florida instigated the revolt by promising freedom to fugitive slaves. By February 1739, at least 69 slaves had escaped to St. Augustine, and rumors circulated "that a Conspiracy was formed by Negroes in Carolina to rise and make their way out of the province." When war between England and Spain broke out in September (see p. 98), 75 Africans rose in revolt and killed a number of whites near the Stono River. According to one account, some of the rebels were Portuguese-speaking Catholics from the Kingdom of Kongo who had been attracted by the prospect of life in Catholic Florida. Displaying their skills as soldiers— decades of brutal slave raiding in Kongo had militarized the society there—the rebels marched toward Florida "with Colours displayed and two Drums beating." White militia killed many of the Stono rebels, preventing a general uprising; after this, frightened whites cut slave imports and tightened plantation discipline.

## William Byrd and the Rise of the Southern Gentry

As the southern colonies became full-fledged slave societies, life changed for whites as well as for blacks. Consider the career of William Byrd II (1674–1744). Byrd's father, a successful planter-merchant in Virginia, hoped to marry his children into the English gentry. To smooth his son's entry into landed society, Byrd sent him to England for his education. But his status-conscious classmates at the Felsted School shunned young Byrd, calling him a "colonial," a first bitter taste of the gradations of rank in English society.

Other English rejections followed. Lacking aristocratic connections, Byrd was denied a post with the Board of Trade, passed over three times for the royal governorship of Virginia, and rejected as a suitor by a rich Englishwoman. In 1726, at age fifty-two, Byrd finally gave up and moved back to Virginia, where he sometimes felt he was "being buried alive." Accepting his lesser destiny as a member of the colony's elite, Byrd built an elegant brick mansion on the family's estate at Westover, sat in "the best pew in the church," and won an appointment to the governor's council.

William Byrd II's experience mirrored that of many planter-merchants, trapped in Virginia and South Carolina by their inferior colonial status. They not only

***Virginian Luxuries*, c. 1810**

This painting by an unknown artist depicts the physical and sexual exploitation inherent in a slave society. On the right, an owner chastises a male slave by beating him with a cane; on the left, ignoring the cultural and legal rules prohibiting sexual intercourse between the races, a white master prepares to bed his black mistress.   Abby Aldrich Rockefeller Folk Art Museum, Williamsburg, VA.

used their wealth to rule over white yeomen families and tenant farmers but also relied on violence to exploit enslaved blacks, the American equivalent of the oppressed peasants of Europe. Planters used Africans to grow food, as well as tobacco; to build houses, wagons, and tobacco casks; and to make shoes and clothes. By making their plantations self-sufficient, the Chesapeake elite survived the depressed tobacco market between 1670 and 1720.

**White Identity and Inequality** To prevent uprisings like Bacon's Rebellion, the Chesapeake gentry found ways to assist middling and poor whites (see Chapter 2). They gradually lowered taxes; in Virginia, for example, the annual head tax (on each adult man) fell from 45 pounds of tobacco in 1675 to just 5 pounds in 1750. They also encouraged smallholders to improve their economic lot by using slave labor, and many did so. By 1770, 60 percent of English families in the Chesapeake owned at least one slave. On the political front, planters now allowed poor yeomen and some tenants to vote. The strategy of the leading families — the Carters, Lees, Randolphs, and Robinsons — was to bribe these voters with rum, money, and the promise of minor offices in county governments. In return, they expected the yeomen and tenants to elect them to office and defer to their rule. This horse-trading solidified the authority of the planter elite, which used its control of the House of Burgesses to limit the power of the royal governor. Hundreds of yeomen farmers benefited as well, tasting political power and garnering substantial fees and salaries as deputy sheriffs, road surveyors, estate appraisers, and grand jurymen.

Even as wealthy Chesapeake gentlemen formed political ties with smallholders, they took measures to set themselves apart culturally. As late as the 1720s, leading planters were boisterous, aggressive men who lived much like the common folk — hunting, drinking, gambling on horse races, and demonstrating their manly prowess by forcing themselves on female servants and slaves. As time passed, however, the planters began — like William Byrd II — to model themselves on the English aristocracy, remaining sexual predators but learning from advice books how to act like gentlemen in other regards: "I must not sit in others' places; Nor sneeze, nor cough in people's faces. Nor with my fingers pick my nose, Nor wipe my hands upon my clothes." Cultivating **gentility** — a refined but elaborate lifestyle — they replaced their modest wooden houses with mansions of brick and mortar. Robert "King" Carter, who owned hundreds of slaves, filled his house — 75 feet long, 44 feet wide, and 40 feet high — with fine furniture and rugs. Planters educated their sons in London as lawyers and gentlemen. But unlike Byrd's father, they expected them to return to America, marry local heiresses, and assume their fathers' roles: managing plantations, socializing with fellow gentry, and running the political system.

Wealthy Chesapeake and South Carolina women likewise emulated the English elite. They read English newspapers and fashionable magazines, wore the finest English clothes, and dined in the English fashion, including an elaborate afternoon tea. To enhance their daughters' gentility (and improve their marriage prospects), parents hired English tutors. Once married, planter women deferred to their husbands, reared pious

**Captain Thomas Smith, *Self-Portrait*, c. 1680**

As the background of this painting suggests, Thomas Smith had military experience, though the details are sketchy (it's thought that he fought under Oliver Cromwell during the Puritan Revolution of the 1640s). An artist as well as a sea captain, Smith moved to Boston and carried with him the Baroque style of painting, which uses light and shadows to create the illusion of forms in space (for example, note the dark shadow that sets off the bottom part of the fort in the background). The last line of the poem visible under the skull shows that Smith, though contemplating death in his advancing years, remained a devout Puritan committed to the Covenant of Grace, hopeful that God would "Crowne me (after Grace) with Glory."    The Worcester Art Museum.

children, and maintained elaborate social networks, in time creating a new ideal: the southern gentlewoman. Using the profits generated by enslaved Africans in the South Atlantic System of commerce, wealthy planters formed an increasingly well-educated, refined, and stable ruling class.

## The Northern Maritime Economy

The South Atlantic System had a broad geographical reach. As early as the 1640s, New England farmers supplied the sugar islands with bread, lumber, fish, and meat. As a West Indian explained, planters "had rather buy foode at very deare rates than produce it by labour, soe infinite is the profitt of sugar works." By 1700, the economies of the West Indies and New England were closely interwoven. Soon farmers and merchants in New York, New Jersey, and Pennsylvania were also ship-ping wheat, corn, and bread to the Caribbean. By the 1750s, about two-thirds of New England's exports and half of those from the Middle colonies went to the British and French sugar islands.

The sugar economy linked Britain's entire Atlantic empire. In return for the sugar they sent to England, West Indian planters received credit—in the form of **bills of exchange**—from London merchants. The planters used these bills to buy slaves from Africa and to pay North American farmers and merchants for their provisions and shipping services. The mainland colonists then exchanged the bills for British manufactures, primarily textiles and iron goods.

**The Urban Economy** | The West Indian trade created the first American merchant fortunes and the first urban industries (Map 3.4). Merchants in Boston, Newport, Providence, Philadelphia, and New York invested their profits in new ships; some set up manufacturing enterprises, including twenty-six refineries that processed raw sugar into finished loaves. Mainland distilleries turned West Indian molasses into rum—producing more than 2.5 million gallons in Massachusetts alone by the 1770s. Merchants in Salem, Marblehead, and smaller New England ports built a major fishing industry by selling salted mackerel and cod to the sugar islands and to southern Europe. Baltimore merchants transformed their town into a major port by developing a bustling export business in wheat, while traders in Charleston shipped deerskins, indigo, and rice to European markets.

As transatlantic commerce expanded—from five hundred voyages a year in the 1680s to fifteen hundred annually in the 1730s—American port cities grew in size and complexity. Seeking jobs and excitement, British and German migrants and young people from the country-side (servant girls, male laborers, and apprentice artisans) flocked to urban areas. By 1750, the populations of New-port and Charleston were nearly 10,000; Boston had 15,000 residents; and New York had almost 18,000. The largest port was Philadelphia, whose population by 1776 had reached 30,000, the size of a large European provincial city. Smaller coastal towns emerged as centers of the lumber and shipbuilding industries. Seventy sawmills lined the Piscataqua River in New Hampshire, providing low-cost wood for homes, warehouses, and especially ship-building. Taking advantage of the Navigation Acts, which allowed colonists to build and own trading vessels, hun-dreds of shipwrights turned out oceangoing vessels, while other artisans made ropes, sails, and metal fittings for the new fleet. By the 1770s, colonial-built ships made up one-third of the British merchant fleet.

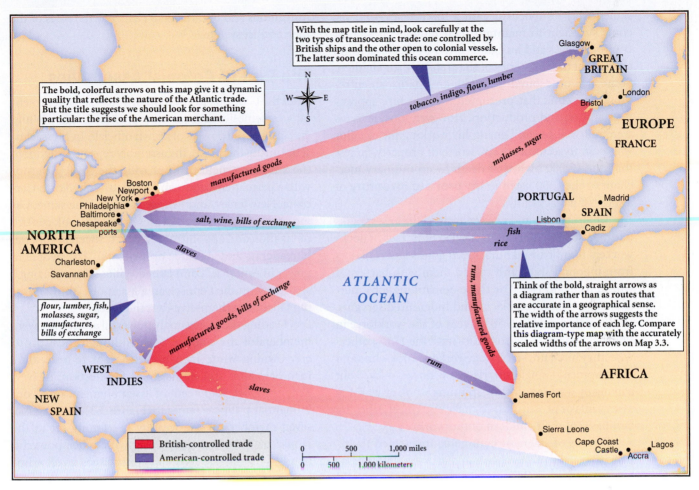

With the map title in mind, look carefully at the two types of transoceanic trade: one controlled by British ships and the other open to colonial vessels. The latter soon dominated this ocean commerce.

The bold, colorful arrows on this map give it a dynamic quality that reflects the nature of the Atlantic trade. But the title suggests we should look for something particular: the rise of the American merchant.

Think of the bold, straight arrows as a diagram rather than as routes that are accurate in a geographical sense. The width of the arrows suggests the relative importance of each leg. Compare this diagram-type map with the accurately scaled widths of the arrows on Map 3.3.

*tobacco, indigo, flour, lumber*
*manufactured goods*
*salt, wine, bills of exchange*
*slaves*
*manufactured goods, bills of exchange*
*molasses, sugar*
*fish*
*rice*
*rum, manufactured goods*
*rum*
*slaves*

*flour, lumber, fish, molasses, sugar, manufactures, bills of exchange*

GREAT BRITAIN
Glasgow
London
Bristol
EUROPE
FRANCE
PORTUGAL
SPAIN
Madrid
Lisbon
Cadiz
AFRICA
James Fort
Sierra Leone
Cape Coast Castle
Accra
Lagos

NORTH AMERICA
Boston
Newport
New York
Philadelphia
Baltimore
Chesapeake ports
Charleston
Savannah
WEST INDIES
NEW SPAIN

ATLANTIC OCEAN

**Legend:**
- British-controlled trade
- American-controlled trade

0   500   1,000 miles
0   500   1,000 kilometers

**MAP 3.4**

**The Rise of the American Merchant, 1750**

Throughout the colonial era, British merchant houses dominated the transatlantic trade in manufactures, sugar, tobacco, and slaves. However, by 1750, American-born merchants in Boston, New York, and Philadelphia had seized control of the commerce between the mainland and the West Indies. In addition, Newport traders played a small role in the slave trade from Africa, and Boston and Charleston merchants grew rich carrying fish and rice to southern Europe.

The South Atlantic System extended far into the interior. A fleet of small vessels sailed back and forth on the Hudson and Delaware rivers, delivering cargoes of European manufactures and picking up barrels of flour and wheat to carry to New York and Philadelphia for export to the West Indies and Europe. By the 1750s, hundreds of professional teamsters in Maryland were transporting 370,000 bushels of wheat and corn and 16,000 barrels of flour to urban markets each year—more than 10,000 wagon trips. To service this traffic, entrepreneurs and artisans set up taverns, horse stables, and barrel-making shops in towns along the wagon roads. Lancaster, in a prosperous wheat-growing area of Pennsylvania, boasted more than 200 German and English artisans and a dozen merchants.

**Urban Society** | Wealthy merchants dominated the social life of seaport cities. In 1750, about 40 merchants controlled more than 50 percent of Philadelphia's trade; they had taxable assets averaging £10,000, a huge sum at the time. Like the Chesapeake gentry, urban merchants imitated the British upper classes, importing architectural design books from England and building Georgian-style mansions to display their wealth. Their wives strove to create a genteel culture by buying fine furniture and entertaining guests at elegant dinners.

Artisan and shopkeeper families, the middle ranks of seaport society, made up nearly half the population. Innkeepers, butchers, seamstresses, shoemakers, weavers, bakers, carpenters, masons, and dozens of other skilled workers toiled to gain a *competency*—an income sufficient to maintain their families in modest comfort. Wives and husbands often worked as a team, and taught the "mysteries of the craft" to their children. Some artisans aspired to wealth and status, an entrepreneurial ethic that prompted them to hire apprentices and expand production. However, most artisans were not well-to-do. During his working life, a tailor was lucky to accumulate £30 worth of property, far less than the £2,000 owned at death by an ordinary merchant or the £300 listed in the **probate inventory** of a successful blacksmith.

Laboring men and women formed the lowest ranks of urban society. Merchants needed hundreds of dockworkers to unload manufactured goods and molasses from inbound ships and reload them with barrels of wheat, fish, and rice. For these demanding jobs merchants used enslaved blacks and indentured servants, who together made up 30 percent of the workforce in Philadelphia and New York City until the 1750s; otherwise, they hired unskilled wageworkers. Poor white and black women—single, married, or widowed—eked out a living by washing clothes, spinning wool, or working as servants or prostitutes. To make ends meet, laboring families sent their children out to work.

Periods of stagnant commerce threatened the financial security of merchants and artisans alike. For laborers, seamen, and seamstresses—whose household budgets left no margin for sickness or unemployment—depressed trade meant hunger, dependence on public charity, and (for the most desperate) petty thievery or prostitution. The sugar- and slave-based South Atlantic System brought economic uncertainty as well as opportunity to the people of the northern colonies.

- How did the South Atlantic System work, and what were its major elements? How did it shape the development of the various colonies?

- What role did Africans play in the expansion of the Atlantic slave trade? What was the role of Europeans?

# The New Politics of Empire, 1713–1750

The South Atlantic System changed the politics of empire. British ministers, pleased with the wealth produced by the trade in slaves, sugar, rice, and tobacco, ruled the colonies with a gentle hand. The colonists took advantage of that leniency to strengthen their political institutions and eventually to challenge the rules of the mercantilist system.

## The Rise of Colonial Assemblies

After the Glorious Revolution of 1688–1689, representative assemblies in America copied the English Whigs and limited the powers of crown officials. In Massachusetts during the 1720s, the assembly repeatedly ignored the king's instructions to provide the royal governor with a permanent salary, and legislatures in North Carolina, New Jersey, and Pennsylvania did the same. Using such tactics, the legislatures gradually took control of taxation and appointments, which angered imperial bureaucrats and absentee proprietors. "The people in power in America," complained William Penn during a struggle with the Pennsylvania assembly, "think nothing taller than themselves but the Trees."

Leading the increasingly powerful assemblies were members of the colonial elite. Although most property-owning white men had the right to vote, only men of wealth and status stood for election. In New Jersey in 1750, 90 percent of assemblymen came from influential political families (Figure 3.3). In Virginia, seven members of the wealthy Lee family sat in the House of Burgesses and, along with other powerful families, dominated its major committees. In New England, affluent descendants of the original Puritans formed a core of political leaders. "Go into every village in New England," John Adams wrote in 1765, "and you will find that the office of justice of the peace, and even the place of representative, have generally descended from generation to generation, in three or four families at most."

However, neither elitist assemblies nor wealthy property owners could impose unpopular edicts on the people. Purposeful crowd actions were a fact of colonial life. An uprising of ordinary citizens overthrew the Dominion of New England in 1689. In New York, mobs closed houses of prostitution; in Salem, Massachusetts, they ran people with infectious diseases out of town; and in New Jersey, in the 1730s and 1740s, mobs of farmers battled with proprietors who were forcing tenants off disputed lands. When officials in Boston restricted the sale of farm produce to a single public market, a crowd destroyed the building, and its members defied the authorities to arrest them. "If you touch One you shall touch All," an anonymous letter warned the sheriff, "and we will show you a Hundred Men where you can show one." These expressions of popular discontent, combined with the growing authority of the assemblies, created a political system that was broadly

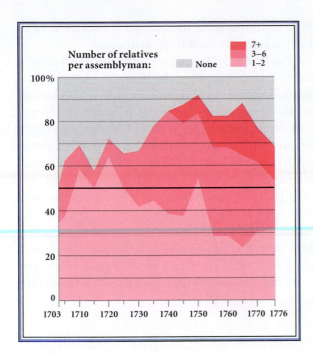

**FIGURE 3.3**

**Family Connections and Political Power, New Jersey, 1700–1776**

As early as 1700, more than 50 percent of the members of the New Jersey assembly came from families with a history of political leadership. By 1750, the percentage whose fathers or other relatives had served in the assembly reached 90 percent; indeed, some members had seven relatives who were (or had been) political leaders, clear testimony of the emergence of powerful political families and an experienced governing elite. However, as the conflict with Britain increased after 1765, voters in New Jersey and elsewhere ousted lukewarm patriots, and new families entered the political ranks.

responsive to popular pressure and increasingly resistant to British control.

## Salutary Neglect

British colonial policy during the reigns of George I (r. 1714–1727) and George II (r. 1727–1760) allowed the rise of American self-government. Royal bureaucrats, pleased by growing trade and import duties, relaxed their supervision of internal colonial affairs. In 1775, British political philosopher Edmund Burke would praise this strategy as **salutary neglect**.

Salutary neglect was a by-product of the political system developed by Sir Robert Walpole, the Whig leader in the House of Commons from 1720 to 1742. By providing supporters with appointments and pensions, Walpole won parliamentary approval for his policies. However, his patronage appointments filled the British government, including the Board of Trade and the colonial bureaucracy, with do-nothing political hacks. When Governor Gabriel Johnson arrived in North Carolina in the 1730s, he vowed to curb the powers of the assembly and "make a mighty change in the face of affairs." Receiving little support from the Board of Trade, Johnson renounced reform and decided "to do nothing which can be reasonably blamed, and leave the rest to time, and a new set of inhabitants."

Walpole's tactics also weakened the empire by undermining the legitimacy of the political system. **Radical Whigs** protested that Walpole had betrayed the Glorious Revolution by using patronage and bribery

**Sir Robert Walpole, the King's Minister**

All eyes are on the secretary of the treasury, Sir Robert Walpole (left), as he offers advice to the Speaker of the House of Commons. A brilliant politician, Walpole used patronage to command a majority in the Commons and also won the confidence of George I and George II, the German-speaking monarchs from the duchy of Hanover. Walpole's personal motto, "Let sleeping dogs lie," helps explain his colonial policy of salutary neglect.   National Trust Photographic Library/Hawksley Studios/The Bridgeman Art Library.

to create a strong Court (or Kingly) Party. The Country Party—whose members were landed gentlemen—likewise warned that Walpole's policies of high taxes and a bloated royal bureaucracy threatened British liberties. Heeding these arguments, colonial legislators complained that royal governors abused their patronage powers. To preserve American liberty, the colonists strengthened the powers of the representative assemblies, unintentionally laying the foundation for the American independence movement (see Comparing American Voices, "The Rise of Colonial Self-Government," pp. 100–101).

## Protecting the Mercantile System

Apart from patronage, Walpole focused on protecting British commercial interests. Initially, Walpole pursued a cautious foreign policy to allow Britain to recover from a generation of war (1689–1713) against Louis XIV of France. But in 1732, he provided a parliamentary subsidy for the new colony of Georgia. Georgia's reform-minded trustees envisioned the colony as a refuge for Britain's poor. To create a society of independent family farmers, the trustees limited most land grants to 500 acres and outlawed slavery.

Walpole had little interest in social reform; he subsidized Georgia to protect the valuable rice-growing colony of South Carolina. The subsidy, however, did exactly the opposite. Britain's expansion into Georgia outraged Spanish officials, who were already angry over British trade tactics in New Spain. British merchants had silently taken over the Andalusian firms that held a monopoly on Spanish-American trade, and now—violating Spanish law—provided many of the slaves and manufactures imported by the Spanish colonies. To counter Britain's commercial imperialism, Spanish naval forces stepped up their seizure of illegal traders, including mutilation of an English sea captain, Robert Jenkins.

**Commercial Aggression** Yielding to parliamentary pressure, Walpole declared war on Spain in 1739. However, the so-called War of Jenkins's Ear (1739–1741) did nothing to undermine Spain's American empire. In 1740, British regulars failed to capture St. Augustine because South Carolina whites, still shaken by the Stono Rebellion, refused to commit militia units to the expedition. A year later, a major British and American assault on the prosperous seaport of Cartagena (in present-day Colombia) also failed. Instead of enriching themselves with Spanish booty, hun-

dreds of troops from the mainland colonies died in the attack, mostly from tropical diseases.

The War of Jenkins's Ear quickly became part of a general European conflict, the War of the Austrian Succession (1740–1748). Massive French armies battled British-subsidized German forces in Europe, and French naval forces roamed the West Indies, vainly trying to conquer a British sugar island. There was little fighting in North America until 1745, when 3,000 New England militiamen, supported by a British naval squadron, captured Louisbourg, a French fortress at the entrance to the St. Lawrence River. To the dismay of New England Puritans, who feared invasion from Catholic Quebec, the Treaty of Aix-la-Chapelle (1748) returned Louisbourg to France. The treaty made it clear to colonial leaders that England would act in its own interests, not theirs.

## The American Economic Challenge

The Walpole ministry had its own complaints about American economic activities. The Navigation Acts stipulated that the colonies were to produce staple crops and to consume British manufactured goods. To enforce the British trade monopoly, Parliament prohibited Americans from selling colonial-made textiles (Woolen Act, 1699), hats (Hat Act, 1732), and iron products such as plows, axes, and skillets (Iron Act, 1750).

**The Politics of Mercantilism** However, the Navigation Acts had a major loophole: They allowed Americans to own ships and transport goods. Colonial merchants exploited those provisions to take control of 75 percent of the transatlantic trade in manufactures and 95 percent of the commerce between the mainland and the British West Indies. Moreover, by the 1720s, the British sugar islands could not absorb all the flour, fish, and meat produced by mainland settlers. So, ignoring Britain's intense rivalry with France, colonial merchants sold their produce to the French sugar islands. Soon French planters were producing low-cost sugar that drove British products off the European market. When American rum distillers began to buy cheap molasses from the French islands, the West Indian "sugar lobby" in London intervened, persuading Parliament to pass the Molasses Act of 1733. The act allowed mainland colonies to export fish and flour to the French islands but—to give a price advantage to British sugar planters—placed a high tariff on French molasses. American merchants and legislators protested that the Molasses Act would cut off molasses

### The Siege and Capture of Louisbourg, 1745

In 1760, as British and colonial troops moved toward victory in the French and Indian War (1754–1763), the London artist J. Stevens sought to bolster imperial pride by celebrating an earlier Anglo-American triumph. In 1745, a British naval squadron led a flotilla of colonial ships and thousands of New England militiamen in an attack on the French fort at Louisbourg, on Cape Breton Island, near the mouth of the St. Lawrence River. After a siege of forty days, the Anglo-American force captured the fort, long considered impregnable. The victory was bittersweet because the Treaty of Aix-la-Chapelle (1748) returned the island to France. Courtesy of the John Carter Brown Library at Brown University.

imports, which would cripple the distilling industry; cut farm exports; and, by slashing colonial income, reduce the mainland's purchases of British goods. When Parliament ignored these arguments, American merchants smuggled in French molasses by bribing customs officials. Luckily for the Americans, sugar prices in Britain rose sharply in the late 1730s, so the act was not rigorously enforced.

The lack of currency in the colonies prompted another conflict with British officials. To pay for British manufactures, American merchants used the bills of exchange and the gold and silver coins earned in the West Indian trade. These payments drained the colonial economy of money, making it difficult for Americans to borrow funds or to buy and sell goods among themselves. To remedy the problem, ten colonial assemblies established public **land banks**, which lent paper money to farmers who pledged their land as collateral for the loans. Farmers used the currency to buy tools or livestock or to pay creditors, thereby stimulating trade. However, some assemblies, particularly the legislature in Rhode Island, issued huge quantities of paper money (which consequently decreased in value) and required merchants to accept it as legal tender. English merchants and other creditors rightly complained about being forced to accept devalued money. So in 1751, Parliament passed the Currency Act, which barred the New England colonies from establishing new land banks and

prohibited the use of publicly issued paper money to pay private debts.

These conflicts over trade and paper money angered a new generation of English political leaders. In 1749, Charles Townshend of the Board of Trade charged that the American assemblies had assumed many of the "ancient and established prerogatives wisely preserved in the Crown"; he vowed to replace salutary neglect with more rigorous imperial control.

The wheel of empire had come full circle. In the 1650s, England had set out to create a centrally managed Atlantic empire and, over the course of a century, achieved the military and economic aspects of that goal. Mercantilist legislation, maritime warfare, commercial expansion, and the forced labor of a million African slaves brought prosperity to Britain. However, internal unrest (the Glorious Revolution) and a policy of salutary neglect had weakened Britain's political authority over its American colonies. Recognizing the threat self-government posed to the empire, British officials in the late 1740s vowed to reassert their power in America—an initiative with disastrous results.

- **How did the ideas and policies of the English Whigs affect British and colonial politics between 1700 and 1760?**

- **What was the British policy of salutary neglect? Why did the British follow this policy and what were its consequences?**

# The Rise of Colonial Self-Government

**B**etween 1700 and 1760, members of the representative assemblies in British North America gradually expanded their authority and power. Their success was the result of greater popular participation in politics and their own political skills. However, the shift in power from imperial appointees to colonial legislators occurred in a piecemeal fashion, as the almost unconscious product of a series of small, seemingly inconsequential struggles. As you read the following correspondence among legislators, governors, and the British officials, look closely at the character of the disputes and how they were resolved.

## Alexander Spotswood

### Confronting the House of Burgesses

As a reward for his military service fighting the forces of Louis XIV of France, Alexander Spotswood became governor of Virginia in 1710. A contentious man, Spotswood was a controversial governor. He told the House of Burgesses to its face that the voters had mistakenly chosen "a set of representatives whom heaven has not generally endowed with the ordinary [intellectual or social] qualifications requisite to legislators." Spotswood set out to reform the voting system that, in his judgment, produced such mediocre representatives. His efforts to oust popular members of the gentry from the House of Burgesses created few friends; in 1722, his enemies in Virginia used their influence in London to have him removed from office.

To ye Council of Trade, Virginia, October 15, 1712
MY LORDS:
. . . The Indians continue their Incursions in North Carolina, and the Death of Colo. Hyde, their Gov'r, which happened the beginning of last Month, increases the misery of that province. . . .

This Unhappy State of her Maj't's Subjects in my Neighbourhood is ye more Affecting to me because I have very little hopes of being enabled to relieve them by our Assembly, which I have called to meet next Week; for the Mob of this Country, having tried their Strength in the late Election and finding themselves able to carry whom they please, have generally chosen representatives of their own Class, who as their principal Recommendation have declared their resolution to raise no Tax on the people, let the occasion be what it will. This is owing to a defect in the Constitution, which allows to every one, tho' but just out of the Condition of a Servant, and that can but purchase half an acre of Land, an equal Vote with the Man of the best Estate in the Country.

The Militia of this Colony is perfectly useless without Arms or ammunition, and by an unaccountable infatuation, no arguments I have used can prevail on these people to make their Militia more Serviceable, or to fall into any other measures for the Defence of their Country.

[From the Journal of the Virginia Council]
December the 17th, 1714
The Governor this day laying before the Council a letter from the Right Honorable the Lords Commissioners for Trade dated the 23d of April 1713 directing him to advise with the Council & to recommend to the Generall Assembly to pass a law for qualifying the Electors & the persons Elected Burgesses to serve in the Generall Assembly of this Colony in a more just & equal manner than the Laws now in force do direct. . . . The Council declare that they cannot advise the Governor to move for any alteration in the present method of Electing of Burgesses, some being of opinion that this is not a proper time, & others that the present manner of electing of Burgesses & the qualifications of the elected is sufficiently provided for by the Laws now in force.

To Mr. Secretary James Stanhope, July 15, 1715
. . . I cannot forbear regretting yt I must always have to do with ye Representatives of ye Vulgar People, and mostly with such members as are of their Stamp and Understanding, for so long as half an Acre of Land (which is of small value in this Country) qualifys a man to be an Elector, the meaner sort of People will ever carry ye Elections, and the humour generally runs to choose such men as are their most familiar Companions, who very eagerly seek to be Burgesses merely for the lucre of the Salary, and who, for fear of not being chosen again, dare in Assembly do nothing that may be disrelished [disapproved] out of the House by ye Common People. Hence it often happens yt what appears prudent and feasible to his Majesty's Governors and Council here will not pass with the House of Burgesses, upon whom they must depend for the means of putting their designs in Execution.

To the Lords Commissioners of Trade, May 23, 1716
... The behaviour of this Gentleman [Philip Ludwell Jr., the colony's Auditor] in constantly opposing whatever I have offered for ye due collecting the Quitt rents [annual feudal dues on land] and regulating the Acc'ts; his stirring up ye humours of the people before the last election of Burgesses; tampering with the most mutinous of that house, and betraying to them the measures resolved on in Council for his Majesty's Service, would have made me likewise suspend him from ye Council, but I find by the late Instructions I have received from his Majesty that Power is taken from ye Governor and transferred upon the majority of that Board [of Councilors], and while there are no less than seven of his Relations there, it is impossible to get a Majority to consent to the Suspension of him.

Sources: R. A. Brock, ed., *The Official Letters of Alexander Spotswood* (Richmond: Virginia Historical Society, 1885), 2: 1–2, 124, 154–155; H. R. MacIlwaine, ed., *Executive Journals of the Council of Colonial Virginia* (Richmond: Virginia State Library, 1928), 3: 392.

## George Clinton

## A Plea for Assistance

George Clinton served as governor of New York from 1744 to 1752. Like many governors during the era of salutary neglect, Clinton owed his appointment to political connections in England. As the second son of the seventh Earl of Lincoln, he would inherit neither the family's estate nor his father's position in the House of Lords; those went to his elder brother. To provide an income for Clinton, his family traded its votes in Parliament for patronage appointments. However, once Clinton was installed as governor of New York, he found himself dependent on the assembly for the payment of his salary—and the salaries of all members of his administration.

My Lords,
    I have in my former letters inform'd Your Lordships what Incroachments the Assemblys of this province have from time to time made on His Majesty's Prerogative & Authority in this Province in drawing an absolute dependence of all the Officers upon them for their Saleries & Reward of their services, & by their taking in effect the Nomination to all Officers....
    1stly, That the Assembly refuse to admit of any amendment to any money bill, in any part of the Bill; so that the Bill must pass as it comes from the Assembly, or all the Supplies granted for the support of Government, & the most urgent services must be lost.
    2ndly, It appears that they take the Payment of the [military] Forces, passing of Muster Rolls into their own

hands by naming the Commissaries for those purposes in the Act.
    3rdly, They by granting the Saleries to the Officers personally by name & not to the Officer for the time being, intimate that if any person be appointed to any Office his Salery must depend upon their approbation of the Appointment....
    I must now refer it to Your Lordships' consideration whether it be not high time to put a stop to these usurpations of the Assembly on His Majesty's Authority in this Province and for that purpose may it not be proper that His Majesty signify his Disallowance of the Act at least for the payment of Saleries.

Source: E. B. O'Callaghan, ed., *Documents Relative to the Colonial History of the State of New York* (Albany, 1860–), 2: 211.

## ANALYZING THE EVIDENCE

- What policies does Spotswood wish to pursue? Why can't he persuade the House of Burgesses to implement them? According to Spotswood, what is wrong with Virginia's political system? How does he propose to reform it?

- Unlike the House of Burgesses, which was elected by qualified voters, the members of the Governor's Council in Virginia were appointed by the king, usually on the governor's recommendation. What is the council's response to the plan to reform the political system? Given Spotswood's description of the incident involving Philip Ludwell, where did the political sympathies of the council lie?

- What were Clinton's complaints about the actions of the New York assembly? Did these actions represent a more or less serious threat to imperial power than the activities of the Virginia Burgesses? Based on their correspondence with the Board of Trade, which governor—Spotswood or Clinton—was the stronger representative of the interests of the crown?

**Bristol Docks and Quay**

Bristol, in southwest England, served as a hub for the trade with Africa, the West Indies, and the American mainland. This detail from an eighteenth-century painting of the bustling seaport shows horses drawing large hogsheads of West Indian sugar to local factories and workers readying smaller barrels of rum and other goods for export to Africa.   Bristol City Museum and Art Gallery/UK Bridgeman Art Library.

## SUMMARY

In this chapter, we examined processes of change in politics and society. The political story began in the 1660s as Britain imposed controls on its American possessions. Parliament passed the Acts of Trade and Navigation to keep colonial products and trade in English hands. Then King James II abolished representative institutions in the northern colonies and created the authoritarian Dominion of New England. Following the Glorious Revolution, the Navigation Acts remained in place and tied the American economy to that of Britain. But the uprisings of 1688–1689 did overturn James II's policy of strict imperial control, restore American self-government, and usher in an era of salutary political neglect.

The social story centers on the development of the South Atlantic System of production and trade, which involved an enormous expansion in African slave raiding; the Atlantic slave trade; and the cultivation of sugar, rice, and tobacco in America. This complex system created an exploited African American labor force in the southern mainland and West Indian colonies and also prosperous communities of European American farmers, merchants, and artisans on the North American mainland. How would the two stories play out? In 1750, slavery and the South Atlantic System seemed firmly entrenched, but the days of salutary neglect appeared numbered.

## CHAPTER REVIEW QUESTIONS

- Describe the dramatic expansion of the British empire in North America in the late seventeenth and early eighteenth centuries. What role did the South Atlantic System play?

- In what ways did politics in the British empire change in the decades following the Glorious Revolution? How do you explain those changes?

# FOR FURTHER EXPLORATION

Atlantic history stands at the center of recent scholarship. See *The Creation of the British Atlantic World* (2005), eds. Elizabeth Mancke and Carole Shammas; *The British Atlantic World, 1500–1800*, 2nd ed. (2009), eds. David Armitage and Michael J. Braddick; and *Atlantic History: A Critical Appraisal* (2009), eds. Jack P. Greene and Philip D. Morgan. Richard Bushman, *King and People in Provincial Massachusetts* (1985), and Brendan McConville, *The King's Three Faces* (2007), explore the decline of British authority.

Betty Wood, *The Origins of American Slavery* (1998), and David Eltis, *The Rise of African Slavery in the Americas* (2000), offer fine surveys. For the diversity and evolution of African bondage, see Ira Berlin, *Many Thousands Gone: The First Two Centuries of Slavery in North America* (1999), and Trevor Burnard, *Mastery, Tyranny, and Desire: Thomas Thistlewood and His Slaves in the Anglo-Jamaican World* (2004). Olaudah Equiano, *The Interesting Narrative of the Life of Olaudah Equiano* (1789, reprint 1995), sketches the emergence of an "African" identity. See also John Thornton, *Africa and Africans in the Making of the Atlantic World, 1400–1800* (1998).

The PBS video *Africans in America, Part 1: Terrible Transformation, 1450–1750,* and the related Web site (**www.pbs.org/wgbh/aia/part1/title.html**) cover the early African American experience. A visual record of the slave experience appears at **hitchcock.itc.virginia .edu/Slavery**. Also see the Library of Congress online exhibit "African American Odyssey" (**memory.loc.gov/ ammem/aaohtml**) and the wide-ranging material on the British slave trade (1600–1807) at **slavetrade .parliament.uk/slavetrade/index.html**.

## TEST YOUR KNOWLEDGE

To assess your command of the material in this chapter, see the Online Study Guide at **bedfordstmartins.com/henretta**.

For Web sites, images, and documents related to topics and places in this chapter, visit **bedfordstmartins.com/makehistory**.

## TIMELINE

| | |
|---|---|
| 1651 | First Navigation Act |
| 1660–1685 | Reign of Charles II, king of England |
| 1663 | Charles II grants Carolina proprietorship |
| 1664 | English capture New Netherland; rename it New York |
| 1681 | William Penn founds Pennsylvania |
| 1685–1688 | Reign of James II, king of England |
| 1686–1689 | Dominion of New England |
| 1688–1689 | Glorious Revolution in England |
| 1689 | William and Mary ascend throne in England Revolts in Massachusetts, Maryland, and New York |
| 1689–1713 | England, France, and Spain at war |
| 1696 | Parliament creates Board of Trade |
| 1705 | Virginia enacts slavery legislation |
| 1714–1750 | British policy of salutary neglect; American assemblies gain power |
| 1720–1742 | Robert Walpole leads Parliament |
| 1720–1750 | African American community forms Rice exports from South Carolina soar Planter aristocracy emerges Seaport cities expand |
| 1732 | Parliament charters Georgia, challenging Spain Hat Act limits colonial enterprise |
| 1733 | Molasses Act threatens distillers |
| 1739 | Stono Rebellion in South Carolina |
| 1739–1748 | War with Spain in the Caribbean and France in Canada and Europe |
| 1750 | Iron Act restricts colonial iron production |
| 1751 | Currency Act prohibits land banks and paper money |

## CHAPTER 4

# Growth and Crisis in Colonial Society, 1720–1765

**In 1736,** Alexander MacAllister left the Highlands of Scotland for the back-country of North Carolina, where his wife and three sisters soon joined him. MacAllister prospered as a landowner and mill proprietor and had only praise for his new home. Carolina was "the best poor man's country," he wrote to his brother Hector, urging him to "advise all poor people . . . to take courage and come." In North Carolina, there were no landlords to keep "the face of the poor . . . to the grinding stone," and so many Highlanders were arriving that "it will soon be a new Scotland." Here, on the far margins of the British empire, people could "breathe the air of liberty, and not want the necessarys of life." Some 300,000 European migrants – primarily Highland Scots, Scots-Irish, and Germans – heeded MacAllister's advice and helped swell the population of Britain's North American settlements from 400,000 in 1720 to almost 2 million by 1765.

The rapid increase in white settlers and the arrival of nearly 300,000 enslaved Africans transformed life throughout British North America. Long-settled towns in New England became overcrowded. Antagonistic ethnic and religious communities jostled uneasily with one another in the Middle Atlantic colonies; in 1742 there were more than fifty German Lutheran and Reformed congregations in Quaker-led Pennsylvania, and by 1748 more than one hundred. By then, the MacAllisters and thousands of other Celtic and German migrants altered the social landscape and introduced religious conflict into the southern backcountry. "Live like Brethren in Unity," Anglican minister Charles Woodhouse advised a Scots-Irish Presbyterian congregation.

Everywhere, two European cultural movements – the Enlightenment and Pietism – changed the tone of intellectual and spiritual life. Advocates of "rational thought" viewed human beings as agents of moral self-determination and urged Americans to fashion a better social order. However, religious pietists outnumbered them and had more influence. Convinced of the weakness of human nature, evangelical ministers told their followers to seek regeneration through divine grace. Amidst this intellectual and religious ferment, migrants and the landless children of long-settled families moved inland and sparked wars with the native peoples and with France and Spain. A generation of dynamic growth produced a decade of deadly warfare that would set the stage for a new era in American history.

**John Collet, *George Whitefield Preaching***

No painting could capture English minister George Whitefield's magical appeal, although this image conveys his open demeanor and religious intensity, as well as his effect on his audiences. When Whitefield spoke to a crowd near Philadelphia, an observer noted that his words were "sharper than a two-edged sword. . . . Some of the people were pale as death; others were wringing their hands . . . and most lifting their eyes to heaven and crying to God for mercy." An astute businessman as well as a charismatic preacher, Whitefield tirelessly promoted the sale of his sermons and books. © Private Collection/The Bridgeman Art Library.

# New England's Freehold Society

In the 1630s, the Puritans had fled England, where a small elite of nobles and gentry owned 75 percent of the arable land and used **leaseholding** tenants and propertyless workers to farm it. In New England, the Puritans created a yeoman society of relatively equal landowning farm families. But by 1750, the migrants' numerous descendants had parceled out the best farmland, threatening the future of the freehold ideal.

## Farm Families: Women in the Household Economy

The Puritans' vision of social equality did not extend to women, and their ideology placed the husband firmly at the head of the household. In *The Well-Ordered Family* (1712), Reverend Benjamin Wadsworth of Boston advised women that being richer, more intelligent, or of higher social status than their husbands mattered little: "Since he is thy Husband, God has made him the head and set him above thee." It was a wife's duty "to love and reverence" her husband.

Women learned this subordinate role throughout their lives. Small girls watched their mothers defer to their fathers, and as young women, they were told to be "silent in company," and saw the courts prosecute many women and few men for the crime of fornication (having sexual intercourse outside of marriage). Soon they found that their marriage portions would be inferior to those of their brothers. Thus, Ebenezer Chittendon of Guilford, Connecticut, left his land to his sons, decreeing that "Each Daughter [shall] have half so much as Each Son, one half in money and the other half in Cattle." Because English law had eliminated most customary restrictions on inheritances, fathers could divide their property as they pleased.

In rural New England, and throughout the colonies, women assumed the role of dutiful helpmeets (helpmates) to their husbands. Farmwives tended gardens that provided fresh vegetables and herbs, and spun thread and yarn from flax and wool and then wove it into cloth for shirts and gowns. They knitted sweaters and stockings, made candles and soap, churned milk into butter and pressed curds into cheese, fermented malt for beer, preserved meats, and mastered dozens of other household tasks. "Notable women"—those who excelled at domestic arts—won praise and high status.

Bearing and rearing children were equally important tasks. Most women in New England married in their early twenties and by their early forties had given birth to six or seven children, delivered with the help of a female neighbor or a midwife. Such large families sapped the physical and emotional strength of most mothers for twenty of their most active years. One Massachusetts mother confessed that she had little time for religious activities because "the care of my Babes takes up so large a portion of my time and attention." Yet most Puritan congregations were filled with women: "In a Church of between *Three* and *Four* Hundred *Communicants*," the eminent minister Cotton Mather noted, "there are but few more than *One* Hundred *Men*; all

The First, Second and Last Scene of Mortality    Prudence Punderson.

### Prudence Punderson (1758–1784), *The First, Second and Last Scenes of Mortality*

This powerful image reveals both the artistic skills of colonial women in the traditional medium of needlework and the Puritans' continuing cultural concern with the inevitability of death. Prudence Punderson, the Connecticut woman who embroidered this scene, rejected a marriage proposal and followed her Loyalist father into exile on Long Island in 1778. Sometime later, she married a cousin, Timothy Rossiter, and bore a daughter, Sophia, who may well be the baby in the cradle being rocked by "Jenny," a slave owned by Prudence's father. Long worried by "my ill state of health" and perhaps now anticipating her own death, Prudence has inscribed her initials on the coffin—and, in creating this embroidery, transformed her personal experience into a broader mediation on the progression from birth, to motherhood, to death.    Connecticut Historical Society.

the Rest are Women." Many women claimed a conversion experience and became full members, revivalist minister Jonathan Edwards suggested, because they feared death during childbirth and because that status meant that "their children may be baptized."

As the size of farms shrank in long-settled communities, many couples chose to have fewer children. After 1750, women in the typical Massachusetts farm village of Andover bore an average of only four children and had time and energy for other tasks. Women in farming families now could make yarn, cloth, or cheese to exchange with neighbors or sell to shopkeepers, raising their families' standard of living. Or, like Susan Huntington of Boston, the wife of a prosperous merchant, they spent more time in "the care & culture of children, and the perusal of necessary books, including the scriptures."

Still, women's lives remained tightly bound by a web of legal and cultural restrictions. Ministers praised women for their piety but excluded them from an equal role in the church. When Hannah Heaton, a Connecticut farmwife, grew dissatisfied with her Congregationalist minister, thinking him unconverted and a "blind guide," she sought out equality-minded Quaker and evangelist Baptist churches that welcomed questioning women such as herself and treated "saved" women equally with men. However, by the 1760s, many evangelical congregations had lost some of their religious zeal and had reinstituted men's dominance over women. "The government of Church and State must be . . . family government" controlled by its "king," declared the Danbury (Connecticut) Baptist Association. Willingly or not, most colonial women abided by the custom that, as essayist Timothy Dwight put it, they should be subservient to their husbands and "employed only in and about the house."

## Farm Property: Inheritance

By contrast, European men who migrated to the colonies escaped many traditional constraints, including the curse of landlessness. "The hope of having land of their own & becoming independent of Landlords is what chiefly induces people into America," an official noted in the 1730s. Owning property gave formerly dependent peasants a new social identity.

Property ownership and family authority were closely related. Most migrating Europeans wanted farms that would provide a living for themselves and ample land for their children. Parents who could not give their offspring land placed these children as indentured servants in more prosperous households. When the inden-

tures ended at age eighteen or twenty-one, propertyless sons faced a decades-long climb up the agricultural ladder, from laborer to tenant and finally to freeholder.

Sons and daughters in well-to-do farm families were luckier: They received a marriage portion when they were between the ages of twenty-three and twenty-five. That portion — land, livestock, or farm equipment — repaid children for their past labor and allowed parents to choose their children's partners, which they did not hesitate to do. Parents' security during old age depended on a wise choice of son- or daughter-in-law. Although the young people could refuse an unacceptable match, they did not have the luxury of falling in love with and marrying whomever they pleased.

Marriage under eighteenth-century English common law was not a contract between equals. A bride relinquished to her husband the legal ownership of all her property. After his death, she received a dower right — the right to use (though not sell), one-third of the family's property; on this widow's death or remarriage, her portion was divided among the children. Thus the widow's property rights were subordinate to those of the family line, which stretched across the generations.

A father's duty was to provide inheritances for his children so that one day they could "be for themselves." Men who failed to do so lost status in the community. Some fathers willed the family farm to a single son and either provided other children with money, an apprenticeship, or uncleared frontier tracts, or required the inheriting son to do so. Other yeomen moved their families to the frontier, where life was hard but land was cheap and abundant. "The Squire's House stands on the Bank of the Susquehannah," traveler Philip Fithian reported from the Pennsylvania backcountry in the early 1760s. "He tells me that he will be able to settle all his sons and his fair Daughter Betsy on the Fat of the Earth."

These farmers' historic achievement was the creation of many communities of independent property owners. A French visitor noted the sense of personal dignity in this rural world, which contrasted sharply with that of European peasants. He found "men and women whose features are not marked by poverty . . . or by a feeling that they are insignificant subjects and subservient members of society."

## Freehold Society in Crisis

How long would this happy circumstance last? Because of rapid natural increase, New England's population doubled each generation, from 100,000 in 1700, to nearly 200,000 in 1725, to almost 400,000 in 1750. Farms had been divided and then subdivided, making them so small—50 acres or less—that parents could provide only one child with an adequate inheritance. In the 1740s, Reverend Samuel Chandler of Andover, Massachusetts, was "much distressed for land for his children," seven of them young boys. A decade later, in nearby Concord, about 60 percent of the farmers owned less land than their fathers had. And overfishing meant that the region's rivers, once overflowing with nutritious fish, had been severely depleted.

Because parents had less to give their sons and daughters, they had less control over their children's lives. The traditional system of arranged marriages broke down, as young people engaged in premarital sex and then used the urgency of pregnancy to win permission to marry. Throughout New England, premarital conceptions rose dramatically, from about 10 percent of firstborn children in the 1710s to more than 30 percent in the 1740s. Given another chance, young people "would do the same again," an Anglican minister observed, "because otherwise they could not obtain their parents' consent to marry."

Even as New England families changed, they maintained the freeholder ideal. Some parents chose to have smaller families and used birth control to do so: abstention, coitus interruptus, or primitive condoms. Other families petitioned the provincial government for frontier land grants and hacked new farms out of the forests of central Massachusetts, western Connecticut, and eventually New Hampshire and Vermont. Still others improved their farms' productivity by replacing the traditional English crops of wheat and barley with high-yielding potatoes and maize (Indian corn). Corn was an especially wise choice: It yielded a hearty food crop for human consumption, and its stalk and leaves furnished feed for cattle and pigs, which provided milk and meat. Gradually, New England changed from a grain to a livestock economy, becoming a major exporter of salted meat to the plantations of the West Indies.

Finally, New England farmers developed the full potential of what one historian has called the "household mode of production." In this system of community exchange, families swapped labor and goods. Women and children worked in groups to spin yarn, sew quilts, and shuck corn. Men loaned neighbors tools, draft animals, and grazing land. Farmers plowed fields owned by artisans and shopkeepers, who repaid them with shoes, furniture, or store credit. Partly because currency was in short supply, no cash changed hands. Instead, farmers, artisans, and shopkeepers recorded debits and credits and "balanced" the books every few years by transferring small amounts of cash. This system

allowed households—and the region's economy—to maximize agricultural output and so preserve the freehold ideal.

- In what ways were the lives of women and men in New England similar? In what ways were they different?

- What was the threat to the freehold ideal in midcentury New England, and what strategies did farming families use to preserve this ideal?

# Toward a New Society: The Middle Colonies, 1720–1765

The Middle colonies—New York, New Jersey, and Pennsylvania—became home to peoples of differing origins, languages, and religions. Scots-Irish Presbyterians, English and Welsh Quakers, German Lutherans and Moravians, and Dutch Reformed Protestants formed ethnic and religious communities that coexisted uneasily.

## Economic Growth and Social Inequality

Ample fertile land attracted migrants to the Middle colonies, and grain exports to Europe and the West Indies financed the colonies' rapid settlement. Between 1720 and 1770, a growing demand for wheat, corn, and flour doubled their prices and brought people and prosperity to the region: The region's population surged from 120,000 in 1720 to 450,000 in 1765 (Figure 4.1).

**Tenancy in New York**  Many migrants refused to settle in New York's fertile Hudson River Valley—and with good reason. There, wealthy Dutch and English families—the Van Rensselaers, Philipses, Livingstons, and Clarks—presided over the huge manors created by the Dutch West India Company and English governors (Map 4.1). Like Chesapeake planters, the New York landlords aspired to live in the same manner as did the European gentry, but they found that few migrants wanted to labor as peasants. To attract tenants, the manorial lords granted long leases, with the right to sell improvements—houses and barns, for example—to the next tenant. Still, the number of tenants rose slowly; the vast 100,000-acre Van Rensselaer estate had only 82 in 1714 and 345 in 1752, with a jump to 700 by 1765.

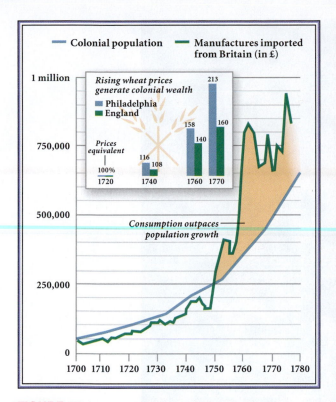

## FIGURE 4.1

### Population Growth, Wheat Prices, and British Imports in the Middle Atlantic Colonies

Wheat prices doubled in Philadelphia between 1720 and 1770 as demand swelled both in Europe and the West Indies. The income earned from the exports of grain and flour paid for English manufactures, which the settlers in the Middle Colonies imported in large quantities after 1750.

Most tenant families hoped that with hard work and ample sales they could eventually buy their own farmsteads. But preindustrial technology during the crucial harvest season limited output. Wheat had to be harvested when it was ripe, but before it sprouted and became useless, yet a worker with a hand sickle could reap only half an acre of wheat, rye, or oats a day. The cradle scythe, a tool introduced during the 1750s, doubled or tripled the amount of grain one worker could cut. Even so, a family with two adult workers could reap only about 12 acres of grain, or roughly 150 to 180 bushels of wheat. After saving enough grain for food and seed, the surplus might be worth £15—enough to buy salt and sugar, tools, and cloth, but little else. The road to landownership was not an easy one.

**Conflict in Pennsylvania** | In Quaker-dominated Pennsylvania and New Jersey, wealth was initially distributed more evenly than in New York. The first migrants arrived with few resources and lived simply in small, one- or two-room houses

## MAP 4.1

### The Hudson River Manors

Dutch and English manorial lords owned much of the fertile east bank of the Hudson River, where they leased farms on perpetual contracts to German tenants and refused to sell land to freehold-seeking migrants from overcrowded New England. This powerful landed elite produced aristocratic-minded Patriot leaders such as Gouverneur Morris and Robert Livingston, as well as prominent American families such as the Roosevelts.

with a sleeping loft, a few benches or stools, and some wooden platters and cups. Only a few wealthy families ate off pewter or ceramic plates imported from England or Holland.

However, the expanding trade in wheat and an

**A Quaker Meeting for Worship**

Quakers dressed plainly and met for worship in unadorned buildings, sitting in silence until inspired by an "inner light." Women spoke during meetings on terms of near-equality to men, a tradition that prepared Quaker women to take a leading part in the nineteenth-century women's rights movement. In this English work, titled *Quaker Meeting*, an elder (his hat on a peg above his head) conveys his thoughts to the congregation.   Museum of Fine Arts, Boston. M. and M. Karolik Collection.

influx of poor settlers sharpened social divisions. By the 1760s, eastern Pennsylvania landowners with large farms were using slaves and poor Scots-Irish migrants to grow wheat. Other ambitious men were buying up land and dividing it into small tenancies, which they let out on profitable leases. Still others were accumulating wealth by providing new settlers with farming equipment, sugar and rum from the West Indies, and financial services. These large-scale farmers, rural landlords, speculators, storekeepers, and gristmill operators formed a distinct class of agricultural capitalists. They built large stone houses for their families, furnishing them with four-poster beds and expensive mahogany tables, on which they laid elegant linen and handsomely decorated Dutch dinnerware.

In contrast, one-half of the Middle colonies' white men owned no land and little personal property. A few propertyless men were the sons of smallholding farmers and would eventually inherit some land. But most were

Scots-Irish or German "inmates"—single men or families, explained a tax assessor, "such as live in small cottages and have no taxable property, except a cow." In the predominantly German township of Lancaster, Pennsylvania, a merchant noted an "abundance of Poor people" who "maintain their Families with great difficulty by day Labour." Although these workers hoped eventually to become landowners, an abrupt and steep rise in land prices prevented many from realizing their dreams.

Some hard-pressed migrants turned to crime, which rose sharply after 1720. Previously, merchant Isaac Norris recalled, "we could Safely go to bed with our doors open but now Robberies, housebreaking, Rapes, & other crimes are become Common." In 1732, the Philadelphia Society of Friends publicly identified the criminals as "the vicious and scandalous Refuse of other Countries," a charge confirmed by recent scholarship. Pennsylvania's religious peoples—Quakers, Mennonites, Amish, Moravians, and Lutherans—broke relatively few laws; those who committed crimes were usually either propertyless individuals, indentured servants, or Scots-Irish (or often all three).

Merchants and artisans took advantage of the ample labor supply to set up an outwork system. They bought wool or flax from farmers and paid propertyless workers and land-poor farm families to spin it into yarn or weave it into cloth. In the 1760s, an English traveler reported that hundreds of Pennsylvanians had turned "to manufacture, and live upon a small farm, as in many parts of England." In the Middle Atlantic as in New England, many communities were now as crowded and socially divided as those in rural England, with many families fearing they were fated to return to the lowly status of the European peasant.

## Cultural Diversity

The Middle Atlantic colonies were not a melting pot. Most European migrants held tightly to their traditions, creating a patchwork of ethnically and religiously diverse communities (Figure 4.2). In 1748, Swedish traveler Peter Kalm counted no fewer than twelve religious denominations in Philadelphia, including Anglicans, Baptists, Quakers, Swedish and German Lutherans, Mennonites, Scots-Irish Presbyterians, and Roman Catholics.

Migrants preserved their cultural identity by marrying within their ethnic groups and maintaining Old World customs. A major exception was the Huguenots, Calvinists who had been expelled from Catholic France in the 1680s and resettled in Holland, England, and the British colonies. Huguenots in American port cities — such as Boston, New York, and Charleston — quickly lost their French identities by intermarrying with other Protestants. More typical were the Welsh Quakers in Chester County, Pennsylvania: Seventy percent of the children of the original Welsh migrants married other Welsh Quakers, as did 60 percent of the third generation.

In Pennsylvania and western New Jersey, Quakers shaped the culture because of their numbers, wealth, and social cohesion. Most Quakers came from English counties with few landlords and brought with them traditions of local village governance, popular participation in politics, and social equality. Because Quakers were also pacifists, Pennsylvania officials bought the land they settled from Native Americans rather than seizing it. However, in 1737, Governor Thomas Penn used sharp tactics to oust the Lenni-Lenape (or Delaware) Indians from a vast area, creating a bitterness that led to war in the 1750s. By that time, Quakers had extended their belief in equality to African Americans. Many Quaker meetings (congregations) condemned slavery, and some expelled members who continued to keep slaves.

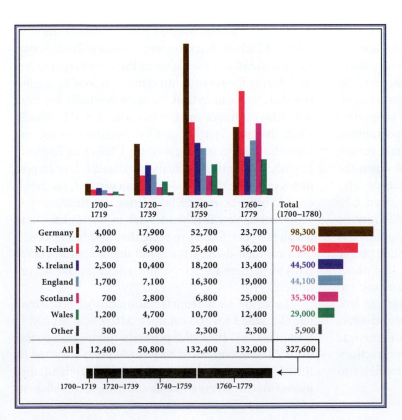

**FIGURE 4.2**

**Estimated European Migration to the British Mainland Colonies, 1700–1780**

After 1720, European migration to British North America increased dramatically, peaking between 1740 and 1780, when more than 264,000 settlers arrived in the mainland colonies. Emigration from Germany peaked in the 1740s, but the number of migrants from Ireland, Scotland, England, and Wales continued to increase during the 1760s and early 1770s. Most migrants, including those from Ireland, were Protestants.  Source: Adapted from Aaron Fogelman, "Migrations to the Thirteen British North American Colonies, 1700–1775: New Estimates," *Journal of Interdisciplinary History* 22 (1992).

| | 1700–1719 | 1720–1739 | 1740–1759 | 1760–1779 | Total (1700–1780) | |
|---|---|---|---|---|---|---|
| Germany | 4,000 | 17,900 | 52,700 | 23,700 | 98,300 | |
| N. Ireland | 2,000 | 6,900 | 25,400 | 36,200 | 70,500 | |
| S. Ireland | 2,500 | 10,400 | 18,200 | 13,400 | 44,500 | |
| England | 1,700 | 7,100 | 16,300 | 19,000 | 44,100 | |
| Scotland | 700 | 2,800 | 6,800 | 25,000 | 35,300 | |
| Wales | 1,200 | 4,700 | 10,700 | 12,400 | 29,000 | |
| Other | 300 | 1,000 | 2,300 | 2,300 | 5,900 | |
| All | 12,400 | 50,800 | 132,400 | 132,000 | 327,600 | |

1700–1719  1720–1739  1740–1759  1760–1779

**The Demory House, c. 1780**

The Demory House lies near the Shenandoah Valley in northwestern Virginia, and was probably built by a migrant from Pennsylvania according to a German design used by both German and Scots-Irish settlers. The house is small but sturdy. It measures 20 feet by 14 feet deep, and has one and a half stories. The two first-floor rooms, a kitchen and a parlor, are separated by an 18 x 18–inch square chimney set in the center of the house, as well as the stairs leading up to the sleeping chamber. Clay and small stones fill the gaps in the exterior walls, which consist of timber planking about 12 inches tall and 6 to 8 inches wide.    © 2003 Copyright and All Rights Reserved by Christopher C. Fennell.

**The German Influx**    The Quaker vision of a "peaceable kingdom" attracted 100,000 German migrants who had fled their homelands because of military conscription, religious persecution, and high taxes. First to arrive, in 1683, were the Mennonites, religious dissenters drawn by the promise of freedom of worship. In the 1720s, a larger wave of German migrants arrived from the overcrowded villages of southwestern Germany and Switzerland. "Wages were far better" in Pennsylvania, Heinrich Schneebeli reported to his friends in Zurich, and "one also enjoyed there a free unhindered exercise of religion." A third wave of Germans and Swiss—nearly 40,000 strong—landed in Philadelphia between 1749 and 1756. Some were redemptioners (indentured servants who migrated as individuals or families) but many more were propertied farmers and artisans in search of better opportunities.

Germans soon dominated many districts in eastern Pennsylvania, and thousands more moved down the fertile Shenandoah Valley into the western backcountry of Maryland, Virginia, and the Carolinas (Map 4.2). Many migrants preserved their cultural identity by settling in Lutheran and Reformed communities. A minister in North Carolina admonished young people "not to contract any marriages with the English or Irish," arguing that "we owe it to our native country to do our part that German blood and the German language be preserved in America." Well beyond 1800, many settlers spoke German, read German-language newspapers, and preserved German farming practices, among which was sending women into the fields to plow and reap.

These settlers were willing colonial subjects of Britain's German-born and German-speaking Protestant monarchs, George I (r. 1714–1727) and George II (r. 1727–1760). They generally avoided politics except to protect their cultural practices; for example, they insisted that married women have the legal right to hold property and write wills, as they did in Germany.

**Scots-Irish Settlers**    Migrants from Ireland, who numbered about 115,000, were the most numerous of the incoming Europeans. Some were Irish and Catholic but most were Scots and Presbyterian, the descendants of the Calvinist Protestants sent to Ireland during the seventeenth century to solidify English rule there. Once in Ireland, the Scots faced hostility from both Irish Catholics and English officials and landlords. Thus, the Irish Test Act of 1704 restricted voting and office-holding to members of the Church of England, English mercantilist regulations placed heavy import duties on linens made by Scots-Irish weavers, and farmers paid heavy taxes. "Read this letter, Rev. Baptist Boyd," a migrant to New York wrote back to his minister, "and tell all the poor folk of ye place that God has opened a door for their deliverance . . . all that a man works for is his own; there are no revenue hounds to take it from us here."

Lured by such reports, thousands of Scots-Irish families sailed for the colonies. Many who landed in Boston in the 1710s settled primarily in New Hampshire. By 1720, most migrated to Philadelphia, attracted by the religious tolerance there. Seeking cheap land, they moved to central Pennsylvania and to the fertile Shenan-

Two groups from Scotland (Scots and Scots Irish) made up about 15 percent of the population and lived primarily in western Pennsylvania, the southern backcountry, and North Carolina.

Those of German ancestry made up about 7 percent of the population and lived mostly in Greater Pennsylvania, which consisted of Penn's colony and the adjacent Shenandoah Valley regions of Maryland and Virginia.

Maps showing dominant ethnic or racial groups can be deceiving because they do not show relative size (a dominant group could include 30 percent or 80 percent of the inhabitants). Moreover, such maps do not reveal if a numerically dominant group enjoys political and economic power or is a subject people, as in the case of enslaved Africans.

People of African origin accounted for 20 percent of the total population and were particularly numerous in the Tidewater regions of Maryland, Virginia, and South Carolina.

Begin with this key. Then look for areas in which a particular group was strongly represented.

**Predominant Ethnic Group**

| | |
|---|---|
| African | Scots-Irish |
| Dutch | Scots |
| English | Swedish |
| German | Welsh |

**MAP 4.2**

### Ethnic and Racial Diversity in the British Colonies, 1775

In 1700, most colonists in British North America were of English origin; by 1775, settlers of English descent constituted only about 50 percent of the total population. African Americans now accounted for one-third of the residents of the South, while tens of thousands of German and Scots-Irish migrants added ethnic and religious diversity in the Middle colonies, the southern backcountry, and northern New England (see Figure 4.2).

doah Valley to the south. Governor William Gooch of Virginia welcomed the Scots-Irish presence to secure "the Country against the Indians." An Anglican planter, however, thought them as dangerous as "the Goths and Vandals of old" had been to the Roman Empire. Like the Germans, the Scots-Irish retained their culture, living in ethnic communities and holding firm to the Presbyterian Church.

## Religious Identity and Political Conflict

In Western Europe, the leaders of church and state condemned religious diversity. "To tolerate all [religions] without controul is the way to have none at all," declared an Anglican clergyman. Orthodox church officials carried such sentiments to Pennsylvania. "The preachers do not have the power to punish anyone, or to force anyone to go to church," complained Gottlieb Mittelberger, an influential German minister. As a re-

sult, "Sunday is very badly kept. Many people plough, reap, thresh, hew or split wood and the like." He concluded: "Liberty in Pennsylvania does more harm than good to many people, both in soul and body."

Mittelberger was mistaken. Although ministers in Pennsylvania could not invoke government authority to uphold religious values, the result was not social anarchy. Instead, religious sects enforced moral behavior through communal self-discipline. Among Quakers, families attended a weekly meeting for worship and a monthly meeting for business, and every three months, a committee reminded parents to provide proper religious instruction. Parents took the committee's words to heart. "If thou refuse to be obedient to God's teachings," Walter Faucit of Chester County admonished his son, "thou will be a fool and a vagabond." The committee also supervised adult behavior; a Chester County meeting, for example, disciplined a member "to reclaim him from drinking to excess and keeping vain company." Significantly, Quaker meetings allowed couples

All the nations and people I had hitherto passed through resemble
own in their manners, customs and lang

## Henry Melchior Muhlenberg
# Cultural Conflict in Pennsylvania

Henry Melchior Muhlenberg (1711–1787) arrived in Pennsylvania in 1742. The first German Lutheran minister in British colonies, he also became the most influential and is known as "the Patriarch of the Lutheran Church in America." Fluent in English and Dutch as well as German, Muhlenberg recorded in his voluminous journals the many conflicts—over religious dogma, Indian affairs, and political allegiance—among the diverse ethnic and religious groups of the Middle colonies.

JULY 17 [1753]. . . . Since the justice of the peace, who is a member of the Presbyterian Church, shares the secret prejudice of his fellow Presbyterians that the German Lutherans retain too much of the papistical [Catholic] leaven, he wrote into the deed of conveyance a derogatory [limiting] clause, stating that the church site is to remain the property of the Lutherans only until a further reformation takes place in our church.

JULY 21 [1753]. . . . Mr. Rose told me that a German married couple lived on this road, in service with a Dutch Reformed man, and that these people had a child to be baptized. Several weeks before, they had walked ten miles to have their child baptized in Neshaminy because it was said that I was going to preach there. But since I had not come, they had asked the Dutch Reformed preacher to baptize their child; but he would not baptize it unless they promised to rear the child in the Reformed religion. And since they neither would nor could promise such a thing, they had returned without having gained their end. . . . I baptized the child to the joy and comfort of the parents.

FEBRUARY 1 [1764]. This afternoon all citizens were summoned to the state house by the governor [who] made a public proclamation:

  1) That it had been learned that a large mob of frontier settlers [the Scots-Irish Paxton Boys], who had killed several Indians in Lancaster, were coming to Philadelphia to kill the Indian families . . . under the protection of the government. . . .
  3) That the governor and *counsel* called upon citizens who were willing to lend armed assistance and resist the rebellion to band themselves together. . . .
As far as I can learn, the opinion and sentiment of various ones of our German citizens is as follows:
  1) They were of the opinion that it could be proved that the Indians who had lived among the so-called Moravian Brethren had secretly killed several settlers.
  2) That the Quakers and Bethlehemites [Moravians] had only used some of the aforesaid Indians as spies and that they had in view only their own selfish interests, without considering at all that they had murdered their fellow Christians.

3) Indeed, [this] . . . explained why the Quakers, etc. in Philadelphia did not exhibit the least evidence of human sympathy, etc. when Germans and other settlers on the frontiers were massacred and destroyed in the most inhuman manner by the Indians. . .
4) Our German citizens . . . would unhesitatingly and gladly pour out their possessions and their blood for our most gracious king [George II, who was also the Prince of Hanover in Germany] and his officers, but they would not wage war against their own suffering fellow citizens for the sake of the Quakers and Moravians and their creatures or instruments, the double-dealing Indians.

OCTOBER 3 [1764]. . . . There was great rejoicing and great bitterness in the political circles of the city, since it was reported that the German church people [the Lutheran and Reformed churches] had gained a victory in the election by putting our *trustee*, Mr. Henry Keppele, into the *assembly*. . . . The English and German Quakers, the Moravians, Mennonites, and Schwenkfelders formed one party, and the English of the High Church and the Presbyterian Church, the German Lutherans, and the German Reformed joined the other party and gained the upper hand—a thing heretofore unheard of.

Source: Henry Melchior Muhlenberg, *The Notebook of a Colonial Clergyman*, trans. and ed. Theodore G. Tappert and John W. Doberstein (Philadelphia: Muhlenberg Press, 1959), 46–47, 50–51, 95–97, 111.

### ANALYZING THE EVIDENCE

- **Why were Germans reluctant to take up arms against the Paxton Boys?**
- **One line of religious division separated sects based primarily on congregations (Quakers, Moravians, Mennonites) from churches with hierarchies and bishops (Anglicans, Presbyterians, Lutherans, Reformed). What else separated these Christians? Why would a Reformed minister refuse to baptize a Lutheran child? Why would a Presbyterian justice of the peace limit the property rights of German Lutherans?**

to marry only if they had land and livestock sufficient to support a family. As a result, the children of well-to-do Friends usually married within the sect, while poor Quakers remained unmarried, wed later in life, or married without permission—in which case they were often ousted from the meeting. These marriage rules helped the Quakers build a self-contained and prosperous community.

In the 1740s, Quaker dominance in Pennsylvania was threatened: The flood of new migrants reduced Quakers to a minority—a mere 30 percent of Pennsylvanians. Moreover, Scots-Irish settlers in central Penn-sylvania were demanding an aggressive Indian policy, challenging the pacifism of the assembly. To retain power, Quaker politicians sought an alliance with German religious groups who also embraced pacifism and voluntary (not compulsory) militia service (see Voices from Abroad, "Henry Melchior Muhlenberg: Cultural Conflict in Pennsylvania," p. 114). But German leaders demanded more seats in the assembly, in which Quakers were overrepresented, and laws that respected their inheritance customs. Other Germans—Lutherans and Baptists—tried to seize control of the assembly by forming a "general confederacy" with Scots-Irish Presbyterians. An observer, noting that "religious zeal is secretly burning," predicted that the scheme was doomed to failure because of "mutual jealousy" (Map 4.3).

By the 1750s, politics throughout the Middle colonies had become a roiling cauldron of such conflicts. In New York, a Dutchman declared that he "Valued English Law no more than a Turd," while in Pennsylvania, Benjamin Franklin disparaged the "boorish" character and "swarthy complexion" of German migrants. The Middle Atlantic's experiment in social diversity prefigured the bitter ethnic and religious tensions that would pervade American society in the centuries to come.

- Who were the new migrants to the Middle colonies? Why did they leave Europe? What were their goals in British North America?

- What were the main issues that divided the ethnic and religious groups of the Middle colonies?

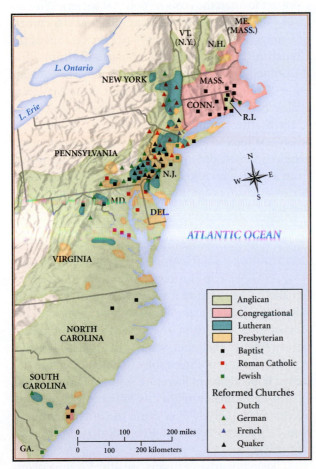

**MAP 4.3**

**Religious Diversity in 1750**

By 1750, religious diversity was on the rise, not only in the multiethnic Middle colonies but in all of British North America. Baptists had increased their numbers in New England, long the stronghold of Congregationalists, and would soon become important in Virginia. Already there were considerable numbers of Presbyterians, Lutherans, and German Reformed in the South, where Anglicanism was the established religion.

# The Enlightenment and the Great Awakening, 1720–1765

Two great European cultural movements reached America between the 1720s and the 1760s: the Enlightenment and Pietism. The Enlightenment, which emphasized the power of human reason to understand and shape the world, appealed especially to urban artisans and well-educated men and women from merchant or planter families. Pietism, an evangelical Christian movement that stressed the individual's personal relationship with God, attracted many more adherents, primarily farmers and urban laborers. Together, the two movements transformed American intellectual and cultural life.

## The Enlightenment in America

To explain the workings of the natural world, some settlers relied on folk wisdom. Swedish migrants in Pennsylvania, for example, attributed magical powers to the great white mullein, a common wildflower, and treated fevers by tying the plant's leaves around their feet and arms. Other settlers relied on religion. As most Christians believed that the earth stood at the center of the universe and that God (and Satan) intervened directly and continuously in human affairs, they were constantly on the watch for signs of God's favor and Satan's wiles.

**The European Enlightenment**    The scientific revolution of the sixteenth and seventeenth centuries challenged both folk and traditional Christian worldviews. In 1543, the Polish astronomer Copernicus published his observation that the earth traveled around the sun, not vice versa. Copernicus's discovery suggested that humans occupied a more modest place in the universe than Christian theology assumed. In the next century Sir Isaac Newton, in his *Principia Mathematica* (1687), used the sciences of mathematics and physics to explain the movement of the planets around the sun. Newton's laws of motion and gravity described how the universe operated by means of natural forces. By accounting for the movement of the planets without recourse to a supernatural being, Newton's work undermined the traditional Christian understanding of the cosmos.

In the century between the *Principia Mathematica* and the French Revolution of 1789, the philosophers of the European Enlightenment used empirical research and scientific reasoning to study all aspects of life, including social institutions and human behavior. Enlightenment thinkers advanced four fundamental principles: the lawlike order of the natural world, the power of human reason, the "natural rights" of individuals (including the right to self-government), and the progressive improvement of society.

English philosopher John Locke was a major contributor to the Enlightenment. In his *Essay Concerning Human Understanding* (1690), Locke stressed the impact of environment and experience on human behavior and beliefs. He argued that the character of individuals and societies was not fixed but could be changed through education, rational thought, and purposeful action. Locke's *Two Treatises of Government* (1690) advanced the revolutionary theory that political authority was not given by God to monarchs, as James II had insisted (see Chapter 3). Instead, it derived from social compacts that people made to preserve their "natural rights" to life, liberty, and property. In Locke's view, the people should have the power to change government policies—or even their form of government.

Locke's ideas and those of other Enlightenment thinkers (arriving in America by way of books and educated migrants) caused some clergymen to respond by devising a rational form of Christianity. Rejecting supernatural interventions and a vengeful Calvinist God, Congregationalist minister Andrew Eliot maintained that "there is nothing in Christianity that is contrary to reason." Reverend John Wise of Ipswich, Massachusetts, used Locke's philosophy to defend the vesting of power in ordinary church members. Just as the social compact formed the basis of political society, Wise argued, so the religious covenant among the lay members of a congregation made them—not the bishops of the Church of England or even ministers like himself—the proper interpreters of religious truth. The Enlightenment influenced Puritan minister Cotton Mather as well. When a measles epidemic ravaged Boston in the 1710s, Mather thought that only God could end it; but when smallpox struck a decade later, he used his newly acquired knowledge of inoculation—gained in part from a slave, who told him of the practice's success in Africa—to advocate this scientific preventive for the disease.

**Franklin's Contributions**    Benjamin Franklin was the exemplar of the American Enlightenment. Born in Boston in 1706 to devout Calvinists and apprenticed as a youth to a printer, Franklin was a self-educated man. While working as a printer and journalist in Philadelphia, he formed a "club of mutual improvement" that met weekly to discuss "Morals, Politics, or Natural Philosophy." These discussions, as well as Enlightenment literature (rather than the Bible), shaped Franklin's thinking. As Franklin explained in his *Autobiography* (1771), "From the different books I read, I began to doubt of Revelation [God-revealed truth]."

Like many urban artisans, wealthy Virginia planters, and affluent seaport merchants, Franklin became a deist. **Deism** was a way of thinking, not an established religion. "My own mind is my own church," said deist Thomas Paine. "I am of a sect by myself," added Thomas Jefferson. Influenced by Enlightenment science, deists such as Jefferson believed that a Supreme Being (or Grand Architect) created the world, then allowed it to operate by natural laws, and did not intervene in history or in people's lives. Rejecting the divinity of Christ and the authority of the Bible, deists relied on "natural

**Benjamin Franklin's Influence**

Benjamin Franklin's work as a scientist and inventor not only won the admiration of eighteenth-century European scientists but also captivated subsequent generations of Americans. This painted panel (c. 1830) from a fire engine of the Franklin Volunteer Fire Company of Philadelphia depicts Franklin's 1752 experiment in which he demonstrated the presence of electricity in lightning.    National Museum of American History, Smithsonian Institution.

reason," their innate moral sense, to define right and wrong (see Comparing American Voices, "Evangelical Religion and Enlightenment Rationalism," pp. 118–119). Thus Franklin, a onetime slave owner, came to question the morality of slavery, repudiating it once he recognized the parallels between racial bondage and the colonies' political bondage to Britain.

Franklin popularized the practical outlook of the Enlightenment in *Poor Richard's Almanack* (1732–1757), an annual publication that was read by thousands. He also founded the American Philosophical Society (1743–present) to promote "useful knowledge." Adopting this goal in his own life, Franklin invented bifocal lenses for eyeglasses, the Franklin stove, and the lightning rod. His book on electricity, published in England in 1751, won praise as the greatest contribution to science since Newton's discoveries. Inspired by Franklin, ambitious printers in America's seaport cities published newspapers and gentlemen's magazines, the first significant

nonreligious periodicals to appear in the colonies. The European Enlightenment, then, added a secular dimension to colonial cultural life, foreshadowing the great contributions to republican political theory by American intellectuals of the revolutionary era: John Adams, James Madison, and Thomas Jefferson.

## American Pietism and the Great Awakening

As educated Americans turned to deism, thousands of other colonists embraced Pietism, a Christian movement originating in Germany around 1700 and emphasizing pious behavior (hence the name). In its emotional worship services and individual striving for a mystical union with God, Pietism appealed to believers' hearts rather than their minds. In the 1720s, German migrants carried Pietism to America, sparking a religious **revival** in Pennsylvania and New Jersey, where Dutch minister

Thus I have given you, I think, the Substance of the Arguments both sides of that great and important Quest

# Evangelical Religion and Enlightenment Rationalism

Two great historical movements—Enlightenment thought and pietistic religion—swept across British North America in the eighteenth century and offered radically different—indeed, almost completely contradictory—worldviews. Pietism sparked religious revivals based on passion and emotion, while Enlightenment rationalism encouraged personal restraint and intellectual logic. Both movements shaped American cultural development: Pietism transformed American religious life, and Enlightenment thinking influenced the principles of the American government.

## Sarah Lippet

### Death as a Passage to Life

Sarah Lippet was a longtime member of the Baptist church of Middletown in eastern New Jersey. She died in October 1767, at the age of sixty-one; fellow parishioners reported her sentiments as she lay, for four days, on her deathbed.

All my lifetime I have been in fears and doubts, but now am delivered. He hath delivered them who through fear of death were all their lifetime subject to bondage. For the love I have for Christ I am willing to part with all my friends to be with Him, for I love Him above all; yet it is nothing in me, for I know if I had my desert I should be in Hell. I believe in Christ, and I know that I put my whole trust in Him, and he that believeth in Him shall not be ashamed nor be confounded. . . .

Why do you mourn when I rejoice? You should not; it is no more for me to die and leave my friends for the great love I have for Christ than for me to go to sleep. I have no fears of death in my mind. Christ has the keys of death and hell, and blessed are the dead that die in the Lord. I can't bear to see a tear shed. You should not mourn. . . .

Source: "The Triumphant Christian," in John E. Stillwell, ed., *Historical and Genealogical Miscellany* (New York, 1964), 3: 465–466.

## Nathan Cole

### The Struggle for Salvation

Connecticut farmer Nathan Cole found God after listening to a sermon by George Whitefield, the great English evangelist. But Cole's spiritual quest was not easy. He struggled for two years before coming to believe that he was saved.

[After hearing Whitefield] I began to think I was not Elected, and that God made some for heaven and me for hell. And I thought God was not Just in so doing. . . . My heart then rose against God exceedingly, for his making me for hell;

Now this distress lasted Almost two years—Poor Me—Miserable me. . . . I was loaded with the guilt of Sin. . . .

Hell fire was most always in my mind; and I have hundreds of times put my fingers into my pipe when I have been smoking to feel how fire felt: And to see how my Body could bear to lye in Hell fire for ever and ever. . . . And while these thoughts were in my mind God appeared unto me and made me Skringe: before whose face the heavens and the earth fled away; and I was Shrinked into nothing; I knew not whether I was in the body or out, I seemed to hang in open Air before God, and he seemed to Speak to me in an angry and Sovereign way[:] what won't you trust your Soul with God; My heart answered O yes, yes, yes. . . .

When God disappeared or in some measure withdrew, every thing was in its place again and I was on my Bed. . . . I was set free, my distress was gone, and I was filled with a pineing desire to see Christs own words in the bible; . . . I got the bible up under my Chin and hugged it; it was sweet and lovely; the word was nigh [near] me in my hand, then I began to pray and to praise God.

Source: "The Spiritual Travels of Nathan Cole, 1741" in *The Great Awakening: Documents on the Revival of Religion, 1740–1745*, ed. Richard L. Bushman (New York: Atheneum, 1970), 68–70.

## Benjamin Franklin

### The Importance of a Virtuous Life

Franklin stood at the center of the American Enlightenment. In his *Autobiography*, he outlined his religious views and his human-centered moral principles.

My Parents had early given me religious Impressions, and brought me through my Childhood piously in the Dissenting Way. But I was scarce 15 when, after doubting by turns of several Points as I found them disputed in the different Books I read, I began to doubt of Revelation itself. Some Books against Deism fell into my Hands. . . . It happened that they wrought an Effect on me quite contrary to what was intended by them: For the Arguments of the Deists [that were quoted in those books] appeared to me much Stronger than the Refutations. In short I soon became a thorough Deist. . . .

I grew convinc'd that Truth, Sincerity & Integrity in Dealings between Man & Man, were of the utmost Importance to the Felicity of Life, and I form'd written Resolutions, (which still remain in my Journal Book) to practice them ever while I lived. . . .

About the Year 1734. There arrived among us from Ireland, a young Presbyterian Preacher named Hemphill, who delivered with a good Voice, & apparently extempore, most excellent Discourses, which drew together considerable Numbers of different Persuasions, who join'd in admiring them. Among the rest I became one of his constant Hearers, his Sermons pleasing me as they had little of the dogmatical kind, but inculcated strongly the Practice of Virtue, or what in the religious Stile are called Good Works. Those however, of our Congregation, who considered themselves as orthodox Presbyterians, disapprov'd his Doctrine, and were join'd by most of the old Clergy, who arraign'd him of Heterodoxy before the Synod, in order to have him silenc'd. I became his zealous Partisan. . . .

I never was without some religious Principles; I never doubted, for instance, the Existance of the Deity, that he made the World, & govern'd it by his Providence; that the most acceptable Service of God was the doing Good to Man; that our Souls are immortal; and that all Crime will be punished & Virtue rewarded either here or hereafter; these I esteem'd the Essentials of every Religion.

Source: Louis P. Masur, ed., *The Autobiography of Benjamin Franklin, with Related Documents*, 2nd ed. (Boston: Bedford/St. Martin's, 2003), 73–74, 93–94, 108.

## John Wise
### The Primacy of Human Reason and Natural Laws

Reverend John Wise (1652–1725) served for many years as a pastor in Ipswich, Massachusetts. A graduate of Harvard College, Wise used the Enlightenment doctrines of John Locke and Samuel von Pufendorf to justify the democratic structure of New England Congregational churches.

I Shall disclose several Principles of Natural Knowledge; plainly discovering the Law of Nature; or the true sentiments of Natural Reason, with Respect to Mans Being and Government. . . . I shall consider Man in a state of Natural Being, as a Free-Born Subject under the Crown of Heaven, and owing Homage to none but God himself. It is certain Civil Government in General, is a very Admirable Result of Providence, and an Incomparable Benefit to Mankind, yet must needs be acknowledged to be the Effect of Humane Free-Compacts and not of Divine Institution; it is the Produce of Mans Reason, of Humane and Rational Combinations, and not from any direct Orders of Infinite Wisdom. . . .

The Prime Immunity in Mans State, is that he is most properly the Subject of the Law of Nature. He is the Favourite Animal on Earth; in that this Part of Gods Image, viz. Reason is Congenate with his Nature, wherein by a Law Immutable, Instampt upon his Frame, God has provided a Rule for Men in all their Actions; obliging each one to the performance of that which is Right, not only as to Justice, but likewise as to all other Moral Vertues, which is nothing but the Dictate of Right Reason founded in the Soul of Man. . . .

The Second Great Immunity of Man is an Original Liberty Instampt upon his Rational Nature. He that intrudes upon this Liberty, Violates the Law of Nature. . . .

The Third Capital Immunity belonging to Mans Nature, is an equality amongst Men; Which is not to be denied by the Law of Nature, till Man has Resigned himself with all his Rights for the sake of a Civil State; and then his Personal Liberty and Equality is to be cherished, and preserved to the highest degree.

Source: John Wise, *A Vindication of the Government of New England Churches* (Boston: J. Allen, for N. Boone, 1717), 32–40.

## ANALYZING THE EVIDENCE
- All of these writers declare a belief in God. How, then, do their beliefs and outlooks differ?
- According to these authors, what is the role of "faith" and of "reason" in their religious lives?
- How would the various writers determine what was "right," or morally correct? What are the sources on which they would rely?
- John Wise asserts that civil government (political institutions) is the "Produce of Mans Reason . . . and not from any direct Orders of Infinite Wisdom." Would Nathan Cole and Sarah Lippet agree?

**Enlightenment Philanthropy: Pennsylvania Hospital, Philadelphia**

Using public funds and private donations, Philadelphia reformers built this imposing structure in 1753. The new hospital embodied two principles of the Enlightenment: that purposeful actions could improve society, and that the products of these actions should express reason and order, exhibited here in the building's symmetrical facade. Etchings like this one from the 1760s (*A Perspective View of the Pennsylvania Hospital*, by John Streeper and Henry Dawkins) circulated widely and bolstered Philadelphia's reputation as the center of the American Enlightenment.   Historical Society of Pennsylvania, Philadelphia.

Theodore Jacob Frelinghuysen preached passionate sermons to German settlers and encouraged church members to spread the message of spiritual urgency. A decade later, William Tennent and his son Gilbert copied Frelinghuysen's approach and led revivals among Scots-Irish Presbyterians throughout the Middle Atlantic region.

**Jonathan Edwards's Calvinism** | Simultaneously, an American-born Pietist movement appeared in New England. The original Puritans were intensely pious Christians, but their spiritual zeal had faded over the decades. In the 1730s, Jonathan Edwards restored that zeal to Congregational churches in the Connecticut River Valley. Edwards was born in 1703, the only son among the eleven children of Timothy and Esther Stoddard Edwards. His father was a poorly paid rural minister, but his mother was the daughter of Solomon Stoddard, a famous Puritan preacher who taught that a compassionate God would give sainthood to more than a select few.

As a young man, Edwards rejected Stoddard's thinking. Inspired by the harsh theology of John Calvin, he preached that men and women were helpless creatures, completely dependent on the mercy of God. In his most famous sermon, "Sinners in the Hands of an Angry God" (1741), Edwards declared: "There is Hell's wide gaping mouth open; and you have nothing to stand upon, nor any thing to take hold of: there is nothing between you and Hell but the air; 'tis only the power and mere pleasure of God that holds you up." According to one observer, the response was electric: "There was a great moaning and crying through the whole house. What shall I do to be saved—oh, I am going to Hell."

Surprisingly, Edwards contributed to Enlightenment thought, accepting Locke's argument in the *Essay Concerning Human Understanding* (1690) that

**Jonathan Edwards (1703–1758)**
From this engraving, based on a picture by Charles Willson Peale, it is easy to imagine that Edwards's direct gaze at the viewer was the same one experienced by the preacher's congregation in Northampton, Massachusetts, as he urged them to be "born again and made new creatures." Edwards was then in his late-forties and at the height of his powers as a scholar—but not as a pastor. When Edwards restricted full church membership to "Saints"—the Calvinist "elect"—his congregation voted 200 to 23 in 1750 to dismiss the great preacher and philosopher. Impoverished, Edwards moved to the frontier town of Stockbridge, where he ministered, without great success, to the Housatonic Indians. © Bettmann/Corbis.

ideas are the product of experience as conveyed by the senses. However, Edwards also argued that people's beliefs depended on their passions. Edwards used his theory of knowledge to justify his preaching: Vivid words would "fright persons away from Hell" and promote conversions. News of Edwards's success stimulated religious fervor up and down the Connecticut River Valley.

**Whitefield's Great Awakening** English minister George Whitefield transformed the local revivals of Edwards and the Tennents into a Great Awakening. After Whitefield had his personal awakening upon reading the German Pietists, he became a follower of John Wesley, the founder of English Methodism. In 1739, Whitefield carried Wesley's fervent message to America, where he attracted huge crowds of "enthusiasts" (as conservative ministers contemptuously labeled them) from Georgia to Massachusetts. "Religion is become the Subject of most Conversations," the *Pennsylvania Gazette* reported. "No books are in Request but those of Piety and Devotion." Whitefield's preaching so impressed Benjamin Franklin that when the revivalist asked for contributions, Franklin emptied the coins in his pockets "wholly into the collector's dish, gold and all." By the time Whitefield reached Boston, Reverend Benjamin Colman reported, the people were "ready to receive him as an angel of God."

Whitefield had a compelling presence. "He looked almost angelical; a young, slim, slender youth . . . cloathed with authority from the Great God," wrote a Connecticut farmer. Like most evangelical preachers, Whitefield did not read his sermons but spoke from memory. He gestured eloquently, raised his voice for dramatic effect, and at times assumed a female persona—as a woman in labor struggling to deliver the word of God. When the young preacher told his spellbound listeners that they had sinned and must seek salvation, some suddenly felt a "new light" within them. As "the power of god come down," Hannah Heaton recalled, "my knees smote together . . . [and] it seemed to me I was a sinking down into hell . . . but then I resigned my distress and was perfectly easy quiet and calm . . . [and] it seemed as if I had a new soul & body both." Strengthened and self-confident, the so-called New Lights were eager to spread Whitefield's message.

## Religious Upheaval in the North

Like all cultural explosions, the Great Awakening was controversial. Conservative ministers—passionless Old Lights, according to the evangelists—condemned the "cryings out, faintings and convulsions" in revivalist meetings and the New Lights' claims of "working Miracles or speaking with Tongues." Boston minister Charles Chauncy attacked the New Lights for allowing women to speak in public: It was "a plain breach of that commandment of the LORD, where it is said, Let your WOMEN keep silence in the churches." In Connecticut, Old Lights persuaded the legislature to prohibit evangelists from speaking to a congregation without the minister's permission. Although Whitefield insisted, "I am no *Enthusiast*," he found many pulpits closed to him when he returned to Connecticut in 1744. But the New Lights refused to be silenced. Dozens of farmers, women, and artisans roamed the countryside, condemning the Old Lights as "unconverted" and willingly accepting imprisonment: "I shall bring glory to God in my bonds," a dissident preacher wrote from jail.

The Great Awakening undermined legally established churches and their tax-supported ministers. In New England, New Lights left the Congregational Church and founded 125 "separatist" churches that supported their ministers through voluntary contributions (Figure 4.3). Other religious dissidents joined Baptist congregations, which also condemned government support of churches: "God never allowed any civil state upon earth to impose religious taxes," declared Baptist preacher Isaac Backus. In New York and New Jersey, the Dutch Reformed Church split in two as New Lights refused to accept doctrines imposed by conservative church authorities in Holland.

Indeed, the Great Awakening challenged the authority of all ministers, whose status rested on respect for their education and knowledge of the Bible. In an influential pamphlet, *The Dangers of an Unconverted Ministry* (1740), Gilbert Tennent asserted that ministers' authority should come not from theological knowledge but from the conversion experience. Reaffirming Martin Luther's belief in the priesthood of all Christians, Tennent suggested that anyone who had felt God's redeeming grace could speak with min-

isterial authority. Isaac Backus likewise celebrated a spiritual democracy, noting with approval that "the common people now claim as good a right to judge and act in matters of religion as civil rulers or the learned clergy." Proving his point were revivalists like Sarah Harrah Osborne, a New Light "exhorter" in Rhode Island, who refused "to shut up my mouth . . . and creep into obscurity" when silenced by her minister. This subversive, critical spirit soon found other targets. Jonathan Edwards spoke for many farm families when he charged that the money-grubbing practices of merchants and land speculators were more suitable "for wolves and other beasts of prey, than for human beings."

As religious enthusiasm spread, churches founded new colleges to educate their young men and to train ministers. New Light Presbyterians established the College of New Jersey (Princeton) in 1746, and New York Anglicans founded King's College (Columbia) in 1754. Baptists set up the College of Rhode Island (Brown) in 1764; two years later, the Dutch Reformed Church subsidized Queen's College (Rutgers) in New Jersey. However, the main intellectual legacy of the Great Awakening was not education for the privileged few but a new sense of authority among the many. A European visi-

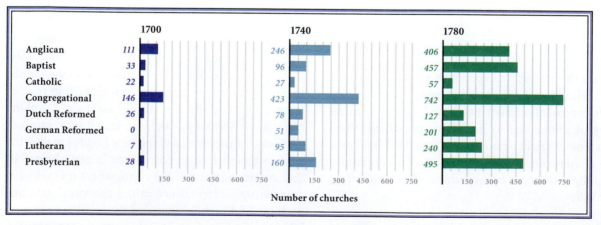

**FIGURE 4.3**

**Church Growth by Denomination, 1700–1780**

In 1700, and again in 1740, the Congregationalist and Anglican churches had the most members. By 1780, however, largely because of their enthusiastic evangelical message, Presbyterian and Baptist congregations outnumbered those of the Anglicans. The growth of immigrant denominations, such as the German Reformed and Lutheran, was equally impressive.

tor to Philadelphia remarked in surprise, "The poorest day-laborer . . . holds it his right to advance his opinion, in religious as well as political matters, with as much freedom as the gentleman."

## Social and Religious Conflict in the South

In the southern colonies, where the Church of England was legally established, religious enthusiasm triggered social conflict. Anglican ministers generally ignored the spiritual needs of African Americans and landless whites, who numbered 40 percent and 20 percent of the population, respectively. Middling white freeholders (35 percent of the residents) formed the core of most Church of England congregations. But prominent planters (just 5 percent) held the real power, using their control of parish finances to discipline ministers. One clergyman complained that dismissal awaited any minister who "had the courage to preach against any Vices taken into favor by the leading Men of his Parish."

**The Presbyterian Revival** Soon, a democratization of religion challenged the dominance of both the Anglican Church and the planter elite. In 1743, bricklayer Samuel Morris, inspired by reading George Whitefield's sermons, led a group of Virginia Anglicans out of their congregation. Seeking a deeper religious experience, Morris invited New Light Presbyterian Samuel Davies to lead their prayer meetings. Davies's sermons, filled with erotic devotional imagery and urging Christians to feel "ardent Passion," sparked Presbyterian revivals across the Tidewater region, threatening the social authority of the Virginia gentry. Traditionally, planters and their well-dressed families arrived at Anglican services in fancy carriages drawn by well-bred horses, and flaunted their power by marching in a body to their honored places in the front pews. Such ritual displays of the gentry's superiority were meaningless if freeholders attended other churches. Moreover, religious pluralism threatened the tax-supported status of the Anglican Church.

To halt the spread of New Light ideas, Virginia governor William Gooch denounced them as "false teachings," and Anglican justices of the peace closed Presbyterian churches. This harassment kept most white yeomen and poor tenant families in the Church of England; so did the fact that many well-educated Presbyterian ministers did not preach in the "enthusiastic" style preferred by illiterate farmers.

**The Baptist Insurgency** New Light Baptist ministers did not hesitate to reach out to ordinary folk. During the 1760s, their vigorous preaching and democratic message converted thousands of white farm families. The Baptists were radical Protestants whose central ritual was adult (rather than infant) baptism. Once men and women had experienced the infusion of grace—had been "born again"—they were baptized in an emotional public ceremony, often involving complete immersion in water.

Even slaves were welcome at Baptist revivals. During the 1740s, George Whitefield had urged Carolina planters to bring their slaves into the Christian fold, but white opposition and the Africans' commitment to their ancestral religions kept the number of converts low. However, in the 1760s, native-born African Americans in Virginia welcomed the Baptists' message that all people were equal in God's eyes. Sensing a threat to the system of racial slavery, the House of Burgesses imposed heavy fines on Baptists who preached to slaves without their owners' permission.

The Baptists' insurgency posed other threats to gentry authority. Baptist preachers repudiated social distinctions and urged followers to call one another "brother" and "sister." They also condemned the planters' dissolute lifestyle. As planter Landon Carter complained, the Baptists were "destroying pleasure in the Country; for they encourage ardent Prayer . . . & an intire Banishment of *Gaming, Dancing,* & Sabbath-Day Diversions." The gentry responded with violence. Hearing Baptist Dutton Lane condemn "the vileness and danger" of drunkenness and whoring, planter John Giles took the charge personally: "I know who you mean! and by God I'll demolish you." In Caroline County, an Anglican posse attacked Brother John Waller at a prayer meeting. Waller "was violently jerked off the stage; they caught him by the back part of his neck, beat his head against the ground, and a gentleman gave him twenty lashes with his horsewhip."

Despite these attacks, Baptist congregations multiplied. By 1775, about 15 percent of Virginia's whites and hundreds of enslaved blacks had joined Baptist churches. To signify their state of grace, some Baptist men "cut off their hair, like Cromwell's round-headed chaplains." Others forged a new evangelical masculinity—"crying, weeping, lifting up the eyes, groaning" when touched by the Holy Spirit but defending themselves with vigor.

"Not able to bear the insults" of a heckler, a group of Baptists "took [him] by the neck and heels and threw him out of doors," setting off a bloody brawl.

The Baptist revival in the Chesapeake challenged customary authority in families and society but did not overturn it. Rejecting the pleas of evangelical women, Baptist men kept church authority in the hands of "free born male members"; and Anglican slaveholders retained control of the political system. Still, the Baptist insurgency infused the lives of poor tenant families with spiritual meaning and empowered yeomen to defend their economic interests. Moreover, as Baptist ministers spread Christianity among slaves, the cultural gulf between blacks and whites shrank, undermining one justification for slavery and giving some blacks a new religious identity. Within a generation, African Americans would develop distinctive versions of Protestant Christianity.

- In what ways did the Enlightenment and the Great Awakening prompt Americans to challenge traditional sources of authority?
- How did the Baptist insurgency in Virginia challenge conventional assumptions about race, gender, and class?

# The Midcentury Challenge: War, Trade, and Social Conflict, 1750–1765

Between 1750 and 1765, three significant events transformed colonial life. First, Britain went to war against the French in America, sparking a worldwide conflict: the Great War for Empire. Second, a surge in trade boosted colonial consumption but caused Americans to become deeply indebted to British creditors. Third, westward migration sparked warfare with Indian peoples, violent disputes between settlers and land speculators, and backcountry rebellions against eastern-controlled governments.

## The French and Indian War

By 1754, France and Britain had laid claim to the vast area between the Appalachian Mountains and the Mississippi River, but few Europeans had moved there (Map 4.4). Though terrain prevented easy access from Britain's seaboard colonies, the Iroquois and their native allies actively expelled white intruders.

However, the strategy the Indians had been using to obtain guns and other goods—playing off the French against the British—was breaking down. The Europeans resented the rising cost of the play-off "gifts," and the Indians faced increasing Anglo-American demands for their lands. In the late 1740s, the Mohawks rebuffed attempts by Sir William Johnson, a British agent and land speculator, to settle Scottish migrants west of Albany. The Iroquois also responded angrily when Virginia governor Robert Dinwiddie, in partnership with Virginia speculators and London merchants, formed the Ohio Company in 1749 and successfully petitioned the king for a grant of 200,000 acres. The land lay in the upper Ohio River Valley, an area the Iroquois controlled through alliances with the Delaware and Shawnee peoples. "We don't know what you Christians, English and French intend," the outraged Iroquois complained. "[W]e are so hemmed in by both, that we have hardly a hunting place left."

**The Albany Congress** To mend relations with the Iroquois, the British Board of Trade called a meeting at Albany in June 1754. At the Albany Congress, British colonial delegates denied having designs on Iroquois lands and sought the Indians' aid against New France. Though small in numbers, the French colony had a broad reach. In the 1750s, the 15,000 French farm families along the St. Lawrence River supplied the fur-trading settlements of Montreal and Quebec and the hundreds of fur traders, missionaries, and soldiers who lived among the western Indian peoples.

To counter French expansion, Benjamin Franklin proposed a "Plan of Union," calling for a continental assembly to manage trade, Indian policy, and defense in the West. But neither Franklin's scheme nor a Board of Trade proposal for a political "union between ye Royal, Proprietary, & Charter Governments" was in the cards. The British ministry worried that union would spark demands for independence; the Americans, warned one official, felt themselves "intitled to a greater measure of Liberty than is enjoyed by the people of England." For their part, colonial leaders feared that a consolidated government would undermine the authority of their assemblies.

French authorities, alarmed as the Iroquois were by the Ohio Company's land grant, sought to stop Anglo-American settlers from pouring into the Ohio River Valley by building a series of forts. One of these, Fort Duquesne, stood where the Monongahela and Allegheny rivers join to form the Ohio River at present-day Pittsburgh. To reassert British claims, Governor

**Hudson Bay**

**Labrador Sea**

HUDSON'S BAY COMPANY

NEW FRANCE

Ft. Louisbourg

Ft. Beauséjour

Quebec

ME.
(MASS.)

Port Royal

Montreal

St. Lawrence R.

Lake Superior

Ft. Frontenac

Ft. Oswego

Lake Huron

Ft. Ticonderoga
N.H.

Boston

Ft. Stanwix

MASS.

R.I.

L. Ontario

N.Y.

Albany

CONN.

Lake Michigan

Detroit

Lake Erie

New York

N.J.

PENN.

Philadelphia

NORTH AMERICA

Mississippi R.

Ft. Duquesne

MD. DEL.

Ft. Cumberland

OHIO
COMPANY
OF
VIRGINIA

VA.

Williamsburg

LOUISIANA

Ohio R.

BRITISH

N.C.

S.C.

**ATLANTIC
OCEAN**

Santa Fe

GA.

Charleston

Savannah

0    250    500 miles
0  250  500 kilometers

Natchez

SPANISH FLORIDA

St. Augustine

New Orleans

| French claims |
| British claims |
| Spanish claims |
| Disputed British-French claims |
| Disputed British-Spanish claims |
| ♠ Major fort |
| ■ French outposts and settlements |

San Antonio

Rio Grande

**Gulf of Mexico**

NEW
SPAIN

Mexico City

**MAP 4.4**

**European Spheres of Influence in North America, 1754**

In the mid-eighteenth century, France, Spain, and the British-owned Hudson Bay Company laid claim to the vast areas of North America still inhabited primarily by Indian peoples. British settlers had already occupied much of the land east of the Appalachian Mountains. To safeguard their lands west of the mountains, Native Americans played off one European power against another. As a British official remarked: "To preserve the Ballance between us and the French is the great ruling Principle of Modern Indian Politics." When Britain expelled France from North America in 1763, Indians had to face encroaching Anglo-American settlers on their own.

Dinwiddie dispatched an expedition led by Colonel George Washington, a young Virginia planter and Ohio Company stockholder. In July 1754, French troops seized Washington and his men, prompting Virginian and British expansionists to demand war. Henry Pelham, the British prime minister, urged calm: "There is such a load of debt, and such heavy taxes already laid upon the people, that nothing but an absolute necessity can justifie our engaging in a new War."

**The War Hawks Win** | Pelham could not control the march of events. In Parliament, two expansionist-minded war hawks — rising British statesman William Pitt and Lord Halifax, the new head of the Board of Trade — persuaded Pelham to launch an American war. In June 1755, British and New England troops captured Fort Beauséjour in the disputed territory of Nova Scotia (which the French called Acadia). Soldiers from Puritan Massachusetts then forced nearly

**Braddock's Defeat and Death, July 1755**

In May 1755 General Edward Braddock led a force of 1,500 British regulars and Virginia militiamen out of Fort Cumberland in western Maryland, intending to oust the French from Fort Duquesne, 50 miles to the west. As Braddock neared the fort, the French garrison of 200 troops and about 600 Indian allies — mostly Potawotomis, Ottawas, Shawnees, and Delawares — set out to ambush his force. Instead, they unexpectedly met the British along a narrow roadway. As the French and Indians fanned out to attack from the woods, the British troops (George Washington reported) "were struck with such a panic that they behaved with more cowardice than it is possible to conceive. The officers behaved gallantly, in order to encourage their men, for which they suffered greatly." The British casualties — 450 killed, 500 wounded — included General Braddock, pictured above, who later died from his wounds.    © Chicago History Museum, USA/The Bridgeman Art Library International.

10,000 French settlers from their lands, arguing they were "rebels" without property rights, and deported them to France, the West Indies, and Louisiana (where "Acadians" was turned into "Cajuns"). English and Scottish Protestants took over the farms the French Catholics left behind.

This Anglo-American triumph was quickly offset by a stunning defeat. In July 1755, a French and Indian force attacked and routed 1,500 British regulars and Virginia militiamen advancing on Fort Duquesne. The attackers slew the British commander, General Edward Braddock, and killed or wounded more than half of his troops. "We have been beaten, most shamefully beaten, by a handfull of Men," George Washington complained bitterly as he led the survivors back to Virginia.

## The Great War for Empire

By 1756, the American conflict had spread to Europe, where it was known as the Seven Years' War, and pitted Britain and Prussia against France, Spain, and Austria. When Britain mounted major offensives in India, West Africa, and the West Indies as well as in North America, the conflict became the Great War for Empire. Since 1700, Britain had reaped huge profits from its overseas trading empire; now it vowed to crush France, the main obstacle to further British expansion.

William Pitt emerged as the architect of the British war effort. Pitt, the grandson of the East Indies merchant Thomas "Diamond" Pitt, was a committed expansionist with a touch of arrogance. "I know that I can save this country and that I alone can," he boasted. In fact, Pitt was a master of both commercial and military strategy, and planned to cripple France by seizing its colonies. In designing the campaign against New France, Pitt exploited a demographic advantage: In North America, George II's 2 million subjects outnumbered the French 14 to 1. To mobilize the colonists, Pitt paid half the cost of their troops and supplied them with arms and equipment, at a cost of £1 million a year. He also committed a fleet of British ships and 30,000 British soldiers to the conflict in America.

Beginning in 1758, the powerful Anglo-American forces moved from one triumph to the next. They forced the French to abandon Fort Duquesne (renamed Fort Pitt) and then captured Fort Louisbourg, a stronghold at the mouth of the St. Lawrence. In 1759, an armada led by British general James Wolfe sailed down the St. Lawrence and took Quebec, the heart of France's American empire. The Royal Navy prevented French rein-forcements from crossing the Atlantic, allowing British forces to complete the conquest of Canada in 1760 by capturing Montreal (Map 4.5).

Elsewhere, the British likewise had great success. From Spain, the British won Cuba and the Philippine Islands. Fulfilling Pitt's dream, the East India Company ousted French traders from India, and British forces seized French Senegal in West Africa. They also captured the rich sugar islands of Martinique and Guadeloupe in the French West Indies, but at the insistence of the West Indian sugar lobby (which wanted to protect its monopoly), the ministry returned the islands to France. In vain, William Burke (cousin to writer and philosopher Edmund Burke) argued that it was "by Means of the *West Indian* Trade that a great Part of *North America* is at all enable to trade with us." Despite the controversial decision to retain Canada rather than the sugar islands, the Treaty of Paris of 1763 confirmed Britain's triumph. It granted Britain sovereignty over half the continent of North America, including French Canada, all French territory east of the Mississippi River, Spanish Florida, and the recent conquests in Africa and India. Britain had forged a commercial and colonial empire that was nearly worldwide.

Britain's territorial acquisitions alarmed Indian peoples from New York to the Mississippi, who preferred the presence of a few French fur traders to an influx of thousands of Anglo-American settlers. To encourage the French to return, the Ottawa chief Pontiac declared, "I am French, and I want to die French." Neolin, a Delaware prophet, went further; he taught that the Indians' decline stemmed from their dependence on European goods, guns, and rum. He called for the expulsion of all white-skinned invaders: "If you suffer the English among you, you are dead men. Sickness, smallpox, and their poison [rum] will destroy you entirely." In 1763, inspired by Neolin's nativist vision, Pontiac led a major uprising by a group of loosely confederated tribes (stretching geographically from the New York Senecas to the Minnesota Chippewas). Indian forces seized nearly every British military garrison west of Fort Niagara, besieged the fort at Detroit, and killed or captured more than 2,000 settlers. But the Indian alliance gradually weakened, and British military expeditions defeated the Delawares near Fort Pitt and broke the siege of Detroit. In the peace settlement, Pontiac and his allies accepted the British as their new political "fathers." In return, the British issued the Proclamation of 1763, which prohibited white settlements west of the Appalachians. It was an edict that the colonists would ignore.

**MAP 4.5**

**The Anglo-American Conquest of New France**

After full-scale war with France began in 1756, it took almost three years for the British ministry to equip colonial forces and dispatch a sizable army to far-off America. In 1758, British and colonial troops attacked the heartland of New France, capturing Quebec in 1759 and Montreal in 1760. This conquest both united and divided the allies. Colonists celebrated the great victory: "The Illuminations and Fireworks exceeded any that had been exhibited before," reported the *South Carolina Gazette*. However, British officers had little respect for colonial soldiers. Said one, "[They are] the dirtiest, most contemptible, cowardly dogs you can conceive."

## British Industrial Growth and the Consumer Revolution

Britain owed its military and diplomatic success to its unprecedented economic resources. Since 1700, when it had wrested control of many oceanic trade routes from the Dutch, Britain had become the dominant commercial power in the Atlantic and Indian oceans. By 1750, it was also becoming the first country to use new manufacturing technology and work discipline to expand output. This combination of commerce and industry would soon make Britain the most powerful nation in the world.

Mechanical power was key to Britain's Industrial Revolution. British artisans designed and built water mills and steam engines that efficiently powered a wide array of machines: lathes for shaping wood, jennies and looms for spinning and weaving textiles, and hammers for forging iron. Compared with traditional manufacturing methods, the new power-driven machinery produced woolen and linen textiles, iron tools, furniture, and chinaware in greater quantities—and at lower cost. Moreover, the entrepreneurs running the new workshops drove their employees hard, forcing them to keep pace with the machines and work long hours. To market the abundant factory-produced goods, English and Scottish merchants extended credit to colonial shopkeepers for a full year instead of the traditional six months. Americans soon were purchasing 30 percent of all British exports.

To pay for British manufactures, mainland colonists increased their exports of tobacco, rice, indigo, and wheat. In Virginia, farmers moved into the Piedmont, the region of plains and rolling hills inland from the flat

Tidewater counties. Using credit advanced by Scottish merchants, planters bought land, slaves, and equipment to grow tobacco, which they exported to expanding markets in France and central Europe (see Reading American Pictures, "Selling Virginia Tobacco in Britain," p. 130). In South Carolina, rice planters enhanced their luxurious lifestyle by using British government subsidies to develop indigo plantations. By the 1760s, they were exporting the deep blue dye to English textile factories and 65 million pounds of rice a year to Holland and southern Europe. Simultaneously, New York, Pennsylvania, Maryland, and Virginia became the breadbasket of the Atlantic world, supplying Europe's exploding population with wheat. In Philadelphia, export prices for wheat jumped almost 50 percent between 1740 and 1765.

Americans used profits from agriculture to buy English manufactures, often on credit. Although this "consumer revolution" raised living standards, it landed many consumers—and the colonies as a whole—in debt (Figure 4.4). Even during the wartime boom of the 1750s, exports paid for only 80 percent of British imports. Britain financed the remaining 20 percent—the Americans' trade deficit—through the extension of credit and Pitt's military expenditures. When the military subsidies ended in 1763, the colonies fell into an economic recession. Merchants looked anxiously at their overstocked warehouses and feared bankruptcy. "I think we have a gloomy prospect before us," a Philadelphia trader noted in 1765, "as there are of late some

Persons failed, who were in no way suspected." The increase in transatlantic trade had made Americans more dependent on overseas credit and markets.

## The Struggle for Land in the East

In good times and bad, the population continued to grow, intensifying the demand for arable land. Consider the experience of Kent, Connecticut, founded in 1738 by descendants of the original Puritan migrants. Like earlier generations, they had moved inland to establish new farms, but Kent stood at the colony's western boundary. To provide for the next generation, many Kent families joined the Susquehanna Company (1749), which speculated in lands in the Wyoming Valley in present-day northeastern Pennsylvania. As settlers took up farmsteads there, the company urged the Connecticut legislature to claim the region on the basis of Connecticut's "sea-to-sea" royal charter of 1662. However, Charles II had also granted the Wyoming Valley to William Penn, and the Penn family had sold farms there to Pennsylvania residents. By the late 1750s, settlers from Connecticut and Pennsylvania were at war, burning down their rivals' houses and barns.

Simultaneously, three distinct but related land disputes broke out in the Hudson River Valley (Map 4.6). Dutch tenant farmers, Wappinger Indians, and migrants from Massachusetts asserted ownership rights to lands long claimed by manorial families such as the Van

**FIGURE 4.4**

**Mainland Population and British Imports**

Around 1750, British imports were growing at a faster rate than the American population, indicating that the colonists were consuming more per capita. But Americans went into debt to pay for these goods, running an annual trade deficit with their British suppliers that by 1772 created a cumulative debt of £2 million.

# Selling Virginia Tobacco in Britain

Tobacco was a big business in England in the 1760s, and the competition among tobacco sellers was keen. To attract customers to his shop, London grocer George Farr commissioned an engraver to create this advertising card, which wittily made a pun on his name. Other tobacco shops issued similar trade cards for their brands of "sweet-scented Virginia tobacco." Even more interesting than the explosion of commercial advertising in the mid-eighteenth century is the imagery used by Farr and other sellers, which both shows and conceals a great deal about the origins of the tobacco sold in Britain.

*The Finest Tobacco by Farr*, London, c. 1750–1770.
Library of Congress.

## ANALYZING THE EVIDENCE

- Why is the central figure an African king or prince sitting on a throne? What would such a figure have to do with the sale of Virginia tobacco in London? And why might an African man be wearing a Native American headdress?

- Farr's trade card does not depict a Virginia plantation with enslaved African workers cultivating the crop. Rather, it shows a cherub-like African child with one hand resting on a tobacco cask and the other holding a tobacco plant. How might an English consumer interpret this image of tobacco production? Why might a tobacco seller such as Farr choose to include a child in his advertisement?

- An English street ballad of 1676 condemned tobacco smoke, alleging that "cursed Pagans did, Devise this stinke," which for a long time had been "from Christians hid." Why did the ballad use religion to attack tobacco smokers? How does this advertisement of the 1760s, with its exotic imagery, address that issue?

- Observe the two ships in the background with flags waving. Why might they have been depicted in this advertisement?

- Neither African in Farr's advertisement is clothed. Another trade card shows a powerfully built, semi-naked African man pointing to a tobacco ad and a well-dressed British man smoking a pipe. What power relations are suggested by such interracial images of dress and undress? What might they convey about the ideology of the British empire?

**MAP 4.6**

**Westward Expansion and Land Conflicts, 1750–1775**

Between 1750 and 1775, the mainland colonial population more than doubled—from 1.2 million to 2.5 million—triggering westward migrations and legal battles over land, which had become increasingly valuable. Violence broke out in eastern areas, where tenant farmers and smallholders contested landlords' property claims based on ancient titles; and in the backcountry, where migrating settlers fought with Indians, rival claimants, and the officials of eastern-dominated governments.

Rensselaers and the Livingstons. When the manorial lords turned to the legal system to uphold their claims, Dutch and English farmers in Westchester, Dutchess, and Albany counties rioted to close the courts. In response, New York's royal governor ordered British general Thomas Gage and two regiments of troops to assist local sheriffs and manorial bailiffs: They suppressed the tenant uprisings, intimidated the Wappingers, and evicted the Massachusetts squatters.

Other land disputes erupted in New Jersey and the southern colonies, where landlords and English aristocrats had successfully revived legal claims based on long-dormant seventeenth-century charters. One court decision allowed Lord Granville, the heir of an original

Carolina proprietor, to collect an annual tax on land in North Carolina; another decision awarded ownership of the entire northern neck of Virginia (along the Potomac River) to Lord Fairfax.

The revival of these proprietary claims by manorial lords and English nobles testified to the rising value of land along the Atlantic coastal plain. It also reflected the maturity of the colonial courts, which now had enough authority to uphold property rights. And it underscored the increasing similarities between rural societies in Europe and America. To avoid the status of European peasants, native-born yeomen and tenant families joined the stream of European migrants searching for cheap land near the Appalachian Mountains.

## Western Rebels and Regulators

As would-be landowners moved westward, they sparked conflicts over Indian policy, political representation, and debts. During the war with France, Delaware and Shawnee warriors had exacted revenge for Thomas Penn's land swindle of 1737 by destroying frontier farms in Pennsylvania and killing hundreds of residents. Scots-Irish settlers demanded the expulsion of all Indians, but Quaker leaders refused. So in 1763, a group of Scots-Irish frontiersmen called the Paxton Boys massacred 20 members of the peaceful Conestoga tribe. When Governor John Penn tried to bring the murderers to justice, 250 armed Scots-Irish advanced on Philadelphia. Benjamin Franklin intercepted the angry mob at Lancaster and arranged a truce, averting a battle with the militia. Prosecution of the Paxton Boys failed for lack of witnesses, and the Scots-Irish dropped their demands that the Indians be expelled; but the episode left a legacy of racial hatred and political resentment.

**The South Carolina Regulators** Violence also broke out in the backcountry of South Carolina, where land-hungry Scottish and Anglo-American settlers clashed repeatedly with Cherokees during the war with France. After the fighting ended in 1763, a group of landowning vigilantes known as the Regulators tried to suppress outlaw bands of whites that were stealing cattle. The Regulators also had political demands: that the eastern-controlled government provide western districts with more courts, fairer taxation, and greater representation in the assembly. "We are *Free-Men*—British Subjects—Not Born *Slaves*," declared a Regulator manifesto. Fearing slave revolts, the lowland rice planters who ran the South Carolina assembly compromised with the vigilantes rather than fighting them. In 1767, the assembly created western

**A Hudson River Manor**

Philipse Manor (just up the Hudson from present-day New York City) encompassed 90,000 acres, and included mills and warehouses as well as a grand house. In this unattributed painting dated 1783, the artist has dressed the women in the foreground in classical costumes, thereby linking the Philipses to the noble families of the Roman republic. To preserve their aristocratic lifestyle and the quasi-feudal leasehold system of agriculture, the Philipses joined with other Hudson River manorial lords to suppress tenant uprisings in the 1760s. During the American Revolution, the family remained loyal to the king and Patriot tenants took control of the manor.   Historic Hudson Valley, Tarrytown, New York.

courts and reduced the fees for legal documents; but it refused to reapportion the legislature or lower western taxes. Like the Paxton Boys in Pennsylvania, the South Carolina Regulators won attention to backcountry needs but failed to wrest power from the eastern elite.

**Civil Strife in North Carolina** | In 1766, a more radical Regulator movement arose in North Carolina. When the economic recession of the early 1760s brought a sharp fall in tobacco prices, many farmers could not pay their debts. When creditors sued these farmers for payment, judges directed sheriffs to seize the debtors' property and sell it to pay debts and court costs. Many backcountry farmers — including evangelical Baptist, German pietist, and Scots-Irish Pres-

byterian migrants — denounced the merchants' lawsuits, both because they generated high fees for lawyers and court officials and because they violated rural customs, which allowed loans to remain unpaid in hard times. Others ended up in jail for resisting court orders.

To save their farms from grasping creditors and tax-hungry officials, North Carolina's debtors defied the government's authority. Disciplined mobs of farmers intimidated judges, closed courts, and freed their comrades from jail. Significantly, the Regulators proposed a coherent set of reforms, including lower legal fees and tax payments in the "produce of the country" rather than in cash. In addition, they demanded greater representation in the assembly and a just revenue system that would tax each person "in proportion to the profits aris-

**Governor Tryon and the Regulators Meet at Hillsborough, 1768**
Orange County, North Carolina, was home to the Sandy Creek Association, led by Herman Husband, a powerful advocate of social justice and the Regulator movement. Accused of corruption by the Associators, Orange County Sheriff Edmund Fanning assailed its members as "Rebels, Insurgents . . . [who should] be shot, hang'd, &c. as mad Dogs," and arrested Husband and two other leaders. To preserve order at Husband's trial, Governor William Tryon led a militia force of 1,400 to Hillsborough, where they confronted 800 Regulators. Only a set of judicious, politically driven decisions defused the potentially violent confrontation shown in the engraving. The judges acquitted Husband of "inciting to riot" but convicted his two associates (whose fines were promptly suspended by the governor). The court also convicted Sheriff Fanning of extortion, while fining him only 3 pennies. With each side claiming victory, the crisis eased but its underlying causes remained. In 1771, Tryon and the Regulators engaged in a pitched battle near the Alamance River, twenty miles west of Hillsborough.   Picture Research Consultants and Archives.

ing from his estate." All to no avail. In May 1771, Royal Governor William Tryon moved to suppress the Regulators. Mobilizing British troops and the eastern militia, Tryon defeated a large Regulator force at the Alamance River. When the fighting ended, 30 men lay dead, and Tryon summarily executed seven insurgent leaders. Not since Bacon's Rebellion in Virginia in 1675 and the colonial uprisings during the Glorious Revolution of 1688 (see Chapter 2) had an American domestic dispute caused so much bloodshed and political agitation.

In 1771, as in 1675 and 1688, colonial conflicts became linked with imperial politics. In Connecticut, Reverend Ezra Stiles defended the North Carolina Regulators. "What shall an injured & oppressed people do,"

he asked, "[when faced with] Oppression and tyranny?" Stiles's remarks reflected growing resistance to recently imposed British policies of taxation and control. The American colonies still depended primarily on Britain for their trade and military defense. However, by the 1760s, the mainland settlements had evolved into complex societies with the potential to exist independently. British policies would determine the direction the maturing colonies would take.

- **What impact did the Industrial Revolution in England have on the American colonies?**

- **What were the causes of unrest in the American backcountry in the mid-eighteenth century?**

## SUMMARY

In this chapter, we observed dramatic changes in British North America between 1720 and 1765. An astonishing surge in population—from 400,000 to almost 2 million—was the combined result of natural increase, European migration, and the African slave trade. Three other transatlantic influences were equally important: The European Enlightenment, European Pietism, and British consumer goods altered the cultural landscape.

We watched the colonists confront three major regional challenges. In New England, crowded towns and ever-smaller farms threatened the yeoman ideal of independent farming, prompting families to limit births, move to the frontier, or participate in an "exchange" economy. In the Middle Atlantic colonies, Dutch, English, German, and Scots-Irish residents maintained their religious and cultural identities, leading to bruising ethnic conflicts. Finally, westward migration into the backcountry and the Ohio River Valley set off battles with Indian peoples, civil unrest among whites, and, ultimately, the Great War for Empire. In the aftermath of the fighting, Britain stood triumphant in Europe and America.

## CHAPTER REVIEW QUESTIONS

- How did the three mainland regions in British North America—New England, the Middle colonies, and the South—become more like one another between 1720 and 1750? In what ways did they become increasingly different? From these comparisons, what conclusions can you draw about the character of American society in the mid-eighteenth century?

- Compare and contrast the ethnic complexity of the Middle colonies with the racial (and, in the backcountry, the ethnic) diversity of the southern colonies. What conflicts did this diversity cause?

# FOR FURTHER EXPLORATION

Individual lives illuminate the social history of early America. In *A Midwife's Tale: The Life of Martha Ballard* (1990), Laurel Thatcher Ulrich vividly pictures women's experiences on the Maine frontier. See also the PBS video *A Midwife's Tale* and the related Web site (**www.pbs.org/amex/midwife**) as well as **www.DoHistory.org**. Benjamin Franklin's *Autobiography* (1771) describes his Enlightenment sensibilities. See also the Library of Congress exhibit, "Benjamin Franklin . . . in His Own Words" (**www.loc.gov/exhibits/treasures/franklin-home.html**), and "The Electric Franklin" site (**www.ushistory.org/franklin**). A failed quest for self-betterment is recounted in *The Infortunate: The Voyage and Adventures of William Moraley* (1992), edited by Susan E. Klepp and Billy G. Smith.

Fine studies of religious leaders are Harry S. Stout's *The Divine Dramatist: George Whitefield* (1991) and George M. Marsden's *Jonathan Edwards* (2003). The Web site of Yale's Jonathan Edwards Center has many resources (**edwards.yale.edu**).

For more information on the Scots-Irish, see Patrick Griffin, *The People with No Name* (2001); on migrant Germans, read Aaron Spencer Fogleman, *Hopeful Journeys* (1996); and on Highland Scots, consult Colin G. Calloway, *White People, Indians, and Highlanders* (2008).

Other important studies include Jane T. Merritt, *At the Crossroads: Indians & Empires on a Mid-Atlantic Frontier* (2003); John Oliphant, *Peace and War on the Anglo-Cherokee Frontier, 1756–63* (2001); and Richard Middleton, *Pontiac's War* (2007). Also see *The War That Made America*, a PBS series on the French and Indian War, and the related Web site (**www.thewarthatmadeamerica.org**).

## TEST YOUR KNOWLEDGE

To assess your command of the material in this chapter, see the Online Study Guide at **bedfordstmartins.com/henretta**.

For Web sites, images, and documents related to topics and places in this chapter, visit **bedfordstmartins.com/makehistory**.

## TIMELINE

| | |
|---|---|
| **1710s–1730s** | Enlightenment ideas spread from Europe to America |
| | Germans and Scots-Irish settle in Middle Colonies |
| | Theodore Jacob Frelinghuysen preaches Pietism to German migrants |
| **1730s** | William and Gilbert Tennent lead Presbyterian revivals among Scots-Irish |
| | Jonathan Edwards preaches in New England |
| **1739** | George Whitefield sparks Great Awakening |
| **1740s–1760s** | Conflict between Old Lights and New Lights |
| | Shortage of farmland in New England threatens freehold ideal |
| | Growing ethnic and religious pluralism in Middle Atlantic colonies |
| | Religious denominations establish colleges |
| **1743** | Benjamin Franklin founds American Philosophical Society |
| | Samuel Morris starts Presbyterian revivals in Virginia |
| **1749** | Virginia speculators create Ohio Company; Connecticut farmers form Susquehanna Company |
| **1750s** | Industrial Revolution begins in England |
| | Consumer purchases increase American imports and debt |
| **1754** | French and Indian War begins |
| | Iroquois and colonists meet at Albany Congress; Franklin's Plan of Union |
| **1756** | Britain begins Great War for Empire |
| **1759–1760** | Britain completes conquest of Canada |
| **1760s** | Land conflict along New York and New England border |
| | Baptist revivals win converts in Virginia |
| **1763** | Pontiac's Rebellion leads to Proclamation of 1763 |
| | Treaty of Paris ends Great War for Empire |
| | Scots-Irish Paxton Boys massacre Indians in Pennsylvania |
| **1771** | Royal governor puts down Regulator revolt in North Carolina |

# PART

# 2

# THE NEW REPUBLIC, 1763–1820

"The American war is over," Philadelphia Patriot Benjamin Rush declared in 1787, "but this is far from being the case with the American Revolution. On the contrary, nothing but the first act of the great drama is closed. It remains yet to establish and perfect our new forms of government." As will be seen in Part 2, the job was even greater than Rush imagined. The republican revolution—which began with the Patriot resistance movement of 1765 and took shape with the Declaration of Independence in 1776—reached far beyond politics. It challenged many of the values and institutions of the colonial social order and forced Americans to consider fundamental changes in their economic, religious, and cultural practices. Here, in summary, are the main themes of our discussion of America's emerging political and social order.

**GOVERNMENT**

. . . [political] experiments . . . stretched over an entire generation

## Creating Republican Institutions

Once Americans had repudiated their allegiance to Britain and its monarch, they had to create new systems of government. In 1776, no one knew how the states should go about setting up republican institutions. Nor did Patriot leaders know if there should be a permanent central authority along the lines of the Continental Congress. It would take experiments that stretched over an entire generation to find out. It would take even longer to assimilate a new American institution—the political party—into the workings of the new government. However, by 1820, difficult years of political conflict, compromise, and constitutional revision had resulted in republican national and state governments that commanded the allegiance of their citizens.

**DIPLOMACY**

. . . wars against Britain divided the new nation's white citizens into bitter factions

## Contending with Foreign Entanglements

To create and preserve their new republic, Americans of European descent fought two wars against Great Britain, an undeclared war against France, and many battles with Indian peoples. The expansion of American sovereignty and settlements into the trans-Appalachian west was a cultural disaster for Indian peoples, who were brutally displaced from their lands. The wars against Britain divided the new nation's white citizens into bitter factions—Patriots against Loyalists in the War of Independence, and prowar Republicans versus antiwar Federalists in the War of 1812—and expended much blood and treasure. Despite these wars, by 1820, the United States had emerged as a strong independent state with internationally accepted boundaries. Freed from a half century of entanglement in European wars and diplomacy, its people began to exploit the riches of the continent.

## ECONOMY

**. . . merchants financed a banking system and . . . manufacturing**

## Expanding Commerce and Manufacturing

By the 1760s, the expansion of farming and commerce had established the foundation for a vigorous national economy. Beginning in the 1780s, northern merchants financed a banking system and organized a rural system of manufacturing. Simultaneously, state governments used charters and other privileges to assist businesses and to improve roads, bridges, and waterways. Meanwhile, southern planters continued to use enslaved African Americans and exported a new staple crop—cotton—to markets in the North and in Europe. Many yeomen farm families migrated westward to grow grain; while workers in the East turned out raw materials such as leather and wool for burgeoning manufacturing enterprises, and made shoes, textiles, tinware, and other handicrafts for market sale. By 1820, the young American republic was on the verge of achieving economic as well as political independence.

## SOCIETY

**Americans confronted . . . divisions of gender, race, religion, and class**

## Defining Liberty and Equality

As Americans confronted the challenges of creating and sustaining a republican society, they became increasingly conscious of long-standing (but previously little-examined) divisions of gender, race, religion, and class. They disagreed over fundamental issues such as legal equality for women, the status of slaves, the meaning of free speech and religious liberty, and the extent of public responsibility for social inequality. As we shall see, political leaders managed to resolve some of these disputes. Legislatures abolished slavery in the North, broadened religious liberty by allowing freedom of conscience, and, except in New England, ended the system of legally established churches. However, Americans continued to argue over social equality, in part because their republican creed placed family authority in the hands of men and political power in the hands of propertied individuals: This arrangement denied power and status not only to slaves but also to free blacks, women, and middling and poor white men.

## CULTURE

**. . . an American [was] . . . a republican, a Protestant, and an enterprising individual**

## Forging Pluralism and National Identity

The British colonies in North America contained a diversity of peoples and ways of life. This complexity inhibited the effort to define an American culture and identity. Native Americans still lived in their own clans and nations; and black Americans, one-fifth of the enumerated population, were developing a distinct African American culture. White Americans were enmeshed in vigorous regional cultures—New England, Middle Atlantic, and Southern—and in strong ethnic communities—English, Scottish, Scots-Irish, German, and Dutch. However, over time, political institutions began to unite Americans of diverse backgrounds, as did increasing participation in the market economy and in evangelical Protestant churches. By 1820, to be an American meant, for many members of the dominant white population, to be a republican, a Protestant, and an enterprising individual in a capitalist-run market system.

# THE NEW REPUBLIC, 1763–1820

| | GOVERNMENT | DIPLOMACY | ECONOMY | SOCIETY | CULTURE |
|---|---|---|---|---|---|
| **1763** | • Stamp Act Congress (1765)<br>• Committees of correspondence<br>• First Continental Congress (1774) | • Treaty of Paris (1763) gives Britain control of Canada, Florida, and parts of India | • Merchants defy Sugar and Stamp Acts<br>• Boycotts spur Patriot women to make textiles | • Artisans win political influence<br>• Quebec Act (1774) allows Catholicism | • Patriots call for American unity<br>• Concept of popular sovereignty takes hold |
| **1775** | • Second Continental Congress (1775)<br>• States institute republican constitutions | • Independence declared (1776)<br>• French provide secret aid to Patriots<br>• Treaty of Alliance with France (1778) | • Manufacturing expands during war<br>• Cutoff of trade and severe inflation threaten economy<br>• War debt grows | • Judith Sargent Murray writes *On the Equality of the Sexes* (1779)<br>• Emancipation of slaves begins in the North | • Thomas Paine's *Common Sense* (1776) calls for a republic<br>• Fall in European migration (1775–1820) enhances American identity |
| **1780** | • Articles of Confederation ratified (1781)<br>• Legislatures emerge as supreme in states<br>• Philadelphia convention drafts U.S. Constitution (1787) | • Treaty of Paris (1783)<br>• Britain restricts U.S. trade with West Indies<br>• U.S. government signs treaties with Indian peoples | • Bank of North America founded (1781)<br>• Commercial recession (1783–1789)<br>• Land speculation increases in West | • Virginia enacts religious freedom legislation (1786)<br>• Politicians and ministers deny vote to women; praise republican motherhood | • Noah Webster defines American English<br>• State cessions and land ordinances create national domain in West<br>• Many German settlers keep own language |
| **1790** | • Conflict over Alexander Hamilton's economic policies<br>• First national parties: Federalists and Republicans | • Wars between France and Britain<br>• Jay Treaty, Pinckney Treaty (both 1795)<br>• Undeclared war with France (1798) | • First Bank of the United States (1792–1811)<br>• States charter business corporations<br>• Outwork system grows | • Bill of Rights ratified (1791)<br>• Creation of French Republic (1793) sparks ideological debate<br>• Sedition Act limits freedom of press | • Indians form Western Confederacy (1790)<br>• Second Great Awakening (1790–1860)<br>• Political divisions emerge between South and North |
| **1800** | • Jefferson's "Revolution of 1800" reduces activism of national government<br>• Chief Justice Marshall asserts federal judicial powers | • Napoleonic Wars (1802–1815)<br>• Haitian rebellion and independence<br>• Louisiana Purchase (1803)<br>• Embargo Act (1807) | • Cotton output and demand for African labor expands<br>• Farm productivity improves<br>• Embargo encourages U.S. manufacturing | • New Jersey retracts suffrage for propertied women (1807)<br>• Atlantic slave trade legally ends (1808) | • Tenskwatawa and Tecumseh revive Western Indian Confederacy<br>• Free blacks enhance sense of African American identity |
| **1810** | • Triumph of Republican Party and end of Federalist Party<br>• State constitutions democratized | • War of 1812 (1812–1815)<br>• John Quincy Adams makes border treaties<br>• Monroe Doctrine (1823) | • Second Bank of the United States chartered (1816–1836)<br>• Supreme Court guards property<br>• Emergence of a national economy | • Suffrage for white men expands<br>• American Colonization Society (1817)<br>• Missouri Compromise (1819–1821) | • War of 1812 tests national unity<br>• Religious benevolence engenders social reform movements |

## CHAPTER 5

# Toward Independence: Years of Decision, 1763-1776

**As the Great War** for Empire ended in 1763, Massachusetts soldier Seth Metcalf celebrated the triumph of British arms. Metcalf thanked "the Great Goodness of God" for the "General Peace" that was so "percularly Advantageous to the English Nation." Just two years later, Metcalf was less optimistic. "God is angry with us of this land," the pious Calvinist wrote in his journal, "and is now Smiting [us] with his Rod Especially by the hands of our Rulers."

The rapid disintegration of the bonds uniting Britain and America — an event that

Metcalf ascribed to Divine Providence — mystified many Americans. How had it happened, asked the president of King's College in New York, that such a "happily situated" people were ready to "hazard their Fortunes, their Lives, and their Souls, in a Rebellion"? White Americans lived in a prosperous, self-governing society, with little to gain and much to lose by rebelling. Or so it seemed before the British government began to reform the imperial system. As Metcalf noted apprehensively in 1765: "This year Came an act from England Called the Stamp Act . . . which is thought will be very oppressive."

Inspired by the great gains of the wars in India, Africa, and the Americas, British leaders envisioned a new type of empire. In place of the existing loosely governed commercial system, they advocated centralized administration by Parliament and authoritarian regimes in their far-flung colonies. And they were especially concerned about the settlers in America, who, according to former Georgia governor Henry Ellis, and now an adviser to the ministry, felt themselves "entitled to a greater measure of Liberty than is enjoyed by the people of England."

Ireland had been closely ruled for decades, and recently the East India Company set up dominion over millions of non-British peoples. Britain's American possessions were likewise filled with aliens and "undesirables": "French, Dutch, Germans innumerable, Indians, Africans, and a multitude of felons from this country," as one member of Parliament put it. Consequently, declared Lord Halifax, "The people of England" considered Americans "as foreigners."

Contesting that status, Pennsylvanian John Dickinson argued that his fellow colonists were "not [East Indian] Sea Poys, nor Marattas, but *British subjects* who are born to liberty, who know its worth, and who prize it high." Thus was the stage set for a struggle between the conceptions of identity — and empire — held by British ministers and American Patriots.

**British Troops Occupy Concord, 1775**

On the night of April 18, 1775, hundreds of British troops marched out of Boston in search of Patriot arms and munitions, and by morning they had reached the nearby towns of Lexington and Concord. The raid led to violent and deadly confrontations with the Patriot militia, an outcome indicated by the unknown artist's depiction of a graveyard in the foreground of this painting. Courtesy, Concord Museum.

# Imperial Reform, 1763–1765

The Great War for Empire of 1754–1763 spurred movements for reform throughout the Atlantic world (Map 5.1). Charles III (r. 1759–1788) of Spain created disciplined military forces in his American possessions, imposed higher taxes on his colonial subjects, and dispatched imperial bureaucrats to rule them. In Britain, the war created an enormous debt, prompting George III (r. 1760–1820) and his ministers to expand the British fiscal-military state to America. Parliament quickly replaced salutary neglect (which had emphasized trade and colonial self-government) with imperial administration (which focused on regulation and taxation).

## The Legacy of War

The war strained the ties between Britain and its North American colonies. British generals and American leaders disagreed on military strategy, and the presence of 30,000 British troops revealed sharp cultural differences. The arrogance of British officers shocked many Americans: British soldiers "are but little better than slaves to their officers," declared a Massachusetts militiaman. The hostility was mutual. British general James Wolfe complained that colonial troops came from the dregs of society and that "there was no depending on them in action."

**Disputes over Trade and Troops**   The war also exposed the ineffectiveness of the royal governors. In theory, the governors had extensive political powers, including command of the provincial militia; in reality, they shared power with the colonial assemblies, which outraged British officials. The Board of Trade complained that in Massachusetts "almost every act of executive and legislative power is ordered and directed by votes and resolves of the General Court." To enforce the collection of trade duties, which colonial merchants had evaded for decades by bribing customs officials, Parliament passed the Revenue Act of 1762. The ministry also instructed the Royal Navy to seize American vessels carrying food crops from the mainland colonies to the French West Indies. It was absurd, declared a British politician, that French armies attempting "to Destroy one English province . . . are actually supported by Bread raised in another."

Britain's military victory brought a fundamental shift in policy: a new peacetime deployment of a 10,000-man army in North America. King George III wanted military commands for his friends, and the king's ministers feared a possible rebellion by the 60,000 French residents of Canada, Britain's newly conquered colony. Native Americans were also a concern: Pontiac's Rebellion had nearly overwhelmed Britain's frontier forts. Moreover, only a substantial military force would deter land-hungry whites from defying the Proclamation of 1763 and settling west of the Appalachian Mountains (see Chapter 4). Finally, British politicians worried about the colonists' loyalty now that they no longer faced a threat from French Canada. "The main purpose of Stationing a large Body of Troops in America," declared treasury official William Knox, "is to secure the Dependence of the Colonys on Great Britain." By stationing an army in America, the British ministry signaled its readiness to subdue restless Frenchmen, unruly Indians, or rebellious colonists.

**The National Debt**   But troops cost money, which was in short supply. Britain's national debt had soared from £75 million in 1756 to £133 million in 1763 and was, an observer noted, "becoming the alarming object of every British subject." And with good reason: Interest on the war debt consumed 60 percent of the nation's budget. To restore fiscal stability, British prime minister Lord Bute decided to raise taxes. The Treasury opposed a higher tax on land, which would primarily affect the gentry and aristocracy, who had great influence in Parliament. So Bute taxed those with little political power—the poor and middling classes—by imposing higher import duties on tobacco and sugar, thus raising their cost to consumers. The ministry likewise increased excise levies—essentially sales taxes—on salt, beer, and distilled spirits, placing more war costs on the king's ordinary subjects. Left unresolved was the question of taxing the American colonists, who, like Britain's poor, had little influence in Parliament.

To collect the taxes—old and new—the government doubled the size of the tax bureaucracy (Figure 5.1). Customs agents patrolled the coasts of southern Britain, seizing tons of contraband French wines and Flemish textiles. Convicted smugglers faced heavy penalties, including death or forced "transportation" to America as indentured servants. (Despite protests by the colonial assemblies, nearly fifty thousand English criminals of all descriptions had already been shipped to America to be sold as indentured servants.)

The price of empire abroad had turned out to be a larger government and higher taxes at home, an outcome that confirmed the worst fears of the British opposition parties, the Radical Whigs and the Country Party.

**MAP 5.1**

**Eurasian Trade and European Colonies, c. 1770**

By 1770, the Western European nations that had long dominated maritime trade had created vast colonial empires and spheres of influence. Spain controlled the western halves of North and South America. Portugal owned Brazil, and Holland ruled Indonesia. Britain, a newer imperial power, boasted settler societies in North America, rich sugar islands in the West Indies, slave ports in West Africa, and a growing presence on the Indian subcontinent. Only France had failed to acquire and hold on to a significant colonial empire. (To trace changes in empire and trade routes, see Map 1.3 on p. 20 and Map 2.2 on p. 48.)

Military spending
Civil spending
Net tax income
(£ sterling, millions)

War of the
Spanish
Succession,
1702–1713

War of the
Austrian
Succession,
1740–1748

Seven
Years' War,
1756–1763

American War
of Independence,
1775–1783

**FIGURE 5.1**

### The Cost of Empire, 1690–1790

It cost money to build and maintain an empire. As Britain built a great navy, subsidized the armies of European allies, and fought four wars against France and Spain between 1702 and 1783, military expenditures soared. Tax revenues did not keep pace, so the government created a large national debt by issuing bonds for millions of pounds. This policy created a class of wealthy financiers, led to political protests, and eventually prompted attempts to tax the American colonists.

Members of those parties complained that the huge war debt placed the nation at the mercy of the "monied interests," the banks and financiers who reaped millions of pounds' interest from government bonds. They further charged that the tax bureaucracy was filled with political appointees, "worthless pensioners and place-men." To reverse the growth of government power—and the threat to personal liberty and property rights—British reformers demanded that Parliament represent a broader spectrum of the property-owing classes. The Radical Whig John Wilkes condemned **rotten boroughs**—sparsely populated, aristocratic-controlled electoral districts—and demanded greater representation for rapidly growing commercial and manufacturing cities. In domestic affairs as in colonial policy, the war had transformed British political life.

## George Grenville: Imperial Reformer

A member of Parliament since 1741, George Grenville was widely conceded to be "one of the ablest men in Great Britain." But when he became prime minister in 1763, the nation was mired in debt and British subjects were paying at least five times as much in taxes as free Americans. Grenville decided that new revenue would have to come from America (Map 5.2).

For Grenville, increased revenue required imperial reform. He began by passing the Currency Act of 1764, which banned the American colonies from treating paper money as legal tender. Colonial shopkeepers,

**George Grenville, Architect of the Stamp Act**

This 1763 portrait of the British prime minister suggests Grenville's energy and ambition. As events were to show, he was determined to reform the imperial system and to ensure that the colonists shared the cost of the empire.    The Earl of Halifax, Garrowby, Yorkshire.

The Treaty of Paris allowed the British-run Hudson's Bay Company to expand its territory and influence.

To see the growth of the British Empire between 1713 and 1763, compare this map with Map 3.2 on page 81. Notice particularly the changes in the value of exports and the size and composition of the population in the three main colonial regions. What were the social and political implications of these changes?

Britain gained much more American territory from the Treaty of Paris (1763) than it had from the Treaty of Utrecht (1713). The new treaty gave Britain control of Spanish Florida and all of New France east of the Mississippi River.

**British Colonies: Comparisons**

Royal   Proprietary   Corporate

|  | Population White (in 1770) | Population Black (in 1770) | Average Annual Exports (in 1770) | Exports per White (shillings)* |
|---|---|---|---|---|
| West Indian islands | 40,000 | 330,000 | £1,856,000 | 928s. |
| Southern mainland | 600,000 | 394,000 | £1,703,776 | 57s. |
| Northern mainland | 1,092,000 | 45,000 | £1,105,376 | 21s. |

*20 shillings = £1 (one English pound); £1 = about $400 in 2010 prices.

In 1763, West Indian sugar was still Britain's primary colonial export crop, but its value was now less than the combined worth of the tobacco, rice, and flour exported from the mainland colonies.

**MAP 5.2**

**Britain's American Empire in 1763**

The Treaty of Paris gave Britain control of the eastern half of North America and returned a few captured sugar islands in the West Indies to France. To protect the empire's new mainland territories, British ministers dispatched troops to Florida and Quebec. They also sent troops to uphold the terms of the Proclamation of 1763, which prohibited Anglo-American settlement west of the Appalachian Mountains.

planters, and farmers had used local currency—which had the same face value as gold or silver coins but was worth less—to pay their debts to British merchants. The Currency Act ensured that merchants would be paid in good money, boosting their profits and British wealth.

**The Sugar Act** | Grenville also won parliamentary approval of the Sugar Act of 1764 to replace the widely ignored Molasses Act of 1733 (see Chapter 3). The prime minister understood the pattern of colonial trade: He knew that mainland settlers had

to sell at least some of their wheat, fish, and lumber in the French sugar islands to accumulate funds to buy British manufactures. He therefore resisted demands from British sugar planters, who wanted to stop this trade by levying a heavy duty of 6 pence per gallon on French molasses; instead, he settled on a duty of 3 pence per gallon and tightened customs enforcement.

This carefully crafted policy garnered little support in America. New England merchants—among them John Hancock of Boston—had made their fortunes smuggling French molasses. In 1754, Boston merchants paid customs duties on a mere 400 hogsheads of molasses, yet they imported 40,000 hogsheads for use by 63 Massachusetts distilleries. Publicly, the merchants claimed that the Sugar Act would wipe out the French trade and ruin the distilling industry; privately, they vowed to evade the duty by smuggling or by bribing officials.

**Constitutional Conflict** More important, the merchants' political allies raised constitutional objections to the Sugar Act. In Massachusetts, the leader of the assembly argued that the new legislation was "contrary to a fundamental Principall of our Constitution: That all Taxes ought to originate with the people." In Rhode Island, governor Stephen Hopkins warned: "They who are taxed at pleasure by others cannot possibly have any property, and they who have no property, can have no freedom." The Sugar Act raised other constitutional issues as well. Merchants prosecuted under the act would be tried by a **vice-admiralty court**, a tribunal run by a British-appointed judge. American assemblies had long opposed vice-admiralty courts, and had found ways to have merchants accused of Navigation Acts violations tried by local common-law courts, where they often were acquitted by friendly juries. The Sugar Act closed this legal loophole by extending the jurisdiction of the vice-admiralty courts to all customs offenses.

The new taxes and courts imposed by the Sugar Act revived old American fears. The influential Virginia planter Richard Bland admitted that the colonies were subject to the Navigation Acts, which restricted their manufactures and commerce. But he also believed that the American settlers "were not sent out to be the Slaves but to be the Equals of those that remained behind." John Adams, the young Massachusetts lawyer defending John Hancock on a charge of smuggling, argued that the vice-admiralty courts diminished this equality by "degrad[ing] every American . . . below the rank of an Englishman."

While the logic of the Americans' arguments appeared compelling, some of their facts were wrong. The Navigation Acts certainly favored British merchants and manufacturers. However, accused smugglers in Britain were also tried in vice-admiralty courts, so there was no discrimination against Americans. The real issue was the exercise of the growing power of the British state. Americans had lived for decades under an administrative policy of salutary neglect and benefited from an "unwritten constitution" that assumed the king's officials would seek political compromises with colonial leaders. Now they saw that the new imperial regime would deprive them "of some of their most essential Rights as British subjects," as a committee of the Massachusetts assembly put it.

For their part, British officials not only insisted on the supremacy of parliamentary laws, they also denied that colonists enjoyed the traditional legal rights of Englishmen. Responding to the Massachusetts assembly's claim that there should be no taxation without representation, royal governor Francis Bernard denied that Americans possessed that constitutional right: "The rule that a British subject shall not be bound by laws or liable to taxes, but what he has consented to by his representatives must be confined to the inhabitants of Great Britain only." To Bernard, Grenville, and other imperial reformers, Americans were second-class subjects of the king, with rights limited by the Navigation Acts, parliamentary laws, and British interests.

## An Open Challenge: The Stamp Act

Another new tax, the Stamp Act of 1765, sparked the first great imperial crisis. The new levy was to cover part of the cost of keeping British troops in America — some £225,000 a year (about $90 million today). The act would require a tax stamp (as proof the tax had been paid) on all court documents, land titles, contracts, newspapers, and other printed items. A similar stamp tax in England yielded £290,000 a year; Grenville hoped the American levy would raise £60,000. Knowing that some Americans would oppose the tax on constitutional grounds, the prime minister first raised the issue explicitly in the House of Commons: Did any member doubt "the power and sovereignty of Parliament over every part of the British dominions, for the purpose of raising or collecting any tax?" No one rose to object.

Confident of Parliament's support, Grenville then threatened to impose the stamp tax unless colonists paid the troops' expenses, which were for the colonists' own defense. London merchants — serving as agents for the colonial legislatures — protested that Americans lacked a continent-wide body to raise such funds. Colonial representatives had met officially only once, at the Albany Congress of 1754, and not a single assembly had accepted the Congress's proposal for a continental union (see Chapter 4). Benjamin Franklin, in Britain as the agent of the Pennsylvania assembly, proposed another solution to Grenville's challenge: American representation in Parliament. "If you chuse to tax us," he wrote, "give us Members in your Legislature, and let us be one People."

With the exception of William Pitt, British politicians rejected Franklin's idea as too radical. They argued that the colonists already had **virtual representation** in Parliament because some of its members were transatlantic merchants and West Indian sugar planters. Colonial leaders were equally skeptical of Franklin's plan. Americans were "situate at a great Distance from their Mother Country," the Connecticut assembly declared, and therefore "cannot participate in the general Legislature of the Nation."

Grenville then urged adoption of the Stamp Act, both to raise revenue and to assert a constitutional principle: "the Right of Parliament to lay an internal Tax upon the Colonies." The House of Commons ignored American opposition and passed the act by an overwhelming majority of 205 to 49. At the request of General Thomas Gage, the British military commander in America, Parliament also passed the Quartering Act, which required colonial governments to provide barracks and food for British troops. Finally, Parliament approved Grenville's proposal that violations of the Stamp Act be tried in vice-admiralty courts.

The design for reform was complete. Using the doctrine of parliamentary supremacy, Grenville had begun to fashion a centralized imperial system in America much like that already in place in Ireland: British officials would govern the colonies with little regard for the local assemblies. Consequently, the prime minister's plan provoked a constitutional confrontation on both the specific issues of taxation, jury trials, and military quartering as well as the general question of representative self-government.

- What were the goals of British imperial reformers?
- Why did the colonists object to the new taxes in 1764 and again in 1765? What arguments did they use? How did these conflicts turn into a constitutional crisis?

**The Intensity of Patrick Henry**
This portrait, painted when Patrick Henry was in his sixties, captures the Patriot's enduring seriousness and intensity. As an orator, Henry drew on evangelical Protestantism to create a new mode of political oratory. "His figures of speech . . . were often borrowed from the Scriptures," a contemporary noted, and his speeches mirrored "the earnestness depicted in his own features." Mead Art Museum, Amherst College. Bequest of Herbert L. Pratt.

his successor, Charles Townshend. They organized protests, violent as well as peaceful, and fashioned a compelling ideology of resistance.

## Politicians Protest and the Crowd Rebels

Virginians took the lead. In May 1765, Patrick Henry, a hotheaded young member of the House of Burgesses, condemned Grenville's legislation and attacked George III for supporting it. Comparing the king to Charles I, whose tyranny had led to his overthrow and execution in the 1640s, Henry seemed to call for a new republican revolution. These remarks, which bordered on treason, frightened the burgesses; nonetheless, they condemned the Stamp Act as "a manifest Tendency to Destroy American freedom." In Massachusetts, James Otis, another republican-minded firebrand, persuaded the House of Representatives to call a meeting of all the mainland colonies "to implore Relief" from the act.

# The Dynamics of Rebellion, 1765–1770

In the name of reform, Grenville had thrown down the gauntlet to the Americans. The colonists had often resisted unpopular laws and aggressive governors, but they had faced an all-out attack on their institutions only once before—in 1686, when James II had unilaterally imposed the Dominion of New England. Now the danger to colonial autonomy was even greater because both the king and Parliament backed reform. But the Patriots, as the defenders of American rights came to be called, met the challenge posed by Grenville and

**Protesting the Stamp Act in Portsmouth, New Hampshire**
Throughout the colonies, disciplined mobs protesting the Stamp Act forced stamp distributors to resign their offices. In this engraving, protesters in the small city of Portsmouth, New Hampshire, stone an effigy of the distributor as other members of the mob carry off a coffin representing the death of American "Liberty."
Picture Research Consultants & Archives.

**The Stamp Act Congress** | Nine assemblies sent delegates to the Stamp Act Congress, which met in New York City in October 1765. The congress protested the loss of American "rights and liberties," especially the right to trial by jury. And it challenged the constitutionality of both the Stamp and Sugar Acts by declaring that only the colonists' elected representatives could tax them. Still, moderate-minded delegates wanted compromise, not confrontation. They assured Parliament that Americans "glory in being subjects of the best of Kings" and humbly petitioned for repeal of the Stamp Act. Other influential Americans favored active (but peaceful) resistance; they organized a boycott of British goods.

Popular opposition took a violent form, however. When the Stamp Act went into effect on November 1, 1765, disciplined mobs demanded the resignation of stamp-tax collectors. In Boston, a group calling itself the **Sons of Liberty** burned an effigy of collector Andrew Oliver and then destroyed Oliver's new brick warehouse. Two weeks later, Bostonians attacked the house of Lieutenant Governor Thomas Hutchinson, long known as a defender of social privilege and imperial authority, breaking his furniture, looting his wine cellar, and setting fire to his library.

Wealthy merchants and Patriot lawyers, such as John Hancock and John Adams, encouraged the mobs, which were usually led by middling artisans and minor merchants. "Spent the evening with the Sons of Liberty," Adams wrote in his diary, "John Smith, the brazier [metalworker], Thomas Crafts, the painter, Edes, the printer, Stephen Cleverly, the brazier; Chase, the dis-

tiller; [and] Joseph Field, Master of a vessel." Some of these men knew one another through their work; others were drinking buddies at the taverns that became centers of Patriot agitation.

In New York City, nearly three thousand shopkeepers, artisans, laborers, and seamen marched through the streets breaking windows and crying "Liberty!" Resistance to the Stamp Act spread far beyond the port cities: In nearly every colony, angry crowds—the "rabble," their detractors called them—intimidated royal officials. Near Wethersfield, Connecticut, 500 farmers seized tax collector Jared Ingersoll and forced him to resign his office in "the Cause of the People."

**The Motives of the Crowd** | Such crowd actions were common in both Britain and America. Every November 5, Protestant mobs on both sides of the Atlantic celebrated Guy Fawkes Day, marking the anniversary of the failure of a 1605 Catholic plot to blow up the Houses of Parliament. Colonial crowds also regularly destroyed brothels and rioted against the impressment (forced service) of merchant seamen by the Royal Navy. Governments tolerated the mobs because they usually did little damage and because, short of calling out the militia, they had no means of stopping them.

But if rioting was traditional, its political goals were new. In New York City, for example, the leaders of the Sons of Liberty were Isaac Sears and Alexander McDougall, minor merchants who were also Radical Whigs. They feared that imperial reform would undermine political liberty. But many artisans and their journeymen joined the protests because low-priced imports of British shoes and other manufactures (like low-priced Chinese imports today) threatened their livelihoods. Other rioters feared new taxes and a parasitic British governing elite. One knowledgeable colonist observed that "the people of America . . . never would submit to be taxed that a few may be loaded with palaces and Pensions . . . while they cannot support themselves and their needy offspring with Bread."

Beliefs of many sorts—as well as a simple quest for excitement—motivated other protesters. Roused by the Great Awakening, evangelical Protestants resented arrogant British military officers and corrupt royal bureaucrats. In New England, where people and memories had long lives, rioters invoked the antimonarchy sentiments of their great-grandparents. An anonymous letter sent to a Boston newspaper promising to save "all the Freeborn Sons of America" was signed "Oliver Cromwell," the English republican revolutionary of the 1650s. Finally, the mobs also included apprentices, day laborers, and unemployed sailors—young men looking for excitement and, when fortified by drink, eager to resort to violence.

Nearly everywhere popular resistance nullified the Stamp Act. Fearing an assault on Fort George, New York lieutenant governor Cadwallader Colden called on General Gage to use his small military force to protect the stamps. Gage refused. "Fire from the Fort might disperse the Mob, but it would not quell them," he told Colden, and the result would be "an Insurrection, the Commencement of Civil War." Frightened collectors gave up their tax stamps, and angry Americans forced officials to accept legal documents without the stamp. This popular insurrection gave a democratic cast to the emerging Patriot movement. "Nothing is wanting but your own Resolution," declared a New York rioter, "for great is the Authority and Power of the People."

Because transatlantic communication took months, the British response to the Stamp Act Congress, the economic boycott, and the riots would not be known until the spring of 1766. However, royal officials in America already sensed the loss of the popular support that had sustained the empire for three generations. Lamented a customs collector in Philadelphia: "What can a Governor do without the assistance of the Governed?"

## The Ideological Roots of Resistance

American resistance began in the seaports because British policies directly affected the economic lives of the residents. The Sugar Act raised the cost of molasses for urban distillers; the Stamp Act taxed the newspapers and legal documents created by urban printers, lawyers, and merchants; and the flood of British manufactures threatened the jobs of seaport artisans. According to one pamphleteer, Americans were being compelled to give the British "our money, as oft and in what quantity they please to demand it."

But some Americans couched their resistance in constitutional terms. Many were lawyers or well-educated merchants and planters. Composing pamphlets of remarkable political sophistication, they gave the resistance movement its rationale, its political agenda, and its leaders.

Patriot writers drew on three intellectual traditions. The first was English common law, the centuries-old body of legal rules and procedures that protected the lives and property of the monarch's subjects. In the famous *Writs of Assistance* case of 1761, Boston lawyer James Otis invoked English legal precedents to challenge a general search warrant allowing customs officials to conduct wide-ranging inspections. As practitioners of English common law, Otis and his colleagues believed in trial by jury and generally opposed the judge-run vice-admiralty courts. In demanding a jury trial for John Hancock in the late 1760s, John Adams made reference to the Magna Carta (1215), the ancient document that, said Adams, "has for many Centuries been esteemed by Englishmen, as one of the . . . firmest Bulwarks of their Liberties." Other lawyers protested that new strictures violated specific "liberties and privileges" embodied in colonial charters and in Britain's "ancient constitution." They objected as well when the ministry declared that colonial judges served "at the pleasure" of royal governors, claiming that tenure would undermine the independence of the judiciary.

A second major intellectual resource for Patriot authors was the rationalist thought of the Enlightenment. Virginia planter Thomas Jefferson invoked David Hume and Francis Hutcheson, Enlightenment philosophers who applied reason in their critiques of traditional political practices and social ills. Jefferson and other Patriots also drew on the writings of John Locke, who had argued that all individuals possessed certain "natural rights"—life, liberty, and property—which governments must protect (see Chapter 4). And they turned as well to the works of French philosopher Montesquieu, who had maintained that a "separation of powers" among government departments prevented arbitrary rule.

The republican and Whig strands of the English political tradition provided a third ideological source for American Patriots. Puritan New England had long venerated the Commonwealth era (1649–1660), when England had been a republic (see Chapter 2). After the Glorious Revolution of 1688–1689, many colonists praised the English Whigs for creating a constitutional monarchy that prevented the king from imposing taxes and other measures. Beginning in the 1750s, Samuel Adams and other colonial leaders also applauded Britain's Radical Whigs for denouncing political corruption and the scheming of royal officials. Joseph Warren, a physician and a Radical Whig Patriot, suggested that the Stamp Act was part of a ministerial plot "to force the colonies into rebellion," and justify the use of "military power to reduce them to servitude."

Such arguments—widely publicized in newspapers and pamphlets—gave intellectual substance to the Patriot movement and turned a series of impromptu riots, tax protests, and boycotts of British manufactures into a formidable political force.

## Parliament Compromises, 1766

When news of the Stamp Act riots and the boycott reached Britain, Parliament was already in turmoil. Disputes over domestic policy had led George III to dismiss Grenville as prime minister (Table 5.1). However, Grenville's allies demanded that imperial reform continue, if necessary at gunpoint. They wanted to uphold the constitutional supremacy of Parliament and its status as one of the few powerful representative bodies in eighteenth-century Europe. "The British legislature," declared Chief Justice Sir James Mansfield, "has authority to bind every part and every subject, whether such subjects have a right to vote or not."

Three other parliamentary factions pushed for repeal of the Stamp Act. The Old Whigs, now led by Lord Rockingham, the new prime minister, had long maintained that America was more important for its "flourishing and increasing trade" than its tax revenues. A

second group—acting at the behest of a committee of merchants in Liverpool, Bristol, and Glasgow—protested that the American trade boycott was cutting deeply into British exports. "The Avenues of Trade are all shut up," a Bristol merchant told Parliament: "We have no Remittances and are at our Witts End for want of Money to fulfill our Engagements with our Tradesmen." Finally, former prime minister William Pitt and his allies in Parliament argued that the Stamp Act was a mistake and insisted it "be repealed absolutely, totally, and immediately." Pitt tried to draw a subtle distinction between taxation and legislation: Parliament lacked the authority to tax the colonies, he said, but its power over America was "sovereign and supreme, in every circumstance of government and legislation whatsoever." As Pitt's ambiguous formula suggested, the Stamp Act raised the difficult constitutional question of the extent of Parliament's sovereign powers.

Rockingham, a young and inexperienced minister facing complex issues, decided on compromise. To mollify the colonists and help British merchants, he repealed the Stamp Act and reduced the duty on molasses imposed by the Sugar Act to a penny a gallon. Then he pacified imperial reformers and hard-liners with the Declaratory Act of 1766, which explicitly reaffirmed Parliament's "full power and authority to make laws and statutes . . . to bind the colonies and people of America . . . in all cases whatsoever." By swiftly ending the Stamp Act crisis, Rockingham hoped it would be forgotten just as quickly.

## Charles Townshend Steps In

Often the course of history is changed by a small event—an illness, a personal grudge, a chance remark. That was the case in 1767, when Rockingham's ministry collapsed over domestic issues and George III named William Pitt to head a new government. Pitt, chronically ill with gout (a painful disease of the joints) and often absent from parliamentary debates, left chancellor of the exchequer Charles Townshend in command. Pitt was sympathetic toward America; Townshend was not. As a member of the Board of Trade, Townshend had sought restrictions on the colonial assemblies and strongly supported the Stamp Act. So, in 1767, when former prime minister Grenville demanded in Parliament that the colonists pay the costs of the British troops in America, Townshend made an unplanned and fateful decision. He promised to find a new source of revenue in America.

The new tax legislation, the Townshend Act of 1767, had both fiscal and political goals. The duties the

**TABLE 5.1**

**Ministerial Instability in Britain, 1760–1782**

| Leading Minister | Dates of Ministry | American Policy |
|---|---|---|
| Lord Bute | 1760–1763 | *Mildly reformist* |
| George Grenville | 1763–1765 | **Ardently reformist** |
| Lord Rockingham | 1765–1766 | Accommodationist |
| William Pitt / Charles Townshend | 1766–1770 | **Ardently reformist** |
| Lord North | 1770–1782 | **Coercive** |

THE REPEAL. — or the Funeral Procession, of MISS AMERIC-STAMP.

**Celebrating Repeal**

This British cartoon mocking supporters of the Stamp Act — "The Repeal, or the Funeral Procession of Miss Americ-Stamp" — was probably commissioned by merchants trading with America. Preceded by two flag bearers, George Grenville, the author of the legislation, carries a miniature coffin (representing the act) to a tomb, as a dog urinates on the leader of the procession. Two bales on the wharf, labeled "Stamps from America" and "Black cloth return'd from America," testify to the failure of the act.   The Granger Collection, New York.

statute imposed on colonial imports of paper, paint, glass, and tea, would raise about £40,000 a year. Though Townshend did allocate some of this revenue for American military expenses, he earmarked most of it to pay the salaries of royal governors, judges, and other imperial officials. Once freed from financial dependence on the American assemblies (that had previously paid them), royal appointees could enforce parliamentary laws and carry out the king's instructions. To strengthen imperial power further, Townshend devised the Revenue Act of 1767, which created a board of customs commissioners in Boston and vice-admiralty courts in Halifax, Boston, Philadelphia, and Charleston. By using parliamentary taxes to finance imperial administration, Townshend intended to undermine American political institutions.

The full implications of Townshend's policies became clear when the New York assembly refused to comply with the Quartering Act of 1765. Fearing an unlimited drain on its treasury, the assembly first denied General Gage's requests for barracks and supplies, then offered limited assistance. Townshend demanded full compliance and Parliament threatened to raise the funds by placing a special duty on New York's imports and exports. The Earl of Shelburne, the new secretary of state, went even further: He wanted to appoint a military governor authorized to seize funds from New York's treasury and "to act with Force or Gentleness as circumstances might make necessary." Townshend decided on a less provocative, but equally coercive measure: the Restraining Act of 1767, which suspended the New York assembly. Faced with the loss of self-government, New Yorkers reluctantly appropriated funds to quarter the troops.

The Restraining Act raised the stakes of the contest. Previously, the British Privy Council had invalidated about 5 percent of laws enacted by colonial legislatures, such as those establishing land banks. Townshend's Restraining Act went much further, declaring that the very existence of American representative assemblies depended on the will of Parliament.

## America Debates and Resists Again

The Townshend duties revived the constitutional debate over taxation. During the Stamp Act crisis, some Americans, including Benjamin Franklin, distinguished between external and internal taxes. They suggested that external duties on trade (such as those long mandated by the Navigation Acts) were acceptable to Americans, but that direct, or internal, taxes were not. Townshend thought this distinction was "perfect nonsense," but he indulged the Americans and laid duties only on trade.

**A Second Boycott and the Daughters of Liberty** Even so, most colonial leaders rejected the legitimacy of Townshend's measures. They agreed with lawyer John Dickinson, author of *Letters from a Farmer in Pennsylvania* (1768), that the real issue was the *intention* of the legislation. Because the Townshend duties were designed to raise revenue (not to regulate trade), they were taxes imposed without consent. In February 1768, the Massachusetts assembly circulated a letter condemning the Townshend Act, and Boston and New York merchants began a new boycott of British goods. Throughout Puritan New

England, ministers and public officials discouraged the purchase of "foreign superfluities" and promoted the domestic manufacture of cloth and other necessities.

American women, ordinarily excluded from public affairs, became crucial to the nonimportation movement through their production of **homespun** cloth. During the Stamp Act boycott of 1765, the wives and daughters of Patriot leaders had made more yarn and cloth, but the Townshend boycott mobilized women of other social groups. Pious farmwives spun yarn at the homes of their ministers. In Berwick, Maine, "true Daughters of Liberty" celebrated American products by "drinking rye coffee and dining on bear venison." Other women's groups supported the boycott with charitable work, spinning flax and wool for the needy. Just as Patriot men followed tradition by joining crowd actions, so women's protests reflected their customary concern for the well-being of the community.

Newspapers celebrated these exploits of the Daughters of Liberty. One Massachusetts town proudly claimed an annual output of 30,000 yards of cloth; East Hartford, Connecticut, reported 17,000 yards. This surge in domestic production did not offset the loss of British imports, which had averaged about 10 million yards of cloth annually, but it brought thousands of women into the public arena.

The boycott mobilized many American men as well. In the seaport cities, the Sons of Liberty published the names of merchants who imported British goods and harassed their employees and customers. By March 1769, the nonimportation movement had spread to Philadelphia; two months later, the members of the Virginia House of Burgesses vowed not to buy dutied articles, luxury goods, or imported slaves. Reflecting colonial self-confidence, Benjamin Franklin called for a return to the pre-1763 mercantilist system: "Repeal the laws, renounce the right, recall the troops, refund the money, and return to the old method of requisition."

**Britain Threatens Coercion** American resistance only increased British determination. When the Massachusetts assembly's letter opposing the Townshend duties reached London, Lord Hillsborough, the secretary of state for American affairs, branded it "unjustifiable opposition to the constitutional authority of Parliament." To strengthen the "Hand of Government" in Massachusetts, Hillsborough dispatched General Thomas Gage and 4,000 British troops to Boston (Map 5.3). Once in Massachusetts, Gage accused its leaders of "Treasonable and desperate Resolves" and advised the ministry to "Quash this Spirit at a Blow." In 1765, American resistance to the Stamp Act had sparked a parliamentary debate; in 1768, it provoked a plan for military coercion.

## Lord North Compromises, 1770

At this critical moment, the ministry's resolve faltered. A series of harsh winters and dry summers in Great Britain had cut grain output and raised food prices. In Scotland and northern England, thousands of tenants deserted their farms and boarded ships for America. Food riots spread across the English countryside; there were riots in British-occupied Ireland, too, over its growing military budget.

Adding to the ministry's difficulties was Radical Whig John Wilkes. Supported by associations of mer-

**John Wilkes, British Radical**

Wilkes won fame on both sides of the Atlantic as the author of *North Briton, Number 45* (depicted on the left), which called for major reforms in the British political system. At a dinner in Boston, Radical Whigs raised their wineglasses to Wilkes, toasting him forty-five times! But Wilkes had many enemies in Britain, including the artist who created this image. Wilkes is depicted (in this 1763 caricature by artist William Hogarth) as a cunning demagogue, brandishing the cap of Liberty to curry favor with the mob.    Miriam and Ira D. Wallach Division of Art, Prints and Photographs, The New York Public Library. Astor, Lenox and Tilden Foundations.

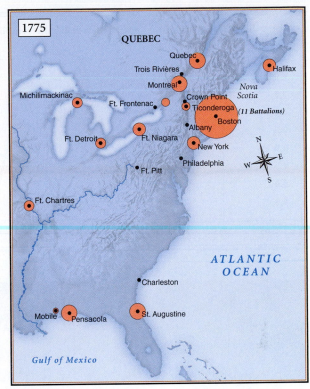

**MAP 5.3**

**British Troop Deployments, 1763 and 1775**

As the imperial crisis deepened, British military priorities changed. In 1763, most British battalions were stationed in Canada to deter Indian uprisings and French Canadian revolts. After the Stamp Act riots of 1765, the British placed large garrisons in New York and Philadelphia. By 1775, eleven battalions of British regulars occupied Boston, the center of the Patriot movement.

chants and artisans, Wilkes attacked government corruption and won election to Parliament. His radical politics endeared him to the American Patriots, who drank toasts to his name and bought teapots and mugs emblazoned with his picture. When Wilkes was imprisoned for libel against Parliament, seven members of an angry London crowd protesting his arrest were killed by troops in the highly publicized Massacre of Saint George's Field.

**Nonimportation Succeeds** | The American trade boycott also bit deeply into the British economy. In 1768, the colonies had cut imports of British manufactures, reducing their trade deficit from £500,000 to £230,000. By 1769, the boycott along with increases in American exports and shipping services gave the mainland colonies a balance-of-payments surplus of £816,000. Hard-hit by these developments, British merchants and manufacturers petitioned Parliament to repeal the Townshend duties. By late 1769, some

ministers felt that the duties were a mistake; also, the king no longer supported Hillsborough's plan to use military force against Massachusetts.

Early in 1770, Lord North became prime minister. A witty man and a skillful politician, North designed a new compromise. Arguing that it was foolish to tax British exports to America (thereby raising their price and decreasing consumption), he persuaded Parliament to repeal most of the Townshend duties. However, North retained the tax on tea as a symbol of Parliament's supremacy. Gratified by the partial repeal, colonial merchants called off the boycott (Figure 5.2).

Even outbreaks of violence did not destroy North's compromise. During the boycott, New York artisans and workers had taunted British troops, mostly with words but occasionally with stones and fists. In retaliation, the soldiers tore down a Liberty Pole (a Patriot flagpole), setting off a week of street fighting. In Boston, friction over constitutional principles and competition between residents and off-duty British soldiers

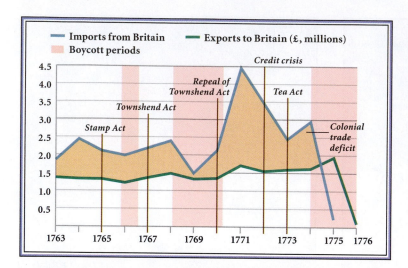

**FIGURE 5.2**

**Trade as a Political Weapon, 1763–1776**

Political upheaval did not affect the mainland colonies' exports to Britain, which rose slightly over the period, but imports fluctuated greatly. The American boycott of 1765–1766 prompted a dip in imports but the second boycott of 1768–1770 led to a sharp drop in imports of British textiles, metal goods, and ceramics. Imports of manufactures soared after the repeal of the Townshend duties, only to plummet when the First Continental Congress proclaimed a third boycott in 1774.

**Patriot Propaganda**

Silversmith Paul Revere issued this engraving of the confrontation between British redcoats and snowball-throwing Bostonians in the days after it occurred. To whip up opposition to the military occupation of their town, Revere and other Patriots labeled the incident "The Boston Massacre." The shooting confirmed their Radical Whig belief that "standing armies" were instruments of tyranny.    Library of Congress.

for jobs triggered a deadly conflict in March 1770, when a group of soldiers fired into a crowd of rowdy demonstrators, killing five men. Convinced of a ministerial conspiracy against liberty, Radical Whigs labeled the incident a "massacre" and filled the popular press with accusations that the British had planned the killings.

**Sovereignty Debated** | Although most Americans remained loyal to the empire, five years of conflict over taxes and constitutional principles had taken their toll. In 1765, American leaders had accepted Parliament's authority; the Stamp Act Resolves had opposed only certain "unconstitutional" legislation. By 1770, the most outspoken Patriots—Benjamin Franklin in Pennsylvania, Patrick Henry in Virginia, and Samuel Adams in Massachusetts—had concluded that the British ruling elite was determined to exploit the colonies for its own benefit. So they repudiated parliamentary supremacy and claimed equality for the American assemblies within the empire. Perhaps thinking of various European "composite monarchies," in which kings ruled far-distant provinces acquired by inheritance or conquest, Franklin suggested that the colonies were now "distinct and separate states" with the "the same Head, or Sovereign, the King."

Franklin's suggestion outraged Thomas Hutchinson, the American-born royal governor of Massachusetts. Hutchinson emphatically rejected the idea of "two independent legislatures in one and the same state." He told the Massachusetts assembly, "I know of no line that can be drawn between the supreme authority of Parliament and the total independence of the colonies."

There the matter rested. The British had twice imposed revenue acts on the colonies, and American Patriots had twice forced a retreat. If Parliament insisted on a policy of constitutional absolutism by imposing taxes a third time, some Americans were prepared to pursue violent resistance. Nor did they flinch when reminded that George III condemned their agitation. As the Massachusetts House replied to Hutchinson, "There is more reason to dread the consequences of absolute uncontrolled supreme power, whether of a nation or a monarch, than those of total independence." Fearful of civil war, Lord North's ministry hesitated to force the issue.

- If Grenville's and Townshend's initiatives had succeeded, how might the character of the British imperial system have changed?

- Weigh the relative importance of economic and ideological motives in promoting the colonial resistance movement. Which was more important? Why?

# The Road to Independence, 1771–1776

Repeal of the Townshend duties in 1770 restored harmony to the British empire, but strong feelings and mutual distrust lay just below the surface. In 1773, those emotions erupted, destroying any hope of compromise. Within two years, the Americans and the British clashed in armed conflict, and Patriot legislators created provisional governments and military forces, the two essentials for independence.

## A Compromise Repudiated

Once aroused, political passions are not easily quieted. In Boston, Samuel Adams and other radical Patriots continued to warn Americans of imperial domination and, late in 1772, persuaded the town meeting to set up a committee of correspondence "to state the Rights of the Colonists of this Province." Soon, eighty Massachusetts towns had similar committees. When British officials threatened to seize the Americans responsible for the burning of the customs vessel *Gaspée* and prosecute them in Britain, the Virginia House of Burgesses and several other assemblies set up their own committees of correspondence.

**The East India Company and the Tea Act** | These committees sprang into action when Parliament passed the Tea Act in May 1773. The act provided financial relief for the East India Company, a royally chartered private corporation that served as the instrument of Britain imperialism. The company was deeply in debt because of military expeditions in India and because high import duties had cut tea consumption in Britain, leaving it with a huge surplus. The Tea Act gave the company a government loan and, to boost its revenue, canceled the import duties on tea the company exported to Ireland and the American colonies. Now even with the Townshend duty of 3 pence a pound on tea, high-quality East India Company tea would cost less than the Dutch tea smuggled into the colonies by American merchants.

Events in far-off Asia thus directly influenced the course of American history. Radical Patriots accused the British ministry of bribing Americans with the cheaper East India Company's tea so they would give up their principled opposition to the tea tax. As an anonymous woman wrote to the *Massachusetts Spy*, "The use of [British] tea is considered not as a private but as a public evil . . . a handle to introduce a variety

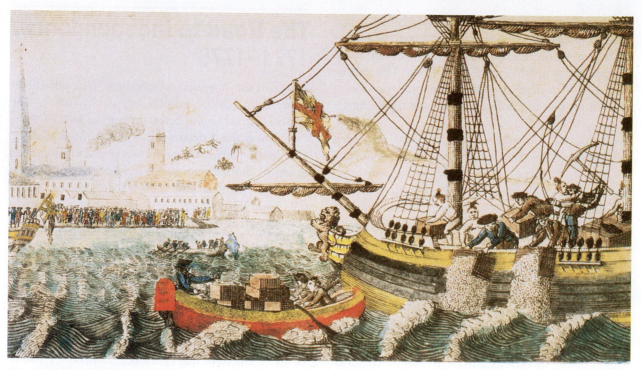

**The Boston Tea Party**

Led by radical Patriots disguised as Mohawk Indians, Bostonians dumped the East India Company's taxed tea into the harbor. The rioters made clear their "pure" political motives by punishing those who sought personal gain: One Son of Liberty who stole some of the tea was "stripped of his booty and his clothes together, and sent home naked." Library of Congress.

of . . . oppressions amongst us." Merchants joined the protest because the East India Company planned to distribute its tea directly to shopkeepers, excluding American wholesalers from the trade's profits. "The fear of an Introduction of a Monopoly in this Country," British general Frederick Haldimand reported from New York, "has induced the mercantile part of the Inhabitants to be very industrious in opposing this Step and added Strength to a Spirit of Independence already too prevalent."

**The Tea Party and the Coercive Acts** | The committees of correspondence organized resistance. They sponsored public bonfires and persuaded their fellow townspeople—sometimes gently, sometimes not—to consign British tea to the flames. When the Sons of Liberty prevented East India Company ships from delivering their cargoes, Royal Governor Hutchinson hatched a scheme to land the tea and collect the tax. When a tea shipment arrived in Boston Harbor on the *Dartmouth*, Hutchinson immediately passed the ship through customs. He intended to order British troops to unload the tea and supervise its sale by auction. To foil the governor's plan, artisans and la-

borers disguised as Indians boarded the *Dartmouth* on December 16, 1773, broke open 342 chests of tea (valued at about £10,000, or about $900,000 today), and threw them into the harbor. "This destruction of the Tea . . . must have so important Consequences," John Adams wrote in his diary, "that I cannot but consider it as an Epoch in History."

The British Privy Council was outraged, as was the king. "Concessions have made matters worse," George III declared. "The time has come for compulsion." Early in 1774, Parliament refused to repeal the American duty on tea; instead, it passed four Coercive Acts to force Massachusetts to pay for the tea and to submit to imperial authority. The Boston Port Bill closed Boston Harbor to shipping; the Massachusetts Government Act annulled the colony's charter and prohibited most town meetings; a new Quartering Act mandated new barracks for British troops; and the Justice Act allowed trials for capital crimes to be transferred to other colonies or to Britain (see Reading American Pictures, "A Political Cartoonist Sounds Off on the Crisis in the Colonies," p. 157).

Patriot leaders throughout the colonies branded the measures "Intolerable" and rallied support for Massachusetts. In Georgia, a Patriot warned the "Freemen

# A Political Cartoonist Sounds Off on the Crisis in the Colonies

**B**ritain's colonial policy between 1763 and 1775 created controversy in Britain as well as in America. George Grenville's ministry enacted the Stamp Act in 1765 only for it to be repealed the next year by Lord Rockingham's government. The conflict over colonial policy split hard-liners who favored coercing the colonies into paying taxes and quartering troops from Old Whigs who favored compromise. The debates roiled the halls of Parliament and spilled onto the pages of London's newspapers, where they took the form of controversial essays and political cartoons, like the one shown here. People of the time immediately understood the meaning—and the political bias—of these cartoons; more than two centuries later, we have to work a bit harder to understand what they are "saying."

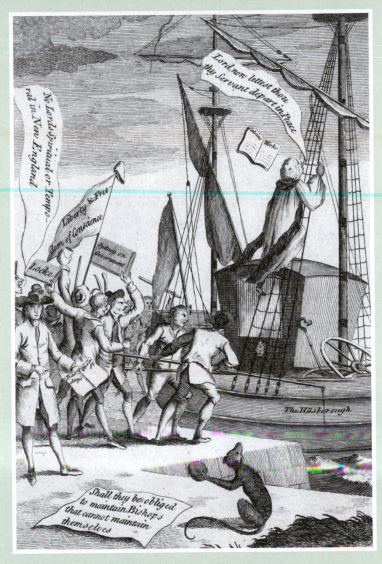

**"An Attempt to Land a Bishop in America," 1768.**
Library of Congress.

## ANALYZING THE EVIDENCE

- "An Attempt to Land a Bishop in America" addressed the proposal (never carried out) to dispatch a bishop of the Church of England to North America to supervise the clergy there. The bishop's jurisdiction would extend not only over Anglican ministers but also over Congregational (Puritan) and Presbyterian clergy. What is the cartoonist's position on the proposal?

- Read the signs and banners carefully. They invoke the name of John Locke, the famed advocate of self-government, and call for "Liberty & Freedom of Conscience." To interpret the words of protest in the balloon on the left—"No Lords Spiritual or Temporal in New England"—think back to the New England Puritans' opinions of bishops (see Chapter 2). What other aspects of the cartoon point

to the artist's stance on the proposal to send a bishop to America?

- The name of the vessel being pushed away from the dock is *The Hillsborough*. When this cartoon was published in 1768, what was the significance of that name to those interested in American affairs?

of the Province" that "every privilege you at present claim as a birthright, may be wrested from you by the same authority that blockades the town of Boston." "The cause of Boston," George Washington declared in Virginia, "now is and ever will be considered as the cause of America." The committees of correspondence had created a firm sense of Patriot unity.

In 1774, Parliament also passed the Quebec Act, which allowed the practice of Roman Catholicism in Quebec. This concession to Quebec's predominantly Catholic population reignited religious passions in New England, where Protestants associated Catholicism with arbitrary royal government and "popish" superstition. Because the act extended Quebec's boundaries into the Ohio River Valley, it likewise angered influential land speculators in Virginia (Map 5.4). Although the ministry did not intend the Quebec Act as a coercive measure, many colonial leaders saw it as further proof of Parliament's intention to control American domestic affairs.

## The Continental Congress Responds

In response to the Coercive Acts, Patriot leaders convened a new continent-wide body, the Continental Congress.

Twelve mainland colonies sent representatives. Four recently acquired colonies—Florida, Quebec, Nova Scotia, and Newfoundland—refused to send delegates, as did Georgia, where the royal governor controlled the legislature. The assemblies of Barbados, Jamaica, and the other sugar islands, although wary of British domination, were even more fearful of revolts by their predominantly African populations and therefore declined to attend.

The delegates who met in Philadelphia in September 1774 had different agendas. Southern representatives, fearing a British plot "to overturn the constitution and introduce a system of arbitrary government," advocated a new economic boycott. Independence-minded representatives from New England demanded political union and defensive military preparations. However, many delegates from the Middle Atlantic colonies favored a political compromise.

Led by Joseph Galloway of Pennsylvania, these men of "loyal principles" proposed a new political system similar to Benjamin Franklin's proposal at the Albany Congress of 1754: Each colony would retain its assembly to legislate on local matters, and a new continent-wide body would handle general American affairs. The king would appoint a president-general to preside over

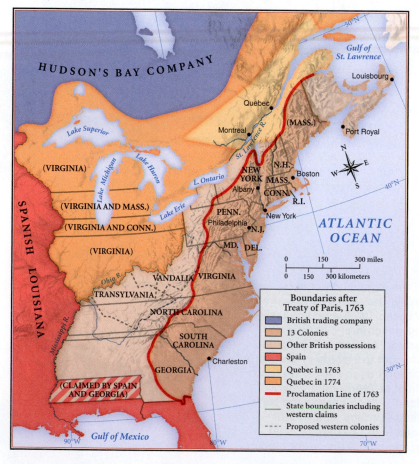

**MAP 5.4**

### British Western Policy, 1763–1774

The Proclamation of 1763 prohibited white settlement west of the Appalachian Mountains. Nonetheless, Anglo-American settlers and land speculators proposed the new colonies of Vandalia and Transylvania to the west of Virginia and North Carolina. When the Quebec Act of 1774 designated most western lands as Indian reserves and vastly enlarged the boundaries of Quebec, this dashed speculators' hopes and eliminated the old sea-to-sea land claims of many seaboard colonies. The act especially angered New England Protestants, who condemned it for allowing French residents to practice Catholicism; and colonial political leaders, who protested its failure to provide Quebec with a representative assembly.

a legislative council selected by the colonial assemblies. Although Galloway's plan gave the council veto power over parliamentary legislation affecting America, the delegates refused to endorse it. With British troops occupying Boston, most thought it was too conciliatory (see Comparing American Voices, "The Debate over Representation and Sovereignty," pp. 160–161).

Instead, a majority of the delegates passed a Declaration of Rights and Grievances, which demanded the repeal of the Coercive Acts. They repudiated the Declaratory Act of 1766, which had proclaimed Parliament's supremacy over the colonies, and stipulated that British control be limited to matters of trade. Finally, the Congress approved a program of economic retaliation: Americans would stop importing British goods in December 1774. If Parliament did not repeal the Coercive Acts by September 1775, the Congress vowed to cut off virtually all colonial exports to Britain, Ireland, and the British West Indies. Ten years of constitutional conflict had culminated in a threat of all-out commercial warfare.

A few British leaders still hoped for compromise. In January 1775, William Pitt, now sitting in the House of Lords as the Earl of Chatham, asked Parliament to renounce its power to tax the colonies and to recognize the Continental Congress as a lawful body. In return for these concessions, he suggested, the Congress should acknowledge parliamentary supremacy and provide a permanent source of revenue to help defray the national debt.

The British ministry rejected Pitt's plan. Twice it had backed down in the face of colonial resistance; a third retreat was impossible. Branding the Continental Congress an illegal assembly, the ministry rejected Lord Dartmouth's proposal to send commissioners to negotiate a settlement. Instead, Lord North set stringent terms: Americans must pay for their own defense and administration and acknowledge Parliament's authority to tax them. To put teeth in these demands, North imposed a naval blockade on American trade with foreign nations and ordered General Gage to suppress dissent in Massachusetts. "Now the case seemed desperate," the prime minister told Thomas Hutchinson, whom the Patriots had forced into exile in London. "Parliament would not—could not—concede. For aught he could see it must come to violence."

## The Rising of the Countryside

The fate of the urban-led Patriot movement would depend on the colonies' large rural population. Most farmers had little interest in imperial affairs. Their lives were deeply rooted in the soil, and their prime allegiance was to family and community. But imperial policies had increasingly intruded into the lives of farm families by sending their sons to war and raising their taxes. In 1754 farmers on Long Island, New York, had paid an average tax of 10 shillings; by 1756, thanks to the Great War for Empire, their taxes had jumped to 30 shillings. Peace brought little relief: The British-imposed Quartering Act kept taxes high, an average of 20 shillings a year, angering farmers in New York and elsewhere.

The urban-led Patriot boycotts of 1765 and 1768 had also raised the political consciousness of rural Americans. When the First Continental Congress called for a new boycott of British goods in 1774, it easily set up a rural network of committees to enforce it. In Concord, Massachusetts, 80 percent of the male heads of families and a number of single women signed a "Solemn League and Covenant" supporting nonimportation. In other farm towns, men blacked their faces, disguised themselves in blankets "like Indians," and threatened violence against shopkeepers who traded "in rum, molasses, & Sugar, &c." in violation of the boycott.

Patriots likewise warned that British measures threatened the yeoman tradition of landownership. In Petersham, Massachusetts, the town meeting worried that new British taxes would drain "this People of the Fruits of their Toil." Arable land was now scarce and expensive in older communities, and in new settlements merchants were seizing farmsteads for delinquent debts. By the 1770s, many northern yeomen felt personally threatened by British policies which, a Patriot pamphlet warned, were "paving the way for reducing the country to lordships" (Table 5.2).

Despite their higher standard of living, southern slave owners had similar fears. Many Virginia Patriots—including Patrick Henry, George Washington, and Thomas Jefferson—speculated in western lands, and they reacted angrily when first the Proclamation of 1763 and then the Quebec Act of 1774 restricted their economic ambitions. Moreover, thanks to their extravagant lifestyle, many Chesapeake planters were deeply in debt to British merchants. Even so, George Washington noted, they lived "genteely and hospitably" and were "ashamed" to adopt frugal ways. Accustomed to being absolute masters on their slave-labor plantations and seeing themselves as guardians of English liberties, planters resented their financial dependence on British creditors and dreaded the prospect of political subservience to British officials.

That danger now seemed real. If Parliament used the Coercive Acts to subdue Massachusetts, then it might turn next to Virginia, dissolving its representative assembly and judicial institutions and assisting British

*Thus I have given you, I think, the Substance of the Arguments
both sides of that great and important Quest*

# The Debate over Representation and Sovereignty

Speaking before the House of Commons, Benjamin Franklin declared that before 1763, Americans had paid little attention to the question of Parliament's "right to lay taxes and duties" in the colonies. The reason was simple, Franklin said: "A right to lay internal taxes was never supposed to be in Parliament, as we are not represented there." Franklin recognized that representation was central to the imperial debate. As the following selections show, the failure to solve the problem of representation—and the closely related issue of parliamentary sovereignty—led to the American rebellion.

## Jared Ingersoll

### Report on the Debates in Parliament (1765)

Connecticut lawyer Jared Ingersoll (1722–1781) served as his colony's agent, or lobbyist, in Britain. In this 1765 letter to the governor of Connecticut, Ingersoll summarizes the debate then underway in Parliament over the Stamp Act. When the act passed, he returned home to become the stamp distributor in Connecticut. A mob forced him to resign that post. Ingersoll later served as a vice-admiralty judge in Philadelphia and, during the revolution, remained loyal to Britain.

The principal Attention has been to the Stamp bill that has been preparing to Lay before Parliament for taxing America. The Point of the Authority of Parliament to impose such Tax I found on my Arrival here was so fully and Universally yielded [accepted], that there was not the least hopes of making any impressions that way. . . .

I beg leave to give you a Summary of the Arguments which are made use of in favour of such Authority. The House of Commons, say they, is a branch of the supreme legislature of the Nation, and which in its Nature is supposed to represent, or rather to stand in the place of, the Commons, that is, of the great body of the people. . . .

That this house of Commons, therefore, is now . . . a part of the Supreme unlimited power of the Nation, as in every State there must be some unlimited Power and Authority. . . .

They say a Power to tax is a necessary part of every Supreme Legislative Authority, and that if they have not that Power over America, they have none, and then America is at once a Kingdom of itself.

On the other hand those who oppose the bill say, it is true the Parliament have a supreme unlimited Authority over every Part and Branch of the Kings dominions and as well over Ireland as any other place.

Yet [they say] we believe a British parliament will never think it prudent to tax Ireland [or America]. Tis true they say, that the Commons of England and of the British Empire are all represented in and by the house of Commons, but this representation is confessedly on all hands by Construction and Virtual [because most British subjects] . . . have no hand in choosing the representatives. . . .

[They say further] that the Effects of this implied Representation here and in America must be infinitely different in the Article of Taxation. . . . By any Mistake an act of Parliament is made that prove injurious and hard the Member of Parliament here [in Britain] sees with his own Eyes and is moreover very accessible to the people. . . . [Also,] the taxes are laid equally by one Rule and fall as well on the Member himself as on the people. But as to America, from the great distance in point of Situation [they are not represented in the same way]. . . .

[Finally, the opponents of the Act say] we already by the Regulations upon their trade draw from the Americans all that they can spare. . . . This Step [of taxation] should not take place until or unless the Americans are allowed to send Members to Parliament. . . .

Thus I have given you, I think, the Substance of the Arguments on both sides of that great and important Question of the right and also of the Expediency of taxing America by Authority of Parliament. . . . [But] upon a Division of the house upon the Question, there was about 250 to about 50 in favour of the Bill.

Source: New Haven Colony Historical Society, *Papers* (1918), 9: 306–315.

## Joseph Galloway

### Plan of Union (1775)

Speaker of the Pennsylvania assembly Joseph Galloway was a delegate to the First Continental Congress, where he proposed a plan that addressed the issue of representation. The colonies would remain British, but operate under a continental government with the power to veto parliamentary laws that affected America. Radical Patriots in the Congress, who favored independence, prevented a vote on Galloway's plan and suppressed mention of it in the records. Galloway remained loyal to the Crown, fought on the British side in the War for Independence, and moved to England in 1778.

If we sincerely mean to accommodate the difference between the two countries, . . . we must take into consideration a number of facts which led the Parliament to pass the acts complained of. . . . [You will recall] the dangerous situation of the Colonies from the intrigues of France, and the incursions of the Canadians and their Indian allies, at the commencement of the last war. . . . Great-Britain sent over her fleets and armies for their protection. . . .

In this state of the Colonies, it was not unreasonable to expect that Parliament would have levied a tax on them proportionate to their wealth, . . . Parliament was naturally led to exercise the power which had been, by its predecessors, so often exercised over the Colonies, and to pass the Stamp Act. Against this act, the Colonies petitioned Parliament, and denied its authority . . . [declaring] that the Colonies could not be represented in that body. This justly alarmed the British Senate. It was thought and called by the ablest men and Britain, a clear and explicit declaration of the American Independence, and compelled the Parliament to pass the Declaratory Act, in order to save its ancient and incontrovertible right of supremacy over all the parts of the empire. . . .

Having thus briefly stated the arguments in favour of parliamentary authority, . . . I am free to confess that the exercise of that authority is not perfectly constitutional in respect to the Colonies. We know that the whole landed interest of Britain is represented in that body, while neither the land nor the people of America hold the least participation in the legislative authority of the State. Representation, or a participation in the supreme councils of the State, is the great principle upon which the freedom of the British Government is established and secured.

I wish to see . . . the right to participate in the supreme councils of the State extended, in some form . . . to America . . . [and therefore] have prepared the draught of a plan for uniting America more intimately, in constitutional policy, with Great-Britain. . . . I am certain when dispassionately considered, it will be found to be the most perfect union in power and liberty with the Parent State, next to a representation in Parliament, and I trust it will be approved of by both countries.

*The Plan*
That the several [colonial] assemblies shall [form an American union and] choose members for the grand council. . . .

That the Grand Council . . . shall hold and exercise all the like rights, liberties and privileges, as are held and exercised by and in the House of Commons of Great-Britain. . . .

That the President-General shall hold his office during the pleasure of the King, and his assent shall be requisite to all acts of the Grand Council, and it shall be his office and duty to cause them to be carried into execution. . . .

That the President-General, by and with the advice and consent of the Grand-Council, hold and exercise all the legislative rights, powers, and authorities, necessary for regulating and administering all the general police and affairs of the colonies. . . .

That the said President-General and the Grand Council, be an inferior and distinct branch of the British legislature, united and incorporated with it, . . . and that the assent of both [Parliament and the Grand Council] shall be requisite to the validity of all such general acts or statutes [that affect the colonies].

Source: Joseph Galloway, *Historical and Political Reflections on the Rise and Progress of the American Rebellion* (London, 1780), 70.

## ANALYZING THE EVIDENCE

- **According to Ingersoll, what were the main arguments of those in Parliament who opposed the Stamp Act? Did those opposing the Stamp Act agree with the act's supporters that Parliament had the right to tax the colonies?**

- **How did Galloway's plan solve the problem of colonial representation in Parliament? How would the British ministers who advocated parliamentary supremacy have reacted to the plan?**

- **The framers of the U.S. Constitution addressed the problem of dividing authority between state governments and the national government by allowing the states to retain legal authority over most matters and delegating limited powers to the national government. Could such a solution have been implemented in the British empire? Why or why not?**

**TABLE 5.2**

**Patriot Resistance, 1762–1776**

| Date | British Action | Patriot Response |
|------|----------------|------------------|
| 1762 | Revenue Act | Merchants complain privately |
| 1763 | Proclamation Line | Land speculators voice discontent |
| 1764 | Sugar Act | Merchants and Massachusetts legislature protest |
| 1765 | Stamp Act | Sons of Liberty riot; Stamp Act Congress; first boycott of British goods |
| 1765 | Quartering Act | New York assembly refuses to fund until 1767 |
| 1767–1768 | Townshend Act; military occupation of Boston | Second boycott of British goods; harassment of pro-British merchants |
| 1772 | Royal commission to investigate *Gaspée* affair | Committees of correspondence form |
| 1773 | Tea Act | Widespread resistance; Boston Tea Party |
| 1774 | Coercive Acts; Quebec Act | First Continental Congress; third boycott of British goods |
| 1775 | British raids near Boston; king's Proclamation for Suppressing Rebellion and Sedition | Armed resistance; Second Continental Congress; invasion of Canada; cutoff of colonial exports |
| 1776 | Military attacks led by royal governors in South | Paine's *Common Sense*; Declaration of Independence |

merchants to seize debt-burdened properties. Consequently, the Virginia gentry supported demands by indebted yeomen farmers to close the law courts, so that they could bargain with merchants over debts without the threat of legal action. "The spark of liberty is not yet extinct among our people," declared one planter, "and if properly fanned by the Gentlemen of influence will, I make no doubt, burst out again into a flame."

## Loyalist Americans

Other "Gentlemen of influence" worried that resistance to Britain would undermine all political institutions and "introduce Anarchy and disorder and render life and property here precarious." Their fears increased when the Sons of Liberty used intimidation and violence to uphold the boycotts. One well-to-do New Yorker complained, "No man can be in a more abject state of bondage than he whose Reputation, Property and Life are exposed to the discretionary violence . . . of the community." As the crisis deepened, such men became Loyalists—so called because they remained loyal to the British crown.

Less affluent Americans also refused to endorse the Patriot cause. In New Jersey and Pennsylvania, thousands of pacifist Quakers and Germans tried to remain neutral. In areas where wealthy landowners became Patriots—the Hudson River Valley of New York, for example—many tenant farmers supported the king because they hated their landlords. Similar social conflicts prompted some Regulators in the North Carolina backcountry and many farmers in eastern Maryland to oppose the Patriots there. Enslaved blacks had little reason to support the cause of their Patriot masters. In November 1774, James Madison reported that some Virginia slaves were planning to escape "when the English troops should arrive."

Prominent Loyalists—royal officials, merchants with military contracts, clergy of the Church of England, and well-established lawyers—tried to mobilize support for the king. Relying on their high status and rhetorical skills, they denounced Patriot leaders as troublemakers and accused them of working toward independence. But Loyalist leaders found relatively few active followers. A Tory association started by the governor of New Hampshire enrolled just fifty-nine members, including fourteen of his relatives. At this crucial juncture, Americans who supported resistance to British rule commanded the allegiance—or at least the acquiescence—of the majority of white Americans.

## Armed Resistance Begins

When the Continental Congress had met in September 1774, Massachusetts was already defying British authority. In August, 150 delegates to an extralegal

Middlesex County Congress had urged Patriots to close the existing royal courts and to transfer their political allegiance to the popularly elected House of Representatives. Subsequently, armed crowds harassed Loyalists and ensured Patriot rule in most of New England.

General Thomas Gage, now the military governor of Massachusetts, tried desperately to maintain imperial power. In September 1774, he ordered British troops in Boston to seize Patriot armories in nearby Charlestown and Cambridge. Following that raid, 20,000 militiamen mobilized to safeguard other Massachusetts military depots. The Concord town meeting raised a defensive force, the famous **Minutemen**, to "Stand at a minutes warning in Case of alarm." Increasingly, Gage's authority was limited to Boston, where it rested on the bayonets of his 3,500 troops. Meanwhile, the Patriot-controlled Massachusetts assembly met in nearby Salem in open defiance of Parliament, collecting taxes, bolstering the militia, and assuming the responsibilities of government.

In London, the colonial secretary, Lord Dartmouth, proclaimed Massachusetts to be in "open rebellion" and ordered Gage to march against the "rude rabble." On the night of April 18, 1775, Gage dispatched seven hundred soldiers to capture colonial leaders and supplies at Concord. Paul Revere and a series of other riders warned Patriots in many towns; at dawn, militiamen confronted the British regulars first at Lexington and then at Concord. Those first skirmishes took a handful of lives, but as the British retreated to Boston, militia from neighboring towns repeatedly ambushed them. By the end of the day, 73 British soldiers were dead, 174 wounded, and 26 missing. British fire had killed 49 Massachusetts militiamen and wounded 39. Too much blood had been spilled to allow another compromise. Twelve years of economic and constitutional conflict had ended in civil violence.

## The Second Continental Congress Organizes for War

A month later, in May 1775, Patriot leaders gathered in Philadelphia for the Second Continental Congress. As the Congress opened, 3,000 British troops attacked American fortifications on Breed's Hill and Bunker Hill overlooking Boston. After three assaults and 1,000 casualties, they finally dislodged the Patriot militia. Inspired by his countrymen's valor, John Adams exhorted the Congress to rise to the "defense of American liberty" by creating a continental army. He nominated George Washington to lead it. After bitter debate, the Congress

approved the proposals, but, Adams lamented, only "by bare majorities."

**Congress versus King George** Despite the bloodshed in Massachusetts, a majority in the Congress still hoped for reconciliation. Led by John Dickinson of Pennsylvania, these moderates won approval of a petition expressing loyalty to George III and asking for repeal of oppressive parliamentary legislation. But Samuel Adams, Patrick Henry, and other zealous Patriots drummed up support for a Declaration of the Causes and Necessities of Taking Up Arms. Americans dreaded the "calamities of civil war," the declaration asserted, but were "resolved to die Freemen rather than to live [as] slaves." George III failed to exploit the divisions among the Patriots; instead, in August 1775, he issued a Proclamation for Suppressing Rebellion and Sedition.

Before the king's proclamation reached America, the radicals in the Congress had won support for an invasion of Canada. Patriot forces easily defeated the British forces at Montreal; but in December 1775, they failed to capture Quebec City and withdrew. Meanwhile, American merchants waged the financial warfare promised at the First Continental Congress by cutting off exports to Britain and its West Indian sugar islands, which were recovering from a series of major El Niño–caused hurricanes. Parliament retaliated with the Prohibitory Act, which outlawed all trade with the rebellious colonies.

**Fighting in the South** Skirmishes between Patriot and Loyalist forces now broke out in the southern colonies. In Virginia, Patriots forced the royal governor, Lord Dunmore, to take refuge on a British warship in Chesapeake Bay. Branding the rebels "traitors," the governor organized two military forces: one white, the Queen's Own Loyal Virginians; and one black, the Ethiopian Regiment, which enlisted 1,000 slaves who had fled their Patriot owners. In November 1775, Dunmore issued a controversial proclamation promising freedom to black slaves and white indentured servants who joined the Loyalist cause. White planters denounced this "Diabolical scheme," claiming it "point[ed] a dagger to their Throats." A new rising of the black and white underclasses, as in Bacon's Rebellion in the 1670s, seemed a possibility. In Fincastle County in southwestern Virginia, Loyalist planter John Hiell urged workers to support the king, promising "a Servant man" that soon "he and all the negroes would get their freedom." Frightened by Dunmore's aggressive tactics, Patriot yeomen and tenants called for a final break with Britain.

**Tryon's Palace in New Bern, North Carolina**

William Tryon, appointed as the royal governor of North Carolina in 1764, was accustomed to living well. Born into a substantial landed-gentry family, he married a London heiress, the daughter of the East India Company's governor of Bombay. Upon his arrival in North Carolina, Tryon persuaded the colony's assembly to appropriate the princely sum of £10,000 to build a mansion for his use. Completed in 1770, the "palace," as critics called it, served as Tryon's home for only a year. After harshly suppressing the Regulator movement in 1771, Tryon was appointed royal governor of New York (he would be the colony's last). Though Tryon's North Carolina mansion burned to the ground in 1798, it was restored in the 1950s, using the original plans.    Tryon's Palace, New Bern, N.C.

In North Carolina, too, military clashes prompted demands for independence. Early in 1776, Josiah Martin, the colony's royal governor, raised a Loyalist force of 1,500 Scottish Highlanders in the backcountry. In response, Patriots mobilized the low-country militia and, in February, defeated Martin's army at the Battle of Moore's Creek Bridge, capturing more than 800 Highlanders. Following this victory, radical Patriots in the North Carolina assembly told its representatives to the Continental Congress to join with "other Colonies in declaring Independence, and forming foreign alliances." In May, the Virginia gentry followed suit: Led by James Madison, Edmund Pendleton, and Patrick Henry, the Patriots met in convention and resolved unanimously to support independence.

## Thomas Paine's *Common Sense*

As radical Patriots edged toward independence, many colonists still retained an affection for the king. Joyous crowds had toasted the health of George III when he ascended the throne in 1760 and again in 1766, when his ministers repealed the Stamp Act. Their loyalty stemmed in part from the character of authority in a patriarchal society. Just as people followed the dictates of elders in town meetings and ministers in churches, so they should obey the king, their imperial "father." Every father was "a king, and governor in his family," as one group of Baptists put it. To deny the king's legitimacy would disrupt the entire social order.

But by late 1775, many Americans were turning against the monarch. As military conflicts escalated, they accused George III of supporting oppressive legislation and ordering armed retaliation. Agitation was especially intense in Philadelphia, where many Quaker and Anglican merchants were either "neutrals" or Loyalists. Artisans, including many Scots-Irish immigrants, became a major force in the city's Patriot movement. Angered by the merchants' passivity and worried that British imports threatened their small-scale manufacturing enterprises, they organized a Mechanics Association to protect America's "just Rights and Privileges." By February 1776, forty artisans sat with forty-seven merchants on the Philadelphia Committee of Resistance.

Cultural and religious motives prompted many Scots-Irish artisans and laborers to become Patriots. They came from Presbyterian families who had fled economic and religious discrimination in British-controlled Ireland, and many had embraced the egalitarian message preached by Gilbert Tennent and other New Light ministers (see Chapter 4). As pastor of Philadelphia's Second Presbyterian Church, Tennent had preached that all men and women were equal before God. Applying this idea to politics, New Light Presbyterians shouted in street demonstrations that they had "no king but King Jesus." Republican philosophy derived from the European Enlightenment also circulated freely among Pennsylvania artisans. Consequently, Patriot leaders Benjamin Franklin and Dr. Benjamin Rush found a receptive audience when they questioned not only the wisdom of George III but the very idea of monarchy.

With popular sentiment in flux, a single brief pamphlet tipped the balance. In January 1776, Thomas Paine published *Common Sense*, a rousing call for independence and a republican form of government. Paine had served as a minor customs official in England until he was fired for joining a protest against low wages. In 1774, Paine, migrated to Philadelphia, where he met Rush and other Patriots who shared his republican sentiments.

In *Common Sense*, Paine launched an assault on the traditional monarchical order in language that stirred popular emotions. "Monarchy and hereditary succession have laid the world in blood and ashes," Paine proclaimed, leveling a personal attack at George III, "the hard hearted sullen Pharaoh of England." Mixing insults with biblical quotations, Paine blasted the British system of "mixed government" among the three estates of king, lords, and commoners. Paine granted that the system "was noble for the dark and slavish times" of the past, but now it yielded only "monarchical tyranny in the person of the king" and "aristocratic tyranny in the persons of the peers."

Paine made a compelling case for American independence by turning the traditional metaphor of patriarchal authority on its head: "Is it the interest of a man to be a boy all his life?" he asked. Within six months, *Common Sense* had gone through twenty-five editions and reached hundreds of thousands of people throughout the colonies. "There is great talk of independence," a worried New York Loyalist noted, "the unthinking multitude are mad for it.... A pamphlet called Com-

**Thomas Paine**

Tom Paine was many things: a failed husband, businessman, and customs agent; a creative inventor and bridge designer; and, most important, a lifelong radical and the author of provocative works that helped change the course of history. In 1776, his pamphlet *Common Sense* sparked Americans to declare independence from Britain. Paine's defense of the French Revolution and attack on monarchy, *The Rights of Man* (1791), won him election to the National Convention, which created the First French Republic. And his *Age of Reason* (1794, 1796), a defense of deism and rational inquiry and a sustained assault on "revealed" religion and Christianity, won him the enmity of devout believers and political conservatives. *Thomas Paine* (oil on canvas), Otis, Bass (1784–1861) / Huntington Library ©The Huntington Library, Art Collections & Botanical Gardens / The Bridgeman Art Library.

mon Sense has carried off . . . thousands." Paine urged Americans to create independent republican states: "A government of our own is our natural right, 'TIS TIME TO PART" (see Voices from Abroad, "Thomas Paine: *Common Sense*," p. 166).

## Independence Declared

Inspired by Paine's arguments and beset by armed Loyalists, Patriot conventions urged a break from Britain. In June 1776, Richard Henry Lee presented Virginia's resolution to the Continental Congress: "That these United Colonies are, and of right ought to be,

All the nations and people I had hitherto passed through resemble
own in their manners, customs and lang

## Thomas Paine
### *Common Sense*

Thomas Paine was a sharp critic and an acute observer. Before arriving in Philadelphia from his native England in mid-1774, Paine had rejected the legitimacy of monarchy. He quickly came to understand the republican spirit of American politics and how this spirit could easily be tapped to create independent governments that might change the course of history. In his widely read political pamphlet *Common Sense* (1776), he showed the colonists that American independence was "natural" and simply "common sense."

In the following pages I offer nothing more than simple facts, plain arguments, and common sense. . . . The sun never shined on a cause of greater worth. 'Tis not the affair of a city, a country, a province, or a kingdom, but of a continent—of at least one eighth part of the habitable globe. 'Tis not the concern of a day, a year, or an age; posterity are virtually involved in the contest, and will be more or less affected, even to the end of time. . . .

We have boasted the protection of Great-Britain, without considering, that her motive was *interest* not *attachment*; that she did not protect us from *our enemies* on *our account*, but from *her enemies* on *her own account*. . . . Our plan is commerce, and that, well attended to, will secure us the peace and friendship of all Europe; because, it is the interest of all Europe to have America a *free port*. Her trade will always be a protection, and her barrenness of gold and silver secure her from invaders. I challenge the warmest advocate for reconciliation, to shew, a single advantage that this continent can reap, by being connected with Great Britain. . . . Our corn will fetch its price in any market in Europe, and our imported goods must be paid for buy them where we will.

Every thing that is right or natural pleads for separation. The blood of the slain, the weeping voice of nature cries, 'TIS TIME TO PART. Even the distance at which the Almighty hath placed England and America, is a strong and natural proof, that the authority of the one, over the other, was never the design of Heaven. . . . There is something very absurd, in supposing a continent to be perpetually governed by an island. In no instance hath nature made the satellite larger than its primary planet, and as England and America, with respect to each other, reverses the common order of nature, it is evident they belong to different systems: England to Europe, America to itself.

But the most powerful of all arguments, is, that nothing but independence, i.e. a continental form of government, can keep the peace of the continent and preserve it inviolate from civil wars. . . . If there is any true cause of fear respecting independence, it is because no plan is yet laid down. Men do not see their way out—Wherefore, . . . I offer the following hints. . . .

Let the assemblies [of the former colonies] be annual, with a President only . . . their business wholly domestic, and subject to the authority of a Continental Congress.

Let each colony be divided into six, eight, or ten convenient districts, each district to send a proper number of delegates to Congress, so that each colony send at least thirty. The whole number in Congress will be at least 390. . . .

But where, say some, is the King of America? I'll tell you. Friend, . . . in America THE LAW IS KING. For as in absolute governments the King is law, so in free countries the law ought to be King; and there ought to be no other. . . . Let the crown at the conclusion of the ceremony, be demolished, and scattered among the people whose right it is. A government of our own is our natural right. . . .

O ye that love mankind! Ye that dare oppose, not only the tyranny, but the tyrant, stand forth! Every spot of the old world is overrun with oppression. Freedom hath been hunted round the globe. Asia, and Africa, have long expelled her.—Europe regards her like a stranger, and England hath given her warning to depart. O! receive the fugitive, and prepare in time an asylum for mankind.

Source: Thomas Paine, *Common Sense* (Philadelphia, 1776).

### ANALYZING THE EVIDENCE

- On what grounds does Paine argue for American independence? Where do you see the influence of Enlightenment thinking in his argument?

- Given that all European nations pursued mercantilist policies, was Paine correct in thinking they would welcome America as a "free port"? How were Europe's monarchies likely to respond to an independent American republic?

- How could Paine celebrate America as a land of freedom and an "asylum for mankind" given the importance of slavery and indentured servitude to its economy? What sort of liberty was Paine championing?

- Why do you think *Common Sense* struck such a chord with Americans throughout the colonies?

**George III, 1771**

King George III was a young man of twenty-seven when the American troubles began in 1765. Six years later, as this portrait by Johann Zoffany suggests, the king had aged. Initially, George had been headstrong and tried to impose his will on Parliament, but he succeeded only in generating political confusion and inept policy. He strongly supported Parliament's attempts to tax the colonies and continued the war in America long after most of his ministers agreed that it had been lost.   The Royal Collection © 2003 Her Majesty Queen Elizabeth II.

free and independent states." Faced with certain defeat, staunch Loyalists and anti-independence moderates withdrew from the Congress, leaving committed Patriots to take the fateful step. On July 4, 1776, the Congress approved the Declaration of Independence (see Documents, p. D-1).

The Declaration's main author, Thomas Jefferson of Virginia, had mobilized resistance to the Coercive Acts with the pamphlet *A Summary View of the Rights of British America* (1774). Now, in the Declaration, he justified independence and republicanism to Americans and the world, by vilifying George III: "He has plundered our seas, ravaged our coasts, burned our towns, and destroyed the lives of our people." Such a prince was a "tyrant," Jefferson concluded, and "is unfit to be the ruler of a free people."

Employing the ideas of the European Enlightenment, Jefferson proclaimed a series of "self-evident" truths: "that all men are created equal"; that they pos-

sess the "unalienable rights" of "Life, Liberty, and the pursuit of Happiness"; that government derives its "just powers from the consent of the governed" and can rightly be overthrown if it "becomes destructive of these ends." By linking these doctrines of individual liberty, **popular sovereignty**, and republican government with American independence, Jefferson established them as the defining political values of the new nation.

For Jefferson, as for Paine, the pen proved mightier than the sword. The Declaration won wide readership and support in France and Germany; at home, it sparked celebrations in rural hamlets and seaport cities, as crowds burned effigies and toppled statues of the king. On July 8, 1776, in Easton, Pennsylvania, a "great number of spectators" heard a reading of the Declaration, "gave their hearty assent with three loud huzzahs, and cried out, 'May God long preserve and unite the Free and Independent States of America.'"

- Why did the Patriot movement wane in the early 1770s? Why did the Tea Act reignite colonial resistance?

- Why did colonial and British leaders fail to reach a political compromise to save the empire?

## SUMMARY

In this chapter we focused on a short span of time — a mere decade and a half — and outlined the plot of a political drama in three acts. In Act I, the Great War for Empire prompts British political leaders to implement a program of imperial reform and taxation. Act II is full of dramatic action, as colonial mobs riot, Patriot pamphleteers articulate ideologies of resistance, and British ministers search for compromise between claims of parliamentary sovereignty and assertions of colonial autonomy. Act III takes the form of tragedy: The once-proud British empire dissolves into civil war, an imminent nightmare of death and destruction.

Why did this happen? More than two centuries later, the answers still are not clear. Certainly, the lack of astute leadership in Britain was a major factor. But British leaders faced circumstances that limited their actions: a huge national debt and deep commitments to both a powerful fiscal-military state and the absolute supremacy of Parliament. Moreover, in America, decades of salutary neglect strengthened Patriots' demands for political autonomy, as did the fears and aspirations of artisans and farmers. The trajectories of their conflicting intentions and ideas placed Britain and its American possessions on course for a disastrous — and fatal — collision.

**Independence Declared**

In this painting by John Trumbull, Thomas Jefferson and the other drafters of the Declaration (John Adams of Massachusetts, Roger Sherman of Connecticut, Robert Livingston of New York, and Benjamin Franklin of Pennsylvania) present the document to John Hancock, the president of the Second Continental Congress. One Patriot observer reported that when the Declaration was read at a public meeting in New York City on July 10, a massive statue of George III was "pulled down by the Populace" and its four thousand pounds of lead melted down to make "Musquet balls" for use against the British troops massed on Staten Island.   Yale University Art Gallery/Art Resource, NY.

## CHAPTER REVIEW QUESTIONS

- Trace the key events in both Britain and America from 1763 to 1776 that forged the Patriot movement. Why did those in Parliament believe that the arguments of the rebellious colonists were not justified? How did the Patriots gain the widespread support of the colonists?

- The narrative suggests that the war for American independence was not inevitable, that the British empire could have been saved. Do you agree? Was there a point during the imperial crisis at which peaceful compromise was possible?

## FOR FURTHER EXPLORATION

Jack P. Greene and J. R. Pole, eds., *The Blackwell Encyclopedia of the American Revolution* (1991), and Barbara DeWolfe, *Discoveries of America: Personal Accounts of British Emigrants* (1997), illuminate the lives and events of the era. A. J. Langguth's *Patriots: The Men Who Started the American Revolution* (1988) should be read in conjunction with Gary B. Nash's *The Unknown American Revolution* (2005).

Edmund Morgan and Helen Morgan explore The *Stamp Act Crisis* (1953), and Philip Lawson's *George Grenville* (1984) examines the man who provoked it. Benjamin Labaree's *The Boston Tea Party* (1979) shows how a "small" event altered the course of history, while David Hackett Fischer explains the rise of the radical Patriots in *Paul Revere's Ride* (1994). For events in Virginia, see Woody Holton, *Forced Founders* (1999), and Michael A. McDonnell, *The Politics of War* (2007).

*Liberty! The American Revolution* (6 hours), a PBS video, has a fine Web site (**www.pbs.org/ktca/liberty/**). For a British perspective, see "This Sceptred Isle: Empire" (**www.bbc.co.uk/radio4/history/empire/regions/americas.shtml**). For links to many document collections, visit **userpages.umbc.edu/~bouton/Revolution.links.htm**. The National Gallery of Art (**www.nga.gov**) has paintings of the period. In *Angel in the Whirlwind: The Triumph of the American Revolution* (1997), Benson Bobrick narrates a grand epic; for more complex analyses, read John Ferling, *A Leap in the Dark: The Struggle to Create the American Republic* (2003), and David Armitage, *The Declaration of Independence: A Global History* (2007).

### TEST YOUR KNOWLEDGE

To assess your command of the material in this chapter, see the Online Study Guide at **bedfordstmartins.com/henretta**.

For Web sites, images, and documents related to topics and places in this chapter, visit **bedfordstmartins.com/makehistory**.

## TIMELINE

| | |
|---|---|
| **1756–1763** | Great War for Empire<br>British national debt doubles |
| **1762** | Revenue Act reforms customs service<br>Royal Navy arrests colonial smugglers |
| **1763** | Treaty of Paris ends war<br>Proclamation Line limits white settlement<br>George Grenville becomes prime minister |
| **1764** | Sugar Act and Currency Act<br>Colonists oppose vice-admiralty courts |
| **1765** | Stamp Act imposes direct tax<br>Quartering Act requires barracks for British troops<br>Sons of Liberty riot<br>Stamp Act Congress meets<br>First American boycott of British goods |
| **1766** | First compromise: Stamp Act repealed; Declaratory Act passed |
| **1767** | Townshend duties<br>Restraining Act suspends New York assembly |
| **1768** | Second American boycott |
| **1769** | Daughters of Liberty make cloth<br>British army occupies Boston |
| **1770** | Second compromise: Partial repeal of Townshend Act<br>Boston "Massacre" |
| **1772** | Committees of correspondence form |
| **1773** | Tea Act assists British East India Company<br>Boston Tea Party |
| **1774** | Coercive Acts punish Massachusetts<br>Quebec Act angers Patriots<br>First Continental Congress meets<br>Third American boycott |
| **1775** | General Gage marches to Lexington and Concord<br>Second Continental Congress creates Continental army<br>Lord Dunmore recruits Loyalist slaves<br>Patriots invade Canada and skirmish with Loyalists in South |
| **1776** | Thomas Paine's *Common Sense*<br>Declaration of Independence |

BOSTON

CHARLES TOWN

## CHAPTER 6

# Making War and Republican Governments, 1776–1789

**When Patriots** in Frederick County, Maryland, demanded his allegiance to their cause in 1776, Robert Gassaway would have none of it. "It was better for the poor people to lay down their arms and pay the duties and taxes laid upon them by King and Parliament than to be brought into slavery and commanded and ordered about [by you]," he told them. The story was much the same in Farmington, Connecticut, where Patriot officials imprisoned Nathaniel Jones and seventeen other men for "remaining neutral." In Pennsylvania, Quakers accused of Loyalism were rounded up, jailed, and charged with treason, and some were hung for aiding the British cause. Everywhere, the outbreak of fighting in 1776 forced families to choose the Loyalist or the Patriot side.

The Patriots' control of most local governments gave them an edge in this battle. Patriot leaders organized militia units and recruited volunteers for the Continental army, a ragtag force that surprisingly held its own on the battlefield. "I admire the American troops tremendously!" exclaimed a French officer. "It is incredible that soldiers composed of every age, even children of fifteen, of whites and blacks, almost naked, unpaid, and rather poorly fed, can march so well and withstand fire so steadfastly."

Military service created political commitment—and vice versa. Patriot leaders encouraged Americans not only to support the war but also to take an active role in government. As the common people entered into politics, the character of political identity changed. Previously, Americans had lived within a social world dominated by the links of family, kinship, and locality; now, republican citizenship emphasized the vertical ties connecting each individual with the state. "From subjects to citizens the difference is immense," remarked South Carolina Patriot David Ramsay. By repudiating monarchical rule and raising a democratic army, the Patriots launched the age of republican revolutions.

Soon republicanism would throw France into turmoil and inspire revolutionaries in Spain's American colonies. The independence of the Anglo-American colonies, remarked the Venezuelan political leader, Francisco de Miranda, who had been in New York and Philadelphia at the end of the American Revolution, "was bound to be . . . the infallible preliminary to our own [independence movement]." The Patriot uprising of 1776 had set in motion a process that by 1826 had replaced an Atlantic colonial system with an American system of new nations.

**The Battle of Bunker Hill**

As British warships and artillery lob cannon balls at Patriot positions, British redcoats advance up the steep slope of Bunker Hill (to the right). It took three assaults and a thousand casualties before they finally dislodged the Patriot militia. The British bombardment ignited fires in nearby Charlestown, which burns in the background. *"Attack on Bunker's Hill, with the Burning of Charles Town,"* American Eighteenth Century. Gift of Edgar Williams and Bernice Chrysler Garbisch. Image © 2005 Board of Trustees, National Gallery of Art, Washington, D.C.

# The Trials of War, 1776–1778

The Declaration of Independence appeared just as the British launched a full-scale military assault. For two years, British troops manhandled the Continental army. A few inspiring American victories kept the rebellion alive, but during the winters of 1776 and 1777, the Patriot cause hung in the balance.

## War in the North

Once the British resorted to military force, few Europeans gave the rebels a chance. The population of Great Britain was 11 million; the colonies, 2.5 million—20 percent of whom were enslaved Africans. Moreover, the British government had access to the immense wealth generated by the South Atlantic System and the emerging Industrial Revolution. Its military budget paid for the most powerful navy in the world, a standing army of 48,000 Britons (with an experienced officer corps), and thousands of German (Hessian) soldiers. Britain also had the support of thousands of American Loyalists and powerful Indian tribes: In the Carolinas, the Cherokees resisted colonists' demands for their lands by allying with the British, as did four of the six Iroquois nations of New York (Map 6.1).

By contrast, the Americans were economically and militarily weak. They lacked a strong central government and a reliable source of tax revenue. Their new Continental army, commanded by General George Washington, consisted of 18,000 poorly trained recruits. The Patriot militia would not march to distant battles, and American officers had never faced a disciplined European army.

To demonstrate Britain's military superiority, the prime minister, Lord North, ordered General William Howe to capture New York City. His strategy was to seize control of the Hudson River and thereby isolate the radical Patriots in New England from the colonies to the south. As the Second Continental Congress declared independence in Philadelphia in July 1776, Howe landed 32,000 troops—British regulars and German mercenaries—outside New York City. In August 1776, Howe defeated the Americans in the Battle of Long Island and forced their retreat to Manhattan Island. There, Howe outflanked Washington's troops and nearly trapped them. Outgunned and outmaneuvered, the Continental army again retreated, eventually crossing the Hudson River to New Jersey. By December, the British army had pushed the rebels across New Jersey and over the Delaware River into Pennsylvania.

**MAP 6.1**

**Patriot and Loyalist Strongholds**

Patriots were in the majority in most of the thirteen mainland colonies and used their control of local governments to funnel men, money, and supplies to the rebel cause. Although Loyalists could be found in every colony, their strongholds were limited to Nova Scotia, eastern New York, New Jersey, and certain areas in the South. However, most Native American peoples favored the British cause and bolstered the power of Loyalist militias in central New York (see Map 6.3) and in the Carolina backcountry.

From the Patriots' perspective, winter came just in time. Following eighteenth-century custom, the British halted their military campaign for the cold months, allowing the Americans to catch them off guard. On Christmas night 1776, Washington crossed the Delaware River and staged a successful surprise attack on Trenton, New Jersey, where he forced the surrender of 1,000 German soldiers. In early January 1777, the Continental army won a small victory at nearby Princeton (Map 6.2). But like bright stars in a dark sky, these minor triumphs could not mask British military superiority. "These are the times," wrote Thomas Paine, "that try men's souls."

**MAP 6.2**

**The War in the North, 1776–1777**

In 1776, the British army drove Washington's forces across New Jersey into Pennsylvania. The Americans counterattacked successfully at Trenton and Princeton and then set up winter headquarters in Morristown. In 1777, British forces stayed on the offensive. General Howe attacked the Patriot capital, Philadelphia, from the south and captured it in early October. Meanwhile, General Burgoyne and Colonel St. Leger launched simultaneous invasions from Canada. With the help of thousands of New England militiamen, American troops commanded by General Horatio Gates defeated Burgoyne in August at Bennington, Vermont, and in October at Saratoga, New York, the military turning point in the war.

# Armies and Strategies

Thanks in part to General Howe, the rebellion survived. Howe had opposed the Coercive Acts of 1774 and still hoped for a political compromise. So he did not try to destroy the American army but simply to show its weakness and persuade the Continental Congress to give up the struggle. Howe's restrained tactics cost Britain the opportunity to nip the rebellion in the bud.

For his part, Washington acted cautiously to avoid a major defeat: "On our Side the War should be defensive," he told Congress. His strategy was to draw the British away from the seacoast, extend their lines of supply, and sap their morale.

Congress had promised Washington a regular force of 75,000 men, but the Continental army never reached even a third of that number. Yeomen refused to be "Haras'd with callouts" that took them away from

***The Battle of Princeton***

Black smoke from burning buildings partially obscures the sun, as the muzzle flash from an American cannon lights up the battlefield. Pursued by Cornwallis after his surprise attack and victory at nearby Trenton, Washington (on horseback to the right of the flag) confronted three regiments of redcoats at Princeton. The Americans had an advantage in numbers and put the British to flight, but only after withstanding the bayonet charge depicted in the right-center of William Mercer's painting.   Library of Congress Manuscript Division. Department of Rare Books and Special Collections.

their families and farms, and would serve only in local militias. When the Virginia gentry imposed a military draft and three years of service on propertyless men—the "Lazy fellows who lurk about and are pests to Society"—they resisted so fiercely that the legislature had to pay them substantial bounties and agree to shorter terms of service. The Continental soldiers recruited in Maryland by General William Smallwood were poor American youths and older foreign-born men, often British ex-convicts and former indentured servants. Most enlisted for the $20 cash bonus (about $2,000 today) and the promise of 100 acres of land.

Molding such recruits into an effective fighting force was nearly impossible. Inexperienced soldiers panicked in the face of a British artillery bombardment or flank attack; and hundreds deserted, unwilling to submit to the discipline of military life. The soldiers who stayed resented the contempt their officers had for the "camp followers," the women who made do with the meager supplies provided to feed and care for the troops.

General Philip Schuyler of New York complained that his troops were "destitute of provisions, without camp equipage, with little ammunition, and not a single piece of cannon."

The Continental army was not only poorly supplied, but held in suspicion by Radical Whig Patriots, who believed that a standing army was a threat to liberty. Even in wartime, they preferred militias to a professional fighting force. Given these handicaps, Washington and his army were fortunate to have escaped an overwhelming defeat.

## Victory at Saratoga

After Howe's dismaying failure to achieve an overwhelming victory, Lord North and his colonial secretary, Lord George Germain launched another major military campaign in 1777. Isolating New England remained the primary goal. To achieve it, Germain planned a three-pronged attack converging on Albany, New York. General John Burgoyne would lead a large contingent of regulars south from Quebec, Colonel Barry St. Leger and a force of Iroquois warriors would attack from the west, and General Howe would lead troops northward from New York City.

Howe had a different plan, which though carried out effectively, led to a disastrous result. He decided to attack Philadelphia, the home of the Continental Congress, hoping to end the rebellion with a single decisive blow. But instead of marching quickly across New Jersey, Howe loaded his troops onto boats and sailed up the Chesapeake Bay to attack Philadelphia from the south. The plan worked. Howe's troops easily outflanked the American positions along Brandywine Creek in Delaware and, in late September, marched triumphantly into Philadelphia. However, the capture of the rebels' capital did not end the uprising; the Continental Congress, determined to continue the struggle, fled into the interior.

Howe's slow campaign against Philadelphia contributed to the defeat of Burgoyne's army at Saratoga. Burgoyne's troops had at first advanced quickly (and successfully) from Quebec, crossing Lake Champlain, overwhelming the American defenses at Fort Ticonderoga in early July, and driving south toward the Hudson River. Then they stalled. Burgoyne—nicknamed "Gentleman Johnny"—was used to high living and had fought in Europe in a leisurely fashion; believing his large army would easily dominate the rebels, he stopped early each day to pitch comfortable tents and eat elaborate dinners with his officers. The American troops led by General Horatio Gates also slowed Burgoyne's progress by felling huge trees in the path of the British force, and by raiding British supply lines to Canada.

At summer's end, Burgoyne's army of 6,000 British and German troops and 600 Loyalists and Indians was stuck near Saratoga, New York. Desperate for food and horses, in August the British raided nearby Bennington, Vermont, but were beaten back by 2,000 American militiamen. Patriot forces to the west in the Mohawk Valley also threw St. Leger and the Iroquois into retreat. Making matters worse, the British commander in New York City recalled 4,000 troops he had sent toward Albany and ordered them to Philadelphia to bolster Howe's force. While Burgoyne waited in vain for help, thousands of Patriot militiamen from Massachusetts, New Hampshire, and New York joined Gates's forces, blocking his advance and retreat in a series of skirmishes that finally gave the British no avenue of escape. They "swarmed around the army like birds of prey," reported an English sergeant, and in October 1777, they forced Burgoyne to surrender.

**Joseph Brant**

Mohawk chief Thayendanegea, known to whites as Joseph Brant, was a devout member of the Church of England and helped to translate the Bible into the Iroquois language. Brant persuaded four of the six Iroquois nations to support Britain in the war. In 1778 and 1779, he led Iroquois warriors and Tory rangers in devastating attacks on American settlements in the Wyoming Valley of Pennsylvania and Cherry Valley in New York. In this 1797 portrait, artist Charles Willson Peale has portrayed Brant with European features. Independence National Historic Park, Philadelphia.

The victory at Saratoga was the turning point of the war. The Patriots captured more than 5,000 British troops, and ensured the diplomatic success of American representatives in Paris, who won a military alliance with France.

## Social and Financial Perils

The Patriots' triumph at Saratoga was tempered by wartime difficulties. A British naval blockade cut off supplies of European manufactures and disrupted the New England fishing industry; meanwhile, the British occupation of Boston, New York, and Philadelphia reduced trade. As unemployed artisans and laborers moved to the countryside, New York City's population declined from 21,000 to 10,000. The British blockade cut tobacco exports in the Chesapeake, so planters grew grain to sell to the contending armies. All across the land, farmers and artisans adapted to a war economy.

With goods now scarce, governments requisitioned military supplies directly from the people. In 1776,

Waßrhaffte Abbildung der Soldaten des Congreßes in Nordamerica, nach der Zeich=
nung eines Deutschen Officiers. Die Weste iß von Leder, mit der Aufschrift Congreß. Die
gantze Kleidung von Zwillich überall mit weißen Franzen beßezt, die Brinkleider gehen bis
auf die Knöchel herunter. Die Meißten laufen barfuß. Ihre Feuer-gewehr sind mit seßr langen
Bayonets versehen, welche Sie auch ßat eines Seiten gewehrs gebrauchen.

**American Militiamen**

Beset by continuing shortages of cloth, the Patriot army dressed in a variety of uniforms and fabrics. This German engraving, taken from a drawing by a Hessian officer, shows two American militiamen (one of them barefoot) wearing hunting shirts and trousers made of ticking, the strong linen fabric often used to cover mattresses and pillows.   Anne S. K. Brown Military Collection, Brown University.

Connecticut officials asked the citizens of Hartford to provide 1,000 coats and 1,600 shirts, and soldiers echoed their pleas. After losing all his shirts "except the one on my back" in the Battle of Long Island, Captain Edward Rogers told his wife that "the making of Cloath . . . must go on." Patriot women responded; in Elizabeth, New Jersey, they promised "upwards of 100,000 yards of linnen and woolen cloth." Other women assumed the burdens of farm work while their men were away at war and acquired a taste for decision-making. "We have sow'd our oats as you desired," Sarah Cobb Paine wrote to her absent husband. "Had I been master I should have planted it to Corn." Their self-esteem boosted by wartime activities, some women expected greater legal rights in the new republican society.

Still, goods remained scarce and pricey. Hard-pressed consumers assailed shopkeepers as "enemies, extortioners, and monopolizers" and called for government regulation. But when the New England states imposed price ceilings in 1777, many farmers and artisans refused to sell their goods. Ultimately, a government official admitted, consumers had to pay the higher market prices "or submit to starving."

Even more frightening, the fighting exposed tens of thousands of civilians to deprivation and death. A British officer, Lord Rawdon, favored giving "free liberty to the soldiers to ravage [the country] at will, that these infatuated creatures may feel what a calamity war is." As British and American armies marched back and forth across New Jersey, they forced Patriot and Loyalist families to flee their homes to escape arrest—or worse. Soldiers and partisans looted farms, and disorderly troops harassed and raped women and girls. "An army, even a friendly one, are a dreadful scourge to any people," wrote one Connecticut soldier. "You cannot imagine what devastation and distress mark their steps."

The war divided many farm communities. Patriots formed committees of safety to collect taxes and seized the property of those who refused to pay. "Every Body submitted to our Sovereign Lord the Mob," lamented a Loyalist preacher. In parts of Maryland, the number of "nonassociators"—those who refused to join either side—was so large that they successfully defied Patriot mobs. "Stand off you dammed rebel sons of bitches," shouted Robert Davis of Anne Arundel County, "I will shoot you if you come any nearer."

**Financial Crisis** | Such defiance exposed the weakness of Patriot governments. Most states were afraid to raise taxes, so officials issued bonds to secure gold or silver from wealthy individuals. When those funds ran out, individual states financed the war by issuing so much paper money—some $260 million all told—that it lost worth, and most people refused to accept it at face value. In North Carolina, even tax collectors eventually rejected the state's currency.

The finances of the Continental Congress collapsed, too, despite the efforts of Philadelphia merchant Robert Morris, the government's chief treasury official. Because Congress lacked the authority to impose taxes, Morris relied on funds requisitioned from the states, but the states paid late or not at all. So Morris secured loans from France and Holland and sold Continental loan certificates to some 13,000 firms and individuals, many of them obscure. Isaac Vanbibber of Maryland bought $116,400 in bonds; Nehemiah Dunham of New Jersey acquired $127,000. All the while, the Congress was issuing paper money—some $200 million between 1776 and 1779—which, like state currencies, quickly fell in value. In 1778, a family needed $7 in Continental bills to buy goods worth $1 in gold or silver. As the exchange

**Paper Currency**

Testifying to their independent status, the new state governments printed their own currencies. Rejecting the English system of pounds and shillings, Virginia used the Spanish gold dollar as its basic unit of currency, although the equivalent in English pounds is also shown. Initially, $1,200 was equal to £360 — a ratio of 3.3 to 1. By 1781, Virginia had printed so much paper money to pay its soldiers and wartime expenses that the value of its currency had depreciated. It now took $40 in Virginia currency to buy the same amount of goods as £1 sterling.   American Numismatic Society, New York City.

rate deteriorated — to 42 to 1 in 1779, 100 to 1 in 1780, and 146 to 1 in 1781 — it sparked social upheaval. In Boston, a mob of women accosted merchant Thomas Boyleston, "seazd him by his Neck," and forced him to sell his wares at traditional prices. In rural Ulster County, New York, women told the committee of safety to lower food prices or "their husbands and sons shall fight no more." As morale crumbled, Patriot leaders feared the rebellion would collapse.

**Valley Forge**   Fears reached their peak during the winter of 1777. While Howe's army lived comfortably in Philadelphia, Washington's army retreated 20 miles to Valley Forge, where 12,000 soldiers and hundreds of camp followers suffered horribly. "The army . . . now begins to grow sickly," a surgeon confided to his diary. "Poor food — hard lodging — cold weather — fatigue — nasty clothes — nasty cookery. . . . Why are we sent here to starve and freeze?" Nearby farmers refused to help. Some were pacifists, Quakers and German sectarians unwilling to support either side. Others looked out for their own families, selling grain for gold from British quartermasters but refusing depreciated Continental currency. "Such a dearth of public spirit, and want of public virtue," lamented Washington. By spring, 1,000 hungry soldiers had deserted, and another 3,000 had died from malnutrition and disease. That winter at Valley Forge took as many American lives as had two years of fighting.

In this dark hour, Baron von Steuben raised the readiness of the American army. A former Prussian military officer, von Steuben was one of a handful of

**A British Camp, c. 1778**

While American troops at Valley Forge took shelter from the cold in tents, British troops stationed just outside New York City (on upper Manhattan Island) lived in simple but well-constructed and warm log cabins. Each hut, built into a slope but including a chimney for indoor heat, housed either a few officers or eight to ten soldiers of the 17th Regiment of Foot. John Ward Dunsmore executed this painting in 1915, basing it on the careful fieldwork of a team of archaeologists.
© Collection of the New-York Historical Society.

republican-minded foreign aristocrats who joined the American cause. Appointed as inspector general of the Continental Army, he instituted a strict drill system and encouraged officers to become more professional. Thanks to von Steuben, the smaller army that emerged from Valley Forge in the spring of 1778 was a much tougher and better-disciplined force.

- **What accounted for British military superiority in the first years of the war? How did the Americans sustain their military effort between 1776 and 1778?**

- **Who was to blame for Britain's failure to win a quick victory over the American rebels: General Howe, General Burgoyne, or the ministers in London? Explain your answer.**

# The Path to Victory, 1778–1783

Wars are often won by astute diplomacy, and so it was with the War of Independence. The Patriots' prospects improved dramatically in 1778, when the Continental Congress concluded a military alliance with France, the most powerful nation in Europe. The alliance gave the Americans desperately needed money, supplies, and, eventually, troops. And it confronted Britain with an international war that challenged its domination of the Atlantic and Indian oceans.

## The French Alliance

France and America were unlikely partners. France was Catholic and a monarchy; the United States was Protestant and a federation of republics. From 1689 to 1763, the two peoples had been enemies: New Englanders had brutally uprooted the French population from Acadia (Nova Scotia) in 1755, and the French and their Indian allies had raided British settlements. But the Comte de Vergennes, the French foreign minister, was determined to avenge the loss of Canada during the Great War for Empire and persuaded King Louis XVI to provide the rebellious colonies with a secret loan and much-needed gunpowder. When news of the rebel victory at Saratoga reached Paris in December 1777, Vergennes sought a formal alliance.

Benjamin Franklin and other American diplomats craftily exploited France's rivalry with Britain to win an explicit commitment to American independence. The Treaty of Alliance of February 1778 specified that once France entered the war, neither partner would sign a separate peace without the "liberty, sovereignty, and independence" of the United States. In return, the Continental Congress agreed to recognize any French conquests in the West Indies. "France and America," warned Britain's Lord Stormont, "were indissolubly leagued for our destruction."

The alliance gave new life to the Patriots' cause. "There has been a great change in this state since the news from France," a Patriot soldier reported from Pennsylvania. Farmers—"mercenary wretches," he called them—"were as eager for Continental Money now as they were a few weeks ago for British gold." Its confidence bolstered, the Continental Congress addressed the demands of the officer corps. Most officers were gentlemen who equipped themselves and raised volunteers; in return, they insisted on lifetime military pensions at half pay. John Adams condemned the officers for "scrambling for rank and pay like apes for nuts," but General Washington urged Congress to grant the pensions: "The salvation of the cause depends upon it." Congress reluctantly granted the officers half pay, but only for seven years.

Meanwhile, the war had become unpopular in Britain. The gentry protested increases in the land tax, and merchants condemned new levies on carriages, wine, and imported goods. "It seemed we were to be taxed and stamped ourselves instead of inflicting taxes and stamps on others," a British politician complained.

At first, George III was determined to crush the rebellion. If America won independence, he warned Lord North, "the West Indies must follow them. Ireland would soon follow the same plan and be a separate state, then this island would be reduced to itself, and soon would be a poor island indeed." Stunned by the defeat at Saratoga, however, the king changed his mind. To thwart an American alliance with France, he authorized North to seek a negotiated settlement. In February 1778, North persuaded Parliament to repeal the Tea and Prohibitory acts and, amazingly, to renounce its power to tax the colonies. But the Patriots, now allied with France and committed to independence, rejected North's overture.

## War in the South

The French alliance did not bring a rapid end to the war. When France entered the conflict in June 1778, it hoped to seize all of Britain's sugar islands. Spain, which joined the war against Britain in 1779, aimed to regain Florida and the fortress of Gibraltar at the entrance to the Mediterranean Sea.

**Britain's Southern Strategy**

For its part, the British government revised its military strategy to defend the West Indies and capture the rich tobacco- and rice-growing colonies: Virginia, the Carolinas, and Georgia. Once conquered, the ministry planned to use the Scottish Highlanders in the Carolinas and other Loyalists to hold them. It had already mobilized the Cherokees and Delawares against the land-hungry Americans and knew that the Patriots' fears of slave uprisings weakened them militarily (Map 6.3). As South Carolina Patriots admitted to the Continental Congress, they could raise only a few recruits "by reason of the great proportion of citizens necessary to remain at home to prevent insurrection among the Negroes."

It fell to Sir Henry Clinton to implement Britain's southern strategy. From the British army's main base in New York City, Clinton launched a seaborne attack on Savannah, Georgia. Troops commanded by Colonel Archibald Campbell captured the town in December 1778. Mobilizing hundreds of blacks to transport supplies, Campbell moved inland and captured Augusta early in 1779. By year's end, Clinton's forces and local Loyalists controlled coastal Georgia, and had 10,000 troops poised for an assault on South Carolina.

### MAP 6.3

**Native Americans and the War in the West, 1778–1779**

Many Indian peoples remained neutral, but others, fearing land-hungry Patriot farmers, used British-supplied guns to raid American settlements. To thwart attacks by militant Shawnees, Cherokees, and Delawares, a Patriot militia led by George Rogers Clark captured the British fort and supply depot at Vincennes on the Wabash River in February 1779. To the north, Patriot generals John Sullivan and James Clinton defeated pro-British Indian forces near Tioga (on the New York–Pennsylvania border) in August 1779 and then systematically destroyed villages and crops throughout the lands of the Iroquois.

In 1780, British forces marched from victory to victory (Map 6.4). In May, Clinton forced the surrender of Charleston, South Carolina, and its garrison of 5,000 troops. Then Lord Charles Cornwallis assumed control of the British forces and, at Camden, defeated an American force commanded by General Horatio Gates, the hero of Saratoga. Only 1,200 Patriot militiamen joined Gates at Camden—a fifth of the number at Saratoga. Cornwallis took control of South Carolina, and hundreds of African Americans fled to freedom behind British lines. The southern strategy was working.

## MAP 6.4

### The War in the South, 1778–1781

Britain's southern military strategy started well. British forces captured Savannah in December 1778, took control of Georgia during 1779, and vanquished Charleston in May 1780. Over the next eighteen months, brutal warfare between the British troops and Loyalist units and the Continental army and militia raged in the interior of the Carolinas and ended in a stalemate. Hoping to break the deadlock, British general Charles Cornwallis carried the battle into Virginia in 1781. A Franco-American army led by Washington and Lafayette, with the help of the French fleet under Admiral de Grasse, surrounded Cornwallis's forces on the Yorktown Peninsula and forced their surrender.

**Admiral Pierre Suffren in India**

The American War for Independence became a worldwide conflict in 1778 when France entered the fight. French and British naval forces and troops clashed in West Africa over control of the slave trade, and in India over access to goods such as textiles, tea, and spices. Here French Admiral Suffren, who spent years in Asia campaigning against the British, exchanges greetings with his Indian ally, Hyder Ali. The ruler of the Indian kingdom of Mysore, Ali led a 1783 revolt against the British. Bridgeman Art Library Ltd.

Then the tide of battle turned. Thanks to another republican-minded European aristocrat, the Marquis de Lafayette, France finally dispatched troops to the American mainland. A longtime supporter of the American cause, Lafayette persuaded King Louis XVI to send General Comte de Rochambeau and 5,500 men to Newport, Rhode Island. There, they threatened the British forces holding New York City.

**Guerrilla Warfare in the Carolinas** Meanwhile, Washington dispatched General Nathanael Greene to recapture the Carolinas, where he found "a country that has been ravaged and plundered by both friends and enemies." Greene put local militiamen, who had been "without discipline and addicted to plundering," under strong leaders and unleashed them on less-mobile British forces. In October 1780, Patriot militia defeated a regiment of Loyalists at King's Mountain, South Carolina, taking about 1,000 prisoners. American guerrillas commanded by the "Swamp Fox," General Francis Marion, also won a series of small but fierce battles. Then, in January 1781, General Daniel Morgan led an American force to a bloody victory at Cowpens, South Carolina. But Loyalist garrisons, helped by the well-organized Cherokees, remained powerful. "We fight, get beaten, and fight again," General Greene declared doggedly. In March 1781, Greene's soldiers fought Cornwallis's seasoned army to a draw at North Carolina's Guilford Court House. Weakened by this **war of attrition**, the British general decided to concede the Carolinas to Greene and seek a decisive victory in Virginia. There, many Patriot militiamen had refused to take up arms, claiming that "the Rich wanted the Poor to fight for them."

Exploiting these social divisions, Cornwallis moved easily through the Tidewater region of Virginia in the early summer of 1781. Reinforcements sent from New York and commanded by General Benedict Arnold, the infamous Patriot traitor, bolstered his ranks. As Arnold and Cornwallis sparred with an American force led by Lafayette near the York Peninsula, Washington was informed that France had finally sent its powerful West Indian fleet to North America, and devised an audacious plan. Feigning an assault on New York City, he secretly marched General Rochambeau's army from Rhode Island to Virginia. Simultaneously, the French fleet took control of Chesapeake Bay. By the time the British discovered Washington's scheme, Cornwallis was surrounded, and his 9,500-man army outnumbered 2 to 1 on land and cut off from reinforcement or retreat by sea. In a hopeless position, Cornwallis surrendered at Yorktown in October 1781.

The Franco-American victory broke the resolve of the British government. "Oh God! It is all over!" Lord North exclaimed. Isolated diplomatically in Europe, stymied militarily in America, and lacking public support at home, the British ministry gave up active prosecution of the war on the American mainland.

## The Patriot Advantage

Angry members of Parliament demanded an explanation. How could mighty Britain, victorious in the Great War for Empire, lose to a motley rebel army? The ministry pointed to a series of blunders by the military leadership. Why had Howe not ruthlessly pursued Washington's army in 1776? Why had Howe and Burgoyne failed to coordinate their attacks in 1777? Why had Cornwallis marched deep into the Patriot-dominated state of Virginia in 1781?

Historians acknowledge British mistakes, but they also attribute the rebels' victory to French aid and the inspired leadership of George Washington. Astutely deferring to elected officials, Washington won the support of the Continental Congress and the state governments. Confident of his military abilities, he pursued a defensive strategy that minimized casualties and maintained the morale of his officers and soldiers through five difficult years of war. Moreover, the Patriots' control of local governments gave Washington a greater margin for error than the British generals had. Local militiamen provided the edge in the 1777 victory at Saratoga, and forced Cornwallis from the Carolinas in 1781.

In the end, it was the American people who decided the outcome, especially the one-third of the white colonists who were zealous Patriots. Tens of thousands of these farmers and artisans accepted Continental bills in payment for supplies, and thousands of soldiers took them as pay—even as the currency literally depreciated in their pockets. Rampant inflation meant that every paper dollar held for a week lost value, imposing a hidden "currency tax" on those who accepted the paper currency. Each individual tax was small—a few pennies on each dollar. But as millions of dollars changed hands multiple times, the currency taxes paid by ordinary citizens financed the American military victory.

## Diplomatic Triumph

After Yorktown, diplomats took two years to conclude a peace treaty. Talks began in Paris in April 1782, but the French and Spanish, still hoping to seize a West Indian island or Gibraltar, stalled for time. Their tactics infuriated American diplomats Benjamin Franklin, John Adams, and John Jay. So the Americans negotiated secretly with the British, prepared if necessary to ignore the Treaty of Alliance and sign a separate peace. British ministers were equally eager: Parliament wanted peace, and they feared the loss of a rich sugar island.

Consequently, the American diplomats secured extremely favorable terms. In the Treaty of Paris, signed in September 1783, Great Britain formally recognized American independence and relinquished its claims to lands south of the Great Lakes and east of the Mississippi River. The British negotiators did not insist on a separate territory for their Indian allies. "In endeavouring to assist you," a Wea Indian complained to a British general, "it seems we have wrought our own ruin." The Cherokees were forced to relinquish claims to 5 million acres—three-quarters of their territory—in treaties with Georgia, the Carolinas, and Virginia.

The Paris treaty also granted Americans fishing rights off Newfoundland and Nova Scotia, prohibited the British from "carrying away any negroes or other property," and guaranteed freedom of navigation on the Mississippi to American citizens "forever." In return, the American government allowed British merchants to pursue legal claims for prewar debts and encouraged the state legislatures to return confiscated property to Loyalists and grant them citizenship.

In the Treaty of Versailles, signed simultaneously, Britain made peace with France and Spain. Neither American ally gained very much. Spain reclaimed Florida from Britain (Map 6.5), but not the strategic fortress at Gibraltar. France received the Caribbean island of Tobago, small consolation for a war that had sharply raised taxes and quadrupled France's national debt. Just six years later, cries for tax relief and political liberty would spark the French Revolution. Only Americans profited handsomely; the treaties gave them independence and access to the trans-Appalachian west.

- **Why did Britain switch to a southern military strategy? Why did that strategy ultimately fail?**

- **Without the French alliance, would the American rebellion have succeeded? Why or why not?**

# Creating Republican Institutions, 1776–1787

When the Patriots declared independence, they confronted the issue of political authority. "Which of us shall be the rulers?" asked a Philadelphia newspaper. The question was multifaceted. Would power reside in the national government or the states? Who would control the new republican institutions: traditional elites or average citizens? Would women have greater political and

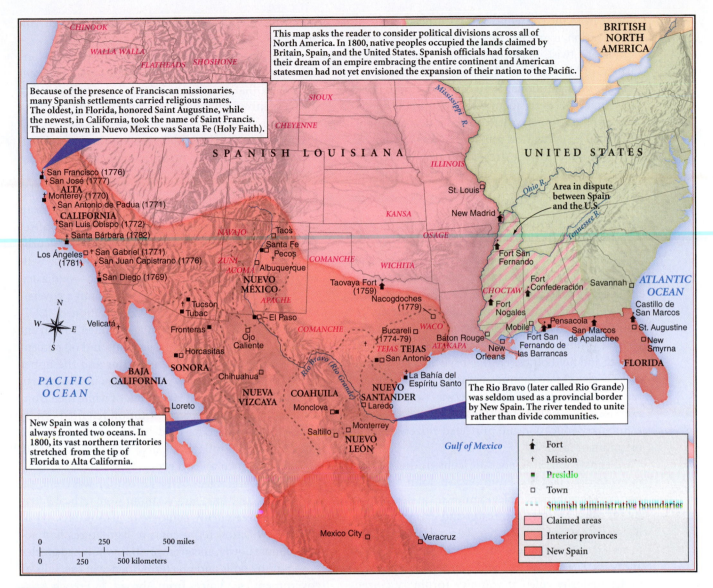

This map asks the reader to consider political divisions across all of North America. In 1800, native peoples occupied the lands claimed by Britain, Spain, and the United States. Spanish officials had forsaken their dream of an empire embracing the entire continent and American statesmen had not yet envisioned the expansion of their nation to the Pacific.

Because of the presence of Franciscan missionaries, many Spanish settlements carried religious names. The oldest, in Florida, honored Saint Augustine, while the newest, in California, took the name of Saint Francis. The main town in Nuevo Mexico was Santa Fe (Holy Faith).

The Rio Bravo (later called Rio Grande) was seldom used as a provincial border by New Spain. The river tended to unite rather than divide communities.

New Spain was a colony that always fronted two oceans. In 1800, its vast northern territories stretched from the tip of Florida to Alta California.

**MAP 6.5**

**New Spain's Northern Empire, 1763–1800**

After Spain acquired Louisiana from France in 1763, Spanish officials tried to create a northern empire. They established missions and forts (presidios) in California, expanded settlements in New Mexico, and (by allying with France during the War of Independence) won Florida back from Britain. However, by the early 1800s Spain's dream of a northern empire had been shattered by Indian uprisings in California and Texas, Napoleon's demand for the return of Louisiana, and the U.S. takeover of Florida.

legal rights? What would be the status of the slaves in the new republic?

## The State Constitutions: How Much Democracy?

In May 1776, the Second Continental Congress urged Americans to reject royal authority and establish republican governments. Most states quickly complied. "Con-

stitutions employ every pen," an observer noted. Within six months, Virginia, Maryland, North Carolina, New Jersey, Delaware, and Pennsylvania had all ratified new constitutions, and Connecticut and Rhode Island had revised their colonial charters to delete references to the king.

**Republicanism** meant more than ousting the king. The Declaration of Independence stated the principle of popular sovereignty: Governments derive "their just powers from the consent of the governed." In the heat of revolution, many Patriots gave this clause a further democratic twist. In North Carolina, the backcountry farmers of Mecklenburg County told their delegates to the state's constitutional convention to "oppose everything that leans to aristocracy or power in the hands of the rich." In Virginia, voters elected a new assembly in 1776 that, an eyewitness remarked, "was composed of men not quite so well dressed, nor so politely educated, nor so highly born" as colonial-era legislatures (Figure 6.1).

**Pennsylvania's Controversial Constitution** | This democratic impulse flowered in Pennsylvania, thanks to a coalition of Scots-Irish farmers, Philadelphia artisans, and Enlightenment-influenced intellectuals. In 1776, these insurgents ousted every officeholder of the Penn family's proprietary government, abolished property ownership as a qualification for voting, and granted all taxpaying men the right to vote and hold office. The Pennsylvania constitution of 1776 also created a unicameral (one-house) legislature with complete power; there was no governor to exercise a veto. Other provisions mandated a system of elementary education and protected citizens from imprisonment for debt.

Pennsylvania's democratic constitution alarmed many leading Patriots. From Boston, John Adams denounced the unicameral legislature as "so democratical that it must produce confusion and every evil work." Along with other conservative Patriots, Adams wanted to restrict office holding to "men of learning, leisure and easy circumstances" and warned of oppression under majority rule: "If you give [ordinary citizens] the command or preponderance in the . . . legislature,

they will vote all property out of the hands of you aristocrats."

To counter the appeal of the Pennsylvania Constitution, Adams published *Thoughts on Government* (1776). In that treatise, he adapted the British Whig theory of mixed government (a sharing of power among the monarch, the Houses of Lords, and the Commons) to a republican society. To disperse authority and preserve liberty, he insisted on separate institutions: Legislatures would make laws, the executive would administer them, and the judiciary would enforce them. Adams also demanded a bicameral (two-house) legislature with an upper house of substantial property owners to offset the popular majorities in the lower one. As further curbs on democracy, he proposed an elected governor with veto power and an appointed—not elected—judiciary.

Conservative Patriots endorsed Adams's governmental system. In New York's Constitution of 1777, property qualifications for voting excluded 20 percent of white men from assembly elections and 60 percent from casting ballots for the governor and the upper house. In South Carolina, elite planters used property rules to disqualify about 90 percent of white men from office holding. The 1778 constitution required candidates for governor to have a debt-free estate of £10,000 (about $700,000 today), senators to be worth £2,000, and assemblymen to own property valued at £1,000.

The political legacy of the Revolution was complex. Only in Pennsylvania and Vermont were radical Patriots able to create truly democratic institutions. Yet in all the new states, representative legislatures had acquired more power, and average citizens now had greater power at the polls and greater influence in the halls of government (see Voices from Abroad, "A French Aristocrat Views Republican Manners," p. 185).

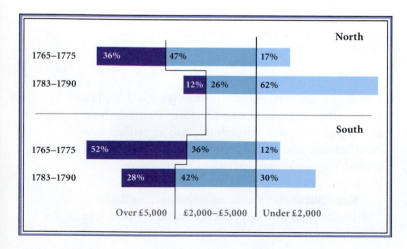

## FIGURE 6.1

### Middling Men Enter the Halls of Government, 1765–1790

Before the Revolution, wealthy men (with assets of £2,000 or more, as measured by tax lists and probate records) dominated most colonial assemblies. The power of money was especially apparent in the southern colonies, where representatives worth at least £5,000 formed a majority of the legislators. However, in the new American republic, the proportion of middling legislators (yeomen farmers and others worth less than £2,000) increased dramatically, especially in the northern states.

Adapted from Jackson T. Main, "Government by the People: The American Revolution and the Democratization of the Legislatures," *William and Mary Quarterly*, 3rd ser., vol. 23 (1966).

# VOICES FROM ABROAD

## François Alexandre Frédéric

## A French Aristocrat Views Republican Manners

**W**hen the French Revolution broke out in 1789, forty-two-year-old François Alexandre Frédéric, duc de la Rochefoucauld-Liancourt, won election to the National Constituent Assembly and served a term as its president. A reformer and a constitutionalist, he was also a monarchist and a confidant of King Louis XVI, who would be executed in 1793. Fearing for his safety, Rochefoucauld fled to England in 1792 and then moved to Philadelphia in 1794. The following year, he and five friends traveled through much of the northern United States and Upper Canada. He published a report of that journey and his speculations on American and Canadian affairs upon his return to Paris in 1799.

We overtook the stage-coach again at the White Horse, where the passengers breakfasted. It appears somewhat strange to Europeans, to see the coachman eat at the same table with the passengers; but it would seem equally strange to Americans, to see the coachman eating by himself. It is futile to argue against the customs of a country; we must submit. Equality, pretended equality, which widely differs from true freedom, is the foundation of this custom, which, in fact, injures nobody. . . .

A spirit, or rather habit of equality, is diffused among this people, as far as it possibly can go. In several inns, especially such as are situate on less frequented roads, the circumstance of our servant not dining with us at the same table excited general astonishment. . . .

The spirit of equality is carried as far as is consistent with order in a great society. The man who is possessed of the greatest wealth, and the most happily circumstanced in every respect, shakes hands with the workman whom he met on his way, converses with him, not under the idea of doing him an honour, as is often the notion elsewhere but from a consciousness, in the first instance, that he may at some future time stand in need of his assistance afterward, without any such interested consideration, but merely through habit, and the force of education, and because he sees in him his fellow-man, only placed in a different situation, to whom he is the less tempted to think himself superior, as it often happens that the now rich man has himself once been in a less enviable situation. . . .

The inferior classes of workmen, down to those who labour in the ports, do not appear to me to be so rustic [unsophisticated, subservient] in America as they generally do in the old world. The reason of this is, without doubt, that they are treated with more civility, and considered by those who employ them as free men with whom they have contracted, rather than as workmen, whom they compel to labour. They are like the workmen of every class, both in town and country, much better paid than in Europe, by

which they are enabled to live well. There is not a family, even in the most miserable hut in the midst of the woods, who does not eat meat twice a day at least, and drink tea and coffee; . . . The shopkeeper and the artisan live much better here than in Europe. . . .

Though there be no distinctions acknowledged by law in the United States, fortune and the nature of professions form different classes. The merchants, the lawyers, the land-owners, who do not cultivate their land themselves (and the number, which is small from the state of Delaware to the north, is great in the states of the south), the physicians, and the clergy, form the first class. The inferior merchants, the farmers, and the artisans, may be included in the second; and the third class is composed of workmen, who let [hire out] themselves by the day, by the month, &c.

In balls, concerts, and public amusements, these classes do not mix; and yet, except the labourer in ports, and the common sailor, every one calls himself, and is called by others, a gentleman; a small fortune is sufficient for the assumption of this title, as it carries men from one class to another. They deceive themselves very much who think that pure republican manners prevail in America.

---

Source: François Alexandre Frédéric, Duc de la Rochefoucauld-Liancourt, *Travels through the United States of America . . . in the Years 1795, 1796, and 1797 . . .*, 2 vols., trans. H. Neuman (London: T. Davison, 1799), 1: 23–24, 68; 2: 215, 671–672.

## ANALYZING THE EVIDENCE

- What is the source of the custom or "habit of equality" that Rochefoucauld finds in the United States?
- How does this French aristocrat explain the paradox of a "spirit of equality" in the midst a society of "different classes" who mostly "do not mix"? How would you explain it?
- What would a society with "pure republican manners" look like?

**John and Abigail Adams**

Both Adamses had strong personalities and often disagreed in private about political and social issues. In 1794, John playfully accused his wife of being a "Disciple of Wollstonecraft," but Abigail's commitment to legal equality for women long predated Mary Wollstonecraft's 1792 treatise, *A Vindication of the Rights of Woman*.    National Portrait Gallery, Smithsonian Institution/Art Resource, NY. / New York State Historical Association.

## Women Seek a Public Voice

The extraordinary excitement of the Revolutionary era tested the dictum that only men could engage in politics. Men controlled all public institutions—legislatures, juries, government offices—but upper-class women engaged in political debate and, defying men's scorn, filled their letters, diaries, and conversations with opinions on public issues. "The men say we have no business [with politics]," Eliza Wilkinson of South Carolina complained in 1783. "They won't even allow us liberty of thought, and that is all I want."

As Wilkinson's remark suggests, women did not insist on civic equality with men; they sought only an end to restrictive customs and laws. Abigail Adams demanded equal legal rights for married women, who under common law could not own property, enter into contracts, or initiate lawsuits. The war bonds she purchased had to be held in a trust run by a male relative. "Men would be tyrants" if they continued to hold such power over women, Adams declared to her husband John, criticizing him and other Patriots for "emanci-

pating all nations" from monarchical despotism while "retaining absolute power over Wives."

Most politicians ignored women's requests, and most men insisted on the traditional sexual and political prerogatives of their sex. Long-married husbands remained patriarchs who dominated their households, and even young men who embraced the republican ideal of "companionate marriage" did not support legal equality for their wives and daughters. Except in New Jersey, which until 1807 allowed unmarried and widowed female property holders to vote, women remained disenfranchised. In the new American republic, only white men enjoyed full citizenship.

Nevertheless, the republican belief in an educated citizenry created opportunities for some women. In her 1779 essay "On the Equality of the Sexes," Judith Sargent Murray argued that men and women had equal capacities for memory and that women had superior imaginations. She conceded that most women were inferior to men in judgment and reasoning, but only from lack of training: "We can only reason from what we know," she argued, and most women had been de-

**Mrs. Mercy Otis Warren**

Dressed in fine silks and lace for this 1763 portrait by John Singleton Copley, Mercy Otis Warren was a woman of means from a highly political family. The sister of one Patriot (the mercurial James Otis) and the wife of another (Dr. James Warren), Mercy demonstrated her Patriot credentials by authoring propaganda plays in the early 1770s, and her Antifederalist beliefs by opposing the Constitution and publishing a three-volume *History of the Rise, Progress, and Termination of the American Revolution* (1805).    Museum of Fine Arts. Bequest of Winslow Warren, 1931. Acc. No. 31.212.

**A Black Loyalist Pass, 1783**

White Patriots claimed their freedom by fighting *against* the British; thousands of black slaves won their liberty by fighting *for* them. This pass certifies that Cato Rammsay (actually Ramsey), "a Negro, resorted to the British Lines" in search of the freedom promised by Virginia Royal Governor Dunmore and British Commander Henry Clinton to slaves who escaped from Patriot owners. Now age forty-five and a "slim fellow," Ramsey had escaped from his owner, John Ramsey of Norfolk, Virginia, in 1776, probably fleeing to Dunmore's ships. Seven years later, he ended up in New York, reunited with his wife, China Godfrey (thirty-five) and their three children: James (twenty), Betsey (fifteen), and Nelly Ramsey (ten), who had fled subsequently from other owners. As the British evacuated New York in 1783, Ramsey and his family were free "to go to Nova Scotia," where they worked as farmers.    Nova Scotia Archives and Record Management, Halifax.

nied "the opportunity of acquiring knowledge." That situation changed in the 1790s, when the attorney general of Massachusetts declared that girls had an equal right to schooling under the state constitution. By 1850, the literacy rates of women and men in the northeastern states were equal, and educated women again challenged their subordinate legal and political status (see Reading American Pictures, "Did the Revolution Promote Women's Rights?" p. 188).

## The Loyalist Exodus

The success of republican institutions was assisted by the departure of 100,000 monarchists, many of whom suffered severe financial losses. John Tabor Kempe, the last royal attorney general of New York, sought compensation of £65,000 sterling (about $4.5 million today) from the British government for lands seized by Patriots,

but only received a mere £5,000. Refugees also suffered psychologically. Loyalists who fled to England complained of "their uneasy abode in this country of aliens," as did many of the evacuees who settled in Canada or the West Indies. An exiled Loyalist woman in Nova Scotia confessed: "[I had] such a feeling of loneliness . . . [that] I sat down on the damp moss with my baby on my lap and cried bitterly."

Some Patriots demanded revolutionary justice: the seizure of all Loyalist property and its distribution to needy Americans. While every state seized some Loyalists' property, American leaders worried that wholesale confiscation would impair the nation's commercial credit and violate its republican principles. In Massachusetts, officials cited the state's constitution of 1780, which protected every citizen "in the enjoyment of his life, liberty, and property, according to the standing laws." When state governments did seize Loyalist property, they

# Did the Revolution Promote Women's Rights?

As the text explains, the republican revolution forced Americans to address the scope of political rights. One question centered on women's claim to equal treatment: Did the doctrines of popular sovereignty and political equality apply to women as well as to men? These two engravings, both published in American magazines, offer evidence that the question was the subject of public debate. Pictures like these pose a twofold challenge to historians—to see them as contemporaries did, and, with the power of hindsight, to place them in a larger historical context. How do these pictures help us understand the status of women in the young republic, both in their own eyes and those of men?

**Frontispiece from *Lady's Magazine*, 1792.**
The Library Company of Philadelphia.

**"Keep Within Compass," c. 1785.** Henry Francis du Pont
Winterthur Museum, Winterthur, Delaware.

## ANALYZING THE EVIDENCE

- The illustration on the left appeared at the front of *The Lady's Magazine and Repository of Entertaining*, published in Philadelphia in 1792. The magazine contained excerpts from Mary Wollstonecraft's *A Vindication of the Rights of Woman* (1792), which explicitly linked women's rights to the republican ideology of the American and French revolutions. What sort of clothing are the women wearing? Why? What does this sort of dress mean ideologically? Do you think this imagery was empowering to women at the time? Why or why not?

- In the engraving on the right, "Keep Within Compass," the first line of the small couplet at the top reads: "How blest the Maid whose bosom no headstrong passion knows." What do the smaller pictures on the lower left and lower right suggest might happen to women who are passionate? What is this engraving urging American women to do? What does it suggest about the thinking and emotions of American men in the new republican era?

often auctioned it to the highest bidders, who were usually wealthy Patriots rather than ambitious yeoman farmers or propertyless foot soldiers. In a few cases, confiscation did produce a democratic result: In North Carolina, about half the new owners of Loyalist lands were small-scale farmers, and in New York, the state government sold farmsteads on the Philipse manor to longtime tenants. When Frederick Philipse III tried to reclaim his estate, the new owners declared they had "purchased it with the price of their best blood," and added, "[We] will never become your vassals again." In general, though, the Revolution did not drastically alter the structure of rural society.

Social turmoil was greater in the cities, where Patriot merchants replaced Tories at the top of the economic ladder. In Massachusetts, the Lowell, Higginson, Jackson, and Cabot families moved their trading enterprises to Boston to fill the vacuum created by the departure of the Loyalist Hutchinson and Apthorp clans. In Philadelphia, small-scale Patriot traders stepped into the void left by the collapse of Anglican and Quaker mercantile firms. The war replaced a traditional economic elite—who invested profits from trade in real estate—with a group of republican entrepreneurs who promoted new trading ventures and domestic manufacturing. This shift facilitated America's economic development in the years to come.

## The Articles of Confederation

As Patriots embraced independence in 1776, they envisioned a central government with limited powers. Carter Braxton of Virginia thought the Continental Congress should "regulate the affairs of trade, war, peace, alliances, &c." but "should by no means have authority to interfere with the internal police [governance] or domestic concerns of any Colony."

That thinking—of a limited central government—informed the Articles of Confederation, which were approved by the Continental Congress in November 1777. The Articles provided for a loose union in which "each state retains its sovereignty, freedom, and independence." As an association of equals, each state had one vote regardless of its size, population, or wealth. Important laws needed the approval of nine of the thirteen states, and changes in the Articles required unanimous consent. Though the Confederation had neither a chief executive nor a judiciary, the government still enjoyed considerable power. The Congress could declare war, make treaties with foreign nations, adjudicate disputes between the states, borrow and print money, and requi-

sition funds from the states "for the common defense or general welfare."

Although the Congress exercised authority from 1776—raising the Continental army, negotiating the treaty with France, and financing the war—the Articles won formal ratification only in 1781. The delay stemmed from conflicts over western lands. The royal charters of Virginia, Massachusetts, Connecticut, and other states set boundaries stretching to the Pacific Ocean. States without western lands—Maryland and Pennsylvania—refused to accept the Articles until the land-rich states relinquished these claims to the Confederation. Threatened by Cornwallis's army in 1781, Virginia gave up its claims, and Maryland, the last holdout, finally ratified the Articles (Map 6.6).

**Continuing Fiscal Crisis**  The Confederation had a major weakness: It lacked the power to tax either the states or the people. By 1780, the central government was nearly bankrupt, and General Washington called urgently for a national tax system; without one, he warned, "our cause is lost." Led by Robert Morris, who became superintendent of finance in 1781, nationalist-minded Patriots tried to expand the Confederation's authority. They persuaded Congress to charter the Bank of North America, a private institution in Philadelphia, arguing that its notes would stabilize the inflated Continental currency. Morris also created a central bureaucracy that paid army expenses, apportioned war costs among the states, and assumed responsibility for the Confederation's debts. He hoped that the existence of a "national" debt would prompt Congress to enact an import duty to pay it off. However, Rhode Island and New York rejected Morris's proposal for an import tax of 5 percent. His state had opposed British import duties, New York's representative declared, and it would not accept them from Congress. To raise revenue, Congress looked to the sale of western lands. In 1783, it asserted that the recently signed Treaty of Paris had extinguished the Indians' rights to those lands and made them the property of the United States.

**The Northwest Ordinance**  Settlers had already moved to the frontier. In 1784, the residents of what is now eastern Tennessee organized a new state, called it Franklin, and sought admission to the Confederation. To preserve its authority over the West, Congress refused to recognize Franklin. Subsequently, Congress created the Southwest and Mississippi Territories (the future states of Tennessee, Alabama, and Mississippi) from lands ceded by North

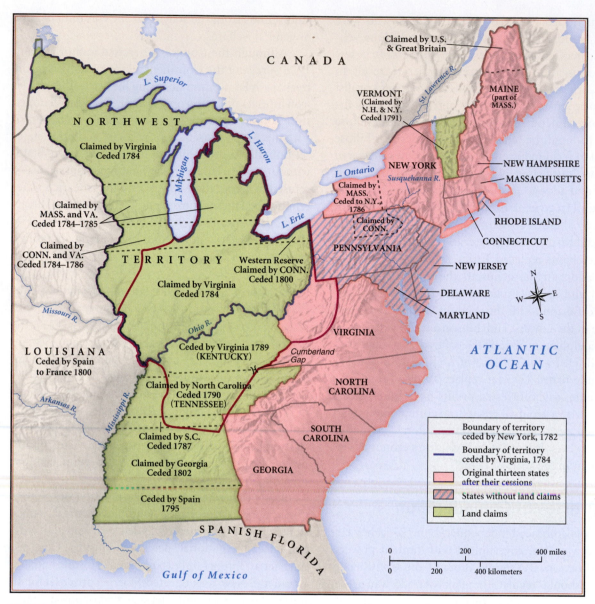

**MAP 6.6**

**The Confederation and Western Land Claims, 1781–1802**

The Congress formed by the Articles of Confederation had to resolve conflicting state claims to western lands. For example, the territories claimed by New York and Virginia on the basis of their royal charters overlapped extensively. Beginning in 1781, the Confederation Congress and, after 1789, the U.S. Congress persuaded all of the states to cede their western claims, creating a "national domain" open to all citizens. In the Northwest Ordinances, the Congress divided the domain north of the Ohio River into territories and set up democratic procedures by which they could eventually join the Union as states. South of the Ohio River, the Congress allowed the existing southern states to play a substantial role in the settling of the ceded lands.

Carolina and Georgia. Because these cessions carried the stipulation that "no regulation . . . shall tend to emancipate slaves," these states and all those south of the Ohio River allowed human bondage.

However, the Confederation Congress banned slavery north of the Ohio River. Between 1784 and 1787, it

issued three important ordinances organizing the "Old Northwest." The Ordinance of 1784, written by Thomas Jefferson, established the principle that territories could become states as their populations grew. The Land Ordinance of 1785 mandated a rectangular-grid system of surveying and specified a minimum price of $1 an acre. It also required that half of the townships be sold in single blocks of 23,040 acres each, which only large-scale speculators could afford, and the rest in parcels of 640 acres each, which restricted their sale to well-to-do farmers (Map 6.7).

Finally, the Northwest Ordinance of 1787 created the territories that would eventually become the states of Ohio, Indiana, Illinois, Michigan, and Wisconsin. The ordinance prohibited slavery and earmarked funds from land sales for the support of schools. It also specified that Congress would appoint a governor and judges to administer each new territory until the population reached 5,000 free adult men, at which point the citizens could elect a territorial legislature. When the population reached 60,000, the legislature could devise a republican constitution and apply to join the Confederation.

The land ordinances of the 1780s were a great and enduring achievement of the Confederation Congress. They provided for orderly settlement and the admission of new states on the basis of equality; there would be no politically dependent "colonies" in the West. But they also extended the geographical division between slave and free areas that would haunt the nation in the coming decades.

## Shays's Rebellion

If the future of the West was bright, postwar conditions in the East were grim. The war had crippled American shipping and cut exports of tobacco, rice, and wheat. The British Navigation Acts, which had nurtured colonial commerce, now barred Americans from legal trade with the British West Indies. Moreover, low-priced British manufactures (and some from India as well) were flooding American markets, driving urban artisans and wartime textile firms out of business. Not until 1800 would white Americans again reach the levels of income and wealth they had enjoyed in 1775.

The fiscal condition of the state governments was dire, primarily because of war debts. Well-to-do merchants and landowners (including Abigail Adams) had invested in state bonds during the war; others had speculated in debt certificates, buying them on the cheap from hard-pressed farmers and soldiers. Now creditors and speculators demanded that the state governments redeem the bonds and certificates quickly and at full value, a policy that would require tax increases and a decrease in the amount of paper currency. Most legislatures refused. The new state constitutions apportioned seats on the basis of population, so many legislators were men of "middling circumstances" from rural com-

munities. By the mid-1780s, such middling farmers and artisans controlled the lower houses of most northern legislatures and formed a sizable minority in southern assemblies. They refused to levy higher taxes to redeem war bonds, instead authorizing new issues of paper currency and allowing debtors to pay private creditors in installments. Although wealthy men deplored these measures as "intoxicating Draughts of Liberty" that destroyed "the just rights of creditors," such political intervention prevented social upheaval.

A case in point was Massachusetts, where lawmakers refused to enact debtor-relief legislation, imposed high taxes to pay off the state's war debt, and cut the supply of paper currency. When cash-strapped farmers could not pay both their taxes and their debts, creditors threatened lawsuits. Debtor Ephraim Wetmore heard a rumor that merchant Stephan Salisbury "would have my Body Dead or Alive in case I did not pay." To protect their livelihoods, farmers called extralegal conventions to protest high taxes and property seizures. Then mobs of angry farmers — including men of high status — closed the courts by force. "[I] had no Intensions to Destroy the Publick Government," declared Captain Adam Wheeler, a former town selectman; his goal was simply to prevent "Valuable and Industrious members of Society [being] dragged from their families to prison" because of their debts. These crowd actions grew into a full-scale revolt led by Captain Daniel Shays, a Continental army veteran.

As a revolt against taxes imposed by a distant government, Shays's Rebellion resembled American resistance to the British Stamp Act. Consciously linking themselves to the Patriot movement, Shays's men placed pine twigs in their hats just as Continental troops had done. "The people have turned against their teachers the doctrines which were inculcated to effect the late revolution," complained Fisher Ames, a conservative Massachusetts lawmaker. Some of the radical Patriots of 1776 likewise condemned the Shaysites: "[Men who] would lessen the Weight of Government lawfully exercised must be Enemies to our happy Revolution and Common Liberty," charged Samuel Adams. To put down the rebellion, the Massachusetts legislature passed the Riot Act and wealthy bondholders equipped a formidable fighting force, which Governor James Bowdoin used to disperse Shays's ragtag army during the winter of 1786–1787.

Although Shays's Rebellion failed, it showed that many middling Patriot families felt that American oppressors had replaced British tyrants. Massachusetts voters turned Governor Bowdoin out of office, and debt-ridden farmers in New York, northern Pennsylvania,

## MAP 6.7

### Land Division in the Northwest Territory

Throughout the Northwest Territory, government surveyors imposed a rectangular grid on the landscape, regardless of the local topography, so that farmers bought neatly defined tracts of land. The right-angled property lines in Muskingum County, Ohio (lower left), contrasted sharply with those in Baltimore County, Maryland (lower right), where—as in most of the eastern and southern states—boundaries followed the contours of the land.

Connecticut, and New Hampshire closed courthouses and forced their governments to provide economic relief. British officials in Canada predicted the imminent demise of the United States; and American leaders urged purposeful action to save their republican experiment. Events in Massachusetts, declared nationalist Henry Knox, formed "the strongest arguments possible" for the creation of "a strong general government."

- What were the main differences between conservative state constitutions, such as those of Massachusetts and New York, and more democratic constitutions, such as Pennsylvania's?

- What were the causes of Shays's Rebellion, and what does it tell us about postwar America?

# The Constitution of 1787

From its creation, the U.S. Constitution was a controversial document, both acclaimed for solving the nation's woes and condemned for perverting its republican principles. Critics charged that republican institutions worked only in small political units—the states. Advocates replied that the Constitution extended republicanism by adding another level of government elected by the people. In the new two-level political federation created by the Constitution, the national government would exercise limited, delegated powers, and the existing state governments would retain authority over all other matters.

## The Rise of a Nationalist Faction

Money questions—debts, taxes, and tariffs—dominated the postwar political agenda. Americans who had served the Confederation as military officers, officials, and diplomats viewed these issues from a national perspective and advocated a stronger central government. George Washington, Robert Morris, Benjamin Franklin, John Jay, and John Adams wanted Congress to control foreign commerce and tariff policy. However, lawmakers in Massachusetts, New York, and Pennsylvania—states with strong commercial traditions—insisted on controlling their own tariffs, both to protect their artisans from low-cost imports and to assist their merchants. Most southern states opposed tariffs because planters wanted to import British textiles and ironware at the lowest possible prices.

Nonetheless, some southern leaders became nationalists because their state legislatures had cut taxes and refused to redeem state war bonds. Such policies, lamented wealthy bondholder Charles Lee of Virginia, led taxpayers to believe they would "never be compelled to pay" the public debt. Creditors also condemned state laws that "stayed" (delayed) the payment of mortgages and other private debts. "While men are madly accumulating enormous debts, their legislators are making provisions for their nonpayment," complained a South Carolina merchant. To undercut the democratic majorities in the state legislatures, creditors joined the movement for a stronger central government.

In 1786, James Madison and other nationalists persuaded the Virginia legislature to call a convention in Annapolis, Maryland, to discuss tariff and taxation policies. When only five state governments sent representatives, the delegates called for another convention in Philadelphia. Spurred on by Shays's Rebellion, nationalists in Congress secured a resolution calling for the convention to revise the Articles of Confederation. Only an "efficient plan from the Convention," a fellow nationalist wrote to James Madison, "can prevent anarchy first & civil convulsions afterwards."

## The Philadelphia Convention

In May 1787, fifty-five delegates arrived in Philadelphia. They came from every state except Rhode Island, where the legislature opposed increasing central authority. Most were strong nationalists; forty-two had served in the Confederation Congress. They were also educated and propertied: merchants, slaveholding planters, and "monied men." There were no artisans, backcountry settlers, or tenants, and only a single yeoman farmer.

Some influential Patriots missed the convention. John Adams and Thomas Jefferson were serving as American ministers to Britain and France, respectively. The Massachusetts General Court rejected Sam Adams as a delegate because he opposed a stronger national government, and his fellow firebrand from Virginia, Patrick Henry, refused to attend because he "smelt a rat."

The absence of experienced leaders and contrary-minded delegates allowed capable younger nationalists to set the agenda. Declaring that the convention would "decide for ever the fate of Republican Government," James Madison insisted on increased national authority. Alexander Hamilton of New York likewise demanded a strong central government to protect the republic from "the imprudence of democracy."

**The Virginia and New Jersey Plans** The delegates elected Washington as their presiding officer and voted to meet behind closed doors. Then — momentously — they decided not to revise the Articles of Confederation but rather to consider the so-called Virginia Plan, a scheme for a powerful national government devised by James Madison. Just thirty-six years old, Madison was determined to fashion national political institutions run by men of high character. A graduate of Princeton, he had read classical and modern political theory and served in both the Confederation Congress and the Virginia assembly. Once an optimistic Patriot, Madison had grown discouraged because of the "narrow ambition" and outlook of state legislators.

Madison's Virginia Plan differed from the Articles of Confederation in three crucial respects. First, the plan rejected state sovereignty in favor of the "supremacy of national authority," including the power to overturn state laws. Second, it called for the national government to be established by the people (not the states) and for national laws to operate directly on citizens of the various states. Third, the plan proposed a three-tier election system in which ordinary voters would elect only the lower house of the national legislature. This lower house would then select the upper house, and both houses would appoint the executive and judiciary.

From a political perspective, Madison's plan had two fatal flaws. First, most state politicians and citizens resolutely opposed allowing the national government to veto state laws. Second, the plan based representation in the lower house on population; this provision, a Delaware delegate warned, would allow the populous states to "crush the small ones whenever they stand in the way of their ambitious or interested views."

So delegates from Delaware and other small states rallied behind a plan devised by William Paterson of New Jersey. The New Jersey Plan gave the Confederation the power to raise revenue, control commerce, and make binding requisitions on the states. But it preserved the states' control of their own laws and guaranteed their equality: As in the Confederation Congress, each state would have one vote in a unicameral legislature. Delegates from the more populous states vigorously opposed this provision. After a month-long debate on the two plans, a bare majority of the states agreed to use Madison's Virginia Plan as the basis of discussion.

This decision raised the odds that the convention would create a more powerful national government. Outraged by this prospect, two New York delegates accused their colleagues of exceeding their mandate to revise the Articles and left the convention. The remaining delegates met six days a week during the summer of

**James Madison, Statesman**

Throughout his long public life, Madison kept the details of his private life to himself. His biography, he believed, should be a record of his public accomplishments, not his private affairs. Future generations celebrated him not as a great man (like Hamilton or Jefferson) or as a great president (like Washington), but as an original and incisive political thinker. The chief architect of the U.S. Constitution and the Bill of Rights, Madison was the preeminent republican political theorist of his generation.   Mead Art Museum, Amherst College.

1787, debating both high principles and practical details. Experienced politicians, they looked for a plan that would be acceptable to most citizens and existing political interests. Pierce Butler of South Carolina invoked a classical Greek precedent: "We must follow the example of Solon, who gave the Athenians not the best government he could devise but the best they would receive."

**The Great Compromise** As the convention grappled with the central problem of the representation of large and small states, the Connecticut delegates suggested a possible solution. They proposed that the national legislature's upper chamber (the Senate) have two members from each state, while seats in the lower chamber (the House of Representatives) be apportioned by population (determined every ten years by a national census). After bitter debate, delegates from the populous states reluctantly accepted this "Great Compromise."

Other state-related issues were quickly settled by restricting (or leaving ambiguous) the extent of central authority. Some delegates opposed a national system of courts, predicting that "the states will revolt at such encroachments" on their judicial authority. This danger led the convention to define the judicial power of the United States in broad terms, vesting it "in one supreme Court" and leaving the new national legislature to decide whether to establish lower courts within the states. The convention also refused to set a property requirement for voting in national elections. "Eight or nine states have extended the right of suffrage beyond the freeholders," George Mason of Virginia pointed out. "What will people there say if they should be disfranchised?" Finally, the convention specified that state legislatures would elect members of the upper house, or Senate, and the states would select the electors who would choose the president. By allowing states to have important roles in the new constitutional system, the delegates hoped that their citizens would accept limits on state sovereignty.

### Negotiations over Slavery

The shadow of slavery hovered over many debates, and Gouverneur Morris of New York brought it into view. Born into the New York aristocracy, Morris had initially opposed Independence because he feared the "domination of a riotous mob." Now a Patriot and a nationalist, he came to Philadelphia convinced that the protection of "property was the sole or primary object of Government & Society." To safeguard property rights, Morris wanted life terms for senators, a property qualification for voting in national elections, and a strong president with veto power. Nonetheless, he rejected the legitimacy of two traditional types of property: the feudal dues claimed by aristocratic landowners and the ownership of slaves. An advocate of **free markets** and personal liberty, Morris condemned slavery as "a nefarious institution."

Many slave-owning delegates from the Chesapeake region—including Madison and George Mason—recognized that slavery contradicted republican principles and hoped for its eventual demise. But these Upper South planters, who owned many slaves, only supported an end to American participation in the Atlantic slave trade—a proposal the South Carolina and Georgia delegates angrily rejected. Unless the importation of African slaves continued, these rice planters and merchants declared, their states "shall not be parties to the Union."

**Gouverneur Morris, Federalist Statesman**

When the war with Britain broke out, Morris had debated joining the Loyalist cause; he was a snob who liked privilege and feared the common people. ("The mob begins to think and reason. Poor reptiles!" he once noted with disdain.) He became a Federalist for much the same reasons. He helped write the Philadelphia constitution and strongly supported the Federalist Party. As American minister to France (1792–1794), Morris took as his mistress the young wife of an aging aristocrat and joined an unsuccessful aristocrat plot to smuggle King Louis XVI out of Paris. National Portrait Gallery, Smithsonian Institution/Art Resource, New York.

At their insistence, the convention denied Congress the power to regulate immigration—and so the slave trade—until 1808 (see Comparing American Voices, "The First National Debate over Slavery," pp. 196–197).

To preserve national unity, the delegates devised other slavery-related compromises. To mollify southern planters, they devised a "fugitive clause" that allowed masters to reclaim enslaved blacks (or white indentured servants) who fled to other states. But in acknowledgment of the antislavery sentiments of Morris and other northerners, the delegates excluded the words *slavery* and *slave* from the Constitution; it spoke only of citizens and "all other Persons." Because slaves lacked the vote, antislavery delegates wanted their census numbers excluded when apportioning seats in Congress. For their part, Southerners—ironically, given that they

*Thus I have given you, I think, the Substance of the Arguments both sides of that great and important Quest...*

# The First National Debate over Slavery

In this part of the text, we trace the impact of republican ideology on American politics and society. What happened when republicanism collided head-on with the well-established practice of slavery? After the Revolution, the Massachusetts courts abolished slavery, but in 1787, slavery was legal in the rest of the Union and was the bedrock of social order and agricultural production in the southern states. A look at the debates on the issue of the African slave trade at the Philadelphia convention and in a state ratifying convention shows that slavery was an extremely divisive issue at the birth of the nation—a dark cloud threatening the bright future of the young republic.

## The Constitutional Convention

Slavery was not a major topic of discussion at the Philadelphia convention, but it surfaced a number of times, notably in the important debate over representation (which produced the three-fifths clause). A discussion of the Atlantic slave trade began when Luther Martin, a delegate from Maryland, proposed a clause allowing Congress to impose a tax on or prohibit the importation of slaves.

Mr. Martin proposed to vary article 7, sect. 4 so as to allow a prohibition or tax on the importation of slaves. . . . [He believed] it was inconsistent with the principles of the Revolution, and dishonorable to the American character, to have such a feature [promoting the slave trade] in the Constitution.

Mr. [John] Rutledge [of South Carolina declared that] religion and humanity had nothing to do with this question. Interest alone is the governing principle with nations. The true question at present is whether the Southern states shall or shall not be parties to the Union. . . .

Mr. [Oliver] Ellsworth [of Connecticut] was for leaving the clause as it stands. Let every state import what it pleases. The morality or wisdom of slavery are considerations belonging to the states themselves. . . . The old Confederation had not meddled with this point, and he did not see any greater necessity for bringing it within the policy of the new one.

Mr. [Charles C.] Pinckney [said] South Carolina can never receive the plan [for a new constitution] if it prohibits the slave trade. In every proposed extension of the powers of Congress, that state has expressly and watchfully excepted that of meddling with the importation of Negroes. . . .

Mr. [Roger] Sherman [of Connecticut] was for leaving the clause as it stands. He disapproved of the slave trade; yet, as the states were now possessed of the right to import slaves, . . . and as it was expedient to have as few objections as possible to the proposed scheme of government, he thought it best to leave the matter as we find it.

Col. [George] Mason [of Virginia stated that] this infernal trade originated in the avarice of British merchants. The British government constantly checked the attempts of Virginia to put a stop to it. The present question concerns not the importing states alone, but the whole Union. . . . Maryland and Virginia, he said, had already prohibited the importation of slaves expressly. North Carolina had done the same in substance. All this would be in vain if South Carolina and Georgia be at liberty to import. The Western people are already calling out for slaves for their new lands, and will fill that country with slaves, if they can be got through South Carolina and Georgia. Slavery discourages arts and manufactures. The poor despise labor when performed by slaves. They prevent the immigration of whites, who really enrich and strengthen a country. . . .

Every master of slaves is born a petty tyrant. They bring the judgment of Heaven on a country. As nations cannot be rewarded or punished in the next world, they must be in this. By an inevitable chain of causes and effects, Providence punishes national sins by national calamities. . . . He held it essential, in every point of view, that the general government should have power to prevent the increase of slavery.

Mr. Ellsworth, as he had never owned a slave, could not judge of the effects of slavery on character. He said, however, that if it was to be considered in a moral light, we ought to go further, and free those already in the country. . . . Let us not intermeddle. As population increases, poor laborers will be so plenty as to render slaves useless. Slavery, in time, will not be a speck in our country. . . .

Gen. [Charles C.] Pinckney [argued that] South Carolina and Georgia cannot do without slaves. As to Virginia, she will gain by stopping the importations. Her slaves will rise in value, and she has more than she wants. It would be unequal to require South Carolina and Georgia to confederate on such unequal terms. . . . He contended that the importation of slaves would be for the interest of the whole Union. The more slaves, the more produce to employ the carrying trade; the more consumption also; and the more of this, the more revenue for the common treasury. . . . [He] should consider a rejection of the [present] clause as an exclusion of South Carolina from the Union.

Source: Max Farrand, ed., *The Records of the Federal Convention of 1787* (New Haven: Yale University Press, 1911), 2: 364–365, 369–372.

## The Massachusetts Ratifying Convention

In Philadelphia, the delegates agreed on a compromise: They gave Congress the power to tax or prohibit slave imports, as Luther Martin had proposed, but withheld that power for twenty years. In the Massachusetts convention, the delegates split on this issue and on many others. They ratified the Constitution by a narrow margin, 187 to 168.

Mr. Neal (from Kittery) [an Antifederalist] went over the ground of objection to . . . the idea that slave trade was allowed to be continued for 20 years. His profession, he said, obliged him to bear witness against any thing that should favor the making merchandize of the bodies of men, and unless his objection was removed, he could not put his hand to the constitution. Other gentlemen said, in addition to this idea, that there was not even a proposition that the negroes ever shall be free: and Gen. Thompson exclaimed— "Mr. President, shall it be said, that after we have established our own independence and freedom, we make slaves of others? Oh! Washington . . . he has immortalized himself! but he holds those in slavery who have a good right to be free as he is. . . ."

On the other side, gentlemen said, that the step taken in this article, towards the abolition of slavery, was one of the beauties of the constitution. They observed, that in the confederation there was no provision whatever for its ever being abolished; but this constitution provides, that Congress may after twenty years, totally annihilate the slave trade. . . .

Mr. Heath (Federalist): . . . I apprehend that it is not in our power to do any thing for or against those who are in slavery in the southern states. No gentleman within these walls detests every idea of slavery more than I do: it is generally detested by the people of this commonwealth, and I ardently hope that the time will soon come, when our brethren in the southern states will view it as we do, and put a stop to it; but to this we have no right to compel them.

Two questions naturally arise: if we ratify the Constitution, shall we do any thing by our act to hold the blacks in slavery or shall we become the partakers of other men's sins? I think neither of them: each state is sovereign and independent to a certain degree, and they have a right, and will regulate their own internal affairs, as to themselves appears proper. . . . We are not in this case partakers of other men's sins. . . .

The federal convention went as far as they could; the migration or immigration &c. is confined to the states, now existing only, new states cannot claim it. Congress, by their ordnance for erecting new states, some time since, declared that there shall be no slavery in them. But whether those in slavery in the southern states, will be emancipated after the year 1808, I do not pretend to determine: I rather doubt it.

Source: Jonathan Elliot, ed., *The Debates . . . on the Adoption of the Federal Constitution* (Philadelphia: J. B. Lippincott, 1836), 1: 103–105, 107, 112, 117.

## ANALYZING THE EVIDENCE

- At the constitutional convention in Philadelphia, what were the main arguments for and against federal restrictions on the Atlantic slave trade? How do you explain the position taken by the Connecticut delegates in Philadelphia and Mr. Heath in the Massachusetts debate?

- Why did George Mason, a Virginia slave owner, demand a prohibition of the Atlantic slave trade?

- What evidence of regional tensions appears in the documents? Several men from different states— Mason from Virginia, Ellsworth from Connecticut, and Heath from Massachusetts—offered predictions about the future of slavery. How accurate were they?

considered slaves property—demanded that slaves be counted in the census the same as full citizens, so as to increase the South's representation. Ultimately, the delegates agreed that each slave would count as three-fifths of a free person for purposes of representation and taxation, a compromise that helped southern planters dominate the national government until 1860.

**National Authority** | Having addressed the concerns of small states and slave states, the convention created a powerful—and procreditor—national government. The Constitution declared that congressional legislation was the "supreme" law of the land. The national government was provided with broad powers of taxation, military defense, and external commerce and the authority to make all laws "necessary and proper" to implement those and other provisions. To assist creditors and establish the new government's fiscal integrity, the Constitution required the United States to honor the existing national debt and prohibited the states from issuing paper money or enacting "any Law impairing the Obligation of Contracts."

The proposed constitution was not a "perfect production," Benjamin Franklin admitted, as he urged the delegates to sign it in September 1787. But the great statesman confessed his astonishment at finding "this system approaching so near to perfection." His colleagues apparently agreed; all but three signed the document.

## The People Debate Ratification

The procedure for ratifying the new constitution was as controversial as its contents. Knowing that Rhode Island (and perhaps other states) would reject it, the delegates did not submit the Constitution to the state legislatures for their unanimous consent, as required by the Articles of Confederation. Instead, they arbitrarily declared that it would take effect when ratified by conventions in nine of the thirteen states. Because of its nationalist sympathies, the Confederation Congress winked at this extralegal procedure; surprisingly, most state legislatures also winked and called ratification conventions.

As the constitutional debate began in early 1788, the nationalists seized the initiative with two bold moves. First, they called themselves **Federalists**, suggesting that they supported a federal union—a loose, decentralized system—and obscuring their commitment to a strong national government. Second, they launched a coordinated campaign in pamphlets and newspapers to explain and justify the Philadelphia constitution.

**The Antifederalists** | The opponents of the Constitution, the Antifederalists, had diverse backgrounds and motives. Some, like Governor George Clinton of New York, feared that state governments would lose power. Rural democrats protested that the proposed document, unlike most state constitutions, lacked a declaration of individual rights; they also feared that the central government would be run by wealthy men. "Lawyers and men of learning and monied men expect to be managers of this Constitution," worried a Massachusetts farmer. "[T]hey will swallow up all of us little folks . . . just as the whale swallowed up Jonah." Giving political substance to these fears, Melancton Smith of New York argued that the large electoral districts prescribed by the Constitution would restrict office-holding to wealthy men, whereas the smaller districts used in state elections usually produced legislatures "composed principally of respectable yeomanry." John Quincy Adams agreed: If only "*eight* men" would represent Massachusetts, "they will infallibly be chosen from the aristocratic part of the community."

Smith summed up the views of Americans who held traditional republican values. To keep government "close to the people," they wanted the states to remain small sovereign republics tied together only for trade and defense—not the "United States" but the "States United." Citing the French political philosopher Montesquieu, Antifederalists argued that republican institutions were best suited to small polities, a localist perspective that shaped American thinking well into the twentieth century. "No extensive empire can be governed on republican principles," declared James Winthrop of Massachusetts. Patrick Henry worried that the Constitution would re-create British rule: high taxes, an oppressive bureaucracy, a standing army, and a "great and mighty President . . . supported in extravagant munificence." As another Antifederalist put it, "I had rather be a free citizen of the small republic of Massachusetts than an oppressed subject of the great American empire."

In New York, where ratification was hotly contested, James Madison, John Jay, and Alexander Hamilton defended the proposed constitution in a series of eighty-five essays, collectively titled *The Federalist*. This work influenced political leaders throughout the country and subsequently won acclaim as an important treatise of practical republicanism. Its authors denied that a centralized government would lead to domestic tyranny. Drawing on Montesquieu's theories and John Adams's *Thoughts on Government*, Madison, Jay, and Hamilton pointed out that authority would be divided among the president, a bicameral legislature, and a judiciary. Each branch of government would "check and balance" the others and so preserve liberty.

In "Federalist No. 10," Madison challenged the view that republican governments only worked in small polities, arguing that a large state would better protect republican liberty. It was "sown in the nature of man," Madison wrote, for individuals to seek power and form factions. Indeed, "a landed interest, a manufacturing interest, a mercantile interest, a moneyed interest, with many lesser interests, grow up of necessity in civilized nations." A free society should welcome all factions but keep any one of them from becoming dominant — something best achieved in a large republic. "Extend the sphere and you take in a greater variety of parties and interests," Madison concluded, inhibiting the formation of a majority eager "to invade the rights of other citizens."

### The Constitution Ratified

The delegates debating these issues in the state ratification conventions included untutored farmers and middling artisans as well as educated gentlemen. Generally, backcountry delegates were Antifederalists, while those from coastal areas were Federalists. In Pennsylvania, Philadelphia merchants and artisans joined commercial farmers to ratify the Constitution. Other early Federalist successes came in four less-populous states — Delaware, New Jersey, Georgia, and Connecticut — where delegates hoped that a strong national government would offset the power of large neighboring states (Map 6.8).

The Constitution's first real test came in January 1788 in Massachusetts, a hotbed of Antifederalist sentiment. Influential Patriots, including Samuel Adams and Governor John Hancock, opposed the new constitution, as did many followers of Daniel Shays. But Boston artisans, who wanted tariff protection from British imports, supported ratification. To win over other delegates, Federalist leaders assured the convention that they would enact a national bill of rights. By a close vote of 187 to 168, the Federalists carried the day.

Spring brought Federalist victories in Maryland, South Carolina, and New Hampshire, reaching the nine-state quota required for ratification. But it took the powerful arguments advanced in *The Federalist* and more promises of a bill of rights to secure the Constitution's adoption in the essential states of Virginia and New York. The votes were again close: 89 to 79 in Virginia and 30 to 27 in New York.

Testifying to their respect for popular sovereignty and majority rule, most Americans accepted the verdict of the ratifying conventions. "A decided majority" of the New Hampshire assembly had opposed the "new system," reported Joshua Atherton, but now they said, "It is adopted, let us try it." In Virginia, Patrick Henry vowed to "submit as a quiet citizen" and fight for amendments "in a constitutional way."

Unlike France, where the Revolution of 1789 divided the society into irreconcilable factions for generations, the American Constitutional Revolution of 1787 created a national republic based on broad popular support. Federalists celebrated their triumph by organizing great processions in the seaport cities. By marching in an orderly fashion — in conscious contrast to the riotous Revolutionary mobs — Federalist-minded citizens affirmed their allegiance to a self-governing but elite-ruled republican nation.

- According to the nationalists, what were the central problems of the Articles of Confederation? How did the delegates to the Philadelphia convention address them?

- How did the Philadelphia convention resolve the three controversial issues of the representation of large and small states, state power, and slavery?

- Who were the Antifederalists and why did they oppose the Constitution?

## SUMMARY

In this chapter, we examined the unfolding of two related sets of events. The first was the war between Britain and its rebellious colonies that began in 1776 and ended in 1783. The two great battles of Saratoga (1777) and Yorktown (1781) determined the outcome of that conflict. Surprisingly, given the military might of the British empire, both were American victories. These triumphs testify to the determination of George Washington, the resilience of the Continental army, and support for the Patriot cause from hundreds of local militias and tens of thousands of taxpaying citizens.

This popular support reflected the Patriots' second success: building effective institutions of republican government. These elected institutions of local and state governance evolved naturally out of colonial-era town meetings and representative assemblies. They were defined in the state constitutions written between 1776 and 1781 and their principles informed the first national constitution, the Articles of Confederation. Despite the challenges posed by conflicts over suffrage, women's rights, and fiscal policy, these self-governing political institutions carried the new republic successfully though the war-torn era and laid the foundation for the Constitution of 1787, the national charter that endures today.

**MAP 6.8**

**Ratifying the Constitution of 1787**

In 1907, geographer Owen Libby mapped the votes of members of the state conventions that ratified the Constitution. His map showed that most delegates from seaboard or commercial farming districts (which sent many delegates to the conventions) supported the Constitution, while those from sparsely represented, subsistence-oriented backcountry areas opposed it. Subsequent research has confirmed Libby's socio-economic interpretation of the voting patterns in North and South Carolina and in Massachusetts. However, other states' delegates were influenced by different factors. For example, in Georgia, delegates from all regions voted for ratification.

# CHAPTER REVIEW QUESTIONS

- The text states that Saratoga was the turning point of the War of Independence. Do you agree? Explain your answer.

- How revolutionary was the American Revolution? What political, social, and economic changes did it produce? What stayed the same?

- Why was the Constitution a controversial document even as it was being written?

- Both the Federalists and the Antifederalists claimed to represent the true spirit of the Revolution. Which group do you think was right? Why?

## FOR FURTHER EXPLORATION

The essays in *Empire and Nation: The American Revolution in the Atlantic World* (2005), edited by Eliga H. Gould and Peter S. Onuf, assess the impact of the revolution. For vivid accounts of the war, see John C. Dann, ed., *The Revolution Remembered: Eyewitness Accounts of the War for Independence* (1980).

Colin G. Calloway, *The American Revolution in Indian Country* (1995); Sylvia R. Frey, *Water from the Rock* (1991); and *Paths to Freedom: Manumission in the Atlantic World* (2009), edited by Rosemary Brana-Shute and Randy J. Sparks, study the revolution's impact on Native and African peoples. A data-rich source is "Africans in America: Revolution" (**www.pbs.org/wgbh/aia/part2/title.html**).

Three studies of women are Carol Berkin, *Revolutionary Mothers* (2005); Clare A. Lyons, *Sex Among the Rabble* (2006); and Cynthia Kierner, *Southern Women in Revolution, 1776–1800* (1998). For an intriguing portrait of "Deborah Sampson, Continental Soldier," go to **forum-network.org/lecture/masquerade-deborah-sampson-continental-soldier**.

Woody Holton, *Unruly Americans and the Origins of the Constitution* (2007), explores the events of the 1780s, while Catherine Drinker Bowen's *Miracle at Philadelphia* (1966) offers a dramatic portrayal of the convention. Jack Rakove's *Original Meanings: Politics and Ideas in the Making of the Constitution* (1996) and Saul Cornell's *The Other Founders* (1999) explore the ideologies of the Framers and their Antifederalist opponents. Also see the online exhibit "Religion and the Founding of the American Republic" (**www.loc.gov/exhibits/religion/rel03.html**), and Susan Juster, *Doomsayers: Anglo-American Prophecy in the Age of Revolution* (2003).

## TEST YOUR KNOWLEDGE

To assess your command of the material in this chapter, see the Online Study Guide at **bedfordstmartins.com/henretta**.

For Web sites, images, and documents related to topics and places in this chapter, visit **bedfordstmartins.com/makehistory**.

## TIMELINE

| | |
|---|---|
| **1776** | Second Continental Congress declares independence |
| | Howe forces Washington to retreat from New York and New Jersey |
| | Pennsylvania approves democratic state constitution |
| | John Adams publishes *Thoughts on Government* |
| **1777** | Articles of Confederation create central government |
| | Patriot women contribute to war economy |
| | Howe occupies Philadelphia (September) |
| | Gates defeats Burgoyne at Saratoga (October) |
| | Severe inflation of paper currency begins |
| **1778** | Franco-American alliance (February) |
| | Lord North seeks political settlement; Congress rejects negotiations |
| | British adopt southern strategy; capture Savannah (December) |
| **1779** | British and American forces battle in Georgia |
| **1780** | Clinton seizes Charleston (May) |
| | French troops land in Rhode Island |
| **1781** | Cornwallis invades Virginia (April); surrenders at Yorktown (October) |
| | States finally ratify Articles of Confederation |
| | Substantial Loyalist emigration |
| **1783** | Treaty of Paris (September 3) officially ends war |
| **1784–1785** | Congress enacts political and land ordinances for new states |
| **1786** | Nationalists hold convention in Annapolis, Maryland |
| | Shays's Rebellion roils Massachusetts |
| **1787** | Congress passes Northwest Ordinance |
| | Constitutional convention in Philadelphia |
| **1787–1788** | Jay, Madison, and Hamilton write *The Federalist* |
| | Eleven states ratify U.S. Constitution |

An EMBLEM of AMERICA.

# CHAPTER 7

# Politics and Society in the New Republic, 1787–1820

**Like an earthquake**, the American Revolution shook the European monarchical order, and its aftershocks reverberated for decades. By "creating a new republic based on the rights of the individual, the North Americans introduced a new force into the world," the eminent German historian Leopold von Ranke warned the king of Bavaria in 1854, a force that might cost the monarch his throne. Before 1776, "a king who ruled by the grace of God had been the center around which everything turned. Now the idea emerged that power should come from below [from the people]."

Other republican-inspired upheavals—England's Puritan Revolution of the 1640s and the French Revolution of 1789—ended in political chaos and military rule. Similar fates befell many Latin American republics that won independence from Spain in the early nineteenth century. But the American states escaped both social anarchy and military dictatorship. Having been raised in a Radical Whig political culture that viewed standing armies and powerful generals as instruments of tyranny, General George Washington left public life in 1783 to manage his plantation, astonishing European observers but bolstering the authority of elected Patriot leaders. "'Tis a Conduct so novel," American painter John Trumbull reported from London, that it is "inconceivable to People [here]."

The great task of fashioning representative republican governments absorbed the energy and intellect of an entire generation and was rife with conflict. Seeking to perpetuate the elite-led polity of the colonial era, Federalists celebrated "natural aristocrats" such as Washington and condemned the radical republicanism of the French Revolution. In response, Jefferson and his Republican followers claimed the Fourth of July as their holiday and "we the people" as their political language. "There was a grand democrat procession in Town on the 4th of July," came a report from Baltimore: "All the farmers, tanners, black-smiths, shoemakers, etc. were there . . . and afterwards they went to a grand feast."

Many people of high status worried that the new state governments were too attentive to the demands of such ordinary workers and their families. When considering a bill, Connecticut conservative Ezra Stiles grumbled, every elected official "instantly thinks how it will affect his constituents" rather than how it would enhance the general welfare. What Stiles criticized as irresponsible, however, most Americans welcomed. The concerns of ordinary citizens were now paramount, and traditional elites trembled.

### An Emblem of America, 1800

In the first years of independence, citizens of the United States searched for a symbolic representation of their new nation. This engraving shows many of the choices: Should the symbol of "America" have an ideological meaning, as in the Goddess of Liberty? Or should it be represented by national heroes, as in the stone Memorial to Washington? Or should America's symbol be found among its unique features, such as Niagara Falls (pictured in the background) or the presence of Africans and Indians (as represented by the black youth to the right and the spear-brandishing figure in front of the falls)? Or, finally, should its symbol be the national flag? Courtesy of the John Carter Brown Library at Brown University.

# The Political Crisis of the 1790s

The final decade of the eighteenth century brought fresh challenges for American politics. The Federalists split into two factions over financial policy and the French Revolution, and their leaders, Alexander Hamilton and Thomas Jefferson, offered contrasting visions of the future. Would the United States remain an agricultural nation governed by local officials, as Jefferson hoped? Or would Hamilton's vision of a strong national government and an economy based on manufacturing become reality?

## The Federalists Implement the Constitution

The Constitution expanded the dimensions of political life by allowing voters to choose national leaders as well as local and state officials. The Federalists swept the election of 1788, winning forty-four seats in the House of Representatives; only eight Antifederalists won election. As expected, members of the Electoral College chose George Washington as president (see Reading American Pictures, "Creating a National Political Tradition," p. 205). John Adams received the second-highest number of electoral votes and became vice president.

**Devising the New Government** | Once the military savior of his country, Washington now became its political father. At age fifty-seven, the first president possessed great personal dignity and a cautious personality. To maintain continuity, he adopted many of the administrative practices of the Confederation and asked Congress to reestablish the existing executive departments: Foreign Affairs (State), Finance (Treasury), and War. He initiated one important practice: The Constitution required the Senate's approval for the appointment of major officials, but Washington insisted that the president had sole authority to remove them, thereby ensuring the executive's control of the bureaucracy. To head the Department of State, Washington chose Thomas Jefferson, a fellow Virginian and an experienced diplomat. For secretary of the treasury, he turned to Alexander Hamilton, a lawyer and his former military aide. The president designated Jefferson, Hamilton, and Secretary of War Henry Knox as his cabinet, or advisory body.

The Constitution mandated a supreme court, but the Philadelphia convention gave Congress the task of creating a national court system. The Federalists wanted strong national institutions, and the Judiciary Act of 1789 reflected their vision. The act established a federal district court in each state and three circuit courts to hear appeals from the districts, with the Supreme Court having the final say. The Judiciary Act also specified that cases arising in state courts that involved federal laws could be appealed to the Supreme Court. This provision ensured that federal judges would have the final say on the meaning of the Constitution.

**The Bill of Rights** | The Federalists kept their promise to add a declaration of rights to the Constitution. James Madison, now a member of the House of Representatives, submitted nineteen amendments to the First Congress; by 1791, ten had been approved by Congress and ratified by the states. These ten amendments, known as the Bill of Rights, safeguard fundamental personal rights, including freedom of speech and religion, and mandate legal procedures, such as trial by jury. By protecting individual citizens, the amendments eased Antifederalists' fears of an oppressive national government and secured the legitimacy of the Constitution. They also addressed the issue of federalism: the proper balance between the authority of the national and state governments. But that question was constantly contested until the Civil War and remains important today.

## Hamilton's Financial Program

George Washington's most important decision was choosing Alexander Hamilton as secretary of the treasury. An ambitious self-made man of great intelligence, Hamilton married into the Schuyler family, influential Hudson River Valley landowners, and was a prominent lawyer in New York City. At the Philadelphia convention, he condemned the "democratic spirit" and called for an authoritarian government and a president with near-monarchical powers.

As treasury secretary, Hamilton devised bold policies to enhance national authority and to assist financiers and merchants. He outlined his plans in three path-breaking reports to Congress: on public credit (January 1790), on a national bank (December 1790), and on manufactures (December 1791). These reports outlined a coherent program of national mercantilism—government-assisted economic development.

## Creating a National Political Tradition

"Four score and seven years ago our fathers brought forth, upon this continent, a new nation. . . ." So Abraham Lincoln began his famous address at Gettysburg in 1863. In fact, although the American Patriots founded a new republic in 1776, it became a *nation*, with a sense of national consciousness, only in subsequent decades. How did America's nationhood develop? The sheer act of living together and addressing common problems created a foundation for nationhood. But graphic representations such as these engravings shaped the national identity and created a sense of political continuity.

**Washington's Journey from Mount Vernon.**
Library of Congress.

**"Independence Declared 1776. The Union Must Be Preserved."** Library of Congress.

### ANALYZING THE EVIDENCE

- George Washington—as myth and symbol—had a lot to do with creating America's sense of nationhood. How is Washington portrayed in the image on the left? It depicts his journey from Virginia to New York in 1789 to assume the presidency. Pay attention to the symbols in the engraving—the laurel wreaths, the American flags, the eagle—and to the fact that Washington is riding a horse, long a symbol of authority and aristocratic power. What do these symbols suggest about Washington? About the presidency? How might

they conflict with America's republican self-image?

- In the Gettysburg Address, Lincoln speaks reverently of "our fathers" bringing forth a new nation. The banner in the engraving of Washington, which was created in 1845, reads: "THE DEFENDER OF THE MOTHERS WILL BE THE PROTECTOR OF THE DAUGHTERS." What is the significance of the use of family imagery by Lincoln and the engraver? How does this imagery "make personal" the concept of the nation?

- The engraving on the right, from 1839, supports the incumbent president, Martin Van Buren (center left). He firmly clasps the hand of Andrew Jackson, his predecessor, political ally, and the author of the famous toast "The Union Must Be Preserved," which was directed against John C. Calhoun and his writings on nullification. What use does the engraver make of Washington and the presidents (arrayed at the top) who followed him? How might this imagery have helped to create a national political tradition?

**Public Credit: Redemption and Assumption**    The financial and social implications of Hamilton's "Report on the Public Credit" made it instantly controversial. Hamilton asked Congress to redeem at face value the $55 million in Confederation securities held by foreign and domestic investors (Figure 7.1). His reasons were simple: As an underdeveloped nation, the United States needed good credit to secure loans from Dutch and British financiers. However, Hamilton's redemption plan would give enormous profits to speculators, who had bought up depreciated securities. For example, the Massachusetts firm of Burrell & Burrell had paid $600 for Confederation notes with a face value of $2,500; it stood to reap a profit of $1,900. Such windfall gains offended a majority of Americans, who condemned the speculative practices of capitalist financiers. Equally controversial was Hamilton's proposal to pay the Burrells and other note holders with new interest-bearing securities, thereby creating a permanent **national debt**.

Hamilton's plan for a national debt owned mostly by the wealthy reawakened the fears of Radical Whigs and "Old Republicans." Speaking for the Virginia House of Burgesses, Patrick Henry condemned this plan "to erect, and concentrate, and perpetuate a large monied interest" and warned that it would prove "fatal to the existence of American liberty." James Madison challenged the morality of Hamilton's plan. He demanded that Congress recompense those who originally owned Confederation securities: the thousands of shopkeepers, farmers, and soldiers who had bought or accepted them during the dark days of the war. However, it would have been difficult to trace the original owners; moreover, nearly half the members of the House of Representatives owned Confederation securities and would profit personally from Hamilton's plan. Melding practicality with self-interest, the House rejected Madison's suggestion.

Hamilton then proposed that the national government further enhance public credit by assuming the war debts of the states. This assumption plan, costing $22 million, also favored well-to-do creditors such as Abigail Adams, who had bought depreciated Massachusetts government bonds with a face value of $2,400 for only a few hundred dollars and would reap a windfall profit. Still, Adams was a long-term investor, not a speculator like Assistant Secretary of the Treasury William Duer. Knowing Hamilton's intentions in advance, Duer and his associates secretly bought up $4.6 million of the war bonds of southern states at bargain rates. Congressional critics condemned Duer's speculation. They also pointed out that some states had already paid off their war debts; in response, Hamilton promised to

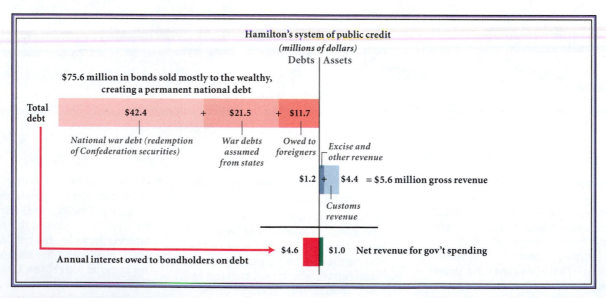

**FIGURE 7.1**

**Hamilton's Fiscal Structure, 1792**

As treasury secretary, Alexander Hamilton established a national debt by issuing government bonds and using the proceeds to redeem Confederation securities and assume the war debts of the states. To pay the annual interest due on the bonds, he used the revenue from excise taxes and customs duties. Hamilton deliberately did not attempt to redeem the bonds because he wanted to tie the interests of the wealthy Americans who owned them to the new national government.

reimburse those states. To win the votes of congressmen from Virginia and Maryland, the treasury chief arranged another deal: He agreed that the permanent national capital would be built along the Potomac River, where suspicious southerners could easily watch its operations. Such astute bargaining gave Hamilton the votes he needed to enact his redemption and assumption plans.

**Creating a National Bank** In December 1790, Hamilton issued a second report asking Congress to charter the Bank of the United States, which would be jointly owned by private stockholders and the national government. Hamilton argued that the bank would provide stability to the specie-starved American economy by making loans to merchants, handling government funds, and issuing bills of credit. These potential benefits persuaded Congress to grant Hamilton's bank a twenty-year charter and send the legislation to the president for his approval.

At this critical juncture, Secretary of State Thomas Jefferson joined with James Madison to oppose Hamilton's financial initiatives. Jefferson had already condemned Duer and the "corrupt squadron of paper dealers" who speculated in southern war bonds. Now he charged that Hamilton's national bank was unconstitutional. "The incorporation of a Bank," Jefferson told President Washington, was not a power expressly "delegated to the United States by the Constitution." Jefferson's argument rested on a *strict* interpretation of the national charter. Hamilton preferred a *loose* interpretation; he told Washington that Article 1, Section 8, empowered Congress to make "all Laws which shall be necessary and proper" to carry out the provisions of the Constitution. Agreeing with Hamilton, the president signed the legislation.

**Raising Revenue through Tariffs** Hamilton now sought revenue to pay the annual interest on the national debt. At his insistence, Congress imposed excise taxes, including a duty on whiskey distilled in the United States. These taxes would yield $1 million a year. To raise another $4 million to $5 million, the treasury secretary proposed higher tariffs on foreign imports. Although Hamilton's "Report on Manufactures" (1791) urged the expansion of American manufacturing, he did not support high **protective tariffs** that would exclude foreign products. Rather, he advocated moderate **revenue tariffs** that would pay the interest on the debt and other government expenses. To counter objections that "national tax collectors" would impair the "sovereignty" of the states, Hamilton selected respected state officials, including some Antifederalists, for many customhouse positions.

Hamilton's scheme worked brilliantly. As American trade increased, customs revenue rose steadily and paid down the national debt. Because import duties covered federal government expenses, they also encouraged rapid settlement of the West. Congress sold land in the national domain at ever-lower prices, an outcome opposed by Hamilton and favored by his Jeffersonian opponents. Regardless, the treasury secretary had devised a strikingly modern and successful fiscal system. Since the "commencement of the funding system," entrepreneur Samuel Blodget Jr. declared in 1801, "the country prospered beyond all former example."

## Jefferson's Agrarian Vision

Hamilton paid a high political price for his success. As Washington began his second four-year term in 1793, Hamilton's financial measures had split the Federalists into bitterly opposed factions. Most northern Federalists supported the treasury secretary, while most southern Federalists joined a group headed by Madison and Jefferson. By 1794, the two factions had acquired names. Hamiltonians remained Federalists; the allies of Madison and Jefferson called themselves Democratic Republicans or simply Republicans.

Thomas Jefferson spoke for southern planters and western farmers. Well-read in architecture, natural history, agricultural science, and political theory, Jefferson embraced the optimism of the Enlightenment. He believed in the "improvability of the human race" and deplored the corruption and social divisions that threatened its progress. Having seen the poverty of laborers in British factories, Jefferson doubted that wageworkers had the economic and political independence needed to sustain a republican polity.

Jefferson therefore set his democratic vision of America in a society of independent yeoman farm families. "Those who labor in the earth are the chosen people of God," he wrote in *Notes on the State of Virginia* (1785). The grain and meat from their homesteads would feed European nations, which "would manufacture and send us in exchange our clothes and other comforts." Jefferson's notion of an international division of labor resembled that proposed by Scottish economist Adam Smith in *The Wealth of Nations* (1776).

Turmoil in Europe brought Jefferson's vision closer to reality. The French Revolution began in 1789; four years later, the First French Republic (1792–1804) went to war against a British-led coalition of monarchies. As fighting disrupted European farming, wheat prices

**Two Visions of America**

Thomas Jefferson (left) and Alexander Hamilton confront each other in these portraits, as they did in the political battles of the 1790s. Jefferson was pro-French, Hamilton pro-British. Jefferson favored farmers and artisans; Hamilton supported merchants and financiers. Jefferson believed in democracy and rule by legislative majorities; Hamilton argued for strong executives and judges. Still, in the contested presidential election of 1800, Hamilton (who detested candidate Aaron Burr) threw his support to Jefferson and secured the presidency for his longtime political foe.    The White House Historical Association (White House Collection). / Yale University Art Gallery/Art Resource, NY.

leaped from 5 to 8 shillings a bushel and remained high for twenty years, bringing substantial profits to Chesapeake and Middle Atlantic farmers. "Our farmers have never experienced such prosperity," remarked one observer. Simultaneously, a boom in the export of raw cotton, fueled by the invention of the cotton gin and the mechanization of cloth production in Britain, boosted the economies of Georgia and South Carolina. As Jefferson had hoped, European markets brought prosperity to American agriculture.

## The French Revolution Divides Americans

American merchants profited even more handsomely from the European war. In 1793, President Washington issued a Proclamation of Neutrality, allowing U.S. citizens to trade with all belligerents. As neutral carriers, American merchant ships claimed a right to pass through Britain's naval blockade of French ports, and American firms quickly took over the lucrative sugar trade between France and its West Indian islands. Commercial earnings rose spectacularly, averaging $20 million annually in the 1790s—twice the value of cotton and tobacco exports. As the American merchant fleet increased from 355,000 tons in 1790 to 1.1 million tons in 1808, northern shipbuilders and merchants provided work for thousands of shipwrights, sailmakers, dockhands, and seamen. Carpenters, masons, and cabinetmakers in Boston, New York, and Philadelphia easily found work building warehouses and fashionable "Federal-style" town houses for newly affluent merchants. In Philadelphia, a European visitor reported, "a great number of private houses have marble steps to the street door, and in other respects are finished in a style of elegance."

**Ideological Politics** As Americans profited from Europe's struggles, they argued passionately over its ideologies. Most Americans had welcomed the French Revolution of 1789 because it abolished feudalism and established a constitutional monarchy. The creation of the First French Republic was more controversial. Urban artisans applauded the end of the monarchy and embraced the democratic, socially egalitarian ideology of the radical Jacobins. Like the Jacobins, they formed political clubs and began to address one another as "citizen." However, Americans with strong religious beliefs condemned the new French government for closing Christian churches and promoting a rational religion based on "natural morality." Fearing social revolution at home, wealthy Americans condemned Robespierre and his vengeance-minded followers for executing King Louis XVI and 3,000 aristocrats (see Voices from Abroad, "Peter Porcupine Attacks Pro-French Americans," p. 209).

Their fears were well founded, because Hamilton's economic policies quickly sparked a domestic insurgency. In 1794, western Pennsylvania farmers, already angered by the state's conservative fiscal policies, mounted the so-called Whiskey Rebellion to protest Hamilton's excise tax on spirits. This tax had cut demand for the corn whiskey the farmers distilled and bartered for eastern manufactures. Like the Sons of Liberty in 1765 and the Shaysites in 1786, the Whiskey Rebels assailed the tax collectors who sent the farmers' hard-earned money to a distant government. But the protesters also waved banners proclaiming the French revolutionary slogan "Liberty, Equality, Fraternity!" To deter popular rebellion and uphold national authority, President Washington raised an army of 12,000 troops and dispersed the Whiskey Rebels.

# VOICES FROM ABROAD

## William Cobbett

## Peter Porcupine Attacks Pro-French Americans

The Democratic Republican followers of Thomas Jefferson declared that "he who is an enemy to the French Revolution, cannot be a firm republican." William Cobbett, a British journalist who settled in Philadelphia and wrote under the pen name "Peter Porcupine," contested this definition of republicanism. A strong supporter of the Federalist Party, Cobbett regularly attacked its Republican opponents in caustic and widely read pamphlets and newspaper articles. Here he evokes the horrors of the Terror in France, which took the lives of thousands of aristocrats and their supporters, and warns that the triumph of doctrinaire republicans would bring the same fate to the United States.

France is a republic, and the decrees of the Legislators were necessary to maintain it a republic. This word outweighs, in the estimation of some persons (I wish I could say they were few in number), all the horrors that have been and that can be committed in that country. One of these modern republicans will tell you that he does not deny that hundreds of thousands of innocent persons have been murdered in France; that the people have neither religion nor morals; that all the ties of nature are rent asunder; . . . that its riches, along with millions of the best of the people, are gone to enrich and aggrandize its enemies; that its commerce, its manufactures, its sciences, its arts, and its honour, are no more; but at the end of all this, he will tell you that it must be happy, because it is a republic. I have heard more than one of these republican zealots declare, that he would sooner see the last of the French exterminated, than see them adopt any other form of government. Such a sentiment is characteristic of a mind locked up in a savage ignorance.

Shall we say that these things never can take place among us? . . . We are not what we were before the French revolution. Political projectors from every corner of Europe, troublers of society of every description, from the whining philosophical hypocrite to the daring rebel, and more daring blasphemer, have taken shelter in these States.

We have seen the guillotine toasted to three times three cheers. . . . And what would the reader say, were I to tell him of a Member of Congress, who wished to see one of these murderous machines employed for lopping off the heads of the French, permanent in the State-house yard of the city of Philadelphia?

If these men of blood had succeeded in plunging us into a war; if they had once got the sword into their hands, they would have mowed us down like stubble. The word Aristocrat would have been employed to as good account here, as ever it had been in France. We might, ere this, have seen our places of worship turned into stables; we might have seen the banks of the Delaware, like those of the Loire, covered with human carcasses, and its waters tinged with blood: ere this we might have seen our parents butchered, and even the head of our admired and beloved President rolling on a scaffold.

I know the reader will start back with horror. His heart will tell him that it is impossible. But, once more, let him look at the example before us. The attacks on the character and conduct of the aged Washington, have been as bold, if not bolder, than those which led to the downfall of the unfortunate French Monarch [Louis XVI, executed in 1793]. Can it then be imagined, that, had they possessed the power, they wanted the will to dip their hands in his blood?

Source: William Cobbett, *Peter Porcupine in America*, ed. David A. Wilson (Ithaca: Cornell University Press, 1994), 150–154.

### ANALYZING THE EVIDENCE

- What horrors does Cobbett describe? Why does he believe a similar fate could befall the United States? What has happened to the republicanism embraced by Americans in 1776?

- By 1796, Americans had a long tradition of political violence, including Indian massacres, bitter fighting among Patriots and Loyalists during the American Revolution, and Shays's Rebellion. Do those episodes give credence to Cobbett's warning that a bloodbath might "take place among us"? Or was he exaggerating the danger?

- Why were Americans generally able to resolve their political disputes peacefully, while the French took up arms to do so? If 100,000 diehard Loyalists had not fled the United States, would the outcome have been different?

**Federalist Gentry**

A prominent New England Federalist, Oliver Ellsworth served as chief justice of the United States from 1796 to 1800. His wife, Abigail Wolcott Ellsworth, was a member of a well-connected Connecticut family. In 1792, portraitist Ralph Earl captured the aspirations of the Ellsworths by painting them in fine clothes and prominently displaying their mansion (it can be seen through the window). Like other Federalists who tried to reconcile their wealth and social authority with republican values, Ellsworth dressed with restraint and his manners, remarked Timothy Dwight, were "wholly destitute of haughtiness and arrogance." Wadsworth Athenaeum/Art Resource, NY.

**Jay's Treaty** | Britain's maritime strategy intensified political divisions in America. Beginning in late 1793, the British navy seized 250 American ships carrying French sugar and other goods. Hoping to protect merchant property through diplomacy, Washington dispatched John Jay to Britain. But Jay returned with a controversial treaty that ignored the American claim that "free ships make free goods" and accepted Britain's right to stop neutral ships. The treaty also required the U.S. government to make "full and complete compensation" to British merchants for pre–Revolutionary War debts owed by American citizens. In return, the agreement allowed Americans to submit claims for illegal seizures and required the British to remove their troops and Indian agents from the Northwest Territory. Despite Republican charges that Jay's Treaty was too conciliatory, the Senate ratified it in 1795, but only by the two-thirds majority required by the Constitution. As long as the Federalists were in power, the United States would have a pro-British foreign policy.

## The Rise of Political Parties

The appearance of Federalists and Republicans marked a new stage in American politics — what historians call the First Party System. Colonial legislatures had factions based on family, ethnicity, or region, but they did not have organized political parties. Nor did the new state and national constitutions make any provision for political societies. Indeed, most Americans believed that parties were dangerous because they looked out for themselves rather than serving the public interest. Thus, Senator Pierce Butler of South Carolina criticized his congressional colleagues as "men scrambling for partial advantage, State interests, and, in short, a train of narrow, impolitic measures."

But pursuit of the public interest collapsed in the face of sharp conflicts over Hamilton's fiscal policies. Most merchants and creditors supported the Federalist party, as did wheat-exporting slaveholders in the Tidewater districts of the Chesapeake. The emerging Republican coalition was more diverse. It included southern tobacco and rice planters, debt-conscious western farmers, Germans and Scots-Irish in the southern backcountry, and subsistence farmers in the Northeast.

Party identity crystallized in 1796. To prepare for the presidential election, Federalist and Republican leaders called caucuses in Congress and conventions in the states. They mobilized popular support by organizing public festivals and processions: The Federalists held banquets in February to celebrate Washington's birthday, and the Republicans marched through the streets on July 4 to honor the Declaration of Independence.

In the election, voters gave Federalists a majority in Congress and made John Adams president. Adams continued Hamilton's pro-British foreign policy and strongly criticized French seizures of American merchant ships. When the French foreign minister Talleyrand solicited a loan and a bribe from American diplomats to stop the seizures, Adams charged that Talleyrand's agents, whom he dubbed X, Y, and Z, had insulted America's honor. In response to the XYZ Affair, Congress cut off trade with France in 1798 and authorized American privateering (licensing private ships to seize French vessels). This undeclared maritime war cut off American trade with the French West Indies and resulted in the capture of nearly 200 French and American merchant vessels.

## Constitutional Crisis and the "Revolution of 1800"

Ominously, the Federalists' attacks against the French Republic prompted domestic protests and governmental repression. When Republican-minded immigrants from Ireland vehemently attacked Adams's policies, a Federalist pamphleteer responded in kind: "Were I president, I would hang them for otherwise they would murder me." To silence the critics, the Federalists enacted three coercive laws limiting individual rights and threatening the fledgling party system. The Naturalization Act lengthened the residency requirement for American citizenship from five to fourteen years, the Alien Act authorized the deportation of foreigners, and the Sedition Act prohibited the publication of insults or malicious attacks on the president or members of Congress. "He that is not for us is against us," thundered the Federalist *Gazette of the United States*. Using the Sedition Act, Federalist prosecutors arrested more than twenty Republican newspaper editors and politicians, accused them of sedition, and convicted and jailed a number of them.

This repression sparked a constitutional crisis. Republicans charged that the Sedition Act violated the First Amendment's prohibition against "abridging the freedom of speech, or of the press." However, they did not appeal to the Supreme Court because the Court's power to review congressional legislation was uncertain and because most of the justices were Federalists. Instead, Madison and Jefferson looked to the state legislatures. At their urging, the Kentucky and Virginia legislatures issued resolutions in 1798 declaring the Alien and Sedition Acts to be "unauthoritative, void, and of no force." The resolutions set forth a **states' rights** interpretation of the Constitution, asserting that the states had a "right to judge" the legitimacy of national laws.

The conflict over the Sedition Act set the stage for the presidential election of 1800. Jefferson, once opposed on principle to political parties, now asserted that they

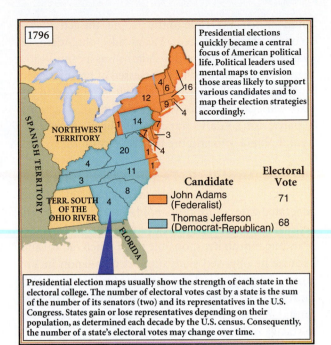

1796

Presidential elections quickly became a central focus of American political life. Political leaders used mental maps to envision those areas likely to support various candidates and to map their election strategies accordingly.

| Candidate | Electoral Vote |
|---|---|
| John Adams (Federalist) | 71 |
| Thomas Jefferson (Democrat-Republican) | 68 |

Presidential election maps usually show the strength of each state in the electoral college. The number of electoral votes cast by a state is the sum of the number of its senators (two) and its representatives in the U.S. Congress. States gain or lose representatives depending on their population, as determined each decade by the U.S. census. Consequently, the number of a state's electoral votes may change over time.

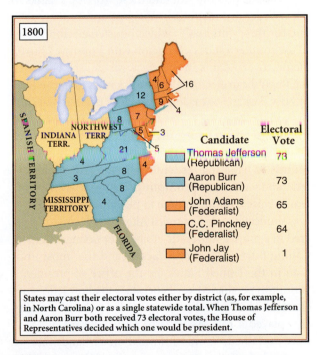

1800

| Candidate | Electoral Vote |
|---|---|
| Thomas Jefferson (Republican) | 73 |
| Aaron Burr (Republican) | 73 |
| John Adams (Federalist) | 65 |
| C.C. Pinckney (Federalist) | 64 |
| John Jay (Federalist) | 1 |

States may cast their electoral votes either by district (as, for example, in North Carolina) or as a single statewide total. When Thomas Jefferson and Aaron Burr both received 73 electoral votes, the House of Representatives decided which one would be president.

**MAP 7.1**

**The Presidential Elections of 1796 and 1800**

Both elections pitted Federalist John Adams of Massachusetts against Republican Thomas Jefferson of Virginia, and both saw voters split along regional lines. Adams carried every New England state and, reflecting Federalist strength in maritime and commercial areas, the eastern districts of the Middle Atlantic states; Jefferson won most of the agricultural-based states of the south and west (Kentucky and Tennessee). New York was the pivotal swing state. It gave its twelve electoral votes to Adams in 1796 and, thanks to the presence of Aaron Burr on the Republican ticket, bestowed them on Jefferson in 1800.

could "watch and relate to the people" the activities of an oppressive government. Meanwhile, John Adams re-evaluated his foreign policy. Adams was a complicated man—easily offended but possessed of great integrity and a strong will. Rejecting Hamilton's advice to declare war against France (and benefit from an upsurge in patriotism), Adams put country ahead of party and used diplomacy to end the maritime conflict.

**The Election of 1800** Despite Adams's statesmanship, the campaign of 1800 degenerated into a bitter, no-holds-barred contest. The Federalists launched personal attacks on Jefferson, branding him an irresponsible pro-French radical and, because he opposed state support of religion in Virginia, "the arch-apostle of irreligion and free thought." Both parties changed state election laws to favor their candidates, and rumors circulated of a Federalist plot to stage a military coup.

The election did not end these worries. Thanks to a low Federalist turnout in Virginia and Pennsylvania and the three-fifths rule (which boosted electoral votes in the southern states), Jefferson won a narrow 73 to 65 victory over Adams in the electoral college. However, the Republican electors also gave 73 votes to Aaron Burr of New York, who was Jefferson's vice presidential running mate (Map 7.1). The Constitution specified that in the case of a tie vote, the House of Representatives would choose between the candidates. For thirty-five rounds of balloting, Federalists in the House blocked Jefferson's election, prompting rumors that Virginia would raise a military force to put him into office.

Ironically, arch-Federalist Alexander Hamilton ushered in a more democratic era by supporting Jefferson. Calling Burr an "embryo Caesar" and the "most unfit man in the United States for the office of president," Hamilton persuaded key Federalists to allow Jefferson's election. The Federalists' concern for political stability also played a role. As Senator James Bayard of Delaware explained, "It was admitted on all hands that we must risk the Constitution and a Civil War or take Mr. Jefferson."

Jefferson called the election the "Revolution of 1800," and so it was. The bloodless transfer of power showed that popularly elected governments could be changed in an orderly way, even in times of bitter partisan conflict. In his inaugural address in 1801, Jefferson praised this achievement, declaring, "We are all Republicans, we are all Federalists." Defying the predictions (and hopes) of European conservatives, the American republican experiment of 1776 had survived a quarter century of economic and political turmoil.

- What was Hamilton's vision of the future? What policies did he implement to achieve it? How was Jefferson's vision different?
- What were the consequences of the French Revolution in American life and politics?

# The Westward Movement and the Jeffersonian Revolution

The United States "is a country in flux," a visiting French aristocrat observed in 1799, and "that which is true today as regards its population, its establishments, its prices, its commerce will not be true six months from now." Indeed, the American republic was beginning a period of dynamic expansion, much of it to the west. Between 1790 and 1810, farm families settled as much land as they had during the entire colonial period. George Washington, himself a speculator in western lands, noted approvingly that the Sons of Liberty were quickly becoming "the lords and proprietors of a vast tract of continent." And the *New-York Evening Post* declared: "It belongs of right to the United States to regulate the future destiny of North America."

## The Expanding Republic and Native American Resistance

In the Treaty of Paris of 1783, Great Britain gave up its claims to the trans-Appalachian region and, said one British diplomat, left the Indian nations "to the care of their [American] neighbours." *Care* was hardly the right word: Many white Americans wanted to destroy native communities. "Cut up every Indian Cornfield and burn every Indian town," proclaimed Congressman William Henry Drayton of South Carolina, so that their "nation be extirpated and the lands become the property of the public." Other leaders, including Henry Knox, Washington's first secretary of war, favored assimilating native peoples into Euro-American society. Knox proposed the division of tribal lands among individual Indian families, who would become citizens of the various states.

**Conflict over Land Rights** As in the past, the major struggle between natives and Europeans centered on land rights. Invoking the Paris treaty and regarding Britain's Indian allies as conquered peoples, the U.S. government asserted both sovereignty over and ownership of the trans-Appalachian west. Indian nations rejected both claims, pointing out they had not been conquered and had not signed the Paris treaty. "Our lands are our life and our breath," declared Creek chief Hallowing King, "if we part with them, we part with our blood." Brushing aside such objections and threatening military action, U.S. commissioners forced the pro-British Iroquois peoples— Mohawks, Onondagas, Cayugas, and Senecas—to cede huge tracts in New York and Pennsylvania in the Treaty of Fort Stanwix (1784). New York land speculators used liquor and bribes to take a million more acres, confining the once powerful Iroquois to reservations—essentially colonies of subordinate peoples.

American negotiators used similar tactics to grab western lands. In 1785, they persuaded the Chippewas, Delawares, Ottawas, and Wyandots to sign treaties giving away most of the future state of Ohio. The tribes quickly repudiated the agreements, justifiably claiming they were made under duress. To defend their lands, they joined with the Shawnee, Miami, and Potawatomi peoples in the Western Confederacy. Led by Miami chief Little Turtle, confederacy warriors crushed American expeditionary forces sent by President Washington in 1790 and 1791.

Fearing an alliance between the Western Confederacy and the British in Canada, Washington doubled the size of the U.S. Army and ordered General "Mad Anthony" Wayne to lead a new expedition. In August 1794, Wayne defeated the Confederacy in the Battle of Fallen Timbers (near present-day Toledo, Ohio). However, continuing Indian resistance forced a compromise. In the Treaty of Greenville (1795), American negotiators acknowledged Indian ownership of the land and, in return for various payments, the Western Confederacy ceded most of Ohio (Map 7.2). The Indian peoples also agreed to accept American sovereignty, placing themselves "under the protection of the United States, and no other Power whatever." These American advances caused Britain to agree, in Jay's Treaty (1795), to reduce its trade and military aid to Indians in the trans-Appalachian region.

The Greenville Treaty sparked a wave of white migration. By 1805, the new state of Ohio had more than 100,000 residents. Thousands more farm families moved into the future states of Indiana and Illinois, sparking new conflicts with native peoples over land

**MAP 7.2**

**Indian Cessions and State Formation, 1776–1840**

By virtue of the Treaty of Paris (1783) with Britain, the United States claimed sovereignty over the entire trans-Appalachian west. The Western Confederacy contested this claim, but the U.S. government upheld it with military force. By 1840, armed diplomacy had forced most Native American peoples to move west of the Mississippi River. White settlers occupied their lands, formed territorial governments, and eventually entered the Union as members of separate—and equal—states. By 1860, the trans-Appalachian region constituted an important economic and political force in American national life.

**Treaty Negotiations at Greenville, 1795**

In 1785, Indian tribes in the Northwest Territory formed the Western Confederacy to prevent white settlement north of the Ohio River. After Indian triumphs in battles in the early 1790s, an American victory at the Battle of Fallen Timbers (1794) and the subsequent Treaty of Greenville (1795) opened up the region for white farmers. However, the treaty recognized many Indian rights because it was negotiated between relative equals on the battlefield. The artist suggests this equality: Notice the height and stately bearing of the Indian leaders — ninety of whom signed the document — and their placement slightly in front of the General Anthony Wayne and his officers.   Unknown, *Treaty of Greenville*, n.d., Chicago Historical Society.

and hunting rights. Declared one Delaware Indian: "The Elks are our horses, the buffaloes are our cows, the deer are our sheep, & the whites shan't have them."

**Assimilation Rejected**  To prevent such conflicts, the U.S. government had encouraged Native Americans to assimilate into white society. The goal, as one Kentucky Protestant minister put it, was to make the Indian "a farmer, a citizen of the United States, and a Christian." Most Indians rejected wholesale assimilation; even those who joined Christian churches retained many ancestral values and religious beliefs. To think of themselves as individuals or members of a nuclear family, as white Americans were demanding, meant

repudiating the clan, the very essence of Indian life. To preserve "the old Indian way," many native communities expelled white missionaries and forced Christianized Indians to participate in tribal rites. As a Munsee prophet declared, "There are two ways to God, one for the whites and one for the Indians."

A few Indian leaders sought a middle path in which new beliefs overlapped with old practices. Among the Senecas, the prophet Handsome Lake encouraged traditional animistic rituals that gave thanks to the sun, the earth, water, plants, and animals. But he included Christian elements in his teachings — the concepts of heaven and hell, and an emphasis on personal morality — to deter his followers from alcohol, gambling, and witchcraft. Handsome Lake's teachings divided the Senecas into hostile factions. Led by Chief Red Jacket, traditionalists condemned European culture as evil and demanded a complete return to ancestral ways.

Most Indians also rejected the efforts of American missionaries to turn warriors into farmers and women into domestic helpmates. Among eastern woodland peoples, women grew corn, beans, and squash—the mainstays of the Indians' diet—and land cultivation rights passed through the female line. Consequently, women exercised considerable political influence, which they were eager to retain. Nor were Indian men interested in becoming farmers. When war raiding and hunting were no longer possible, they turned to grazing cattle and sheep.

## Migration and the Changing Farm Economy

Native American resistance slowed the advance of white settlers but did not stop it. Nothing "short of a Chinese Wall, or a line of Troops," Washington declared, "will restrain . . . the Incroachment of Settlers, upon the Indian Territory." During the 1790s, two great streams of migrants moved out of the southern states (Map 7.3).

**Southern Migrants** One stream, composed primarily of white tenant farmers and struggling yeomen families, flocked through the Cumberland Gap into Kentucky and Tennessee. "Boundless settlements open a door for our citizens to run off and leave us," a worried Maryland landlord lamented, "depreciating all our landed property and disabling us from paying taxes." In fact, many migrants were fleeing from this planter-controlled society. They wanted more freedom and hoped to prosper by growing cotton and hemp, which were in great demand.

Many settlers in Kentucky and Tennessee lacked ready cash to buy land. Like the North Carolina Regulators in the 1770s, poorer migrants claimed a customary right to occupy "back waste vacant Lands" sufficient "to provide a subsistence to themselves and their Posterity." Virginia legislators, who administered the Kentucky Territory, had a more elitist vision. Although they allowed poor settlers to buy up to 1,400 acres of land at reduced prices, they sold or granted huge tracts of

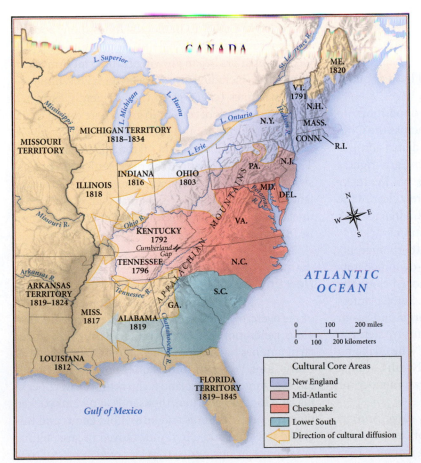

**MAP 7.3**

**Regional Cultures Move West, 1790–1820**

By 1790, four core cultures had developed in the long-settled states along the Atlantic seaboard. Between 1790 and 1820, migrants from these four regions carried their cultures into the trans-Appalachian west. New England customs and institutions were a dominant influence in upstate New York and along the Great Lakes, while the Lower South's hierarchical system of slavery and heavy concentration of African Americans shaped the character of the new states along the Gulf of Mexico. The pattern of cultural diffusion was more complex in the Ohio and Tennessee river valleys, which were settled by migrants from various core regions.

**An Indian Log House in Georgia, 1791**

The Indian peoples of the southeastern United States—the Cherokees, Creeks, Choctaws, and Chickasaws—quickly adopted European practices that fit easily into their relatively settled, agricultural-based way of life. This sturdy Creek log cabin was based on a Scots-Irish or German design and sat adjacent to the family's cornfields, visible in the background.    Library of Congress Prints and Photographs Division.

100,000 acres to twenty-one groups of speculators and leading men. When Kentucky became a state in 1792, this landed elite owned one-fourth of the state, while half the white men owned no land and lived as quasi-legal squatters or tenant farmers.

Widespread landlessness—and opposition to slavery—prompted a new migration across the Ohio River into the future states of Ohio, Indiana, and Illinois. In a free community, thought Peter Cartwright, a Methodist lay preacher from southwestern Kentucky who moved to Illinois, "I would be entirely clear of the evil of slavery . . . [and] could raise my children to work where work was not thought a degradation."

Meanwhile, a second stream of southern migrants from the Carolinas, composed of slave-owning planters and enslaved African Americans, moved along the coastal plain toward the Gulf of Mexico. Some planters set up new estates in the interior of Georgia and South Carolina, while others moved into the future states of Alabama, Mississippi, and Louisiana. "The Alabama Feaver rages here with great violence," a North Carolina planter remarked, "and has carried off vast numbers of our Citizens."

Cotton was the key to this migratory surge. Around 1750, the demand for raw wool and cotton increased dramatically as water-powered spinning jennies, weav-ing mules, and other technological innovations boosted textile production in England. South Carolina and Georgia planters began growing cotton, and American inventors—including Connecticut-born Eli Whitney—built machines (called gins) that efficiently extracted seeds from strands of cotton. To grow more cotton, white planters imported about 115,000 Africans between 1776 and 1808, when Congress cut off the Atlantic slave trade. The cotton boom financed the rapid settlement of Mississippi and Alabama—in a single year, a government land office in Huntsville, Alabama, sold $7 million of uncleared land—and the two states entered the Union in 1817 and 1819, respectively.

**Exodus from New England**    As southerners moved across the Appalachians and along the Gulf Coast, a third stream of migrants flowed out of the overcrowded communities of New England. Previous generations of Massachusetts and Connecticut farm families had moved north and east, settling New Hampshire, Vermont, and Maine. Now, in a vast self-directed surge, New England farmers moved west. Seeking land for their children, thousands of parents packed their wagons with tools and household goods and migrated to New York. Often they moved in large family or religious groups, as one traveler noted in central New

York: "The town of Herkimer is entirely populated by families come from Connecticut. We stayed at Mr. Snow's who came from New London with about ten male and female cousins." By 1820, almost 800,000 New Englanders lived in a string of settlements stretching from Albany to Buffalo, and many others had traveled on to Ohio and Indiana. Soon, much of the Northwest Territory consisted of New England communities that had moved inland.

In New York, as in Kentucky, well-connected speculators snapped up much of the best land. In the 1780s, financier Robert Morris acquired 1.3 million acres of central New York. The Wadsworth family bought thousands of acres in the Genesee region, hoping to re-create the leasehold manorial system of the Hudson River Valley. To attract tenants, the Wadsworths leased farms rent-free for the first seven years, after which they charged rents. Imbued with the "homestead" ethic, many New England families preferred to buy farms. They signed contracts with the Holland Land Company, a Dutch-owned syndicate of speculators, which allowed settlers to pay for their farms as they worked them.

**Innovation on Eastern Farms**  The new farm economy in New York, Ohio, and Kentucky forced major changes in eastern agriculture. Unable to compete with lower-priced western grains, farmers in New England switched to potatoes, which were high yielding and nutritious. To make up for the labor of sons and daughters who had moved inland, Middle Atlantic farmers bought more efficient farm equipment. They replaced metal-tipped wooden plows with cast-iron models that dug deeper and required a single yoke of oxen instead of two. Such changes in crop mix and technology kept production high.

Easterners also adopted the progressive farming methods touted by British agricultural reformers. "Improvers" in Pennsylvania doubled their average yield per acre by rotating their crops and planting nitrogen-rich clover to offset nutrient-hungry wheat and corn. Yeomen farmers diversified production by raising sheep and selling the wool to textile manufacturers. Many farmers adopted a year-round planting cycle, sowing corn in the spring for animal fodder and then planting winter wheat in September for market sale. Women and girls milked the family cows and made butter and cheese to sell in the growing towns and cities.

Whether hacking fields out of western forests or carting manure to replenish eastern soils, farmers now worked harder and longer, but their increased productivity brought them a better standard of living. Westward migration—the settlement and exploitation of Indian lands—boosted the farming economy throughout the country.

## The Jeffersonian Presidency

From 1801 to 1825, three Republicans from Virginia—Thomas Jefferson, James Madison, and James Monroe—each served two terms as president. Supported by farmers in the South and West and strong Republican majorities in Congress, this "Virginia Dynasty" completed what Jefferson had called the Revolution of 1800. It reversed many Federalist policies and actively supported westward expansion.

When Jefferson took office in 1801, he inherited an old international conflict. Beginning in the 1780s, the Barbary States of North Africa had raided merchant ships in the Mediterranean, and like many European nations, the United States had paid an annual bribe to protect its vessels. Initially Jefferson refused to pay this "tribute" and ordered the U.S. Navy to attack the pirates' home ports. However, to avoid an all-out war, which would have increased taxes and the national debt, Jefferson agreed to pay tribute at a lower rate.

At home, Jefferson inherited a national judiciary filled with Federalist appointees, including the formidable John Marshall of Virginia, the new chief justice of the Supreme Court. To add more Federalist judges, the outgoing Federalist Congress had passed the Judiciary Act of 1801. The act created sixteen new judgeships and various other positions, which President Adams filled at the last moment with "midnight appointees." The Federalists "have retired into the judiciary as a stronghold," Jefferson complained, "and from that battery all the works of Republicanism are to be beaten down and destroyed."

Jefferson's fears were soon realized. When Republican legislatures in Kentucky and Virginia repudiated the Alien and Sedition Acts as unconstitutional, Marshall declared that only the Supreme Court held the power of constitutional review. The Court claimed this authority for itself when James Madison, the new secretary of state, refused to deliver the commission of William Marbury, one of Adams's midnight appointees. In *Marbury v. Madison* (1803), Marshall asserted that Marbury had the right to the appointment but that the Court did not have the constitutional power to enforce it. In defining the Court's powers, Marshall voided a section of the Judiciary Act of 1789, in effect asserting the Court's authority to review congressional legislation and interpret the constitution. "It is emphatically the province and duty of the judicial department to

THE RESIDENCE OF DAVID TWINING. 1787.

**Edward Hicks, *The Residence of David Twining***

Hicks painted this farm around 1845, as he remembered it from his childhood in the 1780s (he is the young lad standing next to Elizabeth Twining). By the 1780s, Bucks County in Pennsylvania had been settled by Europeans for more than a century. The county's prosperous Quaker farmers had built large and comfortable clapboard-covered houses, commodious barns, and solid fences. They hired workers, such as the black plowman in the painting, to cultivate their spacious well-manured fields and tend their cattle and sheep. Like many other rural easterners, they had become commercial farmers who sold their grain, meat, hides, and wool into the market economy.   Courtesy of the Abby Aldrich Rockefeller Folk Art Museum, Williamsburg, VA.

say what the law is," the chief justice declared, directly challenging the Republican view that the state legislatures had that power.

Ignoring this setback, Jefferson and the Republicans reversed other Federalist policies. When the Alien and Sedition Acts expired in 1801, Congress branded them unconstitutional political repression and refused to extend them. It also amended the Naturalization Act, restoring the original waiting period of five years for resident aliens to become citizens. Charging the Federalists with grossly expanding the national government's size and power, Jefferson had the Republican Congress

shrink it. He abolished all internal taxes, including the excise tax that had sparked the Whiskey Rebellion of 1794. To quiet Republican fears of a military coup, Jefferson reduced the size of the permanent army. He also secured repeal of the Judiciary Act of 1801, ousting forty of Adams's midnight appointees. Still, Jefferson retained competent Federalist officeholders, removing only 69 of 433 properly appointed Federalists during his eight years as president.

Jefferson likewise governed tactfully in fiscal affairs. He tolerated the economically important Bank of the United States, which he had once condemned as

**BOMBARDMENT OF TRIPOLI.**

**America in the Middle East, 1804**

To protect American merchants from capture and captivity in the Barbary States, President Thomas Jefferson sent in the U.S. Navy. This 1846 lithograph, created by the famous firm of Currier & Ives, depicts one of the three attacks on the North African port of Tripoli by Commodore Edward Preble in August 1804. As the USS *Constitution* and other large warships lob shells into the city, small American gunboats defend the fleet from Tripolitan gunboats. "Our loss in Killed & Wounded has been considerable," Preble reported, and "the Enemy must have suffered very much . . . among their Shipping and on shore."
The Granger Collection, New York.

unconstitutional. But he chose as his secretary of the treasury Albert Gallatin, a fiscal conservative who believed that the national debt was "an evil of the first magnitude." By limiting expenditures and using customs revenue to redeem government bonds, Gallatin reduced the debt from $83 million in 1801 to $45 million in 1812. With Jefferson and Gallatin at the helm, the nation's fiscal affairs were no longer run in the interests of northeastern creditors and merchants.

## Jefferson and the West

Jefferson had long championed settlement of the West. He celebrated the yeoman farmer in *Notes on the State of Virginia*; wrote one of the Confederation's western land

ordinances; and supported Pinckney's Treaty (1795), the agreement between the United States and Spain that reopened the Mississippi River to American trade and allowed settlers to export crops via the Spanish-held port of New Orleans.

As president, Jefferson pursued policies that made it easier for farm families to acquire land. In 1796, a Federalist-dominated Congress had set the price of land in the national domain to $2 per acre; by the 1830s, Jefferson-inspired Republican Congresses had enacted more than three hundred laws that cut the cost to $1.25, eased credit terms, and allowed illegal squatters to buy their farms. Eventually, in the Homestead Act of 1862, Congress gave farmsteads to settlers for free.

**Toussaint L'Ouverture, Haitian Revolutionary and Statesman**

The American Revolution of 1776 constituted a victory for republicanism; the Haitian revolt of the 1790s represented a triumph of liberty over slavery and a demand for racial equality. After leading the black army that ousted French planters and British invaders from Haiti, Toussaint formed a constitutional government in 1801. A year later, when French troops invaded the island, he negotiated a treaty that halted Haitian resistance in exchange for a pledge that the French would not reinstate slavery. Subsequently, the French seized Toussaint and imprisoned him in France, where he died in 1803.    Snark/Art Resource, New York.

**The Louisiana Purchase** | International events challenged Jefferson's vision of westward expansion. In 1799, Napoleon Bonaparte seized power in France and sought to reestablish France's American empire. In 1801, he coerced Spain into signing a secret treaty that returned Louisiana to France and restricted American access to New Orleans, violating Pinckney's Treaty. Napoleon also launched an invasion to restore French rule in Haiti (then called Saint-Domingue), once the richest sugar colony in the Americas. After a massive slave revolt had convulsed the island in 1791, touching off years of civil war and Spanish and British invasions, black Haitians led by Toussaint L'Ouverture—himself a former slave-owning planter—seized control of the country in 1798. Now Napoleon wanted it back, to profit from its wealth and "to destroy the new Algiers that has been growing up in the middle of America."

Napoleon's actions in Haiti and Louisiana prompted Jefferson to question his pro-French foreign policy. "The day that France takes possession of New Orleans, we must marry ourselves to the British fleet and nation," the president warned, dispatching James Monroe to Britain to negotiate an alliance. To keep the Mississippi River open to western farmers, Jefferson told Robert Livingston, the American minister in Paris, to negotiate the purchase of New Orleans.

Jefferson's diplomacy yielded a magnificent prize: the entire territory of Louisiana. By 1802, the French invasion of Haiti was faltering in the face of disease and determined black resistance, a new war threatened in Europe, and Napoleon feared an American invasion of Louisiana. Acting with characteristic decisiveness, the French ruler offered to sell the entire territory of Louisiana for $15 million (about $500 million today). "We have lived long," Livingston remarked to Monroe as they concluded the Louisiana Purchase in 1803, "but this is the noblest work of our lives."

The Louisiana Purchase forced Jefferson to reconsider his strict interpretation of the Constitution. He had long believed that the national government possessed only the powers expressly delegated to it in the Constitution, but there was no provision for adding new territory. So Jefferson pragmatically accepted a loose interpretation of the Constitution and used its treaty-making powers to complete the deal with France. The new western lands, Jefferson wrote, would be "a means of tempting all our Indians on the East side of the Mississippi to remove to the West."

**Secessionist Schemes** | The acquisition of Louisiana brought new political problems. Some New England Federalists, fearing that western expansion would hurt their region and party, talked openly of leaving the Union and forming a confederacy of northeastern states. The secessionists won the support of Aaron Burr, the ambitious vice president. After Alexander Hamilton accused Burr of planning to destroy the Union, the two fought an illegal pistol duel that led to Hamilton's death.

This tragedy propelled Burr into another secessionist scheme, this time in the southwest. When his term as vice president ended in 1805, Burr moved west to avoid prosecution. There, he conspired with General James Wilkinson, the military governor of the Louisiana Territory, either to seize territory in New Spain or

**A Mandan Village**

This Mandan settlement in North Dakota, painted by George Catlin around 1837, resembled those in which the Lewis and Clark expedition spent the winter of 1804–1805. Note the palisade of logs that surrounds the village, as protection from the Sioux and other marauding Plains peoples, and the solidly built mud lodges that provided warm shelter from the bitter cold of winter. Smithsonian American Art Museum, Washington, D.C./Art Resource.

establish Louisiana as a separate nation. But Wilkinson, himself a Spanish spy and incipient traitor, betrayed Burr and arrested him. In a highly politicized trial presided over by Chief Justice John Marshall, the jury acquitted Burr of treason.

The Louisiana Purchase had increased party conflict and generated secessionist schemes in both New England and the southwest. Such sectional differences would continue, challenging Madison's argument in "Federalist No. 10" that a large and diverse republic was more stable than a small one.

**Lewis and Clark Meet the Mandan and Sioux** A scientist as well as a statesman, Jefferson wanted information about Louisiana: its physical features, plant and animal life, and native peoples. He was also worried about intruders: The British-run Hudson's Bay Company and Northwest Company were actively trading for furs on the Upper Missouri River. So in 1804, Jefferson sent his personal secretary, Meriwether Lewis, to explore the region with William Clark, an army officer. From St. Louis, Lewis, Clark, and their party of American soldiers and frontiersmen traveled up the Missouri for 1,000 miles to the fortified, earth-lodge towns of the Mandan and Hidatsa peoples (near present-day Bismarck, North Dakota), where they spent the winter.

The Mandans lived primarily by horticulture, growing corn, beans, and squash. They had acquired horses by supplying food to nomadic Plains Indians and se-

cured guns, iron goods, and textiles by selling buffalo hides and dried meat to European traders. However, the Mandans (and neighboring Arikaras) had been hit hard by the smallpox epidemics that swept across the Great Plains in 1779–1781 and 1801–1802. Now they were threatened by Sioux peoples: Teton, Yanktonai, and Oglala. Originally, the Sioux had lived in the prairie and lake region of northern Minnesota. As their numbers rose and fish and game grew scarce, the Sioux moved westward, acquired horses, and hunted buffalo, living as nomads in portable skin tepees. The Sioux became ferocious fighters who tried to reduce the Mandans and other farming tribes to subject peoples. According to Lewis and Clark, they were the "pirates of the Missouri." Soon the Sioux would dominate the buffalo trade throughout the Upper Missouri region.

In the spring of 1805, Lewis and Clark began an epic 1,300-mile trek into unknown country. Their party now included Toussaint Charbonneau, a French Canadian fur trader, and his Shoshone wife, Sacagawea, who served as a guide and translator. After following the Missouri River to its source on the Idaho-Montana border, they crossed the Rocky Mountains, and—venturing far beyond the Louisiana Purchase—traveled down the Columbia River to the Pacific Ocean. Nearly everywhere, Indian peoples asked for guns so they could defend themselves from other armed tribes. In 1806, Lewis and Clark capped off their pathbreaking expedition by providing Jefferson with the first maps of the immense wilderness and a detailed account of its natural resources

**MAP 7.4**

**U.S. Population Density in 1803 and the Louisiana Purchase**

When the United States purchased Louisiana from France in 1803, much of the land to its east—the vast territory between the Appalachian Mountains and the Mississippi River—remained in Indian hands. The equally vast lands beyond the Mississippi were virtually unknown to Anglo-Americans, even after the epic explorations of Meriwether Lewis and William Clark, and Zebulon Pike. Still, President Jefferson predicted quite accurately that the huge Mississippi River Valley "from its fertility . . . will ere long yield half of our whole produce, and contain half of our whole population."

and inhabitants (Map 7.4). Their report prompted some Americans to envision a nation that would span the continent.

- Was there anything the Western Indian Confederacy could have done to limit white expansion and preserve Indian lands? Explain your position.

- Why did Jefferson support westward expansion? Why did eastern farm families leave their communities to go west? Were their reasons the same as Jefferson's?

# The War of 1812 and the Transformation of Politics

The Napoleonic Wars that ravaged Europe after 1802 brought new attacks on American merchant ships. American leaders struggled desperately to protect the nation's commerce while avoiding war. When this effort finally failed, it sparked dramatic political changes that destroyed the Federalist Party and split the Republicans into National and Jeffersonian factions.

# Conflict in the Atlantic and the West

As Napoleon conquered European countries, he cut off their commerce with Britain and seized American merchant ships that stopped in British ports. The British ministry responded with a naval blockade and seized American vessels carrying sugar and molasses from the French West Indies. The British navy also searched American merchant ships for British deserters and used these raids to replenish its crews, a practice known as impressment. Between 1802 and 1811, British naval officers impressed nearly 8,000 sailors, including many U.S. citizens. In 1807, American anger boiled over when a British warship attacked the U.S. Navy vessel *Chesapeake*, killing three, wounding eighteen, and seizing four alleged deserters. "Never since the battle of Lexington have I seen this country in such a state of exasperation as at present," Jefferson declared.

**The Embargo of 1807** | To protect American interests, Jefferson pursued a policy of peaceful coercion. Working closely with his secretary of state, James Madison, he devised the Embargo Act of 1807, which prohibited American ships from leaving their home ports until Britain and France stopped restricting U.S. trade. The embargo was a creative diplomatic measure, probably inspired by the boycotts of the 1760s and 1770s. But it overestimated the reliance of Britain and France on American shipping, and it underestimated the resistance of merchants, who feared the embargo would ruin them. "All is astonishment and alarm," exclaimed Virginia merchant Robert Gamble, "and God knows when the evil is to subside."

In fact, the embargo cut the American gross national product by 5 percent and weakened the entire economy. Exports plunged from $108 million in 1806 to $22 million in 1808, hurting farmers as well as merchants. "All was noise and bustle" in New York City before the embargo, one visitor remarked; afterward, everything was closed up as if "a malignant fever was raging in the place."

Despite popular discontent over the embargo, voters elected Republican James Madison to the presidency in 1808. A powerful advocate for the Constitution, the architect of the Bill of Rights, and a prominent congressman and party leader, Madison had served the nation well. But John Beckley, a loyal Republican, worried that Madison would be "too timid and indecisive as a statesman," and events proved him right. Acknowledging the embargo's failure, Madison replaced it with new economic restrictions, which also failed to protect American commerce. "The Devil himself could not tell which government, England or France, is the most wicked," an exasperated congressman declared.

**Western War Hawks** | Republican congressmen from the West were certain that Britain was the primary offender. They pointed to its trade with Indians in the Ohio River Valley in violation of the Treaty of Paris and Jay's Treaty. Bolstered by British guns and supplies, the Shawnee war chief Tecumseh [ta-KUM-sa] revived the Western Confederacy in 1809. His brother, the prophet Tenskwatawa [tens-QUA-ta-wa], provided the confederacy with a powerful nativist ideology. He urged Indian peoples to shun Americans, "the children of the Evil Spirit . . . who have taken away your lands"; renounce alcohol; and return to traditional ways. The Shawnee leaders found their greatest support among Kickapoo, Potawatomi, Winnebago, Ottawa, and Chippewa warriors, westerners who lacked knowledge of the strength and numbers of the advancing Americans. They flocked to Tenskwatawa's holy village, Prophetstown, near the juncture of the Tippecanoe and Wabash rivers in the Indiana Territory.

As Tecumseh mobilized the western Indian peoples for war, William Henry Harrison, the governor of the Indiana territory, decided on a preemptive strike. In November 1811, when Tecumseh went south to seek support from the Chickasaws, Choctaws, and Creeks, Harrison took advantage of his absence and attacked Prophetstown. The governor's 1,000 troops and militiamen traded heavy casualties with the confederacy's warriors at the Battle of Tippecanoe and then destroyed the holy village.

With Britain assisting Indians in the western territories and seizing American ships in the Atlantic, Henry Clay of Kentucky, the new Speaker of the House of Representatives, and John C. Calhoun, a rising young congressman from South Carolina, pushed Madison toward war. Like other Republican "war hawks" from the West and South, they wanted to seize territory in British Canada and Spanish Florida. With national elections approaching, Madison issued an ultimatum to Britain. When Britain failed to respond quickly, the president asked Congress for a declaration of war. In June 1812, a sharply divided Senate voted 19 to 13 for war, and the House of Representatives concurred, 79 to 49.

The causes of the War of 1812 have been much debated. Officially, the United States went to war because Britain had violated its commercial rights as a neutral

**Tenskwatawa, "The Prophet," 1830**
Tenskwatawa added a spiritual dimension to Native American resistance by urging a holy war against the invading whites and calling for a return to sacred ancestral ways. His dress reflects his teachings: Note the animal-skin shirt and the heavily ornamented ears. However, some of Tenskwatawa's religious rituals reflected the influence of French Jesuits; he urged his followers to finger a sacred string of beads (such as those in his left hand) that were similar to the Catholic rosary, thereby "shaking hands with the Prophet." Whatever its origins, Tenskwatawa's message transcended the cultural differences among Indian peoples and helped his brother Tecumseh create a formidable political and military alliance.     Smithsonian American Art Museum, Washington, D.C./ Art Resource.

nation. But the Federalists in Congress who represented the New England and Middle Atlantic merchants voted against the war; and in the election of 1812, those regions cast their 89 electoral votes for the Federalist presidential candidate, De Witt Clinton of New York. Madison amassed most of his 128 electoral votes in the South and West, where voters and congressmen strongly supported the war. Many historians therefore argue that the conflict was actually "a western war with eastern labels" (see Comparing American Voices, "Factional Politics and the War of 1812," pp. 226–227).

## The War of 1812

The War of 1812 was a near disaster for the United States, both militarily and politically. An invasion of British Canada in 1812 quickly ended in a retreat to Detroit. Nonetheless, the United States stayed on the offensive in the West. In 1813, American raiders burned the Canadian capital of York (present-day Toronto), Commodore Oliver Hazard Perry defeated a small British flotilla on Lake Erie, and General William Henry Harrison overcame a British and Indian force at the Battle of the Thames, taking the life of Tecumseh, now a British general.

In the East, political divisions prevented a major invasion of Canada. New England Federalists opposed the war and prohibited their states' militias from attacking Canada. Boston merchants and banks refused to lend money to the federal government, making the war difficult to finance. In Congress, Daniel Webster, a dynamic young politician from New Hampshire, led Federalists opposed to higher tariffs and national conscription of state militiamen.

Gradually, the tide of battle turned in Britain's favor. When the war began, American privateers had captured scores of British merchant vessels, but the Royal Navy soon seized the initiative. By 1813, a flotilla of Brit-

**Counting Scalps**

Effective propaganda usually contains a grain of truth, in this case the Indian warriors' practice of scalping their wartime victims. Entitled "A scene on the frontiers as practiced by the humane British and their worthy allies!", this cartoon by Philadelphia artist William Charles accuses the British of paying Indians to kill — and then mutilate — American soldiers. "Bring me the scalps, and the King our master will reward you," says the British officer in the cartoon. The verse at the bottom urges "Columbia's Sons" to press forward their attacks; otherwise, "The Savage Indian with his Scalping knife, / Or Tomahawk may seek to take your life."   Library of Congress.

ish warships was disrupting American commerce and threatening seaports along the Atlantic coast. In 1814, a British fleet sailed up the Chesapeake Bay, and troops stormed ashore to attack Washington City. Retaliating for the destruction of York, the invaders burned the U.S. Capitol and government buildings. After two years of fighting, the United States was stalemated along the Canadian frontier, on the defensive in the Atlantic, and its new capital city lay in ruins. The only U.S. victories came in the Southwest. There, a rugged slave-owning planter named Andrew Jackson and a force of Tennessee militiamen defeated British- and Spanish-supported Creek Indians in the Battle of Horseshoe Bend (1814) and forced the Indians to cede 23 million acres of land (Map 7.5).

**Federalists Oppose the War** | American military setbacks increased opposition to the war in New England. In 1814, Massachusetts Federalists called for a convention "to lay the foundation for a radical reform in the National Compact." When New England Federalists met in Hartford, Connecticut, some delegates proposed secession, but most wanted to revise the Constitution. To end Virginia's domination of the presidency, the Hartford Convention proposed a constitutional amendment limiting the office to a single four-year term and rotating it among citizens from different states. The convention also suggested amendments restricting commercial embargoes to sixty days and requiring a two-thirds majority in Congress to declare war, prohibit trade, or admit a new state to the Union.

As a minority party in Congress and the nation, the Federalists could prevail only if the war continued to go badly — a very real prospect. The war had cost $88 million, raising the national debt to $127 million. And now, as Albert Gallatin warned Henry Clay in May 1814, Britain's triumph over Napoleon in Europe meant that a "well organized and large army is [now ready] . . . to act immediately against us." When an attack from Canada came in the late summer of 1814, only an American naval victory on Lake Champlain stopped the British from marching down the Hudson River Valley. A few months later, thousands of seasoned British troops landed outside New Orleans, threatening

# Factional Politics and the War of 1812

In the quarter-century following the ratification of the U.S. Constitution, American leaders had to deal with the wars of the French Revolution and Napoleon. These European conflicts posed two dangers to the United States. First, the naval blockades imposed by the British and the French hurt American commerce and prompted calls for a military response. Second, European ideological and political struggles intensified party conflicts in the United States. On three occasions, the American republic faced danger from the combination of an external military threat and internal political turmoil. In 1798, the Federalist administration of John Adams almost went to war with France to help American merchants and to undermine the Republican Party. In 1807, Thomas Jefferson's embargo on American commerce shocked Federalists and sharply increased political tensions. And, as the following selections show, these political divisions during the War of 1812 threatened the very existence of the American republic.

## George Washington
### Farewell Address, 1796

Washington's support for Alexander Hamilton's economic policies promoted political factionalism. Ignoring his own role in creating that political divide, Washington condemned factionalism and, as his presidency proceeded, tried to stand above party conflicts. In his farewell address, Washington warned Americans to stand united and avoid the "Spirit of Party."

A solicitude for your welfare [prompts me] . . . to offer . . . the disinterested warnings of a parting friend, who can possibly have no personal motive to bias his counsels. . . .

The Unity of Government which constitutes you one people . . . is a main Pillar in the Edifice of your real independence . . . your tranquility at home; your peace abroad. . . . But it is easy to foresee, that, from different causes, and from different quarters, much pains will be taken, many artifices employed, to weaken in your minds the conviction of this truth. . . .

I have already intimated to you the danger of parties in the State, with particular reference to founding them on geographical discriminations. Let me now take a more comprehensive view, and warn you, in the most solemn manner, against the baneful effects of the Spirit of Party, generally.

This spirit, unfortunately, is inseparable from our nature, having its root in the strongest passions of the human mind. It exists under different shapes, in all governments, more or less stifled, controlled or repressed; but in those of the popular form, it is seen in its greatest rankness, and is truly their worst enemy.

The alternate dominion of one faction over another, sharpened by the spirit of revenge . . . , is itself a frightful despotism; but this leads at length to a more formal and permanent despotism.

Source: James D. Richardson, ed., *A Compilation of the Messages and Papers of the Presidents, 1789–1896* (Washington, D.C.: U.S. Government Printing Office, 1896), 1: 213–215.

## Josiah Quincy et al.
### Federalists Protest "Mr. Madison's War"

Washington's warning was to no avail. The parties – and the nation – divided sharply over the War of 1812. As Congress debated the issue of going to war against Great Britain, Josiah Quincy and other antiwar Federalist congressmen published a manifesto that questioned the justifications for the war offered by President Madison and the military strategy proposed by Republican war hawks.

How will war upon the land [an invasion of British Canada] protect commerce upon the ocean? What balm has Canada for wounded honor? How are our mariners benefited by a war which exposes those who are free, without promising release to those who are impressed?

But it is said that war is demanded by honor. Is national honor a principle which thirsts after vengeance, and is appeased only by blood? . . . If honor demands a war with England, what opiate lulls that honor to sleep over the wrongs done us by France? On land, robberies, seizures, imprisonments, by French authority; at sea, pillage, sinkings, burnings, under French orders. These are notorious. Are they unfelt because they are French? . . .

There is . . . a headlong rushing into difficulties, with little calculation about the means, and little concern about the consequences. With a navy comparatively [small], we are about to enter into the lists against the greatest marine [power] on the globe. With a commerce unprotected and spread over every ocean, we propose to make a profit by privateering, and for this endanger the wealth of which we are honest proprietors. An invasion is threatened of the [British colonies in Canada, but Britain] . . . without putting a new ship into commission, or taking another soldier into pay, can spread alarm or desolation along the extensive range of our seaboard. . . .

What are the United States to gain by this war? Will the gratification of some privateersmen compensate the nation for that sweep of our legitimate commerce by the extended marine of our enemy which this desperate act invites? Will Canada compensate the Middle states for [the loss of] New York; or the Western states for [the loss of] New Orleans?

Let us not be deceived. A war of invasion may invite a retort of invasion. When we visit the peaceable, and as to us innocent, colonies of Great Britain with the horrors of war, can we be assured that our own coast will not be visited with like horrors?

Source: *Annals of Congress*, 12th Cong., 1st sess., vol. 2, cols. 2219–2221.

## Hezekiah Niles

## A Republican Defends the War

In 1814, what the Federalists feared had come to pass: British ships blockaded American ports, and British troops invaded American territory. In January 1815, Republican editor Hezekiah Niles used the pages of his influential Baltimore newspaper, *Niles' Weekly Register*, to explain current Republican policies and blame the Federalists for American reverses.

It is universally known that the causes for which we declared war are no obstruction to peace. The practice of blockade and impressment having ceased by the general pacification of Europe, our government is content to leave the principle as it was. . . .

We have no further business in hostility, than such as is purely defensive; while that of Great Britain is to humble or subdue us. The war, on our part, has become a contest for life, liberty and property—on the part of our enemy, of revenge or ambition. . . .

What then are we to do? Are we to encourage him by divisions among ourselves—to hold out the hope of a separation of the states and a civil war—to refuse to bring forth the resources of the country against him? . . . I did think that in a defensive war—a struggle for all that is valuable—that all parties would have united. But it is not so—every measure calculated to replenish the treasury or raise men is opposed [by Federalists] as though it were determined to strike the "star spangled banner" and exalt the bloody cross. Look at the votes and proceedings of congress—and mark the late spirit [to secede from the Union] . . . that existed in Massachusetts, and see with what unity of action every thing has been done [by New England Federalists] to harass and embarrass the government. Our loans have failed; and our soldiers have wanted their pay, because those [New England merchants] who had the greater part of the monied capital covenanted with each other to refuse its aid to the country. They had a right, legally, to do this; and perhaps, also, by all the artifices of trade or power that money gave them, to oppress others not of their "stamp" and depress the national credit—but history will shock posterity by detailing the length to which they went to bankrupt the republic. . . .

To conclude—why does the war continue? It is not the fault of the government—we demand no extravagant thing. I answer the question, and say—*it lasts because Great Britain depends on the exertions of her "party" in this country to destroy our resources, and compel "unconditional submission."*

Thus the war began, and is continued, by our divisions.

Source: *Niles' Weekly Register*, January 28, 1815.

## ANALYZING THE EVIDENCE

- According to Washington, what is the ultimate cause of political factionalism? Why does Washington believe that factionalism is most dangerous in "popular"—that is, republican—governments?

- What specific dangers did Josiah Quincy and the Federalists foresee with regard to Republican war policies? Read the section on the War of 1812 in the text, and then discuss the accuracy of their predictions.

- According to Hezekiah Niles, by 1815, what were the war goals of the Republican administration? How had those goals changed since the start of the war? Niles charged the Federalists and their supporters with impeding the American war effort. What were his specific charges? Did they have any merit? How might the Federalists have defended their stance with respect to the war?

**MAP 7.5**

**The War of 1812**

Unlike the War of Independence, the War of 1812 had few large-scale military campaigns. In 1812 and 1813, most of the fighting took place along the Canadian border, as small American military forces attacked British targets with mixed success (nos. 1–4). The British took the offensive in 1814, launching a successful raid on Washington, but their attack on Baltimore failed, and they suffered heavy losses when they invaded the United States along Lake Champlain (nos. 5–7). Near the Gulf of Mexico, American forces moved from one success to another: General Andrew Jackson defeated the pro-British Creek Indians at the Battle of Horseshoe Bend, won a victory in Pensacola, and, in the single major battle of the war, routed an invading British army at New Orleans (nos. 8–10).

***Battle of New Orleans,* by Jean-Hyacinthe de Laclotte (detail)**
As their artillery (right center) bombarded the American lines, British infantry attacked the center of General Andrew Jackson's line of troops. At the same time, a column of redcoats (foreground) tried to breach the right flank of the American fortifications. Secure behind their battlements, Jackson's forces repelled the assaults, taking thousands of prisoners and leaving the ground littered with British casualties.
New Orleans Museum of Art, gift of Edgar William and Bernice Chrysler Garbisch.

American control of the Mississippi River. With the nation politically divided and under attack from north and south, Gallatin feared that "the war might prove vitally fatal to the United States."

Fortunately for the young American republic, by 1815 Britain wanted peace. The twenty-year war with France had sapped its wealth and energy, so it began negotiations with the United States in Ghent, Belgium. At first, the American commissioners—John Quincy Adams, Gallatin, and Clay—demanded territory in Canada and Florida, while British diplomats sought an Indian buffer state between the United States and Canada. Both sides quickly realized that these objectives were not worth the cost of prolonged warfare. The Treaty of Ghent, signed on Christmas Eve 1814, retained the prewar borders of the United States.

That result hardly justified three years of warfare, but before news of the treaty reached the United States, a final military victory lifted Americans' morale. On January 8, 1815, General Jackson's troops crushed the British forces attacking New Orleans. Fighting from carefully constructed breastworks, the Americans rained "grapeshot and cannister bombs" on the massed British formations. The British lost 700 men, and 2,000 more were wounded or taken prisoner; just 13 Americans died, and only 58 suffered wounds. A newspaper headline proclaimed: "Almost Incredible Victory!! Glorious News." The victory made Jackson a national hero, redeemed the nation's battered pride, and undercut the Hartford convention's demands for constitutional revision.

## The Federalist Legacy

The War of 1812 ushered in a new phase of the Republican political revolution. Before the conflict, Federalists had strongly supported Alexander Hamilton's program of national mercantilism—a funded debt, a central bank, and tariffs—while Jeffersonian Republicans had opposed it. After the war, the Republicans split into two camps. Led by Henry Clay, National Republicans pursued Federalist-like policies. In 1816, Clay pushed legislation through Congress creating the Second Bank of the United States and persuaded President Madison to sign it. In 1817, Clay won passage of the Bonus Bill, which created a national fund for roads and other internal improvements. Madison vetoed it. Reaffirming traditional Jeffersonian Republican principles, he argued that the national government lacked the constitutional authority to fund internal improvements.

Meanwhile, the Federalist Party crumbled. As one supporter explained, the National Republicans in the eastern states had "destroyed the Federalist party by the adoption of its principles" while the favorable farm policies of Jeffersonians maintained the Republican Party's dominance in the South and West. "No Federal character can run with success," Gouverneur Morris of New York lamented, and the election of 1818 proved him right: Republicans outnumbered Federalists 37 to 7 in the Senate and 156 to 27 in the House. Westward expansion and the success of Jefferson's Revolution of 1800 had shattered the First Party System.

**Marshall's Federalist Law**   However, the Federalists' nationalist policies lived on thanks to John Marshall's long tenure on the Supreme Court. Appointed chief justice by President John Adams in January 1801, Marshall had a personality and intellect that allowed him to dominate the Court until 1822 and strongly influence its decisions until his death in 1835. Winning the support of Joseph Story and other National Republican justices, Marshall shaped the evolution of the Constitution.

Three principles informed Marshall's jurisprudence: judicial authority, the supremacy of national laws, and traditional property rights (Table 7.1). Marshall claimed the right of judicial review for the Supreme Court in *Marbury v. Madison* (1803), and the Court frequently used that power to overturn state laws that, in its judgment, violated the Constitution.

**Asserting National Supremacy**   The important case of *McCulloch v. Maryland* (1819) involved one such law. When Congress created the Second Bank of the United States in 1816, it allowed the bank to set up state branches that competed with state-chartered banks. To enhance the competitiveness

| TABLE 7.1 | | | |
|---|---|---|---|
| **Marshall's Principles and the Major Decisions of the Marshall Court** | | | |
| | **Date** | **Case** | **Significance of Decision** |
| **Judicial Authority** | 1803 | *Marbury v. Madison* | Asserts principle of judicial review |
| **Property Rights** | 1810 | *Fletcher v. Peck* | Protects property rights through broad reading of Constitution's contract clause |
| | 1819 | *Dartmouth College v. Woodward* | Safeguards property rights, especially of chartered corporations |
| **Supremacy of National Law** | 1819 | *McCulloch v. Maryland* | Interprets Constitution to give broad powers to national government |
| | 1824 | *Gibbons v. Ogden* | Gives national government jurisdiction over interstate commerce |

*John Marshall*, **by Chester Harding, c. 1830**

Even at the age of seventy-five, John Marshall (1755–1835) had a commanding personal presence. After he became chief justice of the U.S. Supreme Court in 1801, Marshall elevated the Court from a minor department of the national government to a major institution in American legal and political life. His decisions on judicial review, contract rights, the regulation of commerce, and national banking permanently shaped the character of American constitutional law. *John Marshall*, 1830 (oil on canvas), Chester Harding (1792–1866). The Bridgeman Art Library.

of Maryland's banks, the state legislature imposed a tax on notes issued by the Baltimore branch of the Second Bank. The Second Bank refused to pay, claiming that the tax infringed on national powers and was therefore unconstitutional. The state's lawyers then invoked Jefferson's argument: that Congress lacked the constitutional authority to charter a national bank. Even if a national bank was legitimate, the lawyers argued, Maryland could tax its activities within the state.

Marshall and the nationalist-minded Republicans on the Court firmly rejected both arguments. The Second Bank was constitutional, said the chief justice, because it was "necessary and proper," given the national government's control over currency and credit. Like Alexander Hamilton, Marshall was a loose constructionist: If the goal of a law is "within the scope of the Constitution," he believed, then "all means which are appropriate" to secure that goal are also constitutional.

The Marshall Court again asserted the dominance of national over state statutes in *Gibbons v. Ogden* (1824). The decision struck down a New York law granting a monopoly to Aaron Ogden for steamboat passenger service across the Hudson River to New Jersey. Asserting that the Constitution gave the federal government authority over interstate commerce, the chief justice sided with Thomas Gibbons, who held a federal license to run steamboats between the two states.

### Upholding Vested Property Rights

Finally, Marshall used the Constitution to uphold Federalist notions of property rights. During the 1790s, Jefferson Republicans had celebrated "the will of THE PEOPLE," prompting Federalists to worry that popular sovereignty would result in a "tyranny of the majority." If state legislatures enacted statutes infringing on the property rights of wealthy citizens, Federalist judges vowed to void them.

Marshall was no exception. Determined to protect individual property rights, he invoked the contract clause of the Constitution to do it. The contract clause (in Article I, Section 10) prohibits the states from passing any law "impairing the obligation of contracts." Economic conservatives at the Philadelphia convention had inserted the clause to prevent "stay" laws, which kept creditors from seizing the lands and goods of delinquent debtors. In *Fletcher v. Peck* (1810), Marshall greatly expanded its scope. The Georgia legislature had granted a huge tract of land to the Yazoo Land Company. When a new legislature canceled the grant, alleging fraud and bribery, speculators who had purchased Yazoo lands appealed to the Supreme Court to uphold their titles. Marshall did so by ruling that the legislative grant was a contract that could not revoked. His decision was controversial and far-reaching. It limited state power; bolstered vested property rights; and, by protecting out-of-state investors, promoted the development of a national capitalist economy.

The Court extended its defense of vested property rights in *Dartmouth College v. Woodward* (1819). Dartmouth College was a private institution created by a royal charter issued by King George III. In 1816, New Hampshire's Republican legislature enacted a statute converting the school into a public university. The Dartmouth trustees opposed the legislation and hired Daniel Webster to plead their case. A renowned constitutional lawyer and a leading Federalist, Webster cited the Court's decision in *Fletcher v. Peck* and argued that the royal charter was an unalterable contract. The Marshall Court agreed and upheld Dartmouth's claims.

### The Diplomacy of John Quincy Adams

Even as John Marshall incorporated important Federalist principles into the American legal system, voting citizens and political leaders embraced the outlook of the Republican Party. The political career of John Quincy Adams was a case in point. Although he was the son of Federalist president John Adams, John Quincy Adams had joined the Republican Party before the War of 1812. He came to national attention for his role in negotiating the Treaty of Ghent, which ended the war.

Adams then served brilliantly as secretary of state for two terms under James Monroe (1817–1825). Ignoring Republican antagonism toward Great Britain, in 1817 Adams negotiated the Rush-Bagot Treaty, which limited American and British naval forces on the Great Lakes. In 1818, he concluded another agreement with Britain setting the forty-ninth parallel as the border between Canada and the lands of the Louisiana Purchase. Then, in the Adams-Onís Treaty of 1819, Adams persuaded Spain to cede the Florida territory to the United States (Map 7.6). In return, the American government accepted Spain's claim to Texas and agreed to a compromise on the western boundary for the state of Louisiana, which had entered the Union in 1812.

Finally, Adams persuaded President Monroe to declare American national policy with respect to the Western Hemisphere. At Adams's behest, Monroe warned Spain and other European powers to keep their hands off the newly independent republics in Latin America. The American continents were not "subject for further colonization," the president declared in 1823—a policy that thirty years later became known as the Monroe Doctrine. In return, Monroe pledged that the United States would not "interfere in the internal concerns" of European nations. Thanks to John Quincy Adams, the United States had successfully asserted its diplomatic leadership in the Western Hemisphere and won international acceptance of its northern and western boundaries.

The appearance of political consensus after two decades of bitter party conflict prompted observers to dub James Monroe's presidency the "Era of Good Feeling." This harmony was real but transitory. The Republican Party was now split between the National faction, led by Clay and Adams, and the Jeffersonian faction, soon to be led by Martin Van Buren and Andrew Jackson. The two groups differed sharply over federal support for roads and canals and many other issues. As the aging Jefferson himself complained, "You see so many of these new [National] republicans maintaining in Congress the rankest doctrines of the old federalists." This divi-

**MAP 7.6**

**Defining the National Boundaries, 1800–1820**

After the War of 1812, American diplomats negotiated treaties with Great Britain and Spain that defined the boundaries of the Louisiana Purchase, with British Canada to the north and New Spain (which in 1821 became the independent nation of Mexico) to the south and west. These treaties eliminated the threat of border wars with neighboring states for a generation, giving the United States a much-needed period of peace and security.

sion in the Republican Party would soon produce the Second Party System, in which national-minded Whigs and state-focused Democrats would confront each other. By the early 1820s, one cycle of American politics and economic debate had ended, and another was about to begin.

- **Was the War of 1812 "necessary"? If so, why? If not, why did it occur?**

- **How did the decisions of the Supreme Court between 1801 and 1820 alter the nation's understanding of the Constitution? How did they change American society?**

- **Explain the causes of the rise and fall of the Federalist Party. Why was the Republican triumph so complete?**

## SUMMARY

In this chapter, we traced three interrelated themes: public policy, westward expansion, and party politics. We began by examining the contrasting public policies advocated by Alexander Hamilton and Thomas Jefferson. A Federalist, Hamilton supported a strong national government and created a fiscal infrastructure (the national debt, tariffs, and a national bank) to spur trade and manufacturing. By contrast, Jefferson wanted to preserve the authority of state governments, and he envisioned an America enriched by farming rather than industry.

Jefferson and the Republicans promoted a westward movement that transformed the agricultural economy and sparked new wars with the Indian peoples. Expansion westward also shaped American diplomatic and military policy, leading to the Louisiana Purchase, the War of 1812, and the treaties negotiated by John Quincy Adams.

Finally, there was the unexpected rise of the First Party System. As Hamilton's policies split the political elite, the French Revolution divided Americans into hostile ideological groups. The result was two decades of bitter conflict and controversial measures: the Federalists' Sedition Act, the Republicans' Embargo Act, and Madison's decision to go to war with Britain. Although the Federalist Party faded away, it left as its enduring legacy Hamilton's financial innovations and John Marshall's constitutional jurisprudence.

## CHAPTER REVIEW QUESTIONS

- What impact did the two great developments of this period — the French Revolution and subsequent war in Europe, and the westward expansion of the United States across the North American continent — have on each other?

- Explain the rise and fall of the First Party System. How did the policies pursued by Republican presidents between 1801 and 1825 differ from those implemented by Hamilton and the Federalists during the 1790s? Why did the Federalist agenda fall out of favor? What legacy did the Federalists leave?

# FOR FURTHER EXPLORATION

James Roger Sharp, *American Politics in the Early Republic* (1993), and Thomas P. Slaughter, *The Whiskey Rebellion* (1986), describe the perils of the 1790s. For the impact of the French Revolution, see "Liberty, Equality, Fraternity" (**chnm.gmu.edu/revolution**). Rosemarie Zagarri, *A Woman's Dilemma* (1995), and Linda Kerber, *No Constitutional Right to Be Ladies* (1999), discuss women's political lives.

For the writings of Washington and Jefferson, go to **www.virginia.edu/gwpapers** and **etext.virginia.edu/jefferson/quotations**. See also Annette Gordon-Reed, *Thomas Jefferson and Sally Hemings* (1997), and Ron Chernow, *Alexander Hamilton* (2004). David McCullough's *John Adams* (2001) draws material from the Adams Papers (**www.masshist.org/digitaladams/aea**). On the election of 1800, consult John Ferling, *Adams vs. Jefferson* (2004), and James Horn et al., eds., *The Revolution of 1800* (2002).

Gregory Evans Dowd, *A Spirited Resistance* (1992), and the "Chickasaw Historical Research Page" (**www.chickasawhistory.com**) survey Native Americans. Colin G. Calloway, *One Vast Winter Count* (2003), and Douglas Seefeldt et al., eds., *Across the Continent* (2005), cover the latest Lewis and Clark scholarship. See also **www.pbs.org/lewisandclark**. Theda Perdue, *Cherokee Women* (1998), and William G. McLoughlin, *Cherokee Renascence in the New Republic* (1986), explore cultural interaction.

Ralph Ketcham's *Presidents Above Party* (1984) probes the political world. For the War of 1812, see Donald R. Hickey, *The War of 1812* (1989), and "The War of 1812" site at **www.warof1812.ca/index.html**. R. Kent Newmyer, *The Supreme Court Under Marshall and Taney* (1968), concisely analyzes constitutional change.

## TEST YOUR KNOWLEDGE

To assess your command of the material in this chapter, see the Online Study Guide at **bedfordstmartins.com/henretta**.

For Web sites, images, and documents related to topics and places in this chapter, visit **bedfordstmartins.com/makehistory**.

## TIMELINE

| | |
|---|---|
| 1783 | Treaty of Paris allows settlement of west |
| 1784 | Iroquois peoples cede lands in New York |
| 1787 | Northwest Ordinance |
| 1789 | Judiciary Act establishes federal courts<br>French Revolution begins |
| 1790 | Hamilton's public credit system approved |
| 1790–1791 | Western Confederacy defeats U.S. armies |
| 1791 | Bill of Rights ratified<br>Bank of the United States chartered |
| 1792, 1796 | Kentucky joins Union; Tennessee follows<br>French Republic formed |
| 1793 | Madison and Jefferson found Republican Party<br>War between Britain and France |
| 1794 | Whiskey Rebellion<br>Battle of Fallen Timbers |
| 1795 | Jay's Treaty with Great Britain<br>Pinckney's Treaty with Spain<br>Greenville Treaty accepts Indian land rights |
| 1798 | XYZ Affair<br>Alien, Sedition, and Naturalization Acts<br>Kentucky and Virginia resolutions |
| 1800 | Jefferson elected president 1801<br>John Marshall becomes chief justice |
| 1801–1807 | Gallatin reduces national debt |
| 1802–1807 | France and Britain seize American ships |
| 1803 | Louisiana Purchase<br>*Marbury v. Madison* asserts judicial review |
| 1804–1806 | Lewis and Clark explore West |
| 1807 | Embargo Act cripples American shipping |
| 1808 | Madison elected president |
| 1809 | Tecumseh and Tenskwatawa revive Western Confederacy |
| 1812–1815 | War of 1812 |
| 1817–1825 | Era of Good Feeling |
| 1819 | Adams-Onís Treaty<br>*McCulloch v. Maryland*; *Dartmouth College v. Woodward* |

## CHAPTER 8

# Creating a Republican Culture, 1790–1820

**By the 1820s**, a sense of optimism pervaded America's white citizenry. The new nation, a Kentucky judge declared in a Fourth of July speech, "already exhibits many signs that it is the promised land of civil liberty, and of institutions designed to liberate and exalt the human race." White Americans had good reason to feel fortunate. They lived under a representative republican government, free from arbitrary taxation and from domination by an established church. The deaths of former presidents John Adams and Thomas Jefferson on July 4, 1826—the fiftieth anniversary of the Declaration of Independence—seemed to many Americans a sure sign that God looked with favor on their experiment in self-government.

Inspired by their political freedom, many citizens sought to extend republican principles throughout their society. But what *were* those principles? For entrepreneurial-minded merchants, farmers, and political leaders, republicanism meant the advance of **capitalism**: They wanted governments to solidify capitalist cultural values and create a dynamic market economy. Using their influence in state legislatures, they secured mercantilist policies that assisted private businesses and, they claimed, enhanced the "common wealth." Other Americans celebrated republican social values. In the North, they championed democratic republicanism: equality in family and social relationships. In the South, where class and race sharply divided society, politicians and pamphleteers endorsed an aristocratic republicanism that stressed liberty for whites rather than equality for all.

Yet another vision of American republicanism emerged during the massive religious revival that swept the nation between 1790 and 1850. The document that founded the national republic, the U.S. Constitution of 1787, is thoroughly secular, containing no reference to God and only mentioning religion to prohibit religious tests for holding federal office. But, as Alexis de Tocqueville reported in *Democracy in America* (1835), the Second Great Awakening gave "the Christian religion . . . a greater influence over the souls of men" than in any other country. The resulting religious enthusiasm—what Methodist Bishop McIlvaine praised as "the quickening of the people of God to a spirit and walk becoming the gospel"—prompted political activism on many fronts, from abolitionism, to temperance, to a condemnation of Sunday mail delivery. For those who embraced the Awakening, the United States was both a great experiment in republican government and a Christian civilization that would redeem the world—a moral mission that, for better or worse, would inform American diplomacy in the centuries to come.

**The Fourth of July in Philadelphia, c. 1811**

By the early nineteenth century, the Fourth of July celebration of American independence had become a popular holiday, especially among Jeffersonian Republicans. (Federalists commemorated Washington's birthday.) This detail from a painting by John Lewis Krimmel links the new nation to the Greek and Roman republics through architecture (the building and the statue), notes its social diversity (by including blacks as well as whites), and hints at the tenor of its social life. The young man buying an alcoholic drink and flirting with the young mother may well engage in some rowdy behavior before Independence Day is over. Pennsylvania Academy of the Fine Arts, Philadelphia. (detail) From the estate of Paul Beck Jr.

# The Capitalist Commonwealth

If "the quick succession of sensations and ideas constitute life," observed a French visitor to the United States, "here one lives a hundred fold more than elsewhere; here, all is circulation, motion, and boiling agitation." Boiling agitation was especially evident in the Northeast, where republican state legislatures actively promoted banking and commerce. "Experiment follows experiment; enterprise follows enterprise," another European traveler noted, and "riches and poverty follow." Of the two, riches were readily apparent. Beginning around 1800, the average per capita income of Americans increased by more than 1 percent a year—more than 30 percent in a single generation.

## Banks, Manufacturing, and Markets

America was "a Nation of Merchants," a British visitor reported from Philadelphia in 1798, "keen in the pursuit of wealth in all the various modes of acquiring it." And acquire it they did, making spectacular profits as the wars triggered by the French Revolution (1793–1815) crippled European merchant firms. Fur trader John Jacob Astor and merchant Robert Oliver became the nation's first millionaires. Oliver first worked for an Irish-owned linen firm in Baltimore and then achieved affluence by trading West Indian coffee and sugar. Astor, who migrated from Germany to New York in 1784, became wealthy carrying furs from the Pacific Northwest to markets in China.

**Banking and Credit** To finance such mercantile ventures, Americans needed banks. Before the Revolution, farmers relied on government-sponsored land banks for loans, while merchants arranged partnerships or obtained credit from British suppliers. During the War for Independence, Philadelphia merchants persuaded the Confederation Congress to charter the Bank of North America in 1781, and traders in Boston and New York soon founded similar lending institutions. "Our monied capital has so much increased from the Introduction of Banks, & the Circulation of the Funds," Philadelphia merchant William Bingham boasted in 1791, "that the Necessity of Soliciting Credits from England will no longer exist."

That same year, Federalists in Congress chartered the First Bank of the United States to issue notes and make commercial loans. The bank's profits averaged a handsome 8 percent annually; by 1805, it had branches

**A Cloth Merchant, 1789**
Originally a prosperous storekeeper in New Milford, Connecticut, Elijah Boardman (1760–1832) eventually became a U.S. senator. Like other American traders, he had imported huge quantities of cloth from Britain. When the wars of the 1790s cut off trade, some merchants financed the domestic production of textiles. Others, including Boardman, turned to land speculation. In 1795, he joined the Connecticut Land Company and bought huge tracts in Connecticut's Western Reserve, including the present towns of Medina, Palmyra, and Boardman, Ohio. Ralph Earl painted this portrait in 1789.    Elijah Boardman, the Metropolitan Museum of Art, New York, Bequest of Susan W. Tyler, 1979.

in eight seaport cities. However, Jeffersonians attacked the bank as unconstitutional and claimed that it promoted "a consolidated, energetic government supported by public creditors, speculators, and other insidious men lacking in public spirit of any kind." When the bank's twenty-year charter expired in 1811, Jeffersonian Republicans refused to renew it. To provide credit, merchants, artisans, and farmers persuaded state legislatures to charter banks. By 1816, when Congress (now run by National Republicans) chartered the Second Bank of

**The China Trade**

Following the Revolution, New England merchants traded actively with the major Asian manufacturing centers of China and India. In this painting by George Chinnery (1774–1852), the American flag flies prominently, alongside other national banners, in front of the warehouse district in Canton (modern Guangzhou). There, merchants exchanged bundles of American furs for cargoes of Chinese tea, silks, and porcelain plates, cups, and serving dishes.   Bridgeman Art Library Ltd.

the United States, there were 246 state-chartered banks with tens of thousands of stockholders and $68 million in banknotes in circulation. But these state banks were often shady operations that issued notes without adequate specie reserves and made ill-advised loans to insiders.

Dubious banking policies helped bring on the Panic of 1819 (just as they caused the financial crisis of 2008). But the most important cause was an abrupt 30 percent drop in world agricultural prices after the Napoleonic Wars. In Charleston, South Carolina, in 1818, the price for a pound of raw cotton fell from 34 cents to 15 cents. As their income plummeted, planters and farmers could not pay their debts to their suppliers and banks. Many state banks went bust; those that were still solvent in 1821 had just $45 million in circulation. The panic gave Americans their first taste of a **business cycle**, the periodic expansion and contraction

of output and jobs inherent to an unregulated market economy.

**Rural Manufacturing**  The Panic of 1819 revealed that artisans and yeomen were now part of the market economy. Before 1800, many artisans worked part-time and sold their handicrafts locally; thus, a French traveler in central Massachusetts found many houses "inhabited by men who are both cultivators and artisans." Other artisans bartered products with neighbors. Clockmaker John Hoff of Lancaster, Pennsylvania, exchanged his fine, wooden-cased instruments for a dining table, a bedstead, and labor on his small farm. By 1820, many artisans — shipbuilders in seacoast towns, ironworkers in Pennsylvania and Maryland, and shoemakers in Massachusetts — had expanded their output and were selling their products throughout the nation.

**The Yankee Peddler, c. 1830**

Even in 1830, most Americans lived too far from a market town to go there regularly to buy goods. Instead, they purchased their tinware, clocks, textiles, and other manufactures from peddlers, often from New England, who traveled far and wide in small horse-drawn vans like the one visible through the doorway in this painting.   Courtesy IBM Corporation, Armonk, New York.

American entrepreneurs encouraged this expansion by developing rural manufacturing networks like those in Europe (see Chapter 1). Enterprising merchants bought raw materials, hired workers in farm families to process them, and sold the finished manufactures in regional or national markets. "Straw hats and Bonnets are manufactured by many families," an official in Maine noted in the 1810s. Merchants shipped these products — shoes, brooms, and palm-leaf hats as well as cups, baking pans, and other tin utensils — to stores in seaport cities. And New England peddlers, who quickly acquired the dubious reputation of being hard-bargaining "Yankees," sold them throughout the rural South.

This business expansion resulted from innovations in organizing production and in marketing; new technology played only a minor role. During the 1780s, New England and Middle Atlantic merchants built water-powered mills to run machines that combed wool — and later cotton — into long strands. But until the 1820s, they used the household-based outwork system for the next steps in the process: Farm women and children spun the machine-combed strands into thread and yarn on foot-driven spinning wheels, and men in other households used foot-powered looms to weave the yarn into cloth. In 1820, more than 12,000 household workers labored full-time weaving woolen cloth, which was then pounded flat and given a smooth finish in water-powered fulling mills. However, the transfer of spinning and weaving to factories was already in full swing; the number of water-driven cotton spindles soared from 8,000 in 1809 to 333,000 in 1817.

The growth of manufacturing offered farm families new opportunities — and new risks. Ambitious New

England farmers switched from growing crops for subsistence to raising livestock for sale. They sold meat, butter, and cheese to city markets and cattle hides to the booming shoe industry. "Along the whole road from Boston, we saw women engaged in making cheese," a Polish traveler reported. Other farm families raised sheep and sold raw wool to textile manufacturers. Processing these raw materials invigorated many farming towns. In 1792, Concord, Massachusetts, had one slaughterhouse and five small tanneries; a decade later, the town boasted eleven slaughterhouses and six large tanneries.

As the rural economy churned out more goods, it altered the environment. Foul odors from stockyards and tanning pits wafted over Concord and many other leather-producing towns. To secure hemlock bark to process stiff hides into pliable leather, tanners cut down thousands of acres of trees each year. More trees fell to the ax to create pasturelands for huge herds of livestock—dairy cows, cattle, and especially sheep. By 1850, most of the forests in southern New England and eastern New York were gone: "The hills had been stripped of their timber," New York's *Catskill Messenger* reported, "so as to present their huge, rocky projections." Scores of textile milldams dotted New England's rivers, altering their flow and preventing fish—already severely depleted from decades of overfishing—from reaching upriver spawning grounds. Even as the income of many farmers rose, the quality of their natural environment deteriorated.

In the new capitalist-run market economy, rural parents and their children worked longer and harder. They made yarn, hats, and brooms during the winter and then turned to their regular farming chores during the warmer seasons. More important, these farm families now depended on their wage labor and market sales to purchase the textiles, shoes, and hats they had once made for themselves. The new productive system made families and communities more efficient and prosperous—and more dependent on a market they could not control.

## Building a Transportation Infrastructure

The expansion of the market depended on improvements in transportation. Between 1793 and 1812, the Massachusetts legislature granted charters to more than one hundred private turnpike companies. These charters gave the companies special legal status and often included monopoly rights to a transportation route.

Pennsylvania issued fifty-five charters, including one to the Lancaster Turnpike Company. The company built a 65-mile graded and graveled road between Lancaster and Philadelphia, which quickly boosted the regional economy. Although turnpike investors received only about "three percent annually," Henry Clay estimated, society as a whole "actually reap[ed] fifteen or twenty percent." A farm woman knew what Clay meant: "The turnpike is finished and we can now go to town at all times and in all weather." New turnpikes soon connected dozens of inland market centers to seaport cities.

Water transport was the quickest and cheapest way to get goods to market, so state governments and private entrepreneurs improved water transport by dredging shallow rivers and constructing canals to bypass waterfalls or rapids. Settlers took matters into their own hands. In the rapidly growing states of Kentucky and Tennessee and in southern Ohio, Indiana, and Illinois, settlers paid premium prices for farmland near the great Ohio and Mississippi rivers and their tributaries. And speculators bought up property in the cities along their banks: Cincinnati, Louisville, Chattanooga, and St. Louis. Farmers and merchants built barges to carry cotton, surplus grain, and meat downstream to New Orleans, which by 1815 was handling about $5 million in agricultural products yearly.

## Public Enterprise: The Commonwealth System

Legislative support for road and canal companies reflected the ideology of mercantilism: government-assisted economic development. Just as the British Parliament had used the Navigation Acts to spur prosperity, so American legislatures enacted laws "of great public utility" that would increase the "common wealth." These statutes generally took the form of special charters that bestowed legal privileges. For example, most transportation charters included the power of eminent domain, which allowed turnpike, bridge, and canal corporations to force the sale of privately owned land along their routes. State legislatures also aided capitalist flour millers and textile manufacturers, who flooded adjacent farmland as they built dams to power their water-driven machinery. In Massachusetts, the Mill Dam Act of 1795 deprived farmers of their traditional right under common law to stop the flooding and forced them to accept "fair compensation" for their lost acreage. Judges approved this state-ordered shift in property rights. "The establishment of a great mill-power for manufacturing purposes," Justice Lemuel Shaw

*View of Cincinnati,* **by John Caspar Wild, c. 1835**
Thanks to its location on the Ohio River (a tributary of the Mississippi), Cincinnati quickly became one of the major processing centers for grain and hogs in the trans-Appalachian west. By the 1820s, passenger steamboats and freight barges connected the city with Pittsburgh to the north and the ocean port of New Orleans far to the south.   Museum of Fine Arts, Boston, M. and M. Karolik Collection.

intoned, was "one of the great industrial pursuits of the commonwealth."

Critics condemned the privileges given to private enterprises as "Scheme[s] of an evident antirepublican tendency," as some "freeholder citizens" in Putney, Vermont, put it. The award of "peculiar privileges" to corporations, they argued, not only violated the "equal rights" of all citizens but also lessened the power of the government. As a Pennsylvanian explained, "Whatever power is given to a corporation, is just so much power taken from the State." Nonetheless, judges in state courts, following the lead of John Marshall's Supreme Court (see Chapter 7), consistently upheld corporate charters and grants of eminent domain to private transportation companies. "The opening of good and easy internal communications is one of the highest duties of government," declared a New Jersey judge.

State mercantilism soon spread beyond transportation. Following Jefferson's embargo of 1807, which cut off goods and credit from Europe, the New England states awarded charters to two hundred iron-mining, textile-manufacturing, and banking companies, and Pennsylvania granted more than eleven hundred. By 1820, innovative state governments had created a republican political economy: a commonwealth system that funneled state aid to private businesses whose projects would improve the general welfare.

- How did promoters of mercantilism (the commonwealth system) use state and national governments to promote economic growth?

- Why did many Americans believe that the granting of special privileges and charters to private businesses violated republican principles?

# Toward a Democratic Republican Culture

After independence, many Americans in the northern states embraced a democratic republicanism that celebrated political equality and social mobility. These citizens, primarily members of the emerging **middle class**, redefined the nature of the family and of education by seeking more egalitarian marriages and more affectionate ways of rearing their children.

## Opportunity and Equality– for White Men

Between 1780 and 1820, hundreds of well-educated visitors agreed, almost unanimously, that the American social order was genuinely different from that of Europe. In his famous *Letters from an American Farmer* (1782), French-born essayist J. Hector St. Jean de Crèvecoeur wrote that European society was composed "of great lords who possess everything, and of a herd of people who have nothing." By contrast, the United States had "no aristocratical families, no courts, no kings, no bishops."

The absence of a hereditary aristocracy encouraged Americans to condemn inherited social privilege and to extol legal equality. "The law is the same for everyone [in America,]" noted one European traveler. Yet citizens of the new republic willingly accepted social divisions that reflected personal achievement. As individuals used their "talents, integrity, and virtue" to amass wealth, their social standing rose—a phenomenon that astounded many Europeans. "In Europe to say of someone that he rose from nothing is a disgrace and a reproach," remarked a Polish aristocrat. "It is the opposite here. To be the architect of your own fortune is honorable. It is the highest recommendation."

Some Americans from long-distinguished families felt threatened by the *nouveau riche* and their ideology of wealth-driven social mobility. "Man is estimated by dollars," complained Nathaniel Booth, whose high-status family had once dominated the small Hudson River port town of Kingston, New York. However, for most white men, a merit-based system meant the opportunity to better themselves (Map 8.1).

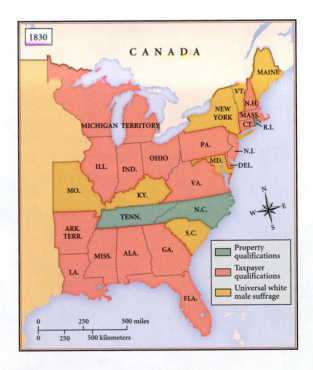

**MAP 8.1**

## The Expansion of Voting Rights for White Men, 1800 and 1830

Between 1800 and 1830, the United States moved steadily toward political equality for white men. Many existing states revised their constitutions and replaced a property qualification for voting with a less-restrictive criterion (the voter must have paid taxes or have served in the militia). Some new states in the West extended the suffrage to all adult white men. As parties sought votes from a broader electorate, the tone of politics became more open and competitive—swayed by the interests and values of ordinary people.

Old cultural rules—and new laws—denied such chances to most women and African American men. When women and free blacks invoked the republican principle of equality and asked for voting rights, male legislators wrote explicit race and gender restrictions into the law. In 1802, Ohio disenfranchised African Americans, and the New York constitution of 1821 imposed a property-holding requirement on black voters. A striking case of sexual discrimination occurred in New Jersey, where the state constitution of 1776 had granted **suffrage** to all property holders. As Federalists and Republicans competed for power, they ignored customary gender rules and urged property-owning single women and widows to vote. Sensing a threat to men's monopoly on politics, the New Jersey legislature in 1807 limited voting rights to white men only. To justify the exclusion of women, legislators invoked both biology and custom: "Women, generally, are neither by nature, nor habit, nor education, nor by their necessary condition in society fitted to perform this duty with credit to themselves or advantage to the public."

## Toward a Republican Marriage System

The controversy over women's political rights mirrored a debate over authority within the household. British and American husbands had long claimed patriarchal power and firm legal control of the family's property. But as John Adams lamented in 1776, the republican principle of equality had "spread where it was not intended," encouraging his wife and other women to speak out on politics and to demand legal and financial rights. Patriot author and historian Mercy Otis Warren maintained that patriarchy was not a "natural" rule but a social contrivance and could be justified only "for the sake of order in families."

Economic and cultural changes also eroded customary paternal authority. In colonial America, most property-owning parents had arranged their children's marriages to protect the family's welfare. They looked for a son- or daughter-in-law with moral values and financial resources; physical attraction and emotional

***The Wedding,* 1805**
Bride and groom stare intently into each other's eyes as they exchange vows, suggesting that their union was a love match, not a marriage based on economic calculation. The plain costumes of the guests and the sparse furnishings of the room suggest that the unknown artist may have provided us with a picture of a rural Quaker wedding.   Philadelphia Museum of Art.

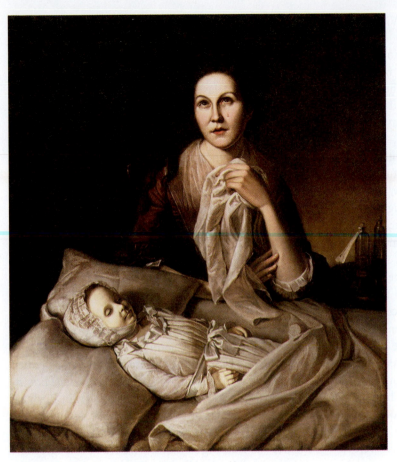

**A Tragedy Sentimentalized in Art**

When the infant daughter of artist Charles Willson Peale died in 1772, he captured his wife's emotions in this painting, *Mrs. Rachel Brewer Peale with Daughter (Rachel Weeping)*. Although Rachel Peale looks toward heaven, she is not praying; the emphasis is on her emotional state, her intense feelings of sorrow over the loss of her child. This focus on personal experience was a hallmark of sentimentalism. Philadelphia Museum of Art.

compatibility between the young people were secondary considerations. But as landholdings shrank in long-settled communities, many yeomen fathers lost control over their children's marriages because they had no farms to hand down. Young men and women chose their own partners, influenced by a new cultural attitude: **sentimentalism**.

**The Impact of Sentimentalism** Sentimentalism originated in Europe as part of the Romantic movement and, after 1800, spread quickly through all classes of American society. Rejecting the Enlightenment's emphasis on rational thought, sentimentalism celebrated the importance of "feeling"—a physical, sensuous appreciation of God, nature, and fellow humans. This new emphasis on deep emotional feelings infused German and English literary works, pop-

ular theatrical melodramas, and the emotional rhetoric of revivalist preachers.

As the hot sentimental passions of the heart overwhelmed the cool rational logic of the mind, a new consent-based marriage system appeared. Magazines praised marriages "contracted from motives of affection, rather than of interest," and many young people looked for a relationship based on intimacy and a spouse who was, as Eliza Southgate of Maine put it, "calculated to promote my happiness." As young people fell in love and married, many fathers saw their roles change from authoritarian patriarchs to watchful paternalists. To guard against free-spending sons-in-law, wealthy fathers often placed their daughters' inheritance in a legal trust. Wrote one Virginia planter to his lawyer: "I rely on you to see the property settlement properly drawn before the marriage, for I by no means consent that Polly shall be left to the Vicissitudes of Life."

As voluntary agreements between individuals, love marriages conformed more closely to republican principles than did arranged matches. In theory, such **companionate marriages** gave wives and husbands "true equality, both of rank and fortune," as one Boston man suggested. In practice, though, husbands continued to dominate most marriages, both because male authority was deeply ingrained in cultural mores and because under American common law, as Abigail Adams complained, husbands had "sovereign authority" over the family's property. Moreover, the new love-based marriage system discouraged parents from protecting young wives, and governments refused to prevent domestic tyranny. As one lawyer noted, women who would rather "starve than submit" to their husbands were left to their fate. The marriage contract "is so much more important in its consequences to females than to males," a young man at the Litchfield Law School in Connecticut astutely observed in 1820, for "they subject themselves to his authority. He is their all—their only relative—their only hope" (see Comparing American Voices, "The Trials of Married Life," pp. 248–249).

Young adults who chose partners unwisely were severely disappointed when their spouses failed as providers or faithful companions. Before 1800, little could be done; officials granted divorces only in cases of neglect, abandonment, or adultery—serious offenses against the moral order of society. After 1800, most divorce petitions cited emotional problems. One woman complained that her husband had "ceased to cherish her," while a man grieved that his wife had "almost broke his heart." Responding to changing cultural values, several states expanded the legal grounds for divorce to include drunkenness and personal cruelty.

## Republican Motherhood

Traditionally, American women had spent their active adult years working as farm wives and bearing and nurturing children. But by the 1790s, the birthrate in the northern states was dropping dramatically. In the farming village of Sturbridge in central Massachusetts, women who married before 1750 usually had eight or nine children; by contrast, those who married around 1810 had an average of six children. In the growing seaport cities, native-born white women bore an average of only four children.

The United States was among the first nations to experience this sharp decline in the birthrate—what historians call the demographic transition. There were several causes. Beginning in the 1790s, thousands of young men migrated to the trans-Appalachian west, which increased the number of never-married women in the East and delayed marriage for many more. Women who married in their late twenties had fewer children. In addition, white couples in the urban middle classes deliberately limited the size of their families. Fathers wanted to leave their children an adequate inheritance; mothers, influenced by new ideas of individualism and self-achievement, did not want to spend their entire adulthood rearing children. After having four or five children, these couples used birth control or abstained from sexual intercourse.

Women's lives also changed because of new currents in Christian social thought. Traditionally, many religious writers had suggested that women were morally inferior to men and often were sexual temptresses. But by 1800, Protestant ministers were blaming men for sexual misconduct and claiming that purity and spirituality were part of women's nature. Influential laymen echoed that thinking. In his *Thoughts on Female Education* (1787), Philadelphia physician Benjamin Rush argued that a young woman should ensure her husband's "perseverance in the paths of rectitude" and receive intellectual training so that she would be "an agreeable companion." Rush called for loyal "republican mothers" who would instruct "their sons in the principles of liberty and government."

Christian ministers readily embraced the idea of **republican motherhood**. "Preserving virtue and instructing the young are not the fancied, but the real 'Rights of Women,'" Reverend Thomas Bernard told the Female Charitable Society of Salem, Massachusetts. He urged his audience to dismiss the public roles for women, such as voting or serving on juries, that English feminist Mary Wollstonecraft had advocated in *A Vindication of the Rights of Woman* (1792). Instead, women should care for their children, a responsibility that gave them "an extensive power over the fortunes of man in every generation."

## Raising Republican Children

Republican values changed assumptions about inheritance and child rearing. English common law encouraged primogeniture, the inheritance of the family's property by the eldest son (see Chapter 1). After the Revolution, most state legislatures enacted statutes that required that the estates of fathers who died without wills be divided equally among all the offspring. Most American parents applauded these statutes be-

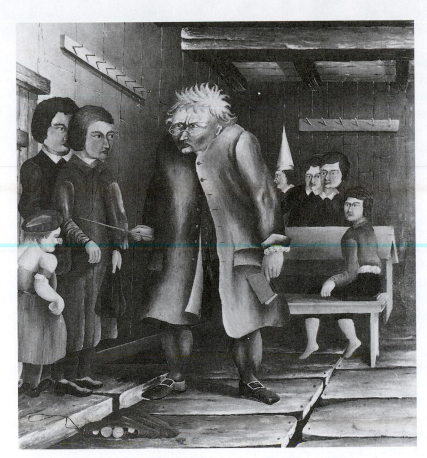

**The Battle over Education**

Here an unknown artist pokes fun at a tyrannical schoolmaster and, indirectly, at the strict approach to child rearing taken by evangelical authors, parents, and teachers. The students' faces reflect the artist's own rationalist outlook. One minister who had been influenced by the Enlightenment suggested that we see in young children's eyes "the first dawn of reason, beaming forth its immortal rays." Copyright The Frick Collection, New York City.

cause they had already begun to treat their children equally and respectfully.

**Two Modes of Parenting** Indeed, many European visitors believed that republican parents gave their children too much respect and freedom. Because of the "general ideas of Liberty and Equality engraved on their hearts," a Polish aristocrat suggested around 1800, American children had "scant respect" for their parents. Several decades later, a British traveler stood dumbfounded as an American father excused his son's "resolute disobedience" with a smile and the remark "A sturdy republican, sir." The traveler guessed that American parents encouraged such independence to prepare youth to "go their own way" in the world.

Permissive child rearing was not universal. Foreign visitors interacted primarily with well-to-do members of Episcopal or Presbyterian churches. Such parents often followed the teachings of rationalist religious writers influenced by John Locke and other Enlightenment thinkers. According to these authors, children were "rational creatures" who should be encouraged to act appropriately by means of advice and praise. The parents' role was to develop their child's conscience, self-discipline, and sense of responsibility. This rationalist method of child rearing was widely adopted by families in the rapidly expanding middle class.

By contrast, many yeomen and tenant farmers, influenced by the Second Great Awakening, raised their children in an authoritarian fashion. Evangelical Baptist and Methodist writers insisted that children were "full of the stains and pollution of sin" and needed strict rules and harsh discipline. Fear was a "useful and necessary principle in family government," John Abbott, a minister, advised parents; a child "should submit to your authority, not to your arguments or persuasions." Abbott told parents to instill humility in children and to teach them to subordinate their personal desires to God's will (see Reading American Pictures, "Changing Middle-Class Families: Assessing the Visual Record," p. 250).

**Debates over Education** Although families provided most moral and intellectual training, independence prompted a greater emphasis on schooling. Bostonian Caleb Bingham, an influential textbook author, called for "an equal distribution of knowledge to make us emphatically a 'republic of

# COMPARING AMERICAN VOICES

# The Trials of Married Life

**A**s the text explains, the ideal American marriage of the early nineteenth century was republican (a contract between equals) and romantic (a match in which mutual love was foremost). Were these ideals attainable, given the social authority of men and the volatility of human passions? Letters, memoirs, and diaries are excellent sources for answering these questions. These selections from the personal writings of a variety of American women offer insights into the new system of marriage and how changes in cultural values intersected with individual lives.

## Emma Hart Willard

### The Danger of High Expectations

Born in Connecticut in 1787, Emma Hart married John Willard in 1809. An early proponent of advanced education for women, she founded female academies in Middlebury, Vermont (1814), and Waterford and Troy, New York (1821). She wrote this letter to her sister, Almira Hart, in 1815.

You think it strange that I should consider a period of happiness as more likely than any other to produce future misery. I know I did not sufficiently explain myself. Those tender and delicious sensations which accompany successful love, while they soothe and soften the mind, diminish its strength to bear or to conquer difficulties. It is the luxury of the soul; and luxury always enervates. . . . This life is a life of vicissitude.

[Suppose] you are secured to each other for life. It will be natural that, at first, he should be much devoted to you; but, after a while, his business must occupy his attention. While absorbed in that he will perhaps neglect some of those little tokens of affection which have become necessary to your happiness. His affairs will sometimes go wrong, . . . and he may sometimes hastily give you a harsh word or a frown.

But where is the use, say you, of diminishing my present enjoyment by such gloomy apprehensions? Its use is this, that, if you enter the marriage state believing such things to be absolutely impossible, if you should meet them, they would come upon you with double force.

The planter's bride, who leaves a numerous and cheerful family in her paternal home, little imagines the change which awaits her in her own retired residence. She dreams of an independent sway over her household, devoted love and unbroken intercourse with her husband, and indeed longs to be released from the eyes of others, that she may dwell only beneath the sunbeam of his. And so it was with me. . . .

There we were together, asking for nothing but each other's presence and love. At length it was necessary for him to tear himself away to superintend his interests. . . . But the period of absence was gradually protracted; then a friend sometimes came home with him, and their talk was of crops and politics, draining the fields and draining the revenue. . . . A growing discomfort began to work upon my mind. I had undefined forebodings; I mused about past days; my views of life became slowly disorganized; my physical powers enfeebled; a nervous excitement followed: I nursed a moody discontent. . . .

If the reign of romance was really waning, I resolved not to chill his noble confidence, but to make a steadier light rise on his affections. . . . This task of self-government was not easy. To repress a harsh answer, to confess a fault . . . in gentle submission, sometimes requires a struggle like life and death; but these . . . efforts are the golden threads with which domestic happiness is woven. . . . How clear is it, then, that woman loses by petulance and recrimination! Her first study must be self-control, almost to hypocrisy. A good wife must smile amid a thousand perplexities.

## Caroline Howard Gilman

### Female Submission in Marriage

Born in Boston in 1794, Caroline Howard married in 1819 and moved to Charleston, South Carolina, with her husband, Samuel Gilman, a Unitarian minister. A novelist, she published *Recollections of a Housekeeper* (1835), a portrait of domestic life in New England, and *Recollections of a Southern Matron* (1838), a fictional account from which this selection is taken.

## Martha Hunter Hitchcock

### Isolation, Unmentionable Sorrows, and Suffering

Martha Hunter Hitchcock married a doctor in the U.S. Army. These excerpts from letters to her cousins Martha and Sarah Hunter describe her emotional dependence on her husband and her unhappy life. The letters are in the collection of the Virginia Historical Society.

To Martha Hunter, 1840:

If I had never married how much of pain, and dissatisfaction, should I have escaped—at all events I should never have known what jealousy is. You must not betray me, dear cousin, for despite all my good resolutions, I find it impossible always to struggle against my nature—the school of indulgence, in which I was educated, was little calculated to teach me, those lessons of forbearance, which I have had to practice so frequently, since my marriage—it is ungrateful in me to murmur, if perchance a little bitter is mingled in my cup of life.

To Sarah Hunter, 1841:

I have lived so long among strangers since my marriage, that when I contrast it with the old warm affection, in which I was nurtured, the contrast is so terrible, that I cannot refrain from weeping at the thought of it—I hope my dear cousin, that yours, will be a happier destiny than mine, in that respect—only think of it! Nearly a year and a half have passed away, since I have seen, a single relation!

To Martha Hunter, 1845:

Uneasiness about [my daughter] Lillie, and very great sorrows of my own, which I cannot commit to paper, have almost weighed me down to the grave; and indeed, without any affectation, I look forward to that, as the only real rest, I shall ever know.

To Martha Hunter, 1846:

Lillie had the scarlet fever, during our visit to Alabama, and she has never recovered from the effects of it—My life is a constant vigil—and there is nothing which wearies mind, and body, so much, as watching a sickly child. . . . All this I have to endure, and may have to suffer more for I know not, what Fate may have in store for me.

## Elizabeth Scott Neblett

# My Seasons of Gloom and Despondency

Elizabeth Scott Neblett lived with her husband and children in Navarro County, Texas. In 1860, she reflected in her diary on her bouts of depression and the difficulties of wives and husbands in understanding each other's inner lives.

It has now been almost eight years since I became a married woman. Eight years of checkered good and ill, and yet thro' all it seems the most of the ill has fallen to my lot, until now my poor weak cowardly heart sighs only for its final resting place, where sorrow grief nor pain can never reach it more.

I feel that I have faithfully discharged my duty towards you and my children, but for this I know that I deserve no credit nor aspire to none; my affection has been my prompter, and the task has proven a labor of love. You have not rightly understood me at all times, and being naturally very hopeful you could in no measure sympathize with me during my seasons of gloom and despondency. . . . But marriage is a lottery and that your draw proved an unfortunate one on your part is not less a subject of regret with me than you. . . .

It is useless to say that during these eight years I have suffered ten times more than you have and ten times more than I can begin to make you conceive of, but of course you can not help the past, nor by knowing my suffering relieve it, but it might induce you to look with more kindness upon [my] faults. . . . The 17th of this month I was 27 years old and I think my face looks older than that, perhaps I'll never see an other birth day and I don't grieve at the idea.

Source: All of the selections are abridged versions of materials in Anya Jabour, ed., *Major Problems in the History of American Families and Children* (Boston: Houghton Mifflin, 2005), 108–113.

## ANALYZING THE EVIDENCE

- What problems do these women share? How might their problems reflect larger social and economic changes in nineteenth-century America?

- Was Emma Willard correct? Did the emotional problems experienced by these women stem, at least in part, from their overly optimistic expectations of love-based marriage? Or was something else the cause of their unhappiness?

- What was Caroline Gilman's advice to wives? Did the other women follow her advice?

- Do these selections suggest that most American women had unfulfilled marriages? Or were these isolated cases? Would you expect to find more records of unhappy marriages than happy ones?

# Changing Middle-Class Families: Assessing the Visual Record

Throughout the text, we have discussed and analyzed American families—white yeomen families, enslaved African American families, and now republican families. These two images allow us to compare two families of similar status: the Cheneys (top), a well-to-do family typical of the colonial era; and the Caverlys (bottom), a nineteenth-century middle-class family. Families being the basic social unit of society, comparing depictions of them allows us to see change over time and understand how shifts in personal relationships alter the nature of society.

## ANALYZING THE EVIDENCE

- Count the number of children in each painting and look closely at their mothers. What impact would multiple pregnancies have on a mother's health? Given the data on birthrates discussed in the text, how many more children is Mrs. Caverly likely to bear? Why might she, like many other white nineteenth-century women, have had fewer children than Mrs. Cheney had?

- How are the children posed in each painting? What do their poses reveal about adults' perceptions of children? In the paintings, is there evidence of change in that thinking from the colonial era to the nineteenth century?

- Though Mrs. Caverly is shown looking toward her husband, there is a Bible on the table next to her; her husband is shown reading a newspaper. What do these clues suggest about women's and men's roles in the 1830s? From your reading of the text, how do these symbolic actions reflect important social and cultural values of the time?

- Whom do you see first when you look at the painting of the Cheneys? Is there a similar visual center in the image of the Caverlys? Notice the differences in the physical settings and in the placement of the family members, and compare the two backgrounds: Why is one plain and gray, and the other decorated and filled with objects? What do the differences tell you about the changing values of the middle class?

**The Cheneys, c. 1795.** National Gallery of Art, Washington, Gift of Edgar Williams and Bernice Chrysler Garbisch.

**The Caverlys, 1836.** Fenimore House Museum, New-York State Historical Association.

**Women's Education**
Even in education-conscious New England, during the colonial era few girls attended free public primary schools for more than a few years. After 1800, as this detail from *Scenes from a Seminary for Young Ladies* (c. 1810–1820) indicates, some girls stayed in school into their teenage years and studied a wide variety of subjects, including geography. Many graduates of these female academies became teachers, a new field of employment for women.   The St. Louis Art Museum, Purchase Funds Given by Decorative Arts Society.

letters.'" Both Thomas Jefferson and Benjamin Rush proposed ambitious schemes for a comprehensive system of primary and secondary schooling, followed by college training for bright young men. They also envisioned a university in which distinguished scholars would lecture on law, medicine, theology, and political economy.

To ordinary citizens, whose teenage children had to work, talk of secondary and college education smacked of elitism. Farmers, artisans, and laborers wanted elementary schools that would instruct their children in the "three Rs": reading, 'riting, and 'rithmetic. In New England, locally funded public schools offered most boys and some girls basic instruction in reading and writing. In other regions, there were few publicly funded schools, and only 25 percent of the boys and perhaps 10 percent of the girls attended private institutions or had personal tutors. Even in New England, only a small percentage of young men and almost no young women went on to grammar school (high school), and less than 1 percent of men attended college. "Let anybody show what advantage the poor man receives from colleges," an anonymous "Old Soldier" wrote to the *Maryland Gazette*. "Why should they support them, unless it is to serve those who are in affluent circumstances, whose children can be spared from labor, and receive the benefits?"

Although many state constitutions encouraged support for education, few legislatures acted until the 1820s. Then a new generation of reformers, primarily merchants and manufacturers, raised educational standards by certifying qualified teachers and appointing statewide superintendents of schools. To encourage self-discipline and individual enterprise in students, the reformers chose textbooks such as *The Life of George Washington* (c. 1800). Its author, Parson Mason Weems,

used examples of events from Washington's life to praise honesty and hard work and to condemn gambling, drinking, and laziness. Believing that patriotic instruction would foster shared cultural ideals, reformers required the study of American history. Thomas Low recalled his days as a New Hampshire schoolboy: "We were taught every day and in every way that ours was the freest, the happiest, and soon to be the greatest and most powerful country of the world."

**Promoting Cultural Independence** Like Caleb Bingham, writer Noah Webster believed that education should raise the nation's intellectual reputation. Asserting that "America must be as independent in *literature* as she is in politics," he called on his fellow citizens to free themselves "from the dependence on foreign opinions and manners, which is fatal to the efforts of genius in this country." Webster's *Dissertation on the English Language* (1789) helpfully defined words according to American usage. With less success, it proposed that words be spelled as they were pronounced, that *labour* (British spelling), for example, be spelled *labur*. Still, Webster's famous "blue-back speller," a compact textbook first published in 1783, sold 60 million copies over the next half-century and served the needs of Americans of all backgrounds. "None of us was 'lowed to see a book," an enslaved African American recalled, "but we gits hold of that Webster's old blue-back speller and we . . . studies [it]."

Despite Webster's efforts, a republican literary culture developed slowly. Ironically, the most successful writer in the new republic was Washington Irving, an elitist-minded Federalist. His whimsical essay and story collections—for example, *Salmagundi* (1807) and *The Sketch Book of Geoffrey Crayon* (1819–1820), which included "Rip Van Winkle" and "The Legend of Sleepy Hollow"—sold well in America and won praise abroad. Frustrated by the immaturity of American cultural life, Irving lived for seventeen years in Europe, reveling in its aristocratic culture and intense intellectuality.

Apart from Irving, no American author was well known in Europe or, indeed, in the United States. "Literature is not yet a distinct profession with us," Thomas Jefferson told an English friend. "Now and then a strong mind arises, and at its intervals from business emits a flash of light. But the first object of young societies is bread and covering." Not until the 1830s and 1840s would American authors achieve a professional identity and make a significant contribution to Western literature (see Chapter 11).

- Did American culture become more democratic— for men and for women—in the early nineteenth century? If so, why? If not, why not?

- How did republican ideas shape parent-child interactions, marriage relationships, and intellectual life?

# Aristocratic Republicanism and Slavery

Republicanism in the South differed significantly from that in the North. Enslaved Africans constituted one-third of the South's population and exposed an enormous contradiction in white Americans' ideology of freedom and equality. "How is it that we hear the loudest yelps for liberty among the drivers of Negroes?" British author Samuel Johnson had chided the American rebels in 1775, a point that some Patriots took to heart. "I wish most sincerely there was not a Slave in the province," Abigail Adams confessed to her husband, John. "It always appeared a most iniquitous Scheme to me—to fight ourselves for what we are daily robbing and plundering from those who have as good a right to freedom as we have."

## The Revolution and Slavery, 1776–1800

In fact, the whites' struggle for independence had raised the prospect of freedom for blacks. As the Revolutionary War began, a black preacher in Georgia told his fellow slaves that King George III "came up with the Book [the Bible], and was about to alter the World, and set the Negroes free." Similar rumors, probably prompted by

royal governor Lord Dunmore's proclamation of 1775 (see Chapter 5), circulated among slaves in Virginia and the Carolinas, prompting thousands of African Americans to flee behind British lines. Two neighbors of Richard Henry Lee, a Virginia Patriot, lost "every slave they had in the world," as did many other planters. In 1781, when the British army evacuated Charleston, more than 6,000 former slaves went with them; another 4,000 left from Savannah. All told, 30,000 blacks may have fled their owners. Hundreds of freed black Loyalists settled permanently in Canada. More than 1,000 others, poorly treated in British Nova Scotia, sought a better life in Sierra Leone, West Africa, a settlement founded by English antislavery organizations.

**Manumission and Gradual Emancipation** | Yet thousands of African Americans supported the Patriot cause. Eager to raise their social status, free blacks in New England volunteered for military service in the First Rhode Island Company and the Massachusetts "Bucks." In Maryland, a significant number of slaves took up arms for the rebels in return for the promise of freedom. Enslaved Virginians struck informal bargains with their Patriot owners, trading loyalty in wartime for the hope of liberty. In 1782, the Virginia assembly passed a **manumission** act, which allowed individual owners to free their slaves; within a decade, planters had released 10,000 slaves.

Quakers took the lead in condemning slavery. Beginning in the 1750s, Quaker evangelist John Woolman urged Friends to free their slaves, and many did so. Rapidly growing evangelical churches, especially Methodists and Baptists, initially advocated emancipation and admitted both enslaved and free blacks to their congregations. In 1784, a conference of Virginia Methodists declared that slavery was "contrary to the Golden Law of God on which hang all the Law and Prophets."

Enlightenment philosophy challenged the widespread belief among whites that Africans were inherently inferior to Europeans. John Locke had argued that ideas were not innate but stemmed from a person's experiences in the world. Accordingly, Enlightenment-influenced Americans suggested that the debased condition of blacks reflected their oppressive captivity: "A state of slavery has a mighty tendency to shrink and contract the minds of men." Defying popular opinion, Quaker philanthropist Anthony Benezet declared that African Americans were "as capable of improvement as White People" and funded a Philadelphia school for their education.

These religious and intellectual currents encouraged legal change. In 1784, judicial rulings abolished

**Republican Families . . . and Servants**
Around 1828, an unidentified artist painted this York, Pennsylvania, family with an African American servant. The husband and wife embody a republican companionate-style marriage (the artist gives equal emphasis to the wife and the husband) in which the mother takes the leading role in rearing and educating the children. Befitting its upper-middle-class status, the family employs an African American woman as a domestic servant and nanny—common occupations among free black women of the time.   Courtesy of The St. Louis Art Museum.

slavery in Massachusetts; over the next twenty years, every state north of Delaware enacted gradual emancipation legislation (Map 8.2). These laws recognized white property rights by requiring slaves to buy their freedom by years—even decades—of additional labor. For example, the New York Emancipation Act of 1799 allowed slavery to continue until 1828 and freed slave children only at the age of twenty-five. Subsequent legislation allowed enslaved people to marry and live where they pleased. Still, as late as 1810, almost 30,000 blacks in the northern states—nearly one-fourth of the African Americans living there—were still enslaved. Those blacks who were free faced severe prejudice from whites

who feared job competition and racial melding. Even as Massachusetts ended slavery, the legislature reenacted an old law that prohibited whites from marrying blacks, mulattos, or Indians.

**Slavery Defended** | The contradiction in American republican ideology between liberty and property rights was greatest in the South, where enslaved African Americans represented a huge financial investment. Some Chesapeake tobacco planters, moved by evangelical religion or an oversupply of workers, manumitted their slaves or allowed them to buy their freedom by working as artisans or laborers. Such measures gradually brought freedom to one-third of the African Americans in Maryland. Farther south, slavery remained ascendant. When the Virginia legislature allowed manumission in 1782, planters feared it would lead to emancipation. Hundreds of slave owners signed petitions demanding protection of "the most valuable and indispensible Article of our Property, our Slaves," and legislators forbade further manumissions. Following the lead of Thomas Jefferson, who owned more than a hundred slaves, they now argued that slavery was a "necessary evil" required to maintain white supremacy and the luxurious planter lifestyle. In North Carolina, legislators condemned private Quaker manumissions as "highly criminal and reprehensible." And the slave-hungry rice- and cotton-growing states of South Carolina and Georgia reopened the Atlantic slave trade. Between 1790 and 1808, merchants in Charleston and Savannah imported about 115,000 Africans, selling thousands to French and American planters in Louisiana (Table 8.1).

All debate in the South over emancipation ended in 1800, when Virginia authorities thwarted an uprising planned by Gabriel Prosser, an enslaved artisan, and hanged him and thirty of his followers. "Liberty and equality have brought the evil upon us," a letter to the *Virginia Herald* proclaimed, denouncing such doctrines as "dangerous and extremely wicked." To preserve their privileged social position, southern leaders redefined republicanism by limiting its principles of individual liberty and legal equality to whites, creating what historians call a *herrenvolk* ("master race") republic.

## The North and South Grow Apart

European visitors to the United States agreed that North and South had distinct characters. A British observer said that New England was home to religious "fanaticism" but that "the lower orders of citizens" there had "a better education, [and were] more intelligent, and

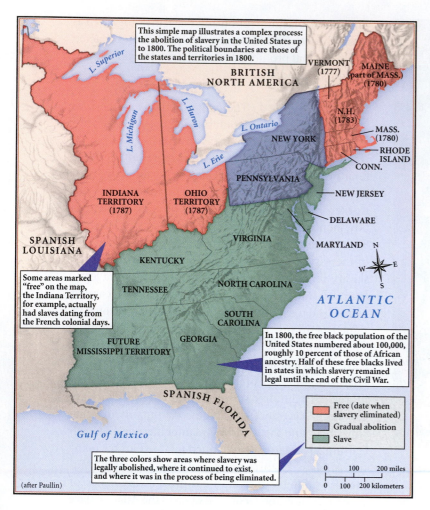

This simple map illustrates a complex process: the abolition of slavery in the United States up to 1800. The political boundaries are those of the states and territories in 1800.

Some areas marked "free" on the map, the Indiana Territory, for example, actually had slaves dating from the French colonial days.

In 1800, the free black population of the United States numbered about 100,000, roughly 10 percent of those of African ancestry. Half of these free blacks lived in states in which slavery remained legal until the end of the Civil War.

The three colors show areas where slavery was legally abolished, where it continued to exist, and where it was in the process of being eliminated.

(after Paullin)

| | |
|---|---|
| 🟥 | Free (date when slavery eliminated) |
| 🟦 | Gradual abolition |
| 🟩 | Slave |

0    100    200 miles
0    100    200 kilometers

**MAP 8.2**

## The Status of Slavery, 1800

In 1775, racial slavery was legal in all of the British colonies in North America. By the time the states achieved their independence in 1783, most African Americans in New England had also been freed. By 1800, all of the states north of Maryland had provided for the gradual abolition of slavery, but the process was slow and not completed until the 1830s. Some slave owners in the Chesapeake region also manumitted their slaves, leaving only the whites of the Lower South firmly committed to racial bondage.

**TABLE 8.1**

### African Slaves Imported into the United States, by Region of Departure and Ethnicity, 1776–1809

| Region of Departure | Ethnicity | Number | Percentage of Imported Slaves |
|---|---|---|---|
| Senegambia | Mandinka, Fulbe, Serer, Jola, Wolof, Bambara | 8,000 | 7 |
| Sierra Leone | Vai, Mende, Kpelle, Kru | 18,300 | 16 |
| Gold Coast | Ashanti, Fanti | 15,000 | 13 |
| Bight of Benin, Bight of Biafra | Ibo, Ibibio | 5,700 | 5 |
| West Central Africa | Kongo, Tio, Matamba | 37,800 | 33 |
| Southeast Africa | Unknown | 1,100 | 1 |
| Other or unknown | | 28,700 | 25 |
| **Total** | | **114,600** | **100** |

NOTE: Recent research suggests that 433,000 enslaved Africans arrived in British North America and the United States between 1607 and 1820: 33,200 before 1700; 278,400 from 1700 to 1775; 114,600 from 1776 to 1809; and 7,000 from 1810 to 1819. The numbers are extrapolated from known voyages of 65,000 Africans. Ethnicity should be considered very tentative because slaves from many regions left from the same port and because the regional and ethnic origins of 28,700 slaves (25 percent) are not known.

SOURCE: Aaron S. Fogleman, "From Slaves, Convicts, and Servants to Free Passengers: The Transformation of Immigration in the Era of the American Revolution," *Journal of American History* 85 (June 1998), table 1 and table A.6.

**Aristocratic Republicanism in South Carolina**

The money that paid for Drayton Hall came originally from raising cattle in South Carolina for sale in the West Indies. At his death in 1717, Thomas Drayton left an estate that included 1,300 cattle and 46 slaves (both Native American and African). His third son, John (1715–1779), used his inheritance to buy slaves, and create a rice-growing plantation along the Ashley River. The design of the home he erected on the site, Drayton Hall (built 1738–1742), was inspired by Andrea Palladio, the Italian Renaissance architect who celebrated the concepts of classical Roman proportion and decoration in his widely read *The Four Books of Architecture* (1516).   Photo courtesy of Drayton Hall.

better informed" than those he met in the South. "The state of poverty in which a great number of white people live in Virginia" surprised the Marquis de Chastellux. Other visitors to the South commented on the rude manners, heavy drinking, and weak work ethic of its residents. White tenants and smallholding farmers seemed only to have a "passion for gaming at the billiard table, a cock-fight or cards," and planters squandered their wealth on extravagant lifestyles while their slaves endured bitter poverty.

Some southerners worried that human bondage corrupted their society by encouraging ignorance and poverty among whites. A South Carolina merchant observed, "Where there are Negroes a White Man despises to work, saying what, will you have me a Slave and work like a Negroe?" Meanwhile, wealthy planters wanted a compliant labor force content with the drudgery of agricultural work. Consequently, they trained most of their slaves as field hands, allowing only a few to learn the arts of the blacksmith, carpenter, or bricklayer. Able

to hire tutors for their own children, well-to-do planters did little to provide other whites with elementary schooling. In 1800, elected officials in Essex County, Virginia, spent about 25 cents per person for local government, including schools, while their counterparts in Acton, Massachusetts, allocated about $1 per person. This difference in support for education mattered: By the 1820s, nearly all native-born men and women in New England could read and write, while more than one-third of white southerners could not.

**Slavery and National Politics**   As the northern states ended human bondage, the South's commitment to slavery became a political issue. At the Philadelphia convention in 1787, northern delegates had reluctantly accepted clauses allowing slave imports for twenty years and guaranteeing the return of fugitive slaves (see Chapter 6). Seeking even more protection for their "peculiar institution," southerners in the new national legislature won approval of

James Madison's resolution that "Congress have no authority to interfere in the emancipation of slaves, or in the treatment of them within any of the States."

Nonetheless, slavery remained a contested issue. The black slave revolt in Haiti brought 6,000 white and free mulatto refugees to the United States in 1793, and their stories of atrocities frightened American slave owners. Meanwhile, northern politicians assailed the British impressment of American sailors as just "as oppressive and tyrannical as the slave trade" and demanded the end of both. When Congress outlawed the Atlantic slave trade in 1808, some northern representatives demanded an end to the trade in slaves between states. In response, southern leaders defended their labor system. "A large majority of people in the Southern states do not consider slavery as even an evil," declared one congressman. The South's political clout—its domination of the presidency and the Senate—ensured that the national government would protect slavery. American diplomats vigorously demanded compensation for slaves freed by British troops during the War of 1812, and Congress enacted legislation upholding slavery in the District of Columbia.

**African Americans Speak Out**    Heartened by the end of the Atlantic slave trade, black abolitionists spoke out. In speeches and pamphlets Henry Sipkins and Henry Johnson condemned slavery as "relentless tyranny." In their view, slavery—not freedom—was the central legacy of American colonial and revolutionary history. For inspiration, they looked to the Haitian Revolution, which overthrew slavery; for collective support, they joined together in secret societies, such as Prince Hall's African Lodge of Freemasons in Boston and affiliated lodges in other northern cities. Along with white antislavery advocates, black abolitionists hoped that slavery would die out naturally as the tobacco economy declined. Their hopes quickly faded as the cotton boom increased the demand for slaves, and Louisiana (1812), Mississippi (1817), and Alabama (1819) joined the Union with state constitutions that permitted slavery.

These events prompted a group of influential white Americans to found the American Colonization Society in 1817. According to Henry Clay—a society member, Speaker of the House of Representatives, and a slave owner—racial bondage had placed his state of Kentucky "in the rear of our neighbors . . . in the state of agriculture, the progress of manufactures, the advance of improvement, and the general prosperity of society." Slaves had to be freed, Clay and other colonizationists argued, and sent back to Africa. Clay feared that

emancipation without removal would prompt racial chaos—"a civil war that would end in the extermination or subjugation of the one race or the other." But few planters responded to the society's plea and, from among the 1.5 million African Americans in the United States in 1820, it resettled only about 6,000 in Liberia, the society's colony on the west coast of Africa.

Most free blacks strongly opposed such colonization schemes. As Bishop Richard Allen of the African Methodist Episcopal Church put it, "[T]his land which we have watered with our tears and our blood is now our mother country." Allen spoke from experience. Born into slavery in Philadelphia in 1760 and sold to a farmer in Delaware, Allen grew up in bondage. In 1777, Freeborn Garretson, an itinerant preacher, converted Allen to Methodism and convinced Allen's owner that on Judgment Day, slaveholders would be "weighted in the balance, and . . . found wanting." Allowed to buy his freedom, Allen enlisted in the Methodist cause, becoming a "licensed exhorter" and then a regular minister in Philadelphia. In 1795, Allen formed a separate black congregation, the Bethel Church; in 1816, he became the first bishop of a new denomination: the African Methodist Episcopal Church. Two years later, 3,000 African Americans met in Allen's church to condemn colonization and to claim American citizenship. Sounding the principles of democratic republicanism, they vowed to defy racial prejudice and advance in American society using "those opportunities . . . which the Constitution and the laws allow to all."

## The Missouri Crisis, 1819–1821

The failure of colonization set the stage for a major battle over slavery. In 1818, Congressman Nathaniel Macon of North Carolina warned slave owners that radical members of the "bible and peace societies" hoped to use the national government to raise "the question of emancipation." And so they did. When Missouri applied for admission to the Union in 1819 with a constitution that allowed slavery, Congressman James Tallmadge of New York intervened: He would support Missouri's constitution only if it banned the entry of new slaves and provided for the emancipation of existing bondspeople. Missouri whites rejected Tallmadge's proposals, and the northern majority in the House of Representatives blocked the territory's admission.

White southerners were horrified. "It is believed by some, & feared by others," Alabama senator John Walker reported from Washington, that Tallmadge's amendment was "merely the entering wedge and that it points already to a total emancipation of the blacks." Mis-

**Reverend Richard Allen and the African Methodist Episcopal Church**

One of the best-known African Americans in the early republic, Richard Allen founded a separate congregation for Philadelphia's black Methodists, the Bethel Church. Working with other ministers in 1816, he created the first independent black religious domination in the United States—the African Methodist Episcopal (AME) Church—and became its first bishop.    Library of Congress. / The Mount Bethel African Methodist Episcopal Church.

sissippi congressman Christopher Rankin accused his northern colleagues of coercion: "You conduct us to an awful precipice, and hold us over it." To underline their commitment to slavery, southerners used their power in the Senate — where they held half the seats — to withhold statehood from Maine, which was seeking to separate itself from Massachusetts.

**Constitutional Issues**    In the ensuing debate, southerners advanced three constitutional arguments. First, invoking the principle of "equal rights," they argued that Congress could not impose conditions on Missouri that it had not imposed on other territories seeking statehood. Second, they maintained that the Constitution guaranteed a state's sovereignty with respect to its internal affairs and domestic institutions, such as slavery and marriage. Finally, they insisted that Congress had no authority to infringe on the property rights of individual slaveholders. In their view, the United States was a confederation of semi-sovereign states with limited national powers. Beyond that, southern leaders reaffirmed their commitment to human bondage. Abandoning the argument that slavery was a "necessary evil," they now invoked religion to champion it as a "positive good." "Christ himself gave a sanction to slavery," declared Senator William Smith of South Carolina. "If it be offensive and sinful to own slaves," a prominent Mississippi Methodist added, "I wish someone would just put his finger on the place in Holy Writ."

Controversy raged in Congress and the press for two years before Henry Clay put together a series of political agreements known collectively as the Missouri Compromise. Faced with unwavering southern opposition to Tallmadge's amendment, a group of northern congressmen deserted the antislavery coalition. They accepted a deal that allowed Maine to enter the Union as a free state in 1820 and Missouri to follow as a slave state in 1821. This agreement preserved a balance in the Senate between North and South and set a precedent for future admissions to the Union. For their part, southern senators accepted the prohibition of slavery in the vast northern section of the Louisiana Purchase, the lands north of latitude 36°30' outside the boundaries of Missouri (Map 8.3).

As they had in the Philadelphia Convention of 1787, white politicians had preserved the Union by compromising over slavery. Now the task was more difficult. The delegates in Philadelphia had resolved their sectional differences in two months; it took Congress two years to work out the Missouri Compromise, which even then did not command universal support. "If we yield now, beware," the *Richmond Enquirer* warned as southern congressmen agreed to exclude slavery from most of the Louisiana Purchase. "What is a *territorial* restriction to-day becomes a *state* restriction tomorrow." The fates of the western lands, enslaved blacks, and the Union itself were now inextricably intertwined, raising the specter of civil war and the end of the American republican experiment. As the aging Thomas

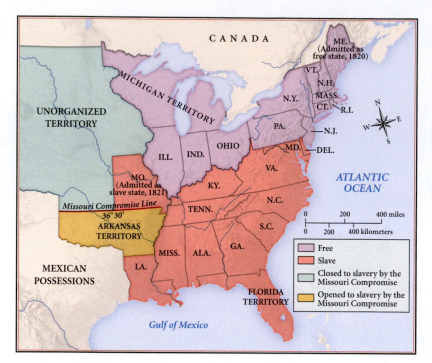

**MAP 8.3**

**The Missouri Compromise, 1820–1821**

The Missouri Compromise resolved for a generation the issue of slavery in the lands of the Louisiana Purchase. The agreement prohibited slavery north of the Missouri Compromise line (36°30' north latitude), with the exception of the state of Missouri. To maintain an equal number of senators from free and slave states in the U.S. Congress, the compromise provided for the nearly simultaneous admission to the Union of Missouri and Maine.

Jefferson exclaimed during the Missouri crisis, "This momentous question, like a fire-bell in the night, awakened and filled me with terror."

- **How did the aristocratic republicanism of the South differ from the democratic republicanism of the North?**

- **What compromises over slavery did the members of Congress make to settle the Missouri crisis? Who benefited most from the agreement?**

# Protestant Christianity as a Social Force

Throughout the colonial era, religion played a role in American life that was significant but not overwhelming. Then, beginning around 1790, religious revivals planted the values of Protestant Christianity deep in the national character and gave a spiritual dimension to American republicanism. These revivals especially changed the lives of blacks and of women. Thousands of African Americans became Baptists and Methodists and created a powerful institution: the black Christian church. Evangelical Christianity also gave rise to new public roles for white women, especially in the North, and set in motion long-lasting movements for social reform.

## A Republican Religious Order

The demand for greater liberty unleashed by the republican revolution of 1776 forced American lawmakers to devise new relationships between church and state. Previously, only the Quaker- and Baptist-controlled governments of Pennsylvania and Rhode Island had rejected a legally **established church** and compulsory religious taxes. Then, a convergence of factors—Enlightenment principles, wartime needs, and Baptist ideology—eliminated most state support for religion and encouraged voluntary church membership.

**Religious Freedom** | Events in Virginia revealed the dynamics of change. In 1776, James Madison and George Mason advanced Enlightenment ideas of religious toleration as they sought to persuade the state's constitutional convention to guarantee all Christians the "free exercise of religion." This measure would end the privileged legal status of the Anglican Church. The delegates, many of whom were Anglicans, accepted this provision in part because they needed the support of Presbyterians and Baptists in the independence struggle. The Baptists also opposed the use of taxes to support religion, even their own. They convinced lawmakers to reject a tax bill (which was supported by George Washington and Patrick Henry) that would have funded all Christian churches. Instead, in 1786, the Virginia legislature enacted Thomas Jefferson's Bill for Establishing Religious Freedom, which made all churches equal in the eyes of the law and granted direct financial support to none.

Elsewhere, the old order of a single established church crumbled away. In New York and New Jersey, the sheer number of denominations—Episcopalian, Presbyterian, Dutch Reformed, Lutheran, and Quaker, among others—prevented lawmakers from agreeing on an established church or compulsory religious taxes. Congregationalism remained the official church in the New England states until the 1830s, but members of other denominations could now pay taxes to their own churches.

**Church-State Relations** | Few influential Americans wanted a complete separation of church and state because they believed that religious institutions promoted morality and respect for governmental authority. "Pure religion and civil liberty are inseparable companions," a group of North Carolinians advised their minister. "It is your particular duty to enlighten mankind with the unerring principles of truth and justice, the main props of all civil government." Accepting this premise, most state governments indirectly supported churches by exempting their property and ministers from taxation.

Freedom of conscience also came with sharp cultural limits. In Virginia, Jefferson's Bill for Establishing Religious Freedom prohibited religious requirements for holding public office, but other states discriminated against those who were not Protestant Christians. The North Carolina Constitution of 1776 disqualified from public employment any citizen "who shall deny the being of God, or the Truth of the Protestant Religion, or the Divine Authority of the Old or New Testament." No Catholics or Jews need apply. New Hampshire's constitution contained a similar provision until 1868.

Americans influenced by Enlightenment deism and by evangelical Protestantism condemned these religious restrictions. Jefferson, Franklin, and other American intellectuals maintained that God had given humans the power of reason so that they could determine moral truths for themselves. To protect society from "ecclesiastical tyranny," they demanded complete freedom of conscience. Many evangelical Protestants also demanded religious liberty; their goal was to protect their churches from an oppressive government. Isaac Backus, a New England minister, warned Baptists not to incorporate their churches or accept public funds because that might lead to state control. In Connecticut, a devout Congregationalist welcomed "voluntarism," the uncoerced funding of churches by their members; it allowed the laity to control the clergy, he said, thereby supporting self-government and "the principles of republicanism."

## The Second Great Awakening

Overshadowing such debates, a decades-long series of religious revivals—the Second Great Awakening—made the United States a genuinely Christian society. The most successful churches were those that preached spiritual equality and governed themselves democratically. Because bishops and priests controlled it, the Roman Catholic Church attracted few Protestants, who preferred Luther's doctrine of the priesthood of all believers. When some Catholics in Norfolk, Virginia, proposed in 1818 that "all Pastors should be appointed by

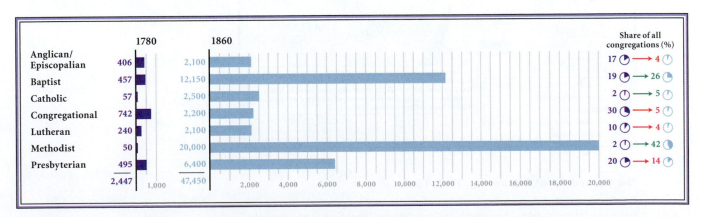

**FIGURE 8.1**

**Number of Church Congregations by Denomination, 1780 and 1860**

The growth of evangelical churches, Methodist and Baptist, transformed American Christianity during the first half of the nineteenth century. Also noteworthy was the surge in the number of Catholic congregations, the result of immigration from Ireland and Germany after 1830.

their respective congregations," they were denounced by church authorities. Nor did the Catholic Church appeal to the unchurched—the great number of Americans who simply ignored religious institutions. Likewise, few Americans joined the Protestant Episcopal Church, the successor to the Church of England, because wealthy lay members dominated many congregations and it, too, had a hierarchy of bishops (Figure 8.1). The Presbyterian Church attracted more adherents, in part because its churches elected laymen to the synods, the congresses that determined doctrine and practice.

**Evangelical Churches** | Evangelical Methodist and Baptist churches were by far the most popular. The Baptists boasted a republican church organization, with self-governing congregations.

Both Baptists and Methodists developed an egalitarian religious culture marked by communal singing and emotional services (see Voices from Abroad, "Frances Trollope: A Camp Meeting in Indiana," p. 261). These denominations came to the fore in the 1790s, as they evangelized the cities and the backcountry of New England. A new sect of Universalists, who repudiated the Calvinist doctrine of predestination and preached universal salvation, also gained tens of thousands of converts, especially in Massachusetts and northern New England. After 1800, enthusiastic camp meetings swept the frontier regions of South Carolina, Tennessee, Ohio, and Kentucky. The largest gathering, at Cane Ridge in Kentucky in 1801, lasted for nine electrifying days and nights and attracted almost 20,000 people (Map 8.4). With these revivals, Baptist and Methodist preachers

**MAP 8.4**

**The Second Great Awakening, 1790–1860**

The Second Great Awakening lasted for decades and invigorated churches in every part of the nation. The revivals in Kentucky and New York State, though, were particularly influential. As thousands of farm families migrated to the west, they carried with them the religious excitement generated by the Cane Ridge revival in Kentucky in 1801. And, between 1825 and 1835, the area along the Erie Canal in New York witnessed such fervor that it came to be known as the Burned-over District.

## Frances Trollope
# A Camp Meeting in Indiana

**F**rances Trollope, a successful English author and the mother of novelist Anthony Trollope, lived for a time in Cincinnati, where she owned a bazaar that sold imported goods from Europe. Unsuccessful as a storekeeper, she won great acclaim as a social commentator. Her critical-minded study, *Domestic Manners of the Americans* (1832), was a bestseller in Europe and the United States. Here Trollope provides a vivid description of a revivalist meeting in Indiana around 1830.

The prospect of passing a night in the back-woods of Indiana was by no means agreeable, but I screwed my courage to the proper pitch, determined to see with my own eyes, and hear with my own ears, what a camp meeting really was. . . . We reached the ground about an hour before midnight, and the approach to it was highly picturesque. The spot chosen was the verge of an unbroken forest, where a space of about twenty acres appeared to have been partially cleared for the purpose. Tents of different sizes were pitched very near together in a circle round the cleared space. . . .

Four high frames, constructed in the form of altars, were placed at the four corners of the inclosure; on these were supported layers of earth and sod, on which burned immense fires of blazing pine-wood. On one side a rude platform was erected to accommodate the preachers, fifteen of whom attended this meeting, and with very short intervals for necessary refreshment and private devotion, preached in rotation, day and night, from Tuesday to Saturday.

When we arrived, the preachers were silent; but we heard issuing from nearly every tent mingled sounds of praying, preaching, singing, and lamentation. . . . The floor [of one tent] was covered with straw, which round the sides was heaped in masses, that might serve as seats, but which at that moment were used to support the heads and arms of the close-packed circle of men and women who knelt on the floor.

Out of about thirty persons thus placed, perhaps half a dozen were men. One of these [was] a handsome-looking youth of eighteen or twenty. . . . His arm was encircling the neck of a young girl who knelt beside him, with her hair hanging dishevelled upon her shoulders, and her features working with the most violent agitation; soon after they both fell forward on the straw, as if unable to endure in any other attitude the burning eloquence of a tall grim figure in black, who, standing erect in the center, was uttering with incredible vehemence an oration that seemed to hover between praying and preaching; his arms hung stiff and immoveable by his side, and he looked like an ill-constructed machine, set in action by a movement so violent as to threaten its own destruction, so jerkingly, painfully, yet rapidly, did his words tumble out; the kneeling circle ceasing not to call, in every variety of tone, on the name of Jesus. . . .

One tent was occupied exclusively by Negroes. They were all full-dressed, and looked exactly as if they were performing a scene on a stage. One woman wore a dress of pink gauze trimmed with silver lace; another was dressed in pale yellow silk; one or two had splendid turbans; and all wore a profusion of ornaments. The men were in snow-white pantaloons, with gay colored linen jackets. One of these, a youth of coal–black comeliness, was preaching with the most violent gesticulations. . . .

At midnight, a horn sounded through the camp . . . to call the people from private to public worship; and we presently saw them flocking from all sides to the front of the preacher's stand. . . . about two thousand persons. . . .

One of the preachers began in a low nasal tone, and, like all other Methodist preachers, assured us of the enormous depravity of man. . . . Above a hundred persons, nearly all females, came forward, uttering howlings and groans so terrible that I shall never cease to shudder when I recall them. They appeared to drag each other forward, and on the word being given, "let us pray," they fell on their knees . . . and they were soon all lying on the ground in an indescribable confusion of heads and legs.

Source: Frances Trollope, *Domestic Manners of the Americans* (London: Whittaker, Treacher, 1832), 139–142.

### ANALYZING THE EVIDENCE

- What is Trollope's opinion about what she witnessed? Did she see what she expected to see? What clues does the narrative provide?

- Who attended the camp meeting? How would you explain the different dress and deportment of the African American believers?

- How did the worship at this nineteenth-century camp meeting differ from that in a New England Congregational church in the eighteenth century? How do you explain the difference?

- How does Trollope characterize the theology of the Methodist preacher? How did it differ from that of earlier Calvinists who believed in predestination?

reshaped the spiritual landscape throughout the South. Offering a powerful emotional message and the promise of religious fellowship, revivalists attracted both unchurched individuals and pious families searching for social ties as they migrated to new communities.

The Second Great Awakening transformed the denominational makeup of American religion. The important churches of the colonial period — the Congregationalists, Episcopalians, and Quakers — grew slowly through natural increase, while Methodist and Baptist churches expanded spectacularly by winning converts. In rural areas, their preachers followed a circuit, "riding a hardy pony or horse" with their "Bible, hymn-book, and Discipline" to visit existing congregations on a regular schedule. They began new churches by searching out devout families, bringing them together for worship, and then appointing lay elders to lead the congregation and enforce moral discipline. Soon, they were the largest denominations.

To attract converts, evangelical ministers copied the "practical preaching" techniques of George Whitefield and other eighteenth-century revivalists (see Chapter 4). They spoke from memory in plain language and often with a flamboyant style and theatrical gestures. "Preach without papers," advised one minister. "[S]eem earnest & serious; & you will be listened to with Patience, & Wonder."

In the South, evangelical religion was initially a disruptive force because many ministers spoke of spiritual equality and criticized slavery. Husbands and planters grew angry when their wives became more assertive and when blacks joined their congregations. To retain white men in their churches, Methodist and Baptist preachers gradually adapted their religious message to justify the authority of yeomen patriarchs and slave-owning planters. One Baptist minister declared that a man was naturally at "the head of the woman," and a Methodist conference proclaimed "that a Christian slave must be submissive, faithful, and obedient."

**Black Christianity**   Other evangelists persuaded planters to spread Protestant Christianity among their African American slaves. During the eighteenth century, most blacks had maintained the religious practices of their African homelands, giving homage to African gods and spirits or practicing Islam. "At the time I first went to Carolina," remembered Charles Ball, a former slave, "there were a great many African slaves in the country. . . . Many of them believed there were several gods [and] I knew several . . . Mohamedans [Muslims]." Beginning in the mid-1780s, Protestant evangelists converted hundreds of African Americans along the James River in Virginia and throughout the Chesapeake and the Carolinas.

Subsequently, black Christians adapted Protestant teachings to their own needs. They generally ignored the doctrines of original sin and Calvinist predestination as well as biblical passages that encouraged unthinking obedience to authority. Some African American converts envisioned the Christian God as a warrior who had liberated the Jews. Their own "cause was similar to the Israelites," preacher Martin Prosser told his fellow slaves as he and his brother Gabriel plotted rebellion in Virginia in 1800. "I have read in my Bible where God says, if we worship him, . . . five of you shall conquer a hundred and a hundred of you a hundred thousand of our enemies." Confident of a special relationship with God, Christian slaves prepared themselves spiritually for emancipation, the first step in their journey to the Promised Land.

## Religion and Reform

Influenced by republican ideology, many whites also rejected the Calvinists' emphasis on human depravity and weakness; instead, they celebrated human reason and free will. In New England, many educated Congregationalists discarded the mysterious concept of the Trinity — Father, Son, and Holy Spirit — and, taking the name Unitarians, worshipped a "united" God and promoted rational thought. "The ultimate reliance of a human being is, and must be, on his own mind," argued William Ellery Channing, a famous Unitarian minister. A children's catechism conveyed the denomination's optimistic message: "If I am good, God will love me, and make me happy."

Other New England Congregationalists softened Calvinist doctrines. Lyman Beecher, the preeminent Congregationalist clergyman of the early nineteenth century, accepted the traditional Christian belief that people had a natural tendency to sin; but, rejecting predestination, he affirmed the capacity of all men and women to choose God. By embracing the doctrine of free will, Beecher testified to the growing belief that people could shape their destiny. "Free Will" Baptists held similar views.

**Benevolence and Reform**   Reflecting this optimism, Reverend Samuel Hopkins linked individual salvation to religious benevolence — the practice of disinterested virtue. As the Presbyterian minister John Rodgers explained, fortunate individuals who had received God's grace had a duty "to dole out charity to their poorer brothers and sisters." Heed-

**Women in the Awakening**

The Second Great Awakening was a pivotal moment in the history of American women. In this detail from *Religious Camp Meeting*, painted by J. Maze Burbank in 1839, all the preachers are men, but women fill the audience and form the majority of those visibly "awakened." By transforming millions of women into devout Christians, the revival movement filled Protestant churches with dedicated workers, teachers, and morality-minded mothers. When tens of thousands of these women also joined movements for temperance, abolition, and women's rights, they spurred a great wave of social reform.   Old Dartmouth Historical Society/New Bedford Whaling Museum, New Bedford, Massachusetts.

ing this message, pious merchants in New York City founded the Humane Society and other charitable organizations. Devout women aided their ministers by holding prayer meetings and providing material aid to members and potential converts. By the 1820s, so many Protestant men and women had embraced benevolent reform that conservative church leaders warned them not to neglect spiritual matters. Still, improving society was a key element of the new religious sensibility. Said Lydia Maria Child, a devout Christian social reformer: "The only true church organization [is] when

heads and hearts unite in working for the welfare of the human-race."

By the 1820s, Protestant Christians were well positioned to undertake that task. Unlike the First Great Awakening, which split churches into warring factions, the Second Great Awakening fostered cooperation among denominations. Religious leaders founded five interdenominational societies: the American Education Society (1815), the Bible Society (1816), the Sunday School Union (1824), the Tract Society (1825), and the Home Missionary Society (1826). Based in eastern cities—New York, Boston, and Philadelphia—these societies ministered to the nation, dispatching hundreds of missionaries to the West and distributing thousands of religious pamphlets.

Increasingly, Protestant ministers and laypeople saw themselves as part of a united religious movement that could change the course of history. "I want to see our state evangelized," declared a churchgoer near the Erie Canal (where the fires of revivalism were so hot that it was known as the "Burned-over District"): "Suppose the great State of New York in all its physical, political, moral, commercial, and pecuniary resources should come over to the Lord's side. Why it would turn the scale and could convert the world. I shall have no rest until it is done."

Because the Second Great Awakening aroused such enthusiasm, religion became an important new force in political life. On July 4, 1827, Reverend Ezra Stiles Ely called on the members of the Seventh Presbyterian Church in Philadelphia to begin a "Christian party in politics." Ely's sermon that day, "The Duty of Christian Freemen to Elect Christian Rulers," proclaimed a religious goal for the American republic—an objective that Thomas Jefferson and John Adams would have found strange and troubling. The two founders had both died precisely a year before, on July 4, 1826, the fiftieth anniversary of the Declaration of Independence. They had gone to their graves believing that America's mission was to spread political republicanism. In contrast, Ely urged the United States to become an evangelical Christian nation dedicated to religious conversion at home and abroad: "All our rulers ought in their official capacity to serve the Lord Jesus Christ." Similar calls for a union of church and state would again be made by evangelical Christians during the Third (1880–1900) and Fourth (1970–present) Great Awakenings.

## Women's New Religious Roles

The upsurge in religious enthusiasm prompted women to demonstrate their piety and even to found new sects. Mother Ann Lee organized the Shakers in Britain and then, in 1774, migrated to America, where she attracted numerous recruits; by the 1820s, Shaker communities dotted the American countryside from New Hampshire to Indiana. Jemima Wilkinson, a young Quaker woman in Rhode Island, found inspiration by reading George Whitefield's sermons. After experiencing a vision that she had died and been reincarnated as Christ, Wilkinson declared herself the "Publick Universal Friend," dressed in masculine attire, and preached a new gospel. Her

**Mrs. Juliann Jane Tillman, 1844**

In 1837, Mrs. Tillman explained in a newspaper article that she "was strangely wrought upon" and "went to God" for help. Soon, "what seemed to be an angel made his sudden appearance, and in his hand was a roll . . . on which was written, 'Thee I have chosen to preach my gospel without delay.'" After much anguish and more supernatural visitations, Mrs. Tillman overcame strong personal doubts – and the equally strong opposition of male ministers and laity – and began to preach in the African Methodist Episcopal Church. Library of Congress Prints and Photographs Division. Reproduction Number: LC-USZ62-54596 (2-21).

teachings blended the Calvinist warning of "a lost and guilty, gossiping, dying World" with Quaker-inspired plain dress, pacifism, and abolitionism. Wilkinson's charisma initially won scores of converts, but her radical lifestyle and ambiguous gender aroused hostility, and her sect dwindled away.

**A Growing Public Presence**   The few female-led sects had less impact than the activities of thousands of women in mainstream churches. For example, women in New Hampshire managed more than fifty local "cent" societies to raise funds for the Society for Promoting Christian Knowledge, New York City women founded the Society for the Relief of Poor Widows, and young Quaker women in Philadelphia ran the Society for the Free Instruction of African Females.

Women took charge of religious and charitable enterprises because they were excluded from other public roles and because of their numbers. After 1800, more than 70 percent of the members of New England Congregational churches were women. The predominance of women prompted Congregational ministers to end traditional gender-segregated prayer meetings, and evangelical Methodist and Baptist preachers actively promoted mixed-sex praying. "Our prayer meetings have been one of the greatest means of the conversion of souls," a minister in central New York reported in the 1820s, "especially those in which brothers and sisters have prayed together."

Far from leading to sexual promiscuity, as critics feared, mixing men and women promoted greater self-discipline. Believing in female virtue, many young women and the men who courted them now postponed sexual intercourse until after marriage — previously a much rarer form of self-restraint. In Hingham, Massachusetts, and many other New England towns, more than 30 percent of the women who married between 1750 and 1800 bore a child within eight months of their wedding day; by the 1820s, the rate had dropped to 15 percent.

As women claimed more spiritual authority, men tried to curb their power. In the North as in the South, evangelical Baptist churches that had once advocated spiritual equality now prevented women from voting on church matters or offering public testimonies of faith. These activities, one layman declared, were "directly opposite to the apostolic command in [Corinthians] xiv, 34, 35, 'Let your women learn to keep silence in the churches.'" Another man claimed, "Women have a different *calling*. That they *be chaste, keepers at home* is the Apostle's direction." But such injunctions merely changed the focus of women's religious activism. Embracing the idea of republican motherhood, Christian women throughout the United States founded maternal associations to encourage proper child rearing. By the 1820s, *Mother's Magazine* and other newsletters, widely read in hundreds of small towns and villages, were giving women a sense of shared purpose and identity.

Religious activism also advanced female education, as churches sponsored academies where girls from the middling classes received intellectual and moral instruction. Emma Willard, the first American advocate of higher education for women, opened the Middlebury Female Seminary in Vermont in 1814 and later founded girls' academies in Waterford and Troy, New York. Beginning in the 1820s, women educated in these seminaries and academies displaced men as public-school teachers, in part because they accepted lower pay

than men would. Female schoolteachers earned from $12 to $14 a month with room and board — less than a farm laborer. But as schoolteachers, women had an acknowledged place in public life — a status that previously had been beyond their reach.

Just as the ideology of democratic republicanism had expanded voting rights and the political influence of ordinary white men in the North, so the values of Christian republicanism had bolstered the public authority of middling women. The Second Great Awakening made Americans a fervently Protestant people. Along with the values of republicanism and capitalism, this religious impulse formed the core of an emerging national identity.

- **Which American churches were the most republican in their institutions and ideology?**

- **Why did Protestant Christianity and Protestant women emerge as forces for social change?**

## SUMMARY

Like all important ideologies, republicanism has many facets. We have explored three of them in this chapter. We saw how state legislatures created capitalist commonwealths in which governments actively supported private businesses that contributed to the public welfare. This republican-inspired policy of state mercantilism remained dominant until the 1840s, when it was replaced by classical liberal doctrines.

We also saw how republicanism influenced social and family values. The principle of legal equality encouraged social mobility among white men and prompted men and women to seek companionate marriages. Republicanism likewise encouraged parents to provide their children with equal inheritances and to allow them to choose their marriage partners. In the South, republican doctrines of liberty and equality coexisted uneasily with slavery and ultimately applied only to the white population.

Finally, we observed the complex interaction of republicanism and religion. Stirred by republican principles, many citizens joined democratic and egalitarian denominations, particularly Methodist and Baptist churches. Inspired by "benevolent" ideas and the enthusiastic preachers of the Second Great Awakening, many women devoted their energies to religious purposes and social reform organizations. The result of all these initiatives — in economic policy, social relations, and religious institutions — was the creation of a distinctive American republican culture.

# CHAPTER REVIEW QUESTIONS

- Explain how the republican ideas of the Revolutionary era shaped American society and culture in the late eighteenth and early nineteenth centuries. What regional differences in the social development of republicanism emerged? How can we account for these differences?

- Trace the relationship between America's republican culture and the surge of evangelism called the Second Great Awakening. In what ways are the goals of the two movements similar? How are they different?

- The text argues that a distinct American identity had begun to emerge by 1820. How would you describe this identity? What were the forces that helped create unity? And what were the points of contention?

# FOR FURTHER EXPLORATION

Jeffrey L. Pasley et al., eds., *Beyond the Founders* (2004), shows how ordinary citizens promoted a democratic polity. Rosemarie Zagarri, *Revolutionary Backlash* (2007), demonstrates its limited inclusion of women. Jack Larkin, *The Reshaping of Everyday Life, 1790–1840* (1997), and **memorialhall.mass.edu/collection/index.html** explore changes in material culture. See also Patrick Griffin, *American Leviathan: Empire, Nation, and Revolutionary Frontier* (2007).

Nancy Cott analyzes cultural shifts in *Public Vows: A History of Marriage and the Nation* (2000). For family life on the Maine frontier, see Laurel Thatcher Ulrich, *A Midwife's Tale: The Life of Martha Ballard* (1990), as well as the related Web sites, **www.pbs.org/wgbh/ amex/midwife** and **www.DoHistory.org**.

Jan Lewis's *The Pursuit of Happiness* (1983) discusses the paternalistic slave-owning gentry of the Upper South; James David Miller, *South by Southwest: Planter Emigration and Identity in the Slave South* (2002), explores their move to the Mississippi Valley. For slavery, consult Douglas R. Egerton, *Gabriel's Rebellion: The Virginia Slave Conspiracies of 1800 and 1802* (1995); Randolph Ferguson Scully, *Religion and the Making of Nat Turner's Virginia* (2008); and the Web site at **www .disc.wisc.edu/slavedata**.

In *The Democratization of American Christianity* (1987), Nathan Hatch traces the impact of evangelical Protestantism. Other fine studies include Mark A. Noll, *America's God: From Jonathan Edwards to Abraham Lincoln* (2003), and Bernard Weisberger, *They Gathered at the River* (1958).

## TEST YOUR KNOWLEDGE

To assess your command of the material in this chapter, see the Online Study Guide at **bedfordstmartins.com/henretta**.

For Web sites, images, and documents related to topics and places in this chapter, visit **bedfordstmartins.com/makehistory**.

## TIMELINE

| | |
|---|---|
| **1782** | St. Jean de Crèvecoeur publishes *Letters from an American Farmer*<br>Virginia manumission law (repealed 1792) |
| **1783** | Noah Webster publishes his "blue-back" speller |
| **1784** | Slavery abolished in Massachusetts; other northern states begin gradual emancipation |
| **1787** | Benjamin Rush writes *Thoughts on Female Education* |
| **1790s** | States grant corporations charters and special privileges<br>Private companies build roads and canals to facilitate trade<br>Merchants develop rural outwork system<br>Chesapeake blacks adopt Protestant beliefs<br>Parents limit family size as farms shrink<br>Second Great Awakening expands church membership |
| **1791** | Congress charters First Bank of the United States |
| **1792** | Mary Wollstonecraft, *A Vindication of the Rights of Woman* |
| **1795** | Massachusetts Mill Dam Act |
| **1800** | Gabriel Prosser plots slave rebellion in Virginia |
| **1800s** | Rise of sentimentalism and of companionate marriages<br>Women's religious activism; founding of female academies<br>Religious benevolence sparks social reform |
| **1801** | Cane Ridge revival in Kentucky |
| **1807** | New Jersey ends voting by propertied women |
| **1816** | Congress charters Second Bank of the United States |
| **1817** | Prominent whites create American Colonization Society |
| **1819** | Plummeting agricultural prices set off financial panic |
| **1819–1821** | Missouri Compromise |
| **1820s** | States reform public education<br>Women become schoolteachers |

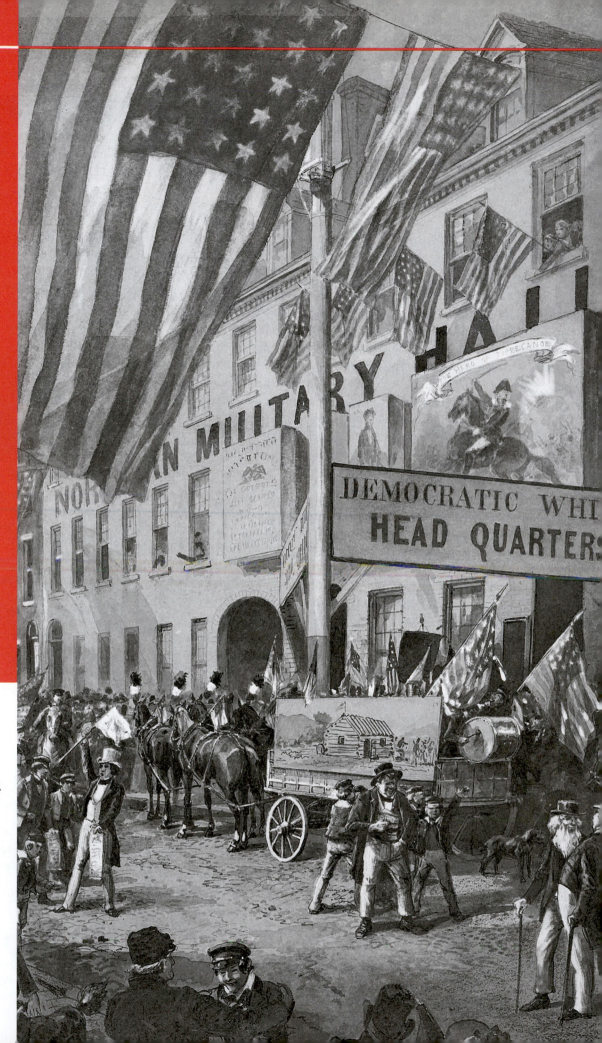

# PART

# 3

# OVERLAPPING REVOLUTIONS, 1820–1860

"The procession was nearly a mile long . . . [and] the democrats marched in good order to the glare of torches," a French visitor remarked in amazement during the election of 1832. "These scenes belong to history . . . the wondrous epic of the coming of democracy." As we will see in Part 3, history was being made in many ways between 1820 and 1850. A series of overlapping revolutions were transforming American society. One was political: the creation of a genuinely democratic polity. The second was economic: In 1820, the United States was predominantly an agricultural nation; by 1850, the northern states boasted one of the world's foremost industrial economies. Third, there was far-reaching social and cultural change, including the Second Great Awakening, great movements of social reform, and the advent of a complex intellectual culture. These transformations affected every aspect of life in the North and Midwest and brought important changes in the South as well. Here, in brief, is an outline of that story.

**ECONOMY**

**Advances in . . . production, transportation, and trade transformed the nation's economy**

## Making an Economic Revolution

Impressive advances in industrial production, transportation, and trade transformed the nation's economy. Factory owners used high-speed machines and a new system of labor discipline to boost the output of goods dramatically. Manufacturers produced 5 percent of the country's wealth in 1820 and nearly 20 percent by 1850. And thanks to enterprising merchants and entrepreneurs, who developed a network of canals and an integrated system of markets, they now sold their products throughout an expanding nation.

**SOCIETY**

**The new economy created a class-based society**

## Forging a New Class Structure

The new economy created a class-based society in the North and Midwest. A wealthy elite of merchants, manufacturers, bankers, and entrepreneurs rose to the top of the social order. To maintain social stability, they adopted a paternalistic program of benevolent reform. But an expanding urban middle class created a distinct material and religious culture and lent support to movements for radical social reform. A mass of propertyless workers, including impoverished immigrants from Germany and Ireland, joined enslaved African Americans at the bottom of the social order. The growth of large cities, primarily in the North, fostered the emergence of new urban and popular cultures. Meanwhile, slavery expanded in numbers and scope as planters created new plantations as far south and west as Texas.

## GOVERNMENT

... party competition engaged the energies of the electorate

## CULTURE

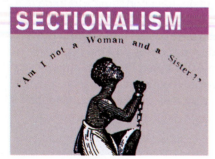

... a series of reform movements ... swept across America

## SECTIONALISM

Slavery ... increasingly divided the nation

## Creating a Democratic Polity

The rapid growth of white male suffrage and political parties sparked the creation of a competitive and responsive democratic polity. Interest groups created various short-lived organizations, notably the Anti-Masonic, Workingmen's, and Liberty parties. Farmers, workers, and entrepreneurs persuaded governments to improve transportation, shorten workdays, and award valuable corporate charters. Catholic immigrants from Ireland and Germany entered local and state politics to protect their cultures from restrictive legislation advocated by Protestant nativists and reformers.

With Andrew Jackson at its head, the Democratic Party led a political and constitutional revolution that cut government aid to financiers, merchants, and corporations. To contend with the Democrats, the Whig Party devised a competing program that stressed economic development, moral reform, and individual social mobility. This party competition engaged the energies of the electorate and helped to unify a fragmented social order.

## Reforming People and Institutions

Between 1820 and 1850, a series of reform movements, many with religious roots and goals, swept across America. Ministers and pious church members embarked upon a program of Benevolent Reform, preaching the gospel of temperance, Sunday observance, prison reform, and many other causes. A few Americans pursued their social dreams in utopian communities, but most reformers worked within the existing society. Then, abolitionists and women's rights activists demanded radical social changes: the immediate end of slavery and the overthrow of the patriarchal legal order. However, southern planters increasingly defended slavery as a "positive good" and restated their commitment to a society based on white supremacy and forced labor.

## Compromising over Slavery

The economic revolution and social reform sharpened sectional divisions: The North developed into an urban industrial society based on free labor, whereas the South remained a rural agricultural society dependent on slavery. Beginning in the 1820s, the two sections fought over economic policy. Northern manufacturers, workers, and farmers won protective tariffs, which southern planters bitterly opposed. Eventually, there was a sectional compromise, as the North accepted tariff reductions. The sections clashed again over the expansion of slavery into Missouri and once again political leaders devised a compromise solution. But slavery—and the social and economic differences it symbolized—increasingly divided the nation.

The economic and cultural transformation of the North and, to a lesser extent, of the Midwest made those regions increasingly different from the South. And the democratic political revolution that affected all sections injected greater volatility and potential for conflict into the political system.

# OVERLAPPING REVOLUTIONS, 1820–1860

| | ECONOMY | SOCIETY | GOVERNMENT | CULTURE | SECTIONALISM |
|---|---|---|---|---|---|
| **1820** | • Waltham textile factory opens (1814)<br>• Erie Canal completed (1825)<br>• Market economy expands nationwide<br>• Cotton belt emerges in South | • Business class develops<br>• Rural women and girls recruited as factory workers<br>• Mechanics form craft unions<br>• Waged work increases | • Spread of universal white male suffrage<br>• Rise of Andrew Jackson and Democratic Party<br>• Anti-Masonic Party rises and declines | • American Colonization Society (1817)<br>• Benevolent reform movements<br>• Revivalist Charles G. Finney<br>• Emerson and transcendentalism | • Missouri crisis and compromise (1819–1821)<br>• David Walker's *Appeal . . . to the Colored Citizens of the World* (1829)<br>• Domestic slave trade moves African Americans west |
| **1830** | • Protective tariffs (1828, 1832) trigger nullification crisis<br>• Boom in cotton output<br>• Panic of 1837<br>• U.S. textiles compete with British<br>• Canal systems link eastern United States | • Charles G. Finney leads revivals<br>• Depression (1837–1843) shatters labor movement<br>• New urban popular culture appears | • Indian Removal Act (1830)<br>• Whig Party forms (1834)<br>• Second Party System emerges<br>• Jackson destroys Second Bank and expands executive power | • Joseph Smith founds Mormonism<br>• Temperance crusade expands<br>• Middle-class culture spreads<br>• Female Moral Reform Society (1834) | • Ordinance of Nullification (1832) and Force Bill (1833)<br>• W. L. Garrison forms American Anti-Slavery Society (1833)<br>• Texas independence |
| **1840** | • Irish immigrants join labor force<br>• *Commonwealth v. Hunt* (1842) assists unions, but workers remain "servants"<br>• Machine tool industry expands | • Working-class districts emerge in cities<br>• Irish and German inflow sparks nativist movement | • Log cabin campaign (1840) mobilizes voters<br>• Tyler's policies disrupt Whig agenda | • Fourierist and other communal settlements founded<br>• Mormons resettle in Utah<br>• Seneca Falls women's convention (1848) | • Slavery defended as a "positive good"<br>• Anti-Slavery Liberty Party (1840)<br>• Abolitionist movement splinters |
| **1850** | • Cincinnati emerges as hog processing center<br>• McCormick, Deere, and other manufacturers set up in Midwest<br>• Severe financial panic shakes economy (1857) | • Immigrants replace women in textile industry<br>• Free labor ideology justifies growing inequality<br>• New York City leads urban growth | • Ethnocultural issues shape politics<br>• Conflict over polygamy in Utah Territory<br>• Laws expand property rights of married women | • Minstrelsy rules popular culture<br>• Public education expands with women as teachers | • Majority of enslaved African Americans live in Deep South<br>• South remains rural and agricultural; North urbanizes and industrializes |

ART IS THE HANDMAID OF HUMAN GOOD. · LOWELL ·

## CHAPTER 9

# Economic Transformation, 1820–1860

**In 1804**, life turned grim for eleven-year-old Chauncey Jerome of Connecticut. His father died suddenly, and Jerome faced indentured servitude on a nearby farm. Knowing that few farmers "would treat a poor boy like a human being," Jerome bought out his indenture by making dials for clocks and then worked as a clockmaker for Eli Terry. A manufacturing wizard, Terry used water power to drive precision saws and woodworking lathes. Soon his shop was turning out thousands of tall case clocks with wooden works. Then, in 1816, Terry patented an enormously popular desk clock with brass parts; his business turned Litchfield, Connecticut, into the clock-making center of the United States. In 1816, Jerome set up his own clock factory. By organizing work more efficiently and using new machines that made interchangeable metal parts, he drove down the price of a simple clock from $20 to $5 and then to less than $2. By the 1840s, he was selling his clocks in England, the hub of the Industrial Revolution; two decades later, his workers were turning out 200,000 clocks a year, clear testimony to American industrial enterprise. By 1860, the United States was not only the world's leading exporter of cotton and wheat but also the third-ranked manufacturing nation behind Britain and France.

"Business is the very soul of an American: the fountain of all human felicity," author Francis Grund observed shortly after arriving from Europe. "It is as if all America were but one gigantic workshop, over the entrance of which there is the blazing inscription, 'No admission here, except on business.'" Stimulated by the entrepreneurial culture of early nineteenth-century America, thousands of artisan-inventors like Chauncey Jerome and thousands of merchants propelled the country into a new economic era. Two great changes defined that era: the **Industrial Revolution** (the growth and mechanization of industry) and the **Market Revolution** (the expansion and integration of markets).

Not all Americans embraced the new ethic of enterprise, and many did not share in the new prosperity. The increase in manufacturing, commerce, and finance created a class-divided society that challenged the founders' vision of an agricultural republic with few distinctions of wealth. As the philosopher Ralph Waldo Emerson warned in 1839: "The invasion of Nature by Trade with its Money, its Credit, its Steam, [and] its Railroad threatens to . . . establish a new, universal Monarchy."

**Technology Celebrated**

Artists joined manufacturers in praising the new industrial age. In this 1836 painting of the city seal of Lowell, Massachusetts, a cornucopia (horn of plenty) spreads its bounty over the symbols of the city's economic wealth. The artist implies that the bales of raw cotton in the foreground will be transformed in the water-powered textile factories into smooth cloth, for shipment to far-flung markets via the new railroad system. The image of technologically driven prosperity was deceptive. Two years earlier, 2,000 women textile workers had gone on strike in Lowell, claiming that their wages failed to provide a decent standard of living. Private Collection/Picture Research Consultants & Archives.

# The American Industrial Revolution

Industrialization came to the United States between 1790 and 1860, as merchants and manufacturers reorganized work routines, built factories, and exploited an ever-wider range of natural resources. Thanks to **mass production**, goods that once had been luxury items became part of everyday life (Figure 9.1). The rapid construction of turnpikes, canals, and railroads by state governments and private entrepreneurs, working together in the Commonwealth System (see Chapter 8), allowed manufactures to be sold throughout the land.

## The Division of Labor and the Factory

The increase of production stemmed initially from changes in the organization of work. Consider the shoe industry: Traditionally, New England shoemakers had turned leather hides into finished shoes and boots in small wooden shacks called "ten-footers," where they worked at their own pace. During the 1820s and 1830s, merchants in Lynn, Massachusetts, undermined the businesses of these independent artisans by introducing an outwork system and a **division of labor**. The merchants hired semiskilled journeymen and set them up in large shops cutting leather into soles and uppers. They sent out the upper sections to dozens of rural

Massachusetts towns, where women binders sewed in fabric linings. The manufacturers then had other journeymen attach the uppers to the soles and return the shoes to the central shop for inspection, packing, and sale. The new system turned employers into powerful "shoe bosses" and eroded workers' wages and independence. But the expansion of shoe production created jobs, and the division of labor both increased output and cut prices.

For products not suited to the outwork system, manufacturers created the modern **factory**, which concentrated production under one roof. For example, in the 1830s, Cincinnati merchants built large slaughterhouses that processed thousands of hogs every month. The technology remained simple: A system of overhead rails moved the hog carcasses past workers. The division of labor made the difference. One worker split the animals, another removed the organs, and others trimmed the carcasses into pieces. Packers then stuffed the pork into barrels and pickled it to prevent spoilage. Reported journalist and landscape architect Frederick Law Olmsted:

> We entered an immense low-ceiling room and followed a vista of dead swine, upon their backs, their paws stretching mutely toward heaven. Walking down to the vanishing point, we found there a sort of human chopping-machine where the hogs were converted into commercial pork. . . . Plump falls the hog upon the table, chop, chop; chop, chop; chop, chop,

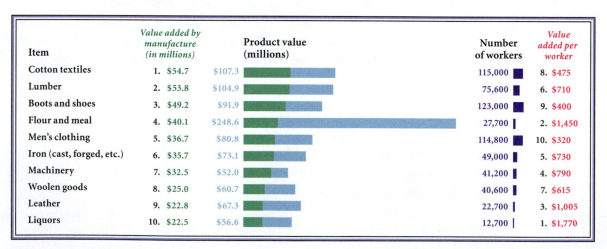

| Item | Value added by manufacture (in millions) | Product value (millions) | | Number of workers | Value added per worker |
|---|---|---|---|---|---|
| Cotton textiles | 1. $54.7 | $107.3 | | 115,000 | 8. $475 |
| Lumber | 2. $53.8 | $104.9 | | 75,600 | 6. $710 |
| Boots and shoes | 3. $49.2 | $91.9 | | 123,000 | 9. $400 |
| Flour and meal | 4. $40.1 | $248.6 | | 27,700 | 2. $1,450 |
| Men's clothing | 5. $36.7 | $80.8 | | 114,800 | 10. $320 |
| Iron (cast, forged, etc.) | 6. $35.7 | $73.1 | | 49,000 | 5. $730 |
| Machinery | 7. $32.5 | $52.0 | | 41,200 | 4. $790 |
| Woolen goods | 8. $25.0 | $60.7 | | 40,600 | 7. $615 |
| Leather | 9. $22.8 | $67.3 | | 22,700 | 3. $1,005 |
| Liquors | 10. $22.5 | $56.6 | | 12,700 | 1. $1,770 |

**FIGURE 9.1**

**Leading Branches of Manufacture, 1860**

In 1860, three industries—boots and shoes, cotton textiles, and men's clothing—each employed more than 100,000 workers. However, three other industries with fewer employees—those engaged in the distilling of liquor, the tanning of leather, and the milling of flour—had the highest productivity, with each worker adding more than $1,000 in value to the finished goods. Source: Adapted from Douglass C. North, *Growth and Welfare in the American Past*, 2nd ed. (Paramus, NJ: Prentice Hall, 1974), table 6.1.

## Pork Packing in Cincinnati

The only modern technology in this Cincinnati pork-packing plant was the overhead pulley that carried hog carcasses past the workers. The plant's efficiency came from its organization, a division of labor in which each worker performed a specific task. Plants such as this one pioneered the development of the moving assembly line, which would reach a high level of sophistication in the early twentieth century, in Henry Ford's automobile factories.   Cincinnati Museum Center.

fall the cleavers. . . . We took out our watches and counted thirty-five seconds, from the moment when one hog touched the table until the next occupied its place.

The Cincinnati system was so efficient—with "disassembly" lines processing sixty hogs an hour—that by the 1840s the city was known as "Porkopolis." By 1850, factories were slaughtering 334,000 hogs a year.

Other factories boasted impressive new technology. In the 1780s, Oliver Evans, a prolific Delaware inventor, built a highly automated flour mill driven by waterpower. His machinery lifted the wheat to the top of the mill, cleaned the grain as it fell into hoppers, ground it into flour, and then cooled the flour as it was poured into barrels. Evans's factory, remarked one observer, "was as full of machinery as the case of a watch." It needed only six men to mill 100,000 bushels of wheat

a year—perhaps ten times as much as they could grind in a traditional mill.

By the 1830s, a new "mineral" economy began to emerge. Manufacturers increasingly ran their machinery with coal-burning stationary steam engines rather than with water power. And they now fabricated metal products—iron, brass, and copper—as well as pork, leather, wool, cotton, and other agricultural goods. In Chicago, Cyrus McCormick used power-driven machines to make parts for farm reapers, which workers assembled on a conveyor belt (see Reading American Pictures, "American Technology Dramatically Increases Farm Productivity," p. 276). In Hartford, Connecticut, Samuel Colt built an assembly line to produce his invention, the six-shooter revolver. These advances in technology and factory organization alarmed British observers: "The contriving and making of machinery has become so common in this country . . . [that] it is

# American Technology Dramatically Increases Farm Productivity

A central aspect of the economic transformation of the mid-nineteenth century was the increased productivity brought about by replacing human muscles with power-driven machinery. As factories installed waterwheels and steam engines to provide power to spinning and weaving machines, the output of woolen and cotton cloth increased dramatically. But what impact did machines have on farming, the dominant occupation in the United States at the time? How did farmers' productivity improve?

**Wheat Farming at Bishop Hill, Illinois.** Bishop Hill Historic Site/Illinois Historic Preservation Agency.

**Diagram of McCormick's Reaper from *The Cultivator*, May 1846.** Wisconsin Historical Society.

## ANALYZING THE EVIDENCE

- The picture at the top shows the wheat harvest at Bishop Hill, a religious community founded in Illinois in 1848 by Swedish Pietists. What tools are the men using to cut the wheat? What are the women's tasks? These communalists certainly harvested more wheat than an individual farm family would reap, but did they do it more efficiently?

- Now look at the picture of McCormick's reaper, taken from an advertisement in a farm journal. Using this machine, the farmer and his son could cut as much grain in a day as the seven men with scythes at Bishop Hill (though the farmer would still have to hire workers to collect it). How did the reaper achieve such a dramatic increase in productivity? What costs did it add to the farm budget?

- Look closely at the reaper in the advertisement. What is the purpose of the letters inscribed on each part of the machine? What does this tell you about the standardization of parts that was crucial to the Industrial Revolution? Why do you think the McCormick Company provided this information to potential buyers?

to be feared that American manufacturers will become exporters not only to foreign countries, but even to England."

## The Textile Industry and British Competition

British textile manufacturers were particularly worried about American competition. They persuaded the British government to prohibit the export of textile machinery and the emigration of **mechanics** (skilled craftsmen who invented and improved tools for industry). Lured by the prospect of higher wages, though, thousands of British mechanics disguised themselves as ordinary laborers and sailed to the United States. By 1812, at least three hundred British mechanics worked in the Philadelphia area alone.

Samuel Slater, the most important émigré mechanic, came to America in 1789 after working for Richard Arkwright, who had invented the most advanced British machinery for spinning cotton. A year later, Slater reproduced Arkwright's innovations in merchant Moses Brown's cotton mill in Providence, Rhode Island, beginning the American Industrial Revolution.

In competing with British mills, American manufacturers had the advantage of an abundance of natural resources. The nation's farmers produced huge amounts of cotton and wool, and the fast-flowing rivers that cascaded down from the Appalachian foothills to the Atlantic coastal plain provided a cheap source of energy. From Massachusetts to Delaware, these waterways were soon lined with industrial villages and textile mills as large as 150 feet long, 40 feet wide, and four stories high (Map 9.1).

**American and British Advantages** Still, British producers easily undersold their American competitors. Thanks to cheap transatlantic shipping and low interest rates in Britain, they could import raw cotton from the United States, manufacture it into cloth, and sell it in America at a bargain price. Moreover, thriving British companies could slash prices to drive fledgling American firms out of business. The most important British advantage was cheap labor: Britain had a larger population—about 12.6 million in 1810 compared to 7.3 million Americans—and thousands of landless laborers willing to take low-paying factory jobs. To offset these advantages, American entrepreneurs won help from the federal government: In 1816, 1824, and 1828, Congress passed tariff bills that taxed imported cotton and woolen cloth. But in the 1830s, Congress reduced the tariffs because southern planters, western farmers, and urban consumers demanded access to inexpensive imports.

**MAP 9.1**

### New England's Dominance in Cotton Spinning, 1840

Although the South grew the nation's cotton, it did not process it in the years before the Civil War. Entrepreneurs in Massachusetts and Rhode Island built most of the factories that spun and wove raw cotton into cloth. The new factories made use of the abundant waterpower available in New England and the region's surplus labor force. Initially, factory managers hired young farm women to work the machines; later, they would rely on immigrants from Ireland and the French-speaking province of Quebec in Canada.

**Number of Spindles in Operation, 1840**
- Under 5,000
- 5,000–25,000
- 25,000–100,000
- 100,000–250,000
- 250,000–500,000

**A Textile Operative at Work**

Powered by water or steam driving a system of leather belts, the looms of the mid-nineteenth century wove cloth much faster and with far less effort than traditional treadle-driven handlooms. However, these new looms required constant attention to repair broken threads, reload shuttles, and prevent imperfections. In this rare daguerreotype of 1850, the young, frail-looking operative moves a lever that will tighten the weave, a task she will repeat many times over the course of her twelve-hour workday.    American Textile History Museum.

## Better Machines, Cheaper Workers

American producers used two other strategies to compete with their British rivals. First, they improved on British technology. In 1811, Francis Cabot Lowell, a wealthy Boston merchant, toured British textile mills, secretly making detailed drawings of their power machinery. Paul Moody, an experienced American mechanic, then copied the machines and improved their design. In 1814, Lowell joined with merchants Nathan Appleton and Patrick Tracy Jackson to form the Boston Manufacturing Company. Having raised the staggering sum of $400,000, they built a textile plant in Waltham, Massachusetts — the first American factory to perform all the operations of clothmaking under one roof. Thanks to Moody's improvements, Waltham's power looms operated at higher speeds than British looms and needed fewer workers.

The second strategy was to tap a cheaper source of labor. In the 1820s, the Boston Manufacturing Company recruited thousands of young women from farm families, appealing to the women by providing them with rooms in boardinghouses and with evening lectures and other cultural activities. To reassure parents about their daughters' moral welfare, the mill owners enforced strict curfews, prohibited alcoholic beverages, and required regular church attendance. At Lowell (1822), Chicopee (1823), and other sites in Massachusetts and New Hampshire, the company built new cotton factories that used this labor system, known as the Waltham Plan.

By the early 1830s, more than 40,000 New England women were working in textile mills. As an observer noted, the wages were "more than could be obtained by the hitherto ordinary occupation of housework," the living conditions were better than those in crowded farmhouses, and the women had greater independence. Lucy Larcom became a Lowell textile operative at age eleven to support herself and not be "a trouble or burden or expense" to her widowed mother. Other women operatives used wages to pay off their father's farm mortgages, send brothers to school, or accumulate a marriage dowry for themselves.

Some operatives just had a good time. Susan Brown, who worked as a Lowell weaver for eight months, spent half her earnings on food and lodging and the rest on plays, concerts, lectures, and a two-day excursion to Boston. Like most textile workers, Brown soon tired of the rigors of factory work and the never-ceasing clatter of the machinery, which ran twelve hours a day, six days a week. After she quit, she lived at home for a time and then moved to another mill. Whatever the hardships, waged work gave young women a sense of freedom. "Don't I feel independent!" a woman mill worker wrote to her sister. "The thought that I am living on no one is a happy one indeed to me." The owners of the Boston Manufacturing Company were even happier. By combining tariff protection with improved technology and cheap female labor, they could undersell their British rivals. Their textiles were also cheaper than those made in New York and Pennsylvania, where farmworkers were better paid than in New England and textile wages consequently were higher. Manufacturers in those states garnered profits by using advanced technology to produce higher-quality cloth. Even Thomas Jefferson, the great champion of yeoman farming, was impressed. "Our manufacturers are now very nearly on a footing with those of England," he boasted in 1825.

## American Mechanics and Technological Innovation

By the 1820s, American-born artisans had replaced British immigrants at the cutting edge of technological innovation. Though few mechanics had a formal education, they nevertheless commanded respect as "men professing an ingenious art." In the Philadelphia region, the remarkable Sellars family produced the most important inventors. Samuel Sellars Jr. invented a machine for twisting worsted woolen yarn to give it an especially smooth surface. His son John improved the efficiency of the waterwheels powering the family's sawmills and built a machine to weave wire sieves. John's sons and grandsons ran machine shops that turned out riveted leather fire hoses, papermaking equipment, and eventually locomotives. In 1824, the Sellars family and other mechanics founded the Franklin Institute in Philadelphia. Named after Benjamin Franklin, whom the mechanics admired for his work ethic and scientific accomplishments, the institute published a journal; provided high-school-level instruction in chemistry, mathematics, and mechanical design; and organized exhibits of new products. Craftsmen in Ohio and other states established similar institutes to disseminate technical knowledge and encourage innovation. Between 1820 and 1860, the number of patents issued by the U.S. Patent Office rose from two hundred to four thousand a year.

American craftsmen pioneered in the development of **machine tools**—machines that made parts for other machines. A key innovator was Eli Whitney (1765–1825), the son of a middling New England farm family. At the age of fourteen, Whitney began fashioning nails and knife blades; later, he made women's hatpins. Aspiring to wealth and status, Whitney won admission to Yale College and subsequently worked as a tutor on a Georgia cotton plantation. Using his expertise in making hatpins, he built a simple machine that separated the seeds in a cotton boll from the delicate fibers, work

**Eli Whitney**

Eli Whitney posed for this portrait in the 1820s, when he had achieved prosperity and social standing as the inventor of the cotton gin and other machines. Whitney's success prompted the artist—his young New Haven, Connecticut, neighbor Samuel F. B. Morse—to turn his creative energies from painting to industrial technology. By the 1840s, Morse had devised the first successful commercial telegraph. Yale University Art Gallery/Art Resource, NY.

previously done by hand in a labor-intensive process. Although Whitney patented his cotton engine (or "gin," as it became known), other manufacturers improved on his design and captured the market.

Still seeking his fortune, Whitney decided in 1798 to manufacture military weapons. He eventually designed and built machine tools that could rapidly produce interchangeable musket parts, bringing him the wealth and fame that he had long craved. After Whitney's death in 1825, his partner John H. Hall built an array of metal-working machine tools, such as turret lathes, milling machines, and precision grinders.

Technological innovation now swept through American manufacturing. Mechanics in the textile industry invented lathes, planers, and boring machines that turned out standardized parts for new spinning jennies and weaving looms. Despite being mass-produced, these jennies and looms were precisely made and operated at higher speeds than British equipment. The leading inventor was Richard Garsed: He nearly doubled the

**A New England Mill, 1850**
This five-story woolen mill towers over the small houses of a New England village and assumed an equally dominant role in the lives of its people. As the population grew and farms shrank in size, rural folk took up work as artisans, out-workers, and factory laborers. Courtesy of The George Eastman House International Museum of Photography. All rights reserved.

speed of the power looms in his father's Delaware factory and patented a cam-and-harness device making it possible for damask and other elaborately designed fabrics to be machine-woven. Meanwhile, the mechanics employed by Samuel W. Collins built a machine for pressing and hammering hot metal into dies, or cutting forms. Using this machine, a worker could make three hundred ax heads a day—compared to twelve using traditional methods. In Richmond, Virginia, Welsh- and American-born mechanics at the Tredegar Iron Works produced great quantities of low-cost parts for complicated manufacturing equipment at a rapid rate. As a group of British observers noted admiringly, many American products were made "with machinery applied to almost every process . . . all reduced to an almost perfect system of manufacture."

As mass production spread, the American Industrial Revolution came of age. The sheer volume of output elevated products such as Remington rifles, Singer sewing machines, and Yale locks into household names in the United States and abroad. After winning praise at the Crystal Palace Exhibition in London in 1851—the first major international display of industrial goods—Remington, Singer, and other American firms became multinational businesses, building factories in Great Britain and dominating some European markets. By 1877, the Singer Manufacturing Company controlled 75 percent of the world market for sewing machines.

## Wageworkers and the Labor Movement

As the Industrial Revolution gathered momentum, it changed the nature of work and of workers' lives. From the early to the mid-nineteenth century, many American **craft workers** espoused **artisan republicanism**, an ideology based on liberty and equality. They saw themselves as a group of small-scale producers, equal to one another and free to work for themselves. The poet Walt Whitman summed up their outlook: "Men must be masters, under themselves."

**Free Workers Form Unions**   However, as the outwork and factory systems spread, more and more workers became wage earners who labored under the direction of an employer. Unlike young women, who embraced factory work because it freed them from parental control and domestic service, men bridled at their status as supervised wage workers. To assert their independent status, male wage workers rejected the traditional terms of *master* and *servant*; instead, they used the Dutch word *boss* to refer to their employer. And lowly apprentices refused to allow their masters to control their private (nonwork) lives. Still, as hired hands, apprentices and journeymen received meager wages and had little job security. The artisan-republican ideal, a by-product of the American Revolution, found itself

**Woodworker, c. 1850**

Skilled furniture makers took great pride in their work, which was often intricately designed and beautifully executed. To underline the dignity of his occupation, this woodworker poses in formal dress and proudly displays the tools of his craft. A belief in the value of their labor was an important ingredient of the artisan-republican ideology held by many workers.   Library of Congress.

challenged by the harsh reality of waged work—labor as a commodity—in an industrializing capitalist society.

Some journeymen wage earners worked in carpentry, stonecutting, masonry, and cabinetmaking—traditional crafts that required specialized skills. Their strong sense of identity, or trade consciousness, enabled these workers to form unions and bargain with their master-artisan employers over low wages and long hours, which restricted their family life and educational opportunities. Before 1800, the building trades' workday was twelve hours—6:00 A.M. to 6:00 P.M.—with an hour each for breakfast and lunch. By the 1820s, masters were demanding shorter meal breaks and longer workdays during the summer (when it stayed light longer), while offering the old daily pay rate. In response, 600 carpenters in Boston went on strike in 1825. The Boston protest failed, but by the mid-1830s, many building-trades workers had won a ten-hour workday. In 1840, craft workers in St. Louis secured a ten-hour day, and President Van Buren issued an executive order setting a similar workday for federal workers.

Artisans in other occupations were less successful in preserving their pay and working conditions. As aggressive entrepreneurs and machine technology changed the nature of production, shoemakers, hatters, printers, furniture makers, and weavers faced falling income, unemployment, and loss of status. To avoid the regimentation of factory work, some artisans in these trades moved to small towns or set up specialized shops. In New York City, 800 highly skilled cabinetmakers owned small shops that made fashionable or custom-made furniture. In status and income, they outranked a much larger group of 3,200 semitrained, wage-earning workers—disparagingly called "botches"—who made cheaper factory-produced tables and chairs. The new industrial system had divided the traditional artisan class into self-employed craftsmen and wage-earning workers.

When wage earners banded together to form unions, they faced a legal hurdle: English and American common law branded such organizations as illegal "combinations." As a Philadelphia judge put it, unions were "a government unto themselves" and unlawfully interfered with a "master's" authority over his "servant." Between 1806 and 1847, there were at least twenty-three legal cases accusing unions of "conspiring" to raise wages and thereby injuring employers. In 1835, the New York Supreme Court found that a shoemakers' union had illegally caused "an industrious man" to be "driven out of employment" because he would not join the union. "It is important to the best interests of society that the price of labor be left to regulate itself," the court declared. The following year, clothing manufacturers in New York City agreed to dismiss workers who belonged to the Society of Journeymen Tailors and circulated a list—a so-called **blacklist**—of the society's members.

**Labor Ideology** | Despite such obstacles, journeymen shoemakers founded a mutual benefit society in Lynn, Massachusetts, in 1830, and similar organizations soon appeared in other shoemaking centers. "The division of society into the producing and non-producing classes," the journeymen explained, had made workers like themselves into a mere "commodity." As another group of workers explained, "The capitalist has no other interest in us, than to get as much labor out of us as possible. We are hired men, and hired men, like hired horses, have no souls." Indeed, workers were "slaves in the strictest sense of the word," declared Lowell textile workers. Still, they admitted: "We are not a quarter as bad off as the slaves of the south. . . . They can't vote nor complain and we can." To exert more pressure on their capitalist employers, in

1834, local unions from Boston to Philadelphia formed the National Trades Union, the first regional union of different trades.

Workers found considerable popular support for their cause. When a court in New York City upheld a conspiracy verdict against a tailors' union, tailors circulated handbills warning that the "Freemen of the North are now on a level with the slaves of the South," and a mass meeting of 27,000 people denounced the decision. In 1836, local juries hearing conspiracy cases acquitted shoemakers in Hudson, New York; carpet makers in Thompsonville, Connecticut; and plasterers in Philadelphia. Even when workers were convicted, judges refrained from handing out jail sentences and imposed only light fines; thus, labor organizers were not deterred. Then, in *Commonwealth v. Hunt* (1842), Chief Justice Lemuel Shaw of the Massachusetts Supreme Judicial Court upheld the right of workers to form unions. Shaw's decision overturned common-law precedents by ruling that a union was not an inherently illegal organization and could strike to enforce a **closed-shop** agreement that limited employment to union members. But many judges continued to resist unions by issuing **injunctions** forbidding strikes.

Union leaders took the artisan republicanism of craft workers and expanded it to include wage workers. Arguing that wage earners were becoming "slaves to a monied aristocracy," they condemned the new factory system in which "capital and labor stand opposed." To create a just society in which workers could "live as comfortably as others," they advanced a **labor theory of value**. Under this theory, the price of goods should reflect the labor required to make them, and the income from the goods' sale should go primarily to the producers, not to factory owners, middlemen, or storekeepers. "All who sell ought to have lawful gain," conceded minister Ezra Stiles Ely, but not at the expense of a widowed mother of ten unable to support herself by making "common shirts." Ely added that "the poor who perform the work, ought to receive at least half of that sum which is charged" to the consumer. Union activists agreed. Appealing to the spirit of the American Revolution, which had destroyed the aristocracy of birth, they called for a new revolution to demolish the aristocracy of capital. Union men organized nearly fifty strikes for higher wages in 1836.

Women textile operatives were equally active. Competition in the woolen and cotton textile industries was fierce because the mechanization of production caused output to grow faster than demand. As prices fell, manufacturers' revenues declined. To maintain profits, employers reduced workers' wages and imposed tougher work rules. In 1828, women mill workers in Dover, New Hampshire, struck against new rules and won some relief; six years later, 800 Dover women walked out again, to protest wage cuts. In Lowell, 2,000 women operatives backed a strike by withdrawing their savings from an employer-owned bank. "One of the leaders mounted a pump," the *Boston Transcript* reported, "and made a flaming . . . speech on the rights of women and the iniquities of the 'monied aristocracy.'" When conditions did not improve, young New England women refused to enter the mills. Impoverished Irish (and later French Canadian) immigrants took their places.

By the 1850s, workers in many mechanized industries faced unemployment as the supply of manufactures exceeded the demand for them. In 1857, industrial overproduction coincided with a financial panic sparked by the bankruptcies of several railroads. As the economy went into a recession, unemployment rose to 10 percent and reminded Americans of the social costs of the new—and otherwise very successful—system of industrial production.

- How did American textile manufacturers compete with British manufacturers? How successful were they?

- In what ways did the emerging industrial economy conflict with artisan republicanism? How did wage laborers respond to the new economy?

# The Market Revolution

As American factories and farms turned out more goods, legislators and businessmen created faster and cheaper ways to get those products to consumers. Beginning in the late 1810s, they constructed a massive system of canals and roads that linked the states along the Atlantic coast with the new states in the trans-Appalachian west. This transportation system set in motion both a crucial market revolution and a great migration of people. By 1860, nearly one-third of the nation's citizens lived in the Midwest (the five states carved out of the Northwest Territory—Ohio, Indiana, Illinois, Michigan, and Wisconsin—along with Missouri, Iowa, and Minnesota), where they created both a complex economy and a society that increasingly resembled those of the Northeast.

# The Transportation Revolution Forges Regional Ties

With the Indian peoples in retreat, slave-owning planters from the Lower South settled in Missouri (admitted to the Union in 1821) and pushed on to Arkansas (admitted in 1836). Simultaneously, yeomen families from the Upper South joined migrants from New England and New York in farming the fertile lands of the Great Lakes basin. Once Indiana and Illinois were settled, land-hungry farmers poured into Michigan (1837), Iowa (1846), and Wisconsin (1848) (see Voices from Abroad, "Ernst Stille: German Immigrants in the Midwest," p. 284). To meet the demand for cheap farmsteads, Congress in 1820 reduced the price of federal land from $2.00 an acre to $1.25 — just enough to cover the cost of the survey and sale. For $100, a farmer could buy 80

acres, the minimum required under federal law. By the 1840s, this generous policy had enticed about 5 million people to states and territories west of the Appalachians (Map 9.2).

To link the settler communities, state governments chartered private companies to build toll roads, or turnpikes. In 1806, Congress approved funds for a National Road, constructed of compacted gravel, to tie the Midwest to the seaboard states. The project began in Cumberland in western Maryland in 1811; reached Wheeling, Virginia (now West Virginia), on the Ohio River in 1818; and ended in Vandalia, Illinois, in 1839. The National Road and other interregional highways carried migrants and their heavily loaded wagons westward; along the way, these migrants passed livestock herds heading in the opposite direction, destined for eastern markets.

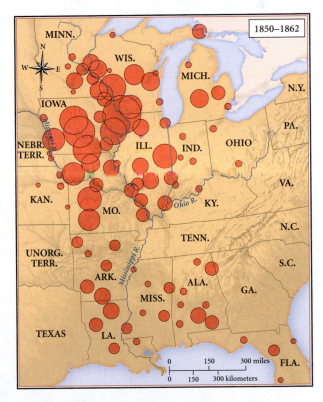

**MAP 9.2**

**Western Land Sales, 1830–1839 and 1850–1862**

The federal government set up local land offices to sell farmsteads to settlers. During the 1830s, the offices sold huge amounts of land in the corn and wheat belt of the Old Northwest (Ohio, Indiana, Illinois, and Michigan) and the cotton belt of the Old Southwest (especially Alabama and Mississippi). By the 1850s, most sales of government land were in the upper Mississippi River Valley (particularly Iowa and Wisconsin). Each circle centers on a government land office and indicates the relative amount of land sold at that office.

All the nations and people I had hitherto passed through resembled[...] own in their manners, customs and lang[...]

# Ernst Stille
# German Immigrants in the Midwest

**B**etween 1830 and 1860, German immigrants flooded into the midwestern states. Among them were twenty-three members of the interrelated Stille and Krumme families from the Prussian province of Westphalia in northwestern Germany. Most of the migrating Stilles and Krummes were younger sons and daughters, who could not hope to inherit farms or make good marriages if they stayed in Westphalia. The letters of Ernst Stille reveal the opportunities—and the hardships—of working life in America during the Market Revolution.

Cincinäti, May 20th 1847

Dearest friends and relatives,

I can't neglect sending a short letter from a foreign country to you in the Fatherland. . . . We went from Bremen to Neu Orleans in 2 months. . . . The trip from Neu Orleans to Cincinäti took 12 days. When I got here there was little work and wage in the city since it was the worst time of the whole year that there is, but I was lucky enough to get a job with Fr. Lutterbeck from Ladbergen [a village near his home in Prussia]. . . . In April all the brickmakers started to work again, many Germans work this trade and earn a good wage and I set to work at this too and earn a dollar a day, of that I have to pay 7 dollars a month for board and washing. . . . We make 8,500 bricks a day and it's hard work but when we start at 4 o'clock in the morning we can be finished by 3 o'clock, if I can stay healthy I will keep working here since if you're healthy and can stand the work, it pays the best.

The only people who are really happy here are those who were used to work in Germany and with toil and great pains could hardly earn their daily bread. When people like that come here, even if they don't have any money, they can manage, they rent a room and the husband goes to work, earns his dollar a day and so he can live well and happily, with a wife and children. But a lot of people come over here who were well off in Germany but were enticed to leave their fatherland by boastful and imprudent letters from their friends or children and thought they could become rich in America, this deceives a lot of people, since what can they do here, if they stay in the city they can only earn their bread at hard and unaccustomed labor? If they want to live in the country and don't have enough money to buy a piece of land that is cleared and has a house then they have to settle in the wild bush and have to work very hard to clear the trees out of the way so they can sow and plant. . . .

Here in Cincinati I know a lot of people who have made it by working hard, like Ernst Lots for example he does very well he also owns a brickyard and earns good money. . . .

Cincinäti, July 10th 1848

At the beginning of April, I started working for Ernst Lots in the brickyard. . . . In the winter no one can work at this trade because of the snow and ice, then there's a huge number of idle people. The main work in the winter is with fat livestock, brought in from the country in large herds, on the outer edge of the city there are large buildings where about 1000 a day are slaughtered and cleaned, then they're brought into the city where they are cut up and salted and put in barrels that's how they're sent from here to other countries. This is a pretty hard and dirty job, that's why most people would rather do nothing for ¼ year than do this, but if you want to put up with this you can earn 1 to 1½ dollars a day.

I also want to let you know that I got married on the 4th of May of this year, to Heinriette Dickmans, the daughter of one of Dieckman's tenants in Leeden [another village in Prussia]. She is 20 years old, left on the same day from Bremerhafen as we went on board but she went via Baltimore. I didn't know her before, neither in Germany nor here, but I got to know her this spring through her uncle Rudolph Expel from Lienen, a good friend of mine who also works for Ernst Lots, who is his son-in-law.

Source: Walter D. Kamphoefner, Wolfgang Helbid, and Ulrike Sommer, eds., *News from the Land of Freedom: German Immigrants Write Home*, trans. Susan Carter Vogel (Ithaca, N.Y.: Cornell University Press, 1991), 83–87.

## ANALYZING THE EVIDENCE

- What does it suggest about the immigrant experience that so many people from a cluster of villages in Prussia ended up in Cincinnati, Ohio? Is that common to the immigrant experience?

- What is Ernst Stille's opinion about what it takes to be successful in America? What may have determined whether he achieved his dream of owning a farm?

- Would Stille's letters encourage other Germans to come to Ohio? Why or why not?

**The Erie Canal**

This pastoral view of the Erie Canal near Lockport, New York, painted by artist John William Hill, only hints at this waterway's profound impact on American life. Without the canal, the town in the background would not exist and farmers such as the man in the foreground would only have local markets for their cattle and grain. By 1860, the success of the Erie Canal had resulted in the construction of a vast system of canals. This infrastructure was as important to the nation as the railroad network of the late nineteenth century and the interstate highway and airport transportation systems of the late twentieth century.
© Bettmann/Corbis

**Canals and Steamboats Shrink Distance** Even on well-built gravel roads, overland travel was slow and expensive. To carry people, crops, and manufactures to and from the Midwest, public money and private businesses developed a water-borne transportation system of unprecedented size, complexity, and cost. The key event was the New York legislature's 1817 decision to build the Erie Canal, a 364-mile waterway to connect the Hudson River and Lake Erie. At the time, the longest artificial waterway in the United States was just 28 miles long—a reflection of the huge capital cost of canals and the lack of American engineering expertise. But New York's ambitious project had three things working in its favor: the vigorous support of New York City's merchants, who wanted access to western markets; the backing of New York's governor, De Witt Clinton, who persuaded the legislature to finance the waterway from tax revenues, tolls, and bond sales to foreign investors; and the relatively gentle terrain west of Albany. Even so, the task was enormous. Workers—many of them Irish immigrants—had to dig out millions of cubic yards of soil, quarry thousands of tons of rock to build the huge locks that raised and lowered the boats, and construct vast reservoirs to ensure a steady supply of water.

The first great engineering project in American history, the Erie Canal altered the ecology of an entire region. As farming communities and market towns sprang up along the waterway, settlers cut down millions of trees to provide wood for houses and barns and to open the land for growing crops and grazing animals. Cows and sheep foraged in pastures that had recently been forests occupied by deer and bears, and spring rains caused massive erosion of the denuded landscape.

Whatever its environmental consequences, the Erie Canal was an instant economic success. The first 75-mile section opened in 1819 and quickly yielded enough revenue to repay its construction cost. When workers finished the canal in 1825, a 40-foot-wide ribbon of water stretched from Buffalo, on the eastern shore of Lake Erie, to Albany, where it joined the Hudson River for the 150-mile trip to New York City. The canal's water "must be the most fertilizing of all fluids," suggested novelist Nathaniel Hawthorne, "for it causes towns with their masses of brick and stone, their churches and theaters, their business and hubbub, their luxury and refinement, their gay dames and polished citizens, to spring up."

The Erie Canal brought prosperity to the farmers of central and western New York and the entire Great Lakes basin. Northeastern manufacturers shipped clothing, boots, and agricultural equipment to farm families; in return, farmers sent grain, cattle, and hogs as well as raw materials (leather, wool, and hemp, for example) to eastern cities and foreign markets. One-hundred-ton freight barges, each pulled by two horses, moved along the canal at a steady 30 miles a day, cutting transportation costs and accelerating the flow of goods. In 1818, the mills in Rochester, New York, processed 26,000 barrels of flour for export east; ten years later, their output soared to 200,000 barrels; and by 1840, it was at 500,000 barrels.

The spectacular benefits of the Erie Canal prompted a national canal boom. Civic and business leaders in Philadelphia and Baltimore proposed waterways to link their cities to the Midwest. Copying New York's fiscal innovations, they persuaded their state governments to invest directly in canal companies or to force state-chartered banks to do so. They also won state guarantees that encouraged British and Dutch investors; as one observer noted in 1844, "The prosperity of America, her railroads, canals, steam navigation, and banks, are the fruit of English capital." Soon, artificial waterways connected the farms and towns of the Great Lakes region with the great port cities of New York, Philadelphia, and Baltimore (via the Erie, Pennsylvania, and Chesapeake and Ohio canals). And every year, 25,000 farmer-built flatboats carried produce to New Orleans, via the Ohio and Mississippi rivers. In 1848, the com-

pletion of the Michigan and Illinois Canal, which linked Chicago to the Mississippi River, completed an inland all-water route from New York City to New Orleans (Map 9.3).

The steamboat, another product of the industrial age, ensured the economic success of the Midwest's river-borne transportation system. In 1807, engineer-inventor Robert Fulton built the first American steamboat, the *Clermont*, which he piloted up the Hudson River. To navigate shallow western rivers, engineers broadened steamboats' hulls to reduce their draft and enlarge their cargo capacity. These improved vessels halved the cost of upstream river transport and, along with the canals, dramatically increased the flow of goods, people, and news. In 1830, a traveler or a letter from New York could reach Buffalo or Pittsburgh by water in less than a week and Detroit or St. Louis in two weeks. In 1800, the same journeys had taken twice as long.

The state and national governments played key roles in developing interregional transportation and communication systems. State legislatures subsidized canals, while the national government created a vast postal system, the first network for the exchange of information. Thanks to the Post Office Act of 1792, there were more than eight thousand post offices by 1830, and the mails safely delivered thousands of letters and

**MAP 9.3**

**The Transportation Revolution: Roads and Canals, 1820–1850**

By 1850, the United States had an efficient system of water-borne transportation composed of three distinct parts. A system of short canals and navigable rivers carried cotton, tobacco, and other products from the countryside of the southern seaboard states into the Atlantic commercial system. A second system, centered on the Erie, Chesapeake and Ohio, and Pennsylvania Mainline canals, linked the major seaport cities of the Northeast to the vast trans-Appalachian region. Finally, a set of regional canals in the Old Northwest connected most of the Great Lakes region to the Ohio and Mississippi rivers and the port of New Orleans.

banknotes worth millions of dollars. The U.S. Supreme Court, headed by John Marshall, likewise encouraged interstate trade by striking down state restrictions on commerce. In *Gibbons v. Ogden* (1824), the Court voided a New York law that created a monopoly on steamboat travel into New York City and established federal authority over interstate commerce (see Chapter 7). That decision meant that no local or state monopolies—or tariffs—would impede the flow of goods, services, and news across the nation.

**Railroads Foster Regional Ties** | By the 1850s, railroads—another technological innovation—were on their way to replacing canals as the core of the national transportation system (Map 9.4). In 1852, canals carried twice the tonnage transported by railroads. Then, capitalists in Boston, New York, and London invested heavily in railroad routes; by 1860, railroads were the main carriers of wheat and freight from the Midwest to the Northeast. Serviced by a vast network of locomotive and freight-car repair shops,

**MAP 9.4**

**Railroads of the North and South, 1850 and 1861**

In the decade before the Civil War, entrepreneurs in the Northeast and the Midwest financed thousands of miles of new railroad lines, creating an extensive and dense transportation system that stimulated economic development. The South built a more limited system of railroads. In all regions, railroad companies used different track gauges, which prevented the efficient flow of traffic.

the Erie Railroad, the Pennsylvania Railroad, the New York Central Railroad, and the Baltimore and Ohio Railroad connected the Atlantic ports — New York, Philadelphia, and Baltimore — with the rapidly expanding Great Lakes cities of Cleveland and Chicago.

The railroad boom of the 1850s expanded commerce into a vast territory around Chicago. Trains carried huge quantities of lumber from Michigan to the treeless prairies of Indiana, Illinois, Iowa, and Missouri, where settlers built 250,000 new farms (covering 19 million acres) and hundreds of small towns. The rail lines moved millions of bushels of wheat to Chicago for transport by boat or rail to eastern markets. Increasingly, they also carried livestock to Chicago's slaughterhouses. In Jacksonville, Illinois, a farmer decided to feed his entire corn crop of 1,500 bushels "to hogs & cattle, as we think it is more profitable than to sell the corn." A Chicago newspaper boasted, "In ancient times all roads led to Rome; in modern times all roads lead to Chicago."

Initially, midwestern settlers relied on manufactured goods made in Britain or in the Northeast. They bought high-quality shovels and spades fabricated at the Delaware Iron Works and the Oliver Ames Company in Easton, Massachusetts; axes forged in Connecticut factories; and steel horseshoes manufactured in Troy, New York. But by the 1840s, midwestern entrepreneurs were also producing such goods as machine tools, hardware, furniture, and especially agricultural implements. Working as a blacksmith in Grand Detour, Illinois, John Deere made his first steel plow out of old saws in 1837; ten years later, he opened a factory in Moline, Illinois, that mass-produced the plows. Stronger than the existing cast-iron models built in New York, Deere's steel plows allowed midwestern farmers to cut through the thick sod of the prairies. Other midwestern companies — McCormick and Hussey, for example — mass-produced self-raking reapers that enabled farmers to harvest 12 acres of grain a day (rather than the 2 acres that could be cut by hand). With the harvest bottleneck removed, midwestern farmers planted more acres and shipped vast quantities of wheat and flour to the East and Europe. Flour soon accounted for 10 percent of all American exports.

Extra-regional trade also linked southern cotton planters to northeastern textile plants and foreign markets. This commerce in raw cotton bolstered the wealth of the South but did not transform the economic and social order there as it did in the Midwest. With the exception of Richmond, Virginia, and a few other places, southern planters did not invest their cotton profits in manufacturing. Lacking cities, factories, and highly trained workers, the South remained tied to agriculture, even as the commerce in wheat, corn, and livestock promoted diversified economies in the Northeast and Midwest.

## The Growth of Cities and Towns

The expansion of industry and trade dramatically increased America's urban population. In 1820, there were only 58 towns with more than 2,500 inhabitants in the United States; by 1840, there were 126 such towns, located mostly in the Northeast and Midwest. During those two decades, the total number of city dwellers grew more than fourfold, from 443,000 to 1,844,000.

The fastest growth occurred in the new industrial towns that sprouted along the "fall line," where rivers began their rapid descent from the Appalachian Mountains to the coastal plain. In 1822, the Boston Manufacturing Company expanded north from its base in Waltham and built a complex of mills in a sleepy Merrimack River village that quickly became the bustling textile factory town of Lowell, Massachusetts. The towns of Hartford, Connecticut; Trenton, New Jersey; and Wilmington, Delaware, also became urban centers as mill owners exploited the waterpower of their rivers and recruited workers from the countryside.

Western commercial cities such as Pittsburgh, Cincinnati, and New Orleans grew almost as rapidly. These cities expanded initially as transit centers — the points at which goods were transferred from farmers' rafts and wagons to boats or railroads. As the midwestern population grew during the 1830s and 1840s, St. Louis, Detroit, and especially Buffalo and Chicago emerged as dynamic centers of commerce. "There can be no two places in the world," journalist Margaret Fuller wrote from Chicago in 1843, "more completely thoroughfares than this place and Buffalo. . . . The life-blood [of commerce] rushes from east to west, and back again from west to east." To a German visitor, Chicago seemed "for the most part to consist of shops . . . [as if] people came here merely to trade, to make money, and not to live." Chicago's merchants and bankers developed the marketing, provisioning, and financial services essential to farmers and small-town shopkeepers in the surrounding countryside. "There can be no better [market] any where in the Union," declared a farmer in Paw Paw, Illinois.

These midwestern commercial hubs quickly became manufacturing centers as well. Capitalizing on the cities' locations as key junctions for railroad lines and steamboats, entrepreneurs built warehouses, flour mills, packing plants, and machine shops, creating work for hundreds of artisans and factory laborers. In 1846,

Cyrus McCormick moved his reaper factory from western Virginia to Chicago to be closer to his midwestern customers. By 1860, St. Louis and Chicago had become the nation's third and fourth largest cities, respectively, after New York and Philadelphia (Map 9.5).

The old Atlantic seaports—Boston, Philadelphia, Baltimore, Charleston, and especially New York City—remained important for their foreign commerce and, increasingly, as centers of finance and manufacturing. New York City and nearby Brooklyn grew at a phenomenal rate: Between 1820 and 1860, their combined populations increased nearly tenfold to 1 million people, thanks to the arrival of tens of thousands of German and Irish immigrants. Drawing on this abundant labor, New York became a center of small-scale manufacturing and the ready-made clothing industry, which relied on thousands of low-paid seamstresses. "The wholesale clothing establishments are . . . absorbing the business of the country," a "Country Tailor" complained to the *New York Tribune*, "casting many an honest and hardworking man out of employment [and helping] . . . the large cities to swallow up the small towns."

New York's growth stemmed primarily from its dominant position in foreign and domestic trade. It had the best harbor in the United States and, thanks to the Erie Canal, was the best gateway to the Midwest and the best outlet for western grain. Exploiting the city's prime location, in 1818 four Quaker merchants founded the Black Ball Line to carry cargo, people, and mail between New York and the European ports of Liverpool, London, and Le Havre, establishing the first transatlantic shipping service to run on a regular schedule. New York merchants likewise dominated trade with the newly independent South American nations of Brazil, Peru, and Venezuela. New York–based traders took over the cotton trade by offering finance, insurance, and shipping to export merchants in southern ports. By 1840, the port of New York handled almost two-thirds of foreign imports into the United States, almost half of all foreign trade, and much of the immigrant traffic.

- What roles did state and national government play in the development of America's transportation networks?

- Describe the different types of cities that emerged in the United States in the first half of the nineteenth century. How do you explain the differences in their development?

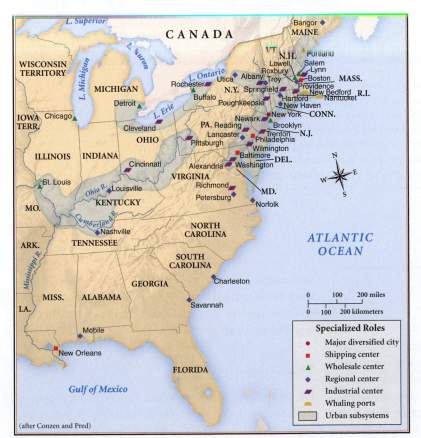

(after Conzen and Pred)

**Specialized Roles**
- ● Major diversified city
- ■ Shipping center
- ▲ Wholesale center
- ◆ Regional center
- ◣ Industrial center
- ▬ Whaling ports
- ▢ Urban subsystems

**MAP 9.5**

**The Nation's Major Cities, 1840**

By 1840, the United States boasted three major conglomerations of cities. The long-settled ports on the Atlantic—from Boston to Baltimore—served as centers for import merchants, banks, insurance companies, and manufacturers of ready-made clothing, and their reach extended far into the interior—nationwide in the case of New York City. A second group of cities stretched along the Great Lakes and included the wholesale distribution hubs of Buffalo, Detroit, and Chicago, as well as the manufacturing center of Cleveland. A third urban system extended along the Ohio River, comprising the industrial cities of Pittsburgh and Cincinnati and the wholesale centers of Louisville and St. Louis.

**Hartford Family**

Completely at home in their elegant drawing room, this elite family in Hartford, Connecticut, enjoys the fruits of the father's business success. As the father lounges in his silk robe, his eldest son (and presumptive heir) adopts an air of studied nonchalance and his daughter fingers a piano, signaling her musical accomplishments. A diminutive African American servant (her size suggesting her status) serves fruit to the lavishly attired woman of the house. The drawing room in such houses was usually sumptuously appointed, with a decor reflecting both the owners' prosperity and their aesthetic and cultural interests.    © White House Historical Association/ Photo by National Geographic Society.

# New Social Classes and Cultures

The Industrial Revolution and the Market Revolution improved the lives of many Americans by enabling them to live in larger houses, cook on iron stoves, and wear better-made clothes. But especially in the cities, the new economic order spawned distinct social classes: a small but wealthy industrial and commercial elite, a substantial middle class, and a mass of propertyless wage earners. By creating a class-divided society, industrialization posed a momentous challenge to America's republican ideals.

## The Business Elite

Before industrialization, white Americans thought of their society in terms of rank: "Notable" families had higher status than families of the "lower orders." Yet in many rural areas, people of different ranks shared a common culture. Gentlemen farmers talked easily with yeomen about crop yields, while their wives conversed about the art of quilting. In the South, humble tenants and aristocratic slave owners enjoyed the same amusements: gambling, cockfighting, and horse racing. Rich and poor attended the same Quaker meetinghouse or Presbyterian church. "Almost everyone eats, drinks, and dresses in the same way," a European visitor to Hartford, Connecticut, reported in 1798, "and one can see the most obvious inequality only in the dwellings."

The Industrial Revolution shattered this agrarian social order and fragmented society into distinct classes and cultures. As millions of Americans moved to large cities, they accentuated the differences between rural and urban life. Moreover, the urban economy made a few city residents — the merchants, manufacturers, bankers, and landlords who made up the business elite — very rich. In 1800, the top 10 percent of the nation's families owned about 40 percent of the wealth; by 1860, the richest 10 percent held nearly 70 percent of the wealth. In New York, Chicago, Baltimore, and New Orleans, the superrich — the top 1 percent — owned more than 40 percent of all tangible property (land and buildings, for example) and an even higher share of intangible property (stocks and bonds).

Government tax policies facilitated the accumulation of wealth. In an era before federal taxes on individual and corporate income, the U.S. Treasury raised most of its revenue from tariffs — regressive taxes on textiles and other imported goods purchased mostly by ordinary citizens. State and local governments also favored the wealthier classes. They taxed real estate (farms, city lots, and buildings) and tangible personal property (furniture, tools, and machinery), but almost never taxed stocks and bonds or the inheritances the rich passed on to their children.

As cities expanded in size and wealth, affluent families consciously set themselves apart. They dressed in well-tailored clothes, rode in fancy carriages, and bought expensively furnished houses tended by butlers, cooks, and other servants. The women no longer socialized with those of lesser wealth, and the men no longer labored side by side with their employees. Instead, they became managers and directors and relied on trusted subordinates to supervise hundreds of factory operatives. Increasingly, merchants, manufacturers, and bankers placed a premium on privacy and lived in separate neighborhoods, often at the edge of the city. The geographic isolation of privileged families and the massive flow of immigrants into separate districts divided cities spatially along lines of class, race, and ethnicity.

## The Middle Class

Standing between wealthy owners and propertyless wage earners was a growing middle class — the social product of the economic revolution. The "middling class," a Boston printer explained, was made up of "the farmers, the mechanics, the manufacturers, the traders, who carry on professionally the ordinary operations of buying, selling, and exchanging merchandize." Other members of this new social group — building contractors, lawyers, surveyors, and so on — suddenly found their services in great demand and financially profitable. Middling business owners, white-collar clerks, and professionals were most numerous in the Northeast, where in the 1840s they numbered about 30 percent of the population. But they also could be found in the agrarian South. The cotton boomtown of Oglethorpe, Georgia (population 2,500), boasted eighty "business houses" and eight hotels in 1854.

The emergence of the middle class reflected a dramatic rise in urban prosperity. Between 1830 and 1857, the per capita income of Americans increased by about 2.5 percent a year, a remarkable rate that has never since been matched. This surge in income, along with an abundance of inexpensive mass-produced goods, fostered a distinct middle-class urban culture. Middle-class husbands earned enough to save about 15 percent of their income, which they used to buy well-built houses in a "respectable part of town." They purchased handsome clothes and drove to work and play in smart carriages. Middle-class wives became purveyors of genteel culture, buying books, pianos, lithographs, and comfortable furniture for their front parlors. Upper-middle-class families hired Irish or African American domestic servants, while less prosperous ones enjoyed the comforts provided by new industrial goods. The middle class outfitted their residences with furnaces (both to warm the entire house and heat water for bathing), cooking stoves with ovens, and Singer's treadle-operated sewing machines. Some urban families now kept their perishable food in iceboxes, which ice-company wagons periodically refilled, and bought many varieties of packaged goods. As early as 1825, the Underwood Company of Boston was marketing jars of well-preserved Atlantic salmon.

If material comfort was one distinguishing mark of the middle class, moral and mental discipline was another. Middle-class writers denounced carnivals and festivals as a "chaos of sin and folly, of misery and fun" and, by the 1830s, had managed to suppress them. Ambitious parents were equally concerned with their children's moral and intellectual development. To help their

[Fig. 130. Plain Timber Cottage-Villa.]

[Fig. 131. Principal Floor.]

### Architecture for the Emergent Middle Class

This dwelling was well suited for a "farmer of wealth" or a middle-class suburbanite, according to Alexander Downing, author of *The Architecture of Country Houses* (1850). The exterior of the house exhibited "a considerable degree of elegance," while the interior boasted a substantial drawing room and dining room, for the entertainment of guests, and a parlor for more intimate conversations among family and friends. Downing's books and similar style manuals by other authors helped define the culture of the growing middle class and diffuse it across the nation. Andrew J. Downing, *The Architecture of Country Houses*, 1850.

offspring succeed in life, middle-class parents often provided them with a high school education (in an era when most white children received only five years of schooling), and stressed the importance of discipline and hard work. American Protestants had long believed that diligent work in an earthly "calling" was a duty owed to God. Now the business elite and the middle class gave this idea a secular twist by celebrating work as the key to individual social mobility and national prosperity.

Benjamin Franklin gave classical expression to the secular work ethic in his *Autobiography*, which was published in full in 1818 (thirty years after his death) and immediately found a huge audience. Heeding Franklin's suggestion that an industrious man would become a rich one, tens of thousands of young American men saved their money, adopted temperate habits, and aimed to rise in the world. There was an "almost universal ambition to get forward," observed Hezekiah Niles, editor of *Niles' Weekly Register*. Warner Myers, a Philadelphia housepainter, raised funds from family, friends, and personal loans and became a builder, constructing sixty houses and garnering ample profits. Countless magazines, children's books, self-help manuals, and novels recounted the stories of similar individuals. The **self-made man** became a central theme of American popular culture and inspired many men (and a few women) to seek wealth. Just as the yeoman ethic had united the social ranks in pre-1800 America, the gospel of personal achievement linked the upper and middle classes of the new industrializing society.

## Urban Workers and the Poor

As thoughtful business leaders surveyed society, they concluded that the yeoman farmer and artisan-republican ideal—a social order of independent producers—was no longer possible. "Entire independence ought not to be wished for," Ithamar A. Beard, the paymaster of the Hamilton Manufacturing Company (in Lowell, Massachusetts), told a mechanics' association in 1827. "In large manufacturing towns, many more must fill subordinate stations and must be under the immediate direction and control of a master or superintendent, than in the farming towns."

Beard had a point. In 1840, all of the nation's slaves and about half of its white workers were laboring for others. The bottom 10 percent of wage earners consisted of casual workers, who were hired on a short-term basis for the most arduous jobs. Poor women washed clothes; their husbands and sons carried lumber and bricks for construction projects, loaded ships, and dug out dirt and stones to build canals. When they could find jobs, these men earned "their dollar per diem," a longtime resident told readers of the *Baltimore American*, but he cautioned that they could never save enough "to pay rent, buy fire wood and eatables" when the harbor or the job market froze up. During business depressions, casual laborers bore the brunt of unemployment; even in good times, their jobs were temporary and dangerous.

Other laborers had greater security of employment, but few were prospering. In Massachusetts in 1825, an unskilled worker earned about two-thirds as much as a mechanic did; two decades later, it was less than half as much. A journeyman carpenter in Philadelphia reported that he was about "even with the World" after several years of work but that many of his coworkers were in debt. The 18,000 women who made men's clothing in New York City in the 1850s earned just a few pennies a day, less than $80 a year. Such meager wages barely paid for food and rent, so poorer workers could not take advantage of the rapidly falling prices of manufactured goods. Only the most fortunate working-class families could afford to educate their children, buy apprenticeships for their sons, or accumulate small dowries for their daughters. Most families sent ten-year-old children out to work, and the death of a parent often threw the survivors into dire poverty. As a charity worker noted, "What can a bereaved widow do, with 5 or 6 little children, destitute of every means of support but what her own hands can furnish (which in a general way does not amount to more than 25 cents a day)?"

Impoverished workers congregated in dilapidated housing in bad neighborhoods. Single men and women lived in crowded boardinghouses, while families jammed themselves into tiny apartments in the basements and attics of small houses. As immigrants poured in after 1840, urban populations soared, and developers squeezed more and more dwellings and foul-smelling outhouses onto a single lot. Venturing into the New York City slums in the 1850s, shocked state legislators found gaunt, shivering people with "wild ghastly faces" living amid "hideous squalor and deadly effluvia, the dim, undrained courts oozing with pollution, the dark, narrow stairways, decayed with age, reeking with filth, overrun with vermin."

Many wage earners sought solace in alcohol. Beer and rum had long been standard fare in American rituals: patriotic ceremonies, work breaks, barn raisings, and games. But during the 1820s and 1830s, the consumption of intoxicating beverages reached new heights, even among the elite; alcoholism killed Daniel Tompkins, vice president under James Monroe, and undermined Henry Clay's bid for the presidency. Heavy drinking was especially devastating for wage earners, who could ill afford its costs. Although Methodist artisans and ambitious craft workers swore off liquor to protect their work skills, health, and finances, other workers drank heavily on the job—and not just during the traditional 11 A.M. and 4 P.M. "refreshers." A baker recalled how "one man was stationed at the window to watch, while the rest drank." Long before the arrival of spirit-drinking Irish and beer-drinking German immigrants, grogshops dotted almost every block in working-class districts and were centers of disorder. Unrestrained drinking by young men led to fistfights, brawls, and robberies. The urban police, mostly low-paid watchmen and untrained constables, were unable to contain the lawlessness.

## The Benevolent Empire

The disorder among wage earners alarmed the rising middle classes, who wanted safe cities and a disciplined workforce. To improve the world around them, many upwardly mobile men and women embraced religious benevolence. Led by Congregational and Presbyterian ministers, they created organizations of conservative social reform that historians call the **Benevolent Empire**. The reformers' goal was to restore "the moral government of God" by reducing intemperance and poverty, explained Presbyterian minister Lyman Beecher. Reform-minded individuals first regulated their own behavior and then tried to control the lives of working people. They would regulate popular behavior—by persuasion if possible, by law if necessary.

The Benevolent Empire targeted age-old evils such as drunkenness, adultery, prostitution, and crime, but its methods were new. Instead of relying on church sermons and persuasion by community leaders, the reformers created large-scale organizations to combat evil: the Prison Discipline Society and the American Society for the Promotion of Temperance, among many others. Each organization had a managing staff, a network of hundreds of chapters, thousands of volunteer members, and a newspaper.

Often acting in concert, these benevolent groups worked to improve society. First, they encouraged people to lead well-disciplined lives and acquire "regular habits." They persuaded local governments to ban carnivals of drink and dancing, such as Negro Election Day (festivities in which African Americans symbolically took over the government), which had been enjoyed by whites as well as blacks. Second, they devised new institutions to help the needy and control the unruly. Reformers provided homes of refuge for abandoned children and asylums for the insane, who previously had been confined by their families in attics and cellars. They campaigned to end corporal punishment of criminals and to rehabilitate them in new, specially designed penitentiaries.

Women formed a crucial part of the Benevolent Empire. Since the 1790s, upper-class women had sponsored charitable organizations such as the Society for

**An Inside View of the Benevolent Empire**

Early-nineteenth-century reformers condemned corporal punishment. So they built prisons designed to rehabilitate criminals and turn them into responsible citizens. As this folk painting by a Massachusetts penitentiary inmate suggests, prison officials imposed tight discipline. The inmates marched in silence: In line with the latest penal theories, prisoners were not allowed to speak with one another, the silence key to encouraging them to reflect on their crimes and express repentance.    Courtesy David A. Schorsch.

the Relief of Poor Widows with Small Children, which was founded in 1797 in New York by Isabella Graham, a devout Presbyterian widow. Her daughter Joanna Bethune set up other charitable institutions, including the Orphan Asylum Society and the Society for the Promotion of Industry, which found jobs for hundreds of poor women as spinners and seamstresses.

Some reformers believed that the decline of the traditional Christian observation of the Sabbath (Sunday) as a day of rest was the greatest threat to the "moral government of God." As the market revolution spread, merchants and storekeepers conducted business on Sundays, and urban saloons provided drink and entertainment. To halt these activities, Lyman Beecher and other ministers founded the General Union for Promoting the Observance of the Christian Sabbath in 1828. General Union chapters, replete with women's auxiliaries, sprang up from Maine to Cincinnati and beyond. To rally Chris-

tians, the General Union demanded Congress repeal an 1810 law allowing mail to be transported—though not delivered—on Sundays. Members boycotted shipping companies that did business on the Sabbath and campaigned for municipal laws forbidding games and festivals on the Lord's day.

The Benevolent Empire's efforts to impose its Sabbatarian values provoked opposition from workers and freethinkers. Men who labored twelve to fourteen hours a day, six days a week wanted the freedom to spend their one day of leisure as they wished. To keep goods moving, shipping company managers demanded that the Erie Canal provide lockkeepers on Sundays; using laws to enforce a particular set of moral beliefs was "contrary to the free spirit of our institutions," they said. When evangelical reformers proposed teaching Christianity to slaves, they aroused hostility among white southerners. This popular resistance by workers and planters limited the success of the initiatives of the Benevolent Empire.

## Charles Grandison Finney: Revivalism and Reform

Presbyterian minister Charles Grandison Finney found a new way to propagate religious values. Finney was not part of the traditional religious elite. Born into a poor farming family in Connecticut, he had planned to become a lawyer and rise into the middle class. But in 1823, Finney underwent an intense conversion experience and chose the ministry as his career. Beginning in towns along the Erie Canal, the young minister conducted emotional revival meetings that stressed conversion rather than doctrine. Repudiating Calvinist beliefs, he preached that God would welcome any sinner who submitted to the Holy Spirit. Finney's ministry drew on—and greatly accelerated—the Second Great Awakening, the wave of Protestant revivalism that had begun after the Revolution (see Chapter 8).

**Evangelical Beliefs** Finney's central message was that "God has made man a moral free agent" who could choose salvation. This doctrine of free will was particularly attractive to members of the new middle class, who had already chosen to improve their material lives. But Finney also had great success in converting people at both ends of the social spectrum, from the haughty rich who had placed themselves above God, to the abject poor who seemed lost to drink and sloth. Finney celebrated their common fellowship in Christ and identified them spiritually with pious middle-class respectability.

Finney's most spectacular triumph came in 1830, when he moved his revivals from small towns to Rochester, New York, now a major milling and commercial city on the Erie Canal. Preaching every day for six months and promoting group prayer meetings in family homes, Finney won over the influential merchants and manufacturers of Rochester, who pledged to reform their lives and those of their workers. They promised to attend church, give up intoxicating beverages, and work hard. To encourage their employees to do the same, wealthy businessmen founded a Free Presbyterian church—"free" because members did not have to pay for pew space. Other Evangelical Protestants founded churches to serve transient canal laborers, and pious businessmen set up a savings bank to encourage thrift among the working classes. Meanwhile, Finney's wife, Lydia, and other middle-class women carried the Chris-

**Charles Grandison Finney, Evangelist (1792–1875)**
When an unknown artist painted this flattering portrait in 1834, Finney was forty-two years old and at the height of his career as an evangelist. Handsome and charismatic, Finney had just led a series of enormously successful revivals in Rochester, New York, and other cities along the Erie Canal. In 1835, he established a theology department at newly founded Oberlin College in Ohio, where he trained a generation of ministers and served as president from 1851 to 1866.   Oberlin College Archives.

tian message to the wives of the unconverted, set up Sunday schools for poor children, and formed the Female Charitable Society to assist the unemployed.

Finney's efforts to create a community of morally disciplined Christians were not completely successful. Skilled workers who belonged to strong craft organizations—boot makers, carpenters, stonemasons, and boatbuilders—protested that they needed higher wages and better schools more urgently than sermons and prayers. Poor people ignored Finney's revival, as did the Irish Catholic immigrants who had recently begun arriving in Rochester and other northeastern cities, bringing with them a hatred of Protestants as religious heretics and political oppressors.

Nonetheless, revivalists from New England to the Midwest copied Finney's evangelical message and techniques. In New York City, wealthy silk merchants Arthur and Lewis Tappan founded a magazine, *The Christian Evangelist*, which promoted Finney's ideas. The revivals swept through Pennsylvania, North Carolina, Tennessee, and Indiana, where, a convert reported, "you could not go upon the street and hear any conversation, except upon religion." The success of the revivals "has been so general and thorough," concluded a Presbyterian general assembly, "that the whole customs of society have changed."

**Temperance** | The **temperance movement** proved to be the most successful evangelical social reform. Soon after evangelical Protestants took over the American Temperance Society in 1832, the organization boasted two thousand chapters and more than 200,000 members. The society employed the methods of the revivals—group confession and prayer, a focus on the family and the spiritual role of women, and sudden emotional conversion—and took them to northern towns and southern villages. On one day in New York City in 1841, more than 4,000 people took the temperance "pledge." Throughout America, the annual consumption of spirits fell dramatically, from an average of 5 gallons per person in 1830 to 2 gallons in 1845.

Evangelical reformers celebrated religion as the key to moral improvement. Laziness and drinking might be cured by self-discipline, as Benjamin Franklin had argued, but people would certainly experience a profound change of heart through religious conversion. Religious discipline and the ideology of social mobility thus served as powerful cements, bonding middle-class Americans and wage-earning citizens to one another in the face of economic divisions created by industrialization, market expansion, and increasing cultural diversity.

## Immigration and Cultural Conflict

Cultural diversity was the result of vast waves of immigrants. Between 1840 and 1860, about 2 million Irish, 1.5 million Germans, and 750,000 Britons poured into the United States. The British migrants were primarily Protestants and relatively prosperous; their ranks included trained professionals, propertied farmers, and skilled workers. Many German immigrants also came from property-owning farming and artisan families and had sufficient resources to move to the midwestern states of Wisconsin, Iowa, and Missouri. Other Germans and most of the Irish settled in the Northeast, where by 1860, they accounted for nearly one-third of white adults. Most immigrants avoided the South because they opposed slavery, feared competition from enslaved workers, and preferred jobs in the northern manufacturing centers.

**Irish Poverty** | The poorest migrants, the Irish peasants and laborers, were fleeing a famine caused by severe overpopulation and a devastating blight that destroyed much of the Irish potato crop. Arriving in dire poverty, the Irish settled mostly in the cities of New England and New York. The men took low-paying jobs as factory hands, construction workers, and canal diggers, while the women became washerwomen and domestic servants. Irish families crowded into cheap tenement buildings with primitive sanitation systems and were the first to die when disease struck a city. In the summer of 1849, a cholera epidemic took the lives of thousands of poor immigrants in St. Louis and New York City.

In times of hardship and sorrow, immigrants turned to their churches. Many Germans and virtually all the Irish were Catholics, and they fueled the growth of the American Catholic Church. In 1840, there were sixteen Catholic dioceses and seven hundred churches; by 1860, there were forty-five dioceses and twenty-five hundred churches. Under the guidance of their priests and bishops, Catholics built an impressive network of institutions—charitable societies, orphanages, militia companies, parochial schools, and political organizations—that helped them maintain both their religion and their German or Irish identity.

**Nativism** | The Protestant fervor stirred up by the Second Great Awakening meant that a barrage of anti-Catholic publications greeted these new immigrants (see Comparing American Voices, "A Debate over Catholic Immigration," pp. 298–299). The artist and inventor Samuel F. B. Morse was a militant critic of Catholicism. In 1834, Morse published *Foreign Conspiracy Against the Liberties of the United States*, which warned of a Catholic threat to American republican institutions. Morse believed that Catholic immigrants would obey the dictates of Pope Gregory XVI (1831–1846), who in an official 1832 papal declaration (encyclical) had condemned liberty of conscience, freedom of publication, and the separation of church and state. Gregory instructed Catholics to repudiate republicanism and acknowledge the "submission due to princes" and to the papacy itself. Republican-minded Protestants of many denominations shared Morse's fears of papal interference in American life and politics, and *Foreign Conspiracy* became their handbook.

The social tensions stemming from industrialization intensified anti-Catholic sentiment. During busi-

**The Drunkard's Progress: From the First Glass to the Grave**
This 1846 lithograph, published by N. Currier, suggests the inevitable fate of those who drink. The drunkard's descent into "Poverty and Disease" ends with "Death by suicide," leaving a grieving and destitute wife and child. Temperance reformers urged Americans to take "The Cold Water Cure" by drinking water instead of alcoholic beverages. To promote abstinence among the young, in 1836 revivalist preacher and temperance lecturer Reverend Thomas Poage Hunt founded the Cold Water Army, an organization that grew to embrace several hundred thousand children, all of whom pledged "perpetual hate to all that can Intoxicate."   Library of Congress.

ness recessions, unemployed Protestant mechanics and factory workers joined mobs that attacked Catholics, accusing them of taking jobs and driving down wages. These cultural conflicts undercut trade unionism, because many Protestant wage earners felt that they had more in common with their Protestant employers than with their Catholic coworkers. Other native-born Protestants formed clubs that called for a halt to immigration. Benevolent-minded Protestants supported the anti-Catholic movement for reasons of public policy. As crusaders for public education, they opposed the diversion of tax resources to Catholic schools; as advocates of temperance and civilized manners, they condemned the rowdyism of drunken Irish men.

In many northeastern cities, religious and cultural tensions led to violence. In 1834, in Charlestown, Massachusetts, a quarrel between Catholic laborers repairing a convent owned by the Ursuline order of nuns and Protestant workers in a neighboring brickyard led to a full-scale riot and the convent's destruction. In 1844, in Philadelphia, riots erupted when the Catholic bishop persuaded public-school officials to use both Catholic and Protestant versions of the Bible. Anti-Irish violence incited by the city's nativist clubs lasted for two months and escalated into open warfare between Protestants and the Pennsylvania militia. Even as the economic revolution brought prosperity to many Americans and attracted millions of immigrants, it divided society along lines of class, ethnicity, and religion.

- What social classes were created by the economic revolution? Describe their defining characteristics.

- What were the main goals of the Benevolent Empire? To what extent were they achieved?

- Weigh the relative importance of the Industrial Revolution and the Market Revolution in changing the American economy.

# A Debate over Catholic Immigration

Between 1776 and 1830, relatively few Europeans immigrated to the United States. Then, as the text explains, an increase in population and in poverty sparked the migration of increasing numbers of Germans (both Catholics and Protestants) and Irish Catholics. The arrival of hundreds of thousands of foreign Catholics in the midst of the intense Protestantism of the Second Great Awakening led to religious riots, the formation of the nativist American Party, and sharp debates in the public press. By using contemporary newspapers and other writings as a source, historians can gain insight into the public rhetoric (and often the private passions) of the time.

## Lyman Beecher

### Catholicism Is Incompatible with Republicanism

Lyman Beecher (1775–1863) was one of the leading Protestant ministers of his generation and the father of a family of Christian social reformers and well-known authors: minister Henry Ward Beecher, Harriet Beecher Stowe (*Uncle Tom's Cabin*), and Catharine Beecher (*A Treatise on Domestic Economy*). In *A Plea for the West* (1835), Lyman Beecher alerted his fellow Protestants to the centralized power of the Roman Catholic Church and its opposition to republican institutions. That opposition was formalized in papal encyclicals issued by Pope Gregory XVI (*Mirari Vos*, 1832) and Pope Pius IX (*Quanta Cura*, 1864), both of which condemned republicanism and freedom of conscience as false political ideologies.

Since the irruption of the northern barbarians, the world has never witnessed such a rush of dark-minded population from one country to another, as is now leaving Europe, and dashing upon our shores. . . .

They come, also, not undirected. There is evidently a supervision abroad—and one here—by which they come, and set down together, in city or country, as a Catholic body, and are led or followed quickly by a Catholic priesthood, who maintain over them in the land of strangers and unknown tongues an [absolute] ascendancy. . . .

The ministers of no Protestant sect could or would dare to attempt to regulate the votes of their people as the Catholic priests can do, who at the confessional learn all the private concerns of their people, and have almost unlimited power over the conscience as it respects the performance of every civil or social duty.

There is another point of dissimilarity of still greater importance. The opinions of the Protestant clergy are congenial with liberty—they are chosen by the people who have been educated as freemen, and they are dependent on them for patronage and support. The Catholic system is adverse to liberty, and the clergy to a great extent are dependent on foreigners [the Pope and church authorities in Rome] opposed to the principles of our government.

Nor is this all—the secular patronage at the disposal of an associated body of men, who under the influence of their priesthood may be induced to act as one . . . would enable them to touch far and wide the spring of action through our cities and through the nation. . . . How many mechanics, merchants, lawyers, physicians, in any political crisis, might they reach and render timid . . . ? How will [the priesthood's] power extend and become omnipresent and resistless as emigration shall quadruple their numbers and action on the political and business men of the nation?

A tenth part of the suffrage of the nation, thus condensed and wielded by the Catholic powers of Europe, might decide our elections, perplex our policy, inflame and divide the nation, break the bond of our union, and throw down our free institutions. . . .

[Catholicism is] a religion which never prospered but in alliance with despotic governments, has always been and still is the inflexible enemy of Liberty of conscience and free inquiry, and at this moment is the main stay of the battle against republican institutions.

Source: Lyman Beecher, *A Plea for the West* (Cincinnati: Truman & Smith, 1835), 72–73, 126, 59–63, 85–86, 59.

## Orestes Brownson

### Catholicism as a Necessity for Popular Government

Like Lyman Beecher, Orestes Brownson was born into the Presbyterian Church, but he quickly grew dissatisfied with its doctrines. After experimenting with Unitarianism, communalism, socialism, and transcendentalism, Brownson converted to Catholicism in 1844. A zealous convert, Brownson defended Catholicism with rigorous, logical, and provocative arguments in this article, "Catholicity Necessary to Sustain Popular Liberty" (1845).

Without the Roman Catholic religion it is impossible to pre-serve a democratic government, and secure its free, orderly, and wholesome action. . . . The theory of democracy is, Construct your government and commit it to the people to be taken care of . . . as they shall think proper.

It is a beautiful theory, and would work admirably, if it were not for one little difficulty, namely, the people are fallible, both individually and collectively, and governed by their passions and interests, which not unfrequently lead them far astray, and produce much mischief.

We know of but one solution of the difficulty, and that is in RELIGION. There is no foundation for virtue but in religion, and it is only religion that can command the degree of popular virtue and intelligence requisite to insure to popular government the right direction. . . . But what religion? It must be a religion which is above the people and controls them, or it will not answer the purpose. It cannot be Protestantism, . . . for Protestantism assumes as its point of departure that Almighty God has indeed given us a religion, but has given it to us not to take care of us, but to be taken care of by us.

[Moreover,] Protestant faith and worship tremble as readily before the slightest breath of public sentiment, as the aspen leaf before the zephyr. The faith and discipline of a sect take any and every direction the public opinion of that sect demands. All is loose, floating, — is here to-day, is there tomorrow, and, next day, may be nowhere. The holding of slaves is compatible with Christian character south of the geographical line, and incompatible north; and Christian morals change according to the prejudices, interests, or habits of the people. . . .

Here, then, is the reason why Protestantism, though it may institute, cannot sustain popular liberty. It is itself subject to popular control, and must follow in all things the popular will, passion, interest, ignorance, prejudice, or caprice.

If Protestantism will not answer the purpose, what religion will? The Roman Catholic, or none. The Roman Catholic religion assumes, as its point of departure, that it is instituted not to be taken care of by the people, but to take care of the people; not to be governed by them, but to govern them. The word is harsh in democratic ears, we admit; but it is not the office of religion to say soft or pleas-ing words. . . . The people need governing, and must be governed, or nothing but anarchy and destruction await them. They must have a master. . . .

Quote our expression, THE PEOPLE MUST HAVE A MASTER, as you doubtless will; hold it up in glaring capitals, to excite the unthinking and unreasoning multitude, and to doubly fortify their prejudices against Catholicity; be mortally scandalized at the assertion that religion ought to govern the people, and then go to work and seek to bring the people into subjection to your banks or moneyed corporations. . . .

The Roman Catholic religion, then, is necessary to sustain popular liberty, because popular liberty can be sus-tained only by a religion free from popular control, above the people, speaking from above and able to command them, and such a religion is the Roman Catholic.

---

Source: Orestes A. Brownson, *Essays and Reviews, Chiefly on Theology, Politics, and Socialism* (New York: D. & J. Sadlier, 1852), 368–370, 372–373, 376, 379–381.

## ANALYZING THE EVIDENCE

- According to Beecher, what specific dangers does Catholicism pose to American republican institutions? Why would he argue that Protestant churches do not pose the same dangers?

- Does Brownson disagree with Beecher's criticism of the social and political impact of Catholicism? If so, why does he disagree? If not, on what basis does he defend the values and practices of the Catholic Church? Explain your answer.

- Given Brownson's statement that "the people must have a master," what would be his view of democracy and popular government?

- Would the leaders of the Protestant Benevolent Empire agree with any aspects of Brownson's social and political philosophy? Why or why not?

**The Philadelphia Riots of 1844**

When riots between nativists and Irish Catholic immigrants broke out in Philadelphia in May 1844, the governor of Pennsylvania called out the militia to restore order. But violence continued. On July 7, battles among Protestants (the well-dressed men in the illustration), Catholics, and state militia left fifteen dead and more than fifty injured. Although the riots were set off by a decision to use both Protestant and Catholic versions of the Bible in the public schools, the causes were more deep-seated. Religious animosities, ethnic differences, and cultural conflicts created an explosive mix that resulted in open warfare. Library of Congress.

## SUMMARY

In this chapter, we examined the causes of the economic transformation of the first half of the nineteenth century. That transformation had two facets: a major increase in production—the Industrial Revolution—and the expansion of commerce—the Market Revolution. Water, steam, and minerals such as coal and iron were crucial ingredients in both revolutions—driving factory machinery, carrying goods to market on canals and rivers, and propelling steamboats and railroad engines.

We also explored the consequences of that transformation: the rise of an urban society, the increasing similarity between the Northeast and Midwest and their growing difference from the South, and the creation of a class-divided society. Seeking to shape the emerging society, benevolent reformers and evangelical revivalists worked to instill moral discipline and Christian values. But artisan republicans, unionized workers, and Irish and German immigrants had their own economic and cultural goals. The result was a fragmented society. Differences of class and culture now split the North just as race and class had long divided the South. As the next chapter suggests, Americans looked to their political system, which was becoming increasingly democratic, to address these divisions. In fact, the tensions among economic inequality, cultural diversity, and political democracy became a troubling—and enduring—part of American life.

## CHAPTER REVIEW QUESTIONS

- In what ways was the economy different in 1860 from what it had been in 1800? How would you explain those differences?

- What was the impact of the economic revolution on the lives of women in various social groups and classes?

- Did the Industrial and Market revolutions make America a more or less republican society? How so?

## FOR FURTHER EXPLORATION

Charles G. Sellers, *The Market Revolution: Jacksonian America, 1815–1846* (1991), and Richard R. John, *Spreading the News: The American Postal System* (1996), explore the social impact of economic change. Laurel Thatcher Ulrich examines the artifacts and myths of *The Age of Homespun* (2001), while David Freeman Hawke surveys technology in the *Nuts and Bolts of the Past* (1988). Also see the Eli Whitney Museum site (**www.eliwhitney.org**). Scott A. Sandage, *Born Losers: A History of Failure in America* (2005), focuses on failed entrepreneurs.

Stephen Aron, *How the West Was Lost* (1996), analyzes economic conflict in Kentucky, and Peter Way, *Common Labor* (1993), describes the hard lives of the men who dug the canals in the trans-Appalachian west. For the Erie Canal, go to **www.nyscanals.gov/cculture/history**. Documents on white pioneers in Michigan, Minnesota, and Wisconsin (1820–1910) are available at **memory.loc.gov/ammem/umhtml/umhome.html**.

Stuart M. Blumin's *The Emergence of the Middle Class* (1989) discusses the formation of urban classes, while Stephen P. Rice, *Minding the Machine* (2004), probes class, languages, and cultures. David Grimsted, *American Mobbing* (1998), explores urban disorder. In *Home and Work* (1990), Jeanne Boydston exposes the impact of the urban market economy on women's lives. For a textile operative's account of mill life, see **www.fordham.edu/halsall/mod/robinson-lowell.html**. For religion and benevolent societies, consult **www.loc.gov/exhibits/religion/rel07.html**, and William R. Hutchison, *Religious Pluralism in America: The Contentious History of a Founding Ideal* (2003).

## TEST YOUR KNOWLEDGE

To assess your command of the material in this chapter, see the Online Study Guide at **bedfordstmartins.com/henretta**.

For Web sites, images, and documents related to topics and places in this chapter, visit **bedfordstmartins.com/makehistory**.

## TIMELINE

| | |
|---|---|
| **1782** | Oliver Evans builds automated flour mill |
| **1790** | Samuel Slater opens spinning mill in Providence, Rhode Island |
| **1792** | Congress passes Post Office Act |
| **1793** | Eli Whitney devises cotton gin |
| **1800–1830** | Shoe entrepreneurs adopt division of labor |
| **1807** | Robert Fulton launches the *Clermont* |
| **1814** | Boston Manufacturing Company opens cotton mill in Waltham, Massachusetts |
| **1816–1828** | Congress levies protective tariffs |
| **1817** | Erie Canal begun (completed in 1825) |
| **1820** | Minimum price for federal land reduced to $1.25 per acre |
| **1820–1840** | Fourfold increase in urban population in Northeast and Midwest |
| **1820s** | New England women take textile jobs<br>Rise of Benevolent Empire leads to conservative social reforms |
| **1824** | *Gibbons v. Ogden* promotes interstate trade |
| **1830s** | Emergence of western commercial cities<br>Labor movement gains strength<br>Urban residence reflects economic class<br>Middle-class culture emerges<br>Growth of temperance movement |
| **1830** | Charles G. Finney begins Rochester revivals |
| **1834** | Local unions form National Trades' Union<br>John Deere invents steel plow |
| **1840s** | Irish and German immigration spark ethnic riots<br>Rise of machine-tool industry |
| **1842** | *Commonwealth v. Hunt* legitimizes trade unions |
| **1848** | Michigan and Illinois Canal completes water route from New York City to New Orleans |
| **1850s** | Expansion of railroads in Northeast and Midwest |
| **1857** | Overproduction and speculation trigger a financial panic |

# A Democratic Revolution, 1820–1844

**Europeans who visited** the United States in the 1830s generally praised its republican society but not its political parties and politicians. "The gentlemen spit, talk of elections and the price of produce, and spit again," Frances Trollope reported in *Domestic Manners of the Americans* (1832). In her view, American politics was the sport of self-serving party politicians who reeked of "whiskey and onions." Other Europeans lamented the low intellectual level of American political debate. The "clap-trap of praise and pathos" from a Massachusetts politician "deeply disgusted" Harriet Martineau, while Basil Hall was astonished by the shallow arguments advanced by the inept "farmers, shopkeepers, and country lawyers" who sat in the New York assembly.

The negative verdict was unanimous. "The most able men in the United States are very rarely placed at the head of affairs," French aristocrat Alexis de Tocqueville concluded in *Democracy in America* (1835). The reason, Tocqueville suggested, lay in the character of democracy itself. Most citizens ignored important policy issues, jealously refused to elect their intellectual superiors, and listened in awe to "the clamor of a mountebank [a charismatic fraud] who knows the secret of stimulating their tastes."

These Europeans were witnessing the American Democratic Revolution. Before 1815, men of great ability had sat in the seats of government, and the prevailing ideology had been republicanism, or rule by "men of TALENTS and VIRTUE," as a newspaper put it. Such republican leaders feared popular rule. So they wrote constitutions with Bills of Rights, bicameral legislatures, and independent judiciaries, and censured men who campaigned for public office as overambitious politicians. Nonetheless, by the 1820s and 1830s, the watchword was *democracy*, which in practice meant rule by party politicians who avidly sought office by rallying supporters through newspapers, broadsides, and great public processions and meetings. Politics increasingly became a sport—a competitive contest for the votes of ordinary men. "That the majority should govern was a fundamental maxim in all free governments," declared Martin Van Buren, the most talented of the middle-class professional politicians. Criticized by one republican-minded Virginian as "too great an intriguer . . . an adroit, dapper, little managing man," Van Buren often pursued selfish goals; but by encouraging ordinary Americans to burn with "election fever" and support party principles, he and other party politicians provided a sense of identity and purpose amid a fragmented social order.

**The Inauguration of President William Henry Harrison, March 4, 1841**

After being sworn into office, President Harrison stands on the steps of the U.S. Capitol (in the red box) reviewing a parade of military units. The short balding man to the right of Harrison is Martin Van Buren, the departing president. Although they could not vote, many women attended the ceremony, both to enjoy the festivities and to show their support for the Whig Party's policies of social and moral reform. Anne S. K. Brown Military Collection, Brown University.

# The Rise of Popular Politics, 1820–1828

Expansion of the **franchise** (the right to vote) dramatically symbolized the Democratic Revolution. By the 1830s, most states allowed most white men to vote. Nowhere else in the world did ordinary farmers and wage earners exercise such political influence. In England, for example, the Reform Bill of 1832 extended the vote to only 600,000 out of 6 million English men—a mere 10 percent.

## The Decline of the Notables and the Rise of Parties

The American Revolution weakened the deferential society of the colonial era, but did not overthrow it. Only two states—Pennsylvania and Vermont—allowed all male taxpayers to vote; even in those states, families of low rank continued to accept the leadership of their social "betters." Consequently, wealthy notables—northern landlords, slave-owning planters, and seaport merchants—dominated the political system in the new republic. And rightly so, thought John Jay, the first chief justice of the Supreme Court. "Those who own the country are the most fit persons to participate in the government of it," Jay declared. Jay and other notables managed local elections by building up an "interest": lending money to small farmers, giving business to storekeepers, and treating their tenants to rum. An outlay of $20 for refreshments, remarked one poll watcher, "may produce about 100 votes." This gentry-dominated system kept men who lacked wealth and powerful family connections from running for office.

**The Rise of Democracy** | The struggle to expand the suffrage began in the 1810s with Maryland reformers invoking the egalitarian language of republicanism: Property qualifications were a "tyranny" because they endowed "one class of men with privileges which are denied to another." To defuse this criticism and deter migration to the West, legislators in Maryland and other seaboard states grudgingly accepted a broader franchise. The new voters quickly changed the tone of politics, rejecting candidates who wore "top boots, breeches, and shoe buckles," their hair in "powder and queues." Instead, they elected men who dressed simply and endorsed democracy.

Smallholding farmers and ambitious laborers in the Midwest and Southwest likewise challenged the old hierarchical order. In Ohio, a traveler reported, "no white man or woman will bear being called a servant." The constitutions of the new states of Indiana (1816), Illinois (1818), and Alabama (1819) prescribed a broad male franchise, and voters usually elected middling men to local and state offices. A well-to-do migrant in Illinois was surprised to learn that the man who plowed his fields "was a colonel of militia, and a member of the legislature." Once in public office, men from modest backgrounds enacted laws that restricted imprisonment for debt, kept taxes low, and allowed farmers to claim squatters' rights to unoccupied land.

By the mid-1820s, many states had given the vote to all white men or to all those who paid taxes or served in the militia. Only a few—North Carolina, Virginia, and Rhode Island—still required the ownership of freehold property for voting. Moreover, between 1818 and 1821, Connecticut, Massachusetts, and New York wrote more democratic constitutions that reapportioned legislative districts on the basis of population and mandated the popular election (rather than the appointment) of judges and justices of the peace.

Democratic politics was contentious and, because it attracted men on the make, often corrupt. Powerful entrepreneurs and speculators—both notables and self-made men—demanded government assistance for their business enterprises and paid bribes to get it. Speculators won land grants by paying off the members of important committees, and bankers distributed shares of stock to key legislators. When the Seventh Ward Bank of New York City received a legislative charter in 1833, the bank's officials set aside one-third of the 3,700 shares of stock for themselves and their friends and almost two-thirds for state legislators and bureaucrats, leaving just 40 shares for public sale.

More political disputes broke out when religious reformers sought laws to enforce the cultural agenda of the Benevolent Empire. In Utica, New York, evangelical Presbyterians called for a town ordinance restricting Sunday entertainment. In response, a member of the local Universalist church—a freethinking Protestant denomination—denounced the measure as coercive and called for "Religious Liberty."

**Parties Take Command** | The appearance of political parties encouraged such debates over government policy. Revolutionary-era Americans had condemned political "factions" as antirepublican and made no mention of political parties in the national and state constitutions. But as the power of notables waned in the 1820s, disciplined political parties appeared in a number of states; usually they were run by professional politicians, often middle-class lawyers and journalists. One observer compared the new organizations to a well-designed textile loom, calling them "machines" that wove the interests of diverse social and economic groups into a coherent legislative program.

Martin Van Buren of New York was the chief architect of the emerging system of party government, at both the state and national levels. The son of a Jeffersonian tavern keeper, Van Buren grew up in the landlord-dominated society of the Hudson River Valley. To get training as a lawyer, he relied on the powerful Van Ness clan; then, determined not to become a dependent "tool" of a notable family, Van Buren repudiated their tutelage. His goal was to create a new political order based on party identity, not family connections. In justifying governments run by party politicians, Van Buren rejected the traditional republican belief that political factions were dangerous. Instead, he claimed that the opposite was true: "All men of sense know that political parties are inseparable from free government," he stated, because they check an elected official's inherent "disposition to abuse power."

Between 1817 and 1821, Van Buren turned his "Bucktail" supporters (so called because they wore a deer's tail on their hats) into the first statewide **political machine**. He purchased a newspaper, the *Albany Argus*, and used it to promote his policies and get out the vote. **Patronage** was an even more important tool. When Van Buren's Bucktails won control of the New York legislature in 1821, they acquired a political interest much greater than that of the notables: the power to appoint some six thousand of their friends to positions in New York's legal bureaucracy of judges, justices of the peace, sheriffs, deed commissioners, and coroners. This **spoils system** was fair, Van Buren suggested, because it "would operate sometimes in favour of one party, and sometimes of another." Party government was thoroughly republican, he added, as it reflected the preferences of a majority of the voters (see Voices from Abroad, "Alexis de Tocqueville: Probing American Politics," p. 306). To ensure the passage of the party's legislative program, Van Buren insisted on disciplined voting as determined by a **caucus**, a meeting of party leaders. On one crucial occasion, the "Little Magician"—a nickname reflecting Van Buren's short stature and political dexterity—gave an elaborate banquet in honor of seventeen New York legislators who sacrificed "individual preferences for the general good" of the party.

## The Election of 1824

The advance of political democracy and party government in the states undermined the traditional notable-dominated system of national politics. After the War of 1812, the aristocratic Federalist Party virtually disappeared, and the Republican Party splintered into competing factions (see Chapter 7). As the election of 1824 approached, five Republican candidates campaigned for the presidency. Three were veterans of President James Monroe's cabinet: Secretary of State John Quincy Adams, the son of former president John Adams; Secretary of War John C. Calhoun; and Secretary of the Treasury William H. Crawford. The other candidates were Henry Clay of Kentucky, the hard-drinking, dynamic Speaker of the House of Representatives; and General Andrew Jackson, now a senator from Tennessee. When the Republican caucus in Congress selected Crawford as the party's official nominee, the other candidates refused to withdraw and took their case to the voters. Thanks to democratic reforms, eighteen of the twenty-four states required popular elections (rather than a vote of the state legislature) to choose their representatives to the electoral college.

Each candidate had strengths. Thanks to his diplomatic successes as secretary of state, John Quincy Adams enjoyed national recognition; and his Massachusetts connection ensured him the electoral votes of New England. Henry Clay based his candidacy on his **American System**, an integrated program of national economic development similar to the Commonwealth System of the state governments. Clay wanted to strengthen the Second Bank of the United States and to use tariff revenues to build roads and canals. His nationalistic program won praise in the West, which needed transportation improvements, but elicited sharp criticism in the South, which relied on rivers to market its cotton and had few manufacturing industries to protect. William Crawford of Georgia, an ideological heir of Thomas Jefferson, denounced Clay's American System as a scheme to "consolidate" political power in Washington. Recognizing Crawford's appeal in the South, John C. Calhoun of South Carolina withdrew from the race and endorsed Andrew Jackson.

As the hero of the Battle of New Orleans, Jackson benefited from the surge of patriotism after the War of 1812. Born in the Carolina backcountry, Jackson had settled in Nashville, Tennessee, where he formed ties to influential families through marriage and a career as an attorney and a slave-owning cotton planter. His rise from common origins symbolized the new democratic

## Alexis de Tocqueville
## Probing American Politics

In 1831, the French aristocrat Alexis de Tocqueville (1805–1859) came to the United States to report on its innovative penal system. But the major product of Tocqueville's nine-month sojourn was *Democracy in America* (1835, 1840), a brilliant analysis of the new republican society. Tocqueville had collected the raw materials for his great study into fourteen notebooks, where he recorded conversations with hundreds of citizens and pondered their significance.

*From a Conversation with Boston intellectual Jared Sparks:*
[Sparks:] The political dogma of this country is that the majority is always right. By and large we are very well satisfied to have adopted it, but . . . sometimes the majority has wished to oppress the minority. . . .

*From a Conversation with Étienne Mazureau, a French-born lawyer in New Orleans:*
[Tocqueville] Q. Before you came under American rule, did you have any of the forms of free government?

[Mazureau] A. No.

Q. Was the change from complete subjection to complete freedom difficult?

A. No. Congress has been careful to give us independence by degrees. At first its rule was almost as absolute as that of our old Governors. Then it gave us the status of a territory. Finally it incorporated us in the Union as an independent State . . . [which promoted our prosperity.]

*From a Conversation with Mr. Guillemain, the French Consul at New Orleans:*
[Tocqueville] Q. Do you think that part of this prosperity is due to the free institutions given to Louisiana?

[Guillemain] A. One must have seen close up as I have for fifteen years the way business is conducted in a little, completely democratic republic, to be convinced that prosperity is not due to political institutions, but is independent of them. You have no idea of such a Bedlam. The people appoint intriguers without talent to office, while outstanding men seldom achieve it. The legislature ceaselessly makes, alters and repeals the laws. . . . The government is a prey to factions. You see what a state of neglect and dirt the town is in; it has a revenue of a million francs. But much squandering of public money prevails. People say that by widening the franchise one increases the independence of the vote. I think the opposite. In all countries the working classes are at the disposition of those who employ them; . . . However . . . prosperity of Louisiana is very great and is perpetually increasing. This government here has the merit of being very weak, and of not hampering any freedom.

*From a Conversation with an Alabama Lawyer:*
[Tocqueville] Q. Do the people choose good representatives?

A. No, in general they choose people on their own level who flatter them. . . .

Q. But from these bad choices there must result bad laws and bad government?

A. Not nearly so much as one might expect at first glance. There are always some men of talent in our assemblies; from the first days these overwhelm the others and absolutely dominate business. It is really they who make and discuss the laws. The rest vote as they do.

*Tocqueville's Reflections:*
The two great social principles which seem to me to rule American society . . . are as follows:

1st. The majority may be mistaken on some points, but finally it is always right. . . .

2nd. Every individual, private person, society, community or nation, is the only lawful judge of its own interest, and provided it does not harm the interests of others, nobody has the right to interfere.

A completely democratic government is so dangerous an instrument that, *even in America*, men have been obliged to take a host of precautions against the errors and passions of Democracy. The establishment of two chambers [in the legislatures], the governor's veto, and above all the establishment of the judges.

Source: Alexis de Tocqueville, *Journey to America*, ed. J. P. Mayer, trans. George Lawrence (Garden City, NY: Anchor Books, 1971), 47, 95, 98–99, 103–104, 148.

### ANALYZING THE EVIDENCE

- Who are Tocqueville's informants? How might their social identity affect their perspective on events?
- According to Tocqueville's sources, what are the strengths and weaknesses of the American political system? What is his view?

age, and his reputation as a "plain solid republican" attracted voters in all regions. Still, Jackson's strong showing surprised most political leaders. The Tennessee senator received 99 of the 261 votes cast by members of the electoral college; Adams garnered 84 votes; Crawford, struck down by a stroke during the campaign, won 41; and Clay finished with 37 (Map 10.1).

Because no candidate received an absolute majority, the Twelfth Amendment to the Constitution (ratified in 1804) specified that the House of Representatives would choose the president from among the three highest vote-getters. This procedure hurt Jackson because many congressmen feared that the rough-hewn "military chieftain" might become a tyrant. Out of the race himself, Henry Clay used his influence as Speaker to thwart Jackson's election. Clay assembled a coalition of congressmen from New England and the Ohio River Valley that voted Adams into the presidency. Adams showed his gratitude by appointing Clay his secretary of state, which was the traditional stepping-stone to the presidency. Clay's appointment was politically fatal for both men: Jackson's supporters accused Clay and Adams of making a secret deal. Condemning what Calhoun labeled a "corrupt bargain" that thwarted the popular mandate for Jackson's election, they vowed to oppose Adams's policies and to prevent Clay's rise to the presidency.

## The Last Notable President: John Quincy Adams

As president, Adams called for bold national leadership. "The moral purpose of the Creator," he told Congress, was to use the president and other public officials to "improve the conditions of himself and his fellow men." Adams called for the establishment of a national university in Washington, extensive scientific explorations in the Far West, and a uniform standard of weights and measures. Most important, he endorsed Henry Clay's American System and its three key elements: protective tariffs to stimulate manufacturing, federally subsidized roads and canals to facilitate commerce, and a national bank to control credit and provide a uniform currency.

**The Fate of Adams's Policies** Manufacturers, entrepreneurs, and farmers in the Northeast and Midwest welcomed Adams's proposals. But his policies won little support in the South, where planters opposed protective tariffs because they raised the price of manufactures. Southern smallholders also feared powerful banks that could force them into bankruptcy. From his deathbed, Thomas Jefferson condemned Adams for promoting "a single and splendid government of aristocracy [of money] . . . riding and ruling over the plundered ploughman and beggared yeomanry."

Other politicians objected to the American System on constitutional grounds. In 1817, President Madison had vetoed the Bonus Bill, which proposed using the national government's income from the Second Bank of the United States to fund improvement projects in the states. Such projects, Madison had argued, were the sole responsibility of the states, a sentiment widely shared among Jeffersonian Republicans. After a trip to Monticello to meet the aging Patriot statesman, Martin Van Buren declared his allegiance to the constitutional "doctrines of the Jefferson School." Now a member of the U.S. Senate, Van Buren joined other Jeffersonian Republicans in defeating most of Adams's proposed subsidies for roads and canals.

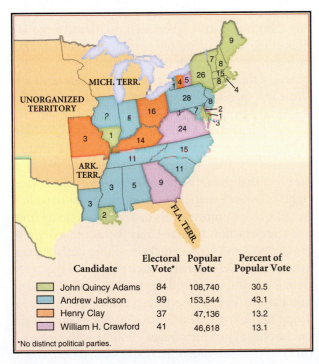

| Candidate | Electoral Vote* | Popular Vote | Percent of Popular Vote |
|---|---|---|---|
| John Quincy Adams | 84 | 108,740 | 30.5 |
| Andrew Jackson | 99 | 153,544 | 43.1 |
| Henry Clay | 37 | 47,136 | 13.2 |
| William H. Crawford | 41 | 46,618 | 13.1 |

*No distinct political parties.

**MAP 10.1**

**The Presidential Election of 1824**

Regional voting was the dominant factor in 1824. John Quincy Adams captured every electoral vote in New England and most of those in New York; Henry Clay carried Ohio and Kentucky, the most populous trans-Appalachian states; and William Crawford took the southern states of Virginia and Georgia. Only Andrew Jackson claimed a national constituency, winning Pennsylvania and New Jersey in the East, Indiana and most of Illinois in the Midwest, and much of the South. Only 356,000 Americans voted, about 27 percent of the eligible electorate.

**John Quincy Adams**

This famous daguerreotype of the former president, taken about 1843 by Philip Haas, conveys his rigid personality and high moral standards. Although these personal attributes hindered Adams's effectiveness as the nation's chief executive, they contributed to his success as an antislavery congressman from Massachusetts in the 1830s and 1840s. The Metropolitan Museum of Art, Gift of I. N. Phelps Stokes, Edward S. Hawes, Alice Mary Hawes, Marion Augusta Hawes, 1937. Photograph © The Metropolitan Museum of Art.

**The Tariff Battle** | The farthest-reaching battle of the Adams administration came over tariffs. The Tariff of 1816 had placed relatively high duties on imports of cheap English cotton cloth, allowing New England textile producers to dominate the market for such goods. In 1824, Adams and Clay secured a new tariff that protected manufacturers in New England and Pennsylvania against imports of iron goods and more expensive English woolen and cotton textiles. Without these tariffs, U.S. producers might have shared the fate of India's once world-dominant textile industry, which was destroyed in the early nineteenth century by cheaper British machine-made imports — thanks to the free trade policies imposed by the British imperial regime.

Recognizing the appeal of tariffs, Van Buren and his Jacksonian allies hopped on the bandwagon. By increasing tariffs on wool, hemp, and other imported raw materials, they hoped to win the support of wool- and hemp-producing farmers in New York, Ohio, and Kentucky for Jackson's presidential candidacy in 1828. The tariff had become a prisoner of politics. "I fear this tariff thing," remarked Thomas Cooper, the president of the College of South Carolina and an advocate of free trade. "[B]y some strange mechanical contrivance [it has become] . . . a machine for manufacturing Presidents, instead of broadcloths, and bed blankets." Disregarding southern protests, northern Jacksonians joined with supporters of Adams and Clay to enact the Tariff of 1828, which raised duties significantly on raw materials, textiles, and iron goods.

The new tariff enraged the South. As the producer of the world's cheapest raw cotton, the South did not need a tariff to protect its main industry. Moreover, by raising the price of manufactures, the tariff cost southern planters about $100 million a year. Planters had to buy either higher-cost American textiles and iron goods, thus enriching northeastern businesses and workers, or highly dutied British imports, thus paying the expenses of the national government. The new tariff was "little less than legalized pillage," an Alabama legislator declared, calling it a "Tariff of Abominations."

Ignoring the Jacksonians' support for the Tariff of 1828, most southerners heaped blame on President Adams. They also criticized Adams's Indian policy. A deeply moral man, the president supported the land rights of Native Americans against expansionist whites. In 1825, U.S. commissioners had secured a treaty from one Creek faction to cede Creek lands in Georgia to the United States for eventual sale to the state's citizens. When the Creek National Council repudiated the treaty, claiming that it was fraudulent, Adams called for new negotiations. In response, Georgia governor George M. Troup attacked the president as a "public enemy . . . the unblushing ally of the savages." Joining with Georgia's congressional delegation, Troup persuaded Congress to extinguish the Creeks' land titles, forcing most Creeks to leave the state.

Elsewhere in the nation, Adams's primary weakness was his out-of-date political style. The last notable to serve in the White House, he acted the part: aloof, moralistic, and paternalistic. When Congress rejected his activist economic policies, Adams questioned the wisdom of the voters and advised elected officials not to be "palsied [enfeebled] by the will of our constituents." Ignoring his waning popularity, the president

A CARTOON COMPARING CONDITIONS UNDER FREE TRADE AND
PROTECTIVE TARIFF

*From "The United States Weekly Telegram," November 5, 1832.*

### The "Tariff of Abominations"

Political cartoons enjoyed wide use in eighteenth-century England and became popular in the United States during the political battles of the First Party System (1794–1815). By the 1820s, American newspapers, which were often subsidized by political parties, published cartoons daily. This political cartoon attacks the tariffs of 1828 and 1832 as hostile to the interests and prosperity of the South. The gaunt figure on the left represents a southern planter, starved by exactions of the tariff, while the northern textile manufacturer has grown stout feasting on the bounty of protectionism.  © Bettmann/Corbis.

# Jackson Forever!
## The Hero of Two Wars and of Or'leans!
# The Man of the People!
#### HE WHO COULD NOT BARTER NOR BARGAIN FOR THE
# PRESIDENCY!

Who, although "*A Military Chieftain*," valued the purity of Elections and of the Electors, **MORE** than the Office of **PRESIDENT** itself! Although the greatest in the gift of his countrymen, and the highest in point of dignity of any in the world,

## BECAUSE
### It should be derived from the
# PEOPLE!

No Gag Laws! No Black Cockades! No Reign of Terror! No Standing Army or Navy Officers, when under the pay of Government, to browbeat, or

## KNOCK DOWN

Old Revolutionary Characters, or our Representatives while in the discharge of their duty.  To the Polls then, and vote for those who will support

# OLD HICKORY
### AND THE ELECTORAL LAW.

### Jackson's Electoral Strategy, 1828

In 1824, Jackson lost the presidency because of an agreement (a "corrupt bargain," according to the Jacksonians) between the supporters of John Quincy Adams and Henry Clay in the House of Representatives. Four years later, supporters of Old Hickory plastered walls with posters celebrating Jackson as "The Man of the People," who would neither "BARTER NOR BARGAIN" for the presidency, saying it should depend only on the vote of the "PEOPLE."
© Collection of the New-York Historical Society.

refused to use patronage to reward his supporters and allowed hostile federal officials to remain in office. Rather than "run" for reelection in 1828, Adams "stood" for it, telling supporters, "If my country wants my services, she must ask for them."

## "The Democracy" and the Election of 1828

Martin Van Buren and the politicians handling Andrew Jackson's campaign had no reservations about running for office. The Little Magician wanted to revive the national political coalition created by Thomas Jefferson; he therefore championed policies that appealed both to northern farmers and artisans (the "plain Republicans of the North") and to southern slave owners and smallholding planters. John C. Calhoun, Jackson's running mate, brought his South Carolina allies into Van Buren's party, and Jackson's close friends in Tennessee rallied voters there and throughout the Old Southwest. By forming a national political party, Jackson's friends hoped to reconcile the diverse economic and social

"interests" that, as James Madison had predicted in "Federalist No. 10," would inevitability exist in a large republic.

At Van Buren's direction, the Jacksonians orchestrated a massive publicity campaign. In New York, fifty newspapers declared their support for Jackson on the same day. Elsewhere, Jacksonians used mass meetings, torchlight parades, and barbecues to celebrate the candidate's frontier origin and rise to fame. With the cry of "Jackson for ever!" they praised "Old Hickory" as a "natural" aristocrat, a self-made man.

The Jacksonians called themselves Democrats or "the Democracy," names that conveyed their egalitarian message. As Thomas Morris told the Ohio legislature, he and his fellow Democrats were fighting for equality: The republic had been corrupted by legislative charters that gave "a few individuals rights and privileges not enjoyed by the citizens at large." Morris promised that the Democracy would destroy such "artificial distinction." Jackson himself declared that "equality among the people in the rights conferred by government" was the "great radical principle of freedom."

Jackson's message of equal rights and popular rule appealed to many social groups. His hostility to business corporations and to Clay's American System won support from northeastern artisans and workers who felt threatened by industrialization. Jackson also captured the votes of Pennsylvania ironworkers and New York farmers who had been enriched by the controversial Tariff of Abominations. Yet, by astutely declaring his preference for a "judicious" tariff that would balance regional interests, Jackson remained popular in the South as well. Old Hickory also garnered votes in the Southeast and Midwest, where his well-known hostility toward Native Americans reassured white farmers seeking Indian removal.

The Democrats' celebration of popular rule carried Jackson into office. In 1824, about one-quarter of the eligible electorate had voted; in 1828, more than one-half went to the polls, and 56 percent voted for the senator from Tennessee (Figure 10.1). Jackson received 178 of 261 electoral votes and became the first president from a trans-Appalachian state (Map 10.2). As the president-elect traveled to Washington, he cut a dignified figure. According to an English observer, he "wore his hair carelessly but not ungracefully arranged, and in spite of his harsh, gaunt features looked like a gentleman and a soldier." Still, Jackson's popularity and sharp temper frightened men of wealth. Senator Daniel Webster of Massachusetts, a former Federalist and now a corporate lawyer, warned his clients that the new president would "bring a breeze with him. Which way it will blow, I cannot tell [but] . . . my fear is stronger than my hope." Supreme Court justice Joseph Story shared Webster's apprehensions. Watching an unruly Inauguration Day crowd climb over the elegant White House furniture to congratulate Jackson, Story lamented that "the reign of King 'Mob' seemed triumphant."

- Was there a necessary connection between the growth of democracy and the emergence of political parties? Explain your answer.

- How do you explain John Quincy Adams's great success as secretary of state (see Chapter 7) and his relative lack of success as president?

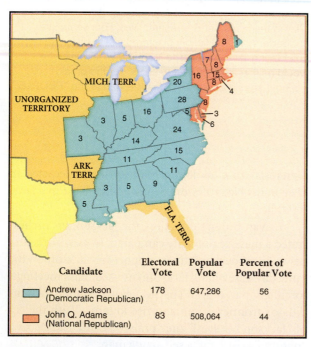

**MAP 10.2**

**The Presidential Election of 1828**

As he did in 1824, John Quincy Adams carried all of New England and some of the Mid-Atlantic states. However, Andrew Jackson swept the rest of the nation and won a resounding victory in the electoral college. More than 1.1 million American men cast ballots in 1828, more than three times the number who voted in 1824.

| Candidate | Electoral Vote | Popular Vote | Percent of Popular Vote |
|---|---|---|---|
| Andrew Jackson (Democratic Republican) | 178 | 647,286 | 56 |
| John Q. Adams (National Republican) | 83 | 508,064 | 44 |

# The Jacksonian Presidency, 1829–1837

American-style political democracy—a broad franchise, a disciplined political party, and policies favoring specific interest groups—ushered Andrew Jackson into office. Jackson used his popular mandate to transform the policies of the national government and the presidency itself. During his two terms in the White House, he enhanced presidential authority, destroyed the nationalistic American System, and established the legitimacy of a new ideology of government. An Ohio supporter summed up Jackson's vision as follows: "the Sovereignty of the People, the Rights of the States, and a Light and Simple Government."

## Jackson's Agenda: Rotation and Decentralization

To make policy, Jackson relied primarily on an informal group of advisors: his so-called "Kitchen Cabinet." Its most influential members were Kentuckians Francis

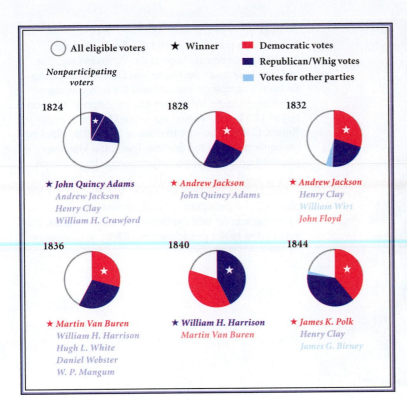

All eligible voters   ★ Winner   Democratic votes
*Nonparticipating voters*   Republican/Whig votes
   Votes for other parties

**1824**
★ **John Quincy Adams**
*Andrew Jackson*
*Henry Clay*
*William H. Crawford*

**1828**
★ **Andrew Jackson**
*John Quincy Adams*

**1832**
★ **Andrew Jackson**
*Henry Clay*
*William Wirt*
*John Floyd*

**1836**
★ **Martin Van Buren**
*William H. Harrison*
*Hugh L. White*
*Daniel Webster*
*W. P. Mangum*

**1840**
★ **William H. Harrison**
*Martin Van Buren*

**1844**
★ **James K. Polk**
*Henry Clay*
*James G. Birney*

**FIGURE 10.1**

**Changes in Voting Patterns, 1824–1840**

Between 1824 and 1840, the proportion of eligible voters who cast ballots in presidential elections increased dramatically from 27 percent to 79 percent, and remained thereafter at that level (note the shrinking white sections of these pie graphs). Voter participation soared first in 1828, when Andrew Jackson and John Quincy Adams contested for the White House, and again in 1840, as competition heated up between Democrats and Whigs, who advocated different policies and philosophies of government. Democrats triumphed in most of these contests because their program appealed to more ordinary citizens than did the policies of their Republican-Whig opponents.

Preston Blair, who edited the *Washington Globe*, and Amos Kendall, who wrote Jackson's speeches; Roger B. Taney of Maryland, who became attorney general, treasury secretary, and then chief justice of the Supreme Court; and, most important, Martin Van Buren, whom Jackson named secretary of state.

Following Van Buren's practice in New York, Jackson used patronage to create a disciplined national party. He rejected the idea of "property in office" (that officials held permanent title to an office) and insisted on a rotation of officeholders, so that when an administration was voted out, its bureaucratic appointees would also have to leave government service. Rotation would not lessen expertise, Jackson insisted, because public duties were "so plain and simple that men of intelligence may readily qualify themselves for their performance." William L. Marcy, a New York Jacksonian, put it bluntly: Government jobs were like the spoils of war, and "to the victor belong the spoils of the enemy." Using the spoils system, Jackson dispensed available government jobs to reward his friends and win backing for his policies.

Jackson's priority was to destroy the American System and all national plans for economic development. As Henry Clay noted apprehensively, the new president wanted "to cry down old [expansive] constructions of the Constitution . . . to make all Jefferson's opinions the articles of faith of the new Church." Declaring that the "voice of the people" called for "economy in the expenditures of the Government," Jackson rejected national subsidies for transportation projects, also on constitutional grounds. In 1830, he vetoed four internal improvement bills, including an extension of the National Road, arguing that they infringed "the reserved powers of states." These vetoes represented an indirect attack on the protective tariffs, another controversial part of the American System, because Clay proposed funding canals and roads with tariff revenues. Jacksonian Senator William Smith of South Carolina agreed, "[D]estroy internal improvements and you leave no motive for the tariff."

## The Tariff and Nullification

In fact, The Tariff of 1828 assisted manufacturers and farmers and had helped Jackson win the presidency. But it saddled him with a major political crisis. There was fierce opposition to high tariffs throughout the South, especially in South Carolina. South Carolina was the only state with an African American majority — 56 percent of the population in 1830 — and its slave owners, like the white sugar planters in the West Indies, feared a black rebellion. They also worried about the legal abolition of slavery. The British Parliament had declared that slavery in the West Indies would end in 1833; South Carolina planters, remembering attempts

CAPITOL

The rejected Minister,
*We never can make him President,
without first making him Vice-president.*

Pub. by H. Austin, N° 214 Broadway, N.Y.

## Who Will Be Jackson's Heir?

Elected vice president in 1828, John C. Calhoun hoped to succeed Jackson in the White House. But he failed to account for Martin Van Buren, who managed Jackson's campaign and claimed the prized office of secretary of state. When Van Buren resigned as secretary in 1831 and Jackson nominated him as minister to Britain, Calhoun sought to destroy his rival by blocking his confirmation in the Senate. The "Little Magician" pounced on this miscalculation, persuading Jackson, already disillusioned by Calhoun's support for nullification, to oust him from the ticket. Van Buren took his place as vice president in 1832, carried into the office—as the cartoonist tells the tale—on Jackson's back, and succeeded to the presidency in 1836.  © Collection of the New-York Historical Society.

to limit slavery in Missouri (see Chapter 8), worried that the U.S. Congress would follow the British lead. So they attacked the tariff, both to lower rates and to discourage attempts to use federal power to attack slavery.

The crisis began in 1832, when high-tariff congressmen ignored southern warnings that they were "endangering the Union" and reenacted the Tariff of Abominations. In response, leading South Carolinians called a state convention, which in November boldly adopted an Ordinance of Nullification declaring the tariffs of 1828 and 1832 to be null and void; prohibiting the collection of those tariffs in South Carolina after February 1, 1833; and threatening secession if federal officials tried to collect them.

South Carolina's act of **nullification** rested on the constitutional arguments developed in *The South Carolina Exposition and Protest* (1828). Written anonymously by Vice President John C. Calhoun, the *Exposition* gave a localist (or sectional) interpretation to the federal union. Because each state or geographic region had distinct interests, localists argued, protective tariffs and other national legislation that operated unequally on the various states lacked fairness and legitimacy—in fact, they were unconstitutional. An obsessive defender of the interests of southern planters, Calhoun

exaggerated the frequency of such legislation, declaring, "Constitutional government and the government of a majority are utterly incompatible."

In developing his interpretation of the Constitution, Calhoun used the arguments first advanced by Jefferson and Madison in the Kentucky and Virginia resolutions of 1798. Because the Constitution had been ratified by conventions in the various states, the resolutions had suggested, sovereignty lay in the states, not in the people. Beginning from this premise, Calhoun developed a states' rights interpretation, arguing that a state convention could declare a congressional law to be unconstitutional and therefore void within the state's borders. Replying to this argument, which had no support in the text of the Constitution, Senator Daniel Webster of Massachusetts presented a nationalist interpretation that celebrated popular sovereignty and Congress's responsibility to secure the "general welfare."

Jackson hoped to find a middle path between Webster's strident nationalism and Calhoun's radical doctrine of localist federalism. The Constitution clearly gave the federal government the authority to establish tariffs, and Jackson vowed to enforce that power, whatever the cost. He declared that South Carolina's Ordi-

**The Great Webster-Hayne Debate, 1830**

The "Tariff of Abominations" sparked one of the great debates in American history. When Senator Robert Y. Hayne of South Carolina (seated in the middle of the picture, with his legs crossed) opposed the federal tariffs by invoking the doctrines of states' rights and nullification, Daniel Webster rose to the defense of the Union. Speaking for two days to a spellbound Senate, Webster delivered an impassioned oration that celebrated the unity of the American people as the key to their freedom. His parting words—"Liberty *and* Union, now and forever, one and inseparable!"—quickly became part of the national memory.   *Webster's Reply to Hayne*, by G. P. A. Healy, City of Boston Art Commission.

nance of Nullification not only violated the letter of the Constitution but also was "unauthorized by its spirit . . . and destructive of the great object for which it was formed." More pointedly, he warned, "Disunion by armed force is treason." At Jackson's request, Congress in early 1833 passed the Force Bill, authorizing the president to use military means to compel South Carolina's obedience to national laws. Simultaneously, Jackson addressed the South's objections to high import duties by winning passage of a new tariff act that, by 1842, reduced rates to the modest levels of 1816. Subsequently, duties remained low because western wheat farmers joined southern planters in advocating cheap imports and warning against retaliatory tariffs by foreign nations. "Illinois wants a market for her agricultural products," declared Senator Sidney Breese in 1846. "[S]he wants the market of the world."

Having won the *political* battle by securing a reduction in duties, the South Carolina convention gave up its *constitutional* demand for the right of nullification. Jackson was satisfied. He had addressed the economic demands of the South while upholding the constitutional principle that no state could nullify a law of the United States—a principle that Abraham Lincoln would embrace to defend the Union during the secession crisis of 1861.

## The Bank War

As the tariff crisis intensified, Jackson faced a major challenge from politicians who supported the Second Bank of the United States. Founded in Philadelphia in 1816 (see Chapter 7), the bank was privately managed and operated under a twenty-year charter from the federal government, which owned 20 percent of its stock. The bank's most important role was to stabilize the nation's money supply, which consisted primarily of notes and bills of credit—in effect, paper money—

issued by state-chartered banks. Those banks promised to redeem the notes on demand with "hard" money—that is, gold or silver coins (also known as specie). By collecting those notes and regularly demanding specie, the Second Bank kept the state banks from issuing too much paper money and depreciating its value.

This cautious monetary policy pleased creditors—the bankers and entrepreneurs in Boston, New York, and Philadelphia, whose capital investments were underwriting economic development. However, ordinary Americans worried that the Second Bank would force the closure of state banks, leaving people holding worthless paper notes. Some politicians opposed the Second Bank because of the arrogance of its president, Nicholas Biddle. "As to mere power," Biddle boasted, "I have been for years in the daily exercise of more personal authority than any President habitually enjoys." Fearing Biddle's influence, bankers in New York and other states wanted the specie owned by the federal government deposited in their own institutions rather than in the Second Bank. Expansion-minded bankers, including friends of Jackson's in Nashville, wanted to escape supervision by any central bank.

### Jackson's Bank Veto

Although the Second Bank had many enemies, a political miscalculation by its friends brought its downfall. In 1832, Henry Clay and Daniel Webster persuaded Biddle to seek an early extension of the bank's charter (which still had four years to run). They had the votes in Congress to enact the required legislation and hoped to lure Jackson into a veto that would split the Democrats just before the 1832 elections.

Jackson turned the tables on Clay and Webster. He vetoed the rechartering bill and issued a masterful veto message that blended constitutional arguments with class rhetoric and patriotic fervor. Adopting Thomas Jefferson's position, Jackson declared that Congress had no constitutional authority to charter a national bank. Then he condemned the bank as "subversive of the rights of the States," "dangerous to the liberties of the people," and a nest of special privilege and monopoly power that promoted "the advancement of the few at the expense of . . . farmers, mechanics, and laborers." Finally, the president noted that British aristocrats owned much of the bank's stock. Such a powerful institution should be "purely American," Jackson declared with patriotic fervor.

Jackson's attack on the bank carried him to victory in 1832. Old Hickory and Martin Van Buren, his longtime ally and new running mate, overwhelmed Henry Clay, who headed the National Republican ticket,

by 219 to 49 electoral votes. Jackson's most fervent supporters were eastern workers and western farmers, who blamed the Second Bank for high urban prices and stagnant farm income. "All the flourishing cities of the West are mortgaged to this money power," charged Senator Thomas Hart Benton, a Jacksonian from Missouri. "They may be devoured by it at any moment." But many of Jackson's other supporters had prospered during a decade of strong economic growth. Along with thousands of middle-class Americans—lawyers, clerks, shopkeepers, and artisans—they wanted an equal opportunity to rise in the world and cheered Jackson's attack on privileged corporations.

### The Bank Destroyed

Early in 1833, Jackson met their wishes by appointing Roger B. Taney, a strong opponent of corporate privilege, as head of the Treasury Department. Taney promptly withdrew the government's gold and silver from the Second Bank. He deposited the specie in various state banks, which critics called Jackson's "pet banks." To justify this abrupt (and probably illegal) transfer, Jackson declared that his reelection represented "the decision of the people against the bank" and gave him a mandate to destroy it. This sweeping claim of presidential power was new and radical. Never before had a president claimed that victory at the polls allowed him to pursue a controversial policy or to act independently of Congress (see Comparing American Voices, "The Character and Goals of Andrew Jackson," pp. 316–317).

The "bank war" escalated into an all-out political battle. In March 1834, Jackson's opponents in the Senate passed a resolution by Henry Clay censuring the president and warning of executive tyranny: "We are in the midst of a revolution, hitherto bloodless, but rapidly descending towards a total change of the pure republican character of the Government, and the concentration of all power in the hands of one man." Jackson remained undeterred by Clay's charges and Congress's censure. "The Bank is trying to kill me but I will kill it," he vowed to Van Buren. And so he did. When the Second Bank's national charter expired in 1836, Jackson prevented its renewal.

Jackson had destroyed both national banking—the handiwork of Alexander Hamilton—and the American System of protective tariffs and internal improvements created by Henry Clay and John Quincy Adams. The result was a profound check on economic activism and innovative policymaking by the national government. "All is gone," observed a Washington newspaper correspondent. "All is gone, which the General Government was instituted to create and preserve."

# Indian Removal

The status of Native American peoples posed an equally complex political problem. By the late 1820s, white voices throughout the South and Midwest were calling for Indian peoples to be resettled west of the Mississippi River. Many eastern supporters of Native Americans also favored resettlement. Removal to the West seemed the only way to protect Indians from alcoholism, financial chicanery, and cultural decline.

However, most Indians did not want to leave their ancestral lands. For centuries Cherokees and Creeks had lived in Georgia, Tennessee, and Alabama; Chickasaws and Choctaws in Mississippi and Alabama; and Seminoles in Florida. During the War of 1812, Andrew Jackson had forced the Creeks to relinquish millions of acres, but Indian tribes still controlled vast tracts and wanted to keep them.

**Cherokee Resistance** | But on what terms? Some Indian peoples had adopted white ways. An 1825 census of the Cherokees revealed that they owned 33 gristmills, 13 sawmills, nearly 2,500 spinning wheels, 760 looms, and 2,900 plows. Many owners were mixed-bloods, the offspring of white traders and Indian women. They had grown up in a bicultural world, knew the political and economic ways of whites, and often favored assimilation into white society. Indeed, some mixed-bloods were indistinguishable from southern planters. James Vann, a Georgia Cherokee, owned more than twenty black slaves, two trading posts, and a gristmill. Forty other mixed-blood Cherokee families each owned twenty or more African American slaves.

To protect their property and the lands of their people, the mixed-bloods sought full integration into American life. In 1821, Sequoyah perfected a system of writing for the Cherokee language; six years later, mixed-bloods devised a new charter of Cherokee government modeled directly on the U.S. Constitution. "You asked us to throw off the hunter and warrior state," Cherokee John Ridge told a Philadelphia audience in 1832. "We did so. You asked us to form a republican government: We did so. . . . You asked us to learn to read: We did so. You asked us to cast away our idols, and worship your God: We did so." Full-blood Cherokees, who made up 90 percent of the population, resisted many of these cultural and political innovations but were equally determined to retain their ancestral lands. "We would not receive money for land in which our fathers and friends are buried," one full-blood chief declared. "We love our land; it is our mother."

What the Cherokees did or wanted carried no weight with the Georgia legislature. In 1802, Georgia had given up its western land claims in return for a federal promise to extinguish Indian landholdings in the state. Now it demanded fulfillment of that pledge. Having spent his military career fighting Indians and seizing their lands, Andrew Jackson gave full support to Georgia. On assuming the presidency, he withdrew the federal troops that had protected Indian enclaves there and in Alabama and Mississippi. The states, he declared, were sovereign within their borders.

**The Removal Act and Its Aftermath** | Jackson then pushed the Indian Removal Act of 1830 through Congress over the determined opposition of evangelical Protestant men—and women. To block removal, Catharine Beecher and Lydia Sigourney

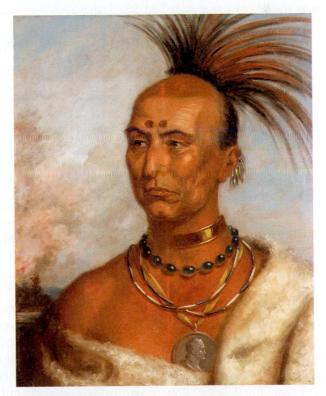

**Black Hawk**

This portrait of Black Hawk (1767–1838), by Charles Bird King, shows the Indian leader as a young warrior, wearing a medal commemorating an early nineteenth-century agreement with the U.S. government. Later, in 1830, when Congress approved Andrew Jackson's Indian Removal Act, Black Hawk mobilized Sauk and Fox warriors to protect their ancestral lands in Illinois. "It was here, that I was born—and here lie the bones of many friends and relatives," the aging chief declared. "I . . . never could consent to leave it." Courtesy Warner Collection of Gulf States Paper Corporation, Tuscaloosa, AL.

# The Character and Goals of Andrew Jackson

From the start of his career, Andrew Jackson was a controversial figure. "Hot-tempered," "Indian-hater," "military despot"—critics hurled many such charges at Jackson, while his friends praised him as an honorable and forthright states-man. His contemporary biographer, the journalist James Parton, found him a man of many faces, an enigma. Others thought they understood his personality and poli-cies: James Hamilton, a loyal Jacksonian and a congressman, recalled Jackson's volatile temper. Henry Clay, his archrival, warned that Jackson's high-handed ac-tions threatened American republican institutions. Even worse, said Philip Hone—a wealthy New York Whig merchant—Jackson and his allies were instigating class warfare. But based on conversations with dozens of Americans, French-man Alexis de Tocqueville offered a more moderate interpretation of the man and his goals.

## James Parton

### From Parton's Preface to *The Life of Andrew Jackson* (1860)

If any one, at the end of a year even, had asked what I had yet discovered respecting General Jackson, I might have answered thus: "Andrew Jackson, I am given to understand, was a patriot and a traitor. He was one of the greatest of generals, and wholly ignorant of the art of war. A writer brilliant, elegant, eloquent, without being able to compose a correct sentence. . . . The first of statesmen, he never devised, he never framed a measure. He was the most candid of men, and was capable of the profoundest dissimulation. A most law-defying, law-obeying citizen. A stickler for discipline, he never hesitated to disobey his superior. A democratic autocrat. An urbane savage. An atrocious saint."

## James Hamilton Jr.

### Hamilton Recalls an Event of 1827, as Jackson Began His Second Campaign for the Presidency

The steamer Pocahontas was chartered by citizens of New Orleans to convey the General and his party from Nashville to that city. She was fitted out in the most sumptuous man-ner. The party was General and Mrs. Jackson, . . . Governor Samuel Houston, Wm. B. Lewis, Robert Armstrong, and others. . . . The only freight was the General's cotton-crop.

During the voyage we stopped at the different towns on the river . . . and at the principal ones, committees addressed the General, to whom he made appropriate replies. In the course of the voyage an event occurred, which I repeat, as it is suggestive of [his] character. A steamer of greater speed than ours, going in the same direction, passed us, crossed our bow; then stopped and let us pass her and then passed

us again in triumph. This was repeated again and again, until the General, being excited by the offensive course, ordered a rifle to be brought to him; hailed the pilot of the other steamer, and swore that if he did the same thing again he would shoot him.

## Philip Hone

### A New York Conservative Ruminates in His Diary on the Jacksonians' Victory in the New York Elections of 1834

I apprehend that Mr. Van Buren [Jackson's vice president and successor] and his friends have no permanent cause of triumph in their victory. They . . . have mounted a vicious horse, who, taking the bit in his mouth, will run away with [them]. . . . This battle had been fought upon the ground of the poor against the rich, and this unworthy prejudice, this dangerous delusion, has been encouraged by the leaders of the triumphant party, and fanned into a flame by the polluted breath of the hireling press in their employ. . . .

The cry of "Down with the aristocracy!" mingled with the shouts of victory, and must have grated on the ears of some of their own leaders like the croaking of the evil-boding raven. They have succeeded in raising this dangerous spirit [of the mob], and have gladly availed themselves of its support to accomplish a temporary object; but can they allay it at pleasure? . . . Eighteen thousand men in New York have voted for the high-priest of the party whose professed design is to bring down the property, the talents, the industry, the steady habits of that class which constituted the real strength of the Commonwealth, to the common level of the idle, the worthless, and the unenlightened. Look to it, ye men of respectability in the Jackson party, are ye not afraid of the weapons ye have used in this warfare?

## Henry Clay

### Clay Introduces a Senate Resolution Censuring Jackson's Actions, December 26, 1833

We are in the midst of a revolution, hitherto bloodless, but rapidly tending toward a total change of the pure republican character of the government, and to the concentration of all power in the hands of one man. The powers of Congress are paralyzed, except when exerted in conformity with his will, by frequent and an extraordinary exercise of the executive veto, not anticipated by the founders of our Constitution, and not practiced by any of the predecessors of the present chief magistrate. . . .

The judiciary has not been exempt from the prevailing rage for innovation. Decisions of the tribunals, deliberately pronounced, have been contemptuously disregarded. And the sanctity of numerous treaties openly violated. Our Indian relations, coeval with the existence of the government, and recognized and established by numerous laws and treaties, have been subverted. . . . The system of protection of improvement lies crushed beneath the veto. The system of protection of American industry [will soon meet a similar fate]. . . . In a term of eight years, a little more than equal to that which was required to establish our liberties [as an independent republican nation between 1776 and 1783], the government will have been transformed into an elective monarchy—the worst of all forms of government.

## Alexis de Tocqueville

### The French Political Philosopher Analyzes Jackson in *Democracy in America* (1835)

Some persons in Europe have formed an opinion of the influence of General Jackson upon the affairs of his country which appears highly extravagant to those who have seen the subject nearer at hand. We have been told that General Jackson has won battles; that he is an energetic man, prone by nature and habit to the use of force, covetous of power and a despot by inclination.

All this may be true; but the inferences which have been drawn from these truths are very erroneous. It has been imagined that General Jackson is bent on establishing a dictatorship in America, introducing a military spirit, and giving a degree of influence to the central authority that cannot but be dangerous to provincial [state] liberties. But in America the time for similar undertakings, and the age for men of this kind, has not yet come; if General Jackson had thought of exercising his authority in this manner, he would infallibly have forfeited his political station and compromised his life; he has not been so imprudent as to attempt anything of the kind.

Far from wishing to extend the Federal power, the President belongs to the party which is desirous of limiting that power to the clear and precise letter of the Constitution and which never puts a construction upon that act favorable to the government of the Union; far from standing forth as the champion of centralization, General Jackson is the agent of the state jealousies; and he was placed in his lofty station by the passions that are most opposed to the central government. It is by perpetually flattering these passions that he maintains his station and his popularity. General Jackson is the slave of the majority: he yields to its wishes, its propensities, and its demands. . . .

General Jackson stoops to gain the favor of the majority. . . . Supported by a power that his predecessors never had, he tramples on his personal enemies, whenever they cross his path. . . . He even treats the national representatives with a disdain approaching to insult; he puts his veto on the laws of Congress and frequently neglects even to reply to that powerful body. . . . The power of General Jackson perpetually increases, but that of the President declines; in his hands the Federal government is strong, but it will pass enfeebled into the hands of his successor.

Sources: James Parton, *The Life of Andrew Jackson. In Three Volumes* (New York: Mason Brothers, 1860), vol. 1, pp. vii–viii; Sean Wilentz, ed., *Major Problems in the Early Republic, 1787–1848* (Lexington, MA: D. C. Heath, 1991), 374 (Hamilton) and 392–393 (Hone); Calvin Colton, ed., *The Life . . . of Henry Clay*, 6 vols. (New York: A. Barnes, 1857), 576–580; Alexis de Tocqueville, *Democracy in America*, abr. by Thomas Bender (New York: Modern Library, 1981), 271–273.

### ANALYZING THE EVIDENCE

- Was Jackson a "democratic autocrat," as Parton puts it? What does he mean by this term? Would the authors of the other excerpts agree with this characterization? Did Jackson instigate class warfare, as Hone suggests?

- In what respects do Clay and Tocqueville agree in their assessment of Jackson and his policies? How do they disagree?

- What did Tocqueville mean by saying that Jackson's power "perpetually increases, but that of the President declines"? Was he correct?

dispatched the Ladies Circular, which urged "benevolent ladies" to use "prayers and exertions to avert the calamity of removal." In response, women from across the nation flooded Congress with petitions. Despite their efforts, Jackson's bill squeaked through the House of Representatives by a vote of 102 to 97.

The Removal Act created the Indian Territory, outside the bounds of any state (on lands in present-day Oklahoma and Kansas). It also promised money and reserved land to Native American peoples who would agree to give up their ancestral holdings east of the Mississippi River. Government officials promised the Indians that they could live on their new land, "they and all their children, as long as grass grows and water runs." But, as one Indian leader noted, in "the wilderness of the West . . . water and timber are scarcely to be

seen." When Chief Black Hawk and his Sauk and Fox followers refused to leave rich, well-watered farmland in western Illinois in 1832, Jackson quickly sent troops to expel them. Following a series of confrontations, the U.S. Army pursued Black Hawk into the Wisconsin Territory and, in the brutal eight-hour Bad Axe Massacre, killed 850 of his 1,000 warriors. Over the next five years, American diplomatic pressure and military power forced seventy Indian peoples to sign treaties and move west of the Mississippi (Map 10.3).

In the meantime, the Cherokees had carried the defense of their lands to the Supreme Court, where they claimed the status of a "foreign nation." In *Cherokee Nation v. Georgia* (1831), Chief Justice John Marshall denied the Cherokees' claim of independence and declared that Indian peoples were "domestic depen-

**MAP 10.3**

**The Removal of Native Americans, 1820–1846**

Beginning in the 1820s, the U.S. government forced scores of Native American peoples to sign treaties that exchanged Indian lands in the East for money and designated reservations west of the Mississippi River. Then, in the 1830s, the government used military force to expel the Cherokees, Chickasaws, Choctaws, Creeks, and many Seminoles from their ancestral homes in the Old Southeast and to resettle them in the Indian Territory, in the present-day states of Oklahoma and Kansas.

**Raising Public Opinion Against the Seminoles**

During the eighteenth century, hundreds of black slaves fled South Carolina and Georgia and found refuge in Spanish Florida, where they lived among and intermarried with the Seminole people. This color engraving from the 1830s — showing red and black Seminoles butchering respectable white families — sought to bolster political support for the forced removal of the Seminoles to the Indian Territory. By the mid-1840s, after a decade of warfare, the U.S. Army had forced 2,500 Seminoles to migrate to Oklahoma. However, another 2,500 Seminoles continued their armed resistance and eventually won a new treaty allowing them to live in Florida.     Granger Collection.

dent nations." However, in *Worcester v. Georgia* (1832), Marshall and the court sided with the Cherokees against Georgia. Voiding Georgia's extension of state law over the Cherokees, the court held that Indian nations were "distinct political communities, having territorial boundaries, within which their authority is exclusive [and is] guaranteed by the United States."

Instead of guaranteeing the Cherokees' territory, the U.S. government took it from them. In 1835, American officials negotiated the Treaty of New Echota with a minority Cherokee faction and insisted that all Cherokees move to the new Indian Territory. When only 2,000 of 17,000 Cherokees had moved by the May 1838 deadline, President Martin Van Buren ordered General Winfield Scott to enforce the treaty. Scott's army rounded up some 14,000 Cherokees and marched them 1,200 miles to the Indian Territory, an arduous journey that became known as the Trail of Tears. Along the way, 3,000 Indians died of starvation and exposure. Once in Oklahoma, the Cherokees excluded anyone of "negro or mullato parentage" from governmental office and thus reaffirmed that full citizenship in their nation was racially defined. Just as the United States was a "white man's country," so Indian Territory would be defined as a "red man's country."

After the Creeks, Chickasaws, and Choctaws moved west of the Mississippi, encouraged by generous gifts of land, the Seminoles were the only numerically significant Indian people remaining in the Old South-

west. After years of warfare, about half the Seminole people moved to Indian Territory. But Seminoles who had intermarried with runaway slaves feared the emphasis on "blood purity" there. During the 1840s, they fought a successful guerrilla war against the U.S. Army and retained their lands in Florida, which was still a sparsely settled frontier region. These Seminoles were the exception, however. The Jacksonians had forced the removal of most eastern Indian peoples.

## The Jacksonian Impact

Jackson's legacy, like that of every other great president, is complex and rich. On the institutional level, he expanded the authority of the nation's chief executive by identifying it with the voice of the people. As Jackson put it, "The President is the direct representative of the American people." Assuming that role during the nullification crisis, he upheld national authority by threatening the use of military force, laying the foundation for Lincoln's defense of the Union a generation later. At the same time (and somewhat contradictorily), Jackson curbed the reach of the national government. By undermining Henry Clay's American System of national banking, protective tariffs, and internal improvements, Jackson reinvigorated the Jeffersonian tradition of a limited and frugal central government (see Reading American Pictures, "Thomas Cole's Political Allegory of Jacksonian America," p. 320).

# Thomas Cole's Political Allegory of Jacksonian America

Andrew Jackson was a polarizing figure whose policies and personality divided Americans. One Jacksonian critic was Thomas Cole (1801–1848). Born in England, Cole came to the United States in 1817 and soon acquired a reputation as a fine landscape painter—a leading member of the so-called Hudson River School. Between 1833 and 1836, Cole executed a series of five large canvases collectively known as *The Course of Empire*, a veiled attack on Jacksonian democracy. (See **en.wikipedia.org/wiki/The_Course_of_Empire**.)

Thomas Cole, *The Course of Empire: The Consummation of Empire.* © Collection of the New-York Historical Society.

## ANALYZING THE EVIDENCE

- Do you recognize the architecture of the buildings? Why would Cole set his allegory in classical Greece or Rome? What political ideologies of the classical world served as models during the Revolutionary era (see Chapter 5)?

- At the lower left of *Consummation*, a red-robed, crowned emperor is borne in triumph on an elephant,

followed by his retainers, officials, and war captives. Cole had read Edward Gibbon's epic history, *The Decline and Fall of the Roman Empire* (1776–1788), which linked Rome's decline to the overthrow of the Roman Republic by Julius Caesar (who was feted in such processions). How might a similar fate befall the American Republic?

- Cole wrote that *The Course of Empire* "anticipated the downfall of pure republican government." *Consummation* offers clues as to the cause of its demise. What is the ideology of "pure republicanism" and how does Cole's imagery suggest its downfall?

**The Taney Court** | Jackson also undermined the constitutional jurisprudence of John Marshall by appointing Roger B. Taney as Marshall's successor. During his long tenure as chief justice (1835–1864), Taney partially reversed the nationalist and vested-property-rights decisions of the Marshall Court and gave constitutional legitimacy to Jackson's policies of states' rights and free enterprise. In the landmark case *Charles River Bridge Co. v. Warren Bridge Co.* (1837), Taney declared that a legislative charter — in this case, to build and operate a toll bridge — did not necessarily bestow a monopoly, and that a legislature could charter a competing bridge to promote the general welfare: "While the rights of private property are sacredly guarded, we must not forget that the community also has rights." This decision directly challenged Marshall's interpretation of the contract clause of the Constitution in *Dartmouth College v. Woodward* (1819), which had stressed the binding nature of public charters (see Chapter 7). By limiting the property claims of existing canal and turnpike companies, Taney's decision allowed legislatures to charter competing railroads that would provide cheaper and more efficient transportation.

The Taney Court also limited Marshall's nationalistic interpretation of the commerce clause by enhancing the regulatory role of state governments. For example, in *Mayor of New York v. Miln* (1837), the Taney Court ruled that New York State could use its "police power" to inspect the health of arriving immigrants. The Court also restored to the states some of the economic powers they had exercised before 1787. In *Briscoe v. Bank of Kentucky* (1837), the justices allowed a bank owned by the state of Kentucky to issue currency, despite the wording of the U.S. Constitution (Article 1, Section 10) that prohibits states from issuing "bills of credit."

**States Revise Their Constitutions** | Inspired by Jackson and Taney's example, Democrats in the various states mounted their own constitutional revolutions. Between 1830 and 1860, twenty states called conventions that wrote new, more democratic constitutions. Most of these constitutions gave the vote to all white men and reapportioned state legislatures on the basis of population. They also brought government "near to the people" by mandating the election, rather than the appointment, of most public officials, including sheriffs, justices of the peace, and judges.

The new constitutions also embodied the principles of **classical liberalism**, or **laissez-faire**, by limiting the government's role in the economy. (Twentieth-century social-welfare liberalism endorses the opposite principle: that government should intervene in economic and social life.) As president, Jackson had destroyed the American System, and his disciples now attacked the state-based Commonwealth System: the use of chartered corporations and state funds to promote economic development. Most Jackson-era constitutions prohibited states from granting special charters to corporations and extending loans and credit guarantees to private businesses. "If there is any danger to be feared in . . . government," declared a New Jersey Democrat, "it is the danger of associated wealth, with special privileges." The revised constitutions also protected taxpayers by setting strict limits on state debt and encouraging judges to enforce them. Said one New York reformer, "We will not trust the legislature with the power of creating indefinite mortgages on the people's property."

"The world is governed too much," the Jacksonians proclaimed as they embraced a small-government, laissez-faire outlook. The first American populists, they celebrated the power of ordinary people to make decisions in the voting booth and the marketplace.

- What were Andrew Jackson's policies on banking and tariffs? Did they help or hurt the American economy? Why?
- Compare and contrast the views of Jackson and John Marshall with respect to the status and rights of Indian peoples.
- How did the constitutional interpretations of the Taney Court and the new Jacksonian state constitutions alter the American legal and constitutional system?

# Class, Culture, and the Second Party System

The rise of the Democracy and Jackson's tumultuous presidency sparked the creation in the mid-1830s of a second national party: the **Whigs**. For the next two decades, Whigs and Democrats competed fiercely for votes and found supporters in different cultural groups. Many evangelical Protestants became Whigs, while most Catholic immigrants and traditional Protestants joined the Democrats. By debating issues of economic policy, class power, and moral reform, party politicians offered Americans a choice between competing programs and political leaders. "Of the two great parties," remarked philosopher and essayist Ralph Waldo Emerson, "[the

Democracy] has the best cause . . . for free trade, for wide suffrage, [but the Whig party] has the best men."

## The Whig Worldview

The Whig Party arose in 1834, when a group of congressmen banded together to oppose Andrew Jackson's policies and his high-handed, "kinglike" conduct. They took the name *Whigs* to identify themselves with the pre-Revolutionary American and British parties — also called Whigs — that had opposed the arbitrary actions of British monarchs. The Whigs accused "King Andrew I" of violating the Constitution by creating a spoils system and undermining elected legislators, who were the true representatives of the sovereign people. One Whig accused Jackson of ruling in a manner "more absolute than that of any absolute monarchy of Europe."

Initially, the Whigs were a diverse group drawn from various political factions. However, under the leadership of Senators Webster of Massachusetts, Clay of Kentucky, and Calhoun of South Carolina, the new party gradually assumed a distinctive stance. Like the Federalists of the 1790s, the Whigs wanted a political world dominated by men of ability and wealth; unlike the Federalists, though, they advocated an elite based on talent, not birth.

The Whigs celebrated the entrepreneur and the enterprising individual: "This is a country of self-made men," they boasted, pointing to the relative absence of permanent distinctions of class and status among white citizens. Embracing the Industrial Revolution, northern Whigs welcomed the investments of "moneyed capitalists," which provided workers with jobs and so "bread, clothing and homes." As Whig congressman Edward Everett told a Fourth of July crowd in Lowell, Massachusetts, there should be a "holy alliance" among laborers, owners, and governments. Many workers agreed, especially those who labored in the New England textile factories and Pennsylvania iron mills that benefited from protective tariffs. To ensure prosperity, Everett and other northern Whigs called for a return to the American System.

**Calhoun's Dissent** | Support for the Whigs in the South — less widespread than that in the North — rested on the appeal of specific policies and politicians. Some southern Whigs were wealthy planters who invested in railroads and banks or sold their cotton to New York merchants. But the majority were yeomen whites who resented the power and policies of low-country planters, most of whom

were Democrats. In addition, some Virginia and South Carolina Democrats became Whigs because, like John C. Calhoun, they favored states' rights and condemned Andrew Jackson's crusade against nullification.

Like Calhoun, most southern Whigs rejected the Whig Party's enthusiasm for high tariffs and social mobility. Calhoun was extremely conscious of class divisions in society. He believed that the northern Whig ideal of equal opportunity was contradicted not only by slavery, which he considered a fundamental American institution, but also by the wage-labor system of industrial capitalism. "There is and always has been in an advanced state of wealth and civilization a conflict between labor and capital," Calhoun declared in 1837. He urged slave owners and factory owners to unite against their common foe: a working class composed of enslaved blacks and propertyless whites.

Most northern Whigs rejected Calhoun's class-conscious social ideology. "A clear and well-defined line between capital and labor" might fit the slave South or class-ridden European societies, Daniel Webster conceded, but in the North "this distinction grows less and less definite as commerce advances." Ignoring the ever-increasing mass of propertyless immigrants and native-born wage workers, Webster focused on the growing size of the northern middle class, whose members generally supported Whig candidates. In the election of 1834, the Whigs won a majority in the House of Representatives by appealing to evangelical Protestants and upwardly mobile families — prosperous farmers, small-town merchants, and skilled industrial workers in New England, New York, and the new communities along the Great Lakes.

**Anti-Masons Become Whigs** | Many Whig voters in 1834 had previously supported the Anti-Masonic Party, a powerful but short-lived political party that formed in the late 1820s. As the name implies, Anti-Masons opposed the Order of Freemasonry. Freemasonry arose in eighteenth-century Europe among men who opposed their monarchical governments and espoused republicanism; it operated as a secret society with complex rituals to avoid police spies. The order spread rapidly in America and attracted political leaders — including George Washington, Henry Clay, and Andrew Jackson — and ambitious businessmen. In New York State alone by the mid-1820s, there were more than 20,000 Masons, organized into 450 local lodges. But after the kidnapping and murder in 1826 of William Morgan, a New York Mason who had threatened to reveal the order's secrets, the Freemasons fell

**Celebrating a Political Triumph, 1836**

To commemorate Martin Van Buren's election in 1836 and to reward friends for their support, the Democratic Party distributed thousands of snuff boxes inscribed with the new president's portrait. By using gifts and other innovative measures to enlist the loyalty of voters, Van Buren and his allies transformed American politics from an upper-class avocation to a democratic contest for votes and power. Collection of Janice L. and David J. Frent.

into disrepute. Thurlow Weed, a newspaper editor in Rochester, New York, spearheaded the Anti-Masonic Party, which condemned the Masons as a secret aristocratic fraternity. To oust Masons from local and state offices, the Anti-Masons nominated their own candidates.

The Whigs recruited Anti-Masons to their party by endorsing the Anti-Masons' support for temperance, equality of opportunity, and evangelical morality. Throughout the Northeast and Midwest, Whig politicians advocated legal curbs on the sale of alcohol and local ordinances that preserved Sunday as a day of worship. The Whigs also won congressional seats in the Ohio and Mississippi valleys, where farmers, bankers, and shopkeepers favored Henry Clay's American System. For these citizens of the growing Midwest, the Whigs' program of government subsidies for roads, canals, and bridges was as important as their moral agenda.

In the election of 1836, the Whig Party faced Martin Van Buren, the architect of the Democratic Party and Jackson's handpicked successor. Van Buren denounced the American System and warned that its revival would promote an oppressive "consolidated government." Po-

sitioning himself as a defender of individual rights, Van Buren condemned the efforts of Whigs and moral reformers to enact state laws imposing temperance and national laws abolishing slavery. "The government is best which governs least" became his motto in economic, cultural, and racial matters.

To oppose Van Buren, the Whigs ran four candidates, each with a strong regional reputation. Their plan was to garner enough electoral votes to throw the contest into the House of Representatives. However, the Whig tally—73 electoral votes collected by William Henry Harrison of Ohio, 26 by Hugh L. White of Tennessee, 14 by Daniel Webster of Massachusetts, and 11 by W. P. Magnum of Georgia—fell far short of Van Buren's 170 votes. Still, the four Whig candidates won 49 percent of the popular vote, showing that the party's message of economic and moral improvement had a broad appeal.

## Labor Politics and the Depression of 1837–1843

As the Democrats battled Whigs on the national level, they faced local challenges from urban artisans and workers. In 1827, artisans and workers in Philadelphia organized the Mechanics' Union of Trade Associations, a group of fifty unions with 10,000 members. The following year, they founded a Working Men's Party to secure "a just balance of power . . . between all the various classes." In their view, the growth of industry and commerce brought prosperity to bankers and entrepreneurs but not to urban artisans and workers, who suffered from rising prices and stagnant wages. To restore the balance, the new party called for the abolition of private banks, chartered monopolies, and debtors' prisons. And it demanded a fairer system of taxation and universal public education.

**Workers Form a Political Party**  By 1833, laborers had established Working Men's Parties in fifteen states. The new parties were locally based but shared a common ideology. They rejected "the glaring inequality of society" that subordinated the interests of workers to those of their employers. "Past experience teaches us that we have nothing to hope from the aristocratic orders of society," declared the New York Working Men's Party. It vowed "to send men of our own description, if we can, to the Legislature at Albany." In Philadelphia, the Working Men's Party elected a number of assemblymen; in 1834, they persuaded the Pennsylvania legislature to authorize tax-supported schools so that workers' children could rise in the world.

Indeed, the workers' ultimate goal was a society without dependent wage earners. In such an artisan republic, said labor intellectual Orestes Brownson, "All men will be independent proprietors, working on their own capitals, on their own farms, or in their own shops." Like the rising middle class, artisan republicans demanded equal rights and equal opportunity. Joseph Weydemeyer, a close friend of Karl Marx, reported from New York in the early 1850s that most American workers "are incipient bourgeois, and feel themselves to be such." Thus William Leggett, a leading member of the New York Loco-Foco (Equal Rights) Party, demanded "a system of legislation which leaves to all the free exercise of their talents and industry." Working Men's candidates won office in many cities, but divisions over policy and the parties' weakness in statewide contests soon took a toll. By the mid-1830s, most politically active workers had joined the Democratic Party and were urging it to eliminate protective tariffs and tax the stocks and bonds of wealthy capitalists.

**Financial Panic and Economic Depression**    At this juncture, the Panic of 1837 threw the American economy—and the union movement—into disarray. The panic began when the Bank of England decided to boost the faltering British economy by sharply curtailing the flow of money and credit to the United States. Since 1822, British manufacturers had extended credit to southern planters to expand cotton production, and British investors had purchased millions of dollars of the canal bonds issued by northern states. Suddenly deprived of British funds, American planters, merchants, and canal corporations had to withdraw gold from domestic banks to pay their commercial debts and interest on their foreign loans. Moreover, as British textile mills drastically reduced their purchases of raw cotton from the South, cotton prices plummeted from 20 cents a pound to 10 cents or less.

Falling cotton prices and the drain of specie to Britain set off a financial panic. On May 8, the Dry Dock Bank of New York City closed its doors, and worried depositors began to withdraw gold and silver coins from other banks. Within two weeks, every bank in the United States had stopped trading specie and curtailed credit, turning a financial panic into an economic crisis. "This sudden overthrow of the commercial credit" had a "stunning effect," observed Henry Fox, the British minister in Washington. "The conquest of the land by a foreign power could hardly have produced a more general sense of humiliation and grief."

A second, longer-lasting downturn began in 1839. To revive the economy after the Panic of 1837, state governments had increased their investments in canals and railroads. As they issued more and more bonds to finance these ventures, bond prices fell sharply in Europe, sparking a four-year-long financial crisis that engulfed state governments in America. Nine states could not meet the interest payments due on their bonds and defaulted, which prompted foreign lenders to cut the flow of new capital to the United States. Bumper crops drove down cotton prices even further, bringing more bankruptcies.

The American economy fell into a deep depression. By 1843, canal construction had dropped by 90 percent and prices had fallen by nearly 50 percent. Unemployment reached almost 20 percent of the workforce in seaports and industrial centers. Minister Henry Ward Beecher described a land "filled with lamentation . . . its inhabitants wandering like bereaved citizens among the ruins of an earthquake, mourning for children, for houses crushed, and property buried forever."

By creating a surplus of unemployed workers, the depression undermined the labor movement. In 1837, six thousand masons, carpenters, and other building-trades workers lost their jobs in New York City, depleting unions' rosters and destroying their bargaining power. By 1843, most local unions and all the national labor organizations had disappeared, along with their newspapers.

## "Tippecanoe and Tyler Too!"

Many Americans blamed the Democrats for the depression of 1837–1843. They criticized Jackson for destroying the Second Bank and directing the Treasury Department to issue a Specie Circular in 1836. The Treasury's document required western settlers to use gold and silver coins to buy farms in the national domain and was believed, albeit mistakenly, to have been primarily responsible for the drain of specie from the economy.

The public turned its anger on Van Buren, who took office just as the panic struck. Ignoring the pleas of influential bankers, the new president refused to revoke the Specie Circular or take actions to stimulate economic activity. Holding to his philosophy of limited government, Van Buren advised Congress that "the less government interferes with private pursuits the better for the general prosperity." As the depression deep-

**Hard Times**

The Panic of 1837 struck Americans hard. As this anti-Democratic political cartoon suggests, unemployed workers turned to drink; women and children begged in the streets; and fearful depositors tried to withdraw funds before banks collapsed. As the plummeting hot-air balloon in the background symbolized, the rising "Glory" of America was crashing to earth.   © Museum of the City of New York, USA /The Bridgeman Art Library.

ened in 1839, this laissez-faire outlook commanded less and less political support. Worse, Van Buren's major piece of fiscal legislation, the Independent Treasury Act of 1840, actually delayed recovery. The act pulled federal specie out of Jackson's pet banks (which had used it to back loans) and placed it in government vaults, where it had little economic impact.

**The Log Cabin Campaign** | Determined to exploit Van Buren's weakness, the Whigs organized their first national convention in 1840 and nominated William Henry Harrison of Ohio for president and John Tyler of Virginia for vice president. A military hero of the Battle of Tippecanoe and the War of 1812, Harrison was well advanced in age (sixty-eight) and had little political experience. But the Whig leaders in Congress, Clay and Webster, wanted a president who would rubber-stamp their program for protective tariffs and a national bank. An unpretentious, amiable man, Harrison told voters that Whig policies were "the only means, under Heaven, by which a poor industrious man may become a rich man without bowing to colossal wealth."

Panic and depression stacked the political cards against Van Buren, but the election turned more on style than on substance. It became the great "log cabin campaign"—the first time two well-organized parties competed for the loyalties of a mass electorate through a new style of campaigning. Whig songfests, parades, and well-orchestrated mass meetings drew new voters into politics. Whig speakers assailed "Martin Van Ruin" as a manipulative politician with aristocratic tastes—a devotee of fancy wines and elegant clothes, as indeed he was. Less truthfully, they portrayed Harrison as a

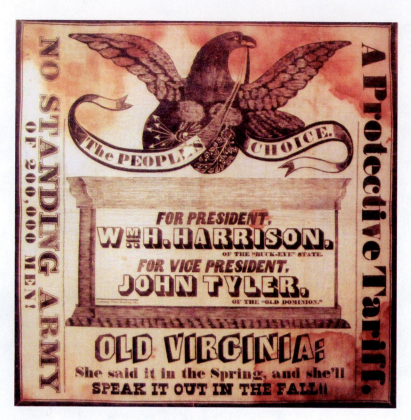

### The Whigs Boost Harrison and Tyler for the White House

In their quest for victory in 1840, Whig political strategists advanced a wide-ranging (and misleading) set of policies. This poster celebrates William Henry Harrison and John Tyler as candidates who would secure protective tariffs for American manufacturers — a policy that appealed to northern voters but one that Tyler opposed. It also promises to cut the size of the U.S. Army, a proposal resisted by General Harrison, victor of the Battle of Tippecanoe. But denouncing a large "Standing Army" would win votes in Virginia, where it recalled the fears of Radical Whig Patriots prior to the American Revolution and remained central to the states' rights ideology espoused by Senator Tyler and other "Old Republicans."    Grouseland Foundation, Inc./Photo courtesy "Fords the Art of Photography," Vincennes, IN.

self-made man who lived contentedly in a log cabin and quaffed hard cider, a drink of the common people. In fact, Harrison's father was a wealthy Virginia planter who had signed the Declaration of Independence, and Harrison himself lived in a series of elegant mansions.

The Whigs boosted their electoral hopes by welcoming women to campaign festivities — a "first" for American politics. Jacksonian Democrats considered politics to be a "manly" affair; they likened politically minded females to "public" women, prostitutes who plied their trade in theaters and other public places. But the Whigs recognized that Christian women from Yankee families, a key Whig constituency, had already entered American public life through the temperance movement and other benevolent activities. In October 1840, Daniel Webster addressed a meeting of twelve hundred Whig women, praised their efforts for moral reform, and urged them to back Whig candidates. "This way of making politicians of their women is something new under the sun," exclaimed one Democrat, who worried that it would bring more Whig men to the polls. And it did: More than 80 percent of the eligible male voters cast ballots in 1840, up from fewer than 60 percent in 1832 and 1836. Heeding the Whigs' campaign

slogan "Tippecanoe and Tyler Too," they voted Harrison into the White House with 53 percent of the popular vote and gave the party a majority in Congress.

### Tyler Subverts the Whig Agenda

Led by Clay and Webster, the Whigs in Congress prepared to reverse the Jacksonian revolution. But their hopes were short-lived; barely a month after his inauguration, Harrison died of pneumonia, and the nation got "Tyler Too." But in what capacity: as acting president or as president? The Constitution was vague on the issue. Ignoring his Whig associates in Congress, who wanted a weak chief executive, Tyler took the presidential oath of office and declared his intention to govern as he pleased. As it turned out, that would not be like a Whig.

Tyler had served in the House and the Senate as a Jeffersonian Democrat, firmly committed to slavery and states' rights. He had joined the Whigs only to protest Jackson's stance against nullification. On economic issues, Tyler shared Jackson's hostility to the Second Bank and the American System. He therefore vetoed Whig bills that would have raised tariffs and created a new national bank. Outraged by this betrayal,

**President John Tyler (1790–1862)**

Both as an "accidental" president and as a man, John Tyler left his mark on the world. His initiative to annex Texas made the election of 1844 into a pivotal contest and led to the war with Mexico in 1846. Tyler's first wife, Letitia, give birth to eight children before dying in the White House in 1842. Two years later, he married twenty-four-year-old Julia Gardiner, who bore him seven more children.   White House Historical Association (White House Collection).

most of Tyler's cabinet resigned in 1842, and the Whigs expelled Tyler from their party. "His Accidency," as he was called by his critics, was now a president without a party.

The split between Tyler and the Whigs allowed the Democrats to regroup. The party vigorously recruited subsistence farmers in the North, smallholding planters in the South, and former members of the Working Men's Parties in the cities. It also won support among Irish and German Catholic immigrants—whose numbers had increased during the 1830s—by backing their demands for religious and cultural liberty, such as the freedom to drink beer and whiskey. A pattern of **ethnocultural politics**, as historians refer to the practice of voting along ethnic and religious lines, now became a prominent feature of American life. Thanks to these urban and rural recruits, the Democrats remained the majority party in most parts of the nation. Their program of equal rights, states' rights, and cultural liberty was more attractive than the Whig platform of economic nationalism, moral reform, temperance laws, and individual mobility.

- How did the ideology of the Whigs differ from that of the Jacksonian Democrats?

- Why did the Working Men's and the Anti-Masonic Parties fail and the Whig Party succeed? What do their respective fates suggest about the nature of the American political system?

## SUMMARY

In this chapter, we have examined the causes and the consequences of the democratic political revolution that accompanied the economic transformation of the early nineteenth century. We saw that the expansion of the franchise weakened the political system run by notables of high status and encouraged the transfer of power to professional politicians—men like Martin Van Buren who were mostly of middle-class origin.

We also witnessed a revolution in government policy, as Andrew Jackson and his Democratic Party dismantled the mercantilist economic system of government-supported economic development. On the national level, Jackson destroyed Henry Clay's

American System; on the state level, Democrats wrote new constitutions that ended the Commonwealth System of government charters and subsidies to private businesses.

Finally, we watched the emergence of the Second Party System. Following the split in the Republican Party during the election of 1824, two new parties—the Democrats and the Whigs—developed on the national level and eventually absorbed the members of the Anti-Masonic and Working Men's Parties. The new party system established universal suffrage for white men and a mode of representative government that was responsive to ordinary citizens. In their scope and significance, these political innovations matched the economic advances of both the Industrial Revolution and the Market Revolution.

## CHAPTER REVIEW QUESTIONS

- How did the Jackson era fundamentally change the American economy, public policy, and society?

- Explain the rise of the Second Party System. How would you characterize American politics in the early 1840s?

- The chapter argues that a democratic revolution swept America in the decades after 1820. What evidence does the text present to support this argument? How persuasive is the evidence?

## FOR FURTHER EXPLORATION

Two new studies of American politics are Sean Wilentz, *The Rise of American Democracy* (2005), and Christian G. Fritz, *American Sovereigns: The People and America's Constitutional Tradition* (2008). See also the classic books by George Dangerfield, *The Era of Good Feelings* (1952), and Alexis de Tocqueville, *Democracy in America* (1835). For concise analyses of the Jackson era, consult Harry L. Watson, *Liberty and Power* (1990); Daniel Feller, *The Jacksonian Promise* (1995); and the essays at **xroads.virginia.edu/~hyper/detoc/home .html**. Richard Hofstadter, *The Idea of a Party System* (1969), lucidly explains the triumph of party politics. See **www.ipl.org/div/potus/jqadams.html** for the election of 1824 and the John Quincy Adams administration. For wonderful political cartoons, go to **loc .harpweek.org**.

Robert V. Remini, *The Life of Andrew Jackson* (1988), highlights Jackson's triumphs and shortcomings. For Jackson's Indian policy, read the novel by Robert J. Conley, *Mountain Windsongs* (1992), and two studies by historians: Sean Michael O'Brien, *In Bitterness and in Tears* (2003), and John Buchanan, *Jackson's Way* (2001). For the Cherokees, see **cherokeehistory.com**. Thomas N. Ingersoll, *To Intermix with Our White Brothers* (2005), discusses Indians of mixed racial heritage.

Major L. Wilson, *The Presidency of Martin Van Buren* (1984), offers a shrewd assessment. For the Whigs, consult Merrill D. Peterson's *The Great Triumvirate: Webster, Clay, and Calhoun* (1987). Sean Wilentz, *Chants Democratic* (1986), covers the ideology of working men.

## TEST YOUR KNOWLEDGE

To assess your command of the material in this chapter, see the Online Study Guide at **bedfordstmartins.com/henretta**.

For Web sites, images, and documents related to topics and places in this chapter, visit **bedfordstmartins.com/makehistory**.

## TIMELINE

| | |
|---|---|
| **1810s** | States expand white male voting rights |
| | Martin Van Buren creates focused party in New York |
| **1825** | John Quincy Adams chosen president by House of Representatives; endorses Henry Clay's American System |
| **1828** | Philadelphia artisans found Working Men's Party |
| | "Tariff of Abominations" raises duties |
| | Andrew Jackson elected president |
| | John C. Calhoun's *South Carolina Exposition and Protest* |
| **1830** | Jackson vetoes National Road bill |
| | Congress enacts Jackson's Indian Removal Act |
| **1831** | *Cherokee Nation v. Georgia* denies Indians' independence, but *Worcester v. Georgia* (1832) upholds their political autonomy |
| **1832** | Massacre of 850 Sauk and Fox warriors at Bad Axe |
| | Jackson vetoes renewal of Second Bank |
| | South Carolina adopts Ordinance of Nullification |
| **1833** | Congress enacts compromise tariff |
| **1834** | Whig Party formed by Clay, Calhoun, and Daniel Webster |
| **1835** | Roger Taney named Supreme Court chief justice |
| **1836** | Van Buren elected president |
| **1837** | *Charles River Bridge* case weakens chartered monopolies |
| | Panic of 1837 derails union movement |
| **1838** | Cherokees die in Trail of Tears march to Indian Territory |
| **1839–1843** | Loans to American states spark international financial crisis and depression |
| **1840** | Whigs win "log cabin" campaign |
| **1841** | John Tyler succeeds William Henry Harrison as president |

Hannah Roberts *Married March 20 1833* Lewis Abbets. 1833.

# Religion and Reform, 1820–1860

**"The spirit of reform** is in every place," declared the children of legal reformer David Dudley Field in their handwritten monthly *Gazette* in 1842:

The labourer with a family says "reform the common schools"; the merchant and the planter say, "reform the tariff," the lawyer "reform the laws," the politician "reform the government," the abolitionist "reform the slave laws," the moralist "reform intemperance," . . . the ladies wish their legal privileges extended, and in short, the whole country is wanting reform.

Like many Americans, the young Fields sensed that the political whirlwind of the 1830s had transformed the way people thought about themselves and about society. Suddenly, thousands of men and women, inspired by the economic progress and democratic spirit of the age and by the religious optimism of the Second Great Awakening, believed that they could improve their personal lives and society as a whole. Some dedicated themselves to the cause of reform. William Lloyd Garrison began as an antislavery advocate and foe of Indian removal and then went on to embrace women's rights, pacifism, and the abolition of prisons. Such obsessive individuals, warned Unitarian minister Henry W. Bellows, were pursuing "an object, which in its very nature is unattainable—the perpetual improvement of the outward condition."

Reform was complex and contradictory. Some reformers wanted to improve society by promoting morality and enforcing social discipline. The first wave of American reformers, the benevolent religious improvers of the 1820s, championed regular church attendance, temperance, and a strict moral code. Their zeal offended many upright citizens: "A peaceable man can hardly venture to eat or drink, . . . to correct his child or kiss his wife, without obtaining the permission . . . of some moral or other reform society," said one.

A second wave of reformers, which arose during the 1830s and 1840s, undertook to liberate people from archaic customs and traditional lifestyles. These reformers were mostly middle-class northerners and midwesterners who promoted a bewildering assortment of radical ideals: extreme individualism, common ownership of property, the immediate emancipation of slaves, and sexual equality. Although their numbers were small, second-wave reformers challenged well-established cultural practices and prompted the horrified opposition of the majority of Americans. As one fearful southerner saw it, radical reformers favored a chaotic world with "No-Marriage, No-Religion, No-Private Property, No-Law and No-Government."

**Hannah Roberts and Lewis Tebbets**
During the 1830s, Joseph H. Davis used bright watercolors to paint scores of family portraits— 150 still survive—that capture the comfortable lives of New England's middle classes. This double portrait commemorates the engagement of a young, well-dressed couple of Berwick, Maine. To emphasize their romantic love, Davis shows them gazing into each other's eyes, their hands linked by a prayer book, a symbol of their education and coming sacred union. Such respectable couples—Lewis Tebbets became a minister of the Methodist Episcopal Church—flocked to hear Ralph Waldo Emerson and other lecturers on the lyceum circuit. Terra Foundation for American Art, Chicago/ Art Resource, NY.

# Individualism: The Ethic of the Middle Class

Those fears were not exaggerated. Rapid economic growth and geographical expansion had weakened traditional institutions, forcing individuals to fend for themselves. In 1835, Alexis de Tocqueville coined the word *individualism* to describe the result. Native-born white Americans were "no longer attached to each other by any tie of caste, class, association, or family," the French aristocrat lamented, and so lived in social isolation. Even as Tocqueville mourned the loss of social ties, the New England essayist and philosopher Ralph Waldo Emerson (1803–1882) celebrated the liberation of the individual. Emerson's vision influenced thousands of ordinary Americans and a generation of important artists; the result was the **American Renaissance**, a remarkable outpouring of first-class novels, poetry, and essays.

## Ralph Waldo Emerson and Transcendentalism

Emerson was the leading voice of **transcendentalism**, an intellectual movement rooted in the religious soil of New England. Its first advocates were Unitarian ministers from well-to-do New England families who questioned the constraints of their Puritan heritage (see Chapter 8). For inspiration, they turned to European romanticism, a new conception of self and society. Romantic thinkers, such as German philosopher Immanuel Kant and English poet Samuel Taylor Coleridge, rejected the ordered, rational world of the eighteenth-century Enlightenment. They embraced human passion and sought deeper insight into the mysteries of existence. By tapping their intuitive powers, the young Unitarians believed, people could come to know the infinite and the eternal.

As a Unitarian, Emerson already stood outside the mainstream of American Protestantism. Unlike most Christians, Unitarians believed that God was a single being, not a trinity of Father, Son, and Holy Spirit. In 1832, Emerson took a more radical step by resigning his Boston pulpit and rejecting all organized religion. He moved to Concord, Massachusetts, and, in influential essays, explored what he called "the infinitude of the private man," the idea of individuality, the radically free person.

The young philosopher argued that people were trapped by inherited customs and institutions. They wore the ideas of earlier times—New England Calvin-

**The Founder of Transcendentalism**

As this painting of Ralph Waldo Emerson by an unknown artist indicates, the young philosopher was an attractive man, his face brimming with confidence and optimism. With his radiant personality and incisive intellect, Emerson deeply influenced dozens of influential writers, artists, and scholars, and enjoyed great success as a lecturer to the emerging middle class.   The Metropolitan Museum of Art, Bequest of Chester Dale, 1962 (64.97.4) Photograph© 1991 The Metropolitan Museum of Art.

ism, for example—as a kind of "faded masquerade," and they needed to shed those values. "What is a man born for but to be a Reformer, a Remaker of what man has made?" Emerson asked. In his view, individuals could be remade only by discovering their "original relation with Nature" and entering into a mystical union with the "currents of Universal Being." The ideal setting for this transcendent discovery was under an open sky, in solitary communion with nature. The revivalist Charles Grandison Finney described his religious conversion in Emersonian terms: an individual in the woods, alone, joining with God in a mystical union.

Emerson's genius lay in his ability to translate such abstract ideas into examples that made sense to middle-class Americans. His essays suggested that nature was saturated with the presence of God, a pantheistic outlook at odds with traditional Christian doctrine. Emerson also warned that the new market society—the focus on work, profits, and consumption—was

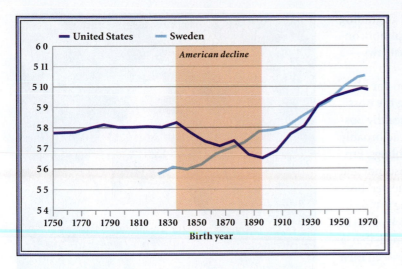

**FIGURE 11.1**

**The Ecology of Health: Average Height of Native-born American and Swedish Men, by Year of Birth, 1750–1970**

American transcendentalists sensed that the new urban and industrial society would damage people's health, and modern research suggests they were right. The average height of men born in the United States from the 1830s to the 1930s (as recorded in military records and other sources) was significantly lower than that of men born between 1750 and 1830. Researchers attribute this decline to the men's childhood experience of less adequate nutrition and greater exposure to infectious diseases in urban areas. However, data from Sweden—a predominantly poor, rural society until 1900—suggests that life in the traditional European agricultural world was equally damaging to people's welfare.   Source: Richard Steckel, "Health and Nutrition in the Preindustrial Era" (Cambridge, MA: National Bureau of Economic Research, Working Paper 8452, 2001).

debasing Americans' spiritual and material lives (Figure 11.1). "Things are in the saddle," he wrote, "and ride mankind."

The transcendentalist message of individual self-realization reached hundreds of thousands of people through Emerson's writings and lectures. Public lectures had become a spectacularly successful way of spreading information and fostering discussion among the middle classes. Beginning in 1826, the lyceum movement—modeled on the public forum of the ancient Greek philosopher Aristotle—arranged lecture tours by hundreds of poets, preachers, scientists, and reformers. The lyceum became an important cultural institution in the North and Midwest—but not in the South, where the middle class was smaller and popular education had a lower priority. In 1839, nearly 150 lyceums in Massachusetts invited lecturers to address more than 33,000 subscribers. Emerson was the most popular speaker, eventually delivering fifteen hundred lectures in more than three hundred towns in twenty states.

Emerson celebrated those who rejected tradition and practiced self-discipline and civic responsibility. His individualistic ethos spoke directly to the experiences of many middle-class Americans, who had left family farms to make their way in the urban world. His pantheistic view of nature encouraged Unitarians in Boston to create the Mount Auburn Cemetery, a beautiful planned landscape of trees and bushes and burial markers for the dead of all faiths; soon there were similar rural cemeteries in many American cities. And Emerson's optimism inspired preachers such as Finney, who told believers to transcend old doctrines

and constraints. "God has made man a moral free agent," Finney declared.

## Emerson's Literary Influence

Emerson sought to remake American literature. In "The American Scholar" (1837), the philosopher issued a literary declaration of independence. He urged American writers to free themselves from the "courtly muse" of Old Europe and instead to find inspiration in the experiences of ordinary Americans: "the ballad in the street; the news of the boat; the glance of the eye; the form and gait of the body."

**Thoreau, Fuller, and Whitman**  One young New England intellectual, Henry David Thoreau (1817–1862), heeded Emerson's call and sought inspiration from the natural world. In 1845, depressed by his beloved brother's death, Thoreau built a cabin near Walden Pond in Concord, Massachusetts, and lived alone there for two years. In 1854, he published *Walden, or Life in the Woods*, an account of his search for meaning beyond the artificiality of civilized society:

> I went to the woods because I wished to live deliberately, to front only the essential facts of life, and see if I could not learn what it had to teach, and not, when I came to die, discover that I had not lived.

*Walden*'s most famous metaphor provides an enduring justification for independent thinking: "If a man does not keep pace with his companions, perhaps it is because he hears a different drummer." Beginning from this premise, Thoreau advocated social nonconformity and civil disobedience against unjust laws — a thoroughgoing individuality.

As Thoreau was seeking self-realization for men, Margaret Fuller (1810–1850) was exploring the possibilities of freedom for women. Born into a wealthy Boston family, Fuller mastered six languages, read broadly in classic literature, and educated her four siblings. Embracing Emerson's ideas, she started a transcendental "conversation," or discussion group, for educated Boston women in 1839. While editing the leading transcendentalist journal, *The Dial*, Fuller published *Woman in the Nineteenth Century* (1844). It proclaimed that a "new era" was changing the relationships between men and women.

Fuller's philosophy began from the transcendental principle that all people — women as well as men — could develop a life-affirming mystical relationship with God. Every woman therefore deserved psychological and social independence: the ability "to grow, as an intellect to discern, as a soul to live freely and unimpeded." She wrote: "We would have every arbitrary barrier thrown down [and] every path laid open to Woman as freely as to Man." Acting on that precept, Fuller became the literary critic of the *New York Tribune* and traveled to Italy to report on the Revolution of 1848. Her adventurous life led to an early death; In 1850, she drowned in a shipwreck en route home to the United States. But Fuller's life and writings inspired a rising generation of women writers and reformers.

Another writer who responded to Emerson's call was the poet Walt Whitman (1819–1892). When Whitman first met Emerson, the poet recalled, he had been "simmering, simmering"; then Emerson "brought me to a boil." Whitman worked as a printer, a teacher, a journalist, an editor of the *Brooklyn Eagle*, and an influential publicist for the Democratic Party. But poetry was the "direction of his dreams." In *Leaves of Grass*, a collection of wild, exuberant poems first published in 1855 and constantly revised and expanded, Whitman recorded in verse his efforts to transcend various "invisible boundaries": between solitude and community, between prose and poetry, even between the living and the dead. At the center of *Leaves of Grass* is the individual — the figure of the poet — "I, Walt." He begins alone: "I celebrate myself, and sing myself." But because he has an Emersonian "original relation" with nature, Whitman claims perfect communion with others: "For every atom belonging to me as good belongs to you." For Emerson, Thoreau, and Fuller, the individual had a divine spark;

***Margaret Fuller, 1848***

At thirty-eight, American social reformer Margaret Fuller moved to Italy, where she reported on the Revolution of 1848 for a New York newspaper. She fell in love there with Thomas Hicks (1823–1890), a much younger American artist. Hicks rebuffed Fuller's romantic advances but painted this flattering portrait, softening her features and giving her a pensive look. Fuller married a Roman nobleman, Giovanni Angelo, Marchese d'Ossoli, and gave birth to a son in September 1848. Two years later, the entire family died in a shipwreck while en route to the United States.   Constance Fuller Threinen.

for Whitman, the collective democracy assumed a sacred character.

The transcendentalists were optimistic but not naive. Whitman wrote about human suffering with passion, and Emerson laced his accounts of transcendence with twinges of anxiety. "I am glad," he once said, "to the brink of fear." Thoreau was gloomy about everyday life: "The mass of men lead lives of quiet desperation." Still, dark murmurings remain muted in their work, overshadowed by assertions that nothing was impossible for the individual who could break free from tradition.

**Darker Visions**   Emerson's writings also influenced two great novelists, Nathaniel Hawthorne and Herman Melville, who had more pessimistic worldviews. Both sounded powerful warnings that unfettered egoism could destroy individuals and those around them.

Hawthorne brilliantly explored the theme of excessive individualism in his novel *The Scarlet Letter* (1850). The two main characters, Hester Prynne and Arthur Dimmesdale, blatantly challenged their seventeenth-century New England community by committing adultery and producing a child. Their decision to ignore social restraints results not in liberation but in degradation: a profound sense of guilt and condemnation by the community.

Herman Melville explored the limits of individualism in even more extreme and tragic terms and emerged as a scathing critic of transcendentalism. His most powerful statement was *Moby Dick* (1851), the story of Captain Ahab's obsessive hunt for a mysterious white whale that ends in death for Ahab and all but one member of his crew. Here, the quest for spiritual meaning in nature brings death, not transcendence, because Ahab, the liberated individual, lacks inner discipline and self-restraint.

*Moby Dick* was a commercial failure. The middle-class audience that devoured sentimental American fiction refused to follow Melville into the dark, dangerous realm of individualism gone mad. What middle-class readers emphatically preferred were the more modest examples of individualism offered by Emerson and Finney: personal improvement through spiritual awareness and self-discipline.

**Brook Farm**   To escape life in America's emerging market society, transcendentalists and other reformers created ideal communities, or utopias. They hoped these planned societies would allow people to realize their spiritual potential. The most important transcendentalist communal experiment was Brook Farm, founded just outside Boston in 1841. Intellectual life at Brook Farm was electric. Emerson, Thoreau, and Fuller were residents or frequent visitors; members recalled that they "inspired the young with a passion for study, and the middle-aged with deference and admiration, while we all breathed the intellectual grace that pervaded the atmosphere."

Whatever its spiritual rewards, Brook Farm was an economic failure. The residents hoped to escape the ups and downs of the market economy by producing their own food and exchanging their surplus milk, vegetables, and hay for manufactures. However, most members were ministers, teachers, writers, and students who had few farming skills; only the cash of affluent residents kept the enterprise afloat. After a devastating fire in 1846, the organizers disbanded the community and sold the farm.

With the failure of Brook Farm, the Emersonians abandoned their quest for a new social system. They accepted the brute reality of the emergent industrial order and tried to reform it, especially through the education of workers and the movement to abolish slavery.

- **What were the main beliefs of transcendentalism, and how did American writers incorporate them into their work?**
- **What is the relationship between transcendentalism and individualism? Between transcendentalism and social reform? Between transcendentalism and the middle class?**

# Rural Communalism and Urban Popular Culture

Even as Brook Farm collapsed, thousands of Americans were joining communal settlements in rural areas of the Northeast and Midwest (Map 11.1). Many communalists were farmers and artisans seeking refuge during the economic depression that began with the Panic of 1837 and lasted seven years. However, these rural utopias were also symbols of social protest and experimentation. By advocating the common ownership of property and unconventional forms of marriage and family life, the communalists challenged capitalist values and traditional gender roles.

Simultaneously, tens of thousands of rural Americans and European immigrants poured into the larger cities of the United States. There, they created a popular culture that challenged some sexual norms, reinforced traditional racist feelings, and encouraged new styles of dress and behavior.

## Mother Ann Lee and the Shakers

The Shakers were the first successful American communal movement. In 1770, Ann Lee Stanley (Mother Ann), a young cook in Manchester, England, had a vision that she was an incarnation of Christ and that sexual lust had caused Adam and Eve to be banished from the Garden of Eden. Four years later, she led a few followers to America, and established a church near Albany, New York. Because of the ecstatic dances that were part of their worship, the sect became known as the Shakers.

After Mother Ann's death in 1784, the Shakers honored her as the Second Coming of Christ, withdrew

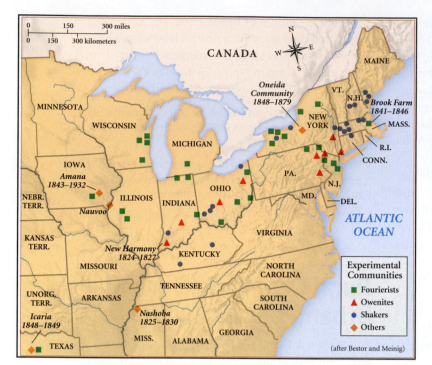

## MAP 11.1

**Major Communal Experiments before 1860**

Some experimental communities settled along the frontier, but the vast majority chose rural areas in well-settled regions of the North and Midwest. Because of their opposition to slavery, communalists usually avoided the South. Most secular experiments failed within a few decades, as the founders lost their reformist enthusiasm or died off; religious communities—such as those of the Shakers and the Mormons—were longer-lived.

from the profane world, and formed disciplined religious communities. Members embraced the common ownership of property; accepted strict oversight by church leaders; and pledged to abstain from alcohol, tobacco, politics, and war. Shakers also repudiated sexual pleasure and marriage. Their commitment to celibacy followed Mother Ann's testimony against "the lustful gratifications of the flesh as the source and foundation of human corruption." The Shakers' theology was as radical as their social thought. They held that God was "a dual person, male and female." This doctrine prompted Shakers to repudiate male leadership and to place community governance in the hands of both women and men—the Eldresses and the Elders.

Shakers founded twenty communities, mostly in New England, New York, and Ohio. Their agriculture and crafts, especially furniture making, acquired a reputation for quality that made most Shaker communities self-sustaining and even comfortable. Because the Shakers disdained sexual intercourse, they relied on conversions and the adoption of thousands of young orphans to increase their numbers. During the 1830s, three thousand adults, mostly women, joined the Shakers, attracted by their communal intimacy and sexual equality. To Rebecca Cox Jackson, an African American seamstress from Philadelphia, the Shakers seemed to be "loving to live forever." As the supply of orphans dried up during the 1840s and 1850s (with the increase in pub-

lic and private orphanages), Shaker communities began to decline. By 1900, the Shakers had virtually disappeared, leaving as their material legacy a distinctive plain but elegant style of wood furniture.

## Arthur Brisbane and Fourierism

As the Shakers' growth slowed during the 1840s, the American Fourierist movement mushroomed. Charles Fourier (1777–1837) was a French reformer who devised an eight-stage theory of social evolution that predicted the imminent decline of individualism and capitalism. According to Arthur Brisbane, the leading disciple of Fourierism in America, Fourier's utopian socialism—a forerunner of class-based **socialism**—would free workers from the "menial and slavish system of Hired Labor or Labor for Wages," just as republicanism had freed Americans from slavish monarchical government. In a Fourierist society, men and women would work for the community, in cooperative groups called phalanxes. The members of a phalanx would be its shareholders; they would own its property in common, including stores and a bank, a school, and a library.

Fourier and Brisbane saw the phalanx as a humane system that would liberate women as well as men. "In society as it is now constituted," Brisbane wrote, individual freedom was possible only for men, while "woman

**Shakers at Prayer**

Most Americans viewed the Shakers with a mixture of fascination and suspicion. They feared the sect's radical aspects—such as a commitment to celibacy and communal property—and considered the Shakers' dancing more an invitation to debauchery than a form of prayer. Those apprehensions surfaced in this engraving, "The Shakers of New Lebanon," New York, which expresses both the powerful intensity and the menacing character of the Shaker ritual. The work of the journalist-engraver Joseph Becker, the picture appeared in *Frank Leslie's Illustrated Newspaper* in 1873.   © Bettmann.

is subjected to unremitting and slavish domestic duties." In the "new Social Order . . . based upon Associated households," men would share women's domestic labor and thereby increase sexual equality.

Brisbane skillfully promoted Fourier's ideas in his influential book *The Social Destiny of Man* (1840), a regular column in Horace Greeley's *New York Tribune*, and hundreds of lectures. Fourierist ideas found a receptive audience among educated farmers and craftsmen, who yearned for economic stability and communal solidarity in the wake of the Panic of 1837. During the 1840s, Fourierists started nearly one hundred cooperative communities, mostly in western New York and the Midwest. However, most of these communities collapsed within a decade because of disputes over work responsibilities and social policies. Fourierism's decline revealed the difficulty of establishing a utopian community in the absence of a charismatic leader or a compelling religious vision.

## John Humphrey Noyes and the Oneida Community

John Humphrey Noyes (1811–1886) was both charismatic and religious. He ascribed the Fourierists' failure to their secular outlook and took as his model the pious Shakers, the true "pioneers of modern Socialism." The Shakers' marriageless society also appealed to Noyes and inspired him to create a community that defined sexuality and gender roles in radically new ways.

**"Bloomerism – An American Custom"**

The hippies of the 1960s weren't the first to draw attention to themselves with their dress (sloppy) and smoking (marijuana). Independent women of the 1850s took to wearing bloomers and puffing on cigars, behaviors that elicited everything from matrons' disapproving stares to verbal and physical assaults from street urchins. Beyond dress and smoking habits, the women's movement questioned existing cultural norms and sought to expand the boundaries of personal freedom. This cartoon appeared in 1851 in *Harper's New Monthly Magazine*, a major periodical of the time.   *Harper's New Monthly Magazine* (August 1851)/ Picture Research Consultants & Archives.

Noyes was a well-to-do graduate of Dartmouth College who joined the ministry after hearing a sermon by Charles Grandison Finney. Dismissed as the pastor of a Congregational church for holding unorthodox beliefs, Noyes turned to perfectionism, an evangelical Protestant movement of the 1830s that attracted thousands of New Englanders who had migrated to New York and Ohio. Perfectionists believed that Christ had already returned to earth (the Second Coming); consequently, according to the Bible, people could aspire to sinless perfection in their earthly lives. Unlike most perfectionists, who lived conventional personal lives, Noyes rejected marriage as the major barrier to perfection. "Exclusiveness, jealousy, quarreling have no place at the marriage supper of the Lamb," Noyes wrote. But instead of the Shakers' celibacy, Noyes and his followers embraced "complex marriage," in which all the members of the community were married to one another.

Noyes's teachings highlighted the growing debate over legal and cultural constraints on women. He rejected monogamy partly to free women from their status as the property of their husbands, as they were by custom and by common law. To give women the time and energy to participate fully in the community, Noyes urged them to avoid multiple pregnancies. He asked men to assist in this effort by avoiding orgasm during intercourse. To raise the community's children, Noyes set up nurseries run by both sexes. Symbolizing the quest for equality, Noyes's women followers cut their hair short and wore pantaloons under calf-length skirts.

In 1839, Noyes set up a perfectionist community near his hometown of Putney, Vermont. When, in the mid-1840s, he introduced the practice of complex marriage, local outrage forced Noyes to relocate the community to an isolated area near Oneida, New York. By the mid-1850s, the Oneida settlement had 200 residents; it became financially self-sustaining when the inventor of a highly successful steel animal trap joined the community. With the profits from trap making, the Oneidians diversified into the production of silverware. When Noyes fled to Canada in 1879 to avoid prosecution for adultery, the community abandoned complex marriage but retained its cooperative spirit. Its members founded Oneida Community, Ltd., a jointly owned silverware-manufacturing company that remained a communal venture until the middle of the twentieth century.

The historical significance of the Oneidians, Shakers, and Fourierists does not lie in their numbers, which were small, or in their fine crafts. Rather, their importance stems from their radical questioning of traditional sexual norms and of the capitalist principles and class divisions of the emerging market society. Their utopian communities stood as countercultural blueprints for a more egalitarian social and economic order.

## Joseph Smith and the Mormon Experience

The Shakers and the Oneidians were radical utopians, but because their communities remained small, they aroused relatively little hostility. The Mormons, members of the Church of Jesus Christ of Latter-day Saints, were religious utopians with a conservative social agenda: to perpetuate close-knit communities and patriarchal power. Because of their cohesiveness and size, the Mormons provoked more animosity than the radical utopians did.

**Joseph Smith** | Like many social movements of the era, Mormonism emerged from religious ferment among families of Puritan descent who lived along the Erie Canal. The founder of the Latter-day Church, Joseph Smith Jr. (1805–1844), was born in Vermont to a poor farming and shop-keeping family that migrated to Palmyra in central New York. In religious experiences that began in 1820, Smith came to believe that God had singled him out to receive a special revelation of divine truth. In 1830, he published *The Book of Mormon*, which he claimed to have translated from ancient hieroglyphics on gold plates shown to him by an angel named Moroni. *The Book of Mormon* told the story of ancient civilizations from the Middle East that had migrated to the Western Hemisphere and of the visit of Jesus Christ, soon after his Resurrection, to one of them. Smith's account explained the presence of native peoples in the Americas and integrated them into the Judeo-Christian tradition.

Smith proceeded to organize the Church of Jesus Christ of Latter-day Saints. Seeing himself as a prophet in a sinful, excessively individualistic society, Smith revived traditional social doctrines, including patriarchal authority within the family. Like many Protestant ministers, he encouraged practices that led to individual success in the age of capitalist markets and factories: frugality, hard work, and enterprise. But Smith also stressed communal discipline to safeguard the Mormon "New Jerusalem" from individualism and rival religious doctrines. His goal was a church-directed society that would ensure moral perfection.

Constantly harassed by hostile anti-Mormons, Smith struggled for years to find a secure home for his new religion. At one point, he identified Jackson County in Missouri as the site of the sacred "City of Zion," and his followers began to settle there. Agitation led by Protestant ministers quickly forced them out: "Mormons were the common enemies of mankind and ought to be destroyed," said one cleric. Smith and his growing congregation eventually settled in Nauvoo, Illinois, a

### A Mormon Man and His Wives

The practice of polygamy split the Mormon community and, because it deviated from traditional religious principles, enraged other Christian denominations. This Mormon household, pictured in the late 1840s, was unusually prosperous, partly because of the labor of the husband's multiple wives. Although the cabin provides cramped quarters for such a large family, it boasts a brick chimney and — a luxury for any pioneer home — a glass window.   Library of Congress.

MAP 11.2

**The Mormon Trek, 1830–1848**

Because of their unorthodox religious views and communal solidarity, Mormons faced hostility first in New York and then in Missouri and Illinois. After founder Joseph Smith Jr. was murdered, Brigham Young led the polygamist faction of Mormons into lands claimed by Mexico and thinly populated by Native Americans. From Omaha, the migrants followed the path of the Oregon Trail to Fort Bridger and then struck off to the southwest. They settled along the Wasatch Range in the basin of the Great Salt Lake in present-day Utah.

town they founded on the Mississippi River (Map 11.2). By the early 1840s, Nauvoo was the largest utopian community in the United States, with 30,000 residents. The rigid discipline and secret rituals of the Mormons — along with their prosperity, hostility toward other sects, and bloc voting in Illinois elections — fueled resentment among their neighbors. That resentment turned to overt hostility when Smith refused to abide by any Illinois law of which he disapproved, asked Congress to turn Nauvoo into a separate federal territory, and declared himself a candidate for president of the United States.

Moreover, Smith claimed to have received a new revelation justifying polygamy, the practice of a man having multiple wives. When leading Mormon men took several wives, they sparked a contentious debate among Mormons and enraged Christians in neighboring towns. In 1844, Illinois officials arrested Smith and charged him with treason for allegedly conspiring to create a Mormon colony in Mexican territory. An anti-Mormon mob stormed the jail in Carthage, Illinois, where Smith and his brother were being held and murdered them.

**Brigham Young and Utah**   Led by Brigham Young, Smith's leading disciple and an energetic missionary, about 6,500 Mormons fled the United States. Beginning in 1845, they crossed the Great Plains into Mexican territory and settled in the Great Salt Lake Valley in present-day Utah. Using cooperative labor and an irrigation system based on communal water rights, the Mormon pioneers quickly spread planned agricultural communities along the base of the Wasatch Range. Many Mormons who rejected polygamy remained in the United States. Led by Smith's son, Joseph Smith III, they formed the Reorganized Church of Jesus Christ of Latter-day Saints and settled throughout the Midwest.

When the United States acquired title to Mexico's northern territories in 1848, the Salt Lake Mormons petitioned Congress to create a vast new state, Deseret, which would stretch from Utah to the Pacific coast. Instead, Congress set up the much smaller Utah Territory in 1850 and named Brigham Young its governor. Young and his associates ruled in an authoritarian fashion, determined to ensure the ascendancy of the Mormon Church and its practices. By 1856, Young and the Utah territorial legislature were openly vowing to resist federal laws that were "of right not in force in this territory." Pressed by Protestant churches to end polygamy and considering the Mormons' threat of nullification "a declaration of war," the administration of President James Buchanan dispatched a small army to Utah. As the "Nauvoo Legion" resisted the army's advance, aggressive Mormon militia massacred a party of 120 California-bound emigrants and murdered suspicious travelers and Mormons seeking to flee Young's regime. Despite this bloodshed, the "Mormon War" ended quietly in June 1858. President Buchanan, a longtime supporter of the white South, feared that the forced abolition of polygamy would serve as a precedent for ending slavery. So he offered a pardon to Utah citizens who would acknowledge federal authority, an offer accepted by Young and other leaders in order to prolong Mormon rule. (To enable Utah to win admission to the Union in 1896, its citizens ratified a constitution that "forever" banned the practice of polygamy. But the state government has never strictly enforced that ban.)

The Salt Lake Mormons had succeeded even as other social experiments had failed. By endorsing private property and individual enterprise, Mormons became prosperous contributors to the new market society. However, their leaders resolutely used strict religious controls to perpetuate patriarchy and communal discipline, reaffirming traditional values. This blend of

**Night Life in Philadelphia**

This watercolor by Russian painter Pavel Svinin (1787–1839) captures the diversity and allure of urban America. A respectable gentleman relishes the delicacies sold by a black oysterman. Meanwhile, a young woman—probably a prostitute—engages the attention of two well-dressed young "swells" outside the Chestnut Street Theatre.   The Metropolitan Museum of Art, Rogers Fund, 1942 (42.95.18). Photograph © 1989 The Metropolitan Museum of Art.

economic innovation, social conservatism, and hierarchical leadership, in combination with a strong missionary impulse, created a wealthy and expansive church that now claims a worldwide membership of about twelve million people.

## Urban Popular Culture

As utopians organized communities in the countryside, rural migrants and foreign immigrants created a new urban culture. In 1800, American cities were overgrown towns with rising death rates: New York had only 60,000 residents, Philadelphia had 41,000, and life expectancy at birth was a mere twenty-five years. Then urban growth accelerated as a huge in-migration outweighed the high death rates. By 1840, New York's population had ballooned to 312,000; Philadelphia and its suburbs had 150,000 residents; and three other cities—

New Orleans, Boston, and Baltimore—each had about 100,000. By 1860, New York had become a metropolis with more than 1 million residents: 813,000 in Manhattan and another 266,000 in the adjacent community of Brooklyn.

**Sex in the City**   These new cities, particularly New York, generated a new urban culture. Thousands of young men and women from rural areas flocked to the city searching for adventure and fortune, but many found only a hard life. Young men labored for meager wages constructing thousands of new buildings each year. Others worked as low-paid clerks or operatives in hundreds of mercantile and manufacturing firms. The young women had an even harder time (see Reading American Pictures, "Looking for Clues in Art about Women's Sphere," p. 342). Thousands toiled as live-in domestic servants, ordered about by the mistress

# Looking for Clues in Art about Women's Sphere

This rather somber painting, *The Intelligence Office*, by William Henry Burr (1849), depicts a scene at an urban employment agency. The woman sitting to the right, dressed in formal satins, is deciding whether to hire the two standing women as domestic servants. What does this picture tell us about social relations in nineteenth-century America? Burr's work also incorporates various hallmarks of the new age: contractual labor relations, then-current forms of communication, and the intensification of class identity. Do you see them?

**A Nineteenth-Century Job Interview.** © Collection of the New-York Historical Society.

## ANALYZING THE EVIDENCE

- Study the applicants' clothing. How does their garb differ from that of the employer? Look carefully at their faces and posture. How do you interpret the attitude of the standing girl, facing outward, looking down? How would you interpret the facial expressions of the women seated in the background?

- What events during the antebellum period forced workers to alter their lifestyle and choices for employment?

- Suppose Burr had been painting in 1749, a century earlier. How would a wealthy village squire or a prosperous merchant go about hiring domestic help? What had changed over the decades? Why did an employer in 1849 need the services of a professional agent?

- How did the women applicants come to use the agent's services? What clue has the artist placed in the picture that suggests an answer?

of the household and often sexually exploited by the master. Thousands more scraped out a bare living as needlewomen in New York's booming clothes manufacturing industry. Unwilling to endure domestic service or subsistence wages, many young girls turned to prostitution. In the 1850s, Dr. William Sanger's careful survey found 6,000 women engaged in commercial sex. Three-fifths of them were native-born whites, and the rest were foreign immigrants; most were between fifteen and twenty years old. Half were or had been domestic servants, half had children, and half were infected with syphilis.

Commercialized sex—and sex in general—formed one facet of the new urban culture. "Sporting men" engaged freely in sexual conquests; otherwise respectable married men kept mistresses in handy apartments; and working men frequented bawdy houses. New York City had some two hundred brothels in the 1820s and five hundred by the 1850s. Prostitutes—so-called "public" women—openly advertised their wares on Broadway, the city's most fashionable thoroughfare, and welcomed clients on the infamous "Third Tier" of the theaters. Many men considered access to illicit sex to be a right. "Man is endowed by nature with passions that must be gratified," declared the *Sporting Whip*, a working-class magazine. Reverend William Berrian, pastor of the ultra-respectable Trinity Episcopal Church, did not disagree; he remarked from the pulpit that he had resorted to "a house of ill-fame" a mere ten times.

Prostitution formed only the tip of the urban sexual iceberg. Freed from family oversight, urban men and women pursued wide-ranging romantic adventures. Men formed homoerotic friendships and relationships; as early as 1800, the homosexual "Fop" was an acknowledged character in Philadelphia. Young people discovered their sexual and social identity by moving from partner to partner until they chanced on an ideal mate. To enhance their allure, they strolled along Broadway in the latest fashions: elaborate bonnets and silk dresses for young women; flowing capes, leather boots, and silver-plated walking sticks for young men. Rivaling the elegance on Broadway was the colorful dress on the Bowery, the broad avenue that ran along the east side of lower Manhattan. By day, the "Bowery Boy" worked as an apprentice or journeyman; by night, he prowled the streets as a "consummate dandy," his hair cropped at the back of his head "as close as scissors could cut," with long front locks "matted by a lavish application of *bear's grease*, the ends tucked under so as to form a roll and brushed until they shone like glass bottles." The "B'hoy," as he was called, cut a dashing figure as he walked along with a "Bowery Gal" in a striking dress

and shawl: "a light pink contrasting with a deep blue" or "a bright yellow with a brighter red."

**Minstrelsy**   Popular entertainment was another facet of the new urban culture. In New York, workingmen could partake of traditional rural blood sports—rat and terrier fights—at Sportsmen Hall, or they could crowd into the pit of the Bowery Theatre to see the "Mad Tragedian," Junius Brutus Booth, deliver a stirring performance of Shakespeare's *Richard III*. Middle-class couples enjoyed evenings at the huge Broadway Tabernacle, where they could hear an abolitionist lecture and see the renowned Hutchinson Family Singers of New Hampshire lead the audience in a roof-raising rendition of their antislavery anthem, "Get Off the Track." Or they could visit the museum of oddities (and hoaxes) created by P. T. Barnum, the great cultural entrepreneur and founder of the Barnum & Bailey Circus.

The most popular theatrical entertainments were the minstrel shows, in which white actors in blackface presented comic routines that blended racist caricature and social criticism. Minstrelsy began around 1830, when a few actors put on blackface and performed song-and-dance routines. The most famous was John Dartmouth Rice, whose "Jim Crow" blended a weird shuffle-dance-and-jump with unintelligible lyrics delivered in "Negro dialect." By the 1840s, there were hundreds of minstrel troupes, including a group of black entertainers, Gavitt's Original Ethiopian Serenaders. The actor-singers' rambling improvised lyrics poked racist fun at the African Americans they caricatured, portraying them as lazy, sensual, and irresponsible while simultaneously using them to criticize white society. Minstrels ridiculed the drinking habits of Irish immigrants, parodied the speech of recent German arrivals, denounced women's demands for political rights, and mocked the arrogance of upper-class men.

**Immigrant Masses and Nativist Reaction**   Still, by performing in blackface, the minstrels declared the importance of being white. In particular, their racism encouraged Irish and German immigrants to identify with the dominant culture of native-born whites, which eased their entry into New York society. By 1855, Irish men and women in New York City numbered 200,000, and Germans 110,000 (Figure 11.2). German-language shop signs filled entire neighborhoods, and German foods (sausages, hamburgers, sauerkraut) and food customs (such as drinking beer in family *biergärten*) became part of the city's culture. The mass of impoverished

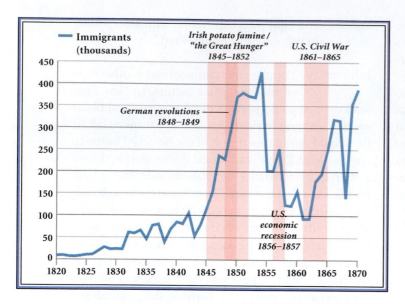

**FIGURE 11.2**

**The Surge in Immigration, 1845–1855**

In 1845, the failure of the potato crop in Ireland prompted the wholesale migration to the United States of peasants from the overcrowded farms of its western counties. Population growth and limited economic prospects likewise spurred the migration of tens of thousands of German peasants, while the failure of the liberal republican political revolution of 1848 prompted hundreds of prominent German politicians and intellectuals to follow them. An American economic recession cut the flow of immigrants, but the booming northern economy during the Civil War again persuaded Europeans to set sail for the United States.

Irish migrants found allies in the American Catholic Church, which soon became an Irish-dominated institution, and the Democratic Party, which gave them a foothold in the political process.

Native-born New Yorkers took alarm as hordes of ethnically diverse migrants altered the city's culture. They organized a nativist movement—a final aspect of the new urban world. Beginning in the mid-1830s, nativists called for a halt to immigration and mounted a cultural and political assault on foreign-born residents (see Chapter 9). Gangs of B'hoys assaulted Irish youths in the streets, employers restricted Irish workers to the most menial jobs, and temperance reformers denounced the German fondness for beer. In 1844, the American Republican Party, with the endorsement of the Whigs, swept the city elections by focusing on the culturally emotional issues of temperance, anti-Catholicism, and nativism (see Comparing American Voices, "Saving the Nation from Drink," pp. 346–347).

In the city, as in the countryside, new values were challenging old beliefs. The sexual freedom celebrated by Noyes at Oneida had its counterpart in commercialized sex and male promiscuity in New York City. Similarly, the disciplined rejection of tobacco and alcohol by the Shakers and the Mormons found a parallel in the Washington Temperance Society and other urban reform organizations. American society was in ferment, and the outcome was far from clear.

- In what respects were the new cultures of the mid-nineteenth century—those of utopian communalists and of urban residents—different from the mainstream culture described in Chapters 8 and 9? How were they alike?

- What accounts for the proliferation of rural utopian communities in nineteenth-century America?

# Abolitionism

Like other reform movements, abolitionism drew on the religious enthusiasm of the Second Great Awakening, and the language of protest changed accordingly. Around 1800, antislavery activists had assailed human bondage as contrary to republicanism and liberty. By the 1830s, white abolitionists were condemning slavery as a sin. Their demands for its immediate end led to fierce political debates, urban riots, and sectional conflicts.

## Black Social Thought: Uplift, Race Equality, and Rebellion

Beginning in the 1790s, leading African Americans in the North advocated a strategy of social uplift. They encouraged free blacks to "elevate" themselves through education, temperance, and hard work. By securing "respectability," they argued, blacks could become the social equals of whites. To promote that goal, black leaders—men such as James Forten, a Philadelphia sailmaker; Prince Hall, a Boston barber; and ministers Hosea Easton and Richard Allen (see Chapter 8)—founded an array of churches, schools, and self-help associations. Capping this effort in 1827, John Russwurm and Samuel D. Cornish of New York published the first African American newspaper, *Freedom's Journal*.

**A Well-Ordered Family**

This lithograph, "The Good Husband," thousands of which were printed by the firm of Currier and Ives, ascribed the family's upper-middle-class lifestyle to the husband and father's "Temperance and Industry." Through such means, the bourgeois values of achievement and respectability achieved a wide circulation and defined the cultural goals embraced by many aspiring American families. Library of Congress Prints and Photographs Division.

America's miserable children from vice" and became a successful author. By 1832, she had published seven books, including *Conversations on Common Things* (1824), an enormously successful treatise on natural science and moral improvement.

In 1841, Dix took up a new cause. Discovering that insane women were jailed alongside male criminals, she persuaded Massachusetts lawmakers to enlarge the state hospital to accommodate indigent mental patients. Exhilarated by that success, Dix began a national movement to establish state asylums for those with mental illnesses. By 1854, she had traveled more than 30,000 miles and had visited eighteen state penitentiaries, three hundred county jails, and more than five hundred almshouses in addition to innumerable hospitals. Issuing dozens of reports, Dix prompted many states to expand their public hospitals and improve their prisons.

Both as reformers and teachers, other northern women transformed public education. From Maine to Wisconsin, women vigorously supported the movement led by Horace Mann to increase elementary schooling and improve the quality of instruction. As secretary of the Massachusetts Board of Education from 1837 to 1848, Mann lengthened the school year; established teaching standards in reading, writing, and arithmetic; and recruited well-educated women as teachers. The intellectual leader of the new women educators was Catharine Beecher, who founded academies for young women in Hartford, Connecticut, and Cincinnati, Ohio. In widely read publications, Beecher argued that "energetic and benevolent women" were better qualified than men were to impart moral and intellectual instruction to the young. By the 1850s, most teachers were women, both because local school boards heeded Beecher's arguments and because they could hire women at lower salaries than men. As secular educators as well as moral reformers, women were now part of American public life.

## Abolitionist Women

Women were central to the antislavery movement. One of the first abolitionists recruited by William Lloyd Garrison was Maria W. Stewart, an African American, who spoke to mixed audiences of men and women in Boston in the early 1830s. As abolitionism blossomed, scores of white women delivered lectures condemning slavery, and thousands more made home "visitations" to win converts to their cause (Map 11.4).

Women abolitionists were particularly aware of the special horrors of slavery for their sex. In her autobiography, *Incidents in the Life of a Slave Girl*, black abolitionist Harriet Jacobs described being forced to

**Sojourner Truth**

Few women had as interesting a life as Sojourner Truth. Born "Isabella" in Dutch-speaking rural New York about 1797, she labored as a slave until emancipated in 1827. Following a religious vision, Isabella moved to New York City, perfected her English, and worked for deeply religious — and ultimately fanatical – Christian merchants. In 1843, seeking further spiritual enlightenment, she took the name "Sojourner Truth" and left New York. After briefly joining the Millerites (who believed the world would end in 1844), Truth won fame as a forceful speaker for abolitionism and woman's rights. This illustration, showing Truth addressing a black audience, suggests her powerful personal presence. Picture Research Consultants & Archives.

have sexual relations with her white owner. "I cannot tell how much I suffered in the presence of these wrongs," she wrote. According to Jacobs and other enslaved women, such sexual assaults were compounded by the cruel treatment they suffered at the hands of their owners' wives, who were enraged by their husbands' promiscuity. In her best-selling novel, *Uncle Tom's Cabin* (1852), Harriet Beecher Stowe charged that one of the greatest moral failings of slavery was the degradation of slave women.

When men challenged their public activism, white abolitionist women grew increasingly conscious of the inferiority of their own social and legal status. In 1836, Congregationalist clergymen in New England assailed

Angelina and Sarah Grimké for addressing mixed male and female audiences. For justification, Sarah Grimké turned to the Bible: "The Lord Jesus defines the duties of his followers in his Sermon on the Mount . . . without any reference to sex or condition," she wrote. "Men and women are CREATED EQUAL! They are both moral and accountable beings and whatever is right for man to do is right for woman." In a pamphlet debate with Catharine Beecher (who believed that women should exercise authority primarily as wives, mothers, and schoolteachers), Angelina Grimké pushed the argument beyond religion by invoking Enlightenment principles to claim equal civic rights for women:

> It is a woman's right to have a voice in all the laws and regulations by which she is governed, whether in Church or State. . . . The present arrangements of society on these points are a violation of human rights, a rank usurpation of power, a violent seizure and confiscation of what is sacredly and inalienably hers.

By 1840, female abolitionists were asserting that traditional gender roles amounted to the "domestic slavery" of women. "How can we endure our present marriage relations," asked Elizabeth Cady Stanton, "[which give a woman] no charter of rights, no individuality of her own?" As another female reformer put it: "The radical difficulty . . . is that women are considered as *belonging* to men" (see Voices from Abroad, "Ernestine Rose: Woman's Rights in America," p. 358). Having acquired a public voice and political skills in the crusade for African American freedom, thousands of northern women now advocated greater rights for themselves.

## The Program of Seneca Falls and Beyond

During the 1840s, women's rights activists devised a pragmatic program of reform. They did not challenge the institution of marriage or the conventional division of labor within the family. Instead, they tried to strengthen the legal rights of married women, especially to allow them to own property. This initiative won crucial support from affluent men, who feared bankruptcy in the volatile market economy and desired to put some family assets in their wives' names. Fathers also wanted to ensure that married daughters had property rights in order to protect them (and their inheritances) from financially irresponsible sons-in-law. These considerations prompted legislatures in three states — Mississippi, Maine, and Massachusetts — to enact married women's property laws between 1839 and 1845. Three years later, women activists in New York won a

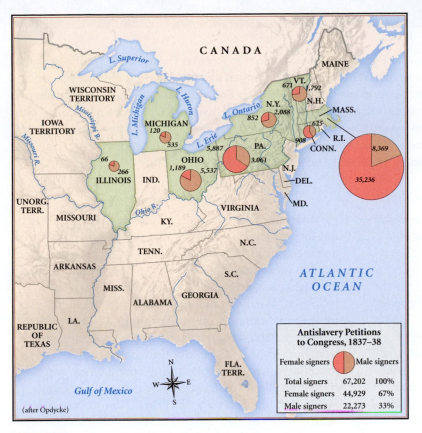

**MAP 11.4**

**Women and Antislavery, 1837–1838**

Beginning in the 1830s, abolitionists and antislavery advocates dispatched dozens of petitions to Congress demanding an end to slavery. Women accounted for two-thirds of the 67,000 signatures on the petitions submitted in 1837–1838, a fact that suggests not only the influence of women in the antislavery movement but also the extent of female organizations and social networks. Lawmakers, eager to avoid sectional conflict, devised an informal agreement (the "gag rule") to table the petitions without discussion.

more comprehensive statute that became the model for fourteen other states. The New York statute of 1848 gave women full legal control over the property they brought to a marriage.

That same year, Elizabeth Cady Stanton and Lucretia Mott organized a gathering of women's right activists in the small New York town of Seneca Falls. Seventy women and thirty men attended the meeting, which issued a rousing manifesto that extended the egalitarian republican ideology of the Declaration of Independence to women. "All men and women are created equal," the Declaration of Sentiments declared, "[yet] the history of mankind is a history of repeated injuries and usurpations on the part of man toward woman [and] the establishment of an absolute tyranny over her." To persuade Americans to right this long-standing wrong, the activists resolved to "employ agents, circulate tracts,

petition the State and National legislatures, and endeavor to enlist the pulpit and the press on our behalf." By staking out claims for equality for women in public life, the Seneca Falls reformers repudiated both the natural inferiority of women and the ideology of separate spheres.

Most men dismissed the Seneca Falls declaration as nonsense, and many women also repudiated the activists and their message. Writing in her diary, one small-town mother and housewife lashed out at the female reformer who "aping mannish manners . . . wears absurd and barbarous attire, who talks of her wrongs in harsh tone, who struts and strides, and thinks that she proves herself superior to the rest of her sex."

Still, the women's rights movement grew in strength and purpose. In 1850, delegates to the first national women's rights convention in Worcester, Massachusetts,

All the nations and people I had hitherto passed through resemble[d] [my] own in their manners, customs and lang[uage]

## Ernestine Rose
## Woman's Rights in America

Ernestine Potowsky Rose was born in Russian Poland in 1810, the daughter of a wealthy rabbi. Facing an arranged marriage, she left her family at the age of seventeen and eventually migrated to England. There she associated with radical Christian reformers and married one of them. In 1836, Rose migrated to New York, where she emerged as a major force in the woman's rights movement. In this 1851 speech, she uses European events to inspire her American colleagues. Rose returned to England in 1869 and died there in 1892.

After having heard the letter read from our poor incarcerated sisters of France, well might we exclaim, Alas poor France! Where is thy glory? Where is the glory of the Revolution of 1848[?]

. . . But need we wonder that France, governed as she is by Russian and Austrian despotism, does not recognize the rights of humanity in the recognition of the Rights of Woman, when even here, in this far-famed land of freedom . . . woman, the mockingly so-called "better half" of man, has yet to plead for her rights. . . . In the laws of the land, she has no rights; in government she has no voice. And in spite of another principle recognized in this Republic, namely, that "taxation without representation is tyranny," she is taxed without being represented. Her property may be consumed by taxes to defray the expenses of that unholy, unrighteous custom called war, yet she has no power to give her vote against it. From the cradle to the grave she is subject to the power and control of man. Father, guardian, or husband, one conveys her like some piece of merchandise over to the other.

At marriage she loses her entire identity, and her being is said to have become merged in her husband. Has nature thus merged it? Has she ceased to exist and feel pleasure and pain? When she violates the laws of her being, does her husband pay the penalty? When she breaks the moral law does he suffer the punishment? When he satisfies his wants, is it enough to satisfy her nature? . . .

But it will be said that the husband provides for the wife, or in other words, he feeds, clothes and shelters her! I wish I had the power to make every one before me fully realize the degradation contained in that idea. Yes! He keeps her, and so he does a favorite horse; by law they are both considered his property. . . .

Not long ago, I saw an account of two offenders, brought before a Justice of New York. One was charged with stealing a pair of boots, for which offense he was sentenced to six months' imprisonment; the other crime was assault and battery upon his wife; he was let off with a reprimand by the judge! . . . The judge showed us the comparative value which he set on these two kinds of property. But then you must remember that the boots were taken by a stranger, while the wife was insulted by her legal owner! . . .

But say some, would you expose woman to the contact of rough, rude, drinking, swearing, fighting men at the ballot box? What a humiliating confession lies in this plea for keeping woman in the background! Is the brutality of some men, then, a reason why woman should be kept from her rights? . . . Carry out the republican principle of universal suffrage, or strike it from your banners and substitute "Freedom and Power to one half of society, and Submission and Slavery to the other." Give women the elective franchise. Let married women have the same right to property that their husbands have. . . .

There is no reason against woman's elevation, but . . . prejudices. The main cause is a pernicious falsehood propagated against her being, namely that she is inferior by her nature. Inferior in what? What has man ever done that woman, under the same advantages could not do? In morals, bad as she is, she is generally considered his superior. In the intellectual sphere . . . there is no need of naming the [Madame] de Staels, . . . the [Mary] Wollstonecrafts, the [Lydia] Sigourneys, the [Fanny] Wrights, the [Harriet] Martineaus, . . . and the [Margaret] Fullers . . . to prove her mental powers, her patriotism, her self-sacrificing devotion to the cause of humanity.

Source: *History of Woman Suffrage*, ed. Elizabeth Cady Stanton, Susan B. Anthony, and Matilda Joslyn Gage (New York: Fowler & Wells, 1887), 1: 237–242.

## ANALYZING THE EVIDENCE

- Rose makes at least four distinct arguments for woman's equality. What are they? Which one is the most convincing? The least powerful?

- How would most American men of this time have justified their privileged legal and social position over women?

The activists' legislative campaign required talented organizers and lobbyists. The most prominent political operative was Susan B. Anthony (1820–1906), who came from a Quaker family and, as a young woman, had acquired political skills in the temperance and antislavery movements. Those experiences, Anthony explained, taught her "the great evil of woman's utter dependence on man." Joining the women's right movement, she worked closely with Elizabeth Cady Stanton. Anthony created an activist network of political "captains," all women, who relentlessly lobbied state legislatures. In 1860, her efforts secured a New York law granting women the right to control their own wages (which fathers or husbands had previously managed); to own property acquired by "trade, business, labors, or services"; and, if widowed, to assume sole guardianship of their children. Genuine individualism for women, the dream of transcendentalist Margaret Fuller, had advanced a tiny step closer to reality. In such small and much larger ways, the midcentury reform movements had altered the character of American culture.

- **Why did religious women such as Mary Walker Ostram and the Grimké sisters become social reformers?**

- **How do you explain the appearance of the women's rights movement? What were the movement's goals, and why did they arouse intense opposition?**

- **What was the relationship between the abolitionist and women's rights movements? Why did women's issues suddenly become so prominent in American culture?**

## SUMMARY

In this chapter, we examined four major cultural movements of the mid-nineteenth century and analyzed the new popular culture in New York City. Our discussion of the transcendentalists highlighted the influence of Ralph Waldo Emerson on the great literary figures of the era; we also linked transcendentalism to the rise of individualism and the character of middle-class American culture.

Our analysis of communal movements probed the efforts of communalists to devise new rules for sexual behavior, gender relationships, and property ownership. We saw in this chapter that successful communal experiments—Mormonism, for example—began with a charismatic leader and a religious foundation and endured if they developed strong, authoritarian institutions.

We also traced the personal and ideological factors that linked the abolitionist and women's rights

**Crusading Women Reformers**

Elizabeth Cady Stanton (1815–1902) and Susan B. Anthony (1820–1906) were a dynamic duo of social reformers. Stanton, the well-educated daughter of a prominent New York judge, was an early abolitionist, and the mother of seven children. Anthony was raised as a Quaker and worked as a teacher and a temperance activist. After meeting in 1851, Stanton and Anthony became friends and co-organizers. From 1854 to 1860, they led a successful struggle to expand New York's Married Women's Property Law of 1848. During the Civil War, they set up the Women's Loyal National League, which helped win passage of the Thirteenth Amendment, ending slavery. In 1866, they joined the American Equal Rights Association, which demanded the vote for women and African Americans.
© Corbis/Bettmann.

hammered out a program of action. The women called on churches to revise notions of female inferiority in their theology. Addressing state legislatures, they proposed laws to guarantee the custody rights of mothers in the event of divorce or a husband's death and to allow married women to institute lawsuits and testify in court. Finally, they began a concerted campaign to win the vote for women. Delegates to the 1851 convention declared that suffrage was "the corner-stone of this enterprise, since we do not seek to protect woman, but rather to place her in a position to protect herself."

movements. Lucretia Mott, Elizabeth Cady Stanton, and the Grimké sisters began as antislavery advocates, but—denied access to lecture platforms by male abolitionists—they became staunch advocates of women's rights. This transition was a logical one: Both enslaved blacks and married women were "owned" by men, either as property or as their legal dependents.

Consequently, the efforts of women's rights activists to abolish the legal prerogatives of husbands were as controversial as the abolitionists' efforts to end the legal property rights of slave owners. As reformers took aim at such deeply rooted institutions and customs, many Americans feared that their activism would not perfect society but destroy it.

## CHAPTER REVIEW QUESTIONS

- Did the era of reform increase or decrease the belief in, and practice of, liberty in American society?

- Explain the relationship between individualism and communalism as presented in the chapter. How were these two movements related to the social and economic changes in America in the decades after 1820?

- Explain the relationship between religion and reform in the decades from 1820 to 1860. Why did many religious people feel compelled to remake society? What was their motivation? How successful were they? Do you see any parallels with social movements today?

## FOR FURTHER EXPLORATION

Ronald Walters, *American Reformers, 1815–1860* (1978), surveys the major reform movements, and Robert H. Abzug, *Cosmos Crumbling* (1994), shows their religious roots. David S. Reynolds, *Walt Whitman's America* (1995), assesses the poet and his society. Charles Capper, *Margaret Fuller* (1992), illuminates Fuller's intellectual milieu, as does Nathaniel Hawthorne's novel, *The Blithedale Romance* (1852). Peter S. Field, in *Ralph Waldo Emerson* (2003), sketches a convincing profile. A good site on transcendentalism is "The Web of American Transcendentalism," found at **www.vcu.edu/engweb/transcendentalism**. For religious utopianism gone mad, read Paul E. Johnson and Sean Wilentz, *The Kingdom of Matthias* (1995).

James B. Stewart, *Holy Warriors* (1976), explores Garrison's abolitionist movement. Also see Mark Perry's study of the Grimké family, *Lift Up Thy Voice* (2001). Stephen B. Oates, *The Fires of Jubilee* (1975), explores the life Nat Turner; Turner's testimony is at **docsouth.unc.edu/neh/turner/menu.html**. *The Narrative of the Life of Frederick Douglass* (1845) is a literary masterpiece. Biographies of abolitionists include John Stauffer, *The Black Hearts of Men* (2001), and Catherine Clinton, *Harriet Tubman* (2004). For antiabolitionism, see Leonard L. Richards, *"Gentlemen of Property and Standing"* (1970), and David Roediger, *The Wages of Whiteness* (1995). Additional material is available from the *Africans in America* series Web site at **www.pbs.org/wgbh/aia/part4/**.

Anne M. Boylan, *The Origins of Women's Activism* (1992), and Mary Ryan, *Women in Public* (1990), explore women's civic activities. Also see Eleanor Flexner, *Century of Struggle* (1959), and the Seneca Falls Women's Rights National Historical Park Web site at **www.nps.gov/wori/index.htm**.

### TEST YOUR KNOWLEDGE

To assess your command of the material in this chapter, see the Online Study Guide at **bedfordstmartins.com/henretta**.

For Web sites, images, and documents related to topics and places in this chapter, visit **bedfordstmartins.com/makehistory**.

## TIMELINE

| | |
|---|---|
| **1826** | Lyceum movement begins |
| **1829** | David Walker's *Appeal . . . to the Colored Citizens of the World* |
| **1830** | Joseph Smith publishes *The Book of Mormon* |
| **1830s** | Emergence of minstrelsy shows; Nativist citizens question immigration policy |
| **1831** | William Lloyd Garrison founds *The Liberator*; Nat Turner's uprising in Virginia |
| **1832** | Ralph Waldo Emerson turns to transcendentalism |
| **1833** | Garrison organizes American Anti-Slavery Society |
| **1834** | New York activists create Female Moral Reform Society |
| **1835** | Abolitionists launch mail campaign; antiabolitionists riot against them |
| **1836** | House of Representatives adopts gag rule; Grimké sisters defend public roles for women |
| **1840** | Liberty Party runs James G. Birney for president |
| **1840s** | Fourierist communities arise in Midwest; Commercialized sex flourishes in New York City |
| **1841** | Transcendentalists found Brook Farm; Dorothea Dix promotes hospitals for mentally ill |
| **1844** | Margaret Fuller publishes *Woman in the Nineteenth Century* |
| **1845** | Henry David Thoreau goes to Walden Pond |
| **1846** | Brigham Young leads Mormons to Salt Lake |
| **1848** | John Humphrey Noyes founds Oneida; Seneca Falls convention proposes women's equality |
| **1850** | Nathaniel Hawthorne's *The Scarlet Letter* |
| **1851** | Herman Melville publishes *Moby Dick* |
| **1852** | Harriet Beecher Stowe writes *Uncle Tom's Cabin* |
| **1855** | Walt Whitman's *Leaves of Grass* |
| **1858** | "Mormon War" over polygamy |

## CHAPTER 12

# The South Expands: Slavery and Society, 1800–1860

**Life in South Carolina** had been good to James Lide. A slave-owning planter who lived near the Pee Dee River, Lide and his wife had raised twelve children. Living in relative comfort, Lide had long resisted the "Alabama Fever" that had prompted thousands of Carolina families to move west. Finally, at age sixty-five, probably seeking land for his many offspring, he moved his slaves and family — including six children and six grandchildren — to a plantation near Montgomery, Alabama. There, the family lived initially in a squalid double log cabin with airholes but no windows. Even as their housing conditions improved, the Lides' family life remained unsettled. "Pa is quite in the notion of moving somewhere," his daughter Maria reported a few years later. Although James Lide lived out his years in Alabama, many of his children did not. In 1854, at the age of fifty-eight, Eli Lide moved to Texas, telling his father, "Something within me whispers onward and onward."

The story of the Lide family was the story of American society. Between 1800 and 1860, white planters from the South as well as yeomen farmers from the North were moving west. The South's "master class was one of the most mobile in history," notes historian James Oakes. The planters' goal was to make the West into a "slave society" similar to those their fathers and grandfathers had built in Virginia and South Carolina. Using the muscles and sweat of a million enslaved African Americans, the planters brought millions of acres into cultivation. By 1840, the South was at the cutting edge of the American Market Revolution. It annually produced and exported 1.5 million bales of raw cotton — over two-thirds of the world's supply — and its economy was larger and richer than that of most nations. "Cotton is King," boasted the *Southern Cultivator*, the leading Georgia farm journal, "and wields an astonishing influence over the world's commerce."

No matter how rich they were, few cotton planters in the southwestern states of Alabama, Mississippi, and Texas lived in elegant houses or led cultured lives. Abandoning the aristocratic gentility of Chesapeake and the Carolinas, these agricultural capitalists wanted to make money. "To sell cotton in order to buy negroes — to make more cotton to buy more negroes, 'ad infinitum,' is the aim . . . of the thorough-going cotton planter," a New England traveler reported from Mississippi in 1835. "His whole soul is wrapped up in

**Generations in Slavery**

In 1862, traveling photographer Timothy O'Sullivan took this picture at the plantation of J. J. Smith in Beaufort, South Carolina. It shows four — perhaps five — generations of a slave family, most of whom were born on the plantation. As you read this chapter, consider whether the experience of this African American family was the exception or the rule. Who might be missing from this family photograph? For example, what happened to the brothers and sisters of the man standing in the back? Library of Congress.

the pursuit." A generation later, Frederick Law Olmsted found that the plantations in Mississippi were large but their owners mostly had "but small and mean residences." Plantation women were especially aware of the loss of genteel surroundings and polite society. Raised in North Carolina, where she was "blest with every comfort, & even luxury," a "discontented" Mary Drake found Mississippi and Alabama "a dreary waste."

Hundreds of thousands of enslaved African Americans in the Lower Mississippi River Valley knew what "dreary waste" really meant: unremitting toil, unrelieved poverty, and profound sadness. Sold south from Maryland, where his family had lived for generations, Charles Ball's father became "gloomy and morose"; when threatened again with sale, he ran off and disappeared. With good reason: On new cotton plantations, slaves labored from "sunup to sundown" and from one end of the year to the other. As one field hand put it, there was "no time off [between] de change of de seasons. . . . Dey was allus clearin' mo' lan' or sump'." Day by day, the forced labor of unwilling black migrants produced the wealth of the Cotton South. Always wanting more, southern planters and politicians plotted to extend their plantation economy across the continent.

# Creating the Cotton South

American slavery took root on the tobacco plantations of the Chesapeake and in the rice fields of the Carolina Low Country. It grew to maturity on the sugar fields of Louisiana, the hemp farms of Kentucky and Tennessee, and especially in the cotton states bordering the Gulf of Mexico: Alabama, Mississippi, and Texas (Figure 12.1). This massive transplantation of slavery led planters to believe that it could keep expanding. "We want land, and have a right to it," declared a Georgia planter on the eve of the Civil War.

## The Domestic Slave Trade

In 1817, when the American Colonization Society began to return a few freed blacks to Africa (see Chapter 8), the southern plantation system was expanding rapidly. In 1790, its western boundary ran through the middle of Georgia; by 1830, it stretched through western Louisiana; by 1860, the slave frontier extended far into Texas (Map 12.1). That advance of 900 miles more than doubled the geographical area cultivated by slave labor and raised the number of slave states from eight in 1800 to fifteen by 1850. The federal government assisted this expansion by buying Louisiana from the French in 1803, removing Native Americans from the southeastern states in the 1830s, and annexing Texas and Mexican lands in the 1840s.

To cultivate this vast area, white planters looked for enslaved laborers first in Africa and then in the Chesapeake region. Between 1776 and 1809, when Congress outlawed the Atlantic slave trade, planters imported about 115,000 Africans. "The Planter will . . . sacrifice every thing to attain Negroes," declared one slave trader. Despite the influx, the demand for labor far exceeded the supply. Consequently, planters imported new African workers illegally, through the Spanish colony of Florida until 1819 and then through the Mexican province of Texas. Yet these Africans—about 50,000 between 1810 and 1869—did not meet the demand.

**The Upper South Exports Slaves** So planters looked to the Chesapeake region, home in 1800 to nearly half of the nation's black population. There, the African American population was growing rapidly from natural increase—an average of 27 percent a decade—and creating a surplus of enslaved laborers. By 1815, so-called Georgia traders had created a large and growing domestic trade in slaves. Between 1818 and 1829, planters in just one Maryland county—Frederick—sold at least 952 slaves to traders or cotton planters. Seventy-five thousand slaves left Virginia during the 1810s and again during the 1820s. The number of unwilling Virginia migrants jumped to nearly 120,000 during the 1830s and then averaged 85,000 during the 1840s and 1850s. In Virginia alone, then, 440,000 African Americans were ripped from com-

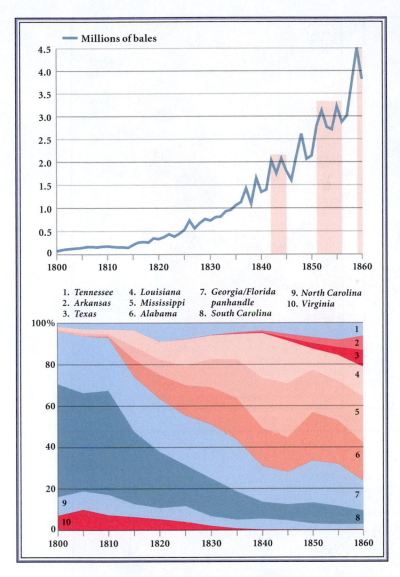

**FIGURE 12.1**

**Cotton Production and Producers, 1800–1860**

Until the mid-1830s, most cotton was grown in Georgia and South Carolina (7 and 8 in the lower graph) and production increased at a steady pace. Then came a series of dramatic changes. By the early 1840s, those south-eastern states grew only one-third of the cotton because planters had moved hundreds of thousands of slaves to the Mississippi Valley (Louisiana, Mississippi, and Alabama — 4, 5, and 6 in the lower graph). Simultaneously, production burst upward in a series of leaps, reaching 2 million bales a year by the mid-1840s, 3 million by the mid-1850s, and 4 million on the eve of the Civil War.   Source: *Historical Statistics of the United States* (Washington, D.C.: U.S. Government Printing Office, 1957), Sec. K 534; lower graph adapted from Alan L. Olmstead and Paul W. Rhode, "'Wait a Cotton Picking Minute': A New View of Slave Productivity" (unpublished paper, 2005), Fig. 5.

munities where their families had lived for three or four generations. By 1860, the "mania for buying negroes" had resulted in a massive forced migration from the Upper South of more than 1 million slaves (Figure 12.2).

This movement of African Americans took two forms: transfer and sale. Looking for new opportunities, thousands of Chesapeake and Carolina planters — men like James Lide — sold their plantations and moved to the Southwest with their slaves. Many other planters in the Old South gave slaves to sons and daughters who were moving west. This transfer of entire or partial plantations accounted for about 40 percent of the African American migrants. The rest — about 60 percent of the one million migrants — were "sold south" through traders. By 1860 a majority of African Americans lived and worked in the Deep South, the lands that stretched from Georgia to Texas.

Just as the Atlantic slave trade was a major eighteenth-century commercial enterprise that enriched English merchants, so the domestic slave trade became a great business between 1800 and 1860. The domestic trade involved both a coastal system through Atlantic seaports and inland routes using rivers and roads. The coastal system sent thousands of slaves to the sugar plantations in Louisiana, the former French territory which entered the Union in 1812. Slave traders scoured the countryside near the port cities of the Chesapeake and the Carolinas — Baltimore, Alexandria, Richmond, Charleston — searching, as one of them put it, for "likely young men such as I think would suit the New Orleans market." Each year, hundreds of muscular young slaves passed through the auction houses of the port cities bound for the massive trade mart in New Orleans. Because this traffic in laborers was highly

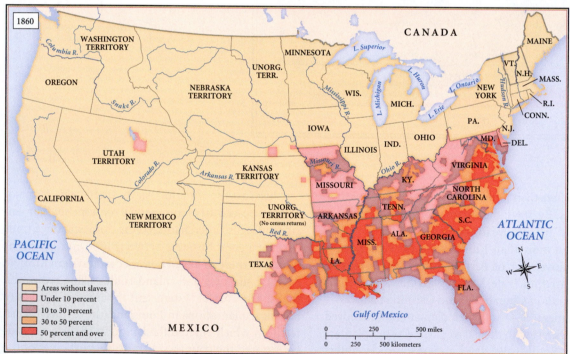

**MAP 12.1**

**Distribution of the Slave Population in 1790, 1830, and 1860**

The cotton boom shifted many African Americans to the Old Southwest. In 1790, most slaves lived and worked on Chesapeake tobacco and Carolina rice and indigo plantations. By 1830, hundreds of thousands of enslaved blacks were laboring on the cotton and sugar lands of the Lower Mississippi Valley and on cotton plantations in Georgia and Florida. Three decades later, the centers of slavery lay along the Mississippi River and in an arc of fertile cotton land—the "black belt"—sweeping from Mississippi through Georgia.

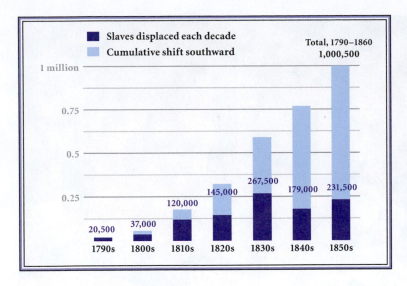

Slaves displaced each decade
Cumulative shift southward

Total, 1790–1860
1,000,500

1 million

0.75

0.5

0.25

267,500

145,000

120,000

179,000   231,500

20,500   37,000

1790s   1800s   1810s   1820s   1830s   1840s   1850s

### FIGURE 12.2

### Forced Migration of Slaves from the Upper South to the Lower South, 1790–1860

The cotton boom that began in the 1810s set in motion a vast redistribution of the African American population. Between 1790 and 1860, white planters moved or sold more than a million slaves from the Upper to the Lower South, a process that broke up families and long-established black communities. Source: Based on data in Robert William Fogel and Stanley L. Engerman, *Time on the Cross* (Boston: Little, Brown, 1974), and Michael Tadman, *Speculators and Slaves: Masters, Traders, and Slaves in the Old South* (Madison: University of Wisconsin Press, 1996).

visible, it elicited widespread condemnation by northern abolitionists.

Sugar was a "killer" crop, and Louisiana (like the eighteenth-century West Indies) soon had a well-deserved reputation among African Americans "as a place of slaughter." Hundreds died each year from disease, overwork, and brutal treatment. Maryland farmer John Anthony Munnikhuysen refused to consent to his daughter Priscilla's marriage to a Louisiana sugar planter, remarking: "Mit has never been used to see negroes flayed alive and it would kill her."

The inland system that sent slaves to the Cotton South was less visible than the coastal trade but much more extensive. It also relied on professional slave traders, who went from one rural village to another buying "young and likely Negroes." The traders then marched their purchases in coffles—columns of slaves bound to one another—to Alabama, Mississippi, and Missouri in the 1830s and to Arkansas and Texas in the 1850s. One slave described the arduous journey: "Dem Speckulators would put the chilluns in a wagon usually pulled by oxens and de older folks was chained or tied together sos dey could not run off." Once a coffle reached its destination, the trader would sell slaves "at every village in the county."

Chesapeake and Carolina planters provided the human cargo. Some planters sold slaves when poor management or their "own extravagances" threw them into debt. "Trouble gathers thicker and thicker around me," Thomas B. Chaplin of South Carolina lamented in his diary. "I will be compelled to send about ten prime Negroes to Town on next Monday, to be sold." Many

### The Internal Slave Trade

Mounted whites escort a convoy of slaves from Virginia to Tennessee in Lewis Miller's *Slave Trader, Sold to Tennessee* (1853). For white planters, the interstate trade in slaves was lucrative; it pumped money into the declining Chesapeake economy and provided young workers for the expanding plantations of the cotton belt. For blacks, it was a traumatic journey, a new Middle Passage that broke up their families and communities. "Arise, Arise and weep no more, dry up your tears, we shall part no more," the slaves sing hopefully as they journey to new lives in Tennessee. Abby Aldrich Rockefeller Folk Art Museum, Williamsburg, VA.

**The Business of Slavery**

In the 1850s, Virginia slaves were still being "sold south." This painting, *Slave Auction in Richmond, Virginia* (1852), captures the pensive and apprehensive emotions of the women and the discontent of the man, none of whom can control their fate. Whites – plantation overseer, slave trader, top-hatted aristocratic planter – lurk in the background, where they are completing the commercial transaction. The illustration on page 369, a public notice for a slave auction to be held in Iberville, Louisiana, advertises "24 Head of Slaves" as if they were cattle – a striking commentary on the business of slavery.   The Granger Collection, New York/Library of Congress.

more planters doubled as slave traders, earning substantial profits by traveling south to sell some of their slaves and those of their neighbors. Prices marched in step with those for cotton; during the boom years of the 1850s, said one planter, a slave "will fetch $1000, cash, quick, this year." Exploiting this demand, Thomas Weatherly of South Carolina drove his surplus slaves to Hayneville, Alabama, where he "sold ten negroes." Colonel E. S. Irvine, a member of the South Carolina legislature and "a highly respected gentleman" in white circles, likewise traveled frequently "to the west to sell a drove of Negroes."

The domestic slave trade was crucial to the prosperity of the South. It provided workers to fell the forests and plant cotton in the Gulf states and bolstered the economy of the Upper South. By selling surplus workers, tobacco, rice, and grain, planters in the Chesapeake and Carolinas added about 20 percent to their income. As a Maryland newspaper remarked in 1858, "[The domestic slave trade serves as] an almost universal resource to raise money. A prime able-bodied slave is worth three times as much to the cotton or sugar planter as to the Maryland agriculturalist."

**The Impact on Blacks** For African American families, the domestic slave trade was a personal disaster that accentuated their status—and vulnerability—as property. On this issue, blacks and whites agreed. W. C. Pennington, a former slave, reflected, "The being of slavery, its soul and its body, lives and moves in the chattel principle, the property principle, the bill of sale principle." A South Carolina master put it more crudely: "[The slave's earnings] belong to *me* because I bought him." Indeed, slave property

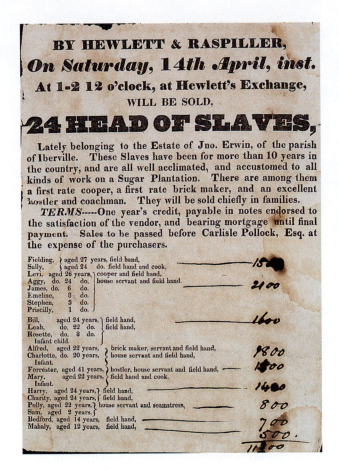

BY HEWLETT & RASPILLER,
On Saturday, 14th April, inst.
At 1-2 12 o'clock, at Hewlett's Exchange,
WILL BE SOLD,

**24 HEAD OF SLAVES,**

Lately belonging to the Estate of Jno. Erwin, of the parish of Iberville. These Slaves have been for more than 10 years in the country, and are all well acclimated, and accustomed to all kinds of work on a Sugar Plantation. There are among them a first rate cooper, a first rate brick maker, and an excellent hostler and coachman. They will be sold chiefly in families.

TERMS-----One year's credit, payable in notes endorsed to the satisfaction of the vendor, and bearing mortgage until final payment. Sales to be passed before Carlisle Pollock, Esq. at the expense of the purchasers.

formed the foundation of the entire southern economic system. As Whig politician Henry Clay observed, the "immense amount of capital which is invested in slave property . . . is owned by widows and orphans, by the aged and infirm, as well as the sound and vigorous. It is the subject of mortgages, deeds of trust, and family settlements." The Whig politician concluded: "I know that there is a visionary dogma, which holds that negro slaves cannot be the subject of property. I shall not dwell long on this speculative abstraction. That is property which the law declares to be property."

As a slave owner, Clay knew that property rights were a key to slave discipline. As one master put it, "I govern them . . . without the whip by stating . . . that I should sell them if they do not conduct themselves as I wish." The threat was effective. "The Negroes here dread nothing on earth so much as this," an observer in Maryland noted. "They regard the south with perfect horror, and to be sent there is considered as the worst punishment that could be inflicted on them."

But thousands of slaves suffered that fate, which destroyed about one in every four slave marriages. "I am Sold to a man by the name of Peterson a trader," lamented a Georgia slave. "My Dear wife for you and my Children my pen cannot Express the griffe I feel to be parted from you all." The trade encompassed children and youth as well as adults; in northern Maryland, boys and girls were sold away at an average age of 17 years. "Dey sole my sister Kate," Anna Harris remembered decades later, "and I ain't seed or heard of her since." The trade also separated almost a third of all slave children under the age of fourteen from one or both of their parents. Sarah Grant remembered, "Mamma used to cry when she had to go back to work because she was always scared some of us kids would be sold while she was away." Well might she worry, for slave traders worked quietly and quickly. "One night I lay down on de straw mattress wid my mammy," Vinny Baker recalled, "an' de nex' mo'nin I woke up an' she wuz gone." When their owner sold seven-year-old Laura Clark and ten other children from their plantation in North Carolina, Clark sensed that she would see her mother "no mo' in dis life."

Despite these sales, 75 percent of slave marriages remained unbroken, and the majority of children lived with one or both parents until puberty. Consequently, the sense of family among African Americans remained strong. Sold from Virginia to Texas in 1843, Hawkins Wilson carried with him a detailed mental picture of his family. Twenty-five years later and now a freedman, Wilson set out to find his "dearest relatives" in Virginia. "My sister belonged to Peter Coleman in Caroline County and her name was Jane. . . . She had three children, Robert, Charles and Julia, when I left — Sister Martha belonged to Dr. Jefferson. . . . Sister Matilda belonged to Mrs. Botts."

During the decades between sale and freedom, Hawkins Wilson and thousands of other African American migrants constructed new lives for themselves in the Mississippi River Valley. Undoubtedly, many of them did so with a sense of foreboding: From personal experience, they knew that their lives could be shaken to the core at any moment. Like Charles Ball, some "longed to die, and escape from the bonds of my tormentors." Even moments of joy were shadowed by the darkness of slavery. Knowing that sales often ended slave marriages, a white minister blessed one couple "for so long as God keeps them together."

Many white planters "saw" only the African American marriages that endured and ignored those they had broken. Accordingly, many slave owners considered themselves benevolent masters, committed to the welfare of "my family, black and white." Some masters gave substance to this paternalist ideal by treating with kindness various "loyal and worthy" slaves — the drivers, the mammy who raised their children, and trusted house servants. By safeguarding the families of these slaves from sale, planters convinced themselves that they "sold south" only "coarse" troublemakers and uncivilized slaves who had "little sense of family." Other owners were more honest about the human cost of their pursuit of wealth. "Tomorrow the negroes are to get off [to Kentucky]," a slave-owning woman in Virginia wrote to a friend, "and I expect there will be great crying and moaning, with children Leaving there mothers, mothers there children, and women there husbands."

Whether or not they acknowledged the slaves' pain, few southern whites questioned the morality of the domestic slave trade. Responding to criticism by abolitionists, the city council of Charleston, South Carolina, declared that slavery was completely consistent "with moral principle and with the highest order of civilization," as was "the removal of slaves from place to place, and their transfer from master to master, by gift, purchase, or otherwise."

## The Dual Cultures of the Planter Elite

A small elite of extraordinarily wealthy planter families stood at the top of southern society. These families — about three thousand in number — each owned more than one hundred slaves and huge tracts of the most fertile lands. Their ranks included many of the richest families in the United States. On the eve of the Civil War, southern planters accounted for nearly two-thirds of all American men with wealth of $100,000 or more.

**The Traditional Southern Gentry** | The westward movement split the plantation elite into two distinct groups: the traditional aristocrats of the Old South, and the upstart capitalist-inclined planters of the cotton states. The Old South gentry, having gained their wealth from tobacco and rice, dominated the Tidewater region of the Chesapeake and the low country of South Carolina and Georgia. During the eighteenth century, these planters built impressive mansions and adopted the manners and values of the English landed gentry (see Chapter 3). Their aristocratic culture survived the revolution of 1776 and soon took on a republican character. Classical republican theory had its roots in the slave-owning societies of Greece and Rome, and had long identified political tyranny (not slavery) as the major threat to liberty. That variety of republican ideology appealed to southern aristocrats, who feared government interference with their property in slaves. To prevent despotic rule by democratic demagogues or radical legislatures, planters demanded

that authority rest in the hands of incorruptible men of "virtue."

Affluent planters cast themselves as the embodiment of this ideal — a republican aristocracy (see Chapter 8). "The planters here are essentially what the nobility are in other countries," declared James Henry Hammond of South Carolina. "They stand at the head of society & politics . . . [and form] an aristocracy of talents, of virtue, of generosity and courage." Wealthy planters criticized the increasingly democratic polity and middle-class society that was developing in the Northeast and Midwest. "Inequality is the fundamental law of the universe," declared one aristocratic-minded planter. Others condemned professional politicians as "a set of demagogues" and questioned the legitimacy of universal suffrage. "Times are sadly different now to what they were when I was a boy," lamented David Gavin, a prosperous South Carolinian. Then, the "Sovereign people, alias mob" had little influence; now they vied for power with the elite. "[How can] I rejoice for a freedom," Gavin demanded to know, "which allows every bankrupt, swindler, thief, and scoundrel, traitor and seller of his vote to be placed on an equality with myself?"

To maintain their privileged identity, aristocratic planters married their sons and daughters to one another and expected them to follow in their footsteps — the men working as planters, merchants, lawyers, newspaper editors, and ministers, and the women hosting plantation balls and church bazaars. To confirm their social preeminence, they lived extravagantly and entertained graciously. James Henry Hammond built a Greek Revival mansion with a center hall 53 feet by 20 feet, its floor embellished with stylish Belgian tiles and expensive Brussels carpets. "Once a year, like a great feudal landlord," a guest recounted, "[Hammond] gave a fete or grand dinner to all the country people."

Rice planters remained at the apex of the plantation aristocracy. In 1860, the fifteen proprietors of the vast plantations in All Saints Parish in the Georgetown district of South Carolina owned 4,383 slaves — nearly 300 apiece — who annually grew and processed 14 million pounds of rice. As inexpensive Asian rice entered the world market in the 1820s and cut their profit margins, Carolina planters sold some slaves and worked the others harder — allowing them to sustain their luxurious lifestyle. The "hospitality and elegance" of Charleston and Savannah impressed savvy English traveler John Silk Buckingham. Buckingham likewise found "polished" families among long-established French Catholic planters in New Orleans and along the Mississippi River: "The sugar and cotton planters live in splendid

**A Louisiana Plantation, 1861**

This view of the St. John plantation in Louisiana by Marie Adrien Persac, a French-born artist, presents an exquisitely detailed but romanticized vision of the planter lifestyle. Well-dressed slaves stand amid neatly spaced rows of cotton as the women of the household prance by on well-groomed horses. Off to the right, smoke rises from the chimneys of a small mill, probably used to process the sugarcane grown elsewhere on the plantation.  Louisiana State University Museum of Art.

edifices, and enjoy all the luxury that wealth can impart" (see Voices from Abroad, "Bernhard, Duke of Saxe-Weimar-Eisenach: The Racial Complexities of Southern Society," p. 372).

In tobacco-growing regions, the lives of the planter aristocracy followed a different trajectory, in part because slave ownership was widely diffused. In the 1770s, about 60 percent of white families in the Chesapeake region owned at least one African American slave. As many wealthy tobacco planters moved their plantations and slaves to the Cotton South, middling planters (who owned between five and twenty slaves) came to dominate the Chesapeake economy. The descendants of the old tobacco aristocracy remained influential, but increasingly as slave-owning grain farmers, lawyers, merchants, industrialists, and politicians. They either hired out slaves they didn't need for their businesses or sold them south or allowed them to purchase their freedom.

**The Ideology and Reality of "Benevolence"** Although the genteel planter aristocracy flourished primarily around the periphery of the South — in Virginia, South Carolina, and Louisiana — its members took the lead in defending slavery. Ignoring the old Jeffersonian response to slavery as a

VOICES
FROM
ABROAD

## Bernhard, Duke of Saxe-Weimar-Eisenach
# The Racial Complexities of Southern Society

In 1825 and 1826, Bernhard, duke of the German principality of Saxe-Weimar-Eisenach, traveled throughout the United States, and published an account of his adventures in 1828. Subsequently, he compiled a distinguished military record serving the king of the Netherlands and then ruled his principality from 1853 until his death in 1862. In this selection from his *Travels*, Bernhard notes the migration to the cotton belt and describes the racial intricacies of New Orleans society.

[On our way to New Orleans] we met several parties of emigrants from the eastern sections of Georgia on their way to Butler County in Alabama. They proposed to settle on lands that they had acquired very cheaply from the federal government. The number of their Negroes, horses, wagons, and cattle showed that these wanderers were well off.

In New Orleans we were invited to a subscription ball. . . . Only good society is invited to these balls. The first to which we came was not very well attended; but most of the ladies were very nice looking and well turned out in the French manner. Their clothing was elegant after the latest Paris fashions. They danced very well and did credit to their French dancing masters. Dancing and some music are the main branches of the education of a Creole [an American-born white] woman. . . .

The native men are far from matching the women in elegance. And they stayed only a short time, preferring to escape to a so-called "Quarterons Ball" which they find more amusing and where they do not have to stand on ceremony. . . .

A "quarteron" (octoroon) is the offspring of a mestizo mother and a white father, just as the mestizo is the child of a mulatto and a white man. The "quarterons" are almost completely white. There would be no way of recognizing them by their complexion, for they are often fairer than the Creoles. Black hair and eyes are generally the signs of their status, although some are quite blond. The ball is attended by the free "quarterons." Yet the deepest prejudice reigns against them on account of their colored origin; the white women particularly feel or affect to feel a strong repugnance to them.

Marriage between colored and white people is forbidden by the laws of the state. Yet the "quarterons," for their part, look upon the Negroes and mulattoes as inferiors and are unwilling to mix with them. The girls therefore have no other recourse than to become the mistresses of white men. The "quarterons" regard such attachment as the equivalent of marriage. They would not think of entering upon it other than with a formal contract in which the man engages to pay a stipulated sum to the mother or father of the girl. The latter even assumes the name of her lover and regards the affair with more faithfulness than many a woman whose marriage was sealed in a church.

Some of these women have inherited from their fathers and lovers, and possess considerable fortunes. Their status is nevertheless always very depressed. They must not ride in the street in coaches, and their lovers can bring them to the balls in their own conveyances only after nightfall. They must never sit opposite a white lady, nor may they enter a room without express permission. . . . But many of these girls are much more carefully educated than the whites, behave with more polish and more politeness, and make their lovers happier than white wives their husbands. And yet the white ladies speak of these unfortunate depressed creatures with great disdain, even bitterness. Because of the depth of these prejudices, many fathers send their daughters, conceived after this manner, to France where good education and wealth are no impediments to the attainment of a respectable place.

Source: C. J. Jeronimus, ed., *Travels by His Highness Duke Bernhard of Saxe-Weimar-Eisenach Through North America in the Years 1825 and 1826*, trans. William Jeronimus (1828; repr., Lanham, Md.: University Press of America, 2001), 296–297, 343, 346–347.

### ANALYZING THE EVIDENCE

- What does this passage suggest about the effect of racial slavery on white marriages?
- Why were France and French fashions so important in the lives of the white and "quarteron" population of New Orleans?
- How does Bernhard's account help explain the values and outlook of the free black population in the South?
- In the United States, the kind of racial mixing Bernhard noted in New Orleans society was unique. Why did it not appear in Charleston, Richmond, and other southern cities?

"misfortune" or a "necessary evil" (see Chapter 8), southern apologists began in the 1830s to argue that slavery was a "positive good" that allowed a civilized lifestyle for whites and provided tutelage for genetically inferior Africans. "As a race, the African is inferior to the white man," declared Alexander Stephens, the future vice president of the Confederacy. "Subordination to the white man, is his normal condition." Apologists depicted planters and their wives as aristocratic models of "disinterested benevolence," who paternalistically provided food and housing for their workers and cared for them in old age. One wealthy Georgian declared, "Plantation government should be eminently patriarchal . . . the *pater-familias,* or head of the family, should, in one sense, be the father of the whole concern, negroes and all."

Those planters who embraced Christian stewardship tried to shape the behavior of their slaves. Some built cabins for their workers and insisted slaves whitewash the cabins regularly. Many others built churches on their plantations, welcomed evangelical preachers, and often required their slaves to attend services. A few encouraged African Americans with spiritual "gifts" to serve as exhorters and deacons. The motives of the planters were mixed. Some acted from sincere Christian belief, while others wanted to counter abolitionist criticism or to use religious teachings to control their workers.

Indeed, religion served increasingly as a justification for human bondage. Protestant ministers in the South pointed out that the Hebrews, God's chosen people, had owned slaves and that Jesus Christ had never condemned slavery. As Hammond told a British abolitionist in 1845: "What God ordains and Christ sanctifies should surely command the respect and toleration of man." But many aristocratic apologists were absentee owners or delegated authority to overseers, and rarely glimpsed the day-to-day brutality of the slave regime. "I was at the plantation last Saturday and the crop was in fine order," an absentee's son wrote to his father, "but the negroes are most brutally scarred & several have run off."

**Cotton Entrepreneurs**   There was much less hypocrisy and far less elegance among the second group of elite planters: the market-driven entrepreneurs of the Cotton South. "The glare of expensive luxury vanishes" in the black soil regions of Alabama and Mississippi, John Silk Buckingham remarked as he traveled through the Cotton South, and aristocratic paternalism vanished as well. A Mississippi planter put it plainly: "Everything has to give way

**The Inherent Brutality of Slavery**

Like all systems of forced labor, American racial slavery relied on physical coercion. Slave owners and overseers routinely whipped slaves who worked slowly or defied their orders. On occasion, they applied the whip with such ferocity that the slave was permanently injured or killed. This photograph of a Mississippi slave named Gordon, taken after he fled to the Union Army in Louisiana in 1863 and published in *Harper's Weekly,* stands as graphic testimony to the inherent brutality of the system.   National Archives.

to large crops of cotton, land has to be cultivated wet or dry, negroes [must] work, hot or cold." Angry at being sold south and pressed to hard labor, many slaves grew "mean" and stubborn. Those who would not labor were subject to the lash. "Whiped all the hoe hands," Alabama planter James Torbert wrote matter-of-factly in his journal. Overseers pushed their workers hard because their salaries often depended on the quantity of cotton they were able "to make for the market." A Mississippi slave recalled, "When I wuz so tired I cu'dnt hardly stan', I had to spin my cut of cotton befor' I cu'd go to sleep. We had to card, spin, an' reel at nite."

Cotton was a demanding crop because of its long growing season. Slaves plowed the land in March;

dropped seeds into the ground in early April; and, once the plants began to grow, continually chopped away the surrounding grasses. In between these tasks, they planted the corn and peas that would provide food for them and the plantation's hogs and chickens. When the cotton bolls ripened in late August, the long four-month picking season began. Slaves in the Cotton South, concluded traveler Frederick Law Olmsted, worked "much harder and more unremittingly" than those in the tobacco regions. Moreover, fewer of them acquired craft skills than in tobacco, sugar, and rice areas, where slave coopers and engineers made casks, processed sugar, and built irrigation systems.

To increase output, profit-conscious cotton planters began during the 1820s to use a rigorous **gang-labor system**. Previously, many planters had either supervised their workers sporadically or assigned them jobs and let them work at their own pace. Now masters with twenty or more slaves organized disciplined teams, or "gangs," supervised by black drivers and white overseers. They instructed the supervisors to work the gangs at a steady pace, clearing and plowing land or hoeing and picking cotton. A traveler in Mississippi described two gangs returning from work:

> First came, led by an old driver carrying a whip, forty of the largest and strongest women I ever saw together; they were all in a simple uniform dress of a bluish check stuff, the skirts reaching little below the knee; . . . they carried themselves loftily, each having a hoe over the shoulder, and walking with a free, powerful swing.

Next marched the plow hands with their mules, "the cavalry, thirty strong, mostly men, but a few of them women." Finally, "a lean and vigilant white overseer, on a brisk pony, brought up the rear."

The cotton planters' quest for profits was ecologically costly. Cotton monoculture and little crop rotation depleted the nutrients in the soil and gradually reduced the output per acre. Still, the crop was a financial bonanza. Because a slave working in a gang finished as much work in thirty-five minutes as a white yeoman planter did in an hour, gang labor became ever more prevalent. In one Georgia county, the percentage of slaves working in gangs doubled between 1830 and 1850 and increased further during the 1850s. As the price of raw cotton surged after 1846, the wealth of the planter class skyrocketed. And no wonder: Nearly 2 million enslaved African Americans now labored on the plantations of the Cotton South and annually produced 4 million bales of the valuable fiber.

## Planters, Smallholding Yeomen, and Tenants

Although the South was a "slave society"—that is, the institution of slavery affected all aspects of life there—most white southerners did not own slaves. The percentage of white families who held blacks in bondage steadily decreased—from 36 percent in 1830, to 31 percent in 1850, to about 25 percent a decade later. However, slave ownership varied by region. In some cotton-rich counties, 40 percent or more of the white families owned slaves; in the hill country near the Appalachian Mountains, the proportion dropped to 10 percent.

**Planter Elites**   Among the privileged minority of 395,000 families who owned slaves in 1860, there was a strict hierarchy. The top one-fifth of these families owned twenty or more slaves. This elite—just 5 percent of the South's white population—dominated the economy, owning over 50 percent of the entire slave population of 4 million, and growing 50 percent of the South's cotton crop. The average wealth of these planters was $56,000 (about $1.5 million today); by contrast, the average southern yeoman or northern farmer owned property worth a mere $3,200.

Substantial proprietors, another fifth of the slave-owning population, held title to six to twenty bondsmen and -women. These middling planters owned almost 40 percent of the slave population and produced more than 30 percent of the cotton. Often they pursued dual careers as skilled artisans or professional men. For example, many of the fifteen slaves owned by Samuel L. Moore worked in his brick factory; the others labored on his Georgia farm. In Macon County, Alabama, James Tolbert owned a plantation that yielded 50 bales of cotton a year; but Tolbert also ran a sawmill, "which pays as well as making Cotton." Dr. Thomas Gale used the income from his medical practice to buy a Mississippi plantation that annually produced 150 bales of cotton. In Alabama, lawyer Benjamin Fitzpatrick used his legal fees to buy ten slaves.

Like Fitzpatrick, many lawyers either owned slaves or managed the affairs of the slave-owning elite. They became well known in their communities by representing merchants and storekeepers in suits for debt, settling disputes over property, and helping smallholders and tenants register their deeds and contracts. Standing at the legal crossroads of their small towns and personally known by many residents, lawyers regularly won election to public office. Less than 1 percent of the male population, in 1828 lawyers made up 16 percent of the Alabama legislature, and an astounding 26 percent in 1849.

**Smallholding Planters and Yeomen** The smallholders who made up the majority of slave owners were much less visible than the wealthy grandees and the middling lawyer-planters. These slave owners held from one to five black laborers in bondage and claimed title to a few hundred acres of land. Some smallholders were well-connected young men who would rise to wealth when their father's death blessed them with more land and slaves. Others were poor but ambitious men trying to pull themselves up by their bootstraps, with the encouragement of elite planters and proslavery advocates. "Ours is a pro-slavery form of Government, and the pro-slavery element should be increased," declared a Georgia newspaper. "We would like to see every white man at the South the owner of a family of negroes."

Taking this advice to heart, aspiring planters saved or borrowed enough to acquire more land and more laborers. Some achieved modest prosperity. One German settler in Alabama reported in 1855 that "nearly all his countrymen" who emigrated with him were now slaveholders. "They were poor on their arrival in the country; but no sooner did they realize a little money than they invested it in slaves," whose labor made them well-to-do.

Bolstered by the patriarchal ideology of the planter class, yeomen farmers ruled their smallholdings with a firm hand. The male head of the household had authority over all the dependents — wives, children, and slaves — and, according to one South Carolina judge, the legal right on his property "to be as churlish as he pleases." The wives of southern yeomen had little power; like women in the North, they lost their legal identity when they married. To express their concerns and interests, many southern women joined churches, where they usually outnumbered men by a margin of two to one. Women especially welcomed the message of spiritual equality preached in evangelical Baptist and Methodist churches, and hoped that the church community would hold their husbands to the same standards of Christian behavior to which they were held. But most churches supported patriarchal rule and told female members to remain in "wifely obedience," whatever the actions of their husbands.

Whatever their authority within the household, most southern yeomen lived and died as hardscrabble farmers. They worked alongside their slaves in the fields, struggled to make ends meet as their families grew, and

moved regularly in search of opportunity. Thus, in 1847, James Buckner Barry left North Carolina with his new wife and two slaves to settle in Bosque County, Texas. There he worked part-time as an Indian fighter while his slaves toiled on a drought-ridden farm that barely kept the family in food. In South Carolina, W. J. Simpson struggled for years as a smallholding cotton planter and then gave up. He hired out one of his two slaves and went to work as an overseer on his father's farm.

Other smallholders fell from the privileged ranks of the slave-owning classes. Selling their land and slaves to pay off debts, they joined the large group of propertyless tenants who farmed the estates of wealthy landlords. In 1860, in Hancock County, Georgia, there were 56 slave-owning planters and 300 propertyless white farm laborers and factory workers; in nearby Hart County, 25 percent of the white farmers were tenants. Across the South, about 40 percent of the white population worked as tenants or farm laborers; as the *Southern Cultivator* observed, they had "no legal right nor interest in the soil [and] no homes of their own."

**Poor Freemen** Propertyless whites enjoyed few of the benefits of slavery and suffered many of its ill consequences. Because hard labor was deemed fit only for enslaved blacks, white workers received little respect. Nor could they hope for a better life for their children, because slave owners refused to pay taxes to fund public schools. Moreover, wealthy planters bid up the price of African Americans, depriving white laborers and tenants of easy access to the slave labor required to accumulate wealth. Finally, planter-dominated legislatures forced all white men — whether they owned slaves or not — to serve in the patrols and militias that deterred black uprisings. For their sacrifices, poor whites gained only the psychological satisfaction that they ranked above blacks. As Alfred Iverson, a U.S. senator from Georgia (1855–1861), explained: A white man "walks erect in the dignity of his color and race, and feels that he is a superior being, with the more exalted powers and privileges than others." To reinforce this sense of racial superiority, planter James Henry Hammond told his poor white neighbors, "In a slave country every freeman is an aristocrat."

Rejecting that half-truth, many southern whites fled planter-dominated counties and sought farms in the Appalachian hill country and beyond — in western Virginia, Kentucky, Tennessee, the southern regions of Illinois and Indiana, and Missouri. Living as yeomen farmers, they used family labor to grow foodstuffs for sustenance. To obtain cash or store credit to buy agricultural implements, cloth, shoes, salt, and other necessities, yeomen families sold their surplus crops, raised hogs for market sale, and—when the price of cotton rose sharply—grew a few bales. Their goals were modest: On the family level, they wanted to preserve their holdings and buy enough land to set up their children as small-scale farmers. As citizens, smallholders wanted to control their local government and elect men of their own kind to public office. However, thoughtful yeomen realized that the cotton revolution had sentenced family farmers to a subordinate place in the southern social order. They could hope for a life of independence and dignity only by moving north or farther west, where labor was "free" and hard work was respectable.

## The Settlement of Texas

By the 1830s, settlers from the South had carried both yeoman farming and plantation slavery into Arkansas and Missouri. Between those states and the Rocky Mountains stretched great grasslands. An army explorer, Major Stephen H. Long, thought the plains region "almost wholly unfit for cultivation" and in 1820 labeled it the Great American Desert. Americans looking for land therefore turned south, to the Mexican province of Texas.

After winning independence from Spain in 1821, the Mexican government encouraged this migration by offering large land grants (and citizenship) to Americans. One early grantee was Moses Austin, an American land speculator who settled smallholding farmers on his vast grant. His son, Stephen F. Austin, acquired even more land from the Mexican government—some 180,000 acres—which he sold to newcomers. By 1835, about 27,000 white Americans and 3,000 African American slaves were raising cotton and cattle in eastern and central Texas. They far outnumbered the 3,000 Mexican residents, who lived primarily near the southwestern Texas towns of Goliad and San Antonio.

When Mexico's central government asserted greater political control over Texas and other provinces in the 1830s, the Americans split into two groups. Members of the "peace party," led by Stephen Austin, accepted Mexican rule but campaigned for greater political autonomy. They wanted Texas to flourish within a decentralized Mexican republic, the sort of "federalism" demanded by the Liberal Party in Mexico and Jacksonian Democrats in the United States. But the "war party," headed mostly by recent migrants from Georgia, demanded independence for Texas. Austin won significant concessions from Mexican authorities, including an exemption from a law ending slavery, but in 1835 Mexico's president, General Antonio López de Santa Anna, nullified them. Santa Anna wanted to impose national authority throughout Mexico. Fearing that outcome, the Texas war party provoked a rebellion that most of the American settlers ultimately supported. On

**Assault on the Alamo**

After a thirteen-day siege, on March 6, 1836, a Mexican army of 4,000 stormed the walls of the small San Antonio fort known as the Alamo (originally a Spanish mission). "The first to climb were thrown down by bayonets . . . or by pistol fire," reported a Mexican officer. After a half-hour of continuous and costly assaults, the attackers won control of a wall. This contemporary woodcut suggests the fierceness of the battle, which took the lives of all 250 Texas defenders; 1,500 Mexicans were killed or wounded in the fighting.   Archives Division, Texas State Library.

**Starting Out in Texas**

Thousands of white farmers, some owning a few slaves, moved onto small farms in Texas and Arkansas during the 1840s and 1850. They lived in crudely built log huts; owned a few cows, horses, and oxen; and eked out a meager living by planting a few acres of cotton in addition to their crops of corn. Their aspirations were simple: to achieve modest prosperity during their lives and to leave their property to their children.   Daughters of the Republic of Texas Library.

March 2, 1836, the American rebels proclaimed the independence of Texas and adopted a constitution legalizing slavery.

President Santa Anna vowed to put down the rebellion. On March 6, he led an army that wiped out the Texan garrison defending the Alamo in San Antonio; then his forces captured Goliad and executed 371 rebel prisoners. Santa Anna thought that he had crushed the rebellion, but New Orleans and New York newspapers romanticized the heroism of the Texans and the deaths at the Alamo of folk heroes Davy Crockett and Jim Bowie. Drawing on anti-Catholic sentiment aroused by Irish immigration, journalists urged Americans to "Remember the Alamo" and depicted the Mexicans as tyrannical butchers in the service of the pope. Scores

of American adventurers, lured by offers of land grants, flocked to Texas to join the rebel forces. Commanded by General Sam Houston, the Texans routed Santa Anna's overconfident army in the Battle of San Jacinto in April 1836, winning de facto independence. The Mexican government refused to recognize the Texas Republic but abandoned efforts to reconquer it.

The Texans voted for annexation by the United States, but President Martin Van Buren refused to bring the issue before Congress. As a Texas diplomat reported, Van Buren and other American politicians feared that annexation would spark a war with Mexico and, beyond that, a "desperate death-struggle . . . between the North and the South [over the extension of slavery]; a struggle involving the probability of a dissolution of the Union."

**The Politics of Democracy**

As American men asserted their claim to a voice in government affairs, politicians catered to their prejudices and preferences. And they took their message to voters, wherever they found them. This detail from George Caleb Bingham's *Stump Speaking* (1855) shows a well-dressed politician on an improvised stage seeking the votes of an audience of farmers—identified by their broad-brimmed hats and casual clothes.    Private Collection/The Bridgeman Art Library Ltd.

## The Politics of Democracy

As national politicians refused admission to Texas, elite planters struggled to control state governments in the Cotton South. Unlike the planter-aristocrats of the eighteenth century, they lived in a republican society with democratic institutions. The Alabama Constitution of 1819 granted suffrage to all white men; it also provided for a **secret ballot**; apportionment based on population; and the election of county supervisors, sheriffs, and clerks of court. Given these democratic provisions, political factions in Alabama had to compete with one another for popular favor. When a Whig newspaper sarcastically asked whether the state's policies should "be governed and controlled by the whim and caprice of the majority of the people," Democrats stood forth as champions of the common folk. They called on "Farmers, Mechanics, laboring men" to repudiate

Whig "aristocrats . . . the soft handed and soft headed gentry."

**The Politics of Taxation** | Whatever the rhetoric, most candidates from both parties were men of substance. In the early 1840s, nearly 90 percent of Alabama's legislators owned slaves, testimony to the power of the slave-owning minority. But relatively few lawmakers—only about 10 percent—were rich planters, a group voters by and large distrusted. "A rich man cannot sympathize with the poor," declared one candidate. Consequently, the majority of elected state officials, and most county officials in the Cotton South, came from the ranks of middle-class planters and planter-lawyers. To curry favor among voters, Alabama Democrats advanced policies that would command popular support, such as low taxes. Their

Whig opponents favored higher taxes, in order to provide government subsidies for banks, canals, roads, and other internal improvements; but they also ran candidates who appealed to the common people.

Regardless of party, Alabama's legislators usually enacted policies supported by slave owners. However, they took care not to anger the mass of yeomen farmers and propertyless whites by favoring too many expensive measures, such as the public works projects favored by the Whigs. "Voting against appropriations is the safe and popular side," one senator declared, and his colleagues agreed; until the 1850s, they rejected most of the bills that would have granted subsidies to railroads, canals, and banks. They also refrained from laying "oppressive" taxes on the people, particularly the poor white majority who owned no slaves. Between 1830 and 1860, the Alabama legislature obtained about 70 percent of the state's revenue from taxes on slaves and land. Another 10 to 15 percent came from levies on carriages, gold watches, and other luxury goods, and on the capital invested in banks, transportation companies, and manufacturing enterprises.

If taxes in Alabama had a democratic thrust, those elsewhere in the South did not. In some states, wealthy planters used their political influence to exempt slave property from taxation. And they shifted the burden of land taxes to backcountry yeomen by taxing farms according to acreage rather than value. Planter-legislators also spared themselves the cost of building fences around their large fields by enacting laws that required yeomen to fence in their livestock. And, during the 1850s, wealthy legislators throughout the South used public funds to subsidize the canals and railroads in which they had invested.

**The Paradox of Southern Prosperity** Seen from one perspective, the southern states' subsidies for transportation were unnecessary. If the South had been a separate nation in 1860, its economy would have been the fourth most prosperous in the world, with a per capita income higher than that of France and Germany. As a contributor to a Georgia newspaper argued in the 1850s, it was beside the point to complain about "tariffs, and merchants, and manufacturers" because "the most highly prosperous people now on earth, are to be found in these very [slave] States."

Yet such arguments tell only part of the story. Many white southerners—especially those who were slave owners—did enjoy higher living standards than other peoples of the world, but most African Americans—30 percent of the population—lived in dire and permanent poverty. And the South's standard of living fell behind that of the North. Both in 1840 and in 1860, the per capita wealth of the South was only 80 percent of the national average, while that in the industrializing Northeast was 139 percent of the average.

Influential southerners blamed the shortcomings of their plantation-based economy on outsiders: "Purely agricultural people," intoned planter-politician James Henry Hammond, "have been in all ages the victims of rapacious tyrants grinding them down." And they steadfastly defended their way of life. "We have no cities—we don't want them," boasted former U.S. senator Louis Wigfall of Texas in 1861. "We want no manufactures: we desire no trading, no mechanical or manufacturing classes. . . . As long as we have our rice, our sugar, our tobacco, and our cotton, we can command wealth to purchase all we want." And so wealthy southerners continued to buy land and slaves, a strategy that brought substantial short-run profits but neglected investments in the great technological innovations of the nineteenth century—water- and steam-powered factories, machine tools, steel plows, and crushed-gravel roads, for example—that would have raised the South's productivity and wealth.

Urban growth—the key to prosperity in Europe and the North—occurred mostly in the commercial cities around the periphery of the South: New Orleans, St. Louis, and Baltimore. Factories—often staffed by slave labor—likewise appeared primarily in the Chesapeake, which had a more diverse economy and a surplus of bound workers. Within the Cotton South, wealthy planters invested in railroads but only to open up new lands for commercial farming; when the Western & Atlantic Railroad reached the Georgia upcountry, the cotton crop quickly doubled. Cotton—and agriculture—remained King.

Slavery also deterred European migrants from settling in the South, because they feared competition from bound labor. Their absence deprived the region of hardworking families and of laborers to drain swamps, dig canals, smelt iron, and work on railroads. When entrepreneurs tried to hire slaves for such tasks, planters replied that "a negro's life is too valuable to be risked" at the dangerous work. Other slave owners feared that hiring out would make their slaves too independent. As a planter explained to Frederick Law Olmsted, such workers "had too much liberty . . . and got a habit of roaming about and taking care of themselves."

Thus, despite its increasing size and booming exports, the South remained an economic colony: Great Britain and the North bought its staple crops and provided its manufactures, financial services, and shipping facilities. In 1860, most southerners—some 84 percent, more than double the percentage in the northern states—still worked in agriculture and southern factories turned out only 10 percent of the nation's manufactured goods. The South's fixation on an "exclusive and exhausting" system of agriculture filled South Carolina textile entrepreneur William Gregg with "dark forebodings." Gregg feared that the combination of cotton and slavery had been to the South

> what the [gold and silver] mines of Mexico were to Spain. It has produced us such an abundant supply of all the luxuries and elegances of life, with so little exertion on our part, that we have become enervated, unfitted for other and more laborious pursuits.

- How would you explain the large and expanding domestic trade in slaves between 1800 and 1860? What combination of factors produced this result?

- By 1860, what different groups made up the South's increasingly complex society? How did these groups interact in the political arena?

# The African American World

By the 1820s, the cultural life of most slaves reflected both the values and customs of their West African ancestors and the language, laws, and religious beliefs of the South's white population. This mix of African and American cultural values persisted for decades because whites discouraged blacks from assimilating and because slaves prized their African heritage.

## Evangelical Black Protestantism

The appearance of black Christianity exemplified the synthesis of African and European cultures. Evangelical Protestantism swept over the white South during the Second Great Awakening, from the 1790s to the 1840s. Baptist and Methodist preachers converted thousands of white families and hundreds of enslaved blacks (see Chapter 8). Until that time, African-born blacks, often identifiable by their ritual scars, had maintained the religious practices of their homelands: Some practiced Islam, but the majority relied on African gods and spirits. As late as 1842, Charles C. Jones, a Presbyterian minister, noted that the blacks on his family's plantation in Georgia believed "in second-sight, in apparitions, charms, witchcraft . . . [and other] superstitions brought from Africa." Fearing "the consequences" for their own

souls if they withheld "the means of salvation" from African Americans, Jones and other zealous white Protestant preachers and planters set out to convert slaves to Christianity.

Other Protestant crusaders came from the ranks of pious black men and women who were swept from the Chesapeake to the Cotton South by the domestic slave trade and carried the evangelical message of emotional conversion, ritual baptism, and communal spirituality with them. Equally important, these crusaders adapted Protestant doctrines to black needs. Enslaved Christians pointed out that blacks as well as whites were "children of God" and should be dealt with according to the Golden Rule—treat others as you would be treated by them. Moreover, black preachers generally ignored the doctrines of original sin and predestination as well as biblical passages that encouraged unthinking obedience to authority. A white minister in Liberty County, Georgia, reported that when he urged slaves to obey their masters, "one half of my audience deliberately rose up and walked off" (see Reading American Pictures, "Slave Life on a Cotton Plantation," p. 381).

**Black Protestantism** Indeed, some African American converts envisioned the deity as the Old Testament warrior who had liberated the Jews and so would also liberate them. Inspired by a vision of Christ, Nat Turner led his bloody rebellion against slavery in Virginia (see Chapter 11). Other black Christians saw themselves as Chosen People: "de people dat is born of God." Charles Davenport, a Mississippi slave, recalled black preachers' "exhort[ing] us dat us was de chillun o' Israel in de wilderness an' de Lawd done sont us to take dis lan' o' milk an' honey."

As successive generations of slaves worshipped a European god, they expressed their Christianity in distinctively African ways. The thousands of African Americans who joined the Methodist Church respected its ban on profane dancing but praised the Lord in the African-derived "ring shout." Minister Henry George Spaulding explained the "religious dance of the Negroes" this way:

> Three or four, standing still, clapping their hands and beating time with their feet, commence singing in unison one of the peculiar shout melodies, while the others walk around in a ring, in single file, joining also in the song.

The songs themselves were usually collective creations, devised spontaneously from bits of old hymns and tunes. Recalled an ex-slave:

# Slave Life on a Cotton Plantation

By the middle decades of the nineteenth century, a majority of enslaved African Americans labored on the cotton plantations that stretched from South Carolina to Texas. What was it like to work and live on a cotton plantation? Historians can consult a mass of evidence to answer this question—the testimonials of escaped slaves, the recollections of former slaves, travelers' accounts, and contemporaneous engravings and photographs. These two images tell a very small part of that story and, like all historical sources, have to be carefully interrogated.

**A Slave Family Picking Cotton.** © Collection of the New-York Historical Society.

## ANALYZING THE EVIDENCE

- Picking the cotton—thousands of small bolls attached to 3-foot-high woody stalks—was a tedious and time-consuming task. The photograph here was taken on a cotton plantation near Savannah, Georgia. Who is harvesting the cotton? (Note the collection bags draped over some of the pickers' shoulders.) Why could this work be done by both sexes and all ages? Why might children have been adept as pickers? Without directly supervising the family's labor, how might the owner have ensured that the work was getting done?

- What does the photo of cotton pickers suggest about women's lives, family relations, and living conditions?

- Why would the planter pictured in *Family Worship in a Plantation in South Carolina*, an engraving printed in a British magazine, have encouraged Christian services? Why might the planter and his wife and children have been attending the service?

- Is it significant that the minister is black? How do we know that he is literate? How is the African American audience reacting to his message?

***Family Worship in a Plantation in South Carolina.*** *The Illustrated London News*/Picture Research Consultants and Archives.

- Would either of these images be used by abolitionists to further their demands for immediate emancipation? Would either be used by authors who defended slavery? Specifically, how might either one be used to attack or defend the slave regime?

We'd all be at the "prayer house" de Lord's day, and de white preacher he'd splain de word and read whar Esekial done say—*Dry bones gwine ter lib ergin.* And, honey, de Lord would come a-shinin' thoo dem pages and revive dis ole nigger's heart, and I'd jump up dar and den and holler and shout and sing and pat, and dey would all cotch de words and I'd sing it to some ole shout song I'd heard 'em sing from Africa, and dey'd all take it up and keep at it, and keep a-addin' to it, and den it would be a spiritual.

By such African-influenced means, black congregations devised a distinctive and joyous brand of Protestant worship to sustain them on the long journey to emancipation and the Promised Land. "O my Lord delivered Daniel," the slaves sang, "O why not deliver me too?"

## Forging Families and Creating Culture

Black Protestantism was one facet of an increasingly homogeneous African American culture in the rural South. Even in South Carolina—a major point of entry for imported slaves—only 20 percent of the black residents in 1820 had been born in Africa. The domestic slave trade mingled blacks from many states, erased regional differences, and prompted the emergence of a core culture in the Lower Mississippi Valley. A prime example was the fate of the Gullah dialect (see Chapter 3). Spoken by blacks in the Carolina low country well into the twentieth century, Gullah did not take root on the cotton plantations of Alabama and Mississippi. There, slaves from Carolina were far outnumbered by migrants

**Black Kitchen Ball**

From time to time, the hardships and demanding work routine of slaves' lives were punctuated by festive celebrations. In this 1838 painting, *Kitchen Ball at White Sulphur Springs*, in Virginia, African Americans dance to the music of a fiddle and a fife (on the right). Note the light complexions and Europeanized features of the most prominent figures, the result of either racial mixing or the cultural perspective of the artist. The painter, Christian Mayr, was born in Germany in 1805 and migrated to the United States in 1833. After working for years as a traveling portrait painter, Mayr settled in New York City in 1845 and died there in 1850.   The North Carolina Museum of Art. Purchased with funds from the State of North Carolina, 52.9.23.

**Antebellum Slave Quarters**

During the colonial period, owners often housed their slaves by gender in communal barracks. In the nineteenth century, slaves usually lived in family units in separate cabins. The slave huts on this South Carolina plantation were sturdily built but had few windows. Inside, they were sparsely furnished.   William Gladstone.

from the Chesapeake, who spoke black English. Like Gullah, black English used double negatives and other African grammatical forms, but consisted primarily of English words rendered with West African pronunciation (for example, with *th* pronounced as *d*—"de preacher").

**African Influences**   As the black population of the Mississippi Valley increased, African influences remained important. At least one-third of the slaves who entered the United States between 1776 and 1809 came from the Congo region of West-Central Africa, and they brought their regional cultures with them. As traveler Isaac Holmes reported in 1821: "In Louisiana, and the state of Mississippi, the slaves . . . dance for several hours during Sunday afternoon. The general movement is in what they call the Congo dance." Similar descriptions of blacks who "danced the Congo and sang a purely African song to the accompaniment of . . . a drum" appeared as late as 1890.

African Americans also continued to respect African incest taboos by shunning marriages between cousins. On the Good Hope Plantation on the Santee River in South Carolina, nearly half of the slave children born between 1800 and 1857 were related by blood to one another; yet when they married, only one of every forty-one unions took place between cousins. This taboo was not copied from white planters: Cousin marriages were frequent among the 440 South Carolina men and women who owned at least 100 slaves in 1860, in part because such unions kept wealth within an extended family.

Unlike white marriages, slave unions were not recognized in law. Southern legislatures and courts prohibited legal marriages among slaves so that their sale would not break a legal bond. Still, many African Americans took marriage vows before Christian ministers. Others publicly marked their married state in ceremonies that included the West African custom of jumping over a broomstick together. Once married, newly arrived young people in the Cotton South whose parents remained in the Chesapeake region often chose older people in their new communities as fictive "aunts" and "uncles." The slave trade had destroyed their family, but not their family values.

The creation of fictive kinship ties was part of a community-building process. Naming children was another. Recently imported slaves frequently gave their children African names. Males born on Friday, for example, were often called Cuffee — the name of that day in several West African languages. Many American-born parents chose names of British origin, but they usually named sons after fathers, uncles, or grandfathers, and daughters after grandmothers. Those transported to the Cotton South often named their children for relatives left behind. Like incest rules and marriage rituals, this intergenerational sharing of names evoked memories of a lost world and bolstered kin ties in the present one.

## Negotiating Rights

By forming stable families and communities, African Americans gradually created a sense of order in the harsh and arbitrary world of slavery. In a few regions, slaves won substantial control over their lives. Blacks in the rice-growing lowlands of South Carolina successfully asserted the right to labor by the "task" rather than to work under constant supervision. Each day, task workers had to complete a precisely defined job — for example, digging up a quarter-acre of land, hoeing half an acre, or pounding seven mortars of rice. By working hard, many finished their tasks by early afternoon, a Methodist preacher reported, and had "the rest of the day for themselves, which they spend in working their own private fields . . . planting rice, corn, potatoes, tobacco &c. for their own use and profit." Slaves on sugar and cotton plantations were less fortunate. There, the gang-labor system imposed a regimented work schedule, and owners prohibited slaves from growing crops on their own. "It gives an excuse for trading," explained one slave owner, "and that encouraged roaming and independence.

Planters worried constantly that enslaved African Americans — a majority of the population in most counties of the Cotton South — would rise in rebellion. Slave owners knew that, legally speaking, they had virtually unlimited power over their slaves. As Justice Thomas Ruffin of the North Carolina Supreme Court wrote in a decision in 1829: "The power of the master must be absolute to render the submission of the slave perfect." But absolute power required brutal coercion, and only

the most hardened or most sadistic masters had the stomach for that. Some southern whites wanted no part of such violence. "These poor negroes, receiving none of the fruits of their labor, do not love work," explained one farm woman, "if we had slaves, we should have to . . . beat them to make use of them."

Moreover, passive resistance by African Americans seriously limited the power of their owners. Slaves slowed the pace of work by feigning illness and "losing" or breaking tools. Some blacks insisted that people be sold "in families." One Maryland slave faced with transport to Mississippi and separation from his wife "neither yields consent to accompany my people, or to be exchanged or sold," his owner reported. Masters ignored such feelings at their peril. A slave (or a relative) might retaliate by setting fire to the master's house and barns, poisoning his food, or destroying crops or equipment. Fear of resistance, as well as the increasingly critical scrutiny of abolitionists, prompted many masters to reduce their reliance on the lash. Instead, they tried to devise "a wholesome and well regulated system" for managing their laborers by using positive incentives like food and special privileges. Noted Frederick Law Olmsted: "Men of sense have discovered that it was better to offer them rewards than to whip them." Nonetheless, owners always had the option of resorting to violence, and many masters continued to assert their power by raping their female slaves.

Slavery remained an exploitative system grounded in fear and coercion. Over the decades, hundreds of individual slaves responded to this violence by attacking their masters and overseers. But only a few blacks — among them Gabriel and Martin Prosser (1800) and Nat Turner (1832) — plotted or mounted mass uprisings that involved taking revenge on their white captors. Most slaves recognized that uprisings would be futile; they lacked the autonomous institutions — such as the communes of peasants or serfs in Europe, for example — needed to organize a successful rebellion. Moreover, whites were numerous, well armed, and determined to maintain their position of racial superiority (see Comparing American Voices, "Slaves and Masters," pp. 386–387).

Escape was equally problematic. Blacks in the Upper South could flee to the North, but only by leaving their family and kin. Slaves in the Lower South could seek freedom in Spanish Florida until 1819, when the United States annexed that territory. Even then, hundreds of blacks continued to flee to Florida, where some intermarried with the Seminole Indians. Elsewhere in the South, small groups of escaped slaves eked out a meager existence in deserted marshy areas or mountain

## CLASS No. 1.

*Comprises those prisoners who were found guilty and executed.*

| Prisoners Names. | Owners' Names. | Time of Commit. | How Disposed of. |
|---|---|---|---|
| Peter | James Poyas | June 18 | |
| Ned | Gov. T. Bennett, | do. | Hanged on Tuesday |
| Rolla | do. | do | the 2d July, 1822, |
| Batteau | do. | do. | on Blake's lands, |
| Denmark Vesey | A free black man | 22 | near Charleston. |
| Jessy | Thos. Blackwood | 23 | |
| John | Elias Horry | July 5 | Do on the Lines near |
| Gullah Jack | Paul Pritchard | do. | Ch.; Friday July 12. |
| Mingo | Wm. Harth | June 21 | |
| Lot | Forrester | 27 | |
| Joe | P. L. Jore | July 6 | |
| Julius | Thos. Forrest | 8 | |
| Tom | Mrs. Russell | 10 | |
| Smart | Robt. Anderson | do. | |
| John | John Robertson | 11 | |
| Robert | do. | do. | |
| Adam | do. | do. | |
| Polydore | Mrs. Faber | do. | Hanged on the Lines |
| Bacchus | Benj. Hammet | do. | near Charleston, |
| Dick | Wm. Sims | 13 | on Friday, 26th |
| Pharaoh | — Thompson | do. | July. |
| Jemmy | Mrs. Clement | 18 | |
| Mauidore | Mordecai Cohen | 19 | |
| Dean | — Mitchell | do. | |
| Jack | Mrs. Purcell | 12 | |
| Bellisle | Est. of Jos. Yates | 18 | |
| Naphur | do. | do. | |
| Adam | do. | do. | |
| Jacob | John S. Glen | 16 | |
| Charles | John Billings | 18 | |
| Jack | N. McNeill | 22 | |
| Cæsar | Miss Smith | do. | |
| Jacob Stagg | Jacob Lankester | 23 | Do. Tues. July 30. |
| Tom | Wm. M. Scott | 24 | |
| William | Mrs. Garner | Aug. 2 | Do. Friday, Aug. 9. |

**"An Account of the Late Intended Insurrection, Charleston, South Carolina"**

In 1820, Charleston had a free black population of 1,500 and an array of African American institutions, including the Brown Fellowship Society (for those of mixed racial ancestry) and an African Methodist Episcopal (AME) church. In 1822, Charleston authorities accused a free black, Denmark Vesey, of organizing a revolt to free the city's slaves. Although historians long accepted the validity of that charge, recent scholarship suggests that Vesey's only offense was antagonizing some whites by claiming his rights as a free man and that the alleged insurrection was a figment of the imagination of fearful slave owners. Regardless, South Carolina officials hanged Vesey and thirty-four alleged co-conspirators and tore down the AME church where they were said to have plotted the uprising.   Rare Book, Manuscript & Special Collections, Duke University Library.

trying to do. Thus, slaves insisted on getting paid for "overwork" and on their right to cultivate a garden and sell its produce. "De menfolks tend to de gardens round dey own house," recalled a Louisiana slave. "Dey raise some cotton and sell it to massa and git li'l money dat way." That money was theirs to do with as they wished. An Alabama slave remembered buying "Sunday clothes with dat money, sech as hats and pants and shoes and dresses." By the 1850s, thousands of African Americans were reaping the small rewards of this underground economy.

Even if their material circumstances improved, however, few slaves accepted the legitimacy of their status. Although he was well fed and never whipped, a former slave explained to an English traveler that he knew he had been oppressed: "I was cruelly treated because I was kept in slavery."

## The Free Black Population

Some African Americans escaped slavery through flight, manumission, or gradual emancipation laws. The proportion of free blacks rose from 8 percent of the African American population in 1790 to about 13 percent between 1820 and 1840, and then fell to 11 percent. Still, in Maryland in 1860, half of all blacks were free and many more were "term" slaves, guaranteed their freedom in exchange for a few more years of work. Nearly half of free blacks in the United States in 1840 (some 170,000) and again in 1860 (250,000) lived in the free states of the North.

**Northern Free Blacks** In the North, few free blacks enjoyed unfettered freedom. Most whites regarded African Americans as their social inferiors and confined them to low-paying jobs. In rural areas, free blacks worked as farm laborers or tenant farmers; in towns and cities, they toiled as domestic servants, laundresses, or day laborers. Only a small number of free African Americans owned land. "You do not see one out of a hundred . . . that can make a comfortable living, own a cow, or a horse," a traveler in New Jersey noted. In addition, northern blacks were usually forbidden to vote, attend public schools, or sit next to whites in churches. Only a few states extended the vote to free blacks, and blacks could testify in court against whites only in Massachusetts. The federal government did not allow free African Americans to work for the postal service, claim public lands, or hold a U.S. passport. As black activist Martin Delaney remarked in 1852: "We are slaves in the midst of freedom."

valleys. However, as Frederick Douglass observed, most slaves were "pegged down to one single spot, and must take root there or die."

Given these limited options, most slaves struggled to build the best possible lives for themselves on the plantations where they lived. Over time, they pressed their owners for a greater share of the product of their labor—much like unionized workers in the North were

# Slaves and Masters

Slavery consisted of a multitude of individual relationships between African Americans and their white owners. But it was also a system of chattel property, forced labor, and sexual abuse. These selections—interviews with former slaves and a diary entry written by a cotton planter—suggest how people's lives were shaped by the slave-master relationship. The Works Project Administration (WPA), a government relief program in the 1930s, conducted hundreds of these interviews, creating a valuable documentary record. However, most of the interviewers were white and the former slaves were very old, so that the resulting stories were less graphic than the actual slave experience.

## Mollie Dawson

### Memories of a Slave Childhood

Mollie Dawson was born into slavery in Texas, where her owner had migrated from Tennessee. When Dawson told her story to a WPA interviewer, she was eighty-five years old.

Dat makes me bo'n in january sometime, of 1852.... Mah maw was de slave of Nath Newman and dat made me his slave. Mah maw's name was Sarah Benjamin. Mah father's name was Carrol Benjamin, and he belonged ter different white folks....

De plantation dat he worked on was j'inin' our'n. I would go ovah ter see him once in a while when I was little, and de last time I goes ovah dar dey whips a man.... Dat was the only slave I ever seed gits a whippin', and I never did wants ter see dis white man anymo'....

Mah mother and father was slavery time married darkies. Dat didn't mean nuthin' dem days, but jest raisin' mo' darkies, and every slave darkie woman had ter do dat whether she wanted to or not. Dey would let her pick out a man, or a man pick him out a woman, and dey was married, and if de woman wouldn't have de man dat picks her, dey would take her ter a big stout high husky nigger somewhere and leave her a few days, jest lak dey do stock now'days, and she bettah begin raisin' chilluns, too....

Mah mother and father never did love each other lak dey ought to, so dey separated as soon as dey was free. Mah father married another woman by law. Mah mother married George Baldwin, and dey lives together fer about twelve years. Dey separated den, and she married Alfred Alliridge and dey lives together till she dies....

I was too young ter do much work durin' slavery time, but I picks lots of cotton, and all de pay we got fer it was a place ter stay, water ter drink, wood ter burn, food ter eat, and clothes ter wear, and we made de food and clothes ourselves. We eats corn pones three times a day, 'ceptin' Sunday and Christmas mornings; Maser Newman lets us have flour fer biscuits, den. In de summah we wore cotton clothes. All of dem was made on de plantation. Some of de women would spin and some would weave and some would make clothes....

Maser Newman was a tall, slender man nearly six foot tall and was blue-eyed. He sho' was good ter all us slaves, but we all knew he means fer us ter work. He never whipped any of us slaves, but he hit one of de men wid a leather line 'bout two times once, 'cause dis slave kinda talked back ter him....

Maser Newman was a slow easy-goin' sort of a man who took everything as it comes, takin' bad and good luck jest alak.... Maser Newman was lots older dan his wife. She was a real young woman, and they 'peared ter think quite a bit of each other.... Maser and Missus Newman jest had two chilluns and both of dem was little girls.... Dey sho' was pretty little gals and dey was smart, too. Dey played wid de little slave chilluns all de time, and course dey was de boss, same as deir mother and father.

Maser Newman was a poor man, compared wid some of de other slave owners. He only had about seven slaves big enough ter work all de year round in de fields.... He didn't have no drivah; he would jest start dem all out ter work, and dey kept at it all day. But he generally worked around pretty close ter dem.

Source: James Mellon, ed., *Bullwhip Days* (New York: Weidenfeld & Nicolson, 1988), 421–428.

## Louisa Picquet

### Sexual Exploitation Under Slavery

Louisa Picquet was born into slavery in Georgia in 1827; around 1840, she became the property of a John Williams of New Orleans. On his death in 1848, she was freed and moved to Ohio with her four children. In 1860, she related the story of her life to Hiram Mattison, a white abolitionist minister, who published it.

Q: How did you say you come to be sold?

A: Well, you see, Mr. Cook [my master] made great parties, and go off to watering-places, and get in debt, and had to break up, and then he took us to Mobile. . . . Then, after a while, the sheriff came from Georgia after Mr. Cook's debts, and found us all, and took us to auction, and sold us. My mother and brother was sold to Texas, and I was sold to New Orleans.

Q: How old were you, then?

A: Well, I don't know exactly, but the auctioneer said I wasn't quite fourteen. . . .

Q: Were there others there white like you?

A: Oh yes, plenty of them. . . . Then I was sold. . . . Mr. Williams allowed that he did not care what they bid, he was going to have me anyhow. Then he bid fifteen hundred. Mr. Horton said 'twas no use to bid anymore, and I was sold to Mr. Williams. I went right to New Orleans then.

Q: Who was Mr. Williams?

A: I didn't know then, only he lived in New Orleans. Him and his wife had parted, some way he had three children, boys. When I was going away I heard someone cryin' and prayin' the Lord to go with her only daughter, and protect me.

Q: Have you never seen her [Picquet's mother] since?

A: No, never since that time. I went to New Orleans, and she went to Texas. So I understood.

A: Mr. Williams told me what he bought me for, soon as we started for New Orleans. He said he was getting old, and when he saw me he thought he'd buy me, and end his days with me. He said if I behave myself he'd treat me well; but, if not, he'd whip me almost to death.

Q: How old was he?

A: He was over forty; I guess pretty near fifty. He was gray-headed. That's the reason he was always so jealous. He never let me go out anywhere. . . .

Q: Had you any children while in New Orleans?

A: Yes, I had four.

Q: Who was their father?

A: Mr. Williams. . . .

Q: Were your children mulattoes?

A: No, sir! They were all white. They look just like him. The neighbors all see that.

Source: H. Mattison, Louisa Picquet, *The Octoroon: Or Inside Views of Southern Life* (New York: Published by the Author, 1861), 17–19.

## Bennet Barrow

### Enforcing Labor Discipline

Bennet Barrow (1811–1854) inherited a substantial cotton plantation in Louisiana. From 1837 to 1845, he kept a diary that consisted of brief remarks on the day's events.

January 1838

14  Appearance of rain—pressed 7 B. [bales of cotton] last Sunday—pressing to day at Gibsons—will ship on Tuesday next 66 B . . . to Gin—On selling from 5 to 11-1/2 cts.—The times are seriously hard all most impossible to raise one dollar . . . great Excitement in Congress, Northern States medling with slavery—first they com'ced by petition—now by openly speaking of the sin of Slavery in the southern states . . . must eventually cause a separation of the Union.

October 1838

12  Clear verry cold morning—hands picked worse yesterday than they have done this year. . . . Whiped near half the hands to day for picking badly & trashy. . . .

26  Clear pleasant weather—Cotton picks very trashy—Whiped 8 or 10 for weight today. . . .

May 1839

21  Clear verry warm—Finished hilling Cotton—Darcas & Fanny are the greatest shirks of any negroes I have—laid up twicet a month—Went to Town—man tried for whipping a negro to Death. trial will continue till to morrow—deserves death—Cleared!

July 1841

18  . . . Received a note from Ruffin stating that several of my negroes were implicated in an intended insurrection on the 1st of August next. . . .

27  Cloudy. Verry warm, Negros all Cleared. But will be tried by the Planters themselves &c.

Source: Edwin Davis Adams, *Plantation Life in the Florida Parishes of Louisiana, 1836–1845 as Reflected in the Diary of Bennet H. Barrow* (New York: AMS Press, 1967 [c. 1943]), 105–106, 133, 135, 148, 236, 237.

## ANALYZING THE EVIDENCE

- How strong is the evidence in these selections? Is there any reason to question its accuracy? Mollie Dawson was eighty-five when she was interviewed. How reliable was her memory? An abolitionist published Louisa Picquet's account as an indictment of slavery. Is his account trustworthy? Is Bennet Barrow's diary a more reliable source than the other two? Explain your answer.

- Were you surprised by any of these accounts? If so, why? What did they tell you about day-to-day life under slavery that you did not know?

- Why do you suppose Picquet was freed in 1848?

**A Master Bridge Builder**

Horace King (1807–1885) was a self-made man of color, a rarity in the nineteenth-century South. Born a slave of mixed European, African, and Native American (Catawba) ancestry, King built major bridges in Georgia, Alabama, and Mississippi during the early 1840s. After winning his freedom in 1846, he built and ran a toll bridge across the Chattahoochee River in Alabama. During the Civil War, King worked as a contractor for the Confederacy; during Reconstruction, he served two terms as a Republican in the Alabama House of Representatives.   Collection of the Columbus Museum, Columbus, Georgia; Museum Purchase.

Of the few African Americans who were able to make full use of their talents, several achieved great distinction. Mathematician and surveyor Benjamin Banneker (1731–1806) published an almanac and helped lay out the new capital in the District of Columbia; Joshua Johnston (1765–1832) won praise for his portraiture; and merchant Paul Cuffee (1759–1817) acquired a small fortune from his business enterprises. More impressive and enduring were the community institutions created by free African Americans. Throughout the North, these largely unknown men and women founded schools, mutual-benefit organizations, and fellowship groups, often called Free African Societies. Discriminated against by white Protestants, they formed their own congregations and a

new religious denomination—the African Methodist Episcopal Church, headed by Bishop Richard Allen (see Chapter 8).

These institutions gave free African Americans a measure of cultural autonomy, even as they institutionalized sharp social divisions among blacks. "Respectable" blacks tried through their dress, conduct, and attitude to win the "esteem and patronage" of prominent whites—first Federalists and then Whigs and abolitionists—who were sympathetic to their cause. Those efforts separated them from impoverished blacks, who distrusted not only whites but also blacks who "acted white."

**Standing for Freedom in the South**   The free black population in the slave states numbered approximately 94,000 in 1810 and 225,000 in 1860. Most of these men and women lived in coastal cities—Mobile, Memphis, New Orleans—and in the Upper South. Partly because skilled Europeans avoided the South, free blacks formed the backbone of the region's urban artisan workforce. African American carpenters, blacksmiths, barbers, butchers, and shopkeepers played prominent roles in the economies of Baltimore, Richmond, Charleston, and New Orleans. But free blacks faced many dangers. Those accused of crimes were often denied a jury trial, and those charged with vagrancy were sometimes forced back into slavery. Other free blacks were simply kidnapped and taken elsewhere by their captors to be sold.

As a privileged group among African Americans, free blacks in the South had divided loyalties. To advance the welfare of their families, they were tempted to distance themselves from plantation slaves and assimilate white culture and values. Indeed, some privileged blacks became adjunct members of the planter class. David Barland, one of twelve children born to a white Mississippi planter and his black slave Elizabeth, himself owned no fewer than eighteen slaves. In neighboring Louisiana, some free blacks supported secession because they owned slaves and were "dearly attached to their native land."

Such men were exceptions. Most free African Americans acknowledged their ties to the great mass of slaves, some of whom were their relatives. "We's different [from whites] in color, in talk and in 'ligion and beliefs," said one. White planters reinforced black unity in the 1840s and 1850s by calling for the reenslavement of free African Americans. Knowing their own liberty was not secure so long as slavery existed, free

**An African American Clergyman**

This flattering portrait is one of two paintings of African Americans by black artist Joshua Johnston (who also went by the surname Johnson). Born into slavery in 1765, Johnston somehow became a free man and a successful artist. In an advertisement in the *Baltimore Intelligence* in 1798, he described himself as a "Portrait Painter . . . a self-taught genius deriving from nature and industry his knowledge of the Art." White merchant families in Maryland and Virginia held Johnston's work in high regard and commissioned most of his thirty or so extant works. Bowdoin College Museum of Art, Brunswick, Maine. Museum Purchase, George Otis Hamlin Fund.

blacks celebrated West Indian Emancipation Day (August 1) and sought freedom for all Americans of African ancestry. As a delegate to the National Convention of Colored People in 1848 put it, "Our souls are yet dark under the pall of slavery." In the rigid American caste system, free blacks stood as symbols of hope to enslaved African Americans and as symbols of danger to most whites.

- Why did certain African cultural practices (the ring shout and incest taboos, for example) persist in the United States while others (ritual scarring, for example) disappeared?

- What were some of the successes of African Americans in the period 1800–1860? In what endeavors did they not succeed?

## SUMMARY

In this chapter, we focused on the theme of an expanding South. Beginning about 1800, planters carried the plantation system from its traditional home in the Upper South to the Mississippi Valley and beyond. Powered by cotton, this movement westward divided the planter elite into aristocratic paternalists and entrepreneurial capitalists, and involved the forced migration of more than 1 million enslaved African Americans.

We also examined the character of white and black societies in the Cotton South. After 1820, less than a third of white families owned slaves and another third were yeoman farmers; propertyless tenant farmers and laborers made up the rest. Many whites joined evangelical Protestant churches, as did blacks, who infused their churches with African modes of expression. Indeed, church and family became core institutions of African American society, providing strength and solace amid the tribulations of slavery. Finally, we explored the initiatives taken by the free black population, in both the northern and southern states, to achieve individual mobility and to build community institutions. These efforts produced a church-based leadership class and a black abolitionist movement.

## CHAPTER REVIEW QUESTIONS

- How did plantation crops and the system of slavery change between 1800 and 1860? Why did these changes occur?

- Why in 1860 did white southerners remain committed to the institution of slavery and its expansion? Based on what you've learned so far in Part 3, compare and contrast society in the American South with that of the North. Is it fair to say that America was, in fact, two distinct societies by 1860?

# FOR FURTHER EXPLORATION

Charlene M. Boyer Lewis explores the lives of the planter class in *Ladies and Gentlemen on Display* (2001). Other studies of slave owners are William Kauffman Scarborough, *Masters of the Big House* (2003), and Jeffrey Robert Young, *Domesticating Slavery* (1999). For the planters' intellectual pursuits, read Michael O'Brien, *Conjectures of Order* (2004). Edward Ball's *Slaves in the Family* (1998) recounts his ancestors' ownership of slaves, their illicit sexual unions, and the family's diverse racial identity. Stephanie McCurry's *Masters of Small Worlds* (1995) evokes the patriarchal lives of yeomen families. For plantation discipline, see Sally E. Hadden, *Slave Patrols* (2001), and John Hope Franklin and Loren Sweninger, *Runaway Slaves* (1999). On slavery's decline in the North, read Joanne Pope Melish, *Disowning Slavery* (1998).

Ira Berlin, *Generations of Captivity* (2003), Adam Rothman, *Slave Country: American Expansion and the Origins of the Deep South* (2005), and Michael Tadman, *Speculators and Slaves* (1996), analyze the changing character of slavery and African American society. See also Charles Joyner, *Down by the Riverside* (1984), and the material at **www.pbs.org/wnet/slavery/about/index.html**. For primary documents on the black Christian church, consult **docsouth.unc.edu/church/index.html**. Marcus Wood, *Blind Memory* (2000), offers many images of slave life, while Walter Johnson, *Soul by Soul* (1999), closely examines the New Orleans slave mart. Two document-rich Web sites are "The African-American Mosaic" at **www.loc.gov/exhibits/african/intro.html** and "Slaves and the Courts, 1740–1860" at **lcweb2.loc.gov/ammem/aaohtml**.

## TEST YOUR KNOWLEDGE

To assess your command of the material in this chapter, see the Online Study Guide at **bedfordstmartins.com/henretta**.

For Web sites, images, and documents related to topics and places in this chapter, visit **bedfordstmartins.com/makehistory**.

## TIMELINE

| | |
|---|---|
| **1810s** | Africans from Congo region influence black culture |
| | Natural increase produces surplus of slaves in Old South |
| | Domestic slave trade expands, disrupting black family life |
| **1812** | Louisiana becomes a state, and its sugar output increases |
| **1817** | Mississippi becomes a state; Alabama follows (1819) |
| **1820s** | Growth in free black population in North and South |
| | Slave-owning gentry in Old South adopt paternalistic ideology |
| | Entrepreneurial planters in Cotton South turn to gang labor |
| | Southern Methodists and Baptists become socially conservative |
| | African Americans adopt Christian beliefs |
| **1830s** | Advocates of slavery argue it is a "positive good" |
| | Boom in cotton production |
| | Percentage of slave-owning white families falls |
| | Yeomen farm families retreat to hill country |
| | Lawyers become influential in southern politics |
| **1840s** | Southern Whigs advocate economic diversification |
| | Gradual emancipation completed in North |
| **1850s** | Cotton prices and production increase; slave prices rise |
| | Southern states subsidize railroads, but industrialization remains limited |

# PART

# 4

# CREATING AND PRESERVING A CONTINENTAL NATION, 1844–1877

Between 1844 and 1877, the United States became a continental nation by fighting—and winning—three wars and creating a stronger central government. In the 1840s, it took over much of western North America through diplomatic negotiations with Great Britain and a war of conquest with Mexico. Geographic expansion sharpened political conflicts between the free and slave states and led to the South's secession in 1861. The Union government consolidated national authority by defeating the secessionists in a long Civil War, freeing millions of slaves, and reconstructing the Union under the ideals of the Republican Party.

Reconstruction included far more than reincorporating the South. After the war, the national government opened up newly acquired western lands for Euro-Americans by conquering Indian peoples and confining them to reservations. These events created new conflicts and systems of race relations. Native Americans found themselves negotiating between policies of "race uplift" and potential citizenship, and their desire to retain their traditional cultural and tribal ties. Meanwhile, Reconstruction offered hope for millions of workers of African ancestry, who fought for a fairer labor system and equal citizenship rights as African *Americans*. The story of these transforming events falls into five interconnected parts.

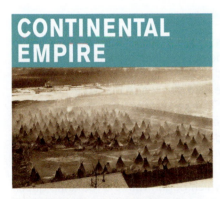

## CONTINENTAL EMPIRE

**The quest for western lands sparked wars against Mexico and . . . Indian peoples**

### Diplomatic and Military Expansion

The romantic spirit of Manifest Destiny pervaded American culture during the 1840s, prompting southerners to push for the annexation of Texas and Midwesterners to demand control over Oregon. Railroad entrepreneurs championed expansionism, as did northeastern merchants eager to expand trade across the Pacific. The quest for western lands sparked wars against Mexico and the Cheyennes, Sioux, and Comanches, among other Indian peoples. The purchase of Russian claims to Alaska, and efforts to acquire overseas coaling stations, marked policymakers' rising interest in foreign markets. On the continent, Anglo-American settlement of California and the Southwest overturned Spanish and Mexican customs and land claims and rapidly opened up the region to white miners, farmers, and ranchers.

## SECTIONALISM

**. . . a downward spiral of conflict . . . ended in the Civil War**

### Secession and Reunion

The Mexican War prompted a decade-long debate over the constitutional status of newly acquired lands. This increasingly bitter political struggle led to the Compromise of 1850, a multifaceted legislative agreement that won little support either in the North or the South. The Kansas-Nebraska Act of 1854 and the 1857 *Dred Scott* decision began a downward spiral of conflict that ended in the Civil War. Though sectional conflict would continue, the Union emerged stronger from the Civil War, as Republican policies bound the nation together. Never again would a region seek to leave the nation and establish its independence.

## GOVERNMENT

**The Civil War greatly enhanced [federal] military power and constitutional authority**

## ECONOMY

**[Republicans] enacted aggressive policies to promote economic development**

## SOCIETY

**Irish, German, and British immigrants prompted a sharp nativist reaction**

## Democracy Challenged

Continental expansion and sectional conflict triggered the disintegration of the Second Party system. As Southern Whigs became Democrats and Northern Whigs turned into Republicans, party allegiances split along sectional lines and created political divisions that persisted well into the twentieth century. Political developments brought about by the Civil War greatly enhanced the military power and the constitutional authority of the national government. Three wartime constitutional amendments changed the nature of federalism by altering the nature of American citizenship — prohibiting slavery, mandating suffrage for black men, and forbidding state action that denied people equal protection under the law. After the war, the U.S. Army remained a significant force, enforcing Reconstruction in the South, suppressing Indian peoples, and upholding legal authority in the West.

## Public Support for Private Enterprise

The Civil War created a powerful American state. To fight the war, the Union government mobilized millions of men and billions of dollars. In the process, it created a modern fiscal system, an elaborate network of national banks, and — for the first time in American history — a significant national bureaucracy. Inspired by Whig ideology, Republican-run Congresses enacted aggressive policies to promote economic development. They granted huge subsidies to railroad companies, protected industries and workers through high protective tariffs, promoted education and economic research, gave western land to farmers and cattlemen, and mapped and distributed western resources, including timber and mineral rights. A great postwar boom in railway construction, land speculation, and agricultural production collapsed in 1873, as a worldwide decline in prices led to a lengthy depression.

## New Peoples, New Statuses

The ethnic composition and racial distinctions of the United States changed dramatically during the decades before, during, and just after the Civil War. Millions of Irish, German, and British immigrants prompted a sharp nativist reaction. Increasingly, the elite classes of the North doubted the wisdom of universal male suffrage. The freedom granted to 4 million African Americans raised a similar issue for southern whites, who maintained their privileged racial status by denying full political and civil rights for freedmen. In the trans-Mississippi West, whites jostled uneasily with conquered Hispanic residents, subject Indian peoples, and despised Chinese immigrants. These decades, which began with the romantic quest for continental empire, ended on the bitter notes of racial struggles and half-won freedoms.

Nonetheless, many European Americans looked back on the era as one of unprecedented progress. The United States had claimed a vast, resource-rich empire in the West. Railroads and industrial cities were growing from Chicago to San Francisco, and merchants and traders looked eagerly across the Pacific. The nation had fought a great war that preserved the Union and vanquished slavery. And America's dynamic postwar economy began to draw immigrants from many continents. These achievements, by no means predictable in 1840, had set the nation on a course toward global power.

# CREATING AND PRESERVING A CONTINENTAL NATION, 1844–1877

| | CONTINENTAL EMPIRE | SECTIONALISM | GOVERNMENT | ECONOMY | SOCIETY |
|---|---|---|---|---|---|
| **1840** | • Texas annexation (1845), acquisition of Oregon (1846), and Mexican War (1846–1848) extend U.S. borders to Pacific<br>• Wars against Seminoles in Florida (1835–1842, 1855–1858) | • Mexican War and Wilmot Proviso (1846) increase sectional conflict<br>• Gold Rush makes California eligible for statehood—free or slave? | • Free-Soil Party (1848)<br>• Seneca Falls convention seeks votes for women (1848) | • Recession causes some states to default on bonds issued to build canals<br>• Walker Tariff (1846) lowers rates, increases trade | • Whites migrate to Oregon and California<br>• Hispanics incorporated as citizens in Southwest |
| **1850** | • President Pierce opens Japan to trade; seeks expansion of American territory and slavery into Caribbean<br>• Comanches and Sioux dominate Great Plains trade in horses and buffalo hides | • Compromise of 1850<br>• Harriet Beecher Stowe's *Uncle Tom's Cabin* (1852)<br>• Kansas-Nebraska Act (1854) and "Bleeding Kansas" | • Whig Party disintegrates; Know-Nothing Party emerges<br>• Republican Party founded (1854)<br>• Rise of southern secessionists | • Surge of cotton output in South<br>• Expansion of farm society into trans-Mississippi west<br>• Railroads and manufacturing intensify in North and Midwest | • Indians resettled throughout West<br>• Arrival of millions of German and Irish immigrants<br>• *Dred Scott* decision (1857) implies slavery throughout United States |
| **1860** | • Union triumphs in Civil War, preserving a continental nation<br>• Secretary of State Seward buys Alaska from Russia (1867)<br>• Homesteaders, cattlemen, and miners settle Plains and West | • South Carolina leads secession movement (1860)<br>• Confederate States of America (1861–1865)<br>• Radical Republicans seek to reconstruct postwar South | • Freedman's Bureau assists ex-slaves<br>• Fourteenth Amendment (1868) extends legal and political rights | • Republicans enact Whigs' policy agenda: Homestead Act (1862), railroad aid, high tariffs, and national banking | • Emancipation Proclamation (1863) and Thirteenth Amendment (1865) end slavery<br>• Blacks in the South struggle for freedom, land, and education |
| **1870** | • Wars against Plains Indians: Cheyennes, Sioux, Apaches, and Nez Perce | • Ku Klux Klan and white vigilantes attack Reconstruction governments<br>• Compromise of 1877 ends Reconstruction | • Fifteenth Amendment (1870) extends vote to black men<br>• Rollback of Republican control of Congress (1874) | • Rise of sharecropping in the South<br>• Depression of 1873 halts railway expansion | • White elites challenge ideal of universal suffrage<br>• Dawes Act (1887) seeks Indian assimilation |

## CHAPTER 13

# Expansion, War, and Sectional Crisis, 1844–1860

**The American expansionist** surge of the 1840s had deep roots. Visionaries had long predicted a glorious expansion across the continent. "It belongs of right to the United States to regulate the future destiny of North America," declared a writer in the *New-York Evening Post* in 1803. Two decades later, politicians had taken up the refrain. "Our natural boundary is the Pacific Ocean," asserted Massachusetts congressman Francis Baylies in 1823. "The swelling tide of our population must and will roll on until that mighty ocean interposes its waters." Yet the creation of a continental republic was far from inevitable; it required a transportation revolution—canals and railways—that would connect far-flung regions, a growing land-hungry population, and a dynamic economy. By the 1840s, all of those factors were in place.

Other obstacles remained. Strong, well-armed Indian peoples controlled the Great Plains, Mexico held sovereignty over Texas and the lands west of the Rocky Mountains, and Great Britain laid claim to the Oregon Country. To extend the American republic would likely involve new Indian wars and armed conflict with Mexico (perhaps aided by France, its creditor) and Great Britain. An ardent imperialist, President James Polk willingly assumed those risks. "I would meet the war which either England or France or all the powers of Christendom might wage," he told Secretary of State James Buchanan in 1846, "and fight until the last man."

Polk's aggressive expansionism sparked fighting abroad and conflict at home. A war with Mexico intended to be "brief, cheap, and bloodless" became, as Senator Thomas Hart Benton of Missouri complained, "long, costly, and sanguinary." Even Polk's great territorial acquisitions—New Mexico, California, the Oregon Country—proved double-edged, because they reignited a bitter debate over the extension of slavery. Southerners threatened to secede from the Union in 1850, Northerners responded with anger, and rhetoric spiraled downward into violence. When Massachusetts Senator Charles Sumner accused Senator Andrew P. Butler of South Carolina in 1856 of taking "the harlot slavery" as his mistress, South Carolina representative Preston Brooks beat Sumner unconscious with a walking cane. As Brooks struck down Sumner in Washington, Axalla Hoole of South Carolina and other proslavery migrants in the Kansas Territory fought armed New England abolitionists. Passion had replaced political compromise as the hallmark of American public life.

### War News from Mexico, 1848

In this painting of men at the "American Hotel," artist Richard Caton Woodville (1825–1855) captures the public's hunger for news of the Mexican War, the first foreign conflict since the War of 1812. As a journalist in Baltimore, Woodville's hometown, noted, "People begin to collect every evening, about 5 o'clock at the telegraph and newspaper offices, waiting for extras and despatches." Note the subordinate placement of African Americans and a woman (in the window at the right edge of the painting). Private Collection, on loan to the National Gallery of Art, Washington, Photograph © 2002 Board of Trustees, National Gallery of Art.

# Manifest Destiny: South and North

The upsurge in violence reflected a generational shift in culture and politics. The Missouri crisis of 1819–1822 (see Chapter 8) had thrown a fright into the nation's leaders. For the next two decades, the professional politicians who managed the Second Party System avoided policies, such as the annexation of the slaveholding Republic of Texas, that would prompt regional strife. Then, during the 1840s, many citizens embraced an ideology of conquest that proclaimed their God-given duty to extend American republicanism and capitalism to the Pacific Ocean. But whose republican institutions and economic system: the hierarchical racial order of the slaveholding South, or the more democratic, reform-minded society of the North and Midwest? Or both? Ultimately, the failure to find a politically acceptable answer to this question would rip the nation apart.

## The Push to the Pacific

As expansionists developed continental ambitions, the term **Manifest Destiny** captured those dreams. John L. O'Sullivan, editor of the *Democratic Review*, coined the phrase in 1845: "Our manifest destiny is to overspread the continent allotted by Providence for the free development of our yearly multiplying millions." Underlying the rhetoric of Manifest Destiny was a sense of Anglo-American cultural and racial superiority: The "inferior" peoples who lived in the Far West — Native Americans and Mexicans — were to be brought under American dominion, taught republicanism, and converted to Protestantism (see Reading American Pictures, "Visualizing 'Manifest Destiny,'" p. 401).

**Oregon** | Land-hungry farmers of the Ohio River Valley had already cast their eyes toward the fertile valleys of the Oregon Country. This region stretched along the Pacific coast between the Mexican province of California and Russian settlements in Alaska and was claimed by both Britain and the United States. Since 1818, a British-American agreement had allowed people from both nations to live there. The British-run Hudson's Bay Company developed a lucrative fur trade north of the Columbia River, while Methodist missionaries and a few hundred Americans settled to the south, in the Willamette Valley (Map 13.1).

In 1842, American interest in Oregon increased dramatically. The U.S. Navy published a glowing report of fine harbors in the Puget Sound, which were already being used by New England merchants trading with China. In the same year, a party of one hundred farmers journeyed along the Oregon Trail, which fur traders and explorers had blazed from Independence, Missouri, across the Great Plains and the Rocky Mountains (Map 13.2). Their letters from Oregon told of a mild climate and rich soil.

"Oregon fever" suddenly raged. A thousand men, women, and children — with a hundred wagons and 5,000 oxen and cattle — had gathered in Independence

**MAP 13.1**

**Territorial Conflict in Oregon, 1819–1846**

As thousands of American settlers poured into the Oregon Country in the early 1840s, British authorities tried to keep them south of the Columbia River. However, the migrants – and fervent midwestern expansionists – asserted that Americans could settle anywhere in the territory, raising the prospect of armed conflict. In 1846, British and American diplomats resolved the dispute by dividing the region at the 49th parallel.

**Settling Oregon**

It did not take long for Americans to populate the Far West and re-create there the small-town life of the eastern states. As early as 1845, as this drawing by a British military officer shows, Oregon City boasted a steepled church, several large merchandise warehouses, and several dozen houses. On the riverbank opposite the town stand several Indians, who had a very different way of life and would be steadily pushed off the lands of their ancestors.   Library of Congress from Henry James Warre, *Sketches from North America and the Oregon Territory* (London: Dickson & Co., 1848).

by late April 1843. As the spring mud dried, they began their six-month trek, hoping to miss the winter snows. Another 5,000 settlers, mostly yeomen farm families from the southern border states (Missouri, Kentucky, and Tennessee), set out over the next two years. These pioneers overcame floods, dust storms, livestock deaths, and a few armed encounters with Indians before reaching the Willamette Valley, a journey of 2,000 miles.

By 1860, about 250,000 Americans had braved the Oregon Trail, with 65,000 heading for Oregon and 185,000 to California. More than 34,000 migrants died in the effort, mostly from disease and exposure; fewer than 500 deaths resulted from Indian attacks. The walking migrants wore paths 3 feet deep, and their wagons carved 5-foot ruts across sandstone formations in southern Wyoming—tracks that are visible today. Women found the trail especially difficult; in addition to their usual chores and the new work of driving wagons and animals, they lacked the support of female kin and the security of their domestic space. About 2,500 women endured pregnancy or gave birth during the long journey, and some did not survive. "There was a woman died in this train yesterday," Jane Gould Tortillott noted in her diary. "She left six children, one of them only two days old."

The 10,000 migrants who made it to Oregon in the 1840s mostly settled in the Willamette Valley. Many families squatted on 640 acres and hoped Congress would legalize their claims so that they could profit from the sale of their surplus acreage to new settlers. They quickly created a race- and gender-defined polity by restricting voting to a "free male descendant of a white man."

**California**   About 3,000 other early pioneers ended up in the Mexican province of California. They left the Oregon Trail along the Snake River, trudged down the California Trail, and settled in the interior along the Sacramento River, where there were few Mexicans. A remote outpost of Spain's American empire, California had been settled only in the 1770s, when Spanish authorities built a chain of presidios— religious missions and forts—along the Pacific coast.

**MAP 13.2**

**The Great Plains: Indian Peoples and Settler Trails**

By the 1850s, the Mormon, Oregon, and Santa Fe trails ran through "Indian Country," the semi-arid, buffalo-filled area of the Great Plains west of the 95th meridian, through the Rocky Mountains. Tens of thousands of Americans set out on these trails to found new communities in Utah, Oregon, New Mexico, and California. This mass migration increasingly exposed Indian peoples to American diseases, guns, and manufactures. But their lives were even more significantly affected by U.S. soldiers, and the traders who provided a ready market for Indian horses and mules, dried meat, and buffalo skins.

After Mexican independence in 1821, the government took over the Franciscan-run missions and freed the 20,000 Indians who had been coerced into working on them. Some mission Indians rejoined their tribes, but many intermarried with mestizos (Mexicans of mixed Spanish and Indian ancestry) and worked on large ranches. To promote California's development, Mexican authorities bestowed large land grants on entrepreneurs, who raised Spanish cattle, prized for their hides and tallow.

## Visualizing "Manifest Destiny"

In 1845, newspaper editor John O'Sullivan coined the term *Manifest Destiny* to describe Americans' suddenly urgent longing to extend the nation to the Pacific Ocean. John Gast's painting, *American Progress* (1872), gave visual form to that aspiration and was widely distributed through color lithographs. What do the details of the painting tell us about the meaning of Manifest Destiny?

**John Gast, *American Progress.*** Library of Congress.

### ANALYZING THE EVIDENCE

- The painting is an allegory: The artist uses symbols to depict America's expansion to the Pacific. The central symbol of the goddess Liberty floats westward, her forehead emblazoned with the "Star of Empire." Why did Gast choose Liberty to lead the republic west? Why is she wearing the Star of Empire? What is the meaning of the "School Book" in her right hand? Of the telegraph lines?

- The painting has three horizontal planes—foreground, middle ground, and background—and each tells a story. What stages of social evolution are pictured in each plane? What symbols of progress does Gast employ? What role does technology play in the artist's rendition of progress?

- Gast also divided the painting into two vertical planes by altering the brightness of the image. What might a transition from light to dark symbolize?

- In the background on the far right stands New York City, with the magnificent Brooklyn Bridge (still under construction in 1872) spanning the East River. Far to the left is the Pacific Ocean. Why did Gast include these elements?

- Aside from the goddess, there are no clearly visible white women in the picture (though two Native American women can be seen in the foreground at left)—nor are there any black men or women. Why might Gast have excluded Euro-American women and African Americans?

**William Henry Jackson, *California Crossing, South Platte River*, detail, 1867**
The South Platte River was wide (stretching from the foreground to the low bluff in the middle of the picture) but shallow, allowing relatively easy passage for the migrants' cattle and covered wagons. During the late spring and early summer, wagon trains often stretched across the Great Plains as far as the eye could see.   National Park Service/ Picture Research Consultants & Archives.

The ranches soon linked California to the American economy. New England merchants dispatched dozens of agents to buy leather for the booming Massachusetts boot and shoe industry and tallow to make soap and candles. Many agents married the daughters of the elite Mexican landowners and ranchers — the Californios — and adopted their manners, attitudes, and Catholic religion. A crucial exception was Thomas Oliver Larkin, a successful merchant in the coastal town of Monterey. Larkin worked closely with Mexican ranchers, but he remained an American in outlook and eventually fostered California's annexation to the United States.

Like Larkin, the American migrants in the Sacramento River Valley did not want to assimilate into Mexican society. Some hoped to emulate the Americans in Texas by colonizing the country and then seeking annexation to the United States. However, in the early 1840s, these settlers numbered only about 1,000; by con-trast, 7,000 Mexicans and 300 American traders lived along the coast.

## The Plains Indians

As the Pacific-bound wagon trains rumbled across Nebraska along the broad Platte River, the migrants encountered the unique ecology of the Great Plains. A vast sea of grass stretched north from Texas to Saskatchewan in Canada, and west from the Missouri River to the Rocky Mountains. Tall grasses flourished in the eastern regions of the future states of Kansas, Nebraska, and the Dakotas, where there was ample rainfall. To the west — in the semiarid region beyond the 100th meridian — the migrants found short grasses that sustained a rich wildlife dominated by buffaloes and grazing antelopes. Nomadic buffalo-hunting Indian peoples roamed the western plains, while the tall grass-

***Comanche Meeting the Dragoons,* 1830s**

In the 1830s, when artist George Catlin accompanied the dragoons of the U.S. Army into Indian Territory, the Comanches were masters of the southern plains. They hunted buffalo, raised horses and mules for sale, and used their skills as horsemen to dominate other Indian peoples and control the passage of Americans along the Santa Fe Trail.   Smithsonian American Art Museum, Washington, D.C. / Art Resource, NY.

lands and river valleys to the east were home to semi-sedentary tribes and, since the 1830s, the Indian peoples whom Andrew Jackson had "removed" to the west. A line of military forts—stretching from Fort Jesup in Louisiana to Fort Snelling in Minnesota—policed the boundary between white America and what Congress in 1834 designated as Permanent Indian Territory.

For centuries, the Indians who lived on the eastern edge of the plains, such as the Pawnees and the Mandan on the Upper Missouri River, subsisted primarily on food crops—corn and beans—supplemented by buffalo meat. They hunted the buffalo on foot, driving them over cliffs or into canyons for the kill. To the south, the nomadic Apaches acquired horses from Spanish settlers in New Mexico. No longer dependent on dogs to move their goods, the Apaches ranged widely across the southern plains. But it was the Comanches, who migrated down the Arkansas River from the Rocky Mountains around 1750, who first developed a specialized horse culture. Fierce warriors and skilled buffalo hunters, the Comanches pushed the Apaches to the southern edge of the plains. Then the Comanches evolved into pastoralists; each Comanche family owned thirty to thirty-five horses or mules, far more than the five or six required for buffalo hunting. They sold both horses and mules to northern Indian peoples and Euro-

American farmers in Missouri and Arkansas. They also exchanged goods with traders and travelers along the Sante Fe Trail, which cut through Comanche and Kiowa territory as it connected Missouri and New Mexico. By the early 1840s, goods worth nearly $1 million moved along the trail each year.

By the 1830s, the Kiowas, Cheyennes, and Arapahos had also adopted this horse culture and, allied with the Comanches, dominated the plains between the Arkansas and Red rivers. With the new culture came sharper social divisions. Some Kiowa men owned hundreds of horses and had several "chore wives" and captive children who worked for them. Poor men, who owned only a few horses, could not find marriage partners and often had to work for their wealthy kinsmen.

However, even as European horses enhanced the mobility and wealth of the Plains Indians, European diseases and guns thinned their ranks. A devastating smallpox epidemic spread northward from New Spain in 1779–1781, taking the lives of half of the Plains Indians. Twenty years later, another smallpox outbreak left dozens of deserted villages along the Missouri River. Smallpox struck the northern plains again from 1837 to 1840, killing half of the Assiniboines and Blackfeet and nearly a third of the Crows and Pawnees. "If I could see this thing, if I knew where it came from, I would go there and fight it," exclaimed a distressed Cheyenne warrior as an epidemic ran through his tribe.

European weapons also altered the geography of native peoples. Around 1750, the Crees and Assiniboines, who lived on the far northern plains, acquired guns by trading wolf pelts and beaver skins to the British-run Hudson's Bay Company. Once armed, they drove the Blackfeet peoples westward into the Rocky Mountains and took control of the Saskatchewan and Upper Missouri River basins. When the Blackfeet obtained guns and horses around 1800, they emerged from the mountains and pushed the Shoshones and Crows to the south. Because horses could not easily find winter forage in the cold, snow-filled plains north of the Platte River, the Blackfeet could not maintain large herds; most families kept five to ten horses and remained hunters, not pastoralists.

The powerful Sioux, who acquired guns and ammunition from French, Spanish, and American traders along the Missouri River, also remained buffalo hunters. As nomadic people who traveled in small groups, the Sioux largely avoided major epidemics and increased their numbers. They kept some sedentary peoples, such as the Arikaras, in subjection and raided others for their crops and horses. By the 1830s, the Sioux were the dominant tribe on the central as well as the northern plains. "Those lands once belonged to the Kiowas and the Crows," boasted the Oglala Sioux chief Black Hawk, "but we whipped those nations out of them, and in this we did what the white men do when they want the lands of the Indians."

The Sioux's prosperity came at the expense not only of other Indian peoples but also of the buffalo, which provided them with a diet rich in protein and with hides and robes to sell. The number of hides and robes shipped down the Missouri River each year by the American Fur Company and the Missouri Fur Company increased from 3,000 in the 1820s, to 45,000 in the 1830s, and to 90,000 annually after 1840. North of the Missouri, the story was much the same. The 24,000 nomadic Indians of that region — Blackfeet, Crees, and Assiniboines — annually killed about 160,000 buffalo. The women dried the meat to feed their people and to sell to white traders and soldiers. They also undertook the arduous work of skinning and tanning the hides, which were used primarily for their own needs — for tepees, buffalo robes, and sleeping covers. But they traded surplus hides and robes, about 40,000 annually, for pots, knives, guns, and other manufactures. As among the Kiowas, trade with Euro-Americans increased social divisions. "It is a fine sight," a traveler noted around 1850, "to see one of those big men among the Blackfeet, who has two or three lodges, five or six wives, twenty or thirty children, fifty to a hundred head of horses; for his trade amounts to upward of $2,000 per year."

Although the Blackfeet, Kiowas, and Sioux contributed to the market economy, its workings remained largely unknown to them. Not understanding the value of their buffalo hides in world markets — as winter clothes, leather accessories, and industrial drive belts — they could not demand the best price. Nor was the future bright, because the Indians' subsistence needs and the overkill for the export trade was cutting the size of the buffalo herds. In the 1820s, the northern herd had numbered more than 5 million; by the late 1860s, it had shrunk to less than 2 million. According to Assiniboines' beliefs, when their cultural hero Inkton'mi taught the people how to kill the buffalo, he said: "The buffalo will live as long as your people. There will be no end of them until the end of time." Rather than a perpetual guarantee, by the 1860s Inkton'mi's words prefigured the end of time — the end of traditional buffalo-hunting and, perhaps, of the Assiniboines as well.

## The Fateful Election of 1844

The election of 1844 changed the American government's policy toward the Great Plains, the Far West, and Texas. Since 1836, when Texas sought annexation, southern leaders had advocated American expansion to extend slavery, only to be rebuffed by cautious party politicians and northern abolitionists. Now rumors swirled that Great Britain wanted California as payment for the large debts owed to British investors; that it was encouraging Texas to remain independent; and that it had designs on Spanish Cuba, which some slave owners wanted to annex to the United States. To thwart such imagined schemes, southern expansionists demanded the immediate annexation of Texas.

At this crucial juncture, Oregon fever and Manifest Destiny altered the political landscape in the North. In 1843, Americans in the Ohio River Valley and the Great Lakes states organized "Oregon conventions," and Democratic and Whig politicians alike called for American control of the entire Oregon Country, from Spanish California to Russian Alaska (which began at 54°40' north latitude). With northerners demanding Oregon, southern Democrats again called for the annexation of Texas. The southerners had the support of President John Tyler, a proslavery zealot. Disowned by the Whigs because of his opposition to Henry Clay's nationalist economic program, Tyler hoped to win reelection in

1844 as a Democrat. To curry favor among northern expansionists of both parties, Tyler proposed to seize all of Oregon.

In April 1844, Tyler and John C. Calhoun, his expansionist-minded secretary of state, sent the Senate a treaty to bring Texas into the Union. But the two major presidential hopefuls, Democrat Martin Van Buren and Whig Henry Clay, opposed Tyler's initiative. Fearful of raising the issue of slavery, they persuaded the Senate to reject the treaty.

Expansion into Texas and Oregon became the central issue in the election of 1844. Most southern Democrats favored expansion and refused to support Van Buren, because of his opposition to annexing Texas. The party also passed over Tyler, whom they did not trust. Instead, the Democrats selected Governor James K. Polk of Tennessee, an avowed expansionist and a slave owner. Known as "Young Hickory" because he was a protégé of Andrew Jackson, Polk shared his mentor's iron will, boundless ambition, and determination to open up lands for white settlement. Accepting the false claim in the Democratic Party platform that both areas already belonged to the United States, Polk campaigned for the "Re-occupation of Oregon and the Re-annexation of Texas." He insisted that the United States claim "the whole of the territory of Oregon" to the Alaskan border. "Fifty-four forty or fight!" became his jingoistic cry.

The Whigs nominated Henry Clay, who again advocated his American System of high tariffs, internal improvements, and national banking. Clay initially dodged the issue of Texas but, seeking southern votes, ultimately supported annexation. Northern Whigs who opposed the admission of a new slave state expressed their disappointment in Clay by casting their ballots for James G. Birney of the Liberty Party (see Chapter 11). Birney garnered less than 3 percent of the national vote but took enough Whig votes in New York to cost Clay that state—and the presidency.

Following Polk's narrow victory, congressional Democrats called immediately for Texas statehood. However, they lacked the two-thirds majority in the Senate needed to ratify a treaty of annexation. So the Democrats admitted Texas using a joint resolution of Congress, which required just a majority vote in each house, and Texas became the twenty-eighth state in December 1845. Polk's strategy of linking Texas and Oregon had put him in the White House and Texas in the Union. Shortly, it would make the expansion of the South—and its system of slavery—the central topic of American politics.

- **What ideas did the term *Manifest Destiny* reflect? Did it cause historical events, such as the new political support for territorial expansion, or was it merely a description of events?**

- **Which of the peoples native to the Great Plains increased in numbers and in wealth between 1750 and 1860? Why did they flourish while other peoples did not?**

# War, Expansion, and Slavery, 1846–1850

The acquisition of Texas whetted Polk's appetite for all the Mexican lands between Texas and the Pacific Ocean. If necessary, he was ready to go to war to get them. What he and many Democrats consciously ignored was the crisis over slavery that this expansion would unleash. Like other American presidents, Polk would learn that war can be a costly military and political option.

## The War with Mexico, 1846–1848

Since gaining independence in 1821, Mexico had not prospered. Its civil wars and political instability resulted in a stagnant economy, a weak government, and modest tax revenues, which were quickly devoured by a bloated bureaucracy and debt payments to European bankers. Although the distant northern provinces of California and New Mexico contributed little to the national economy and remained sparsely settled, with a Spanish-speaking population of only 75,000 in 1840, Mexican officials vowed to preserve their nation's historic boundaries. When its former province of Texas voted to join the American union in July 1845, Mexico broke off diplomatic relations with the United States.

**Polk's Expansionist Program** | President Polk quickly set in motion his plans to acquire Mexico's other northern provinces. He hoped to foment a revolution in California that, like the 1836 rebellion in Texas, would lead to annexation. In October 1845, Secretary of State James Buchanan told merchant Thomas Oliver Larkin, now the U.S. consul in the port of Monterey, to encourage influential Californios to seek independence and union with the United States. To add military muscle to this scheme, Polk ordered American naval commanders to seize San Francisco Bay and California's coastal towns in case of war with Mexico. The president also instructed the War Department to dispatch Captain John C. Frémont and an "exploring" party of heavily armed soldiers into Mexican territory. By December 1845, Frémont's force had reached California's Sacramento River Valley.

With these preparations in place, Polk launched a secret diplomatic initiative: He sent Louisiana congressman John Slidell to Mexico, telling him to secure the Rio Grande boundary and to buy the provinces of California and New Mexico for $30 million. However, Mexican officials declared that the annexation of Texas violated Mexican sovereignty and refused to see Slidell.

Events now moved quickly toward war. Polk ordered General Zachary Taylor and an American army of 2,000 soldiers to occupy disputed lands between the Nueces River (the historic southern boundary of Spanish Texas) and the Rio Grande, which the Republic of Texas had claimed as its border with Mexico. "We were sent to provoke a fight," recalled Ulysses S. Grant, then a young officer serving with Taylor, "but it was essential that Mexico should commence it." When the armies clashed near the Rio Grande in May 1846, Polk deliv-

ered the war message he had drafted long before. Taking liberties with the truth, the president declared that Mexico "has passed the boundary of the United States, has invaded our territory, and shed American blood upon the American soil." Ignoring pleas by some Whigs for a negotiated settlement, an overwhelming majority in Congress voted for war—a decision greeted with great popular acclaim. To avoid a simultaneous war with Britain, Polk retreated from his demand for "fifty-four forty or fight" and accepted a British proposal to divide the Oregon Country at the forty-ninth parallel.

**American Military Successes** Meanwhile, American forces in Texas established their military superiority. Zachary Taylor's army crossed the Rio Grande; occupied the Mexican city of Matamoros; and, after a fierce six-day battle in September 1846, took the interior Mexican town of Monterrey. Two months later, a U.S. naval squadron in the Gulf of Mexico seized Tampico, Mexico's second most important port. By the end of 1846, the United States controlled much of northeastern Mexico (Map 13.3).

**MAP 13.3**

**The Mexican War, 1846–1848**

After moving west from Fort Leavenworth in present-day Kansas, American forces commanded by Captain John C. Frémont and General Stephen Kearney defeated Mexican armies in California in 1846 and early 1847. Simultaneously, U.S. troops under General Zachary Taylor and Colonel Alfred A. Doniphan won victories over General Santa Anna's forces south of the Rio Grande. In mid-1847, General Winfield Scott mounted a successful seaborne attack on Veracruz and Mexico City, ending the war.

**Street Fighting in the Calle de Iturbide, 1846**
Monterrey, which had resisted Spanish troops during Mexico's war for independence (1820–1821), was captured by the Americans only after bloody house-to-house fighting in the Mexican War (1846–1848). Protected by thick walls and shuttered windows, Mexican defenders pour a withering fire on the dark-uniformed American troops and buckskin-clad frontier fighters. A large Catholic cathedral looms in the background, its foundations obscured by the smoke from the Mexicans' cannons.   West Point Museum, United States Military Academy, West Point, N.Y.

Fighting had also broken out in California. In June 1846, naval commander John Sloat landed 250 marines in Monterey and declared that California "henceforward will be a portion of the United States." Almost simultaneously, American settlers in the Sacramento River Valley staged a revolt and, supported by Frémont's force, captured the town of Sonoma, where they proclaimed the independence of the "Bear Flag Republic." To cement these victories, Polk ordered army units to capture Santa Fe in New Mexico and then march to southern California. Despite stiff Mexican resistance,

American forces secured control of California early in 1847.

Polk expected these American victories to end the war, but he had underestimated the Mexicans' national pride and the determination of President Santa Anna. In February 1847 in the Battle of Buena Vista, Santa Anna nearly defeated Taylor's army in northeastern Mexico. To bring Santa Anna to terms, Polk approved General Winfield Scott's plan to attack the Mexican capital. In March 1847, Scott captured the port of Veracruz and, with a force of 14,000 soldiers, began the

260-mile march to Mexico City. Scott's troops crushed Santa Anna's forces and seized the Mexican capital in September 1847. Those defeats cost Santa Anna his presidency, and a new Mexican government made peace with the United States.

## A Divisive Victory

Initially, the war with Mexico sparked an explosion of patriotic support. The *Nashville Union* hailed it as a noble struggle to extend "the principles of free government." However, the war soon divided the nation (see Comparing American Voices, "The Mexican War: Expansion and Slavery," pp. 410–411). Some northern Whigs—among them Charles Francis Adams of Massachusetts (the son of John Quincy Adams) and Chancellor James Kent of New York—opposed the war on moral grounds. It was "causeless & wicked & unjust," declared Kent. Adams, Kent, and other so-called **conscience Whigs** accused Polk of waging a war of conquest to add new slave states and give slave-owning Democrats permanent control of the federal government. The Whig party grew bolder when voters repudiated Polk's war policy in the elections of 1846 and gave them control of Congress. Whig leaders now called for "No Territory"—a Congressional pledge that the United States would not seek any land from the Mexican republic. "Away with this wretched cant about a 'manifest destiny,' a 'divine mission' . . . to civilize, and Christianize, and democratize our sister republics at the mouth of a cannon," declared New York Senator William Duer.

**The Wilmot Proviso** Moreover, Polk's expansionist policies split the Democrats along sectional lines. As early as 1839, Ohio Democrat Thomas Morris had warned that "the power of slavery is aiming to govern the country, its Constitutions and laws." In 1846, David Wilmot, an antislavery Democratic congressman from Pennsylvania, took up that refrain. Wilmot proposed that slavery be prohibited in any territories gained from the war. His plan rallied Whigs and antislavery Democrats in the House of Representatives, which passed the Wilmot Proviso. Congress had begun to divide along sectional lines. "The madmen of the North . . . ," grumbled the *Richmond Enquirer*, "have, we fear, cast the die and numbered the days of this glorious Union." Fearing that outcome, a few proslavery northern senators joined their southern colleagues to kill the proviso.

Fervent Democratic expansionists now became even more aggressive. President Polk, Secretary of State

Buchanan, and Senators Stephen A. Douglas of Illinois and Jefferson Davis of Mississippi called for the annexation of a huge swath of Mexican territory south of the Rio Grande. However, John C. Calhoun and other politicians feared this demand would extend the costly war and require the assimilation of a huge number of Mexicans of mixed Indian and Spanish ancestry. So they favored only the annexation of sparsely settled New Mexico and California. "Ours is a government of the white man," proclaimed Calhoun, and should never welcome "into the Union any but the Caucasian race."

To unify the Democratic Party, Polk and Buchanan abandoned their hyperexpansionist dreams and accepted Calhoun's policy. In February 1848, Polk signed the Treaty of Guadalupe Hidalgo, in which the United States agreed to pay Mexico $15 million in return for more than one-third of its territory. The Senate ratified the treaty in March 1848 (Map 13.4). The same year, Congress created the Oregon Territory, and in 1850 it enacted the Oregon Donation Land Claim Act, which granted farm-sized plots of "free land" to settlers who took up residence before 1854. Soon, treaties with Indian peoples extinguished their titles to much of the new territory. With the settlement of Oregon and the acquisition of New Mexico and California, the first stage of the American conquest of the Far West was complete.

**Free Soil** But the political debate was far from over and dominated the election of 1848. The Senate's rejection of the Wilmot Proviso revived Thomas Morris's charge that white southerners were engaged in a "Slave Power" conspiracy to dominate national life. To thwart any such plan, thousands of ordinary northerners, including farmer Abijah Beckwith of Herkimer County, New York, joined the **free-soil movement**. To Beckwith, slavery was an institution of "aristocratic men" and a danger to "the great mass of the people [because it] . . . threatens the general and equal distribution of our lands into convenient family farms."

The free-soilers quickly organized the Free-Soil Party. The new party abandoned the Liberty Party's emphasis on the sinfulness of slavery and the natural rights of African Americans. Instead, like Beckwith, it depicted slavery as a threat to republicanism and the Jeffersonian ideal of a freeholder society. Their call for free soil, which extended the principle of the Wilmot Proviso, was the first antislavery proposal to attract broad support. Hundreds of men and women in the Great Lakes states joined the free-soil organizations formed by the American and Foreign Anti-Slavery Society. So, too, did Frederick Douglass, the foremost black abolitionist, who attended the convention that estab-

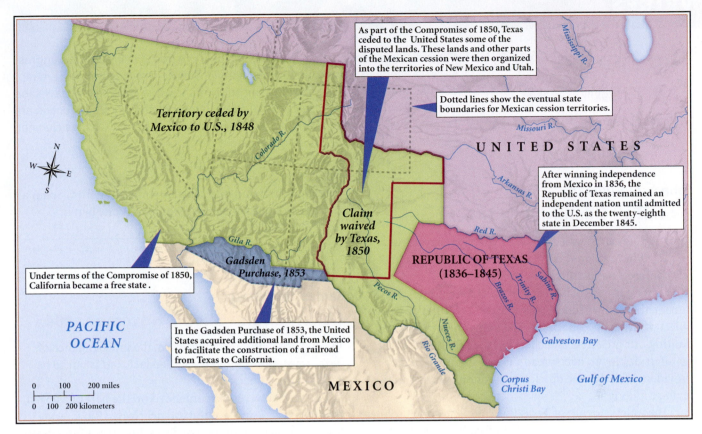

As part of the Compromise of 1850, Texas ceded to the United States some of the disputed lands. These lands and other parts of the Mexican cession were then organized into the territories of New Mexico and Utah.

Dotted lines show the eventual state boundaries for Mexican cession territories.

*Territory ceded by Mexico to U.S., 1848*

After winning independence from Mexico in 1836, the Republic of Texas remained an independent nation until admitted to the U.S. as the twenty-eighth state in December 1845.

*Claim waived by Texas, 1850*

REPUBLIC OF TEXAS (1836–1845)

Under terms of the Compromise of 1850, California became a free state.

*Gadsden Purchase, 1853*

In the Gadsden Purchase of 1853, the United States acquired additional land from Mexico to facilitate the construction of a railroad from Texas to California.

PACIFIC OCEAN

MEXICO

UNITED STATES

Galveston Bay

Corpus Christi Bay

Gulf of Mexico

0   100   200 miles
0   100   200 kilometers

**MAP 13.4**

**The Mexican Cession, 1848**

In the Treaty of Guadalupe Hidalgo (1848), Mexico ceded to the United States its vast northern territories—the present-day states of California, Nevada, Utah, Arizona, New Mexico, and half of Colorado. These new territories, President Polk boasted to Congress, "constitute of themselves a country large enough for a great empire, and the acquisition is second in importance only to that of Louisiana in 1803."

lished the Free-Soil Party in 1848 and endorsed its strategy for broadening the appeal of antislavery. However, William Lloyd Garrison and other radical abolitionists condemned the Free-Soilers' stress on white freehold farming as racist "whitemanism."

**The Election of 1848** The conflict over slavery took a toll on Polk and the Democratic Party. Scorned by Whigs and Free-Soilers and exhausted by his rigorous dawn-to-midnight work regime, Polk declined to run for a second term; he would die just three months after leaving office. In his place, the Democrats nominated Senator Lewis Cass of Michigan, an avid expansionist who had advocated buying Cuba, annexing Mexico's Yucatán Peninsula, and taking all of Oregon. To maintain party unity on the slavery issue, Cass promoted a new idea—squatter sovereignty—Congressional legislation that would al-

low settlers in each territory to determine its status as free or slave.

Cass's doctrine of squatter sovereignty failed to persuade some northern Democrats, who opposed the expansion of slavery into any territories. They joined the Free-Soil Party, as did Martin Van Buren, who became its candidate for president. To attract Whig votes, the Free-Soilers chose conscience Whig Charles Francis Adams for vice president.

The Whigs nominated General Zachary Taylor for president. Taylor was a Louisiana slave owner firmly committed to the defense of slavery in the South but not in the territories, a position that won him support in the north. Moreover, the general's military exploits had made him a popular hero, known affectionately among his troops as "Old Rough and Ready." In 1848, as in 1840, running a military hero worked for the Whigs. Taylor took 47 percent of the popular vote to

Thus I have given you, I think, the Substance of the Arguments
both sides of that great and important Quest

# The Mexican War: Expansion and Slavery

**C**onflict with Mexico prompted debates over the Polk administration's aggressive efforts to acquire territory and spread slavery. The expansionists are represented here by John L. O'Sullivan, the editor of the *United States Magazine and Democratic Review*, and Secretary of State James Buchanan. Polk's critics are the poet Walt Whitman, the editor of the *Brooklyn Eagle*, and Charles Sumner, a future Republican senator from Massachusetts.

## John L. O'Sullivan
### "Manifest Destiny," July 1845

Texas is now ours . . . her star and her stripe may already be said to have taken their place in the glorious blazon of our common nationality. . . .

Other nations [Britain and France] have undertaken to intrude themselves [into Texas affairs] . . . for the avowed object of thwarting our policy and hampering our power, limiting our greatness and checking the fulfillment of our manifest destiny to overspread the continent allotted by Providence for the free development of our yearly multiplying millions. . . .

The independence of Texas was complete and absolute. It was an independence, not only in fact, but of right. No obligation of duty towards Mexico tended in the least degree to restrain our right to [annex it]. . . . What then can be more preposterous than all this clamor by Mexico and the Mexican interest, against Annexation, as a violation of any rights of hers . . . ?

Nor is there any just foundation for the charge that Annexation is a great pro-slavery measure — calculated to increase and perpetuate that institution. Slavery had nothing to do with it. . . . That it will tend to facilitate and hasten the disappearance of Slavery from all the northern tier of the present Slave States, cannot surely admit of serious question. The greater value in Texas of the slave labor now employed in those States, must soon produce the effect of draining off that labor southwardly. . . .

California will, probably, next fall away from the loose adhesion which, in such a country as Mexico, holds a remote province in a slight equivocal kind of dependence on the metropolis. . . . Already the advance guard of the irresistible army of Anglo-Saxon emigration has begun to pour down upon it, armed with the plough and the rifle, and marking its trail with schools and colleges, courts and representative halls, mills and meeting-houses. A population will soon be in actual occupation of California, over which it will be idle for Mexico to dream of dominion. . . . And they will have a right to independence — to self-government . . . a better and a truer right than the artificial title of sovereignty in Mexico, a thousand miles distant, inheriting from Spain a title good only against those who have none better.

---

Source: Sean Wilentz, ed., *Major Problems in the Early Republic, 1787–1848* (D. C. Heath: Lexington, MA, 1991), 525–528.

## James Buchanan
### Letter to John Slidell, November 1845

In your negotiations with Mexico, the independence of Texas must be considered a settled fact, and is not to be called in question. . . .

It may, however, be contended on the part of Mexico, that the Nueces and not the Rio del Norte [Rio Grande], is the true western boundary of Texas. I need not furnish you arguments to controvert this position. . . . The jurisdiction of Texas has been extended beyond that river [the Nueces] and . . . representatives from the country between it and the Del Norte have participated in the deliberations both of her Congress and her Convention. . . .

The case is different in regard to New Mexico. Santa Fe, its capital, was settled by the Spaniards more than two centuries ago; and that province has been ever since in their possession and that of the Republic of Mexico. The Texans never have conquered or taken possession of it. . . . [However,] . . . a great portion of New Mexico being on this side of the Rio Grande and included within the limits already claimed by Texas, it may hereafter, should it remain a Mexican province, become a subject of dispute. . . .

If in adjusting the boundary, the province of New Mexico should be included within the limits of the United States, this would obviate the danger of future collisions. Mexico would part with a remote and disturbed province, the possession of which can never be advantageous to her. . . . It would seem to be equally the interest of both Powers, that New Mexico should belong to the United States. . . .

It is to be seriously apprehended that both Great Britain and France have designs upon California. . . . This Government . . . would vigorously interpose to prevent the latter from becoming either a British or a French Colony. . . .

The possession of the Bay and harbor of San Francisco, is all important to the United States.

The Government of California is now but nominally dependent on Mexico. . . . It is the desire of the President that you shall use your best efforts to obtain a cession of that Province. . . . Money would be no object.

Source: Victoria Bissell Brown and Timothy J. Shannon, eds., *Going to the Source: The Bedford Reader in American History* (Bedford/St Martin's: Boston, 2004), I, 260–262.

## Charles Sumner

### Letter to Robert Winthrop, October 25, 1846

By virtue of an unconstitutional Act of Congress, in conjunction with the de facto government of Texas, the latter was annexed to the United States some time in the month of December, 1845. If we regard Texas as a province of Mexico, its boundaries must be sought in the geography of that republic. If we regard it as an independent State, they must be determined by the extent of jurisdiction which the State was able to maintain. Now it seems clear that the river Nueces was always recognized by Mexico as the western boundary; and it is undisputed that the State of Texas, since its Declaration of Independence, never exercised any jurisdiction beyond the Nueces. . . .

In the month of January, 1846, the President of the United States directed the troops under General Taylor, called the Army of Occupation, to take possession of this region [west of the Nueces river]. Here was an act of aggression. As might have been expected, it produced collision. The Mexicans, aroused in self-defence, sought to repel the invaders. . . .

Here the question occurs, What was the duty of Congress in this emergency? Clearly to withhold all sanction to unjust war,—to aggression upon a neighboring Republic,—to spoliation of fellow-men. Our troops were in danger only because upon foreign soil, forcibly displacing the jurisdiction and laws of the rightful government. . . . The American forces should have been directed to *retreat*, not from any human force, but from *wrongdoing*; and this would have been a true victory.

Alas! This was not the mood of Congress. With wicked speed a bill was introduced, furnishing large and unusual supplies of men and money. . . . This was adopted by a vote of 123 to 67; and the bill then leaped forth, fully armed, as a measure of open and active hostility against Mexico.

Source: Sean Wilentz, ed., *Major Problems in the Early Republic, 1787–1848* (D. C. Heath: Lexington, MA, 1991), 541.

## Walt Whitman

### Editorial in the *Brooklyn Eagle*, September 1, 1847

The question whether or no there shall be slavery in the new territories which . . . we are largely to get through this Mexican war, is a question between *the grand body of white workingmen, the millions of mechanics, farmers, and operatives of our country*, with their interests on the one side— and the interests of the few thousand rich, "polished," and aristocratic owners of slaves at the South, on the other side.

Experience has proved . . . that a stalwart mass of respectable workingmen, cannot exist, much less flourish, in a thorough slave State. Let any one think for a moment what a different appearance New York, Pennsylvania, or Ohio, would present—how much less sturdy independence and family happiness there would be—were slaves the workmen there, instead of each man as a general thing being his own workman. . . .

Slavery is a good thing enough . . . to the rich—the one out of thousands; but it is destructive to the dignity and independence of all who work, and to labor itself. . . . All practice and theory . . . are strongly arrayed in favor of limiting slavery to where it already exists.

Source: Sean Wilentz, ed., *Major Problems in the Early Republic, 1787–1848* (D. C. Heath: Lexington, MA, 1991), 525–528, 541, 543.

### ANALYZING THE EVIDENCE

- **What arguments do Buchanan and Sumner make about the boundaries of Texas, the issue that sparked the fighting? Whose argument is more persuasive?**
- **What are O'Sullivan's and Buchanan's views with respect to California? Do they support or undercut the proposition that the Polk administration undertook an imperialist war of aggression?**
- **O'Sullivan raises the issue of who has a "right" to California. What is your view?**
- **Why does Whitman oppose the expansion of slavery? Given Whitman's views, who might have gotten his vote in the election of 1848? Why?**

**"This Is the House That Polk Built"**

President James Polk's administration started off with a bang—a long-sought Democratic free-trade tariff, a compromise settlement of the Oregon boundary dispute with Great Britain, and a war to seize California and other Mexican provinces. This ambitious agenda promised fame for the president, but the cartoonist pictures Polk as a worried man, afraid that he has built a house of cards that might collapse at any time.    Bettmann/Corbis.

Cass's 42 percent. However, Taylor won a majority in the electoral college (163 to 127) only because Van Buren and the Free-Soil ticket took enough votes in New York to deny Cass a victory there. The bitter debate over the expansion of slavery had changed the dynamics of national politics, as antislavery voters denied the presidency to Clay in 1844 and to Cass in 1848.

## California Gold and Racial Warfare

Even before Taylor took office, events in California took center stage. In January 1848, workers building a mill for John A. Sutter in the Sierra Nevada foothills discovered flakes of gold. Sutter was a Swiss immigrant who had arrived in California in 1839, became a Mexican

citizen, and accumulated an estate in the Sacramento River Valley. He tried to hide the discovery, but by mid-1848 Americans from Monterey and San Francisco were pouring into the foothills, along with hundreds of Indians and Californios and scores of Australians, Mexicans, and Chileans. The gold rush was on. By January 1849, sixty-one crowded ships had left northeastern ports to sail around Cape Horn to San Francisco; by May, twelve thousand wagons had crossed the Missouri River bound for the goldfields (Map 13.5). For Bernard Reid, the overland trip on the Pioneer Line was "a long dreadful dream," beset by cholera, scurvy, and near starvation. Still, by the end of 1849, more than 80,000 people, mostly men, had arrived in California.

**The Forty-Niners** The "forty-niners" lived in crowded, chaotic towns and mining camps amid gamblers, saloon keepers, and prostitutes. They fashioned a rudimentary legal system based on practice in the East and set up "claims clubs" that settled mining disputes. The American miners usually treated fellow whites fairly but ruthlessly expelled Indians, Mexicans, and Chileans from the gold fields or confined them to marginal diggings. When substantial numbers of Chinese migrants arrived in 1850, they were often forced off independent claims and so had to work for wages (see Voices from Abroad, "Norman Assing (Yuan Sheng): Equality for Chinese Immigrants," p. 414).

The first miners to exploit a site often struck it rich. They scooped up the easily reached deposits and left small pickings for later arrivals. His "high hopes" wrecked, one latecomer saw himself and most other California miners as little better than "convicts condemned to exile and hard labor." They were often condemned to disease as well: "Diarrhea was so general during the fall and winter months" and so often fatal, a Sacramento doctor remarked, that it was called "the disease of California." Like many other migrants, William Swain gave up the search for gold; at the end of 1850, he borrowed funds and returned to his wife, infant daughter, and aged mother on a New York farm. "O William," his wife Sabrina had written, "I wish you had been content to stay at home, for there is no real home for me without you."

Thousands of other disillusioned forty-niners were either too ashamed or too tired or too adventurous to go home. Some became wage workers for companies that engaged in hydraulic or underground mining; many others turned to farming. "Instead of going to the mines where fortune hangs upon the merest chance," a frustrated miner advised emigrants, "[you] should at once commence the cultivation of the soil." Farming required

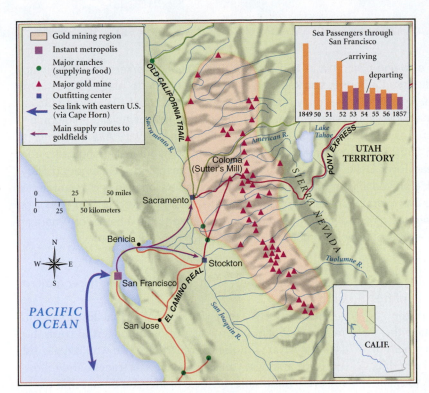

**MAP 13.5**

## The California Gold Rush, 1849–1857

Traveling from all parts of the world — South America, Europe, China, and Australia, as well as the eastern United States — hundreds of thousands of bonanza-seekers converged on the California goldfields. Miners traveling by sea landed at San Francisco, which mushroomed into a substantial city; many other prospectors trekked overland to the goldfields on the Old California Trail. By the mid-1850s, the gold rush was over: Almost as many people were sailing from San Francisco each year as were arriving to seek their fortune.

**California Drinking, 1855**

Men — and women — from around the globe joined the California gold rush in search of easy money. This lithograph by Frank Marryat, *The Bar of a Gambling Saloon*, suggests this geographic diversity by picturing Mexicans, Chinese, and Americans in their national dress. Some patrons drink to their success in the fields or at the gambling tables, while a crowd of men in the adjacent room ogles scantily clad "public women" dancing on a platform. © Collection of the New-York Historical Society, USA /The Bridgeman Art Library.

## Norman Assing (Yuan Sheng)
## Equality for Chinese Immigrants

The arrival in California in 1852 of 20,000 Chinese workers, including many indentured laborers, sparked Anglo-American efforts to restrict Asian immigration. A California assembly committee condemned "coolie labor" and Governor John Bigler suggested legislation to "check this tide of Asiatic immigration." Norman Assing (Yuan Sheng) responded to Bigler in the *Daily Alta California* on May 5, 1852. Like most nineteenth-century Chinese migrants, Assing came from the Pearl River Delta region of southern China (present-day Guangdong Province). He arrived in New York City in 1820, became a Christian and a naturalized citizen, and lived in Charleston, South Carolina. Assing moved to San Francisco and emerged as a prominent merchant and—thanks to his mastery of American culture—the self-appointed spokesman for the Chinese in California.

To His Excellency Gov. Bigler

Sir: I am a Chinaman, a republican, and a lover of free institutions; am much attached to the principles of the Government of the United States, and therefore take the liberty of addressing you as the chief of the government of this state. . . . The effect of your late message has been thus far to prejudice the public mind against my people, to enable those who wait the opportunity to hunt them down, and rob them of the rewards of their toil. . . .

You are deeply convinced you say "that to enhance the prosperity and to preserve the tranquility of this state, Asiatic immigration must be checked." This, your Excellency, is but one step towards a retrograde movement of the government . . . which the citizens of this country ought never to tolerate. It was one of the principal causes of quarrel between you (when colonies) and England; when the latter pressed laws against emigration, you looked for immigration; it came, and immigration made *you what you are*, your nation what it is. . . .

You argue that this is a republic of a particular race that the constitution of the United States admits of no asylum to any other than the pale face. This proposition is false in the extreme; and you know it. The declaration of your independence, and all the acts of your government, your people, and your history, are against you.

It is true, you have degraded the negro because of your holding him in involuntary servitude, and because for the sake of union in some of your states such was tolerated. And amongst this class you would endeavor to place us; and no doubt it would be pleasing to some would-be free-men to mark the brand of servitude upon us. But we would beg to remind you that when your nation was a wilderness, and the nation from whom you sprung *barbarous*, we [Chinese] exercised most of the arts and virtues of civilized life; that we are possessed of a language and literature, and that men skilled in science and the arts are numerous amongst us; that the productions of our manufactories, our

sail and work-shops, form no small share of the commerce of the world. . . .

And we beg to remark, that so far as the history of our race in California goes, it stamps with the test of truth the fact that we are not the degraded race you would make us. We came amongst you as mechanics or traders, and following every honorable business of life. You do not find us pursuing occupations of a degrading character, except you consider labor degrading, which I am sure you do not. . . .

You say "you desire to see no change in the generous policy of this Government as far as regards Europeans." It is out of your power to say, however, in what way or to whom the doctrines of the Constitution shall apply. You have no more right to propose a measure for checking immigration, than you have to assume the right of sending a message to the Legislature on the subject.

As far as regards the color and complexion of our race, we are perfectly aware that our population have been a little more tanned than yours. Your Excellency will discover, however, . . . that as far as the aristocracy of *skin* is concerned, ours might compare with many of the European races; nor do we consider that your Excellency, as a Democrat, will make us believe that the framers of your declaration of rights ever suggested the propriety of establishing an aristocracy of *skin*.

Source: *Daily Alta California*, May 5, 1852.

### ANALYZING THE EVIDENCE

- What are the major arguments Assing uses to defend the rights of Chinese immigrants in California?
- Why does Assing claim that Bigler (and California) cannot limit immigration?
- The Naturalization Act of 1790 limits naturalization to aliens who are "free white persons." How does that law affect Assing's arguments?

arable land, which was owned by Mexican grantees or occupied by Indian peoples. The American arrivals brushed aside both groups, brutally eliminating the Indians and wearing down Mexican claimants with legal tactics and political pressure.

**Racial Warfare and Land Rights** | The subjugation of the Indians came first. When the gold rush began in 1848, there were about 150,000 Indians in California; by 1861, there were only 30,000. As elsewhere in the Americas, European diseases took the lives of thousands of natives. But in California, white settlers also undertook systematic campaigns of extermination and local political leaders did little to stop them: "A war of extermination will continue to be waged . . . until the Indian race becomes extinct," predicted Governor Peter Burnett in 1851. Congress abetted these assaults. At the bidding of white Californians, it repudiated treaties that federal agents had negotiated with 119 tribes, and that provided the Indians with 7 million acres of land. Instead, in 1853, Congress authorized five reservations of only 25,000 acres each and refused to provide the Indians with military protection.

Consequently, some settlers simply murdered Indians to push them off non-reservation lands. The Yuki people, who lived in the Round Valley in northern California, were one target. As the *Petaluma Journal* reported in April 1857: "Within the past three weeks, from 300 to 400 bucks, squaws and children have been killed by whites." Other white Californians turned to slave trading: "Hundreds of Indians have been stolen and carried into the settlements and sold," the state's Indian Affairs superintendent reported in 1856. Labor-hungry farmers quickly put them to work. Indians were "all among us, around us, with no house and kitchen without them," recalled one farmer. Expelled from their lands and widely dispersed, many Indian peoples simply vanished as distinct communities. Those tribes that survived were a shadow of their former selves. In 1854, Round Valley was home to at least 5,000 Yukis; a decade later, only 85 men and 215 women remained.

The Mexicans and Californios who held grants to thousands of acres were harder to dislodge. The Treaty of Guadalupe Hidalgo guaranteed that the land grants made by Spanish and Mexican authorities would be "inviolably respected." Despite the fact that many of the 800 grants in California were either fraudulent or questionable, the Land Claims Commission created by Congress upheld the validity of 75 percent of them. In the meantime, hundreds of Americans had set up farms on the grants, many of which had never been settled. Having come of age in the anti-monopoly Jacksonian

era, these American squatters rejected the notion that so much unoccupied and unimproved land could be held by a few families. They pressured local land commissioners and judges to void suspect grants, with considerable success. Although the squatters failed to secure legislation transferring unoccupied grants to the public domain, the Americans' clamor for land was so intense and their numbers so large that even successful Mexican and Californio claimants decided to sell off their properties at bargain prices.

In northern California, farmers found that they could grow most eastern crops: corn and oats to feed work horses, pigs, and chickens; potatoes, beans, and peas for the farm table; and refreshing grapes, apples, and peaches. Ranchers gradually replaced Spanish cattle with American breeds that yielded more milk and meat, which found a ready market as California's population shot up to 380,000 by 1860 and 560,000 by 1870. Most important, wheat and barley farmers cultivated hundreds of acres, using the latest technology and scores of hired workers to produce huge crops, which San Francisco merchants exported to Europe at high prices. The gold rush gradually turned into a wheat boom.

## 1850: Crisis and Compromise

The rapid settlement of California qualified it for admission to the Union. Hoping to avoid an extended debate over slavery, President Taylor advised the settlers to skip the territorial phase and immediately apply for statehood. When Californians ratified a state constitution prohibiting slavery in November 1849, the president urged Congress to admit California as a free state.

**Constitutional Conflict** | Taylor's effort to avoid sectional conflict failed. California's bid for admission produced passionate debates in Congress and four distinct positions with respect to the expansion of slavery. On the verge of death, John C. Calhoun took his usual extreme stance. Calhoun deeply resented the North's "long-continued agitation of the slavery question." To uphold southern honor (and political power), he proposed a constitutional amendment to create a dual presidency, thus permanently dividing executive power within the national government between the North and the South. Calhoun also advanced the radical argument that Congress had no constitutional authority to regulate slavery in the territories. Slaves were property, Calhoun pointed out, and the Constitution restricted Congress's power to abrogate or limit property rights. That argument ran counter to a half century of practice. Congress had prohibited slavery

**Resolving the Crisis of 1850**
By 1850, Whig Henry Clay had been in Congress for nearly four decades. Now in partnership with fellow Whig Daniel Webster and Democrat Stephen Douglas, Clay fashioned a complex—and controversial—compromise that preserved the Union. In this engraving, he addresses a crowded Senate chamber, with Webster sitting immediately to his left. Clay addresses his remarks to his prime antagonist, Southern nationalist John C. Calhoun, the man with the long white hair at the far right of the picture. Library of Congress Prints and Photographs Division, LC-DIG-ppmsca-09398.

in the Northwest Territory in 1787, and it had extended that ban to most of the Louisiana Purchase in the Missouri Compromise of 1820.

Calhoun's assertion that "slavery follows the flag" won support in the Deep South, but many southerners favored a more moderate proposal to extend the Missouri Compromise line to the Pacific Ocean. This plan won the backing of Pennsylvanian James Buchanan and other influential northern Democrats. It would guarantee slave owners access to some western territory, including a separate state in southern California.

A third alternative was squatter sovereignty. Lewis Cass had advanced this idea in 1848, and Democratic senator Stephen Douglas of Illinois now became its champion. Douglas called his plan popular sovereignty to link it to the ideology of republicanism, which placed ultimate power in the hands of the people (see Chapter 5), and it had considerable appeal. Politicians hoped it would remove the explosive issue of slavery from the national agenda, and local settlers welcomed the power it would give them. However, popular sovereignty was a slippery concept. Could residents accept or ban slavery when a territory was first organized? Or must they delay that decision until a territory had enough people to frame a constitution and apply for statehood? To promote their plan, advocates of popular sovereignty evaded answering such questions.

For their part, antislavery advocates refused to accept any plan for California that might allow slavery there or elsewhere. Senator Salmon P. Chase of Ohio, elected by a Democratic–Free-Soil coalition, and Senator William H. Seward, a New York Whig, urged a fourth position: that federal authorities restrict slavery within its existing boundaries and eventually extinguish it completely. Condemning slavery as "morally unjust, politically unwise, and socially pernicious" and invoking "a higher law than the Constitution," Seward demanded bold action to protect freedom, "the common heritage of mankind."

**A Complex Compromise** Standing on the brink of disaster, senior Whig and Democratic politicians worked desperately to preserve the Union. Aided by Millard Fillmore, who became president in 1850 after Zachary Taylor's sudden death, Whig leaders Henry Clay and Daniel Webster and Democrat Stephen A. Douglas won the passage of five separate laws known collectively as the Compromise of 1850. To mollify the South, the compromise included a new Fugitive Slave Act that gave federal support to slave catchers. To satisfy the North, the legislation admitted California as a free state, resolved a boundary dispute between New Mexico and Texas in favor of New Mexico, and abolished the slave trade (but not slavery) in

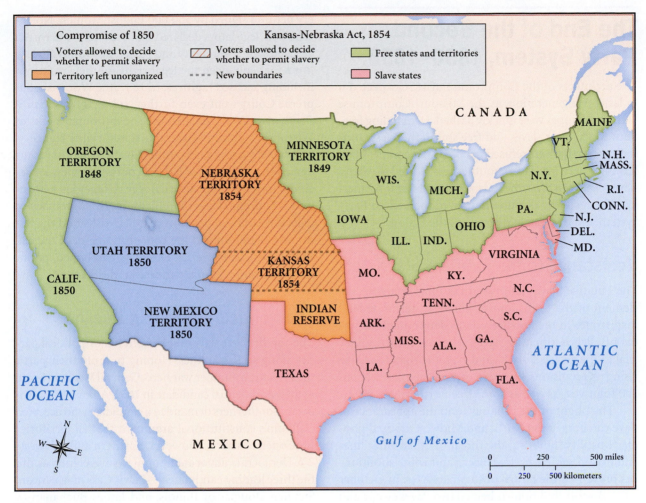

**Compromise of 1850**
- Voters allowed to decide whether to permit slavery
- Territory left unorganized

**Kansas-Nebraska Act, 1854**
- Voters allowed to decide whether to permit slavery
- New boundaries
- Free states and territories
- Slave states

**MAP 13.6**

**The Compromise of 1850 and the Kansas-Nebraska Act of 1854**

The contest over the expansion of slavery involved vast territories. The Compromise of 1850 peacefully resolved the status of the Far West: California would be a free state, and settlers in the Utah and New Mexico territories would vote for or against slavery (the doctrine of popular sovereignty). However, the Kansas-Nebraska Act of 1854 voided the Missouri Compromise (1820) and instituted popular sovereignty in those territories. That decision sparked a bitter local war and revealed a fatal flaw in the doctrine.

the District of Columbia. Finally, the compromise organized the rest of the lands acquired from Mexico into the territories of New Mexico and Utah and, invoking popular sovereignty, left the issue of slavery in their hands (Map 13.6).

The Compromise of 1850 preserved the Union, but only barely. During the debate, South Carolina's governor warned that his state might well secede. He and other militant secessionists (or "fire-eaters") in Georgia, Mississippi, and Alabama organized special conventions to promote the goal of safeguarding "southern rights" by leaving the Union. Georgia congressman Alexander H. Stephens called on the delegates of one such convention to make "the necessary preparations of men and

money, arms and munitions, etc. to meet the emergency." However, a majority of convention delegates remained committed to the Union—though now only conditionally. They agreed to leave the Union if Congress abolished slavery anywhere or refused to grant statehood to a territory with a proslavery constitution. Political wizardry had solved the immediate crisis, but the underlying issues remained unresolved.

- **Why did President Polk go to war with Mexico? Why did the war become so divisive in Congress and the country?**

- **What issues did the Compromise of 1850 resolve? Who benefited more from its terms: the North or the South? Why?**

# The End of the Second Party System, 1850–1858

The architects of the Compromise of 1850 expected it to last for a generation, as the Missouri Compromise had. Their hopes were quickly dashed. Demanding freedom for fugitive slaves and free soil in the West, antislavery northerners refused to accept the compromise. For their part, proslavery southerners plotted to extend slavery into the West, the Caribbean, and Central America. The resulting disputes destroyed the Second Party System and deepened the crisis of the Union.

## Resistance to the Fugitive Slave Act

The Fugitive Slave Act proved the most controversial element of the Compromise. Under its terms, federal magistrates in the northern states determined the status of alleged runaway slaves. The law denied a jury trial to the accused blacks and even the right to testify. Using its provisions, southern owners reenslaved about 200 fugitives (as well as some free northern blacks).

The plight of the runaways and the appearance of slave catchers in the North and Midwest aroused popular hostility. Ignoring the threat of substantial fines and prison sentences, free blacks and white abolitionists prevented the return of fugitive slaves. In October 1850, Boston abolitionists helped two slaves escape and drove a Georgia slave catcher out of town. Rioters in Syracuse, New York, broke into a courthouse, freed a fugitive slave, and accused the U.S. marshal of kidnapping. Abandoning nonviolence, Frederick Douglass declared, "The only way to make a Fugitive Slave Law a dead letter is to make half a dozen or more dead kidnappers." Precisely such a deadly result occurred in Christiana, Pennsylvania, in September 1851. About twenty African Americans exchanged gunfire with Maryland slave catchers, killing two of them. Federal authorities indicted thirty-six blacks and four whites for treason and other crimes. But a Pennsylvania jury acquitted one defendant, and northern public opinion forced the government to drop the charges against the rest.

Harriet Beecher Stowe's novel, *Uncle Tom's Cabin* (1852), boosted opposition to the Fugitive Slave Act and to slavery. Conveying the moral principles of abolitionism in heartrending personal situations, Stowe's melodramatic book evoked empathy for enslaved women and men and outrage toward the internal slave trade. In Britain, the novel sold 1 million copies in eight months and resulted in the Stafford House Address, an antislav-

ery petition signed by 560,000 English women. Northern states' legislators declared that the Fugitive Slave Act violated state sovereignty and passed **personal-liberty laws** that enhanced the legal rights of their residents, including accused fugitives. In 1857, the Wisconsin Supreme Court went even further, ruling in *Ableman v. Booth* that the act violated the constitutional rights of Wisconsin's citizens. Taking a states' rights stance — traditionally a southern position — the Wisconsin court denied the authority of federal courts to review its decision. In 1859, Chief Justice Roger B. Taney led a unanimous Supreme Court in affirming the supremacy of federal courts — a position that has withstood the test of time — and upheld the constitutionality of the act. But by then, as Frederick Douglass had hoped, popular opposition had made the law a "dead letter."

## The Political System in Decline

The conflict over slavery split both major political parties along sectional lines. Hoping to unify their party, the Whigs ran another war hero, General Winfield Scott, as their presidential candidate in 1852. Among the Democrats, southerners demanded a candidate who accepted Calhoun's constitutional argument that all territories were open to slavery. However, northern and midwestern Democrats advocated popular sovereignty, as did the three leading candidates — Lewis Cass of Michigan, Stephen Douglas of Illinois, and James Buchanan of Pennsylvania. Ultimately, the party settled on a compromise candidate, Franklin Pierce of New Hampshire, a congenial man who was sympathetic to the South, and swept to victory. Many Free-Soilers voted for Pierce, reuniting the Democratic Party. The Whig Party fragmented along sectional wings over slavery and would never again wage a national campaign.

As president, Pierce pursued an expansionist foreign policy. To assist northern merchants, who wanted a commercial empire, he negotiated a treaty with Japan. To mollify southern expansionists, who desired a landed empire, he tried to purchase extensive Mexican lands south of the Rio Grande. Ultimately, Pierce settled for a narrow slice of land — the Gadsden Purchase of 1853 — that enabled his negotiator, James Gadsden, to build a transcontinental rail line from New Orleans to California.

Pierce's most controversial initiatives came in the Caribbean and Central America. Southern expansionists had long urged Cuban slave owners to declare independence and join the United States; to assist them, and the American traders who carried thousands of African slaves to Spanish-owned Cuba each year, Pierce covertly supported military expeditions to Cuba and Nicaragua and threatened war with Spain. Northern Democrats in Congress denounced this aggressive diplomacy and reacted strongly when Secretary of State William L. Marcy arranged for American diplomats in Europe to compose the Ostend Manifesto, which urged Pierce to seize Cuba. They denounced the manifesto and scuttled the planters' dreams of American expansion into the Caribbean.

## The Kansas-Nebraska Act and the Rise of New Parties

The Caribbean was a sideshow. The main stage was the trans-Mississippi west, where a major controversy in 1854 destroyed the Second Party System and sent the Union spinning toward disaster. The Missouri Compromise prohibited new slave states in the Louisiana Purchase north of 36°30'. Consequently, southern senators had long prevented the creation of new territories there; it remained Permanent Indian Territory. Now Senator Stephen A. Douglas of Illinois hoped to open it up, so that a transcontinental railroad could link Chicago to California. Without a railroad, Douglas asked, "How are we to develop our immense interests and possessions on the Pacific? . . . The Indian barrier must be removed." Douglas introduced a bill extinguishing Native American rights on the Great Plains, organiz-

ing the large free territory of Nebraska, and opening it up to white settlers.

Southern politicians opposed Douglas's initiative. They hoped to extend slavery throughout the Louisiana Purchase and to have a southern city—New Orleans, Memphis, or St. Louis—as the eastern terminus of a transcontinental railroad. To win their support, Douglas amended his bill so that it explicitly repealed the Missouri Compromise and organized the region on the basis of popular sovereignty. He also agreed to the formation of two territories, Nebraska and Kansas, allowing southerners to hope that Kansas would become a slave state. Knowing that the revised bill would "raise a hell of a storm" in the North, Douglas argued that Kansas was not suited to plantation agriculture and would become a free state. After weeks of bitter debate, the Senate enacted the Kansas-Nebraska Act. In the House of Representatives, sixty-six northern Democrats refused to follow the party line and opposed the act. But Pierce used pressure and patronage to persuade twenty-two of them to change their votes, and the measure squeaked through.

**The American and Republican Parties** The Kansas-Nebraska Act of 1854 was a disaster for the American political system. It finished off the Whig Party and nearly destroyed the Democrats as a national party. Denouncing the act as "part of a great scheme for extending and

### An Excursion of the New York Turners, 1854

Friedrich Ludwig Jahn, a Prussian educator and nationalist, founded the Turner (or gymnastics) movement in 1811. Intended to develop moral character and patriotic élan as well as physical strength among German men, Turner societies advocated public schooling, free speech, and political democracy. Brought to the United States by German refugees from the failed democratic Revolution of 1848, the Turner movement preserved German culture and served as a home for German abolitionists and reformers. Here, some Turners display their physical fitness while others discuss politics, sing German songs, and drink beer.   Museum of the City of New York, The J. Clarence Davies Collection.

perpetuating supremacy of the slave power," northern Whigs and "anti-Nebraska" Democrats abandoned their old parties. They joined with Free-Soilers and abolitionists in a new Republican Party.

The new party was a coalition of "strange, discordant and even hostile elements," one Republican observed, but its leaders were united in opposing slavery. Republicans repudiated slavery because it degraded the dignity of manual labor and drove down the wages and working conditions of free white workers. Like Thomas Jefferson, they praised a society based on "the middling classes who own the soil and work it with their own hands." Abraham Lincoln, an Illinois Whig who became a Republican, conveyed the party's vision of social mobility. "There is no permanent class of hired laborers among us," he declared; every free man had a chance to become a property owner. Ignoring the increasing class divisions in the industrializing North and Midwest, Lincoln and his fellow Republicans celebrated republican liberty and individual enterprise.

The Republicans faced strong competition from the American, or Know-Nothing, Party. The party had its origins in the anti-immigrant and anti-Catholic movements of the 1840s (see Chapter 9). In 1850, these secret nativist societies banded together as the Order of the Star-Spangled Banner; the following year, they formed the American Party. When faced with outsiders' questions, the party's secrecy-conscious members often replied, "I know nothing," hence the nickname. The Know-Nothing Party's program was far from secret, however: It wanted to unite native-born Protestants against the "alien menace" of Irish and German Catholics, prohibit further immigration, and institute literacy tests for voting. In 1854, voters elected dozens of Know-Nothing candidates to the House of Representatives and gave the American Party control of the state governments of Massachusetts and Pennsylvania. The emergence of a major nativist party became a real possibility.

### Bleeding Kansas

Meanwhile, thousands of settlers rushed into the Kansas Territory, putting Douglas's concept of popular sovereignty to the test. On the side of slavery, Missouri senator David R. Atchison encouraged residents of his state to cross temporarily into Kansas to vote in crucial elections there. Opposing Atchison was the abolitionist New England Emigrant Aid Society, which dispatched free-soilers to Kansas. In 1855, the Pierce administration accepted the legitimacy of a proslavery legislature in Lecompton, Kansas, which had been elected by border-crossing Missourians. However, the majority of Kansas residents favored free soil and refused allegiance to the Lecompton government.

In 1856, both sides turned to violence, prompting Horace Greeley of the *New York Tribune* to label the territory "Bleeding Kansas." A proslavery force, seven hundred strong, looted and burned the free-soil town of Lawrence. The attack enraged John Brown, a fifty-six-year-old abolitionist from New York and Ohio, who commanded a free-state militia. Brown was a complex man with a long record of failed businesses, but he had an intellectual and moral intensity that won the trust of influential people. Taking vengeance for the sack of Lawrence, Brown and his followers murdered five proslavery settlers at Pottawatomie. Abolitionists must "fight fire with fire" and "strike terror in the hearts of the proslavery people," Brown declared. The attack on Lawrence and the Pottawatomie killings started a guerrilla war in Kansas that took nearly two hundred lives.

### Armed Abolitionists in Kansas, 1859

The confrontation between North and South in Kansas took many forms. In the spring of 1859, Dr. John Doy (seated) slipped across the border into Missouri and tried to lead thirteen escaped slaves to freedom in Kansas, only to be captured and jailed in St. Joseph, Missouri. The serious-looking men standing behind Doy, well armed with guns and Bowie knives, attacked the jail and carried Doy back to Kansas. The photograph celebrated—and memorialized—their successful exploit. Kansas State Historical Society.

## Buchanan's Failed Presidency

The violence in Kansas dominated the presidential election of 1856. The new Republican Party counted on anger over Bleeding Kansas to boost the party's fortunes. Its platform denounced the Kansas-Nebraska Act and demanded that the federal government prohibit slavery in all the territories. Republicans also called for federal subsidies for transcontinental railroads, reviving a Whig economic proposal popular among midwestern Democrats. For president, the Republicans nominated Colonel John C. Frémont, a free-soiler who had won fame in the conquest of Mexican California.

**The Election of 1856**   The American Party entered the election with equally high hopes, but like the Whigs and Democrats, it split along sectional lines over slavery. The southern faction of the American party nominated former Whig president Millard Fillmore, while the northern contingent endorsed Frémont—thanks to clever maneuvering by Republican politicians. During the campaign, the Republicans won the votes of many Know-Nothing workingmen in the North by demanding a ban on foreign immigrants and high tariffs on foreign manufactures. As a Pennsylvania Republican put it, "Let our motto be, protection to everything American, against everything foreign." In New York, Republicans campaigned on a reform platform designed "to cement into a harmonious mass . . . all of the Anti-Slavery, Anti-Popery and Anti-Whiskey" voters.

The Democrats reaffirmed their support for popular sovereignty and the Kansas-Nebraska Act, and nominated James Buchanan of Pennsylvania. A tall, dignified man and an experienced but unimaginative politician, Buchanan was staunchly prosouthern. He won the three-way race with 1.8 million popular votes (45.3 percent) and 174 electoral votes. Frémont polled 1.3 million popular votes (33.2 percent) and 114 electoral votes; Fillmore won 873,000 popular votes (21.5 percent) but captured only 8 electoral votes.

The dramatic restructuring of parties was now apparent (Map 13.7). With the splintering of the American Party, the Republicans had replaced the Whigs as the second major party. However, Republicans were a sectional party. Frémont had not won a single vote in the South; had he triumphed, a North Carolina newspaper warned, the result would have been "a separation

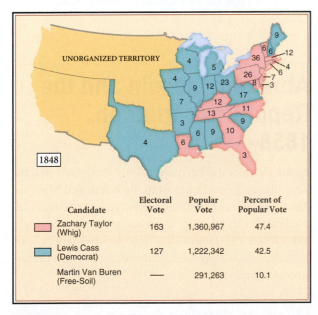

| 1848 | | | |
| --- | --- | --- | --- |
| Candidate | Electoral Vote | Popular Vote | Percent of Popular Vote |
| Zachary Taylor (Whig) | 163 | 1,360,967 | 47.4 |
| Lewis Cass (Democrat) | 127 | 1,222,342 | 42.5 |
| Martin Van Buren (Free-Soil) | — | 291,263 | 10.1 |

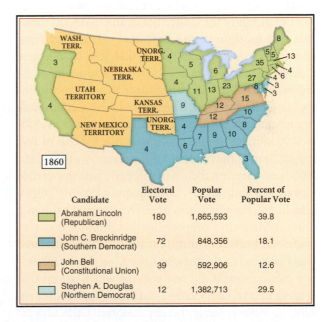

| 1860 | | | |
| --- | --- | --- | --- |
| Candidate | Electoral Vote | Popular Vote | Percent of Popular Vote |
| Abraham Lincoln (Republican) | 180 | 1,865,593 | 39.8 |
| John C. Breckinridge (Southern Democrat) | 72 | 848,356 | 18.1 |
| John Bell (Constitutional Union) | 39 | 592,906 | 12.6 |
| Stephen A. Douglas (Northern Democrat) | 12 | 1,382,713 | 29.5 |

**MAP 13.7**

**Political Realignment, 1848 and 1860**

In the presidential election of 1848, both the Whig and the Democratic candidates won electoral votes throughout the nation. Subsequently, the political conflict over slavery and the Compromise of 1850 destroyed the Whig Party in the South. As the only nationwide party, the Democrats won easily over the Whigs in 1852 and, because of the split between Republicans and Know-Nothings, triumphed in 1856 as well. However, a new regional-based party system had taken shape by 1860 and would persist for the next seventy years—with Democrats dominant in the South and Republicans usually controlling the Northeast, Midwest, and Far West.

of the states." The fate of the republic hinged on President Buchanan's ability to quiet the passions of the past decade and to hold the Democratic Party — the only national party — together.

### Dred Scott: Petitioner for Freedom

Events — and his own values and weaknesses — conspired against Buchanan. In 1856, the Supreme Court decided the case of *Dred Scott v. Sandford*, which raised the controversial issue of Congress's constitutional authority over slavery in the territories. Dred Scott was an enslaved African American who had lived for a time with his owner, an army surgeon, in the free state of Illinois and in the Wisconsin Territory, where the Northwest Ordinance (1787) prohibited slavery. Scott claimed that residence in a free state and a free territory had made him free. Buchanan wanted the Court to reject Scott's appeal and pressured the two justices from Pennsylvania to side with their southern colleagues. Seven of the nine justices issued opinions declaring that Scott was still a slave. But they disagreed on the legal rationale, so the case did not create a binding principle of constitutional law.

Chief Justice Roger B. Taney of Maryland, a slave owner himself, wrote the most influential opinion. He declared that Negroes, whether enslaved or free, could not be citizens of the United States and that Scott therefore had no right to sue in federal court. That argument was controversial, given that free blacks were citizens in many states and therefore had access to the federal courts. But Taney then made two even more controversial claims. First, he endorsed John C. Calhoun's argument that the Fifth Amendment, which prohibited "taking" of property without due process of law, meant that Congress could not prevent southern citizens from carrying their slave property into the territories and owning it there. Consequently, the chief justice concluded, the provisions of the Northwest Ordinance and the Missouri Compromise that prohibited slavery had never been constitutional. Second, Taney declared that Congress could not give to territorial governments any powers that it did not possess, which meant that settlers in a territory could not enact legislation prohibiting slavery. Taney thereby endorsed Calhoun's interpretation of popular sovereignty: Only when settlers wrote a constitution and requested statehood could they prohibit slavery.

In a single stroke, Taney had declared the Republicans' stance against the expansion of slavery to be unconstitutional. The Republicans could never accept the legitimacy of Taney's arguments. Led by Senator Seward of New York, they accused the chief justice and

President Buchanan of participating in the Slave Power conspiracy.

Buchanan then added fuel to the raging constitutional fire. Ignoring reports that antislavery residents held a clear majority in Kansas, he refused to allow a popular vote on the proslavery Lecompton constitution and recommended the admission of Kansas as a slave state. Angered by Buchanan's machinations, Stephen Douglas, the most influential Democratic senator and architect of the Kansas-Nebraska Act, broke with the president and persuaded Congress to deny statehood to Kansas. (Kansas would enter the Union as a free state in 1861.) Still determined to aid the South, Buchanan informed Congress in December 1858 that he was resuming negotiations to buy Cuba. By pursuing a proslavery agenda — first in *Dred Scott* and then in Kansas and Cuba — Buchanan widened the split in his party and the nation.

- **Why did the Compromise of 1850 fail? Would it have succeeded if the Kansas-Nebraska Act of 1854 either had not been enacted or had contained different provisions?**

- **What were the main constitutional arguments advanced during the debate over slavery in the territories? Which of those arguments influenced Chief Justice Taney's opinion in *Dred Scott*?**

# Abraham Lincoln and the Republican Triumph, 1858–1860

As the Democratic Party split along sectional lines, the Republicans gained support in the North and Midwest. Abraham Lincoln of Illinois emerged as the only Republican leader whose policies and temperament might have saved the Union. But few southerners trusted Lincoln, and his presidential candidacy revived secessionist agitation.

## Lincoln's Political Career

The middle-class world of storekeepers, lawyers, and entrepreneurs in the small towns of the Ohio River Valley shaped Lincoln's early career. He came from a hardscrabble yeoman farm family that was continually on the move — from Kentucky, where Lincoln was born in 1809, to Indiana, and then to Illinois. In 1831, Lincoln rejected his father's life as a subsistence farmer and be-

**Abraham Lincoln, 1859**

Lincoln was not a handsome man, and he photographed poorly. His campaign photographs were often retouched to hide his prominent cheekbones and nose. More important, no photograph ever captured Lincoln's complex personality and wit or the intensity of his spirit and intellect. To grasp Lincoln, it is necessary to read his words.   Chicago Historical Society.

Proviso. Lincoln believed that human bondage was unjust but doubted that the federal government had the constitutional authority to tamper with slavery in the South. With respect to the Mexican War, he took a middle ground. Lincoln voted for military appropriations, but he also supported Wilmot's proposal to prohibit slavery in any acquired territories. And he introduced legislation that would require the gradual (and thus compensated) emancipation of slaves in the District of Columbia. Lincoln advocated firm opposition to the expansion of slavery, gradual emancipation, and, to resolve the issue of racial diversity, the colonization of freed blacks in Africa. Both abolitionists and proslavery activists heaped scorn on Lincoln's middle-of-the-road policies, and he lost his bid for reelection. Dismayed by the rancor of ideological debate, he withdrew from politics and prospered as a lawyer representing railroads and manufacturers.

Lincoln returned to the political fray because of the Kansas-Nebraska Act. Shocked by the act's repeal of the Missouri Compromise and Douglas's advocacy of popular sovereignty, Lincoln reaffirmed his position that slavery should be excluded from the territories. Beyond that, he likened slavery to a cancer that had to be cut out if the nation's republican ideals and moral principles were to endure.

**The Lincoln-Douglas Debates** | Abandoning the Whigs, Lincoln quickly emerged as the Republican leader in Illinois. Campaigning for the U.S. Senate against Douglas in 1858, Lincoln explained that the proslavery Supreme Court might soon declare that the Constitution "does not permit a state to exclude slavery from its limits," just as it had decided in *Dred Scott* that "neither Congress nor the territorial legislature" could ban slavery in a territory. In that event, he warned, "we shall awake to the reality . . . that the Supreme Court has made Illinois a slave state." The prospect of slavery spreading into the North informed Lincoln's famous "House Divided" speech. Quoting from the Bible, "A house divided against itself cannot stand," he predicted that American society "cannot endure permanently half slave and half free. . . . It will become all one thing, or all the other."

The Senate race in Illinois attracted national interest because of Douglas's prominence and Lincoln's reputation as a formidable speaker. During a series of seven debates, Douglas declared his support for white supremacy: "This government was made by our fathers, by white men for the benefit of white men," he said, and attacked Lincoln for supporting "negro equality." Lincoln parried Douglas's racist attacks by advocating

came a store clerk in New Salem, Illinois. Socially ambitious, Lincoln sought entry into the middle class by mastering its culture; he joined the New Salem Debating Society, read Shakespeare, and studied law.

Admitted to the bar in 1837, Lincoln moved to Springfield, the new state capital. There, he met Mary Todd, the cultured daughter of a Kentucky banker; they married in 1842. Her tastes were aristocratic; his were humble. She was volatile; he was easygoing, but suffered bouts of depression that tried her patience and tested his character.

**An Ambitious Politician** | Lincoln's ambition was "a little engine that knew no rest," his closest associate remarked, and it propelled him into politics. An admirer of Henry Clay, Lincoln joined the Whig Party and won election to four terms in the Illinois legislature, where he promoted education, banks, canals, and railroads. He became a dexterous party politician, adept in the distribution of patronage and the passage of legislation.

In 1846, the rising lawyer-politician won election to a Congress that was bitterly divided over the Wilmot economic opportunity for free blacks but not equal political rights. Taking the offensive, he asked how Douglas could accept the *Dred Scott* decision (which protected slave owners' property in the territories) yet advocate popular sovereignty (which asserted the settlers' power to exclude slavery). Douglas responded with the so-called Freeport Doctrine: that a territory's residents could exclude slavery by not adopting laws to protect it. That position pleased neither proslavery nor antislavery advocates. Nonetheless, the Democrats won a narrow majority in the state legislature, which reelected Douglas to the U.S. Senate.

## The Union under Siege

The debates with Douglas gave Lincoln a national reputation, and in the election of 1858 the Republican Party won control of the U.S. House of Representatives.

**The Rise of Radicalism** | Shaken by the Republicans' advance, southern Democrats divided again into moderates and fire-eaters. The moderates, who included Senator Jefferson Davis of Mississippi, strongly defended "southern rights"; they demanded ironclad political or constitutional protections for slavery. The fire-eaters—men such as Robert Barnwell Rhett of South Carolina and William Lowndes Yancey of Alabama—repudiated the Union and actively promoted secession. Radical antislavery northerners likewise took a strong stance. Senator Seward of New York declared that freedom and slavery were locked in "an irrepressible conflict," and militant abolitionist John Brown, who had perpetrated the Pottawatomie massacre, showed what that might mean. In October 1859, Brown led eighteen heavily armed black and white men in a raid on the federal arsenal at Harpers Ferry, Virginia. Brown hoped to arm slaves with the arsenal's weapons and mount a major rebellion that would end slavery.

Republican leaders condemned Brown's unsuccessful raid, but Democrats called his plot "a natural, logical, inevitable result of the doctrines and teachings of the Republican party." When the state of Virginia charged Brown with treason and sentenced him to be hanged, transcendentalist reformers Henry David Thoreau and Ralph Waldo Emerson defended him as "an angel of light" and a "saint awaiting his martyrdom." The slaveholding states looked to the future with terror. "The aim of the present black republican organization is the destruction of the social system of the Southern States, without regard to consequences," warned one newspaper. Once Republicans came to power, another cau-

tioned, they "would create insurrection and servile war in the South—they would put the torch to our dwellings and the knife to our throats."

Nor could the South count on the Democratic Party to protect its interests. At the party's convention in April 1860, northern Democrats rejected Jefferson Davis's proposal to protect slavery in the territories, prompting the delegates from eight southern states to quit the meeting. At a second Democratic convention in Baltimore, northern and midwestern delegates nominated Stephen Douglas for president; meeting separately, southern Democrats nominated the sitting vice president, John C. Breckinridge of Kentucky.

**The Election of 1860** | With the Democrats divided, the Republicans sensed victory. They courted white voters with a free-soil platform that opposed both slavery and racial equality: "Missouri for white men and white men for Missouri," declared that state's Republican platform. The national Republican convention chose Lincoln as its presidential candidate because his position on slavery was more moderate than the abolitionist stance taken by the best-known Republicans, Senators William Seward of New York and Salmon Chase of Ohio. Lincoln also conveyed a compelling egalitarian image that appealed to small-holding farmers, wage earners, and Midwestern voters.

The Republican strategy worked. Although Lincoln received only 40 percent of the popular vote, he won every northern and western state except New Jersey, giving him 180 (of 303) electoral votes and an absolute majority in the electoral college. Breckinridge took 72 electoral votes by sweeping the Deep South and picking up Delaware, Maryland, and North Carolina. Douglas won 30 percent of the popular ballot but secured electoral votes only in Missouri and New Jersey. The Republicans had united voters in the Northeast, Midwest, and Pacific Coast behind free soil.

A revolution was in the making. Slavery had permeated the American federal republic so thoroughly that southerners saw it as a natural part of the constitutional order—an order that was now under siege. Fearful of a massive black uprising, Chief Justice Taney recalled "the horrors of St. Domingo [Haiti]." At the very least, warned John Townsend of South Carolina, a Republican administration in Washington would suppress "the inter-State slave trade" and thereby "*cripple this vital Southern institution* of slavery." To many southerners, it seemed time to think carefully about Lincoln's 1858 statement that the Union must "become all one thing, or all the other."

THE NATIONAL GAME. THREE "OUTS" AND ONE "RUN".
ABRAHAM WINNING THE BALL.

**Lincoln on Home Base**

As early as 1860, the language and imagery of sports had penetrated politics. Sporting a long, rail-like bat labeled "EQUAL RIGHTS AND FREE TERRITORY," Abraham Lincoln appears ready to score a victory in the election. His three opponents—from left to right, John Bell (the candidate of a new Constitutional Union party), Stephen A. Douglas, and John C. Breckinridge—will soon be "out." Indeed, according to the pro-Lincoln cartoonist, they were about to be "skunk'd." As Douglas laments, their attempt to put a "short stop" to Lincoln's presidential ambitions had failed. Museum of American Political Life.

- • What was Lincoln's position on slavery during the 1850s? Did it differ from that of Stephen Douglas? Explain your answer.

- • What was the relationship between the collapse of the Second Party System of Whigs and Democrats and the Republican victory in the election of 1860?

## SUMMARY

In this chapter, we examined four related themes: the ideology of Manifest Destiny and the westward movement of Americans in the 1840s, the impact of Ameri-

can traders and settlers on the Great Plains and California Indians, the causes and consequences of the Mexican War (1846–1848), and the disintegration of the Second Party System during the 1850s.

We saw that the determination of Presidents John Tyler and James Polk to add territory and slave states to the Union pushed the United States into the Mexican War and into a new debate over the expansion of slavery. To resolve the resulting crisis, Henry Clay, Daniel Webster, and Stephen Douglas devised the Compromise of 1850. Their efforts were in vain: Anti-slavery northerners defied the Fugitive Slave Act, and expansionist-minded southerners sought new slave states in the Caribbean. *Ideology* (the pursuit of absolutes) replaced *politics* (the art of compromise) as the ruling principle of American political life.

The Second Party System rapidly disintegrated. The Whig Party vanished, and two issue-oriented parties, the nativist American Party and the antislavery Republican Party, competed for its members. As the Republicans gained strength, the Democratic Party splintered into sectional factions over Bleeding Kansas and other slavery-related issues. The stage was set for Lincoln's victory in the climactic election of 1860.

## CHAPTER REVIEW QUESTIONS

● What were the links between the Mexican War of 1846–1848 and Abraham Lincoln's election as president in 1860?

● When and why did the Second Party System of Whigs and Democrats collapse?

● Some historians claim that the mistakes of a "blundering generation" of political leaders led, by 1860, to the imminent breakup of the Union. Do you agree with their assessment? Why or why not?

## FOR FURTHER EXPLORATION

Patricia Nelson Limerick, *The Legacy of Conquest* (1989), highlights social conflicts in the West. See also the PBS documentary *The West* (6 hours) and its Web site (**www.pbs.org/weta/thewest**). For "California as I Saw It," a resource of first-person narratives of California settlers, go to **memory.loc.gov/ammem/cbhtml/cbhome.html**. On early Texas history, see **www.tsl.state.tx.us/treasures**. The PBS documentary *U.S.-Mexican War: 1846–1848* (4 hours) and its Web site (**www.pbs.org/usmexicanwar**) cover both American and Mexican perspectives.

David Potter, *The Impending Crisis, 1848–1861* (1976), covers the political history of the 1850s. John Patrick Daly, *When Slavery Was Called Freedom: Evangelicalism, Proslavery, and the Causes of the Civil War* (2002), and Leonard L. Richards, *The Slave Power: The Free North and Southern Domination, 1780–1860* (2000), offer broad cultural analyses. For good state-focused studies of Virginia and South Carolina, read William A. Link, *Roots of Secession* (2003), and Manisha Sinha, *The Counterrevolution of Slavery* (200 0).

Eric Foner, *Free Soil, Free Labor, Free Men* (1970), covers the ideology of the Republican Party, while Michael Holt's *The Political Crisis of the 1850s* (1978) traces the collapse of the Second Party System. For Lincoln, read Stephen Oates, *With Malice Toward None* (1977). The court's decision in the *Dred Scott* case, as well as links to the justices' concurring and dissenting opinions, can be found at **www.tourolaw.edu/patch/scott**. "*Uncle Tom's Cabin* and American Culture" (**utc.iath.virginia.edu**) places the novel in its literary and cultural context.

## TEST YOUR KNOWLEDGE

To assess your command of the material in this chapter, see the Online Study Guide at **bedfordstmartins.com/henretta**.

For Web sites, images, and documents related to topics and places in this chapter, visit **bedfordstmartins.com/makehistory**.

## TIMELINE

| | |
|---|---|
| **1844** | James Polk elected president |
| **1845** | Texas admitted into Union |
| **1846** | United States declares war on Mexico<br>Treaty with Britain divides Oregon Country<br>Wilmot Proviso approved by House but not by Senate |
| **1847** | American troops capture Mexico City |
| **1848** | Gold found in California<br>Treaty of Guadalupe Hidalgo gives Mexican provinces of California, New Mexico, and Texas to United States<br>Free-Soil Party forms<br>Zachary Taylor elected president |
| **1850** | President Taylor dies; Millard Fillmore assumes presidency<br>Compromise of 1850 preserves Union<br>Northern abolitionists reject Fugitive Slave Act<br>South seeks to acquire Spanish Cuba to expand slavery |
| **1851** | American (Know-Nothing) Party forms |
| **1852** | Harriet Beecher Stowe publishes *Uncle Tom's Cabin* |
| **1854** | Ostend Manifesto urges seizure of Cuba<br>Kansas-Nebraska Act tests policy of popular sovereignty<br>Republican Party forms |
| **1856** | Turmoil in Kansas undermines popular sovereignty<br>James Buchanan elected president |
| **1857** | *Dred Scott v. Sandford* allows slavery in U.S. territories |
| **1858** | President Buchanan backs Lecompton constitution<br>Abraham Lincoln and Stephen Douglas debate in U.S. Senate race |
| **1859** | John Brown raids federal arsenal at Harpers Ferry |
| **1860** | Abraham Lincoln elected president in four-way contest |

# Two Societies at War, 1861–1865

**"What a scene** it was," Union soldier Elisha Hunt Rhodes wrote in his diary at Gettysburg in July 1863. "Oh the dead and the dying on this bloody field." Thousands of men had already died and the slaughter would continue for almost two more years. "What is this all about?" asked Confederate lieutenant R. M. Collins as another gruesome battle ended. "Why is it that 200,000 men of one blood and tongue . . . [are] seeking one another's lives? We could settle our differences by compromising and all be at home in ten days." But, almost inexplicably, there was no compromise. "God wills this contest, and wills that it shall not yet end," President Abraham Lincoln reflected in 1862. Even on the eve of victory in 1865, Lincoln felt the nation in the grip forces beyond human control: "The Almighty has His own purposes."

To explain why southerners seceded and fought to the bitter end is not simple, but racial slavery is an important part of the answer. To southern whites, the Republican victory in 1860 presented an immediate danger to the slave-owning republic that had existed since 1776. Lincoln won not a single electoral vote in the South, and many Republicans vowed to limit (and perhaps even end) the slave system. "We are resisting revolution," leading southerners protested. "[O]ur struggle is for inherited rights." Southerners did not believe Lincoln when he promised not "directly or indirectly, to interfere with the institution of slavery in the States where it exists." To the contrary, a southern newspaper declared: "The mission of the Republican party was to meddle with everything – to meddle with the domestic institutions of other States, and to meddle with family arrangements in their own states – to overthrow Democracy, Catholicism and Slavery." Soon, a southern senator warned, "cohorts of Federal office-holders, Abolitionists, may be sent into [our] midst" to mobilize enslaved blacks. Remembering John Brown's raid, southerners were terrified that federal officials would encourage bloody slave revolts and racial mixture. By *racial mixture*, white southerners meant sexual relations between black men and white women, given that white owners had already fathered untold thousands of children by their enslaved black women. "Better, far better! [to] endure all horrors of civil war," insisted a Confederate recruit from Virginia, "than to see the dusky sons of Ham leading the fair daughters of the South to the altar." To preserve the subordination of blacks and the supremacy of white men, radical southerners chose the dangerous enterprise of secession.

Lincoln and the North would not let them go in peace. Living in a world still ruled by kings and princes, northern leaders believed that the collapse of

**Fields of Death**

Fought with mass armies and new weapons, the Civil War took a huge toll in human lives, as evidenced by this grisly photograph of a small section of the battlefield at Antietam, Maryland. At Shiloh, Tennessee, General Ulysses Grant surveyed a field "so covered with dead that it would have been possible to walk . . . in any direction, stepping on dead bodies, without a foot touching the ground." Library of Congress.

the American Union might destroy for all time the possibility of a democratic republican government. "We cannot escape history," the new president eloquently declared. "We shall nobly save, or meanly lose, the last best hope of earth." A young Union army recruit from Ohio put the issue simply: "If our institutions prove a failure . . . of what value will be house, family, or friends?"

And so came the Civil War. Called the War Between the States by southerners and the War of the Rebellion by northerners, the struggle continued until the great issues of the Union and slavery had finally been resolved. The cost was incredibly high: more American lives lost than the combined total for all the nation's other wars, and a century-long legacy of bitterness between the triumphant North and the vanquished white South.

# Secession and Military Stalemate, 1861–1862

Following Lincoln's election in November 1860, secessionist fervor swept through the Deep South. But veteran party leaders in Washington still hoped to save the Union. In the four months between Lincoln's election and his inauguration on March 4, 1861, they sought a new compromise.

## The Secession Crisis

The Union collapsed first in South Carolina, the home of John C. Calhoun, nullification, and southern rights. Robert Barnwell Rhett and other fire-eaters had demanded secession since the Compromise of 1850, and their goal was now within reach. "Our enemies are about to take possession of the Government," warned one South Carolinian, predicting that those "enemies" would act like a "conqueror." Frightened by that prospect, a special state convention voted unanimously on December 20, 1860, to dissolve "the union now subsisting between South Carolina and other States."

**The Lower South Secedes** | Fire-eaters elsewhere in the Deep South quickly called similar conventions and organized mobs to attack local Union supporters. In early January, white Mississippians joyously enacted a secession ordinance. Within a month, Florida, Alabama, Georgia, Louisiana, and Texas had also left the Union (Map 14.1). In February, the jubilant secessionists met in Montgomery, Alabama, to proclaim a new nation: the Confederate States of America. Adopting a provisional constitution, the delegates named Mississippian Jefferson Davis, a former

U.S. senator and secretary of war, as the Confederacy's president and Georgia congressman Alexander Stephens as vice president.

Secessionist fervor was less intense in the four states of the Middle South (Virginia, North Carolina, Tennessee, and Arkansas), where there were fewer slaves. White opinion was especially divided in the four border slave states (Maryland, Delaware, Kentucky, and Missouri), where yeomen farmers held greater political power. During the 1850s, journalist Hinton Helper of North Carolina had warned yeomen that "the slaveholders . . . have hoodwinked you." Influenced partly by such sentiments, the legislatures of Virginia and Tennessee refused to join the secessionist movement and urged a compromise.

Meanwhile, the Union government floundered. The president declared secession illegal but—in line with his pro-South, states' rights outlook—claimed that the federal government lacked authority to restore the Union by force. Buchanan's timidity prompted South Carolina's new government to demand the surrender of Fort Sumter (a federal garrison in Charleston Harbor) and to cut off its supplies. The president again backed down, refusing to order the navy to escort a supply ship into the harbor.

**The Crittenden Compromise** | Instead, the outgoing president urged Congress to find a compromise. The plan proposed by Senator John J. Crittenden of Kentucky received the most support. Crittenden's plan had two parts. The first, which Congress approved, called for a constitutional amendment to protect slavery from federal interference in any state where it already existed. Crittenden's second provision called for the westward extension of the Missouri Compromise line (36°30' north latitude) to the Califor-

**Agitating for Secession**

Lincoln's election triggered a vigorous response from South Carolina's fire-eaters, who called a secession rally in Charleston. On December 1, 1860, hundreds of well-dressed planters and merchants met at the Mills Hotel to hear prominent secessionists demand withdrawal from the Union. Three weeks later, in a unanimous vote, a special state convention did just that. Library of Congress.

nia border. Slavery would be barred north of the line and protected to the south, including any territories "hereafter acquired," thus raising the prospect of expansion into Cuba or Central America. Congressional Republicans rejected Crittenden's second proposal on strict instructions from Lincoln, the president-elect. With good reason, Lincoln feared that it would prompt new imperialist adventures. "I want Cuba," Senator Albert G. Brown of Mississippi had candidly stated in 1858. "I want Tamaulipas, Potosi, and one or two other Mexican States . . . for the planting or spreading of slav-

ery." In 1787, 1821, and 1850, the North and South had resolved their differences over slavery. In 1861, there would be no compromise.

In his March 1861 inaugural address, Lincoln carefully outlined his views on slavery and the Union. He promised to safeguard slavery where it existed but vowed to prevent its expansion. Beyond that, Lincoln declared that the Union was "perpetual"; consequently, the secession of the Confederate states was illegal. The Republican president declared his intention to "hold, occupy, and possess" federal property in the seceded states and

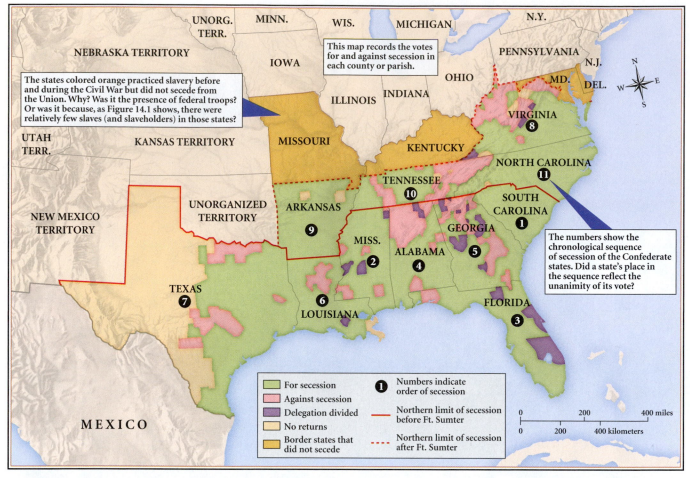

**MAP 14.1**

**The Process of Secession, 1860–1861**

The states of the Lower South had the highest concentration of slaves, and they led the secessionist movement. After the attack on Fort Sumter in April 1861, the states of the Upper South joined the Confederacy. Yeomen farmers in Tennessee and the backcountry of Alabama, Georgia, and Virginia opposed secession but, except in the future state of West Virginia, initially rallied to the Confederate cause. Consequently, the South entered the Civil War with its white population relatively united.

"to collect duties and imposts" there. If military force was necessary to preserve the Union, Lincoln—like Andrew Jackson during the nullification crisis—would use it. The choice was the South's: Return to the Union, or face war.

## The Upper South Chooses Sides

The South's decision came quickly. When Lincoln dispatched an unarmed ship to resupply Fort Sumter, Jefferson Davis and his associates in the Provisional Government of the Confederate States decided to seize the fort. The Confederate forces opened fire on April 12, with ardent fire-eater Edmund Ruffin supposedly fir-

ing the first cannon. Two days later, the Union defenders capitulated. On April 15, Lincoln called 75,000 state militiamen into federal service for ninety days to put down an insurrection "too powerful to be suppressed by the ordinary course of judicial proceedings."

Northerners responded to Lincoln's call to arms with wild enthusiasm. Asked to provide thirteen regiments of volunteers, Republican governor William Dennison of Ohio sent twenty. Many northern Democrats also lent their support. "Every man must be for the United States or against it," Democratic leader Stephen Douglas declared. "There can be no neutrals in this war, only patriots—or traitors." How then might the Democratic Party function as a "loyal opposition," supporting the Union while challenging certain Republican policies? It would not be an easy task.

Whites in the Middle and Border South now had to choose between the Union and the Confederacy, and their decision was crucial. Those eight states accounted for two-thirds of the whites in the slaveholding states, three-fourths of their industrial production, and well over half of their food. They were home to many of the nation's best military leaders, including Colonel Robert E. Lee of Virginia, a career officer whom veteran General Winfield Scott recommended to Lincoln to lead the new Union army. Those states were also geographically strategic. Kentucky, with its 500-mile border on the Ohio River, was essential to the movement of troops and supplies. Maryland was vital to the Union's security because it bordered the nation's capital on three sides.

The weight of its history as a slave-owning colony and state decided the outcome in Virginia. A convention approved secession by a vote of 88 to 55, with dissenters coming mainly from the state's yeomen-dominated northwestern counties. Elsewhere, Virginia whites embraced the Confederate cause. "The North was the aggressor," declared Richmond lawyer William Poague as he enlisted. "The South resisted her invaders." Refusing Scott's offer of the Union command, Robert E. Lee resigned from the U.S. Army. "Save in defense of my native state," Lee told Scott, "I never desire again to draw my sword." Arkansas, Tennessee, and North Carolina quickly joined Virginia in the Confederacy.

Lincoln moved aggressively to hold strategic areas where relatively few whites owned slaves (see Figure 14.1). To secure the railway line connecting Washington to the Ohio River Valley, the president ordered General George B. McClellan to take control of northwestern Virginia. "I am armed like a desperado," wrote a Unionist there. "Friends have become enemies to one another." In October 1861, the yeoman-dominated electorate voted overwhelmingly to set up a separate breakaway territory, West Virginia, which was admitted to the Union in 1863. Unionists also carried the day in Delaware. In Maryland, where slavery was still entrenched, a pro-Confederate mob attacked Massachusetts troops traveling through Baltimore, causing the war's first combat deaths: four soldiers and twelve civilians. When Maryland secessionists destroyed railroad bridges and telegraph lines, Lincoln ordered Union troops to occupy the state and arrest Confederate sympathizers, including legislators. He released them only in November 1861, after Unionists had secured control of Maryland's government.

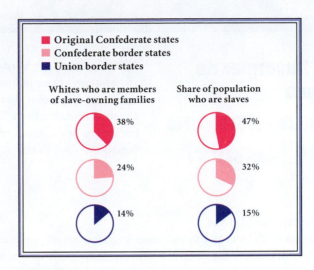

**FIGURE 14.1**

**Slavery and Secession**

As these graphs indicate, the Confederate states that initially seceded from the Union were heavily invested in slavery. Nearly 40 percent of whites in those Deep South states were members of families that owned slaves, who numbered nearly half that region's population. By contrast, only 14 percent of the whites owned slaves in the pro-Union border states, such as Missouri and Maryland, where enslaved people formed only 15 percent of the population.

Lincoln was equally energetic in the Mississippi River Valley. To win control of Missouri (along with the Missouri River and the Upper Mississippi River), Lincoln mobilized the state's German American militia, which strongly opposed slavery; in July, the German Americans defeated a force of Confederate sympathizers commanded by the state's governor. Despite continuing raids by Confederate guerrilla bands, which included the notorious outlaws Jesse and Frank James, the Union retained control of Missouri (see Voices from Abroad, "Ernest Duvergier de Hauranne: Germans and the War in Missouri," p. 434). In Kentucky, secessionist and Unionist sentiment was evenly balanced, so Lincoln moved cautiously. He allowed Kentucky's thriving trade with the Confederacy to continue until Unionists took over the state government in August 1861. When the Confederacy responded to the cutoff of trade by invading Kentucky in September, Illinois volunteers commanded by Ulysses S. Grant drove them out. Mixing military force with political persuasion, Lincoln had kept four border states (Delaware, Maryland, Missouri, and Kentucky) and the northwestern portion of Virginia in the Union.

All the nations and people I had hitherto passed through resembled
own in their manners, customs and lang

## Ernest Duvergier de Hauranne
## Germans and the War in Missouri

Tens of thousands of German immigrants settled in Missouri and other mid-western states in the two decades before the Civil War. As this letter written by Ernest Duvergier de Hauranne indicates, most of them supported the Union cause. A French citizen, Duvergier de Hauranne (1843–1877) traveled widely, and his letters home offer intelligent commentary on American politics and society during the Civil War.

St. Louis, September 12, 1864

Missouri is to all intents and purposes a rebel state, an occupied territory where the Federal forces are really nothing but a garrison under siege; even today it is not certain what would happen if the troops were withdrawn. Party quarrels here are poisoned by class hatreds. Not only are questions of peace and war, of national honor and humiliation, hotly debated, but so is the much more explosive question of slavery versus abolition. . . . It is a war over private interests between two irreconcilable classes. The old Anglo-French families, attached to Southern institutions, harbor a primitive, superstitious prejudice in favor of slavery. Conquered now, but full of repressed rage, they exhibit the implacable anger peculiar to the defenders of lost causes. They no longer have any hope of reviving slavery or their own past fortunes; . . . they seem to be lying low while hoping for an opportunity to take their revenge.

The more recent German population is strongly abolitionist. They have brought to the New World the instincts of European democracy, together with its radical attitudes and all-or-nothing doctrines. Ancient precedents and worn-out laws matter little to them. They have not studied history and have no respect for hallowed injustices; but they do have, to the highest degree, that sense of moral principle which is more or less lacking in American democracy. They aren't afraid of revolution: to destroy a barbarous institution they would, if necessary, take an axe to the foundations of society. Furthermore, their interests coincide with their principles. . . . Even if their democratic beliefs and innate sense of justice did not cause them to rise up against slavery, they would still detest it as an obstacle to their prosperity and as a source of unfair competition with their labor.

The immigrant arrives poor and lives by his work. A newcomer, having nothing to lose and caring little for the interests of established property owners, sees that the subjection of free labor to the ruinous competition of slave labor must be ended. At the same time, his pride rebels against the prejudice attached to work in a land of slavery; he wants to reestablish its value. . . .

There is no mistaking the hatred the two parties, not to say the two peoples, have for each other. . . .

As passions were coming to a boil, the Federal government sent General [John C.] Frémont here as army commander and dictator. . . . An abolitionist and a self-made man, he put himself firmly at the head of the German party, determined to crush the friends of slavery. He formed an army of Germans. . . . He left the abolitionist party in the West organized, disciplined, stronger and more resolute, but he also left the pro-Southern party more exasperated than ever, and society divided, without intermediaries, into two hostile camps. . . .

Everyone is an extremist; between the radical abolitionists and the friends of the South there is no moderate Unionist middle ground. Bands of guerrillas hold the countryside, where they raid as much as they please; politics serves as a fine pretext for looting. Their leaders are officers from the army of the South who receive their orders from the Confederate government. . . . These "bushwackers," who ordinarily rob indiscriminately, maintain their standing as political raiders by occasionally killing some poor, inoffensive person. Finally, people bent on personal vengeance take advantage of the state of civil war: sometimes one hears of villages divided against themselves so bitterly that massacres are carried on from door to door with incredible ferocity. . . . You can see what emotions are still boiling in this region that is supposed to be pacified.

Source: Ernest Duvergier de Hauranne, *A Frenchman in Lincoln's America* (Chicago: Lakeside Press, 1974), 1: 305–309.

### ANALYZING THE EVIDENCE

- According to Duvergier de Hauranne, why did German immigrants oppose slavery? How does his explanation provide insight into the free-soil movement?

- Why, even in 1864, did the federal government lack control over Missouri, a border state that remained in the Union? What clues does Duvergier de Hauranne provide?

- Ethnic rivalries loomed large in the civil warfare in Missouri. As you read the chapter, look for other ethnic conflicts that exploded during the war. Why did they do so?

## Setting War Objectives and Devising Strategies

Speaking as provisional president of the Confederacy in April 1861, Jefferson Davis identified the Confederates' cause with that of the Patriots of 1776: Like their grandfathers, he said, white southerners were fighting for the "sacred right of self-government." The Confederacy sought "no conquest, no aggrandizement . . . ; all we ask is to be let alone." Davis's renunciation of expansion was probably a calculated short-run policy; after all, the slave owners' quest to extend slavery had sparked Lincoln's election and southern secession. Still, this decision simplified the Confederacy's military strategy; it needed only to defend its boundaries to achieve independence. Ignoring strong antislavery sentiment among potential European allies, the Confederate constitution explicitly ruled out gradual emancipation or any other law "denying or impairing the right of property in negro slaves." Indeed, Confederate vice president Alexander Stephens insisted that his nation's "cornerstone rests upon the great truth that the Negro is not equal to the white man, that slavery—subordination to the superior race—is his natural or normal condition."

Lincoln responded to Davis in a speech to Congress on July 4, 1861. He portrayed secession as an attack on popular government, America's great contribution to world history. The issue, Lincoln declared, was "whether a constitutional republic" had the will and the means to "maintain its territorial integrity against a domestic foe." Determined to crush the rebellion, Lincoln rejected General Winfield Scott's strategy of peaceful persuasion through economic sanctions and a naval blockade. Instead, the president insisted on an aggressive military campaign to restore the Union.

**Union Thrusts Toward Richmond** Lincoln hoped that a quick strike against the Confederate capital of Richmond, Virginia, would end the rebellion. Many northerners were equally optimistic. "What a picnic," thought one New York volunteer, "to go down South for three months and clean up the whole business." So in July 1861, Lincoln ordered General Irvin McDowell and an army of 30,000 men to attack General P. G. T. Beauregard's force of 20,000 troops at Manassas, a Virginia rail junction 30 miles southwest of Washington. McDowell launched a strong assault near Manassas Creek (also called Bull Run), but panic swept his troops when the Confederate soldiers counterattacked, shouting the hair-raising "rebel yell." "The peculiar corkscrew sensation that it sends down your backbone under these circumstances can never be told," one Union veteran wrote. "You have to feel it." McDowell's troops—along with the many civilians who had come to observe the battle—retreated in disarray to Washington.

The rout at Bull Run made it clear that the rebellion would not be easily crushed. Lincoln replaced McDowell with General George McClellan and enlisted an additional million men to serve for three years in the newly created Army of the Potomac. A cautious military engineer, McClellan spent the winter of 1861 training the recruits; then, early in 1862, he launched a major offensive. With great logistical skill, the Union general transported 100,000 troops by boat down the Potomac River to the Chesapeake Bay and landed them on the peninsula between the York and James rivers (Map 14.2). Ignoring Lincoln's advice to "strike a blow," McClellan advanced slowly toward the South's capital, allowing the Confederates to mount a counterstrike. To relieve the pressure on Richmond, a Confederate army under Thomas J. "Stonewall" Jackson marched rapidly northward through the Shenandoah Valley in western Virginia and threatened Washington. Lincoln recalled 30,000 troops from McClellan's army to protect the Union capital, and Jackson returned quickly to Richmond to bolster the main Confederate army commanded by General Robert E. Lee. Lee launched a ferocious attack that lasted from June 25 to July 1 and cost the Confederates 20,000 casualties to the Union's 10,000. When McClellan failed to exploit the Confederates' losses, Lincoln ordered a withdrawal and Richmond remained secure.

**Lee Moves North: Antietam** Hoping for victories that would humiliate Lincoln's government, Lee went on the offensive. Joining with Jackson in northern Virginia, he routed Union troops in the Second Battle of Bull Run (August 1862) and then struck north through western Maryland. There, he nearly met with disaster. When Lee divided his force, sending Jackson to capture Harpers Ferry in West Virginia, a copy of Lee's orders fell into McClellan's hands. But the Union general again failed to exploit his advantage, delaying his attack, and allowing Lee's depleted army to occupy a strong defensive position on the high ground west of Antietam Creek, near Sharpsburg, Maryland. Outnumbered 87,000 to 50,000, Lee desperately fought off McClellan's attacks until Jackson's troops arrived and saved the Confederates from a major defeat. Appalled by the Union casualties, McClellan allowed Lee to retreat to Virginia.

The fighting at Antietam was savage. A Wisconsin officer described his men "loading and firing with demoniacal fury and shouting and laughing hysterically."

In September 1862, Union forces halted the Confederate invasion of Maryland with victories at South Mountain and Antietam (11 and 12).

**11** *South Mountain Sept. 14, 1862*

**12** *Antietam Sept. 17, 1862*

Frederick

**MARYLAND**

Baltimore

Harpers Ferry

**WEST VIRGINIA (1863)**

**5** *Winchester May 25, 1862*

*Potomac R.*

*Shenandoah R.*

☆ **Washington, D.C.**

The only major battle of 1861–Bull Run–took place about 30 miles southwest of the Union's capital. It left both armies in disarray.

To relieve pressure on Richmond, Confederate troops under General Stonewall Jackson made a run up the Shenandoah Valley, threatening Washington (4, 5, and 7).

**1** *Bull Run July 21, 1861 Aug. 29–30, 1862*

**10**

*B L U E   R I D G E   M T S .*

**4** *McDowell May 8, 1862*

*Cross Keys June 8, 1862* **7**

**9** *Cedar Mt. Aug. 9, 1862*

**13** *Fredericksburg Dec. 13, 1862*

N W E S

At Fredericksburg (13) in December 1862, Confederate forces repulsed another Union thrust into the heart of Virginia.

0   20   40 miles
0   20   40 kilometers

The Peninsular Campaign (2 and 3; 6 and 8) began in May 1862 as an attempt by the Union armies to take Richmond by moving up the peninsula between the James and York Rivers.

*Rappahannock R.*

Assisted by Jackson's attacks, Lee repulsed the Union assault on Richmond and then advanced toward Washington. After another Confederate victory in the second battle of Bull Run (10) in August 1862, Lee's army moved into Maryland.

**6** *Fair Oaks May 31–June 1, 1862*

**VIRGINIA**

Richmond ☆

*York R.*

*Chesapeake Bay*

**8** *Seven Days June 25–July 1, 1862*

**Union Movements**

| | |
|---|---|
| ⟵ | McDowell |
| ⟵ --- | McClellan |
| ⟵ -·- | Frémont |
| ⟵ -··- | Banks |
| ⟵ -···- | Shields |
| ⟵ ooooo | Pope |
| ⟵ ••••• | Burnside |
| ✸ | Union victory |

**Confederate Movements**

| | |
|---|---|
| ⟵ ••••• | Johnston |
| ⟵ ooooo | Holmes |
| ⟵ --- | Jackson |
| ⟵ | Lee |
| ✺ | Confederate victory |
| +++++ | Railroad |
| ❶ | Sequence of battles |

To help you to follow the sequence of the major battles of the eastern campaigns of 1862, each battle is dated and its place in the chronology denoted by a number in a circle.

**3** *Williamsburg May 5, 1862*

*James R.*

**2** *Siege of Yorktown Apr. 5–May 4, 1862*

Ft. Monroe

**MAP 14.2**

**The Eastern Campaigns of 1862**

Many of the great battles of the Civil War took place in the 125 miles separating the Union capital, Washington, D.C., and the Confederate capital, Richmond, Virginia. During 1862, Confederate generals Thomas Jonathan "Stonewall" Jackson and Robert E. Lee won battles that defended the Confederate capital (3, 6, 8, and 13) and launched offensive strikes against Union forces guarding Washington (1, 4, 5, 7, 9, and 10). They also suffered a defeat—at Antietam (12), in Maryland—that was almost fatal. As was often the case in the Civil War, the victors in these battles were either too bloodied or too timid to exploit their advantage.

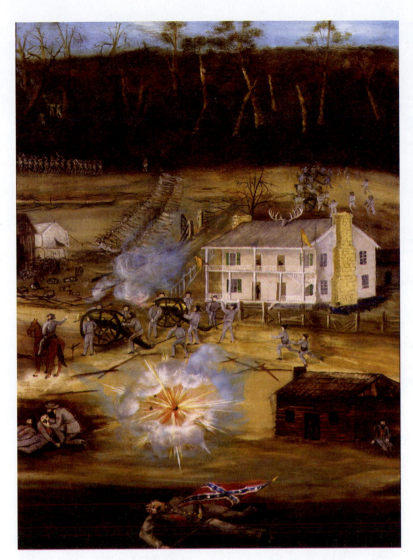

### The Battle of Pea Ridge, Arkansas, March 1862

Pea Ridge was the biggest battle of the Civil War fought west of the Mississippi and was of considerable strategic significance. By routing one Confederate army and holding another to a draw, outnumbered Union forces maintained their control of Missouri—just to the north of the battleground—for the duration of the war. The painting shows the main Confederate advance to the Elkhorn Tavern, a position its troops were not able to hold on the second day of the battle. Each side had about 1,000 men killed or wounded, with another 200 taken prisoner. Museum of the Confederacy, Richmond, Virginia.

A sunken road—nicknamed Bloody Lane—was filled with Confederate bodies two and three deep, and the advancing Union troops knelt on this "ghastly flooring" to shoot at the retreating Confederates. The battle at Antietam on September 17, 1862, remains the bloodiest single day in U.S. military history. Together, the Confederate and Union dead numbered 4,800 and the wounded 18,500, of whom 3,000 soon died. (By comparison, there were 6,000 American casualties on D-Day, which began the invasion of Nazi-occupied France in World War II.)

In public, Lincoln claimed Antietam as a Union victory; privately, he criticized McClellan for not fighting Lee to the bitter end. A masterful organizer of men and supplies, McClellan refused to risk his troops, fearing that heavy casualties would undermine public support for the war. Lincoln was more worried by the prospect of a lengthy war. He dismissed McClellan and began a long search for a more aggressive commanding general. His first choice, Ambrose E. Burnside, proved to be more daring but less competent than McClellan. In December, after heavy losses in futile attacks against well-entrenched Confederate forces at Fredericksburg, Virginia, Burnside resigned his command, and Lincoln replaced him with Joseph "Fighting Joe" Hooker. As 1862 ended, Confederates were optimistic: They had won a stalemate in the East.

**The War in the Mississippi Valley**  During the same months of 1862, Union commanders in the Midwest had been more successful (Map 14.3). Their goal was to control the Ohio, Mississippi, and Missouri rivers, dividing the Confederacy and reducing the mobility of its armies. Because Kentucky did not join the rebellion, the Union already dominated the Ohio River Valley. In February 1862, the

**MAP 14.3**

**The Western Campaigns, 1861–1862**

As the Civil War intensified in 1862, Union and Confederate military and naval forces sought control of the great valleys of the Ohio, Tennessee, and Mississippi rivers. From February through April 1862, Union armies moved south through western Tennessee (1–3 and 5). By the end of June, Union naval forces controlled the Mississippi River north of Memphis (4, 10, and 11) and from the Gulf of Mexico to Vicksburg (6, 7, 9, and 12). These military and naval victories gave the Union control of crucial transportation routes, kept Missouri in the Union, and carried the war to the borders of the states of the Lower South.

Union army used an innovative tactic to take charge of the Tennessee and Mississippi rivers as well. General Ulysses S. Grant used riverboats clad with iron plates to capture Fort Henry on the Tennessee River and Fort Donelson on the Cumberland River. When Grant moved south to seize critical railroad lines, Confederate troops led by Albert Sidney Johnston and P. G. T. Beauregard caught his army by surprise near a small log church named Shiloh. But Grant relentlessly committed troops until he forced a Confederate withdrawal. As the fighting at Shiloh ended on April 7, Grant surveyed a large field "so covered with dead that it would have been possible to walk over the clearing in any direction, stepping on dead bodies, without a foot touching the ground." The cost in lives was horrific, but Lincoln was resolute: "What I want . . . is generals who will fight battles and win victories."

Three weeks later, Union naval forces commanded by David G. Farragut struck the Confederacy from the Gulf of Mexico. They captured New Orleans and took control of fifteen hundred plantations and 50,000 slaves in the surrounding region. The Union now held the South's financial center and largest city and had struck a strong blow against slavery. Workers on many plantations looted their owners' mansions and refused to labor unless they were paid wages. "[Slavery there] is forever destroyed and worthless," declared one Northern reporter. Union victories had significantly undermined Confederate strength in the Mississippi River Valley.

- Why was there no new compromise over slavery in 1861? How important was the conflict at Fort Sumter? Would the Confederacy—and the Union—have decided to go to war in any event?

- In the first years of the war, what were the political and military strategies of each side? Which side was the more successful? Why?

# Toward Total War

The military carnage in 1862 revealed that the war would be long and costly. Grant later remarked that, after Shiloh, he "gave up all idea of saving the Union except by complete conquest." Increasingly, the Civil War resembled the **total wars** that would come in the twentieth century. In such wars, governments mobilized the entire resources of their societies and decreed that the lives and property of enemy civilians were legitimate objects of attack. Aided by the Republican Party and a talented cabinet, Lincoln gradually organized an effective central government able to wage all-out war. Jefferson Davis had less success at harnessing southern resources, because the eleven states of the Confederacy remained suspicious of centralized rule and southern yeomen grew increasingly skeptical of the war effort.

## Mobilizing Armies and Civilians

Initially, patriotic fervor filled both armies with eager young volunteers. One Union recruit recalled that all he heard was "War! War! War!" Even those of sober minds joined up. "I don't think a young man ever went over all the considerations more carefully than I did," reflected William Saxton of Cincinnatus, New York. "It might mean sickness, wounds, loss of limb, and even life itself. . . . But my country was in danger." The southern call for volunteers was even more successful, thanks to its strong military tradition, supply of trained officers, and a culture that stressed duty and honor. "Would you, My Darling, . . . be willing to leave your Children under such a [despotic Union] government?" James B. Griffin of Edgefield, South Carolina, asked his wife. "No—I know you would sacrifice every comfort on earth, rather than submit to it." Enlistments declined, however, as potential recruits learned the realities of mass warfare: epidemic diseases in the camps and wholesale death on the battlefields. Both governments soon faced the need for conscription.

**The Military Draft** | The Confederacy acted first. In April 1862, following the bloodshed at Shiloh, the Confederate Congress imposed the first legally binding draft in American history. New laws required existing soldiers to serve for the duration of the war and demanded three years of military service from all men between the ages of eighteen and thirty-five. In September 1862, after the heavy casualties at Antietam, the age limit jumped to forty-five. The South's draft had two loopholes, both controversial. First, it exempted one white man—the planter, a son, or an overseer—for each twenty slaves, allowing some whites on large plantations to avoid military service. This provision, a legislator from Mississippi warned Jefferson Davis, "has aroused a spirit of rebellion in some places." Second, draftees could hire substitutes. By the time this loophole was closed in 1864, the price of a substitute had risen to $300 in gold, three times the annual wage of a skilled worker. Laborers and yeomen farmers angrily complained that it was "a rich man's war and a poor man's fight."

Consequently, some southerners refused to serve. Because the Confederate constitution vested sovereignty

**Kansas Volunteers, 1862**

When they posed for this tintype photograph in 1862, these men from Company E, 8th Kansas Volunteer Infantry, had marched hundreds of miles through Kentucky and Tennessee in a largely fruitless pursuit of the Confederate Army and wore the look of battle-hardened troops. Some of these volunteers appear to be in their thirties or forties, and perhaps were abolitionist veterans of the civil strife in Bloody Kansas during the 1850s. Kansas State Historical Society.

in the individual states, the government in Richmond could not compel military service. Independent-minded governors such as Joseph Brown of Georgia and Zebulon Vance of North Carolina simply ignored President Davis's first draft call in early 1862. Elsewhere, state judges issued writs of **habeas corpus**—legal instruments used to protect people from arbitrary arrest—and ordered the Confederate army to release reluctant draftees. However, the Confederate Congress overrode the judges' authority to free conscripted men, so the government was able to keep substantial armies in the field well into 1864.

The Union government acted more ruthlessly toward Confederate sympathizers and those who opposed the draft. In Missouri and other border states, Union commanders levied special taxes on southern supporters. Lincoln went further, suspending habeas corpus and, over the course of the war, temporarily imprisoning about 15,000 people without trial. The president placed civilians who discouraged enlistments or resisted the draft under the jurisdiction of military courts, preventing acquittals by sympathetic local juries. But Union governments primarily used incentives

to lure recruits. When the Militia Act of 1862 set local quotas, states, counties, and towns avoided conscription by using cash bounties of as much as $600 (about $11,000 today) and signed up nearly 1 million men. The Union also allowed men to avoid military service by providing a substitute or paying a $300 fee.

When the Enrollment Act of 1863 finally initiated conscription in the North, recent German and Irish immigrants often refused to serve. It was not their war, they said. Northern Democrats used the furor over conscription to bolster support for their party, which increasingly criticized Lincoln's policies. They accused Lincoln of drafting poor whites to liberate blacks, who would then flood the cities and take their jobs. Slavery was nearly "dead," declared a Democratic newspaper in Cincinnati, "[but] the negro is not, there is the misfortune." In July 1863, the immigrants' hostility to conscription and blacks led to riots in New York City. For five days, Irish and German workers ran rampant, burning draft offices, sacking the homes of influential Republicans, and attacking the police. The rioters lynched and mutilated a dozen African Americans, drove hundreds of black families from their homes, and burned

**The Business of Recruiting an Army**

Following the New York City draft riots in July 1863, Union governments used monetary bonuses to induce men to join the army. This painting by George Law shows a recruiting post in 1864. To meet New York's draft quota of 30,000 men, the county and state governments offered volunteers bounties of $300 and $75 — on top of a U.S. government bounty of $302. The total — some $677 — was serious money at a time when the average worker earned $1.70 for a ten-hour day.   Anne S. K. Brown Military Collection, Brown University Library.

down the Colored Orphan Asylum. Lincoln rushed in Union troops who had just fought at Gettysburg; they killed more than a hundred rioters and suppressed the immigrant mobs.

The Union government won greater support among native-born middle-class citizens. In 1861, prominent New Yorkers established the U.S. Sanitary Commission to provide medical services and prevent the spread of epidemic diseases among the troops. Through its network of seven thousand local auxiliaries, the commission collected clothing and food. "I almost weep," reported a local agent, "when these plain rural people come to send their simple offerings to absent sons and brothers." The commission also recruited battlefield nurses and doctors for the Union Army Medical Bureau. Despite these efforts, dysentery, typhoid, and malaria spread through the camps, as did mumps and measles, viruses that were often deadly to rural recruits. Diseases and

infections killed about 250,000 Union soldiers, nearly twice the 135,000 who died in combat. Still, thanks to the Sanitary Commission, Union troops had a far lower mortality rate than soldiers fighting in nineteenth-century European wars. Confederate troops were less fortunate. Thousands of women volunteered as nurses, but the Confederate army's health system was poorly organized. Scurvy was a special problem for southern soldiers, who lacked vitamin C in their diets, and they died from camp diseases at a high rate.

So much death created new industries and cultural rituals. Embalmers devised a zinc chloride fluid to preserve soldiers' bodies, allowing them to be shipped home for burial; this innovation marked the beginning of modern funeral practices. Military cemeteries with hundreds of crosses in neat rows replaced the landscaped "rural cemeteries" in vogue in American cities before the Civil War. And thousands of mothers, wives, and sisters mourned the deaths of fallen soldiers. Facing utter deprivation, working-class women grieved for the loss of a breadwinner; meanwhile, middle-class wives, bound by the affectionate tenets of domesticity, lamented the death of their partner in life. Clothing stores set aside space for black crape "mourning" dresses and other personal accessories of death. The destructive war, in concert with the emerging consumer culture and ethic of domesticity, had produced a new "cult of mourning" among the middle and upper classes.

**Women in Wartime**    As tens of thousands of wounded husbands and sons limped home from the war, their wives and sisters helped them rebuild their lives. Another 200,000 women worked as volunteers in the Sanitary Commission and the Freedman's Aid Society, which collected supplies for liberated slaves.

The war drew more women into the wage-earning work force as nurses, clerks, and factory operatives. Dorothea Dix (see Chapter 11) served as superintendent of female nurses and, by successfully combating the prejudice against women providing medical treatment to men, opened a new occupation to women. Thousands of educated Union women became government clerks, while southern women staffed the efficient Confederate postal service. In both societies, millions of women took over farm tasks; filled jobs in schools and offices; and worked in textile, shoe, and food-processing factories. A few even became spies, scouts, and (disguising themselves as men) soldiers. As Union nurse Clara Barton, who later founded the American Red Cross, recalled, "At the war's end, woman was at least fifty years in advance of the normal position which continued peace would have assigned her."

## Mobilizing Resources

Wars are usually won by the side that possesses greater resources. In that regard, the Union had a distinct advantage. With nearly two-thirds of the nation's popu-

**Hospital Nursing**

Working as nurses in battlefront hospitals, thousands of Union and Confederate women gained firsthand experience of the horrors of war. A sense of calm prevails in this behind-the-lines Union hospital in Nashville, Tennessee, as nurse Anne Belle tends to the needs of soldiers recovering from their wounds. Most Civil War nurses were volunteers; they spent time cooking and cleaning for their patients as well as tending their injuries.    U.S. Army Military History Institute.

lation, two-thirds of the railroad mileage, and accounting for almost 90 percent of the industrial output, the North's economy was far superior to that of the South (Figure 14.2). The North had a further great advantage in the manufacture of cannon and rifles because many of its arms factories were equipped for mass production.

But the Confederate position was far from weak. Virginia, North Carolina, and Tennessee had substantial industrial capacity. Richmond, with its Tredegar Iron Works, was an important manufacturing center, and in 1861 its armory acquired the gun-making machinery from the U.S. armory at Harpers Ferry. The produc-

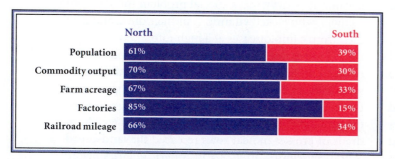

| | North | South |
|---|---|---|
| Population | 61% | 39% |
| Commodity output | 70% | 30% |
| Farm acreage | 67% | 33% |
| Factories | 85% | 15% |
| Railroad mileage | 66% | 34% |

**FIGURE 14.2**

### Economies, North and South, 1860

The military advantages of the North were even greater than this chart suggests. The population figures for the South include slaves, whom the Confederacy feared to arm. Also, the South's commodity output was primarily in farm goods rather than manufactures. Finally, southern factories were much smaller on average than those in the North.    Sources: Stanley Engerman, "The Economic Impact of the Civil War," in *The Reinterpretation of American Economic History*, ed. Robert W. Fogel and Stanley L. Engerman (New York: Harper & Row, 1971); and U. S. census data.

### Richmond: Capital City and Industrial Center

The Confederacy chose Richmond as its capital because of the historic importance of Virginia as the home of Washington, Jefferson, Madison, and Monroe. However, Richmond was also a major industrial center. Exploiting the city's location at the falls of the James River, the city's entrepreneurs had developed a wide range of industries: flour mills, tobacco factories, railroad and port facilities, and, most important, a substantial iron industry. In 1861, the Tredegar Iron Works employed nearly a thousand workers and, as the only facility in the South that could manufacture large machinery and heavy weapons, made a major contribution to the Confederate war effort.   The Library of Virginia.

tion at the Richmond armory, the purchase of Enfield rifles from Britain, and the capture of 100,000 Union guns enabled the Confederacy to provide every infantryman with a modern rifle-musket by 1863.

Moreover, with 9 million people, the Confederacy could mobilize enormous armies. Enslaved blacks, one-third of the population, assisted the war effort by producing food for the army and cotton for export. Confederate leaders counted on **King Cotton** to purchase clothes, boots, blankets, and weapons from abroad. They also saw it as a diplomatic weapon that would persuade Britain and France, whose textile factories needed raw cotton, to assist the Confederacy. British manufacturers had stockpiled cotton, however, and exploited new sources in Egypt and India. Still, the South's hope was partially fulfilled. Although Britain never recognized the Confederacy as an independent nation, it treated the rebel government as a belligerent power — with the right under international law to borrow money

and purchase weapons. The odds, then, did not necessarily favor the Union, despite its superior resources.

**Republican Economic and Fiscal Policies**   To mobilize northern resources, the Republican-dominated Congress enacted a neomercantilist program of government-assisted economic development that far surpassed Henry Clay's American System. The Republicans imposed high tariffs (averaging nearly 40 percent) on various foreign goods, thereby encouraging domestic industries. To boost agricultural output, they offered "free land" to farmers. The Homestead Act of 1862 gave settlers the title to 160 acres of public land after five years of residence. To create an integrated national banking system (far more powerful than the First and Second Banks of the United States), Secretary of the Treasury Salmon P. Chase forced thousands of local banks to accept federal charters and regulations.

Finally, the Republican Congress implemented Clay's program for a nationally financed transportation system. Expansion to the Pacific, the California gold rush, and subsequent discoveries of gold, silver, copper, and other metals in Nevada, Montana, and other western lands had revived demands for such a network. So, in 1862, Congress chartered the Union Pacific and Central Pacific companies to build a transcontinental railroad line and granted them lavish subsidies. This comprehensive economic program won the Republican Party the allegiance of farmers, workers, and entrepreneurs and bolstered the Union's ability to fight a long war.

New industries sprang up to provide the Union army—and its 1.5 million men—with guns, clothes, and food. Over the course of the war, soldiers consumed more than half a billion pounds of pork and other packed meats. To meet this demand, Chicago railroads built new lines to carry thousands of hogs and cattle to the city's ever-larger stockyards and slaughterhouses. By 1862, Chicago had passed Cincinnati as the meatpacking capital of the nation, bringing prosperity to thousands of midwestern farmers and great wealth to Philip D. Armour and other meatpacking entrepreneurs.

Bankers and financiers likewise found themselves pulled into the war effort. The annual spending of the Union government shot up from $63 million in 1860 to more than $865 million in 1864 (Figure 14.3). To raise that enormous sum, the Republicans created a modern system of public finance that secured funds in three ways. First, the government increased tariffs; placed high duties on alcohol and tobacco; and imposed direct taxes on business corporations, large inheritances, and the incomes of wealthy citizens. These levies paid about 20 percent of the cost. Interest-paying bonds issued by the U.S. Treasury financed another 65 percent. The National Banking Acts of 1863 and 1864 forced most banks to buy those bonds; and Jay Cooke, a Philadelphia banker working for the Treasury Department, used newspaper ads and 2,500 subagents to persuade nearly a million northern families to buy them.

The Union paid the remaining 15 percent by printing paper money. The Legal Tender Act of 1862 authorized $150 million in paper currency—soon known as **greenbacks**—and required the public to accept them as legal tender. Like the Continental currency of the Revolutionary era, greenbacks could not be exchanged for specie; however, because they were issued in relatively limited amounts, they only lost a small part of their face value.

If a modern fiscal system was one result of the war, immense concentrations of capital in many industries was another. The task of supplying the huge war machine, an observer noted, gave a few men "the command of millions of money." Such massed financial power threatened not only the prewar society of small producers but also the future of democratic self-government. Americans "are never again to see the republic in which we were born," lamented abolitionist and social reformer Wendell Phillips.

### The South Resorts to Coercion and Inflation

The economic demands on the South were equally great but, true to its states' rights philosophy, the Confederacy initially left most matters to the state governments. However, as the realities of total war became clear, Jefferson Davis's administration took extraordinary measures: It built and

**FIGURE 14.3**

**The High Cost of War: Union Finances, 1860 and 1864**

In 1864, the Union government received almost 5 times as much in tax revenues as it had in 1860, but it spent nearly 14 times as much, mostly to pay soldiers and buy military supplies. In four years, the public debt had risen by a factor of 28, so that in 1864 the interest payment on the debt alone nearly equaled the level of *all* federal government spending in 1860.

**A Southern Refugee Family**

As Union and Confederate armies swept back and forth across northern Virginia and other war zones, the civilian population feared for its property and personal security. Here, two southern women—their husbands presumably away at war—have hitched up their mules and piled their goods and children on a farm wagon in order to flee the fighting. Lucky refugees had relatives in safe areas; others had to rely on the goodwill of strangers.    National Archives.

operated shipyards, armories, foundries, and textile mills; commandeered food and scarce raw materials such as coal, iron, copper, and lead; requisitioned slaves to work on fortifications; and directly controlled foreign trade.

The Confederate Congress and ordinary southern citizens opposed many of Davis's initiatives, particularly those involving taxes. The Congress refused to tax cotton exports and slaves, the most valuable property held by wealthy planters, and the urban middle classes and yeomen farm families refused to pay more than their fair share. Consequently, the Confederacy covered less than 10 percent of its expenditures through taxation. The government paid another 30 percent by borrowing, but wealthy planters and foreign bankers grew increasingly wary of investing in Confederate bonds that might never be redeemed.

So the Confederacy had to pay 60 percent of the war costs by printing paper money. The flood of currency created a spectacular inflation: By 1865, prices had risen to ninety-two times their 1861 level. As food prices soared, riots erupted in more than a dozen southern cities and towns. In Richmond, several hundred women broke into bakeries, crying, "Our children are starving while the rich roll in wealth." In Randolph County, Alabama, women confiscated grain from a government warehouse "to prevent starvation of themselves and their families." As inflation continued, southerners refused to accept paper money, whatever the consequences. When South Carolina storekeeper Jim Harris rejected the currency presented by Confederate soldiers, they raided his storehouse and, he claimed, "robbed it of about five thousand dollars worth of goods." Army supply officers likewise seized goods from merchants and offered payment in worthless IOUs. Facing a public that feared strong government and high taxation, the Confederacy could sustain the war effort only by seizing its citizens' property and by championing white supremacy: President Davis warned that a

Union victory would destroy slavery "and reduce the whites to the degraded position of the African race."

- How did the governments—the Union or the Confederacy—go about mobilizing soldiers, citizens, and resources to wage a total war? How successful were their respective strategies?

- What were the main economic policies enacted by the Republican-controlled Congress?

# The Turning Point: 1863

By 1863, the Lincoln administration had finally created an efficient war machine and a set of strategic priorities. Henry Adams, the grandson of John Quincy Adams and a future novelist and historian, noted the change from his diplomatic post in London: "Little by little, one began to feel that, behind the chaos in Washington power was taking shape; that it was massed and guided as it had not been before." Slowly but surely, the tide of the struggle had turned against the Confederacy.

## Emancipation

When the war began, antislavery Republicans demanded that abolition—as well as restoration of the Union—be a goal of the war. The fighting should continue, said a Massachusetts abolitionist, "until the Slave power is completely subjugated, and *emancipation made certain*." Because slave-grown crops sustained the Confederacy, activists justified black emancipation on military grounds. As Frederick Douglass put it, "Arrest that hoe in the hands of the Negro, and you smite the rebellion in the very seat of its life."

**"Contrabands"** As abolitionists pressed their case, African Americans exploited wartime chaos to seize freedom for themselves. When three slaves reached the camp of Union general Benjamin Butler in Virginia in May 1861, he labeled them "contraband of war" (a term for enemy property that can be legitimately seized, according to international law) and refused to return them. Butler's term stuck, and soon thousands of "contrabands" were camping with Union armies. Near Fredericksburg, Virginia, an average of 200 blacks appeared every day, "with their packs on their backs and handkerchiefs tied over their heads—men, women, little children, and babies." To provide legal status to these fugitives, Congress passed the Confiscation Act in August 1861; it authorized the seizure of property, including slave property, used to support the rebellion.

Radical Republicans—Treasury Secretary Salmon Chase, Senator Charles Sumner of Massachusetts, and Representative Thaddeus Stevens of Pennsylvania—now began to use wartime legislation to destroy slavery. A longtime member of Congress, Stevens was a masterful politician, skilled at fashioning legislation that could win majority support. In April 1862, Stevens and the Radicals persuaded Congress to end slavery in the District of Columbia by providing compensation for owners; in June, Congress outlawed slavery in the federal territories (finally enacting the Wilmot Proviso of 1846); and in July, it passed a second Confiscation Act. This act overrode the property rights of Confederate planters by declaring "forever free" the thousands of fugitive slaves and all slaves captured by the Union army. Emancipation had become an instrument of war.

**The Emancipation Proclamation** Initially, Lincoln had rejected emancipation as a war aim, but faced with thousands of contrabands and Radical Republican pressure, he moved cautiously toward that goal. The president drafted a general proclamation of emancipation in July 1862, and he publicly linked black freedom with the preservation of the Union in August. "If I could save the Union without freeing any slave, I would do it," Lincoln told Horace Greeley of the *New York Tribune*, "and if I could save it by freeing all the slaves, I would do it."

Now he waited for a Union victory. Considering the Battle of Antietam "an indication of the Divine Will," Lincoln issued a preliminary proclamation of emancipation five days later, on September 22, 1862, and based its legal authority on his duty as commander in chief to suppress the rebellion. The proclamation stated that slavery would be legally abolished in all states that remained out of the Union on January 1, 1863. The rebel states could preserve slavery by renouncing secession. None chose to do so.

The proclamation was politically astute. Lincoln conciliated slave owners in the Union-controlled border states, such as Maryland and Missouri, by leaving slavery intact in those states. It also permitted slavery to continue in areas occupied by Union armies: western and central Tennessee, western Virginia, and southern Louisiana. In Indian Territory, also under Union control, most mixed-blood Cherokee slave owners remained committed to the Confederacy. They did not formally free their 4,000 slaves until July 1866, when a new treaty with the U.S. government specified that their ex-slaves "shall have all the rights of native Cherokee."

Consequently, the Emancipation Proclamation did not immediately free a single slave. Yet, as abolitionist Wendell Phillips understood, Lincoln's proclamation had moved slavery to "the edge of Niagara," and it would soon be swept over the brink. Advancing Union troops became the agents of slavery's destruction. "I became free in 1863, in the summer, when the yankees come by and said I could go work for myself," recalled Jackson Daniel of Maysville, Alabama. As Lincoln now saw it, "the old South is to be destroyed and replaced by new propositions and ideas"—a system of free labor.

Emancipation was extraordinarily controversial. In the Confederacy, Jefferson Davis labeled it the "most execrable measure recorded in the history of guilty man"; in the North, it unleashed a racist backlash among white voters. During the elections of 1862, the Democrats denounced emancipation as unconstitutional, warned of slave uprisings, and predicted that freed blacks would take white jobs. Every freed slave, suggested a nativist-minded New Yorker, should "shoulder an Irishman and leave the Continent." Such sentiments propelled Democrat Horatio Seymour into the governor's office in New York; if abolition was a war goal, Seymour argued, the South should not be conquered. According to one observer, many Democrats viewed "every success of the rebels . . . [as] a party victory & hail it with triumph." Their party swept to victory in Pennsylvania, Ohio, and Illinois, and gained thirty-four seats in Congress. But Republicans still held a twenty-five-seat majority in the House and gained five seats in the Senate. Lincoln refused to retreat. Calling emancipation an "act of justice," he signed the final proclamation on New Year's Day 1863. "If my name ever goes into history," he said, "it was for this act."

## Vicksburg and Gettysburg

The Emancipation Proclamation's fate would depend on Republican political success and Union military victories. The outlook was not encouraging on either front. Democrats had made significant gains in 1862, and popular support was growing for a negotiated peace. Two brilliant victories in Virginia by General Robert E. Lee, whose army defeated Union forces at Fredericksburg (December 1862) and Chancellorsville (May 1863), further eroded northern support for the war.

**The Battle for the Mississippi** | At this critical juncture, General Grant mounted a major offensive to split the Confederacy in two. Grant drove south along the west bank of the Mississippi in Arkansas and then crossed the river near Vicksburg, Mississippi. There, he defeated two Confederate armies and laid siege to the city. After repelling Union assaults for six weeks, the exhausted and starving Vicksburg garrison surrendered on July 4, 1863. Five days later, Union forces took Port Hudson, Louisiana (near Baton Rouge), and seized control of the Mississippi River. Grant had taken 31,000 prisoners; cut off Louisiana, Arkansas, and Texas from the rest of the Confederacy; and prompted thousands of slaves to desert their plantations or demand wages.

As Grant had advanced toward Vicksburg in May, Confederate leaders had argued over the best strategic response. President Davis and other politicians wanted to send an army to Tennessee to relieve the Union pressure along the Mississippi River. But General Lee, buoyed by his recent victories, favored a new invasion of the North. That strategy, Lee suggested, would either draw Grant's forces to the east or give the Confederacy a major victory that would destroy the North's will to fight.

**Lee's Advance and Defeat** | Lee won out. In June 1863, he maneuvered his army north through Maryland into Pennsylvania. The Army of the Potomac moved along with him, positioning itself between Lee and Washington, D.C. On July 1, the two great armies met by accident at Gettysburg, Pennsylvania, in what became a decisive confrontation (Map 14.4). On the first day of battle, Lee drove the Union's advance guard to the south of town. But Union commander George G. Meade placed his troops in well-defended hilltop positions and called up reinforcements. By the morning of July 2, Meade had 90,000 troops to Lee's 75,000. Aware that he was outnumbered but intent on victory, Lee ordered assaults on Meade's flanks but failed to turn them.

On July 3, Lee decided on a dangerous frontal assault against the center of the Union line. After the heaviest artillery barrage of the war, Lee sent General George E. Pickett and his 14,000 men to take Cemetery Ridge. When Pickett's men charged across a mile of open terrain, they were met by deadly fire from artillery and massed riflemen; thousands were killed, wounded, or captured. As the three-day battle ended, the Confederates had suffered 28,000 casualties, one-third of the Army of Northern Virginia, while 23,000 of Meade's soldiers lay killed or wounded. Shocked by the bloodletting, Meade allowed the Confederate units to escape. Lincoln was furious. "As it is," the president brooded, "the war will be prolonged indefinitely."

Still, Gettysburg was a great Union victory and, together with the simultaneous triumph at Vicksburg, was the major turning point in the war. Southern armies

**MAP 14.4**

**Lee Invades the North, 1863**

After Lee's victories at Chancellorsville (1) in May and Brandy Station (2) in June, the Confederate forces moved northward, constantly shadowed by the Union army. On July 1, the two armies met accidentally near Gettysburg, Pennsylvania. In the ensuing battle (3), the Union army, commanded by General George Meade, emerged victorious, primarily because it was much larger than the Confederate force and held well-fortified positions along Cemetery Ridge, which gave its units a major tactical advantage.

would never again invade the North, and Southern citizens grew increasingly critical and worried. The Confederate elections of 1863 went sharply against the politicians who supported Jefferson Davis.

Vicksburg and Gettysburg transformed the political and diplomatic situation. In the fall of 1863, Republicans swept state elections in Pennsylvania, Ohio, and New York. In Europe, the victories boosted the leverage of American diplomats. Since 1862, the British-built ironclad cruiser the *Alabama* had sunk or captured more than a hundred Union merchant ships, and the Confederacy was about to accept delivery of two more cruisers. But with a Union victory increasingly likely, the British government decided to stop the flow of advanced weapons to the Confederacy and impound the

warships. British workers and reformers had long condemned slavery; now, because of poor grain harvests, Britain depended on imports of wheat and flour from the American Midwest. King Cotton diplomacy had failed; King Wheat stood triumphant. "Rest not your hopes in foreign nations," President Jefferson Davis advised his people. "This war is ours; we must fight it ourselves."

- **Some historians argue that emancipation happened because thousands of slaves "freed themselves" by fleeing to Union armies. How persuasive is their argument?**

- **Why were the battles at Gettysburg and Vicksburg significant? How did they change the tide of war strategically, diplomatically, and psychologically?**

**Black Soldiers in the Union Army**
Determined to end racial slavery, tens of thousands of African Americans volunteered for service in the Union army in 1864 and 1865, boosting the northern war effort at a critical moment. These proud soldiers were members of the 107th Colored Infantry, stationed at Fort Corcoran near Washington, D.C. In January 1865, their regiment saw action in the daring capture of Fort Fisher, which protected Wilmington, North Carolina, the last Confederate port open to blockade runners.   Library of Congress.

# The Union Victorious, 1864–1865

The Union victories of 1863 meant that the South could not win independence through a decisive military triumph. However, the Confederacy could still hope for a battlefield stalemate and a negotiated peace. To keep the Union in Republican hands, Lincoln faced the daunting task of conquering the South.

## Soldiers and Strategy

Two developments allowed the Union to prosecute the war vigorously: the promotion of aggressive generals and the enlistment of African American soldiers. As early as 1861, free African Americans and fugitive slaves had volunteered for the Union army, both to fight against slavery and, as Frederick Douglass put it, to win "the right to citizenship." But military service for blacks offended many northern whites. "I am as much

opposed to slavery as any of them," a New York soldier wrote to his local newspaper, "but I am not willing to be put on a level with the negro and fight with them." Although Union generals opposed the enlistment of African Americans, doubting that former slaves would make good soldiers, free and contraband blacks formed volunteer regiments in New England, South Carolina, Louisiana, and Kansas.

**The Impact of Black Troops**  The Emancipation Proclamation changed military policy and popular sentiment. The proclamation invited former slaves to serve in the Union army, and northern whites, having suffered thousands of casualties, now accepted that blacks should share in the fighting and dying. The valor of the first African American regiments to go into combat also influenced northern opinion. In 1863, a heroic and costly attack on Fort Wagner, South Carolina, by the Fifty-fourth Massachusetts Infantry convinced Union officers of the value of black soldiers. The Lincoln administration now recruited as many

**Grant Planning a Strategic Maneuver**

On May 21, 1864, the day this photograph was taken, Grant pulled his forces from the Spotsylvania Court House, where a bitter two-week battle (May 8–21) resulted in 18,000 Union and 10,000 Confederate casualties. He moved his army to the southeast, seeking to outflank Lee's forces. Photographer Timothy H. O'Sullivan caught up to the Union high command at Massaponax Church, Virginia, and captured this image of Grant (to the left) leaning over a pew and reading a map held by General George H. Meade. As Grant plots the army's movement, his officers smoke their pipes and read reports of the war in newspapers that had just arrived from New York City. Intercepting Grant's forces, Lee took up fortified positions first at the North Anna River and then at Cold Harbor, where the Confederates scored their last major victory of the war (May 31–June 3).    Library of Congress.

African Americans as it could. By the spring of 1865, nearly 200,000 African Americans were serving the Union. Without black soldiers, the president suggested, "we would be compelled to abandon the war in three weeks."

Military service did not end racial discrimination. Black soldiers were initially paid less than white soldiers ($10 a month versus $13) and won equal pay only by threatening to quit. Moreover, blacks served under white officers in segregated regiments and were used primarily to build fortifications, garrison forts, and guard supply lines. Nonetheless, African Americans continued to volunteer, knowing they were fighting for freedom and a new social order. "Hello, Massa," said one black soldier to his former master, who had been taken prisoner. "Bottom rail on top dis time." The worst fears of the secessionists had come true: Through the agency of the Union army, blacks had risen in a great rebellion against slavery.

**Capable Generals Take Command** | As African Americans bolstered the army's ranks, Lincoln finally found an efficient and ruthless commanding general. In March 1864, Lincoln placed General Ulysses S. Grant in charge of all Union armies; from then on, the president determined overall strategy and Grant implemented it. Lincoln favored a simultaneous advance against the major Confederate armies, a strategy Grant had long favored, in order to achieve a decisive victory before the election of 1864.

Grant knew how to fight a war that relied on industrial technology and targeted an entire society. At Vicksburg, he had besieged the whole city and forced its surrender. Then, in November 1863, he had used railroads to charge to the rescue of an endangered Union army near Chattanooga, Tennessee. Grant believed that the efforts of earlier Union commanders "to conserve life" through cautious tactics had merely prolonged the war. He was willing to accept heavy casualties, a stance that earned him a reputation as a butcher of enemy armies and his own men.

In May 1864, Grant ordered two major offensives. Personally taking charge of the 115,000-man Army of the Potomac, he set out to destroy Lee's force of 75,000 troops in Virginia. And Grant instructed General William Tecumseh Sherman, who shared his harsh outlook, to invade Georgia and take Atlanta. "All that has gone before is mere skirmish," Sherman wrote as he prepared for battle. "The war now begins."

Grant advanced toward Richmond, hoping to force Lee to fight in open fields, where the Union's superior manpower and artillery would prevail. Remembering his tactical errors at Gettysburg, Lee remained in strong defensive positions and attacked only when he held an advantage. The Confederate general seized that opportunity twice, winning costly victories in early May 1864 at the bloody battles of the Wilderness and Spotsylvania Court House. At Spotsylvania, the troops fought at point-blank range; an Iowa recruit recalled "lines of blue and grey [soldiers firing] into each other's faces; for an hour and a half." Despite heavy losses in these battles and then at Cold Harbor, Grant drove on (Map 14.5). His attacks severely eroded Lee's forces, which suffered 31,000 casualties, but Union losses were even higher: 55,000 men.

**Stalemate** | The fighting took a heavy psychological toll. "Many a man has gone crazy since this campaign began from the terrible pressure on mind and body," observed a Union captain. As morale declined, soldiers deserted. In June 1864, Grant laid siege to Petersburg, an important railroad center near

**MAP 14.5**

**The Closing Virginia Campaign, 1864–1865**

Beginning in May 1864, General Ulysses S. Grant launched an all-out campaign against Richmond. By threatening to cut General Robert E. Lee's lines of supply, Grant tried to lure him into open battle. Lee avoided a major test of strength. Instead, he retreated to defensive positions and inflicted heavy casualties on Union attackers at the Wilderness, Spotsylvania Court House, North Anna, and Cold Harbor (1–4). From June 1864 to April 1865, the two armies faced each other across defensive fortifications outside Richmond and Petersburg (5). Grant finally broke this ten-month siege by a flanking maneuver at Five Forks (6). Lee's surrender followed shortly.

Richmond. Protracted trench warfare—foreshadowing that in France in World War I—was devastating. Union and Confederate soldiers built complex networks of trenches, tunnels, and artillery emplacements stretching for 40 miles along the eastern edge of Richmond and Petersburg. Invoking the intense imagery of the Bible, an officer described the continuous artillery barrages and sniping as "living night and day within the 'valley of the shadow of death.'" The stress was especially great for the outnumbered Confederate troops, who spent months in the muddy, hellish trenches without rotation to the rear.

As time passed, Lincoln and Grant felt pressures of their own. The enormous casualties and military stalemate threatened Lincoln with defeat in the November election. The Republican outlook worsened in July, when Jubal Early's cavalry burned the Pennsylvania town of Chambersburg and threatened Washington, forcing Grant to divert troops from the Petersburg campaign. To punish farmers in the Shenandoah Valley who had aided the Confederate raiders, Grant ordered General Philip H. Sheridan to turn the region into "a barren waste." Sheridan's troops conducted a scorched-earth campaign, destroying grain, barns, and gristmills. These tactics, like Early's raid, violated the military norms of the day, which treated civilians as noncombatants. On both sides, rising desperation and anger were changing the definition of conventional warfare.

## The Election of 1864 and Sherman's March

As the siege at Petersburg dragged on, Lincoln's hopes for reelection depended on General Sherman in Georgia. Sherman's army of 90,000 men had advanced methodically toward Atlanta, a railway hub at the heart of the Confederacy. Then, in June 1864, Sherman engaged General Joseph E. Johnson's army of 60,000 in a set battle at Kennesaw Mountain, only to suffer 3,000 casualties—five times the Confederates' losses. By late July, the Union army reached the northern outskirts of Atlanta, but the next month brought little gain. Like Grant, Sherman seemed bogged down in a hopeless campaign.

**The National Union Party versus the Peace Democrats** Meanwhile, the presidential campaign of 1864 was heating up. In June, the Republican Party's convention rebuffed attempts to prevent Lincoln's renomination. It endorsed the president's war strategy, demanded the Confederacy's unconditional surrender, and called for a consti-

tutional amendment to abolish slavery. The delegates likewise embraced Lincoln's political strategy. To attract border-state and Democratic voters, the Republicans took a new name, the National Union Party, and chose Andrew Johnson, a Tennessee slave owner and Unionist Democrat, as Lincoln's running mate.

The Democratic Party met in August and nominated General George B. McClellan for president. Lincoln had twice removed McClellan from military commands: first for an excess of caution and then for his opposition to emancipation. Like McClellan, the Democratic delegates rejected emancipation and condemned Lincoln's repression of domestic dissent. However, they split into two camps over the issue of continuing the war. War Democrats vowed to continue fighting until the Union was restored, while Peace Democrats called for a "cessation of hostilities" and a constitutional convention to negotiate a peace settlement. Although personally a War Democrat, McClellan promised if elected to recommend to Congress an immediate armistice and a peace convention. Hearing this news, Confederate vice president Alexander Stephens celebrated "the first ray of real light I have seen since the war began." He predicted that if Atlanta and Richmond held out, Lincoln would be defeated and McClellan could be persuaded to accept an independent Confederacy.

**The Fall of Atlanta and Lincoln's Victory** Stephens's hopes collapsed on September 2, 1864, as Atlanta fell to Sherman's army. In a stunning move, the Union general pulled his troops from the trenches, swept around the city, and destroyed its rail links to the south. Fearing that Sherman would encircle his army, Confederate general John B. Hood abandoned the city. "Atlanta is ours, and fairly won," Sherman telegraphed Lincoln, sparking hundred-gun salutes and wild Republican celebrations in northern cities. "We are *gaining* strength," Lincoln warned Confederate leaders, "and may, if need be, maintain the contest indefinitely."

A deep pessimism settled over the Confederacy. Mary Chesnut, a plantation mistress and general's wife wrote in her diary, "I felt as if all were dead within me, forever," and foresaw the end of the Confederacy: "We are going to be wiped off the earth" (see Comparing American Voices, "Gender, Class, and Sexual Terror in the Invaded South," pp. 454–455).

Recognizing the dramatic change in the military situation, McClellan repudiated the Democratic peace platform. The National Union Party went on the offensive, attacking McClellan's inconsistency and labeling Peace Democrats as "copperheads" (poisonous snakes) who were hatching treasonous plots. "A man must go for the Union at all hazards," declared a Republican legislator in Pennsylvania, "if he would entitle himself to be considered a loyal man."

Lincoln won a clear-cut victory in November. The president received 55 percent of the popular vote and won 212 of 233 electoral votes. Republicans and National Unionists captured 145 of the 185 seats in the House of Representatives and increased their Senate majority to 42 of 52 seats. Many Republicans owed their victory to the votes of Union troops, who wanted to crush the rebellion and end slavery.

Legal emancipation was already under way at the edges of the South. In 1864, Maryland and Missouri amended their constitutions to end slavery, and the three Confederate states occupied by the Union army — Tennessee, Arkansas, and Louisiana — followed suit. Still, abolitionists worried that the Emancipation Proclamation, which was based on the president's wartime powers, would lose its force at the end of the war. Urged on by Lincoln and National Equal Rights League, the Republican Congress approved the Thirteenth Amendment, ending slavery, in January 1865 and sent it to the states for ratification. Slavery was nearly dead.

**William Tecumseh Sherman**

A man of nervous energy, Sherman smoked cigars and talked continuously. When seated, he crossed and uncrossed his legs incessantly, and a journalist described his fingers as constantly "twitching his red whiskers — his coat buttons — playing a tattoo on the table — or running through his hair." But on the battlefield Sherman was a decisive general who commanded the loyalty of his troops. This 1865 photograph was taken after Sherman's devastating march through Georgia and the Carolinas.   Library of Congress.

**William Tecumseh Sherman: "Hard War" Warrior** | Thanks to William Tecumseh Sherman, the Confederacy was nearly dead as well. As a young military officer stationed in the South, Sherman sympathized with the planter class and felt that slavery upheld social stability. But Sherman believed in the Union. Secession meant "anarchy," he told his southern friends in early 1861: "If war comes . . . I must fight your people whom I best love." Serving under Grant, Sherman distinguished himself at Shiloh and Vicksburg. Taking command of the Army of the Tennessee, he developed the philosophy and tactics of "hard war." "When one nation is at war with another, all the people of one are enemies of the other," Sherman declared, turning his troops loose against civilians suspected of helping Confederate guerrillas. When guerrillas fired on a boat carrying Unionist civilians near Randolph, Tennessee, Sherman sent a regiment to destroy the town, asserting, "We are justified in treating all inhabitants as combatants."

After capturing Atlanta, Sherman decided on a bold strategy. Instead of pursuing the retreating Confederate army northward into Tennessee, he proposed to move south, live off the land, and "cut a swath through to the sea." To persuade Lincoln and Grant to approve his unconventional plan, Sherman argued that his march would be "a demonstration to the world, foreign and domestic, that we have a power [Jefferson] Davis cannot resist." The Union general lived up to his pledge. "We are not only fighting hostile armies," Sherman wrote, "but a hostile people, and must make old and young, rich and poor, feel the hard hand of war." He left Atlanta in flames, and during his 300-mile march to the sea (Map 14.6) his army consumed or demolished everything in its path. A Union veteran wrote, "[We] destroyed all we could not eat, stole their niggers, burned their cotton & gins, spilled their sorghum, burned & twisted their R.Roads and raised Hell generally." Although Sherman's army usually did not harm noncombatants who kept to their peaceful business, the havoc so demoralized Confederate soldiers that many deserted their units and returned home. When Sherman reached Savannah in mid-December, the city's 10,000 defenders left without a fight.

# Gender, Class, and Sexual Terror in the Invaded South

**W**hen the white men of the South marched off to war, they left behind their wives and children. Soon, Confederate women in the border states confronted an enemy army of occupation. Southern women feared sexual abuse by occupying troops, especially as Union armies invaded the Confederacy and exposed women to a dangerous army of destruction. As the following selections show, rules of culture and class (for example, how "gentlemen" should act) and assumptions of male sexual privilege meant these interactions had varied outcomes.

## Cornelia Peake McDonald
### Journal

Cornelia Peake McDonald was the wife of an affluent lawyer in Winchester, Virginia, which was occupied during the Civil War; her nine children were born between 1848 and 1861.

[May 1863] 22nd . . . To day I received another intimation that my house would be wanted for a [Union] regimental hospital. I feel a sickening despair when I think of what will be my condition if they do take it. . . .

    Major Butterworth . . . told me that he was a quarter master, and that he had been sent to inform me that I must give up the house, as they must have it for a hospital. . . . I lost no time in seeking [General] Milroy's presence. . . . "Gen. Milroy," said I. He looked around impatiently. "They have come to take my house from me." . . . [He replied,] "Why should you expect me to shelter you and your family, you who are a rebel, and whose husband and family are in arms against the best government the world ever saw?" . . . "But Gen. Milroy, you are commandant here . . . and you can suffer me to remain in mine, where at least I can have a shelter for my sick children. . . . At last he raised his head and looked in my face. "You can stay but I allow it at the risk of my commission."

Source: *A Woman's Civil War*, ed. Minrose C. Gwin (Madison: University of Wisconsin, 1992), 101, 150–153.

## Judith White Brockenbrough McGuire
### Diary

Judith White Brockenbrough McGuire, of Alexandria, Virginia, spent most of the war as a refugee in Richmond.

June 11, 1865
These particulars . . . I have [heard] from our nephew, J. P. [in occupied central Virginia. He reports that] . . . the

Northern officers seemed disposed to be courteous to the ladies, in the little intercourse which they had with them. General Ferrera, who commanded the negro troops, was humane, in having a coffin made for a young Confederate officer. . . . The surgeons, too, assisted in attending to the Confederate wounded. An officer one morning sent for Mrs. N. [to return an item stolen by Union soldiers]. . . . She thanked him for his kindness. He seemed moved and said, "Mrs. N., I will do what I can for you, for I cannot be too thankful that my wife is not in an invaded country."

Source: Rod Gragg, *The Illustrated Confederate Reader* (Harper & Row: New York, 1989), 88–89.

## Henrietta E. Lee
### Letter to Union General David Hunter

Henrietta E. Lee was the wife of Edmund J. Lee, a wealthy relative of Robert E. Lee. David Hunter was fighting Confederate forces in the Shenandoah Valley.

Shepherdstown, Va., July 20, 1864
General Hunter:
Yesterday your underling, Captain Martindale, of the First New York Calvary, executed your infamous order and burned my house. . . . I, therefore, a helpless woman whom you have cruelly wronged, address you, a Major-General of the United States Army, and demand why this was done? . . .

    A colonel of the Federal Army has stated that you deprived forty of your officers of their commands because they refused to carry out your malignant mischief [of burning]. All honor to their names for this, at least! They are men, and have human hearts and blush for such a commander! . . . Your name will stand on history's pages as the Hunter of weak women, and innocent children.

Source: *The Women of the South in War Times*, comp. Matthew Pace Andrews (Baltimore: Norman, Remington, 1924), 382–383.

## Anna Maria Green

## Diary

Twenty-year-old Anna Maria Green kept a diary as General William Tecumseh Sherman's army of 60,000 men approached Milledgeville, Georgia.

Saturday evening November 19th [1864] — Again we are in a state of excitement caused by the near approach to our town of the enemy. Last night they were two thousand strong at Monticello. . . . Minnie came in to call me to look at a fire in the west. My heart sank, and almost burst with grief as I beheld the horizon crimson and the desolation our hated foe was spreading. Great God! Deliver us, oh! Spare our city. . . .

Nov. 25th Friday evening . . . This morning the last of the vandals left our city and burned the bridge after them — leaving suffering and desolation behind them, and embittering every heart. The worst of their acts was committed to poor Mrs. Nichols — violence done, and atrocity committed that ought to make her husband an enemy unto death. Poor woman. I fear she has been driven crazy.

Source: Rod Gragg, *The Illustrated Confederate Reader* (Harper & Row: New York, 1989), 175–176.

## Unknown Woman

## Letter to Her Daughter

This letter was written by a woman in Columbia, South Carolina.

Columbia March 3, 1865
My dear Gracia
Doubtless your anxiety is very great to hear something about us after the great calamity that has befallen our town. We have lost everything, but thank God, our lives have been spared. Oh Gracia, what we have passed through no tongue can tell, it defies description! . . .

The first regiment sent into the city was what Sherman calls his "Tigers." Whenever he sends these men ahead, he intends to do his worst. . . . The first thing they did was break open the stores and distribute the goods right and left. They found liquor and all became heartily drunk. . . . When night came on, the soldiers . . . fired the houses. It was a fearful sight. . . .

We stayed all night in the street, protected by a Yankee Captain from Iowa who was very kind to us.

Source: Rod Gragg, *The Illustrated Confederate Reader* (Harper & Row: New York, 1989), 189–190.

## Daniel Heyward Trezevant

## Report

Daniel Heyward Trezevant, a doctor in Columbia, South Carolina, wrote a brief report after Sherman's departure.

The Yankees' gallantry, brutality and debauchery were afflicted on the negroes. . . . The case of Mr. Shane's old negro woman, who, after being subjected to the most brutal indecency from seven of the Yankees, was, at the proposition of one of them to "finish the old Bitch," put into a ditch and held under water until life was extinct. . . .

Mrs. T.B.C. was seized by one of the soldiers, an officer, and dragged by the hair and forced to the floor for the purpose of sensual enjoyment. She resisted as far as practical — held up her young infant as a plea for sparing her and succeeded, but they took her maid, and in her presence, threw her on the floor and had connection with her. . . . They pinioned Mrs. McCord and robbed her. They dragged Mrs. Gynn by the hair of her head about the house. Mrs. G. told me of a young lady about 16, Miss Kinsler, who . . . three officers brutally ravished and who became crazy. . . .

Source: Rod Gragg, *The Illustrated Confederate Reader* (Harper & Row: New York, 1989), 192.

## ANALYZING THE EVIDENCE

- Why does General Milroy allow Cornelia McDonald to stay in her home? Was it because they were both members of the American upper classes? Or because the general held cultural values that protected women and children? How do the actions of the "Yankee Captain from Iowa" compare with Milroy's decision? What does the report about Mrs. N. and the kindness of the unnamed officer in the diary of Judith McGuire suggest about that officer's motivation?

- Why did Henrietta E. Lee call herself "helpless"? What did she mean — and what was her aim — in praising the officers allegedly dismissed by General Hunter?

- Although none of these writers used the word *rape* (why not?), we can assume that Mrs. Nichols was raped, as were Miss Kinsler and the enslaved African American maid in Columbia. What about Mrs. T.B.C., Mrs. McCord, and Mrs. Gynn? Should we believe these sources (and other, similar accounts written by whites) when they assert or imply that Union troops raped enslaved women and spared white women?

- What impact might accounts of the Union soldiers' brutality toward women have had on the Confederate army? Were such acts of brutality an inevitable result of the practice of "hard war"?

**MAP 14.6**

**Sherman's March through the Confederacy, 1864–1865**

The Union victory in November 1863 at Chattanooga, Tennessee (2), was almost as critical as the victories in July at Gettysburg and Vicksburg, because it opened up a route of attack into the heart of the Confederacy. In mid-1864, General William Tecumseh Sherman advanced on the railway hub of Atlanta (3 and 4). After finally taking the city in September 1864, Sherman relied on other Union armies to stem General Hood's invasion of Tennessee (5 and 6) while he began his devastating "March to the Sea." By December, he had reached Savannah (7); from there, he cut a swath through the Carolinas (8–10).

Georgia's African Americans treated Sherman as a savior. "They flock to me, old and young," he wrote. "[T]hey pray and shout and mix up my name with Moses . . . as well as 'Abram Linkom,' the Great Messiah of 'Dis Jubilee.'" To provide for the hundreds of blacks now following his army, Sherman issued Special Field Order No. 15, which set aside 400,000 acres of prime rice-growing land for the exclusive use of freedmen. By June 1865, about 40,000 blacks were cultivating "Sherman lands." Many freedmen believed that the lands were to be theirs forever, belated payment for generations of unpaid labor: "All the land belongs to the Yankees now and they gwine divide it out among de coloured people."

In February 1865, Sherman invaded South Carolina to link up with Grant at Petersburg and to punish the instigators of nullification and secession. His troops ravaged the countryside as they cut a narrow swath across the state. After capturing South Carolina's capital, Columbia, they burned the business district, most churches, and the wealthiest residential neighborhoods. "This disappointment to me is extremely bitter," lamented Jefferson Davis. By March, Sherman had reached North Carolina, ready to link up with Grant and crush Lee's army.

**The Confederate Collapse** Grant's war of attrition in Virginia had already exposed a weakness in the Confederacy: rising class resentment among poor whites. Angered by slave owners' exemptions from military service and fearing that the Confederacy was doomed, ordinary southern farmers now repudiated the draft. "All they want is to git you . . . to fight for their infurnal negroes," grumbled an Alabama hill farmer. More and more soldiers fled their units. "I am now going to work instead of to the war," vowed David Harris, another backcountry yeoman. By 1865, at least 100,000 men had deserted from Confederate armies, prompting reluctant Confederate leaders to allow the enlistment of black soldiers and promising freedom to those who served. But the fighting ended too soon to reveal whether any slaves would have fought for the Confederacy.

The symbolic end of the war took place in Virginia. In April 1865, Grant finally gained control of the crucial railroad junction at Petersburg and forced Lee to abandon Richmond. As Lincoln visited the ruins of the Confederate capital and was mobbed by joyful ex-slaves, Grant cut off Lee's escape route to North Carolina. On April 9, almost four years to the day after the attack on Fort Sumter, Lee surrendered at Appomattox Court House, Virginia. By late May, all the

Confederate generals had stopped fighting, and the Confederate army and government simply melted away (Map 14.7).

The hard and bitter conflict was finally over. Union armies had destroyed slavery and the Confederacy; many of the South's factories, railroads, and cities were in ruins, and its farms and plantations had suffered years of neglect. Almost 260,000 Confederate soldiers had paid for secession with their lives. On the other side, more than 360,000 northerners had died for the Union, and thousands more had been maimed (see Reading American Pictures, "What Do Photographs Tell Us about the Civil War?" p. 458). Was it all worth the price? Delivering his second inaugural address in March 1865, Abraham Lincoln could justify the hideous carnage only by alluding to divine providence: "[S]o still it must be said 'the judgments of the Lord are true and righteous altogether.'"

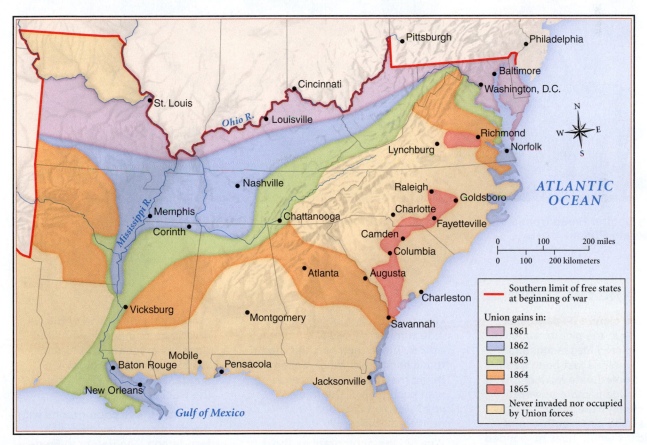

**MAP 14.7**

**The Conquest of the South, 1861–1865**

It took four years for the Union armies to defeat the Confederate forces. Until 1864, most of the South remained in Confederate hands; even at the end of the war, Union armies had never entered many parts of the rebellious states. Most of the Union's territorial gains came on the vast western front, where its control of strategic lines of communication (the Ohio and Mississippi rivers and major railroads) gave its forces a decisive advantage.

# What Do Photographs Tell Us about the Civil War?

The Civil War was the first military conflict recorded extensively by photographers. As the full-page photograph at the beginning of this chapter attests, the results were not pretty. Many Civil War photos portray military encampments and hundreds show the bodies of dead men scattered across fields of battle—grim scenes, indeed. But what was the impact of these photographs of death, given that few of them achieved wide distribution at the time? What insight can other photographs give us into the nature of the conflict?

**A Union Soldier Freed from a Confederate Prison.** © Corbis.

**Captain George A. Custer and a Confederate Prisoner.** Library of Congress.

## ANALYZING THE EVIDENCE

- Study the picture on page 428. Then look at the picture above of the emaciated Massachusetts soldier who has just been freed from a Confederate military prison. Which image is more powerful intellectually? Emotionally? How do you think nineteenth-century Americans would have responded to the two photographs? And how would you explain the Confederates' treatment of that prisoner (who was only one among many)?

- The other photograph above shows Captain (later General) George A. Custer sitting side by side with a captured Confederate officer. These men had just tried to kill each other. What reasons might they have had for behaving with such civility: The rules of war? Respect between two gentlemen-officers?

- Why did the photographer, the famous Mathew Brady, take this picture of Custer and the prisoner? Brady chose his images carefully so that they conveyed a message or a perspective on events. Is the African American boy, the southerner's slave property, a clue to one of the meanings of this picture? What does his presence add to the photograph? What might it suggest about the significance of the war?

- Compare these photographs with the painting by David English Henderson, *The Return to Fredericksburg after the Battle* (p. 459). What are the advantages (and drawbacks) of the two mediums—photography and art—in conveying the experience of war?

**The Harsh Aftermath**

The end of the war was not the end of the suffering, as David English Henderson's *The Return to Fredericksburg after the Battle* (1865) shows. Many southern soldiers and families returned to devastated homes and cities. Shocked by the destruction, the members of this well-to-do family stare blankly into space, unable yet to comprehend how they will rebuild their shattered lives.   Gettysburg National Military Park.

But what of the war's effects on society? A New York census taker suggested that the conflict had undermined "autocracy" and had an "equalizing effect." Slavery was gone from the South, he reflected, and in the North, "military men from the so called 'lower classes' now lead society, having been elevated by real merit and valor." However perceptive these remarks, they ignored the wartime emergence of a new financial aristocracy that would soon preside over what Mark Twain would label the Gilded Age. Nor was the sectional struggle yet concluded. As the North began to reconstruct the South and the Union, it found those tasks to be almost as hard and bitter as the war itself.

- How did the Emancipation Proclamation affect the politics and military affairs of the North?

- What were the strengths and weaknesses of Grant's and Sherman's military strategy and tactics? How were their ways of warfare different from traditional military practice?

## SUMMARY

In this chapter, we surveyed the dramatic events of the Civil War. Looking at the South, we watched the fire-eaters declare secession, form a new Confederacy, and attack Fort Sumter. Subsequently, we saw its generals repulse Union attacks against Richmond and go on the offensive. However, as the war continued, the inherent weaknesses of the Confederacy came to the fore. Enslaved workers fled or refused to work, and yeomen farmers refused to fight for an institution that primarily benefited wealthy planters.

Examining the North, we witnessed its military shortcomings. Its generals—McClellan and Meade—moved slowly to attack and refused to pursue their weakened foes. However, the Union's significant advantages in industrial output, financial resources, and military manpower became manifest over time. Congress created efficient systems of banking and war finance, Lincoln found efficient and ruthless generals, and the emancipation and recruitment of African Americans provided an abundant supply of soldiers determined to end slavery.

We explored the impact of the war on civilians in both regions: the imposition of conscription and high taxes, the increased workload of farm women, and the constant food shortages and soaring prices. Above all else, there was the omnipresent fact of death—a tragedy that touched nearly every family, North and South.

## CHAPTER REVIEW QUESTIONS

- As the Civil War began, politicians and ordinary citizens in both the North and the South were supremely confident of victory. Why did southerners believe they would triumph? Why did the North ultimately win the war?

- In 1860, the institution of slavery was firmly entrenched in the United States; by 1865, it was dead. How did this happen? How did Union policy toward slavery and enslaved people change over the course of the war? Why did it change?

# FOR FURTHER EXPLORATION

Charles P. Roland, *An American Iliad* (1991), and James M. McPherson, *The Battle Cry of Freedom* (1988), are fine histories of the Civil War. Recent important studies include Nicholas Onuf and Peter Onuf, *Nations, Markets, and War* (2006); Drew Gilpin Faust, *This Republic of Suffering: Death and the American Civil War* (2008); and Dora L. Costa and Matthew E. Kahn, *Heroes and Cowards: The Social Face of War* (2008).

For military matters, consult Nancy Scott Anderson and Dwight Anderson, *The Generals: Ulysses S. Grant and Robert E. Lee* (1988); Mark Grimsley, *The Hard Hand of War* (1995); and Gary W. Gallagher, *The Confederate War* (1997). William W. Freehling's *The South vs. the South* (2001) explores anti-Confederate sentiment.

James M. McPherson, *For Cause and Comrades* (1997), presents accounts of ordinary soldiers, as does Ira Berlin et al., eds., *Freedom's Soldiers: The Black Military Experience in the Civil War* (1998). Earl J. Hess, *The Union Soldier in Battle* (1997), vividly describes the smell, sound, and feel of combat, as does Michael Shaara's novel, *Killer Angels* (1974).

For southern women, read Drew Gilpin Faust, *Mothers of Invention* (1996); Laura F. Edwards, *Scarlett Doesn't Live Here Anymore* (2000); and *Mary Chesnut's Civil War*, edited by C. Vann Woodward (1981). See also Jane E. Schultz, *Women at the Front* (2004).

For Civil War photographs from the Library of Congress collection, visit **memory.loc.gov/ammem/cwphtml/cwhome.html**. A fine Web site is "The Valley of the Shadow" (**valley.lib.virginia.edu**), and the companion book by Edward L. Ayers, *In the Presence of Mine Enemies* (2003). For firsthand documents relating to emancipation, see **www.history.umd.edu/Freedmen/home.html**.

## TEST YOUR KNOWLEDGE

To assess your command of the material in this chapter, see the Online Study Guide at
**bedfordstmartins.com/henretta**.

For Web sites, images, and documents related to topics and places in this chapter, visit
**bedfordstmartins.com/makehistory**.

## TIMELINE

| | |
|---|---|
| **1860** | Abraham Lincoln elected president (November 6) |
| | South Carolina secedes (December 20) |
| **1861** | Lincoln inaugurated (March 4) |
| | Confederates fire on Fort Sumter (April 12) |
| | Virginia leaves Union (April 17) |
| | General Butler declares runaway slaves "contraband of war" (May) |
| | Confederates win Battle of Bull Run (July 21) |
| | First Confiscation Act (August) |
| **1862** | Legal Tender Act authorizes greenbacks (February) |
| | Union triumphs at Shiloh (April 6–7) |
| | Confederacy introduces draft (April) |
| | Congress passes Homestead Act (May) |
| | Congress subsidizes transcontinental railroads (July) |
| | Second Confiscation Act (July) |
| | Union halts Confederates at Antietam (September 17) |
| | Preliminary emancipation proclamation (September 22) |
| **1863** | Lincoln signs Emancipation Proclamation (January 1) |
| | Union wins battles at Gettysburg (July 1–3) and Vicksburg (July 4) |
| | Union initiates draft (March), sparking riots in New York City (July) |
| **1864** | Ulysses S. Grant named Union commander (March) |
| | Grant advances on Richmond (May) |
| | William Tecumseh Sherman takes Atlanta (September 2) |
| | Lincoln reelected (November 8) |
| | Sherman marches through Georgia (November and December) |
| **1865** | Congress approves Thirteenth Amendment (January 31) |
| | Robert E. Lee surrenders (April 9) |
| | Lincoln assassinated (April 14) |
| | Thirteenth Amendment ratified (December 6) |

# Reconstruction, 1865–1877

**In 1869,** Wyoming Territory did something few Americans could have imagined before the Civil War: It gave women full voting rights. A few local women's rights advocates supported the measure, but one legislator endorsed it in a spirit of revenge. "Damn it," he said, "if you are going to let the niggers and pigtails [Chinese] vote, we will ring in the women, too." A decade later, similar arguments surfaced in California. "We give negroes, and Chinamen, and everything else, a right to vote," pointed out one delegate to a state constitutional convention. Another challenged him: "Are you going over to that doctrine of the universal brotherhood of man?" He answered, "In regard to women, I am."

In other spheres, as well, "universal brotherhood" was a subject of intense debate. Congress overhauled the Naturalization Act of 1790, which had limited citizenship to immigrants who were "free white persons." The most radical congressmen argued that racial barriers to citizenship should be dropped entirely. But their proposal foundered, largely because of opposition to Chinese immigration. One U.S. senator warned that Chinese American citizenship would put "an end to republican government" on the Pacific coast. In the end, Congress offered citizenship rights to people of African descent, but not to those from Asia.

As these debates suggest, the Civil War opened enormous questions about citizenship and nationhood. Americans engaged in intense, often violent struggles over the postwar order. Slavery was finished—that much was certain—and the South had been forcibly reattached to the Union. But how should the United States reincorporate former rebels into the political system? Could it also define a secure place for four million former slaves? What about immigrants from many parts of the world? And if the United States was no longer a "white man's country," might citizenship extend to women as well as to black men?

Reconstruction is often thought of as something that happened in the South. But events there were part of a much broader transformation. Far beyond the ex-Confederacy, the United States embarked on an ambitious process of nation building. Chapter 16 will explore events in the West. There, the United States knit together a continental empire; military conflict with Native Americans entered its final phase, and the arrival of Asian immigrants raised new issues of citizenship and trade. In Chapter 15, we will focus on events in Washington, D.C., and in the former Confederacy, where freed slaves, former slave owners, and other southerners found their worlds turned upside down.

*Chloe and Sam,* **1882**
**After the Civil War, the country went through the wrenching peacemaking process known as Reconstruction. The struggle between the victorious North and the vanquished Confederacy was fought out on a political landscape, but Thomas Hovenden's painting reminds us of the deeper meaning of Reconstruction: that Chloe and Sam, after lives spent in slavery, might end their days in the dignity of freedom.** Amon Carter Museum of Western Art.

# The Struggle for National Reconstruction

The U.S. Constitution does not address the question of how to restore rebellious states. After the Civil War, the nation had to determine whether the Confederate states, upon seceding, had legally left the Union. If so, then their reentry required action by Congress. If not—if even during secession they had retained their constitutional status—then restoring these states might be an administrative matter, best left to the president. Lack of clarity on this fundamental question made for explosive politics. In the early years of Reconstruction, the president and Congress struggled over who was in charge. Only by winning this fight did Republicans in Congress open the way for the sweeping achievements of radical Reconstruction.

## Presidential Approaches: From Lincoln to Johnson

As wartime president, Lincoln had offered amnesty to all but high-ranking Confederates. When 10 percent of a rebellious state's voters had taken an oath of loyalty, he proposed, the state would be restored to the Union, provided that it approved the Thirteenth Amendment abolishing slavery (see Chapter 14). But Confederate states rejected Lincoln's Ten Percent Plan, and Congress proposed a tougher substitute. The Wade-Davis Bill, passed on July 2, 1864, required an oath of allegiance to the Union by a majority of each state's adult white men, new governments formed only by those who had never taken up arms against the North, and permanent disenfranchisement of Confederate leaders. Lincoln used a **pocket veto** to kill the Wade-Davis Bill; that is, he left it unsigned when Congress adjourned, while initiating talks with congressional leaders aimed at a compromise.

We will never know what would have happened had Lincoln lived. His assassination in April 1865 plunged the nation into political uncertainty and fueled Unionist fury against the South. As a special train bore Lincoln's flag-draped coffin slowly home to Illinois, tens of thousands of Americans lined the railroad tracks to pay respects. Grieving northerners blamed all Confederates for the acts of southern sympathizer John Wilkes Booth and his accomplices in the assassination. At the same time, Lincoln's death left the presidency in the hands of a man utterly lacking in Lincoln's moral sense and political judgment, Vice President Andrew Johnson.

Johnson was a self-styled "common man" from the hills of eastern Tennessee. Trained as a tailor, he built a career on the support of farmers and laborers. Loyal to the Union, Johnson refused to leave the U.S. Senate when Tennessee seceded. After federal forces captured Nashville in 1862, Lincoln appointed Johnson as Tennessee's military governor. In the election of 1864, placing this War Democrat on the Republican ticket had seemed a smart move, designed to promote unity and court southern Unionists. But after Lincoln's death, Johnson's presidency wreaked political havoc. Johnson, who was not even a Republican, often seemed to view ex-Confederates as his friends and abolitionists as his enemies.

In May 1865, with Congress out of session for months to come, Johnson advanced his own version of Reconstruction. He offered amnesty to all southerners who swore allegiance to the United States, except for the highest-ranking Confederates. Johnson appointed provisional governors for the southern states and required only that they revoke secession, repudiate Confederate debts, and ratify the Thirteenth Amendment. Within months, all the former Confederate states had met Johnson's terms and created functioning elected governments.

Many northerners were disgusted with Johnson. "The rebels have gotten back all their rights and have all been pardoned," wrote one angry Union army veteran in Missouri. He called Johnson "a traitor to the loyal people of the Union." Meanwhile, despite military defeat (see Voices from Abroad, "David Macrae: The Devastated South," p. 465), southerners' new legislatures moved to restore slavery in all but name. They enacted laws, known as **Black Codes**, designed to force former slaves back to plantation labor. The codes, for example, imposed severe penalties on blacks who did not hold full-year labor contracts and set up procedures for taking black children away from their parents and apprenticing them to former slave owners. Johnson, moreover, talked tough but then forgave ex-Confederate leaders easily when they appealed for pardons. Emboldened by Johnson's indulgence, ex-Confederates began to filter back into the halls of power. When Georgians elected Alexander Stephens, former vice president of the Confederacy, to represent them in Congress, many outraged Republicans saw this as the last straw.

## Congress versus the President

Under the Constitution, Congress is "the judge of the Elections, Returns and Qualifications of its own Members" (Article 1, Section 5). Using this power, Republican

## David Macrae
## The Devastated South

In this excerpt from *The Americans at Home* (1870), an account of his tour of the United States, Scottish clergyman David Macrae describes the war-stricken South as he found it in 1867–1868, at a time when the crisis over Reconstruction was boiling over.

I was struck with a remark made by a Southern gentleman in answer to the assertion that Jefferson Davis [the president of the Confederacy] had culpably continued the war for six months after all hope had been abandoned.

"Sir," he said, "Mr. Davis knew the temper of the South as well as any man in it. He knew if there was to be anything worth calling peace, the South must win; or, if she couldn't win, she wanted to be whipped—well whipped— thoroughly whipped."

The further south I went, the oftener these remarks came back upon me. Evidence was everywhere that the South had maintained the desperate conflict until she was utterly exhausted. . . . Almost every man I met at the South, especially in North Carolina, Georgia, and Virginia, seemed to have been in the army; and it was painful to find many who had returned were mutilated, maimed, or broken in health by exposure. When I remarked this to a young Confederate officer in North Carolina, and said I was glad to see that he had escaped unhurt, he said, "Wait till we get to the office, sir, and I will tell you more about that." When we got there, he pulled up one leg of his trousers, and showed me that he had an iron rod there to strengthen his limb, and enable him to walk without limping, half of his foot being off. He showed me on the other leg a deep scar made by a fragment of a shell; and these were but two of seven wounds which had left their marks upon his body. When he heard me speak of relics, he said, "Try to find a North Carolina gentleman without a Yankee mark on him."

Nearly three years had passed when I traveled through the country, and yet we have seen what traces the war had left in such cities as Richmond, Petersburg, and Columbia. The same spectacle met me at Charleston. Churches and houses had been battered down by heavy shot and shell hurled into the city from Federal batteries at a distance of five miles. Even the valley of desolation made by a great fire in 1861, through the very heart of the city, remained unbuilt. There, after the lapse of seven years, stood the blackened ruins of streets and houses waiting for the coming of a better day. . . . Over the country districts the prostration was equally marked. Along the track of Sherman's army, especially, the devastation was fearful—farms laid waste, fences burned, bridges destroyed, houses left in ruins, plantations in many cases turned into wilderness again.

The people had shared in the general wreck, and looked poverty-stricken, careworn, and dejected. Ladies who before the war had lived in affluence, with black servants round them to attend to their every wish, were boarding together in half-furnished houses, cooking their own food and washing their own linen, some of them, I was told, so utterly destitute that they did not know when they finished one meal where they were to find the next. . . . Men who had held commanding positions during the war had fallen out of sight and were filling humble situations—struggling, many of them, to earn a bare subsistence. . . . I remember dining with three cultured Southern gentlemen, one a general, the other, I think, a captain, and the third a lieutenant. They were all living together in a plain little wooden house, such as they would formerly have provided for their servants. Two of them were engaged in a railway office, the third was seeking a situation, frequently, in his vain search, passing the large blinded house where he had lived in luxurious ease before the war.

Source: Allan Nevins, ed., *America through British Eyes* (Gloucester, MA: Peter Smith, 1968), 345–347.

### ANALYZING THE EVIDENCE

- In general, we value accounts by foreigners for insights they provide into America that might not be visible to its own citizens. Do you find any such insights in the Reverend Macrae's account of the postwar South?

- The South proved remarkably resistant to northern efforts at reconstruction. Can we find explanations for that resistance in Macrae's account?

- The North quickly became disillusioned with radical Reconstruction (see p. 483). Is there anything in Macrae's sympathetic interviews with wounded southern gentlemen and destitute ladies that sheds light on the susceptibility of many northerners to propaganda depicting a South in the grip of "a mass of black barbarism"?

**Memphis Riot, 1866**

Whites in postwar Memphis, as in much of the South, bitterly resented the presence in their city of former black soldiers mustered out of service with the U.S. Army. On April 30, 1866, when some black veterans — no longer protected by their uniforms — celebrated the end of their Army service by drinking, violence broke out. For three days, whites burned black neighborhoods, churches, and schools, raped several African American women, and killed dozens of black residents. Two whites also died in the rioting, which hardened Northern public opinion and prompted calls for stronger measures to put down ex-Confederate resistance. This tinted illustration is based on a lithograph that appeared in *Harper's Weekly*.
*Harper's Weekly*/Picture Research Consultants & Archives.

majorities in both houses refused to admit southern delegations when Congress convened in December 1865, effectively blocking Johnson's program. Hoping to mollify Congress, some southern states dropped the most objectionable provisions from the Black Codes. But at the same time, antiblack violence erupted in various parts of the South. A Nashville newspaper reported that white gangs were "riding about whipping, maiming and killing all negroes who do not obey the orders of their former masters."

Congressional Republicans concluded that the South planned to circumvent the Thirteenth Amendment. The federal government had to intervene. Back in March 1865, Congress had established the Freedmen's Bureau to aid former slaves. Now, in early 1866, Congress voted to extend the bureau, gave it direct funding for the first time, and authorized its agents to investigate mistreatment of blacks. Even more extraordinary was a civil rights bill that declared formerly enslaved people to be citizens and granted them equal protection and rights of contract, with full access to the courts.

These bills provoked bitter conflict with Johnson, who vetoed them both. Johnson's racism, hitherto publicly muted, now blazed forth: "This is a country for white men, and by God, as long as I am president, it shall be a government for white men." Galvanized, Re-

publicans in Congress gathered two-thirds majorities and overrode both vetoes, passing the Civil Rights Act in April 1866 and the Freedmen's Bureau law four months later. Their resolve was reinforced by continued violence in the South, which culminated in three days of rioting in Memphis, Tennessee, that left forty-six blacks dead and hundreds of African American homes, churches, and schools burned.

**Radical Republicans and the Fourteenth Amendment**   Anxious to protect freedpeople and reassert Republican power in the South, Congress moved to ensure black civil rights. In what became the Fourteenth Amendment to the Constitution, they declared that "all persons born or naturalized in the United States" were citizens. No state could abridge "the privileges or immunities of citizens of the United States"; deprive "any person of life, liberty, or property, without due process of law"; or deny anyone "equal protection of the laws." Johnson was right on one thing: Republicans were tending toward "centralization." In a stunning increase in federal power, the Fourteenth Amendment declared that when people's essential rights were at stake, national citizenship henceforth took precedence over citizenship in a state.

Johnson urged the states not to ratify the amendment, but public opinion had swung against him. In August 1866, Johnson embarked on a disastrous speaking tour, during which he made matters worse by shouting at hecklers and insulting hostile crowds. In the 1866 congressional elections, voters inflicted humiliation on Johnson by giving Republicans a three-to-one majority in Congress.

Power had shifted to the so-called Radical Republicans, who sought sweeping transformations in the defeated South. The Radicals' leader in the Senate was Charles Sumner of Massachusetts, the fiery abolitionist who in 1856 had been nearly beaten to death by South Carolina congressman Preston Brooks. Radicals in the House followed Thaddeus Stevens of Pennsylvania, a passionate advocate of freedpeople's political and eco-nomic rights. With such men at the fore, and with congressional Republicans now numerous and united enough to override Johnson's vetoes on many questions, Republicans proceeded to remake Reconstruction.

## Radical Reconstruction

The Reconstruction Act of 1867, enacted in March, divided the conquered South into five military districts, each under the command of a U.S. general (Map 15.1). To reenter the Union, each former Confederate state had to grant the vote to freedmen and deny it to leading ex-Confederates. Each military commander was required to register all eligible adult males, black as well as white; supervise new state constitutional conventions; and ensure that new constitutions guaranteed black

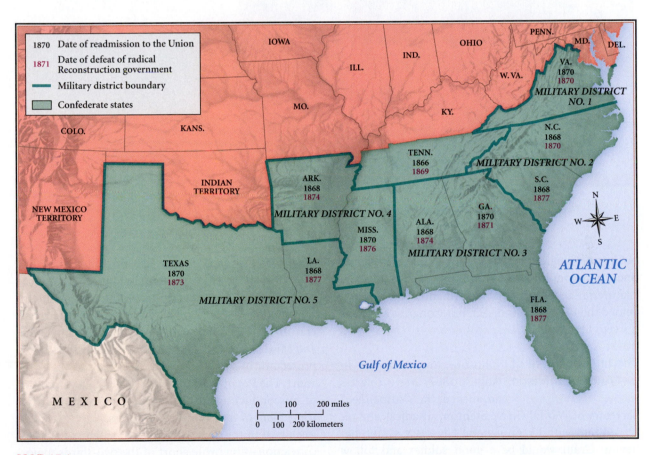

**MAP 15.1**

**Reconstruction**

The federal government organized the Confederate states into five military districts during radical Reconstruction. For the states shown in this map, the first date indicates when that state was readmitted to the Union; the second date shows when Radical Republicans lost control of the state government. All the ex-Confederate states rejoined the Union between 1868 and 1870, but the periods of radical rule varied widely. Republicans lasted only a few months in Virginia; they held on until the end of Reconstruction in Louisiana, Florida, and South Carolina.

**"The First Vote"**

In this pastel drawing, based on an engraving by Alfred Waud that appeared in *Harper's Weekly* in November 1867, the voters shown represent elements of African American political leadership: an artisan with tools, a well-dressed member of the middle class, and a Union soldier. After ratification of the Fifteenth Amendment in 1870, African American men voted in every state of the Union. © Bettmann/Corbis.

**suffrage.** Congress would readmit a state to the Union once these conditions were met and the new state legislature ratified the Fourteenth Amendment. Johnson vetoed the Reconstruction Act, but Congress overrode his veto (Table 15.1).

**The Impeachment of Andrew Johnson** Johnson fought back. In August 1867, after Congress adjourned, he "suspended" Secretary of War Edwin M. Stanton, a Radical, and replaced him with Union general Ulysses S. Grant, believing Grant would be a good soldier and follow orders. Johnson, however, had misjudged Grant, who publicly objected to the president's machinations. When the Senate reconvened in the fall, it overruled Stanton's suspension. Grant, now an open enemy of Johnson, resigned so that Stanton could resume his place as secretary of war. On February 21, 1868, Johnson formally dismissed Stanton. The feisty secretary of war responded by barricading himself in his office, precipitating a crisis.

Three days later, for the first time in U.S. history, legislators in the House of Representatives introduced articles of **impeachment** against the president, employing their constitutional power to charge high federal officials with "Treason, Bribery, or other high Crimes and Misdemeanors." The House serves, in effect, as the prosecutor in such cases, and the Senate serves as the court. The Republican majority brought eleven counts of misconduct against Johnson, most relating to infringement of the powers of Congress. After an eleven-week trial in the Senate, thirty-five senators voted for conviction—one vote short of the two-thirds majority required. Seven Republicans voted for acquittal along with twelve Democrats. The dissenting Republicans felt that removing a president for defying Congress was too damaging to the constitutional system of checks and balances. But despite the president's acquittal, Congress had shown its power. For the brief months remaining in his term, Johnson was largely irrelevant to Reconstruction policy.

| TABLE 15.1 | |
|---|---|
| **Primary Reconstruction Laws and Constitutional Amendments** | |
| **Law (Date of Congressional Passage)** | **Key Provisions** |
| Thirteenth Amendment (December 1865*) | Prohibited slavery |
| Civil Rights Act of 1866 (April 1866) | Defined citizenship rights of freedmen |
| | Authorized federal authorities to bring suit against those who violated those rights |
| Fourteenth Amendment (June 1866†) | Established national citizenship for persons born or naturalized in the United States |
| | Prohibited the states from depriving citizens of their civil rights or equal protection under the law |
| | Reduced state representation in House of Representatives by the percentage of adult male citizens denied the vote |
| Reconstruction Act of 1867 (March 1867) | Divided the South into five military districts, each under the command of a Union general |
| | Established requirements for readmission of ex-Confederate states to the Union |
| Tenure of Office Act (March 1867) | Required Senate consent for removal of any federal official whose appointment had required Senate confirmation |
| Fifteenth Amendment (February 1869‡) | Forbade states to deny citizens the right to vote on the grounds of race, color, or "previous condition of servitude" |
| Ku Klux Klan Act (April 1871) | Authorized the president to use federal prosecutions and military force to suppress conspiracies to deprive citizens of the right to vote and enjoy the equal protection of the law |

*Ratified by three-fourths of all states in December 1865.
†Ratified by three-fourths of all states in July 1868.
‡Ratified by three-fourths of all states in March 1870.

## The Election of 1868 and the Fifteenth Amendment

The impeachment controversy made Grant, already the Union's greatest war hero, a Republican idol as well, and he easily won the party's presidential nomination in 1868. Although he supported radical Reconstruction, Grant also urged reconciliation between the sections. His Democratic opponent, Horatio Seymour, a former governor of New York, almost declined the nomination because he understood that Democrats could not yet overcome the stain of disloyalty. Grant won by an overwhelming margin, receiving 214 out of 294 electoral votes. Republicans retained two-thirds majorities in both houses of Congress.

In February 1869, in the wake of this smashing victory, Republicans produced the last Reconstruction amendment, the Fifteenth. It protected male citizens' right to vote irrespective of race, color, or "previous condition of servitude." Despite Radical Republicans' protests, the amendment left room for a **poll tax** (a tax paid for the privilege of voting) and literacy requirements, both necessary concessions to northern and western states that already relied on such provisions to keep immigrants and the "unworthy" poor from the polls. Congress required the four states remaining under federal control to ratify it as a condition for being readmitted to the Union. A year later, the Fifteenth Amendment became part of the Constitution.

Passage of the Fifteenth Amendment, despite its limitations, was an astonishing feat. Elsewhere in the Western Hemisphere, lawmakers had left emancipated slaves in a condition of semicitizenship, with no voting rights. But, like almost all Americans, congressional Republicans had extraordinary faith in the power of the ballot. African American leaders agreed. "The colored people of these Southern states have cast their lot with the Government," declared a delegate to Arkansas's constitutional convention, "and with the great Republican Party. . . . The ballot is our only means of protection." After the amendment was ratified, hundreds of

**Women's Rights, 1870s**

This engraving of a National Woman's Suffrage Association (NWSA) meeting in the 1870s shows that it was an all women's organization, and female led. The NWSA investigated the "labor question" and called for equal pay for wage-earning women.   The Granger Collection, New York.

thousands of African Americans flocked to the polls across the South, in an atmosphere of collective pride and celebration.

## Woman Suffrage Denied

Northern women had played key roles in the antislavery movement and Union victory. Women's rights leaders, who had campaigned for women's voting rights since the Seneca Falls convention of 1848, fervently hoped that Reconstruction would bring votes for women as well as for black men. As Elizabeth Cady Stanton put it, women could "avail ourselves of the strong arm and the blue uniform of the black soldier to walk in by his side." The addition of a single word in the Fifteenth Amendment would have done it: The protected categories for voting could have read "race, color, *sex*, or

previous condition of servitude." But that word proved impossible to obtain. For the authors of Reconstruction, enfranchising black men had clear benefits. It punished ex-Confederates and ensured Republican support in the South. But a substantial majority of northern voters—all men, of course—opposed women's enfranchisement. Even Radicals feared that this "side issue" would defeat the Fourteenth Amendment and overburden the party's program.

At the May 1869 convention of the Equal Rights Association, black abolitionist and women's rights advocate Frederick Douglass pleaded for white women to understand the plight in which former slaves found themselves, and to allow black male suffrage to take priority. "When women, because they are women, are hunted down, . . . dragged from their homes and hung upon lamp posts, . . . then they will have an urgency to

OUT IN THE COLD.

**"Out in the Cold"**

Though many women, including African American activists in the South, went to the polls in the early 1870s to test whether the new Fourteenth Amendment had given them the vote, federal courts subsequently rejected women's voting rights. Only the Wyoming and Utah territories fully enfranchised women. At the same time, revised naturalization laws allowed immigrant men of African descent—though not of Asian descent—to become citizens. With its crude Irish, African, and Chinese racial caricatures, this 1884 cartoon from the humor magazine *The Judge* echoes the arguments of some white suffragists that though men of races stereotyped as inferior had been enfranchised, white women were not. The woman knocking on the door is also a caricature, with her harsh appearance and masculine style of dress.   Library of Congress.

obtain the ballot equal to our own." Some women's rights leaders joined Douglass in backing the Fifteenth Amendment, even without the word *sex*. But most white women in the audience rebelled. One African American woman remarked that they "all go for sex, letting race occupy a minor position." In her despair, Elizabeth Cady Stanton lashed out against "Patrick and Sambo and Hans and Ung Tung," maligning uneducated freedmen and immigrants who could vote while educated white women could not. Douglass's resolution in support of the Fifteenth Amendment failed, and the convention broke up in bitterness.

At this searing moment, a rift opened in the women's movement. The majority, led by Lucy Stone and Julia Ward Howe, reconciled themselves to disappointment. Organized into the American Woman Suffrage Association, they remained loyal to the Republican Party in hopes that once Reconstruction had been settled, it would be women's turn. A group led by Elizabeth Cady Stanton and Susan B. Anthony struck out in a new direction. They saw that the moment of radical innovation had passed and woman suffrage was unlikely in the near future. Stanton declared that woman "must not put her trust in man." The new organization that she headed, the National Woman Suffrage Association (NWSA) focused exclusively on women's rights and took up the battle for a federal suffrage amendment.

In 1873, NWSA members decided to test the limits of the new constitutional amendments. Suffragists all over the United States, including some African American women in the South, tried to register and vote. Most were turned away. In Rochester, New York, Susan B. Anthony cast a straight Republican ballot and was arrested afterward in her home, by a polite and rather embarrassed U.S. marshal. In one of a series of ensuing lawsuits, suffrage advocate Virginia Minor of Missouri argued that the registrar who rejected her had violated her rights under the Fourteenth Amendment. In *Minor v. Happersett* (1875), the Supreme Court dashed suffragists' hopes. It ruled that suffrage rights were not inherent in citizenship; women were citizens, but state legislatures could deny women the ballot if they wished.

Despite these defeats, radical Reconstruction created the conditions for a high-profile, nationwide movement for women's voting rights. Amid debates over the Fourteenth and Fifteenth Amendments, some Americans argued for the measure as part of a bold expansion of democracy. Others saw white women's votes as a possible counterweight to the votes of African American or Chinese men (while opponents pointed out that black and immigrant women would likely be enfranchised, too). When Wyoming Territory gave women the vote in 1869, its governor received telegrams of congratulation from as far away as Europe. Afterward, contrary to antisuffragist warnings, female voters in Wyoming did not appear to neglect their homes, abandon their children, or otherwise "unsex" themselves. In fact, suffragists argued that women's presence helped make

Wyoming politics less corrupt and more respectable. The goal of votes for women could no longer be dismissed as the absurd notion of a tiny minority. It became a serious issue for national debate.

- **How did Lincoln and Johnson each approach Reconstruction?**

- **Over what issues did Johnson and Congress clash? What measures and policies emerged from that conflict?**

- **What did the supporters of radical Reconstruction do to advance their vision for the postwar South?**

- **How did Reconstruction affect the movement for women's voting rights?**

# The Meaning of Freedom

While political leaders in Washington struggled over Reconstruction, emancipated slaves acted on their own ideas about freedom (see Comparing American Voices, "Freedom," pp. 474–475). Freedom meant many things—the end of punishment by the lash; the ability to move around; the reunion of families; and the opportunity to build schools and churches, and publish and read newspapers. Topmost among freedmen's demands was the right to vote. To achieve a true measure of freedom, former slaves had to overcome both the hostility of former Confederates and the ambivalence of many Unionist allies.

## The Quest for Land

One of freedmen's most pressing goals was landownership. In the chaotic final months of war, freedmen had seized control of plantations where they could. In Georgia and South Carolina, General William Tecumseh Sherman had reserved large coastal tracts for liberated slaves and settled them on forty-acre plots. Sherman simply did not want to be bothered with refugees as his army crossed the region, but the freedmen assumed that Sherman's order meant that the land was theirs. After the war, resettlement became the responsibility of the Freedmen's Bureau. Thousands of rural blacks hoped for land distributions. "I have gone through the country," reported a black spokesman in South Carolina, "and on every side I was besieged with questions: How are we to get homesteads, to get lands?"

Johnson's amnesty plan, enabling pardoned Confederates to recover property seized during the war, blasted freedmen's hopes. In October 1865, Johnson ordered General Oliver O. Howard, head of the Freedmen's Bureau, to restore plantations on the Sea Islands off the South Carolina coast to their white owners. Dispossessed blacks protested: "Why do you take away our lands? You take them from us who have always been true, always true to the Government! You give them to our all-time enemies! That is not right!" Former slaves resisted efforts to evict them. Led by black Union veterans, they fought pitched battles with plantation owners and bands of ex-Confederate soldiers. But white landowners, sometimes aided by federal troops, generally prevailed.

**Freed Slaves and Northerners: Conflicting Goals**  The problem of land was broader than Johnson's policies or even ex-Confederate resistance. A profound gap lay between the goals of freed slaves and those of Republicans in Washington. The economic revolution of the antebellum period had transformed New England and the Mid-Atlantic states. Most congressional leaders believed, following in the tradition of antebellum Whigs, that once slavery was dead, the same kind of economic development would revolutionize the South. Republicans sought to restore cotton as the country's leading export. They envisioned former slaves as wageworkers on cash-crop plantations, not as independent farmers. Only a handful of radicals, like Thaddeus Stevens, argued that freed slaves had already *earned* a right to the land, through what Lincoln once referred to as "four hundred years of unrequited toil." Stevens proposed that large southern plantations be treated as "forfeited estates of the enemy" and broken up into small farms for the former slaves.

Today, most historians of Reconstruction agree with Stevens: Policymakers did not go far enough to ensure freedpeople's economic welfare. Left without land, former slaves were rendered poor and vulnerable. At the time, however, men like Stevens had few allies. Though often accused of harshness toward the defeated Confederacy, most Republicans—even Radicals—recoiled at the idea of confiscating private land. They could not imagine "giving" land to former slaves. The same congressmen, of course, had no difficulty giving homesteaders land on the frontier that had been taken from Indians. But Republicans were deeply reluctant to confiscate white-owned plantations. Some southern Republican state governments did try, without much success, to use tax policy to break up large landholdings and get them into the hands of poorer whites and blacks. In 1869, South Carolina established a land commission to buy property and resell it on easy terms to the landless; about 14,000 black families acquired farms through

**Wage Labor of Former Slaves**
This photograph, taken in South Carolina shortly after the Civil War, shows former slaves leaving the cotton fields. Many freedpeople were organized into work crews probably not that different from earlier slave gangs, although they now labored for wages. Freedmen resisted such working conditions and sought greater freedom from constant threats and oversight.   © Collection of the New-York Historical Society.

the program. But such initiatives were the exception, not the rule.

**Wage Labor and Sharecropping**  Freedmen and freedwomen wanted as much independence of work and life as they could achieve. Obtaining no land, however, most began with few options but to work for former slave owners. Serious conflict ensued. Landowners wanted to retain the old **gang-labor system**, with wages replacing the food, clothing, and shelter that slaves had once received. Southern planters—who had recently scorned the North for the cruelties of the wage-labor system—now embraced waged work with apparent satisfaction. Maliciously comparing freedpeople to free-roaming pigs, landowners told them to "root, hog, or die." Former slaves found themselves with rock-bottom wages, especially in agriculture; it was a shock to find that Emancipation and a "free labor" system did not prevent a hardworking family from nearly starving. African American workers used a variety of tactics to fight back. Some left the fields and traveled long distances to seek work on the railroads or in turpentine and lumber camps. Others organized to bargain for fairer wages. Not only black farmworkers but also factory workers and laundrywomen went on strike.

At the same time, a major conflict raged between employers and freedpeople over the labor of women. In slavery, African American women's bodies had been the sexual property of white men. Protecting black women from such abuse, as much as possible, was a crucial priority for freedpeople. When planters demanded that black women go back into the fields, African Americans resisted resolutely. "I seen on some plantations," one freedman recounted, "where the white men would . . . tell colored men that their wives and children could not live on their places unless they work in the fields. The colored men [answered that] whenever they wanted their wives to work they would tell them themselves."

There was a profound irony in this man's definition of freedom: It designated a wife's labor as her husband's property. In that, of course, freedpeople were adapting to white norms. Some black women asserted their independence and headed their own households—though in a society utterly disrupted by war, this was often a matter of necessity rather than choice. For many freedwomen and freedmen, the opportunity for a stable family life was one of the greatest achievements of emancipation. Many enthusiastically accepted the northern ideal of **domesticity**. Missionaries, teachers, and editors of black newspapers urged men to work diligently and support their families, and women (though many worked for wages) to devote themselves to motherhood and the home. Like their northern allies, many southern African Americans believed domesticity was the key to civilization and progress.

# Freedom

**S**lavery meant one thing to slave owners, something altogether different to slaves. When freedom came, there was no bridging this bottomless gulf. The following documents offer vivid testimony to the bitter legacy of slavery.

## Henry William Ravenel

### Diary Entry, March 8, 1865

Henry William Ravenel was from a (formerly) wealthy plantation family; his diary was written amid the Confederacy's collapse and the aftermath of defeat in South Carolina.

The breath of Emancipation has passed over the country, & we are now in that transition state between the new & the old systems—a state of chaos & disorder. Will the negro be materially benefitted by the change? Will the condition of the country in its productive resources, in material prosperity be improved? Will it be a benefit to the landed proprietors? These are questions which will have their solution in the future. They are in the hands of that Providence which over-ruleth all things for good. It was a strong conviction of my best judgment that the old relation of master & slave, had received the divine sanction & was the best condition in which the two races could live together for mutual benefit. There were many defects to be corrected & many abuses to be remedied. Among these defects I will enumerate the want of legislation to make the marriage contract binding—to prevent the separation of families, & to restrain the cupidity of cruel masters. Perhaps it is for neglecting these obligations that God has seen fit to dissolve that relation. I believe the negro must remain in this country & that his condition although a freed-man, must be to labour on the soil. Nothing but necessity will compel him to labour. Now the question is, will that necessity be so strong as to compel him to labour, which will be profitable to the landed proprietors. Will he make as much cotton, sugar, rice & tobacco for the world as he did previously? They will now have a choice *where* to labour. This will ensure good treatment & the best terms. The most humane, the most energetic & the most judicious managers have the best chances in the race for success. I expect to see a revolution in the ownership of landed estates. Those only can succeed who bring the best capacity for the business. Time will show.

Source: *The Civil War and Reconstruction: A Documentary Collection*, ed. William E. Gienapp (New York: W. W. Norton, 2001), 304–05.

## Edward Barnell Heyward

### Letter, January 22, 1866

This letter is from the son of a South Carolina plantation owner to a friend in the North. Perhaps most telling, in this letter, is Heyward's despair over the future of his former slaves. He believes that, after emancipation, "their best days are over."

My dear Jim

Your letter of date July 1865, has just reached me and you will be relieved by my answers, to find that I am still alive, and extremely glad to hear from you. . . . I have served in the Army, my brother died in the Army, and every family has lost members. No one can know how reduced we are, particularly the refined & educated. . . .

My father had five plantations on the coast, and all the buildings were burnt, and the negroes, now left to themselves, are roaming in a starvation condition . . . like lost sheep, with no one to care for them.

They find the Yankee only a speculator, and they have no confidence in anyone. They very naturally, poor things, think that freedom means doing nothing, and this they are determined to do. They look to the government, to take care of them, and it will be many years, before this once productive country will be able to support itself. The former kind and just treatment of the slaves, and their docile and generous temper, make them now disposed to be [quiet] and obedient: but the determination of your Northern people to give them a place in the councils of the Country and make them the equal of the white man, will at last, bear its fruit, and we may *then* expect them, to rise against the whites, and in the end, be exterminated themselves.

I am now interested in a school for the negroes, who are around me, and will endeavor to do my duty, to them, as ever before, but I am afraid their best days are past. . . .

I feel now that I have *no country*, I *obey* like a subject, but I cannot love such a government. Perhaps the next letter, you get from me, will be from England. . . .

Source: Stanley I. Kutler, ed., *Looking for America: The People's History*, 2nd ed., 2 vols. (New York: W. W. Norton, 1979), 2: 4–6.

## Isabella Soustan
### Letter, July 10, 1865

Isabella Soustan, a freedwoman in Virginia, wrote this letter to her former master not long after the Civil War's end.

I have the honor to appeal to you one more for assistance, Master. I am cramped hear nearly to death and no one ceares for me heare, and I want you if you please Sir, to Send for me. I dont care if I am free. I had rather live with you. I was as free while with you, as I wanted to be. Mas Man you know I was as well Satisfied with you as I wanted to be. Now Affectionate Master pleas, oh, please come or Sind for me. John is still hired out at the same and doing Well and well Satisfied only greaveing about home, he want to go home as bad as I do, if you ever Send for me I will Send for him immediately, and take him home to his kind Master. Mas Man. Pleas to give my love to all of my friends, and especially to my young mistress don't forget to reserve a double portion for yourself. I Will close at present, hoping to bee at your Service Soon yes before yonder Sun Shal rise and set any more.

May I subscribe myself your Most affectionate humble friend and Servt.
Isabella A. Soustan

Source: Leon F. Litwack, *Been in the Storm So Long: The Aftermath of Slavery* (New York: Knopf, 1979), 332.

## Jourdon Anderson
### Letter, August 7, 1865

Anderson had escaped with his family from Tennessee and settled in Dayton, Ohio. He dictated this letter, which then was printed in the *New York Daily Tribune*. Folklorists have recorded the ways that slaves found, even in bondage, for "puttin' down" their masters. But only in freedom – and in a northern state – could Anderson's sarcasm be expressed so openly.

To My Old Master, Colonel P. H. Anderson, Big Spring, Tennessee.

Sir:
I got your letter, and was glad to find that you had not forgotten Jourdon. . . . I thought the Yankees would have hung you long before this, for harboring Rebs. . . .

I want to know particularly what the good chance is you propose to give me. I am doing tolerably well here. I get twenty-five dollars a month, with victuals and clothing; have a comfortable home for Mandy, — the folks here call her Mrs. Anderson, — and the children — Milly, Jane, and Grundy — go to school and are learning well. . . .

Mandy says she would be afraid to go back without some proof that you were disposed to treat us justly and kindly; and we have concluded to test your sincerity by asking you to send us our wages for the time we served you. This will make us forget and forgive old scores, and rely on your justice and friendship in the future. I served you faithfully for thirty-two years, and Mandy twenty years. At twenty-five dollars a month for me and two dollars a week for Mandy, our earnings would amount to eleven thousand six hundred and eighty dollars. Add to this the interest for the time our wages have been kept back, and deduct what you paid for our clothing, and three doctor's visits to me, and pulling a tooth for Mandy, and the balance will show what we are in justice entitled to. Please send the balance by Adams Express, in care of V. Winters, esq., Dayton, Ohio. If you do not pay us for faithful labors in the past we can have little faith in your promises in the future. . . .

In answering this letter, please state if there would be any safety for my Milly and Jane, who are now grown up, and both good-looking girls. . . . I would rather stay here and starve — and die, if it come to that — than have my girls brought to shame by the violence and wickedness of their young masters. You will also please state if there has been any schools opened for the colored children in your neighborhood. The great desire of my life now is to give my children an education, and have them form virtuous habits.

From your old servant,
Jourdon Anderson

P.S. Say howdy to George Carter, and thank him for taking the pistol from you when you were shooting at me.

Source: Leon F. Litwack, *Been in the Storm So Long: The Aftermath of Slavery* (New York: Knopf, 1979), 333–335.

### ANALYZING THE EVIDENCE

- **What were Ravenel's and Heyward's attitudes toward freedmen and freedwomen? How did their views differ, and on what points did they agree?**

- **What predictions do Ravenel and Heyward make about the South's postwar future? How might their expectations have shaped their own actions?**

- **Soustan and Anderson are both writing to men who formerly claimed them as property. How do you account for the differences in their approach and tone? What conditions of life does each writer mention? What conclusions might be drawn from this about the varied postwar experiences of freedpeople?**

Even in rural areas, former slaves refused to work under the conditions of slavery. There would be no gang work, they vowed: no overseers, no whippings, no regulation of their private lives. All across the South, planters who needed labor were forced to yield to what one planter termed "the inveterate prejudices of the freedmen, who desire to be masters of their own time." In a few areas, waged work became the norm—for example, on the giant sugar plantations of Louisiana financed by northern capital. But cotton planters lacked the money to pay wages, and sometimes, in lieu of a straight wage, they offered a share of the crop. Freedmen, in turn, paid their rent in shares of the harvest.

Thus sprang up the distinctive laboring system of cotton agriculture known as **sharecropping**, in which freedmen worked as renters, exchanging their labor for the use of land, house, implements, and sometimes seed and fertilizer. Sharecroppers typically turned over half of their crops to the landlord (Map 15.2). In a credit-starved agricultural region that grew crops for a world economy, sharecropping was an effective strategy, through which laborers and landowners shared risks and returns. But it was a very unequal relationship, given sharecroppers' dire economic circumstances. Starting out penniless, they had no way of making it through the first growing season without borrowing for food and supplies.

Country storekeepers stepped in. Bankrolled by northern suppliers, they furnished the sharecropper with provisions and took as collateral a **lien** on the crop, effectively assuming ownership of the cropper's share and leaving him only the proceeds that remained after

## MAP 15.2

### The Barrow Plantation, 1860 and 1881

This map is a modern redrawing of one that first appeared in the popular magazine *Scribner's Monthly* in April 1881, accompanying an article about the Barrow plantation. The boundary line is the same on both maps because the plantation remained in the same family. Comparing the 1860 map of this central Georgia plantation with the 1881 map reveals the impact of sharecropping on patterns of black residence. In 1860, the slave quarters were clustered near the planter's house. In contrast, by 1881 the sharecroppers were scattered across the plantation's 2,000 acres, having built cabins on the ridges between the low-lying streams. The surname Barrow was common among the sharecropping families, which means almost certainly that they had been slaves who, years after emancipation, still had not moved on. For sharecroppers, freedom meant not only their individual lots and cabins but also the school and church shown on the map.

**Cotton Farmers, Marietta, Georgia, c. 1880**

Before the Civil War, the South had proudly called itself the "Cotton Kingdom": After the war, cotton was still king, but few southerners got rich on cotton profits. Instead, thousands of small-scale farmers, white and black, struggled with plunging crop prices, debt, and taxes on land to support an array of ambitious Reconstruction programs. The farmers here have baled their cotton for market and pose with their wagons in Marietta's courthouse square.   Courtesy Georgia Department of Archives, Vanishing Georgia Collection, cob262.

his debts had been paid. Once indebted at one store, sharecroppers could no longer shop around. They became easy targets for exorbitant prices, unfair interest rates, and crooked bookkeeping. As cotton prices declined during the 1870s, more and more sharecroppers failed to settle accounts and fell into permanent debt. If the merchant was also the landowner or conspired with the landowner, the debt became a pretext for forced labor, or **peonage**, though when things became hopeless, sharecroppers sometimes managed to pull up stakes and move on.

Sharecropping—a product of the struggles of Reconstruction—endured in part because it was a good fit for cotton agriculture. Cotton, unlike sugarcane, could be raised efficiently by small farmers (provided they had the lash of indebtedness always on their backs). We can see this in the experience of other countries that became major producers in response to the global cotton famine set off by the Civil War. In India, Egypt, Brazil, and West Africa, variants of the sharecropping system emerged. Most striking was the adoption everywhere of crop-lien laws, at the behest of international merchants and bankers who put up the capital. Indian and Egyptian villagers got the advances they needed to shift from subsistence agriculture to cotton but at the price of being placed, as in America, perma-

nently under the thumb of furnishing merchants. American planters resisted sharecropping at first because they started at a different place: not traditional, subsistence economies that had to be converted to cotton but a proven plantation system over which they had been absolute masters.

For freedmen, sharecropping was not the worst choice, in a world where former masters threatened to impose labor conditions that were close to slavery (see Reading American Pictures, "Why Sharecropping?" p. 478). But for southern agriculture, the costs were devastating. With farms leased on a year-to-year basis, neither tenant nor owner had much incentive to improve the property. The crop-lien system rested on expensive interest payments—money that might otherwise have gone into agricultural improvements. And sharecropping committed the South inflexibly to cotton, which as a market crop generated the cash required by landlords and furnishing merchants. The result was a stagnant farm economy that blighted the South's future. As Republican governments tried to remake the South, they faced not only the challenges of wartime destruction and widespread poverty but also the failure of their hopes that free labor would create a modern, prosperous South, built in the image of the industrializing North. Instead, a rural economy emerged that remained

# Why Sharecropping?

The account of sharecropping on the neighboring pages describes the experience of hundreds of thousands of ex-slaves and plantation owners. How do we know that our generalizations are true? Or, more concretely, that a sharecropper reading our account might nod and say, "Yes, that's the way it was"? One sliver of evidence is this photograph of a family of freedpeople standing proudly by their new cabin and young cotton crop. In what ways does this contemporary photograph confirm or amplify our account of sharecropping?

**Sharecroppers in Georgia.** Brown Brothers.

## ANALYZING THE EVIDENCE

- The cotton rows go right up to the house. Why might this family not have land set aside for a garden and livestock? What does this suggest about the historians' claim that sharecropping doomed the South to a cash-crop monoculture?

- Note the gent in the background—most likely the landowner—with his handsome horse and carriage. The tenant farmers and children in the foreground look directly at the photographer, yet this man chooses to remain in the background and look straight ahead. Presuming that this man is the landowner, which seems likely, he has probably rented out the cabins and farmland to these tenants but still has the run of the place. What does his presence suggest about the limits of sharecropping as a means of freedpeople achieving independence?

- In the struggle for economic independence, everything was relative. What elements in the photograph suggest that, compared to the lives they knew as slaves or, after emancipation would have faced as day laborers, these farmers might have thought they were not faring so badly? Consult Map 15.2 on page 476 while considering your answer (bearing in mind of course that the family in this photograph did not live on the Barrow plantation).

mired in widespread poverty and based on an uneasy compromise between landowners and laborers.

## Republican Governments in the South

Between 1868 and 1871, all the former Confederate states met congressional stipulations and rejoined the Union. Protected by federal troops, Republican administrations in these states retained power for periods ranging from a few months in Virginia to nine years in South Carolina, Louisiana, and Florida. These governments remain some of the most misunderstood institutions in all U.S. history. Ex-Confederates never accepted their legitimacy. Many contemporaries agreed, focusing particularly on the role of African American Republicans who began to serve in public office. "It is strange, abnormal, and unfit," declared one British visitor to Louisiana, "that a *negro* Legislature should deal . . . with the gravest commercial and financial interests."

During much of the twentieth century, historians echoed such critics, condemning Reconstruction leaders as ignorant and corrupt. These historians shared, at root, the racist assumptions of the British observer: Blacks were simply unfit to legislate. (In the early twentieth century, U.S. historians lived in a country that once again elected, year after year, an all-white Congress; the prospect of a nonwhite president was completely unthinkable.) In fact, Reconstruction governments were ambitious. They were hated, in part, because they undertook impressive reforms in public education, family law, social services, commerce, and transportation. Like their northern allies, southern Republicans admired the economic and social transformations that had occurred in the North before the Civil War, and during Reconstruction they worked energetically to import them.

The southern Republican Party included former Whigs, a few former Democrats, black and white newcomers from the North, and southern African Americans. From the start its leaders faced the dilemma of racial prejudice. In the upcountry, white Unionists were eager to join the party. But in most areas the Republicans also needed African American voters, who constituted a majority of registered voters in Alabama, Florida, South Carolina, and Mississippi.

For a brief moment in the late 1860s, black and white Republicans joined forces through the Union League, a secret fraternal order. Formed in border states and northern cities during the Civil War, the Union League became a powerful political club that spread through the former Confederacy. Functioning as a grassroots wing of Radical Republicanism, league members pressured Congress to uphold justice to freedmen. After blacks won voting rights, the Union League organized meetings at churches and schoolhouses to instruct freedmen on political issues and voting procedures. League clubs also held parades and military drills, giving a public face to the new political order.

The Freedmen's Bureau also supported grassroots Reconstruction efforts. Though some bureau officials were hostile to freedmen and sympathized with planters' interests, most were dedicated, often idealistic men who tried valiantly to reconcile opposing interests. Bureau men kept a sharp eye out for unfair labor contracts and often forced landowners to bargain with workers and tenants. Bureau leaders advised freedmen

**Hiram R. Revels**

In 1870, Hiram R. Revels (1827–1901) was elected to the U.S. Senate from Mississippi to fill Jefferson Davis's former seat. Revels was a free black from North Carolina who had moved to the North and attended Knox College in Illinois. During the Civil War he had recruited African Americans for the Union army and, as an ordained Methodist minister, served as chaplain of a black regiment in Mississippi, where he settled after the war.   The Granger Collection, New York.

**Fisk Jubilee Singers, 1873**

Fisk University in Nashville, Tennessee, was established in 1865 to provide higher education for African Americans from all across the South. When university funds ran short in 1871, the Jubilee Singers choral group was formed and began touring to raise money for the school. They performed African American spirituals and folksongs, such as "Swing Low, Sweet Chariot," arranged in ways that appealed to white audiences, making this music nationally popular for the first time. In 1872 the group performed for President Grant at the White House. Money raised by this acclaimed chorale saved Fisk from bankruptcy. Edmund Havel's portrait of the group was painted during their first European tour.   Fisk University Art Galleries.

on economic matters; provided direct payments to desperate families, especially women and children; and helped establish freedpeople's schools. In cooperation with northern aid societies, the bureau played a key role in founding African American colleges and universities such as Fisk, Tougaloo, and the Hampton Institute. These institutions, in turn, focused first on training teachers. By 1869 there were more than three thousand teachers instructing freedpeople in the South. More than half were themselves black.

Ex-Confederates viewed the Union League, Freedmen's Bureau, and Republican Party as illegitimate forces in southern affairs, and they bitterly resented the political education of freedpeople. They referred to southern whites who supported Reconstruction as **scalawags**—an ancient Scots-Irish term for worthless animals—and they denounced northern whites as **carpetbaggers**, self-seeking interlopers who carried

all their property in cheap suitcases called carpetbags. Such labels glossed over the actual diversity of white Republicans. Many new arrivals from the North, while motivated by personal profit, also brought capital and skills. Interspersed with ambitious schemers were idealists hoping to advance the cause of freedmen's rights. The so-called scalawags were even more varied. Some were former slave owners; others were ex-Whigs or even ex-Democrats drawn to Republicanism as the best way to attract northern capital. But most hailed from the backcountry and wanted to rid the South of its slaveholding aristocracy. They had generally fought against, or at least refused to support, the Confederacy, believing that slavery had victimized whites as well as blacks.

Southern Democrats' contempt for black leaders, whom they regarded as ignorant field hands, was just as misguided as their stereotypes about white Republicans. The first African American leaders in the South

**Outside the Freedmen's Bureau Office, Beaufort, South Carolina**
This photograph, taken in the 1870s, shows how offices of the Freedmen's Bureau became hubs of activity in southern cities and towns. Southerners, both black and white, gathered at the offices to sign contracts, resolve labor disputes, obtain official advice—even get married and mediate family conflicts. Bureau officials, whose numbers were pitifully small in comparison with the scope and number of their duties, had limited resources to address postwar devastation and the arrival of "free labor." Nonetheless, in the power vacuum of the ex-Confederacy, many bureau officials played a central role in restoring order and upholding justice. Miriam and Ira D. Wallach Division of Art, Prints and Photographs, The New York Public Library. Astor, Lenox and Tilden Foundations.

came from the ranks of antebellum free blacks. They were joined by northern blacks who moved south to support Reconstruction. Many were Union veterans; some were employees of the Freedmen's Bureau and northern missionary societies. Others had escaped from slavery and were returning home. One of these ex-slaves was Blanche K. Bruce, who had been tutored on a Virginia plantation by his white father. During the war, Bruce escaped and established a school for freedmen in Missouri. In 1869, he moved to Mississippi and became active in politics; in 1874, he became Mississippi's second black U.S. senator.

During radical Reconstruction, African American speakers, some financed by the Republican Party, fanned out into the old plantation districts and recruited former slaves to participate in politics. Still, few of the new leaders were field hands; most had been preachers or artisans. Literacy helped freedman Thomas Allen, a Baptist minister and shoemaker, win election to the Georgia legislature. "In my county," Allen recalled, "the colored people came to me for instructions, and I gave them the best instructions I could. I took the *New York Tribune* and other papers, and in that way I found out a great deal, and I told them whatever I thought was right." Though never proportionate to their numbers in the population, blacks became officeholders across the South. In South Carolina, African Americans constituted a majority in the lower house of the legislature

**Freedmen's School, Petersburg, Virginia, 1870s**

A Union veteran, returning to Virginia in the 1870s to photograph battlefields, captured this image of an African American teacher and her students at a freedmen's school. Note the difficult conditions in which they study: Many are barefoot, and there are gaps in the walls and floor of the school building. Nonetheless, the students have a few books. Despite poverty and relentless hostility from many whites, freedpeople across the South were determined to get a basic education for themselves and their children. William L. Clements Library, University of Michigan.

in 1868. Over the course of Reconstruction, twenty African Americans served in state administrations as governor, lieutenant governor, secretary of state, or lesser offices. More than six hundred served as state legislators and sixteen as congressmen.

Southern Republicans had big plans. Their Reconstruction governments eliminated property qualifications for the vote and abolished the Black Codes that hemmed in freedpeople. Their new state constitutions expanded the rights of married women, enabling them to hold property and wages independent of their husbands'—"a wonderful reform," one white woman in Georgia wrote, for "the cause of Women's Rights." Like their counterparts in the North, southern Republicans also believed in using government to foster economic growth. They sought to diversify the economy beyond cotton agriculture, and they poured money into railroads and other building projects to expand the region's shattered economy.

In myriad ways, Republicans brought southern state and city governments up to date. They outlawed corporal punishments such as whipping and branding. They established more humane penitentiaries as well as hospitals and asylums for orphans and the disabled. South Carolina offered free public health services, while Alabama provided free legal representation for defendants who could not pay. Some municipal governments paved the streets and installed streetlights. Petersburg, Virginia, established a board of health that offered free medical care during the smallpox epidemic of 1873. Nashville, Tennessee, created soup kitchens for the poor.

Most impressive of all were achievements in public education, where the South had lagged woefully. Republicans viewed education as the foundation of a true democratic order. By 1875, over half of black children were attending school in Mississippi, Florida, and South Carolina. African Americans of all ages rushed to the newly established schools, even when they had to pay tuition. They understood why slaveholders had criminalized slave literacy: The practice of freedom rested on the ability to read newspapers, labor contracts, history books, and the Bible. A school official in Virginia reported that freedpeople were "*crazy to learn.*" One Louisiana man explained why he was sending his children to school, even though he needed their help in the field. It was "better than leaving them a fortune; because if you left them even five hundred dollars, some man having more education than they had would come along and cheat them out of it all." Meanwhile, thousands of white children, particularly girls and the sons of poor farmers and laborers, also benefited from the new public education system. Young white women's graduation from high school, an unheard of occurrence before the Civil War, became accepted and even celebrated in southern cities and towns.

## Building Black Communities

In slavery days, African Americans had built networks of religious worship and mutual aid to sustain one another, but these operated largely underground. After emancipation, southern blacks could engage in open community building. In doing so, they cooperated with northern missionaries and teachers who came to help in the great work of freedom. "Ignorant though they may be, on account of long years of oppression, they exhibit a desire to hear and to learn, that I never imagined," reported African American minister Reverend James Lynch, who had traveled from Maryland to the Deep South. "Every word you say while preaching, they drink down and respond to, with an earnestness that sets your heart all on fire."

Independent churches quickly became central institutions of black life, as blacks across the South left white-dominated congregations, where they had sat in segregated balconies, and built churches of their own. These churches joined their counterparts in the North to become national denominations, including, most prominently, the National Baptist Convention and the African Methodist Episcopal Church. Everywhere, black churches served not only as sites of worship but also as schools, social centers, and meeting halls. Black ministers were community leaders and often political spokesmen as well. As Charles H. Pearce, a Methodist minister in Florida, declared, "A man in this State cannot do his whole duty as a minister except he looks out for the political interests of his people." Calling forth the special destiny of formerly enslaved southerners as the new "Children of Israel," black ministers provided a powerful religious underpinning for the politics of their congregations.

The flowering of southern black churches, schools, newspapers, and civic groups was one of the most enduring initiatives of the Reconstruction era. Dedicated teachers and charity leaders embarked on a project of "race uplift" that never ceased thereafter, while black entrepreneurs were proud to build businesses that served their own communities. The issue of **desegregation** — sharing public facilities with whites — was a trickier one. Some black leaders pressed for desegregated public facilities, but they were keenly aware of the backlash this was likely to provoke. Many freedpeople made it clear that they preferred their children to attend all-black schools, especially if they had encountered hostile or condescending white teachers. Others had pragmatic concerns. Asked whether she wanted her boys to attend an integrated school, one woman in New Orleans said no: "I don't want my children to be pounded by dem white boys. I don't send them to school to fight, I send them to learn."

At the national level, congressmen wrestled with similar issues as they debated an ambitious civil rights bill championed by Radical Republican senator Charles Sumner. Sumner first introduced his bill in 1870, seeking to enforce, among other things, equal access to schools, public transportation, hotels, and churches. Through a series of defeats and delays, the bill remained on Capitol Hill for five years. Opponents charged that shared use of public spaces would lead to race mixing and intermarriage. Some sympathetic Republicans feared a backlash, while others questioned whether, because of the First Amendment, the federal government had the right to regulate churches. On his deathbed in 1874, Sumner exhorted a visitor to remember the civil rights bill: "Don't let it fail." In the end, the Senate removed Sumner's provision for integrated churches, and the House removed the clause requiring integrated schools. But to honor the great Massachusetts abolitionist, Congress passed the Civil Rights Act of 1875. The law required "full and equal" access to jury service and to transportation and public accommodations, irrespective of race. It was the last such act for almost a hundred years — until the Civil Rights Act of 1964.

- In what ways did the freedmen's goal of landownership clash with the goals of northern Republicans and of southerners? What were the results of that clash?

- What were the goals of southern Republican governments? In what ways did they succeed in realizing these aims?

- How did black communities develop during Reconstruction? Based on their collective activities, what priorities did they appear to have had in the wake of emancipation?

# The Undoing of Reconstruction

Sumner's death marked the waning of radical Reconstruction. Leaders of that movement had accomplished more than anyone dreamed a few years earlier. But a chasm had opened between the goals of freedmen, who wanted autonomy, and policymakers, whose first priorities were to reincorporate ex-Confederates into the nation and build a powerful national economy. Meanwhile, the North was flooded with one-sided, often racist reports such as James M. Pike's *The Prostrate State* (1873), which described South Carolina in the grip of "black barbarism." Events of the 1870s deepened the northern public's disillusionment. Scandals rocked the Grant administration, and a sudden economic depression placed severe restraints on both private investment and public spending. At the same time, northern re- solve was worn down by ex-Confederates' continued refusal to accept Reconstruction. Only full-scale military intervention could reverse the situation in the South, and by the mid-1870s the North had no political will- power to renew the occupation. Besieged by economic hardship and ex-Confederate resistance, Reconstruc- tion faltered.

## The Republican Unraveling

Republicans who banked on economic growth to un- derpin their ambitious programs found their hopes dashed by a severe depression that began in 1873. This global downturn affected much of Europe and even touched other parts of the world. In the United States, the initial panic was triggered by the bankruptcy of the Northern Pacific Railroad, backed by leading finan- cier Jay Cooke. Cooke's supervision of Union finances during the Civil War had made him a national hero; his downfall was a shock, and since Cooke was so well connected in Washington, it raised suspicions that Re- publican financial manipulation had caused the de- pression. Grant's officials deepened public resentment toward their party when they rejected pleas to increase the money supply and provide relief from debt and unemployment.

The impact of the depression varied in different parts of the United States. But many farmers found themselves in a terrible plight as crop prices plunged, while industrial workers faced layoffs and sharp re- ductions in pay. Within a year, 50 percent of American iron manufacturing had stopped. By 1877, half the nation's railroad companies had filed for bankruptcy. Rail construction halted. With hundreds of thousands thrown out of work, people took to the road. Wander- ing "tramps," who camped beside railroad tracks and knocked on doors to beg for work and food, became a source of fear and anxiety for prosperous Americans.

In addition to discrediting Republicans, the depres- sion directly undercut their policies, most dramatically in the South. The ex-Confederacy was still recovering from the ravages of war, and the region's new economic and social order, negotiated in the wake of emancipa- tion, remained fragile. The ambitious policies of south- ern Republicans—for education, public health, and grants to railroad builders—cost a great deal of money. Federal support, offered through programs like the Freedmen's Bureau, had begun to fade even before 1873. Republicans had banked on major infusions of

northern and foreign investment capital into the South; for the most part, these failed to materialize. Investors who had sunk money into Confederate bonds, only to have those repudiated, were especially wary. The South's economy grew more slowly than Republicans had hoped, and when the depression hit, growth screeched to a halt. State debts mounted rapidly, and as crushing interest on bonds fell due, public credit collapsed.

Not only had Republican officials failed to antici- pate a severe depression; during the era of generous spending, considerable funds had been wasted or ended up in the pockets of public officials. Corruption was common in an era of railroad building and ambitious public contracts, and some notorious cases in the South rivaled the scandals that would soon be uncovered in Washington, D.C. Two swindlers in North Carolina, one of them a former Union general, were found to have distributed more than $200,000 in bribes and loans to legislators to gain millions in state funds for rail con- struction. Instead of building railroads, they used the money to travel to Europe and speculate in stocks and bonds. Not only Republicans were on the take. "You are mistaken," wrote one Democrat to a northern friend, "if you suppose that all the evils . . . result from the carpetbaggers and negroes. The Democrats are leagued with them when anything is proposed that promises to pay." Bipartisan or not, such corruption severely dam- aged the cause of Reconstruction.

One of the depression's most tragic results was the failure of the Freedman's Savings and Trust Company. This private bank, founded in 1865, had worked closely with the Freedmen's Bureau and Union army across the South. Former slaves associated it with the party of Lincoln, and thousands responded to northerners' call for thrift and savings by bringing their small deposits to the nearest branch. Not only African American farm- ers and entrepreneurs but also churches and charitable groups opened accounts at the bank. But in the early 1870s, the bank's directors sank their money into risky loans and speculative investments. In June 1874, the bank failed.

Some Republicans believed that, because the bank had been so closely associated with the U.S. Army and other federal agencies, Congress had a duty to step in. Even a southern Democratic representative argued that the government was "morally bound to see to it that not a dollar is lost." But in the end, Congress refused to compensate the sixty-one thousand depositors; about half recovered small amounts—averaging $18.51—but the other half received nothing. Abandonment of the bank signaled that the party of Reconstruction was losing its moral leadership.

**The Disillusioned Liberals** | As a result of both the depression and a backlash against the activist government of the postwar years, a revolt took shape inside the Republican Party. It was led by influential intellectuals, journalists, and businessmen who were **classical liberals** — believers in free trade, smaller government, and limited voting rights. Unable to block Grant's renomination in 1872, these dissidents broke away and formed a new party under the name Liberal Republican. Their candidate was Horace Greeley, longtime publisher of the *New York Tribune* and veteran reformer and abolitionist. The Democrats, still in disarray, also nominated Greeley, notwithstanding his editorial diatribes against them. A poor campaigner, Greeley was assailed so bitterly that, as he said, "I hardly knew whether I was running for the Presidency or the penitentiary."

Grant won re-election overwhelmingly, capturing 56 percent of the popular vote and every electoral vote. Yet the Liberal Republicans had managed to shift the terms of political debate. The agenda they had advanced — civil service reform, smaller government, restricted voting rights, and reconciliation with the South — resonated with Democrats, who were working to reclaim their status as a legitimate national party. Democrats had long been the party of limited government, and the rise of Liberal Republicanism provided an opportunity to revive that message. Liberalism thus crossed party lines, uniting disillusioned Republicans with Democrats who denounced government activism, especially social welfare programs. E. L. Godkin of *The Nation* and other classical liberal editors played key roles in turning northern public opinion against Reconstruction. With unabashed elitism, liberals claimed freedmen were unfit to vote. They denounced universal suffrage, which "can only mean in plain English the government of ignorance and vice."

The second Grant administration gave the liberals plenty of ammunition for their anticorruption guns. The most notorious scandal involved Crédit Mobilier, a sham corporation set up by shareholders in the Union Pacific Railroad to secure government grants at an enormous profit. Organizers of the scheme protected it from federal investigation by providing gifts of Crédit Mobilier stock to powerful members of Congress. Another major scandal involved the Whiskey Ring, a network of liquor distillers and treasury agents who defrauded the government of millions of dollars of excise taxes on whiskey. The ringleader was a Grant appointee, and Grant's private secretary, Orville Babcock, had a hand in the thievery. The others went to prison, but Grant stood by Babcock, possibly perjuring himself to save his secretary from jail. The stench of scandal permeated the White House.

## Counterrevolution in the South

While northerners became preoccupied with scandals and the shock of economic depression, ex-Confederates seized the initiative in the South. Most believed (as northern liberals had also begun to argue) that southern Reconstruction governments were illegitimate "regimes." Led by the planters, ex-Confederates staged a massive counterrevolution designed to take back the South.

Insofar as they could win at the ballot box, southern Democrats took that route. They got ex-Confederate voting rights restored and campaigned against "negro rule." But when violence was necessary, southern Democrats used it. Present-day Americans, witnessing violence and political instability in other countries, seldom remember that our own history includes the overthrow of elected governments by paramilitary groups. But this is exactly how Reconstruction ended in many parts of the South. Ex-Confederates organized to terrorize Republicans, especially in districts with large proportions of black voters. Black political leaders were shot, hanged, beaten to death, and in one case even beheaded. Many Republicans, both black and white, went into hiding or fled for their lives. Southern Democrats called this violent process "Redemption."

No one looms larger in this bloody story than Nathan Bedford Forrest, a decorated Confederate general. Born in poverty in 1821, Forrest had scrambled in the booming cotton economy to become a big-time slave trader and Mississippi plantation owner. A fiery champion of secession, Forrest had formed a Tennessee Confederate cavalry regiment, fought bravely at the battle of Shiloh, and won fame as a daring raider. On April 12, 1864, his troopers perpetrated one of the war's worst atrocities, the slaughter of black Union troops at Fort Pillow, Tennessee. Forrest's troops refused to take prisoners, instead shooting down black soldiers as they tried to surrender.

Forrest's determination to uphold white supremacy emerged again after the war's end, altering the course of Reconstruction. William G. Brownlow, elected

**Nathan Bedford Forrest in Uniform, c. 1865**
Before he became Grand Wizard of the Ku Klux Klan, Forrest had been a celebrated cavalry general in the Confederate army. This photograph shows him in uniform before he was mustered out.    Library of Congress.

as Tennessee's Republican governor in 1865, was a tough man, a former prisoner of the Confederates who was not shy about calling his enemies to account. Ex-Confederates struck back with a campaign of terror, targeting especially Brownlow's black supporters. Amid the mayhem, some ex-Confederates formed the first Ku Klux Klan group in late 1865 or early 1866. As it proliferated across the state, the Klan turned to Forrest, who had been trying, unsuccessfully, to rebuild his prewar fortunes. Late in 1866, at a secret meeting in Nashville, Forrest donned the robes of Grand Wizard. His activities are mostly cloaked in mystery, but there is no mistake about his goals: The Klan would strike blows against the despised Republican government of Tennessee.

In many towns, the Klan became virtually identical to the Democratic Party. In fact, Klan members—including Forrest—dominated Tennessee's delegation to the Democratic national convention of 1868. At home, the Klan unleashed a murderous campaign of terror, and though Governor Brownlow responded resolutely, in the end the Republicans cracked. By March 1869, Brownlow retreated to the U.S. Senate. The Klan spread in the meantime to other states, where its members burned freedmen's schools, beat teachers, murdered

and threatened Republican politicians, and attacked Republican gatherings. By 1870, Democrats had seized power in Georgia and North Carolina and were making headway across the South.

In responding to the Klan between 1869 and 1871, the federal government showed it could still exert power effectively in the South. Determined to end Klan violence, Congress held extensive hearings and passed laws designed to put down the Klan and enforce freedmen's rights under the Fourteenth and Fifteenth Amendments. These so-called Enforcement Laws authorized federal prosecutions, military intervention, and martial law to suppress terrorist activities. The Grant administration made full use of these new powers. In South Carolina, where the Klan became deeply entrenched, U.S. troops occupied nine counties, made hundreds of arrests, and drove as many as 2,000 Klansmen from the state.

This assault on the Klan, while raising the spirits of southern Republicans, also revealed how dependent they were on Washington. The potency of the anti-Klan legislation, a Mississippi Republican wrote, "derived alone from its source" in the federal government. "No such law could be enforced by state authority, the local power being too weak." But northern Republicans were growing disillusioned with Reconstruction, and in the South, prosecuting Klansmen was an uphill battle against all-white juries and unsympathetic federal judges. After 1872, prosecutions began to drop off. In the meantime, Texas fell to the Democrats in 1873 and Alabama and Arkansas in 1874.

As the increasingly divided Republicans debated how to respond, voters in the congressional election of 1874 handed the ruling party one of the most stunning defeats of the entire nineteenth century. Responding particularly to the severe depression that gripped the nation, they defeated almost half of the party's 199 representatives in the House. Democrats, who had held 88 seats, now commanded an overwhelming majority of 182. "The election is not merely a victory but a revolution," exulted one Democratic newspaper in New York.

After 1874, with Democrats in firm control of the House, Republicans who tried to shore up their southern wing had limited options. Bowing to election results, the Grant administration began to reject southern Republicans' appeals for aid. Events in Mississippi showed the results. As state elections neared in 1875, paramilitary groups such as the Red Shirts operated openly. Mississippi's Republican governor, Adelbert Ames, a Union veteran from Maine, appealed to the president for federal troops, but Grant refused. "The whole public are tired out with these annual autumnal outbreaks in the South," complained one Grant official, who went on to tell southern Republicans that they were responsible for their own fate. As Mississippi Republicans faced a rising tide of brutal murders, Governor Ames—realizing that nothing could result but further bloodshed—urged his allies to give up the fight. Brandishing guns and stuffing ballot boxes, Democratic "Redeemers" swept the 1875 elections and took control of Mississippi. Thus, by 1876, Reconstruction was largely over. Republican governments, backed by token U.S. military units, remained in only three southern states: Louisiana, South Carolina, and Florida. Elsewhere, former Confederates and their allies were back in power.

**The Supreme Court Rejection of Equal Rights** Northern Democrats and so-called Redeemers in the South played decisive roles in ending Reconstruction. But even though, for the moment, Democrats had won control of the House and ex-Confederates had seized power in southern states, new landmark constitutional amendments and federal laws remained in force. If the Supreme Court had left these intact, subsequent generations of civil rights advocates could have used the federal courts to combat discrimination and violence. Instead, the court closed off this avenue for the pursuit of justice and equal rights, just as it had dashed the hopes of women's rights advocates.

As early as 1873, in a group of decisions known collectively as the *Slaughterhouse Cases*, the Court began to undercut the power of the Fourteenth Amendment. In these cases and a related ruling, *U.S. v. Cruikshank* (1876), the justices argued that the Fourteenth Amendment offered only a few, rather trivial federal protections to citizens (such as access to navigable waterways). In *Cruikshank*—a case that emerged from the massacre of African American farmers by ex-Confederates in Colfax, Louisiana, which was followed by a Democratic political coup—the Court ruled that voting rights remained a state prerogative unless the state *itself* violated those rights. So long as the civil rights of former slaves were being violated by individuals or private groups (including the Klan), that was a state responsibility and beyond federal jurisdiction. Therefore, the Fourteenth Amendment did not protect citizens from armed vigilantes, even if those vigilantes seized political power. The Court thus gutted the Fourteenth Amendment. In the *Civil Rights Cases* (1883), the justices also struck down the Civil Rights Act of 1875. The impact of these decisions endured for decades.

## The Political Crisis of 1877

After the grim election results of 1874, Republicans faced an uphill battle in the presidential election of 1876. Abandoning Grant, they nominated Rutherford B. Hayes, a former Union general who was untainted by corruption and—even more important—was governor of the key swing state of Ohio. Hayes's Democratic opponent was New York governor Samuel J. Tilden, a Wall Street lawyer with a reform reputation. Tilden favored **home rule** for the South, but so, more discreetly, did Hayes. With enforcement on the wane, Reconstruction did not figure prominently in the campaign, and little was said about the states still ruled by Reconstruction governments: Florida, South Carolina, and Louisiana.

Once returns started coming in on election night, however, those three states began to loom very large. Tilden led in the popular vote and seemed headed for victory until sleepless politicians at Republican headquarters realized that the electoral vote stood at 184 to 165, with the 20 votes from Florida, South Carolina, and Louisiana still uncertain. If Hayes took those votes, he would win by a margin of 1. Republicans still controlled the election process in the three states; citing Democratic fraud and intimidation, they certified Republican victories. The "Redeemer" Democrats who had seized the states sent in their own electoral votes, for Tilden. When Congress met in early 1877, it confronted two sets of electoral votes from those states.

The Constitution does not provide for such a contingency. All it says is that the president of the Senate (in 1877, a Republican) opens the electoral certificates before the House (Democratic) and the Senate (Republican) and that "the Votes shall then be counted" (Article 2, Section 1). Suspense gripped the country. There was talk of inside deals, of a new election, even of a violent coup. Finally, Congress appointed an electoral commission to settle the question. The commission included seven Republicans, seven Democrats, and, as the deciding member, David Davis, a Supreme Court justice not known to have fixed party loyalties. Davis, however, disqualified himself by accepting an Illinois seat in the Senate. He was replaced by Republican justice Joseph P. Bradley, and by a vote of 8 to 7, on party lines, the commission awarded the disputed votes to Hayes.

In the House of Representatives, outraged Democrats vowed to stall the final count of electoral votes so as to prevent Hayes's inauguration on March 4. But in the end, they went along—partly because Tilden himself urged that they do so. Hayes had publicly indicated his desire to offer substantial patronage to the South,

**"Grantism"**

President Grant was lampooned on both sides of the Atlantic for the problems of his scandal-ridden administration. The British magazine *Puck* shows Grant barely defying gravity to keep himself and his corrupt subordinates aloft and out of jail. To a great extent, however, the hero of the Union Army remained personally popular at home and abroad. The British public welcomed Grant with admiration on his triumphant foreign tour in 1877. Library of Congress.

including federal funds for education, internal improvements, and economic growth. He promised "a complete change of men and policy"—naively hoping, at the same time, that he could count on support from old-line southern Whigs and protect black voting rights. Hayes was inaugurated on schedule. He expressed hope in his inaugural address that the federal government could protect "the interests of both races carefully and equally." But, setting aside the U.S. troops who were serving on border duty in Texas, only 3,000 Union soldiers remained in the South. As soon as the new president ordered them back to their barracks, the last

Republican administrations in the South fell. Reconstruction had ended.

## Lasting Legacies

In the short run, the fall of the last state Republican governments had little impact on the lives of most southerners. Much of the violent work of "Redemption" had already been done. What mattered was the broad political trend: the long, slow decline of Radical Republican power from the early 1870s through the mid-1880s, and the corresponding rise of ex-Confederate power in the South and Democrats on the national stage. It was obvious to most Americans that so-called Redeemers in the South had assumed power through violence. But many—including prominent classical liberals who shaped public opinion—believed that ex-Confederates had overthrown corrupt, illegitimate governments and that the end justified the means. Those who deplored the results had little political traction. The only remaining question was how far the revolution would be rolled back. In 1884, when Democrats elected their first post–Civil War president, Grover Cleveland, many freedpeople feared that he would seek to repeal the Thirteenth Amendment and reinstate slavery.

But the South never went back to the antebellum status quo. Sharecropping, for all its flaws and injustices, was not slavery. Freedmen and freedwomen managed to resist gang labor and work on their own terms. They had established their right to marry, read and write, worship as they pleased, and travel in search of a better life—rights that were not easily revoked. Across the South, black farmers overcame great odds to buy and work their own land. African American businessmen built thriving enterprises. Parents sacrificed to send their children to school, and a few proudly watched their sons and daughters graduate from college. Black religious and charitable leaders sustained networks of mutual aid. At the grassroots level, Reconstruction never entirely ended.

Reconstruction had also shaken, if not entirely overturned, the legal and political framework that had, since the founding of the United States, made it a white man's country. This was a stunning achievement, and though hostile courts and violent resistance undercut it, no one ever repealed the Thirteenth, Fourteenth, and Fifteenth Amendments. They remained in the Constitution, an enduring statement of belief in equality, even if equality in practice was as yet unfulfilled. It was on this constitutional framework that the civil rights movement of the twentieth century would be built (Chapter 26). Meanwhile, legal cases brought by Asian immigrants, Mexicans in the Southwest, and American-born women would show that the Fourteenth and Fifteenth Amendments had transformed the nature of American citizenship.

In fact, the new federal powers asserted in Reconstruction—what Andrew Johnson disparaged as "centralization"—were in some ways more potent in the West than in the South. Republicans boldly carried their nation-building project into the West, to consolidate a continental empire. U.S. policymakers and

businessmen also developed networks of trade and finance that stretched overseas. Before 1865, Americans had often worried about European interference in their domestic affairs. After the Civil War, Americans seldom brooded over such matters. Instead, the United States proudly began to describe itself as Britain's leading rival, not only in championing Emancipation and other marks of "advancing civilization" but also as a naval and commercial power around the world. Though the cause of freedom did not always advance, the federal powers that had secured emancipation would find new outlets in the postwar era.

- **What factors undermined Republican control of the federal government during the 1870s? What were the consequences of this development for Reconstruction?**

- **How did ex-Confederates achieve their counter-revolution against Reconstruction? What role did northern Democrats and the Supreme Court play in that counterrevolution?**

- **What was the political crisis of 1877, and what were its consequences for Reconstruction?**

- **What economic, social, and political legacies persisted after the end of Reconstruction?**

## SUMMARY

Postwar Republicans confronted two great tasks: restoring the rebellious states to the Union and defining the role of emancipated slaves. After Lincoln's assassination, his successor, Andrew Johnson, hostile to Congress, unilaterally offered the South easy terms for reentering the Union. Exploiting this opportunity, southerners adopted oppressive Black Codes and welcomed ex-Confederates back into power. Congress impeached Johnson, and though failing to convict him, seized the initiative. They placed the South under military rule. In this second, or radical, phase of Reconstruction, Republican state governments tried to transform the South's economic and social institutions. Congress passed innovative civil rights acts and funded new agencies like the Freedmen's Bureau. The Fourteenth Amendment defined U.S. citizenship and asserted that states could no longer limit or supersede it. The Fifteenth Amendment gave full voting rights to formerly enslaved men. Debate over this amendment precipitated a split among women's rights advocates, since women did not win inclusion.

Freedmen found that their goals conflicted with those of Republican leaders, who counted on cotton to fuel economic growth. Like Southern landowners, they envisioned former slaves as wage workers, while freedmen wanted their own land. Sharecropping, which satisfied no one completely, emerged as a compromise suited to the needs of the cotton market and an impoverished, credit-starved region.

Nothing could reconcile ex-Confederates to Republican government, and they staged a violent counterrevolution in the name of white supremacy and "Redemption." Meanwhile, struck by a massive economic depression, Northern voters handed Republicans a crushing defeat in the election of 1874. By 1876, Reconstruction was dead. Rutherford B. Hayes's extremely narrow victory in the presidential election of that year, decided by a federal commission, resulted in the withdrawal of the last Union troops from the South. A series of Supreme Court decisions also undermined the Fourteenth Amendment and civil rights laws, setting up legal parameters through which, over the long term, disenfranchisement and segregation would flourish. Nonetheless, grassroots community-building among African Americans continued in the South, even after national Reconstruction faded.

## CHAPTER REVIEW QUESTIONS

- How might the outcome of Reconstruction have been different had Lincoln lived, or chosen a different vice presidential running mate in 1864?

- What were the goals of Radical Republicans and of freedpeople during Reconstruction? How did these differ, and what were the results?

- Why did Reconstruction falter? To what extent was its failure the result of events in the South, in the North, and in Washington, D.C.?

# FOR FURTHER EXPLORATION

The best modern book on Reconstruction is Eric Foner's major synthesis, *Reconstruction: America's Unfinished Revolution, 1863–1877* (1988). Foner's *Nothing But Freedom* (1983) helpfully places Reconstruction in a comparative context. See also Michael Perman, *Emancipation and Reconstruction,* 2nd ed. (2003). *Black Reconstruction in America* (1935), by African American activist and scholar W. E. B. Du Bois, deserves attention as the first book on Reconstruction that stressed the role of blacks in their own emancipation. On freedmen's experiences, see Leon F. Litwack, *Been in the Storm So Long: The Aftermath of Slavery* (1979). More recent studies include Julie Saville, *The Work of Reconstruction: From Slave to Wage Laborer in South Carolina, 1860–1870* (1994). In *Gendered Strife and Confusion* (1997), Laura F. Edwards explores the impact of ordinary women and men on Reconstruction. For recent views of the Freedmen's Bureau, see Paul A. Cimbala and Randall M. Miller, eds., *The Freedmen's Bureau and Reconstruction* (1999). For national politics, see (in addition to Foner) *The Reconstruction Presidents* (1998), by Brooks D. Simpson. On Americans' fading support for Reconstruction at the national level, see Heather Cox Richardson, *The Death of Reconstruction* (1991), and David W. Blight's sweeping *Race and Reunion* (1991). The site for the PBS documentary *Reconstruction: The Second Civil War* (**www.pbs.org/wgbh/amex/reconstruction/index.html**) features many helpful primary documents and images.

## TIMELINE

| | |
|---|---|
| **1864** | Wade-Davis Bill passed by Congress but killed by Lincoln's pocket veto |
| **1865** | Freedmen's Bureau established<br>Lincoln assassinated; Andrew Johnson succeeds him as president<br>Johnson implements Lincoln's restoration plan |
| **1866** | Civil Rights Act passes over Johnson's veto<br>Republican gains in congressional elections |
| **1867** | Reconstruction Act |
| **1868** | Impeachment crisis<br>Fourteenth Amendment ratified<br>Ulysses S. Grant elected president |
| **1870** | Ku Klux Klan at peak of power<br>Fifteenth Amendment ratified |
| **1872** | Grant reelected |
| **1873** | Panic of 1873 ushers in severe economic depression of 1873–1877 |
| **1874** | Sweeping Democratic gains in congressional election |
| **1875** | Whiskey Ring scandal undermines Grant administration<br>*Minor v. Happersett* Supreme Court rules that Fourteenth Amendment does not extend voting rights to women |
| **1877** | Rutherford B. Hayes becomes president<br>Reconstruction ends |

## TEST YOUR KNOWLEDGE

To assess your command of the material in this chapter, see the Online Study Guide at **bedfordstmartins.com/henretta**.

For Web sites, images, and documents related to topics and places in this chapter, visit **bedfordstmartins.com/makehistory**.

THE GREAT WEST

COPYRIGHTED 1881 BY GAYLORD WATSON

# Conquering a Continent

**On May 10, 1869**, people across the United States poured into the streets for a giant party. In Chicago and other large cities, the racket was incredible. Cannons boomed, church bells rang, train whistles shrilled. New York fired a hundred-gun salute at City Hall. Congregations sang anthems, while the less religious gathered in saloons to celebrate with whiskey. In Philadelphia, joyful throngs at the statehouse reminded one observer of the day, four years earlier, when news had arrived of Lee's surrender. The festivities were triggered by a long-awaited telegraph message: Executives of the Union Pacific and Central Pacific Railroads had driven a golden spike at Promontory Point, Utah, linking up their lines. An unbroken track now stretched from the Atlantic to the Pacific. A journey across the United States, which until recently had taken several months, could now be made in less than a week.

The transcontinental railroad meant economic growth. When they heard the news, San Francisco residents got right to business: After firing a cannon salute, they loaded a shipment of Japanese tea onto a train bound for St. Louis, marking California's first overland delivery to the East. In the coming decades, trade and tourism in areas west of the Mississippi River fueled tremendous economic development. San Francisco, which in 1860 had handled $7.4 million in imports, increased that figure to $49 million by 1890. The new railroad would, as one speaker predicted in 1869, "populate our vast territory" and make America "the highway of nations."

The railroad was a political as well as an economic triumph for the Union. The Republicans who emerged victorious from the Civil War saw themselves as heirs to the American System envisioned by Henry Clay and other antebellum Whigs. They believed that government intervention in the economy was the key to nation building. Unlike the Whigs, whose plans had been stalled by Democratic opposition, Republicans enjoyed a decade of unparalleled power in Washington. They used that power vigorously: Federal spending per person, which skyrocketed during the Civil War, afterward remained well above earlier levels. Republicans argued that industrialization and economic integration were the best guarantors of lasting peace. As a New York minister declared, the transcontinental railroad would "preserve the Union of these states."

The minister was wrong on one point, however. He claimed the railroad was a peaceful achievement, in contrast to battlefield victories that had brought "desolation, devastation, misery, and woe." In fact, creating a conti-

**The Great West**

In the wake of the Civil War, Americans looked westward. Republicans implemented an array of policies to foster economic development and the making of continental fortunes in the "Great West." Ranchers, farmers, and lumbermen cast hungry eyes on the remaining lands held by Native Americans. Steamboats and railroads, both visible in the background of this image, became celebrated as symbols of the expanding reach of U.S. economic might. This 1881 promotional poster illustrates the bountiful natural resources to be found out west, as well as the land available for ranching, farming, and commerce. The men in the lower left corner are surveying land for sale. Library of Congress.

nental empire caused plenty of woe. Incorporating the areas west of the Mississippi into the national economy required the conquest of native peoples and the establishment of friendly conditions for international investors – often at great domestic cost. Conquering the West helped make the United States into a major industrial power, yet it also deepened America's rivalry with the imperial powers of Europe and created new patterns of investment and exploitation in Latin America and Asia.

# The Republican Vision

Reshaping the former Confederacy was only one part of Republicans' plan for a reconstructed nation. They remembered the era after Andrew Jackson's destruction of the Second National Bank as a period of economic chaos, when the United States had become vulnerable to international creditors and market fluctuations. Land speculation on the frontier had provoked dizzying cycles of boom and bust. Failure to fund a transcontinental railroad had left different regions of the country disconnected. This, Republicans believed, had helped trigger the Civil War, and they were determined to take economic policy in a new direction.

Even as the war still raged, the Republican-dominated Congress made vigorous use of federal power, launching the transcontinental rail project, developing a new national banking system, and passing the Homestead Act. Congress also raised the **protective tariff** on a range of manufactured goods, from textiles to steel, and on some agricultural products, like wool and sugar. At federal customhouses in each port, foreign manufacturers who brought merchandise into the United States had to pay import fees. These tariff revenues gave U.S. manufacturers, who did not pay the fees, a competitive advantage in America's giant domestic market.

The massive economic depression that began in 1873 set limits on Republicans' ambitious economic program, just as it hindered their Reconstruction policies in the South. But key policies endured. Tariffs, the national banking system, and public subsidies to railroads, in particular, continued to shape the economy. Though some historians argue that the late nineteenth century was an era of unrestrained capitalism, in which government sat passively by, the industrial United States was actually the product of a massive public-private partnership, in which government played a critical role. Secretary of State William Seward, already

looking abroad for markets and raw materials, provided a blueprint for international trade, resource exploitation, and investment for a century to come.

## Integrating the National Economy

Railroad development in the United States began well before the Civil War, with the first locomotives arriving from Britain in the early 1830s. Unlike canals or roads, railroads offered the promise of year-round, all-weather service. Locomotives could run in the dark and never needed to rest, except to take on coal and water. Steam engines carried them over steep mountains and rocky gorges, where pack animals could find no fodder and canals could never reach. West of the Mississippi, railroads opened vast regions for conquest, farming, trade, and tourism. Railroads "do wonders — they work miracles," declared one booster. Looking back later, a transcontinental railroad executive was only half joking when he said, "[T]he West is purely a railroad enterprise."

Railroads could be run by the government or financed by private investors. Unlike most European countries, the United States chose the private approach, but the federal government provided essential incentives in the form of loans, subsidies, and land grants. States and localities also lured railroads with offers of financial aid, mainly by buying railroad bonds. Without this aid, the rail network would have grown much more slowly and would most likely have concentrated in urban regions. With it, railroads enjoyed an enormous boom. By 1900, virtually no corner of the country lacked rail service (Map 16.1).

Railroad companies transformed American capitalism. They adopted a legal form of organization, the corporation, that enabled them to raise private capital in prodigious amounts. In earlier decades, state legislatures had chartered corporations for specific public purposes, binding these creations to government goals

**MAP 16.1**

**The Expansion of the Railroad System, 1870–1890**

In 1860, the nation had 30,000 miles of rail track; by 1890, it had 167,000 miles. The tremendous burst of construction during the last twenty years of that period essentially completed the nation's rail network, although there would be additional expansion for the next two decades. The main areas of growth were in the South and in the lands west of the Mississippi. Time zones—introduced by the railroad companies in 1883—are marked by the gray lines.

and oversight. But over the course of the nineteenth century, legislatures gradually began to allow any business to become a corporation by simply applying for a state charter. Among the first corporations to become large interstate enterprises, private railroads were much freer than earlier corporations to do as they pleased, and after the Civil War they received lavish grants of public resources with few strings attached. In this, their position was not unlike that of American banks in late 2008, after the big federal bailout: Even critics acknowledged that public aid to these giant companies was good for the economy, but they observed that it also lent government support to fabulous accumulations of private wealth.

**Protective Tariffs and Economic Growth**

Along with the transformative power of railroads, the Republicans' protective tariffs helped build other U.S. industries, including textile and steel manufacturing in the Northeast and Midwest and (through a tariff on imported wool) sheep ranching in the West. Tariffs also funded government itself. In an era when the United States did not levy income taxes on corporations or individuals, tariffs provided the largest share of revenue for the treasury. The Civil War had left the Union with a staggering debt of $2.8 billion. Tariff income—which totaled $2.1 billion during the 1880s alone—erased that debt in two decades and then generated huge surpluses. These paid for a generous

Union veterans' pension program, America's first steel battleships, and other federal projects.

As Reconstruction faltered and southern Democrats returned to Congress, tariffs came under political fire. Democrats argued that they taxed American consumers by denying them access to low-priced imported goods and forcing them to pay subsidies to U.S. manufacturers. Republicans claimed, conversely, that tariffs benefited ordinary workers because they created jobs, blocked low-wage foreign competition, and safeguarded America from the kind of industrial poverty that had arisen in Europe. According to this argument, tariffs helped American men earn enough to support their families; wives could devote themselves to homemaking, and children could go to school, not the factory. Republican campaign pamphlets described lurid conditions in "free trade" England, where women labored in mines and iron forges. For protectionist Republicans, then, high tariffs were akin to the abolition of slavery: They protected the most vulnerable workers and made the economy more just.

In fierce political debates over the tariff, which peaked in the 1880s, both sides were partly right. Protective tariffs did play a powerful role in economic growth. Along with other policies that promoted development, they helped transform the United States from a largely agricultural country into a world industrial power. Eventually, though, even protectionist Republicans had to admit that Democrats had a point: Tariffs had not prevented poverty in the United States. U.S. companies accumulated many benefits from tariffs but failed to pass most of these along to workers, who often toiled long hours for low wages. Furthermore, protective tariffs helped foster **trusts**, corporations that dominated whole sectors of the economy and wielded monopoly or near-monopoly power.

**The Role of Courts** | The rise of railroads and other giant corporations prompted many proposals for government regulation of these monster enterprises. But in this aspect of their economic policies, most historians agree, Republicans did not make government powerful enough. State legislatures did pass hundreds of regulatory laws after the Civil War, but with the federal government asserting new powers, interstate companies challenged such laws in federal courts. In *Munn v. Illinois* (1877), the U.S. Supreme Court acknowledged that states did have the right to regulate those businesses that served important public purposes, such as railroads and grain elevators. However, the justices feared that too many state and local regulations and impediments to business would fragment the national marketplace. Starting in the 1870s, they interpreted the "due process" clause of the new Fourteenth Amendment—which dictated that no state could "deprive any person of life, liberty, or property, without due process of law"—as shielding corporations from excessive regulation. Ironically, the Court refused to use that same amendment to protect freedpeople in the South.

In the Southwest, as well, federal courts promoted economic development at the expense of racial justice. Though the United States had taken control of New Mexico and Arizona after the Mexican War (1846–1848), economic change occurred slowly. In the 1870s, much land remained in the hands of Mexican farmers and ranchers. Many lived as *peónes*, under long-standing agreements with *patrónes*, or landowners, who held large tracts originally granted by the Spanish crown. But the post–Civil War years brought railroads and an influx of land-hungry Anglos. New Mexico's governor reported indignantly that Mexican shepherds were often "asked" to leave their ranges "by a cowboy or cattle herder with a brace of pistols at his belt and a Winchester in his hands."

Existing land claims were so complex that Congress eventually set up a special court to rule on land titles. Between 1891 and 1904, the court invalidated most traditional land claims, including those of *ejidos*, or village commons, in New Mexico. Mexican Americans lost about 64 percent of the contested lands on which the court ruled. In addition, much land was sold or appropriated through legal machinations like those of a notorious group of politicians and lawyers known as the Santa Fe Ring. The result was the displacement of thousands of Mexican American villagers and farmers.

**Silver and Gold** | In an era of nation building, U.S. and European policymakers sought new ways to rationalize economic markets. At a series of conferences, for example, industrializing nations tried to develop an international system of standard measurements and even a unified currency. Though this vision failed as each nation succumbed to self-interest, governments did increasingly agree that, for "scientific" reasons, money should be based on gold, which was thought to have an intrinsic worth above other metals. Great Britain had long been on the **gold standard**, meaning that paper notes from the Bank of England could be backed by gold held in the bank's vaults. During the 1870s and 1880s, the United States, Germany, France, Norway, and other countries also converted to gold.

Before they made the shift, these nations had been on a bimetallic standard: They issued both gold and silver coins, with the respective weights fixed at a relative value. The United States switched to the gold standard in part because treasury officials and financiers were watching developments out west. Geologists accurately predicted the discovery of immense lodes of silver, such as the Comstock Lode found at Virginia City, Nevada, without comparable new gold strikes. A massive influx of silver would clearly upset the long-standing ratio. Thus, with a law that became infamous to later critics as "the Crime of 1873," Congress chose gold. It directed the U.S. Treasury to cease minting silver dollars, and over a six-year period, to retire the **greenbacks** (paper dollars) that had been issued during the Civil War and replace them with notes from an expanded system of national banks. After this process was complete, in 1879, the treasury exchanged such notes for gold on request. (Advocates of bimetallism did achieve one small victory: The Bland-Allison Act of 1878 required the U.S. Mint to coin a modest amount of silver.)

By putting the United States on the gold standard, Republican policymakers sharply limited the nation's money supply, to the level of available gold. The amount of money circulating in the United States had been $30.35 per person in 1865; by 1880, it fell to only $19.36 per person. Today, few economists would sanction such a plan, especially for an economy growing at breakneck speed. They would recommend, instead, increasing money supplies to keep pace with development. But at the time, policymakers were reacting to the antebellum years of rampant speculation and the keenly felt hardships of inflation during the Civil War. The United States, as a developing country, also needed to attract investment capital from Britain, Belgium, and other European nations that were on the gold standard. Making it easy to exchange U.S. bonds and currency for gold encouraged European investors to bring their capital to the United States.

Republican policies fostered exuberant growth and a breathtakingly rapid integration of the economy. Railroads and telegraphs tied the nation together. U.S. manufacturers amassed staggering amounts of capital and built corporations of national and even global scope. To a large extent, the courts rejected federal regulation of these new enterprises. In 1900, census officials reported that "the mainland of the United States is the largest area in the civilized world . . . unrestricted by customs, excises, or national prejudice." With its immense, integrated marketplace of workers, consumers, raw materials, and finished products, the United States was poised to become a mighty industrial power.

## The New Union and the World

The United States emerged from the Civil War with new leverage in its negotiation with European countries, especially Great Britain, whose navy dominated the high seas. Britain, which had permitted Confederate raiding vessels such as the CSS *Alabama* to be built in its shipyards, agreed afterward to submit to arbitration and pay the United States $15.5 million in damages. In the flush of victory, many Americans expected more British or Spanish territories to fall easily into the Union's lap. Senator Charles Sumner initially proposed, in fact, that Britain settle the *Alabama* claims by handing over Canada.

Such grand dreams were a logical extension of pre–Civil War conquests, especially in the Mexican War. With the East now linked to San Francisco by rail, merchants and manufacturers cast their eyes across the Pacific, hungry for trade with Asia. Americans had already established a dominant presence in the Hawaiian Islands, where U.S. whalers and merchant ships stopped for food and repairs. With the advent of steam-powered vessels, both the U.S. Navy and private shippers wanted more refueling points in the Caribbean and Pacific.

Even before the Civil War, these commercial aims had prompted the U.S. government to force Japan to open trade. For two centuries, after unpleasant encounters with Portuguese traders in the 1600s, Japanese leaders had adhered to a policy of strict isolation. Americans, who wanted refueling stations in Japan, argued that international trade would extend what one missionary called "commerce, knowledge, and Christianity, with their multiplied blessings." Whether or not Japan wanted these blessings was irrelevant. In 1854, Commodore Matthew Perry succeeded in getting Japanese officials to sign a treaty at Kanagawa, allowing U.S. ships to refuel at two ports. By 1858, America and Japan had commenced trade, and a U.S. consul took up residence in the Japanese capital, Edo (now known as Tokyo).

Union victory paved the way not only for increased trade with Japan and other parts of Asia but also for economic expansion in Latin America. While the United States was preoccupied with its internal war, France had deposed Mexico's government and installed an emperor. On May 5, 1867, Mexico overthrew the French invaders and executed Emperor Maximilian, events that have been celebrated ever since on Cinco de Mayo. Mexico—the part, that is, that the United States had

**An American Merchant Ship in Yokohama Harbor, 1861**

After the United States forcibly "opened" Japan to foreign trade in 1854, American and European ships and visitors became a familiar sight in the port of Yokohama. In these 1861 prints (which are two panels of a five-panel series), artist Hashimoto Sadahide meticulously details the activity on and around a merchant ship in Yokohama Harbor. On the left goods are carried onto the ship; on the right, two women dressed in Western style watch the arrival of another boat. In the background a steamship flies the French flag. Library of Congress.

not annexed in 1848 — regained independence. But without European backing, Mexico lay open to the economic designs of its increasingly powerful northern neighbor.

U.S. policymakers developed a new model for asserting power in Latin America and Asia, not by direct conquest of land and people but through international trade. The architect of this vision was William Seward, secretary of state from 1861 to 1869, under Lincoln and Johnson. A New Yorker of grandiose ambition and ego, Seward had been Lincoln's main rival for the presidential nomination in 1860. He believed, like many contemporaries, that Asia would soon become "the chief theatre of [world] events" and that trade there was key to America's prosperity. Seward urged the Senate to purchase sites in both the Pacific and the Caribbean for naval bases and refueling stations. When Japan changed policy and tried to close its ports to foreign trade, Seward dispatched U.S. Navy vessels to join those of Britain, France, and the Netherlands. They reopened trade by force. At the same time, Seward urged annexation of Hawaii. He predicted that the United States would one day claim the Philippines and build a canal across the isthmus of Panama.

Seward's short-term achievements were modest. During his term of office, Congress was preoccupied with the Civil War and Reconstruction. After Lee's surrender, Americans had little enthusiasm for further military exploits. Seward achieved only two significant victories. In 1868, he secured congressional approval for the Burlingame Treaty with China, which guaranteed the rights of U.S. missionaries in China and set official terms for the emigration of Chinese laborers, some of whom were already clearing farmland and building railroads across the West. In the same year, Seward negotiated the purchase of Alaska from Russia. After the Senate approved the deal, Seward waxed poetic about his long-term dream:

**Building the Central Pacific Railroad**
In 1865, Chinese workers had labored to build the 1,100-foot-long, 90-foot-high trestle over the divide between the American and Bear rivers at Secret Town in the Sierra Nevada mountains. In 1877, the Chinese workers shown in this photograph by Carleton Watkins were again at work on the site, burying the trestle to avoid replacement of the aging timbers, which had become a fire hazard. University of California at Berkeley, Bancroft Library.

Our nation with united interests blest
Not now content to poise, shall sway the rest;
Abroad our empire shall no limits know,
But like the sea in endless circles flow.

Many Americans scoffed at the purchase of Alaska, a frigid arctic tract that the secretary of state's critics nicknamed "Seward's Icebox." But Seward mapped out a path that his Republican successors would follow thirty years later in an aggressive bid for global power. In the meantime, the United States laid foundations for its military and economic ascendance closer to home, through final conquest of the American West.

- **What factors helped advance the integration of the national economy after the Civil War?**

- **How did the post–Civil War nation's economic goals shape its foreign policy? What role did William Seward play in advancing that policy?**

# Incorporating the West

In the national economy they hoped to build, Republicans made a place for farms as well as factories. They sought to attract families to the West through the Homestead Act, which gave free public plots of 160 acres each to applicants who occupied and improved them. Lincoln administration officials not only promoted the Homestead Act in America but also advertised it in Europe, hoping to attract immigrants to serve in the Union Army and then settle the Great Plains. As early as 1860, Republicans hailed the future of "Uncle Sam's Farm" in popular lyrics written by the abolitionist Hutchinson Family Singers:

A welcome, warm and hearty, do we give the sons of toil,
To come west and settle and labor on Free Soil;

We've room enough and land enough, they needn't
feel alarmed—
Oh! Come to the land of Freedom and vote yourself
a farm.

Republicans hoped that hardworking families would
cross the Mississippi River, claim homesteads, and
help build up a continental empire—especially in the
interior West, which was inhabited by Indian peoples
but remained "empty" on U.S. government survey
maps. They were eager to send miners and ranchers on
the same mission.

Implementing this plan required innovative federal policies. In 1862, Congress created the federal
Department of Agriculture to conduct research and
distribute experimental seeds and advice to farmers.
That same year, through the Morrill Act, Congress set
aside 140 million acres of federal land to be sold by the
states, to raise money for public universities; the goal,
in part, was to foster technical expertise and scientific
research. After the Civil War, Congress funded several
geological surveys, dispatching U.S. Army officers, scientists, artists, and photographers west to map unknown terrain and catalog natural resources. In 1879,
Congress consolidated these efforts into an influential

new bureau in the Department of the Interior, the U.S.
Geological Survey (USGS).

To a large extent, these policies succeeded in incorporating lands west of the Mississippi. European
investors sank millions into mines and cattle operations. Railroads soon crisscrossed the West, and homesteaders and their families filed land claims by the
thousands. The United States began to fully exploit its
continental empire for minerals, lumber, and other
raw materials that European nations obtained through
overseas conquest. But in many parts of the West, dreams
of unlimited growth outran reality. The Great Plains,
in particular, proved resistant to conquest. After prospering in the 1870s, ranchers and farmers faced devastating blizzards and drought in the following decade.
Republicans' bold initiatives proved insufficient to
meet the challenges of life on the plains.

## Cattlemen and Miners

As late as the Civil War years, great bison herds roamed
the western grasslands. But overhunting and the introduction of European animal afflictions, like the
bacterial disease brucellosis, were already decimating

**Cowboys on the Open Range**

Cowboys were really farmhands on horseback, with the skills to work on the range. An ethnically diverse group, including
blacks and Hispanics, they earned $25 a month, plus meals and a bed in the bunkhouse, in return for long hours of gruel-
ing, lonesome work. Cowboys were part of the system of open-range ranching, in which cattle (branded with their owners'
mark) from different ranches grazed together. At roundups, cowboys separated the cattle by owner and branded the
calves.   Library of Congress.

the herds. In the 1870s, hide hunters finished them off so thoroughly that, at one point, fewer than a hundred of the animals remained in U.S. territory. Hunters hidden downwind of a herd, under the right conditions, could kill four or five dozen bison at a time without moving from the spot. One Montana hunter told a visitor that he had killed sixty-three of the animals in less than an hour. Hunters took the hides but left the meat to rot, an act of vast wastefulness that shocked native peoples. An early conservationist called it "butchery [of the] most cruel kind."

Where bison had grazed, ranchers envisioned cow country. South Texas provided an early model for their ambitious plans. By the end of the Civil War, about five million head of longhorn cattle grazed on Anglo ranches there. In 1865, the Missouri Pacific Railroad reached Sedalia, Missouri, far enough west to be accessible as the Confederacy surrendered and Texas reentered the Union. A longhorn worth $3 in Texas might command $40 at Sedalia. With this incentive, Texas ranchers inaugurated the Long Drive, hiring cowboys to herd cattle hundreds of miles north to the new rail lines, which soon extended into Kansas. At Abilene and Dodge City, Kansas, ranchers sold their longhorns, and trail-weary cowboys crowded into saloons. These cattle towns captured the nation's imagination as symbols of the "Wild West." The reality was much less exciting. Cowboys, many of them African American and Hispanic, were actually farmhands on horseback who worked long, harsh hours for low pay.

News of easy money traveled fast. North of Texas, where land remained in the public domain, the grass was free and the rush was on. Open lands drew investors and adventurers eager for a taste of the West. By the early 1880s, as many as 7.5 million cattle were destroying the native grasses and trampling water holes on the plains, creating the conditions for a long-term ecological catastrophe. A cycle of good weather only postponed disaster, which arrived in 1886: record blizzards and bitter cold. An awful scene of rotting carcasses greeted cowhands as they rode onto the range in the spring. Further damaged by a severe drought the following summer, the cattle boom collapsed.

Thanks to new strategies, however, cattle ranching survived and became part of the integrated national economy. Ranchers had abandoned the Long Drive as railroads reached Texas in the 1870s. Meanwhile, northern cattlemen began to fence small areas of land and plant hay. Stockyards appeared beside the rapidly extending railroad tracks. Ranchers brought cattle there for sale, and trains took the gathered animals to giant slaughterhouses in Chicago and other midwestern cen-

**MAP 16.2**

**The Mining Frontier, 1848–1890**

The Far West was America's gold country because of its geological history. Veins of gold and silver form when molten material from the earth's core is forced up into fissures caused by the tectonic movements that create mountain ranges, such as the ones that dominate the far western landscape. It was these veins, the product of mountain-forming activity many thousands of years earlier, that prospectors began to discover after 1848 and furiously exploit. Although widely dispersed across the Far West, the lodes that they found followed the mountain ranges bisecting the region and bypassing the great plateaus not shaped by the ancient tectonic activity.

ters, which turned them into cheap beef for customers back east. Hispanic shepherds from New Mexico also brought sheep to feed on the mesquite and prickly pear that supplanted native grasses. Sheep raising, previously scorned by ranchers as unmanly and threatening to cattle, became a major enterprise in the sparser high country of the Sierras and Rockies.

In these same years, extraction of mineral wealth became the basis for development in the Far West (Map 16.2). In the late 1850s, as easy pickings in the

**Hydraulic Mining**

When surface veins of gold played out, miners turned to hydraulic mining, the modern form of which was invented in California in 1853. The technology was simple, using high-pressure streams of water to wash away hillsides of gold-bearing soil. Although building the reservoirs, piping systems, and sluices cost money, the profits from hydraulic mining helped transform western mining into big business. But, as this daguerreotype suggests, the large scale on which hydraulic mining was done wreaked large-scale havoc on the environment.   Collection of Matthew Isenberg.

California gold rush diminished, prospectors had spread across the West in hopes of striking it rich elsewhere. They had found gold at many sites, including Nevada, the Colorado Rockies, and in South Dakota's Black Hills. As news of each gold strike spread, a wild remote area turned almost overnight into a mob scene of prospectors, traders, prostitutes, and saloon keepers (see Voices from Abroad, "Baron Joseph Alexander von Hübner: A Western Boom Town," p. 503). At community meetings, prospectors would make their own laws, often using them as an instrument for excluding or discriminating against Mexicans, Chinese, and blacks.

At some sites, miners found other metals, including the copper, lead, and zinc that eastern industries demanded. The silver from Nevada's immense Comstock Lode, discovered in 1859, built the boom-

town of Virginia City, which soon acquired fancy hotels, a Shakespearean theater, and even its own stock exchange. In 1870, a hundred saloons operated in Virginia City, brothels lined D Street, and men outnumbered women two to one. In the 1880s, however, as the Comstock Lode played out, Virginia City suffered the fate of many mining camps: It became a ghost town. What remained was a ravaged landscape with mountains of debris, poisoned water sources, and surrounding lands stripped of timber. The insatiable demands of mining triggered the growth of smelting, lumbering, and other industries at many far-flung sites. Comstock, one critic remarked, was "the tomb of the forests of the Sierra." At the same time, booming California created a market for timber and produce from the Pacific Northwest. By the 1880s, Portland

# VOICES FROM ABROAD

## Baron Joseph Alexander von Hübner

## A Western Boom Town

During a leisurely trip around the world in 1871, Baron Joseph Alexander von Hübner, a distinguished Austrian diplomat, traveled across the United States, taking advantage of the newly completed transcontinental railroad to see the Wild West. After observing Mormon life in Salt Lake City, he went northward to Corinne, Utah, near the juncture where the Central Pacific and Union Pacific railroads met. The baron might have arrived with romantic notions of the Wild West popular among Europeans of his class. That was not, however, how he departed.

Corinne has only existed for four years. Sprung out of the earth as if by enchantment, this town now contains upwards of 2,000 inhabitants, and every day increases in importance. It is a victualing center for the advanced posts of the [miners] in Idaho and Montana. A coach runs twice a week to Virginia City and to Helena, 350 and 500 miles to the north. Despite the serious dangers and the terrible fatigue of the journeys, these diligences are always full of passengers. Various articles of consumption and dry goods of all sorts are sent in wagons. The "high road" is but a rough track in the soil left by the wheels of the previous vehicles.

The streets of Corinne are full of white men armed to the teeth, miserable looking Indians dressed in the ragged shirts and trousers furnished by the federal government, and yellow Chinese with a business-like air and hard, intelligent faces. No town in the Far West gave me so good an idea as this little place of what is meant by "border life," the struggle between civilization and savage men and things. . . .

All commercial business centers in Main Street. The houses on both sides are nothing but boarded huts. I have seen some with only canvas partitions. . . . The lanes alongside of the huts, which are generally the resort of Chinese women of bad character, lead into the desert, which begins at the doors of the last houses. . . .

To have on your conscience a number of man-slaughters committed in full day, under the eyes of your fellow citizens; to have escaped the reach of justice by craft, audacity, or bribery; to have earned a reputation for being "sharp," that is, for knowing how to cheat all the world without being caught — those are the attributes of the true rowdy in the Far West. . . . Endowed as they often are with really fine qualities — courage, energy, and intellectual and physical strength — they might in another sphere and with the moral sense which they now lack, have become valuable members of society. But such as they are, these adventurers have a reason for being, a providential mission to fulfill. The qualities needed to struggle with and conquer savage nature have naturally their corresponding defects.

Look back, and you will see the cradles of all civilization surrounded with giants of Herculean strength ready to run every risk and to shrink from neither danger nor crime to attain their ends. It is only by the peculiar temper of the time and place that we can distinguish them from the backwoodsman and rowdy of the United States.

Source: Oscar Handlin, ed., *This Was America* (Cambridge, MA: Harvard University Press, 1949), 313–315.

### ANALYZING THE EVIDENCE

- We read foreign impressions of America to find in them insights that Americans themselves might not have had. In what ways, if any, do you find such insights in Baron von Hübner's account of Corinne?

- The baron describes Corinne as a booming supply center for the hard-rock mining industry of Montana and Idaho. Yet his explanation of Corinne is more romantic. He sees in its activities a "struggle between civilization and savage men and things." Is that a helpful insight for us? Would it have been shared or seen as helpful, say, by a Boston businessman looking to invest in real estate in Corinne?

- The baron is unsparing in his description of the "Chinese women of bad character," "miserable looking" Indians, and other unsavory inhabitants of Corinne. But he makes an exception for the gunmen roaming the streets. Despite their "defects," they have "a providential mission to fulfill." What does he mean by that? Would his view have made sense to the hypothetical Boston businessman mentioned above? Or to other Americans who saw in the West the economic opportunity of a lifetime?

503

and Seattle blossomed into populous and important commercial centers (Map 16.3).

## Homesteaders

Before farmers would settle the western plains, they had to be persuaded that crops would grow there. Powerful interests worked hard to overcome the popular idea that the grassland was the **Great American Desert** (Map 16.4). Railroads, eager to sell land the government had granted them, advertised aggressively. Land speculators, transatlantic steamship lines, and western states and territories joined the campaign. "Why emigrate to Kansas?" asked a testimonial in *Western Trail*, the Rock Island Railroad's gazette. "Because it is the garden spot of the world. Because it will grow anything that any other country will grow, and with less work."

Newcomers found the soil beneath the native prairie grasses deep and fertile. Steel plows enabled them to break through the tough roots, while barbed wire provided cheap, effective fencing against roaming cattle. European immigrants brought strains of hard-kernel wheat that tolerated the extreme temperatures of the plains. As if to confirm the promoters' optimism, a wet cycle occurred between 1878 and 1886, shifting the zone of greater rainfall toward the Rockies. Americans decided that "rain follows the plow." Some attributed the increased rain to soil cultivation and tree planting. Others credited God. As one settler on the southern plains remarked, "The Lord just knowed we needed more land an' He's gone and changed the climate."

The motivation for most settlers, American or European, was to better themselves economically. Union veterans, who received favorable terms in staking homestead claims, played a major role in settling Kansas and other plains states. When a severe depression hit northern Europe in the 1870s, Norwegians and Swedes joined German emigrants in large numbers. At the peak of "American fever" in 1882, more than 105,000 Scandinavians left for the United States. Swedish and Norwegian became the primary languages in parts of Minnesota and the Dakotas.

For African Americans, the plains could represent a promised land of freedom. In 1879, some black communities chose to leave the South in a quest to escape poverty and white vengeance. Some six thousand blacks walked out of Mississippi and Louisiana, most carrying little but the clothes on their backs and faith in God. They called themselves **Exodusters**, participants in a great exodus to the prairie. The 1880 census reported 40,000 blacks in Kansas, by far the largest African American concentration in the West aside from Texas, where

**MAP 16.3**

**The Settlement of the Pacific Slope, 1860–1890**

In 1860, the economic development of the Pacific slope was remarkably uneven—fully under way in northern California and scarcely begun anywhere else. By 1890, a new pattern had begun to emerge, with the swift growth of southern California foreshadowed and the Pacific Northwest incorporated into the regional and national economy.

**MAP 16.4**

**The Natural Environment of the West, 1860s**

As cattle ranchers and homesteaders pushed into the Great Plains and beyond the line of semiaridity, they sensed the overwhelming power of the natural environment. In a landscape without trees for fences and barns, and without adequate rainfall, ranchers and farmers had to relearn their business. The Native Americans peopling the plains and mountains had learned to live in this environment, but their knowledge counted for little against the ruthless pressure of the settlers to domesticate the West.

the expanding cotton frontier attracted hundreds of thousands of black migrants.

For all newcomers, taming the plains differed from "pioneering" in antebellum Iowa or Oregon. Dealers sold big new machines to help with plowing and harvesting. Western wheat traveled by rail to giant grain elevators, and it traded immediately on world markets. Hoping that frontier land values would appreciate rap-

idly, many farmers planned to profit from selling acreage as much as (or more than) from selling their crops. In boom times, many rushed into debt to acquire more land and better equipment. All these enthusiasms—for cash crops, land speculation, borrowed money, and new technology—bore witness to the conviction that farming was, as one agricultural journal remarked, a business "like all other business."

**The Shores Family, Custer County, Nebraska, 1887**
Whether the Shores family came west as Exodusters, we do not know. But in 1887, when this photograph was taken, they were well settled on their Nebraska farm, although still living in sod houses. The matriarch and patriarch of the family, Rachel and Jerry Shores (an ex-slave), are third and second from the right. Nebraska State Historical Society.

**Women in the West** Those who came west to mine ore, to harvest lumber, or to tend cattle were overwhelmingly male, but homesteaders most often arrived as families. Women and children played critical roles in running farms. For this reason, farmers held a special place in Republicans' vision of a transformed nation. According to the ideal of domesticity, which had spread widely in the North before the Civil War, it was a man's devotion to his wife and children that caused him to work hard, be thrifty, and contribute to national progress. Meanwhile, women's commitment to the home, motherhood, and female Christian charity were considered crucial to the improvement of American civilization. Respectable settlers did not, of course, include in this vision of domesticity the thousands of prostitutes who worked in western mining camps and cattle towns.

Domesticity precipitated a political clash with a distinctive religious group that had already conquered part of the West: Mormons, or members of the Church of Jesus Christ of Latter-Day Saints (LDS). Most Americans at the time were deeply hostile to Mormonism, especially the LDS practice of plural marriage—sanctioned by church founder Joseph Smith—through which some Mormon husbands married more than one wife. Mormons had their own view of women's role. In 1870, the Utah legislature granted full voting rights to women. This measure increased LDS power—since most Utah women were Mormons, and many men in mining camps were not—and recognized the central role of women in Mormon life. Amid the upheaval of Reconstruction, **polygamy** and women's voting rights became intertwined political controversies (see Comparing American Voices, "Women's Rights in the West," pp. 508–509).

Utah was not the only place in the West where women found new rights and opportunities. As noted in Chapter 15, legislators in Wyoming Territory were the first to grant women full voting rights, in 1869. Western women also ran for public office and held government posts more often than in other regions of the country. Kansas women took the lead: Starting with Argonia in 1887, six towns elected women as mayors, and Oskaloosa boasted the nation's first all-female city council. Such work was part of a broader pattern of women's employment outside the home. Female lawyers, doctors, and entrepreneurs—even single female ranchers and homesteaders—were not uncommon in the West. A shortage of skilled labor and women's frontier self-reliance may have contributed to this marked trend.

Yet the vast majority of rural women endured considerable frontier hardship. This was especially true of those who bore and raised children on homesteads. For many, life on the plains was monotonous and isolated, especially when prosperity proved elusive. "Such an air of desolation," wrote a woman when she moved to the grasslands of Nebraska. Another, in Texas, spoke of "such a lonely country." In his novel *Giants in the Earth*, O. E. Rolvaag dramatically portrayed the fear and iso-

**Promoting the Prairie, 1870s**

This sketch by Henry Worrall is a classic "booster" image, promoting the plains farming life. After ten years' labor, the woodland farmer will still be poor, as he's spent the time cutting down trees. But after only six years on the prairie, a farmer would see far greater results from his labor: a larger home, vines, orchards, flourishing grain crops, as well as a church and neighbors nearby. And if trees are a necessity, they can be grown quickly: Worrell also claims that one Topeka cottonwood grew 26 feet tall in four years. Such images—accompanied by glowing testimonials from scientists, government experts, and newspaper editors—helped lure farmers to the plains. This image soon found its way onto posters advertising the Atchison, Topeka, and Santa Fe Railway.   Kansas State Historical Society.

lation of late-nineteenth-century Norwegian immigrant women on the Dakota prairie, far from the coastal fishing villages of their childhoods. Farmers' advocates soon warned that many farmwives on the plains were ending up in insane asylums. Though the claim was exaggerated, it circulated widely, suggesting that it resonated with homesteaders' personal experiences.

## Debt and Aridity

Homesteading men suffered alongside women and children. In the late nineteenth century, due to technological innovation and the global expansion of export agriculture, farm products glutted world markets. The result was a long, precipitous drop in crop prices. Wheat, cotton, and corn farmers were especially vulnerable. In some years during the 1880s, the price of corn fell so low that Iowa farmers found it more cost-effective to keep their harvest and burn it in their stoves for winter heat than to sell it.

Farmers faced another problem: They were individual businessmen in a marketplace that rewarded **economies of scale**. Thus, they faced serious disadvantages in negotiating with the railroads and merchant companies that transported and sold their products, as well as bankers and equipment dealers who supplied them with machinery and loans. Many understood their dilemma all too keenly, and in the 1880s farmers in the West and South would build one of the most powerful protest movements in the history of American politics.

In the meantime, farmers on the Great Plains faced the additional challenge of a hostile environment. In the grasslands, a cloud of grasshoppers could descend and

# Women's Rights in the West

In 1870, Utah's territorial legislature granted voting rights to women. The decision was a shock to advocates of women's suffrage in the East: They expected their first big victories would come in New England, not in the West. Furthermore, Utah was overwhelmingly peopled by Mormons—members of the Church of Jesus Christ of Latter Day Saints (LDS). Critics saw Mormonism as a harshly patriarchal religion. They especially loathed the Mormon practice of "plural marriage," in which some Mormon men took more than one wife. Most Easterners thought this practice was barbaric and demeaning to women. Over the next two decades, Republicans pressured Mormons to abolish plural marriage. They also disenfranchised Mormon women and, a few years later, all Mormons; Congress refused to admit Utah as a state. Only after 1890, when the LDS church officially abolished plural marriage, was Utah statehood possible. In 1896, when Utah became a state, women's voting rights were finally reinstated.

**Fanny Stenhouse**

## Exposé of Polygamy: A Lady's Life among the Mormons (1872)

An Englishwoman who converted to the faith and moved to Utah, Stenhouse became disillusioned and published her book to criticize the practice of Mormon polygamy.

How little do the Mormon men of Utah know what it is, in the truest sense, to have a wife, though they have so many "wives," after their own fashion. Almost imperceptibly to the husband, and even the wife herself, a barrier rises between them the very day that he marries another woman. It matters not how much she believes in the doctrine of plural marriages, or how willing she may be to submit to it; the fact remains the same. The estrangement begins by her trying to hide from him all secret sorrow; for she feels that what has been can not be undone now, and she says, "I cannot change it; neither would I if I could, because it is the will of God, and I must bear it; besides, what good will it do to worry my husband with all my feelings?"

. . . A man may have a dozen wives; but from the whole of them combined he will not receive as much real love and devotion as he might from one alone, if he had made her feel that she had his undivided affection and confidence. How terribly these men deceive themselves! When peace, or rather quiet, reigns in their homes, they think that the spirit of God is there. But it is not so! It is a calm, not like the gentle silence of sleep, but as the horrible stillness of death—the death of the heart's best affections, and all that is worth calling love. All true love has fled, and indifference has taken its place. The very children feel it. What do they—what can they care about their fathers? They seldom see them.

Whatever, in the providence of God, may be the action of Congress toward Utah, if the word of a feeble woman can be listened to, let me respectfully ask the Honorable Senators and Representatives of the United States that, in the abolition of Polygamy, if such should be the decree of the nation, let no compromise be made where subtlety can bind the woman now living in Polygamy to remain in that condition.

Source: *Exposé of Polygamy: A Lady's Life among the Mormons*, ed. Linda Wilcox DeSimone (Logan: Utah State University Press, 2008), 72–73, 155.

**Eliza Snow, Harriet Cook Young, Phoebe Woodruff**

## A Defense of Plural Marriage

The vast majority of Mormon women defended their faith and the practice of plural marriage. The statements by Eliza Snow, Harriet Cook Young, and Phoebe Woodruff, below, were made at a public protest meeting in Salt Lake City in 1870. LDS women pointed proudly to their new suffrage rights as proof of their religion's just treatment of women. Why did Mormons, who dominated the Utah legislature, give women full voting rights? In part, they sought to protect their church by increasing Mormon voting power: Most of the non-Mormons were single men who worked on ranches or in mining camps. But the LDS Church also celebrated women's central role in the family and community. Some women achieved prominence as midwives, teachers, and professionals.

*Eliza Snow:* Our enemies pretend that, in Utah, woman is held in a state of vassalage—that she does not act from choice, but by coercion—that we would even prefer life elsewhere, were it possible for us to make our escape. What nonsense! We all know that if we wished we could leave at any time—either go singly, or to rise en masse, and there is no power here that could, or would wish to, prevent us. I will now ask this assemblage of intelligent ladies, do you know of anyplace on the face of the earth, where woman has more liberty, and where she enjoys such high and glorious privileges as she does here, as a latter-day saint? No! The very idea of woman here in a state of slavery is a burlesque on good common sense.

*Harriet Cook Young:* Wherever monogamy reigns, adultery, prostitution and foeticide, directly or indirectly, are its concomitants. . . . The women of Utah comprehend this; and they see, in the principle of plurality of wives, the only safeguard against adultery, prostitution, and the reckless waste of pre-natal life, practiced throughout the land.

*Phoebe Woodruff:* God has revealed unto us the law of the patriarchal order of marriage, and commanded us to obey it. We are sealed to our husbands for time and eternity, that we may dwell with them and our children in the world to come; which guarantees unto us the greatest blessing for which we are created. If the rulers of the nation will so far depart from the spirit and letter of our glorious constitution as to deprive our prophets, apostles and elders of citizenship, and imprison them for obeying this law, let them grant this, our last request, to make their prisons large enough to hold their wives, for where they go we will go also.

Source: Edward W. Tullidge, *Women of Mormondom* (New York: Tullidge & Crandall, 1877), 390–391, 396, 400.

## Susan B. Anthony
## Letter to *The Revolution*, July 5, 1871

National women's suffrage leaders responded awkwardly to the Utah suffrage victory. Being associated with Mormons, they understood, damaged their fragile new movement in the eyes of most Americans. But they tried tentatively to forge alliances with Mormon women they viewed as progressive, as well as dissidents in the church. Suffrage leader Susan B. Anthony traveled to Salt Lake City in 1871 to try to forge alliances with Mormon women, especially dissidents such as Fanny Stenhouse. Anthony expressed strong disapproval of polygamy, but she also tried to change the debate to focus on the vulnerability of all married women to exploitation by their husbands. Her report from Utah, published in her journal *The Revolution*, is below.

Woman's work in monogamy and polygamy is essentially one and the same—that of planting her feet on the solid ground of self-support; . . . there is and can be no salvation for womanhood but in the possession of power over her own subsistence.

The saddest feature here is that there really is nothing by which these women can earn an independent livelihood for themselves and children. No manufacturing establishments; no free schools to teach. Women here, as everywhere, must be able to live honestly and honorably without men, before it can be possible to save the masses of them from entering into polygamy or prostitution, legal or illegal. Whichever way I turn, whatever phase of social life presents itself, the same conclusion comes—independent bread alone can redeem woman from her sure subjection to man. . . .

Here is missionary ground. Not for and "thus saith the Lord," divine rights, canting priests, or echoing priestesses of any sect whatsoever; but for great, god-like, humanitarian men and women, who "feel for them in bonds as bound with them," . . . a simple, loving, sisterly clasp of hands with these struggling women, and an earnest work with them. Not to modify nor ameliorate, but to ABOLISH the whole system of woman's subjection to man in both polygamy and monogamy.

Source: *The Revolution*, 20 July 1871.

## ANALYZING THE EVIDENCE

- What arguments did the Mormon women make in defense of plural marriage? On what grounds did Stenhouse argue for its abolition?

- Susan B. Anthony's letter was published in Boston. How might Mormon women have reacted to it? Would they have been persuaded? How might non-Mormon women have reacted to the statements by Snow, Young, and Woodruff?

- How do you account for the very different experiences of plural marriage described by Stenhouse, on the one hand, and Snow, Young, and Woodruff, on the other?

destroy a crop in a day; a prairie fire or hailstorm could do the job in an hour. In spring, homesteaders could face sudden, terrifying tornados; their winter experiences added the word *blizzard* to the American vocabulary in the 1870s. On the plains, also, farmers did not find what forested land had always provided—ample water and lumber for both fuel and construction. Newly arrived families often cut dugouts into hillsides and then, after a season or two, erected houses made of turf cut from the ground.

Over the long term, homesteaders discovered that the western grasslands did not receive enough rain to grow wheat and other grains. Despite the belief that "rain followed the plow," the cycle of rainfall shifted from wet to dry. "A wind hot as an oven's fury," reported the budding novelist Stephen Crane from Nebraska, "[f]rom day to day . . . raged like a pestilence," destroying the crops and leaving "farmers helpless, with no weapon against this terrible and inscrutable wrath of nature." By the late 1880s, some recently settled lands emptied as homesteaders fled in defeat—50,000 of them from the Dakotas alone. It had become obvious that farming in the arid West required methods other than those used east of the Mississippi.

Clearly, 160-acre homesteads were the wrong size: Farmers needed either small, intensively irrigated plots or immense tracts that could support capital-intensive farming. The latter approach included dry farming, which involved deep planting to bring subsoil moisture to the roots and quick harrowing after rainfalls to turn over a dry mulch that slowed evaporation. Dry farming developed most fully on huge corporate farms in the Red River Valley of North Dakota. But even family farms, the norm elsewhere, could not survive on less than 300 acres of grain crops plus machinery for plowing, planting, and harvesting. Crop prices were too low, and the climate too unpredictable, to allow farmers to get by on less.

In this struggle, settlers regarded themselves as nature's potential conquerors, striving, as one pioneer remarked, "to get the land subdued and the wilde nature out of it." Much about its "wilde nature" was, of course, hidden to these strangers to the plains. They did not know that destroying biodiversity, which was what farming the plains really meant, opened pathways for exotic, destructive pests and weeds, and that plowing under the native bunch grasses rendered the soil vulnerable to erosion. By the turn of the twentieth century, about half the nation's cattle and sheep, one-third of its cereal crops, and nearly three-fifths of its wheat came from the Great Plains. But it was not a sustainable achievement. In the twentieth century, this renowned breadbasket was revealed to be, in the words of one historian, "the largest, longest-run agricultural and environmental miscalculation in American history."

John Wesley Powell, a one-armed veteran of the Battle of Shiloh, predicted this catastrophe from an early date. Powell, employed by the new U.S. Geological Survey, led celebrated expeditions in the West. During one of these, he and his survey team navigated the rapids of the Colorado River in wooden boats through the Grand Canyon. In his *Report on the Lands of the Arid Regions of the United States* (1878), Powell told Congress bluntly that individual 160-acre homesteads would not work in dry regions. Impressed with the success of Mormon irrigation projects in Utah, Powell urged the United States to follow that model. He proposed that the government develop the West's water resources, building dams and canals and organizing landowners into local districts that would operate these democratically. Doubting that rugged individualism would succeed in the West, Powell proposed massive cooperation under government control.

Unfortunately, after heated debate, Congress rejected Powell's plan. His critics accused him of playing into the hands of large ranching corporations; boosters and would-be farmers were not yet willing to give up the dream of small homesteads dotted across the plains. But Powell turned out to be right. Though environmental historians do not always agree with Powell's proposed solution, they point to his *Report on Arid Lands* as a cogent critique of what went wrong on the Great Plains. By 1900, Americans would begin to agree with Powell that the federal government should not sell off this public land but instead hold and manage much of it in trust for the American people. At the same time, federal funding eventually paid for the dams and canal systems that supported intensive agriculture in many parts of the West.

**Yellowstone** | Though it took decades for Americans to accept irrigation and cooperative farming, the conquest of the West precipitated other innovations. So rapid and thorough was the West's incorporation into the national marketplace that some officials began to fear rampant overdevelopment. Amid the heady initiatives of Reconstruction, Congress therefore began to preserve sites of unusual natural splendor. As early as 1864, Congress gave 10 square miles of the Yosemite Valley to California for "public use, resort, and recreation." (In 1890, Yosemite reverted to federal control.) Praising the austere beauty of western landscapes, leading writers urged the United States to create

***The Yo-Hamite Falls,*** *1855*

This is one of the earliest artistic renderings of the Yosemite Valley, drawn, in fact, before the place came to be called Yosemite. The scale of the waterfall, which drops 2,300 feet to the valley below, is dramatized by artist Thomas A. Ayres's companions in the foreground. In this romantic lithograph, one can already see the grandeur of the West that Yosemite came to represent for Americans. University of California at Berkeley, Bancroft Library, Honeyman Collection.

more preserves. Congress responded in 1872 by setting aside 2 million acres of Wyoming's Yellowstone Valley "as a public park or pleasuring ground for the benefit and enjoyment of the people."

Tourism was at least as important a motive for Yellowstone's creation as dawning environmental consciousness. Here, again, railroads played a central role. Jay Cooke, owner of the Northern Pacific Railroad, lobbied Congress vigorously to get Yellowstone established. Luxury Pullman cars soon ushered visitors to Yellowstone's grand hotel, operated by the railroad itself. Thus, tourism became a booming enterprise in parts of the West at the same moment that farming, ranching, and mining did. Yellowstone and Yosemite became symbols of national pride, grander than Europe's castles. Busy urban Americans—especially members of the elite—began to find a refuge in the solitude of the natural parks. The national preserves of the West, as one senator put it, became a "great breathing-place for the national lungs."

The creation of Yellowstone National Park was fraught with complications. No one knew exactly what a "national park" was or how to operate it. The U.S. Army was dispatched to take charge of Yellowstone; only in the 1890s and early 1900s, when Congress established many more parks in the West, did consistent management policies emerge. In the meantime, soldiers spent much of their time evicting native peoples who hunted in the Yellowstone Valley. Congress's stipulation that the government keep the park in a "natural condition" required removing any Indians who might spoil its "natural" qualities. Yet, though native hunting was prohibited, wealthy eastern sportsmen quickly came out to hunt the big-game animals that had sustained Indian peoples like the Crows.

The creation of Yellowstone was an early, important step toward a public ethic of preservation and respect for land and wildlife. At the same time, the eviction of Indians from the park showed how creating small preserves of "uninhabited wilderness" was

**Killing the Bison**

This woodcut shows passengers shooting bison from a Kansas Pacific Railroad train—a small thrill added to the modern convenience of traveling west by rail. By the end of the 1870s, the plains bison shown here, which once numbered in the tens of millions and had been a large part of the Plains Indians' way of life, had been hunted almost to extinction. North Wind Picture Archives.

part of the process of conquest itself. Nothing demonstrated this more dramatically than what took place in Yellowstone in 1877. That year, the federal government forcibly removed the Nez Perce tribe from their ancestral lands in Idaho. Under the leadership of young Chief Joseph, the Nez Perce tried to flee to Canada. After a journey of 1,100 miles, they were forced to surrender just short of the border. On the way, five bands fled across Yellowstone; as Nez Perce warrior Yellow Wolf remembered, they "knew that country well." For thirteen days, Nez Perce men raided the valley for supplies, waylaying several groups of tourists. The following summer, just east of the park border, U.S. troops defeated a desperate group of Bannock Indians who, facing starvation on an assigned reservation, had fled to Yellowstone.

Both conflicts made headlines across the country. Americans, proud of their nation's new "pleasuring ground" at Yellowstone, were startled to find that the park was still a site of native resistance. Throughout the postwar decades, such conflicts reminded Americans that they were not, in fact, "settling" empty territory in the West. They were *unsettling* it from native peoples who already lived there. The drive toward settlement often trumped environmentalism. In 1874, for example, Congress tried to enact America's first wildlife protection bill, seeking to prohibit the killing of female bison by non-Indians. President Grant vetoed the bill. Treaties the United States had signed in 1867 and 1868 promised various Plains Indian tribes that they could live free

and hunt as long as bison ranged "in such numbers as to justify the chase." Grant and the army knew that killing bison would cripple Indian resistance. To complete the work of conquest, the great herds of bison had to vanish from the plains.

- How did cattle ranching develop on the western grasslands and become part of the integrated national economy?

- What factors drew homesteaders to the Great Plains, and what role did they play in the Republicans' vision for the post–Civil War nation?

- What environmental conditions did the homesteaders confront on the Great Plains? How did they respond to those conditions, and what were the consequences of that response?

- What prompted the U.S. government to set aside natural reserves such as Yellowstone? What were the results of that policy?

# A Harvest of Blood: Native Peoples Dispossessed

Before the Civil War, Congress reserved the Great Plains for nomadic peoples. After all, they did not believe the western prairie could be farmed. But in the era of railroads, steel plows, and Union victory, Americans suddenly had the power and desire to incorporate the whole plains. The U.S. Army fought against not only the loosely federated Sioux—who had become the major power on the grasslands—but also many other peoples who had agreed to live on reservations but found conditions so desperate that they fled in protest (Map 16.5). These "reservation wars," caused largely by inconsistencies in federal policy, were messy and bitter. Faced with inconsistent policies, failed military campaigns, a series of army atrocities, and egregious corruption in the Indian Bureau, Americans began to heed reformers who called for a new, more humane policy—one that would destroy native ways of life but "save" Indians themselves.

## The Civil War and Indians on the Plains

In August 1862, the attention of most Unionists and Confederates was riveted on General George McClellan's failed campaign on the Chesapeake Bay peninsula. But in Minnesota, the Dakota Sioux were increasingly restive. In 1858, they had agreed to settle on a strip of land reserved for them by the government, in exchange for receiving regular payments and supplies. But Indian agents, contractors, and even Minnesota's territorial governor pocketed most of the funds meant for the Dakotas. When

**MAP 16.5**

**Indian Country in the West, to 1890**

As settlement pushed onto the Great Plains after the Civil War, native peoples put up bitter resistance but ultimately to no avail. Over a period of decades, they ceded most of their lands to the federal government, and by 1890 they were confined to scattered reservations.

**Enclosed Dakota Camp at Fort Snelling, Minnesota, 1862**

During the trial of Dakota warriors involved in the 1862 rebellion, and through the harsh Minnesota winter that followed, more than a thousand members of the tribe were imprisoned inside an enormous enclosure on Pike Island, across from Fort Snelling, near St. Paul. A measles epidemic broke out in the crowded Dakota camp and dozens died, especially children. Though U.S. soldiers were often unfriendly toward their captives, local sentiment was even more hostile, and troops regularly marched through the camp, in part to protect the Dakota from vigilante violence. In 1863 all members of the tribe were forcibly removed from the state. In November 1862, photographer Benjamin Franklin Upton captured this image of Dakota tents within the Pike Island enclosure. Minnesota Historical Society.

the Dakotas protested that their children were starving, state officials dismissed their appeals. Corruption was so egregious that one leading Minnesota clergyman, Episcopal bishop Henry Whipple, wrote an urgent appeal to President James Buchanan. "A nation which sows robbery," he warned, "will reap a harvest of blood."

Whipple's prediction proved correct: In the summer of 1862, a decade of anger boiled over. In a surprise attack, Dakota warriors fanned out through the Minnesota countryside, killing settlers and burning farms. They planned to sweep eastward to St. Paul but were repulsed at Fort Ridgely and the town of New Ulm. In the end, more than four hundred whites lay dead and thousands had fled. Panicked officials telegraphed for aid, spreading hysteria from Wisconsin to Colorado.

Minnesotans' fierce response to the Dakota uprising set the stage for further conflict. A hastily appointed military court, bent on revenge, sentenced 307 Dakotas to death, making it clear that Indians who rebelled would be treated as criminals rather than captured warriors. Abraham Lincoln, who insisted on reviewing the trial records, commuted most of the sentences but authorized the deaths of 38 Dakota men. They were

hanged just after Christmas 1862 in the largest mass execution in U.S. history. Two months later, Congress canceled all treaties with the Dakotas, revoked their annuities, and expelled them from Minnesota. Faced with these cruel conditions, scattered bands fled farther west to join nonreservation allies.

As this rebellion showed, the Civil War had created two dangerous conditions in the West. First, with the Union Army fighting the Confederacy, western whites felt especially vulnerable to Indian attacks. Second, fearful westerners found that when they chose to, they could fight Indians with minimal federal oversight. In the wake of the Dakota uprising, worried Coloradans favored a military campaign against the Cheyennes — allies of the Sioux — even though the Cheyennes had shown little evidence of hostility. Colorado militia leader John M. Chivington, an aspiring politician, determined to quell public anxiety and make his own career.

In May 1864, Chivington's militia attacked a Cheyenne encampment, shooting down a chief who had made peace terms with the United States. After witnessing this murder, Cheyenne chief Black Kettle surrendered his own band to federal agents, who instructed them to camp in the area of Sand Creek, in eastern Colorado, until a treaty could be signed. On November 29, 1864, Chivington's Colorado militia attacked this camp while most of the warriors were out hunting. They killed Black Kettle and hunted down more than a hundred women, children, and even infants, following an officer's orders to leave none alive. The militia rode back for a celebration in Denver, where they hung Cheyenne scalps (and women's genitals) from the rafters of the Apollo Theater.

The northern plains exploded in conflict. Infuriated by the Sand Creek massacre, Cheyennes carried war pipes to the Arapahos and Sioux, who attacked and burned settlements along the South Platte River. Ordered to subdue these peoples, the U.S. Army failed miserably: Officers were not even able to locate the enemy, who traveled rapidly in small bands and knew the country well. This humiliation was compounded in December 1866 when 1,500 Sioux warriors executed a perfect ambush, luring Captain William Fetterman and 80 soldiers from a Wyoming fort and wiping them out. With this victory the Sioux succeeded in closing the Bozeman Trail, a private road under army protection that had served as the main route into Montana.

General William Tecumseh Sherman, who had taken command of the army in the West, swore to defeat the Plains Indians, "even to their extermination." But the Union hero who had helped defeat the Confederacy met his match on the plains. Another year of fighting proved expensive, exhausting, and inconclusive. In 1868, the Sioux, led by the Oglala band under Chief Red Cloud, told a peace commission they would not sign any treaty unless the United States pledged to abandon all its forts along the Bozeman Trail. The commission agreed. Red Cloud had won.

In the wake of these events, eastern public opinion turned against the Indian wars, which seemed at best ineffective and costly, and at worst brutal. Congress held hearings on the slaughter at Sand Creek. Though Chivington, now a civilian, was never prosecuted, the massacre became an infamous example of western vigilantism. By the time Ulysses Grant entered the White House in 1869, the congressional leaders orchestrating radical Reconstruction in the South also began to seek solutions to the "Indian problem" out West.

## Grant's Peace Policy

When he entered the White House, Ulysses S. Grant inherited an Indian policy in disarray. Federal incompetence was highlighted by yet another mass killing of

friendly Indians in January 1870, this time on the Marias River in Montana, by an army detachment that shot and burned to death 173 Piegan (Blackfoot) women and children. Having run out of other promising options, Grant developed a peace policy for the West, based on recommendations from Christian reformers. He put reformers themselves in charge. These men and women, including many former abolitionists, had created such organizations as the Indian Rights Association and the Women's National Indian Association. They rejected the racism of many westerners and soldiers like General Philip Sheridan, who once declared, "The only good Indians I ever saw were dead."

Reformers argued that native peoples had the innate capacity to become equal with whites. They believed, however, that Indians could achieve that goal only if they were Christianized and educated in white ways. Reformers thus aimed to destroy native languages, cultures, and religions. As one put it, they would "kill the Indian and save the man." Despite their humane intentions, peace advocates' condescension was obvious. They ignored dissenters like Dr. Thomas Bland of the National Indian Defense Association, who suggested that instead of an "Indian problem" there might be a "white problem"—the refusal to permit Indians to live according to their own traditional ways. To most nineteenth-century Americans, such a notion was shocking and uncivilized.

**Indian Boarding Schools** | Reformers focused their greatest energy on educating the next generation. Realizing that **assimilation**, or adoption of white ways, was difficult when children lived at home, agents and missionaries worked hard to enroll children in off-reservation schools. The most famous of these, Pennsylvania's Carlisle School, was founded in 1879. Native families were exhorted, bullied, and bribed into sending their children to such schools, where Indian children were required to speak only English and missionaries forced them to take up white ways. The Lakota boy Plenty Kill, who became one of Carlisle's first students at age eleven and received the new name Luther, remembered his loneliness and terror upon arrival: "The big boys would sing brave songs, and that would start the girls to crying. . . . The girls' quarters were about a hundred and fifty yards from ours, so we could hear them." After having his hair cut short, Plenty Kill felt a profound change in his identity. "None of us slept well that night," he recalled. "I felt that I was no more Indian, but would be an imitation of a white man."

**Indian School**

This photograph was taken at the Riverside Indian School in Anadarko, Oklahoma Territory. The pupils have been shorn of their braids and clothed in Mother Hubbard dresses and shirts and trousers — one step on the journey into the mainstream of white American society. Children as young as five were separated from their families and sent to Indian schools that taught them new skills while pressuring them to abandon traditional Indian ways.    University of Oklahoma, Western History Collections.

Even in the first flush of reform zeal, Grant's peace policy faced daunting hurdles. Most Indian peoples had been yanked off their traditional lands and assigned to barren ground that would have defeated the most enterprising farmer. Poverty and dislocation made Indians especially vulnerable to the ravages of infectious diseases like measles and scarlet fever. In the meantime, Quaker, Presbyterian, and Methodist reformers fought nasty turf battles among themselves and with Catholic missionaries. Also, despite the efforts of reformers, agents and traders continued to skim off money and supplies from the people they were supposed to protect. Rutherford B. Hayes's administration (1877–1881) undertook housecleaning at the Bureau of Indian Affairs, but corruption lingered.

From the Indian point of view, reformers often became just another interest group in a crowded field of whites who sent hopelessly mixed messages. Individual army officers, agents, and missionaries ranged from sympathetic to utterly ruthless. Many times, after chiefs thought they had reached a face-to-face agreement, they found it denied or drastically altered by Congress or the Bureau of Indian Affairs. The Nez Perce chief Joseph observed, "[T]he white people have too many chiefs. They do not understand each other. They do not all talk alike. . . . I cannot understand why so many chiefs are allowed to talk so many different ways, and promise so many different things." A Kiowa chief agreed: "We make but few contracts, and them we remember well. The whites make so many they are liable to forget them. The white chief seems not to be able to govern his braves."

Native peoples were nonetheless forced to accommodate, as independent tribal governance and treaty making came to an end. Back in the 1830s, the U.S. Supreme Court had declared Indians no longer sovereign but rather "domestic dependent nations." On a practical basis, however, officers in the field and the Senate in Washington had continued to negotiate treaties as late as 1869. In 1871, the House of Representatives, long jealous of Senate privileges, passed a bill to abolish all treaty making with Indians. The Senate agreed, provided that existing treaties remained in force. It was one more step in a long, torturous erosion of native rights. Eventually, the U.S. Supreme Court ruled in *Lone Wolf v. Hitchcock* (1903) that Congress could make whatever Indian policies it chose, ignoring all existing treaties. That same year, in *Ex Parte Crow Dog*, the Court ruled that no Indian was a citizen unless Congress designated him so. Indians were henceforth wards of the government. These rulings remained in force until the New Deal of the 1930s.

**Breaking Up Tribal Lands**    While the United States exerted increasing legal power over native peoples, reformers made another effort to assimilate them through the Dawes Severalty Act, passed in 1887. This law had long been the dream of Senator Henry L. Dawes of Massachusetts, a leader of the Indian Rights' Association. Dawes saw the reservation system as an ugly relic of the past. He hoped to break up tribal landholding and give Indians **severalty** (individual ownership of land) by dividing reservations into homesteads, just like those of white farmers in the West. Supporters of the plan believed that ownership of private property would encourage Indians to adopt white ways. It would lead, Dawes wrote, to "a personal sense of independence." Property ownership, echoed another reformer, would make the Indian man "intelligently selfish, . . . with a *pocket that aches to be filled with dollars!*"

The Dawes Act was a disaster. It played into the hands of whites who coveted Indian land: They quickly urged that all reservation lands not needed for allotments be sold to non-Indians. Further, the Bureau of Indian Affairs (BIA) implemented the law carelessly, to the shock of Dawes and other sponsors. In Indian Territory, a government commission seized more than 15 million "surplus" acres from native tribes by 1894. This opened the way for whites to convert the last federal territory set aside for native peoples into the state of Oklahoma. Before the Dawes Act, American Indians had held more than 155 million acres of land across the United States; by 1900, this had dropped to 77 million acres. By the time of the Indian Reorganization

Act of 1934, native peoples had also lost 66 percent of their individually allotted lands through fraud, BIA mismanagement, and pressure to sell to whites.

## The End of Armed Resistance

Despite the glaring flaws that soon became apparent, Americans by the mid-1870s believed they had solved the "Indian problem" in the lands west of the Mississippi. In the Southwest, such formidable peoples as the Kiowas and Comanches had been forced onto designated reservations. The Navajo (or Diné) people, exiled under horrific conditions during the Civil War, were permitted to reoccupy their traditional homeland and abandoned further military resistance. An outbreak among California's Modoc people in 1873—again, humiliating to the army—had at last been subdued. Only

**Little Plume and Yellow Kidney**
Photographer Edward S. Curtis took this photograph of Piegan (Blackfeet) warrior Little Plume and his son Yellow Kidney. Curtis's extensive collection of photographs of Native Americans remains a valuable resource for historians. Curtis, however, altered his images for publication to make his native subjects seem more "authentic": Even though Indians made widespread use of non-native furniture, clothes, and other consumer goods (even Singer sewing machines), Curtis removed those from the frame. He also retouched photographs to remove items such as belts and watches. Note the circular "shadow" here, against the lodge wall, near Little Plume's right arm: The original photograph included a clock.   Library of Congress.

Sitting Bull, a leader of the powerful Lakota Sioux on the northern plains, openly refused to go to a reservation. He often crossed into Canada, where he told reporters that "the life of white men is slavery. . . . I have seen nothing that a white man has, houses or railways or clothing or food, that is as good as the right to move in open country and live in our own fashion."

**Sitting Bull and Custer** In 1874, the Lakotas faced a direct provocation. General George Armstrong Custer, a brash self-promoter who had graduated last in his class at West Point, led an expedition into South Dakota's Black Hills and loudly proclaimed the discovery of gold. Amid the severe depression that began in 1873, prospectors rushed in. The United States, reneging on its 1868 treaty, pressured Sioux leaders to sell the Black Hills, but the chiefs said no. Ignoring this answer, the government demanded in 1876 that all Sioux gather at the federal agencies. The policy backfired: Not only did Sitting Bull and others refuse to report, but other Sioux, Cheyennes, and Arapahos slipped away from reservations to join Sitting Bull.

Amid the nation's centennial celebration in July 1876, Americans received awful news. On June 25–26, General Custer had led 210 men of the Seventh Cavalry in an ill-considered assault on Sitting Bull's camp beside the Little Big Horn River in Montana. In defense, the Sioux and their allies had killed the attackers to the last man. The story of Custer's "last stand" quickly served to justify American conquest. Long after Americans forgot the massacres of Cheyenne women and children at Sand Creek and Piegan people on the Marias River, prints of the Battle of Little Big Horn hung in barrooms across the country. William F. "Buffalo Bill" Cody, in his traveling Wild West performances, enacted a revenge killing of the Cheyenne warrior Yellow Hand, in a tableau that Cody called "first scalp for Custer." Notwithstanding that the tableau featured a white man scalping a Cheyenne, Cody depicted this as a triumph for civilization in the West.

Little Big Horn was the last major military victory of Plains Indians against the U.S. Army. Pursued relentlessly after Custer's defeat, Sioux warriors watched their children starve through a bitter winter. Slowly, families trickled into the agencies, accommodating themselves to life on reservations that the U.S. government fragmented and drastically reduced in size (Map 16.6). The next year the Nez Perce, fleeing desperately for the Canadian border, also surrendered. The last holdout was in the Southwest: Chiricahua Apache leader Geronimo. Like many others, Geronimo had accepted reservation

**MAP 16.6**

**The Sioux Reservations in South Dakota, 1868–1889**

In 1868, when they bent to the demand that they move onto the reservation, the Sioux thought they had gained secure rights to a substantial part of their ancestral hunting grounds. But harsh conditions on reservations led to continuing military conflicts. Land-hungry whites exerted continuous local pressure, and officials in Washington repeatedly changed the terms of Sioux land holdings—always eroding native claims.

life but then took up arms out of sheer desperation. Recalling the desolate land the tribe had been allotted, one Apache said, "[T]here was nothing but cactus, rattlesnakes, heat, rocks, and insects. . . . Many, many of our people died of starvation." The army recruited other Apaches to track Geronimo into the hills; in September 1886, he surrendered for the last time. The Chiracahua Apaches never returned to their homeland. The United States had completed its military conquest of the West.

**Dime Novel Cover, 1872**

During and after the Civil War, publishers found an immense market for two types of cheap, sensational novels: urban detective stories and tales of the frontier. The cover of this 1872 novel is typical of the latter. Dime novel Westerns featured such fictional heroes as Deadwood Dick and alleged "real-life" stories about Jesse James or Buffalo Bill. Such novels did not reflect real life in the West, but they were very popular nationwide, particularly among young people and working-class readers. The "Western," as a later film genre, relied heavily on the stories and stereotypes that dime novels popularized.   Library of Congress.

## Strategies of Survival

Even though the warpath closed, many native peoples continued secretly to practice traditional customs. Away from the disapproving eyes of agents, missionaries, and teachers, they passed on their languages, oral histories, and traditional arts and medicine from each generation to the next. Frustrated missionaries often concluded that little could be accomplished on the reservations because bonds of kinship and custom were so strong. Yet they

had difficulty enrolling students in off-reservation boarding schools because so many parents hated to relinquish their children. Thus, most Indian schools ended up on or near reservations, and white teachers were forced to accept their pupils' continued participation in the rhythms of reservation life.

Selectively, at least, most native peoples accepted some white ways. Many parents urged their sons and daughters to study hard at white-run schools, learn English, and develop skills to help them succeed in the new world that confronted them. Some of these children grew up to be writers and artists who interpreted native experiences for national audiences. Others took up law and medicine. While enrolled at the Carlisle School in Pennsylvania, the son of a Quechan chief from Arizona wrote to the agent on his family's reservation. He warned, in fluent English, that he knew about the agent's thievery and would write to Washington to expose him if he did not stop.

In practice, most native people relied upon both tradition and innovation as they sought the best path forward (see Reading American Pictures, "A Sioux Chief Blends Old and New Ways," p. 521). One of the most famous examples was a Dakota boy named Ohiyesa, who grew up to become Dr. Charles Eastman. Posted to the Pine Ridge Reservation in South Dakota, Eastman practiced medicine side by side with traditional healers, whom he respected. While assimilating to European American culture, Eastman wrote many popular books under his Dakota name, Ohiyesa. He remembered that when he left for boarding school, his father said, "We have now entered upon this life, and there is no going back. . . . Remember, my boy, it is the same as if I sent you on your first war-path. I shall expect you to conquer."

Nothing exemplified this syncretism better than the Ghost Dance movement of the late 1880s, which fostered the hope that native peoples could, through sacred dances, resurrect the bison and create a great storm that would drive whites back across the Atlantic. The Ghost Dance drew on significant Christian elements as well as native ones. As it spread from reservation to reservation — from Paiutes to Arapahos to Sioux — native peoples across the West began to develop new forms of pan-Indian identity and cooperation.

Unfortunately, the outcome of the Ghost Dance movement bore witness to the lethal exertion of authority by misunderstanding whites. When a group of Lakota Sioux Ghost Dancers left their South Dakota reservation after police there killed Sitting Bull in December 1890, they were pursued by the U.S. Seventh Cavalry, in the fear that further spread of the Ghost Dance would provoke war. On December 29, at Wounded Knee Creek,

**"A Close Call"**

Part of the appeal of Buffalo Bill's Wild West, for contemporary audiences, was that it reenacted exploits of his that actually happened or, at any rate, that Buffalo Bill claimed to have happened. In fact, Bill never called the Wild West a "show"; he placed tremendous emphasis on its allegedly authentic re-enactments. In this poster advertising the 1894 season, U.S. troopers are rescuing him in the nick of time from a scalping. Such advertisements contributed to the glorification of wars of conquest against "savages."
Granger Collection, New York.

the army caught up with the fleeing Indians and killed more than 150 Lakota men, women, and children. Like so many others—such as Sand Creek and the killing of Piegan on the Marias River—this massacre could have been avoided if U.S. officials had had a clearer understanding of native viewpoints, and had pursued a fairer and more consistent course of action. The deaths at Wounded Knee stand as a final indictment against decades of relentless U.S. expansion, chaotic and conflicting policies, and bloody mistakes.

Less than two months after the Wounded Knee massacre, General William T. Sherman died in New York. As the nation marked his passing with pomp and speech-making, commentators noted that Sherman's career had paralleled the rise of the United States. Sherman's first military exploits had been against Seminoles in

Florida; later, during the Mexican War (1846–1848), the army sent him west to help claim California. After a stint in civilian life, Sherman returned to the military when the Civil War broke out, warning a friend in Virginia that northerners were "not going to let this country be destroyed." Before war's end, Sherman's name was infamous throughout the South. It was appropriate that this general who helped subdue the South was then sent west to defeat the Sioux and Cheyennes, until he declared that "the Indian question has become one of sentiment and charity, but not of war."

When Sherman had graduated from West Point in 1840, the United States counted twenty-six states, none of them west of Missouri. At his death in 1891, the nation boasted forty-four states, in settled territory stretching to the Pacific coast. The United States now rivaled

# A Sioux Chief Blends Old and New Ways

Late-nineteenth-century Americans developed a keen anthropological interest in Native American cultures, but most also believed that Indians were a "vanishing race," too primitive to survive modern life in an industrial society. Photographers, notably Edward S. Curtis, created individual portraits of people from many different tribes. Wherever possible, Curtis removed from his photographs any objects of modern manufacture (see "Little Plume and Yellow Kidney," p. 517).

The photograph shown here offers a different perspective. Taken by photographer C. G. Morledge in 1891, on the Pine Ridge reservation in South Dakota, it shows the bedroom of Red Cloud, a distinguished chief of the Oglala Lakota (Sioux) tribe. Red Cloud had won a war against the U.S. Army just after the Civil War, and he remained a trusted and powerful leader. He confronted what he saw as meddlesome agents with such tenacity and shrewdness that the Sioux nicknamed Pine Ridge "The Place Where Everything Is Disputed."

**Red Cloud's Bedroom.** Denver Public Library, Western History Division.

## ANALYZING THE EVIDENCE

- As shown in this photograph, Red Cloud's bedroom brings together objects from different traditions. What objects do you see? From what sources did Red Cloud likely obtain them?

- How do you interpret the presence of five American flags? The portrait of Abraham Lincoln (located between the two small flags in the middle)?

- What continuities in Red Cloud's daily life—traditions and practices passed down by his Oglala Lakota elders—might not be reflected in the photo?

521

Britain and Germany as an industrial giant, and its dynamic economy was drawing immigrants from Asia, Latin America, and Eastern and Southern Europe to join those from Africa and Western Europe. Over the span of Sherman's career, the United States had become a major player on the world stage. It had done so, in part, through the kind of fierce military conquest that Sherman himself made famous, as well as through bold expansions of federal power. Because of the conflicts and decisions made in Sherman's lifetime, the children and grandchildren of Civil War heroes inherited a vast empire. In the coming decades, it would be up to them to determine how to use the nation's new power at home and abroad.

- How did the Civil War affect relations between the Sioux and their allies, white settlers, and the U.S. government?

- What effect did Grant's peace policy and subsequent U.S. Indian policy have on native peoples? What role did white reformers play in those policies?

- What were the last acts of native peoples' armed resistance? What were the consequences of that resistance?

- What survival strategies did conquered native peoples develop?

## SUMMARY

Between 1861 and 1877, the United States completed its conquest of the continent. After the Civil War, the expansion of railroads fostered the integration of the national economy. Republicans in the federal government promoted this integration by erecting protective tariffs, while federal courts made rulings that facilitated economic growth and strengthened corporations. To attract foreign investment, Republican policymakers placed the nation on the gold standard. These policymakers also pursued a vigorous foreign policy, acquiring Alaska and asserting U.S. power indirectly through control of international trade in Latin America and Asia.

An important result of economic integration was the incorporation of the Great Plains. Cattlemen built an industry linked to the integrated economy, though in the process nearly driving the native bison to extinction. Homesteaders confronted harsh environmental conditions as they converted the grasslands for agriculture. Republicans championed homesteader families as representatives of domesticity, an ideal opposed to Mormon plural marriage in Utah. Homesteading accelerated the rapid, often violent, transformation of the western environment. Perceiving this transformation, the federal government began setting aside natural preserves such as Yellowstone, often clashing with Native Americans who wished to hunt on the land.

Such conflict over land ultimately led to the conquest of Native Americans. During the Civil War, white settlers clashed with the Sioux and their allies. Grant's peace policy sought to end this conflict by forcing Native Americans to assimilate western practices. Native American armed resistance continued through the 1870s and 1880s, ending with Geronimo's surrender in 1886. Thereafter, Native Americans survived, though not without further conflict, by either secretly continuing their traditions or selectively adopting white ways. Due in part to the determined military conquest of this period, the United States claimed for itself a major role on the world stage.

## CHAPTER REVIEW QUESTIONS

- What national economic development policies did Republicans pursue during the Civil War and Reconstruction? What were the resulting achievements and costs?

- What were some of the impacts of the settlement of the Great Plains and Far West on the natural environment?

- Why did U.S. policies toward Native Americans in this era result in so much continued violence? In what ways did American Indians in the West respond to U.S. encroachment on their traditional lands, and to assimilation efforts?

## FOR FURTHER EXPLORATION

On the subject of the economic consolidation of the West, see William Cronon's *Nature's Metropolis* (1991). John Stover's *American Railroads*, 2nd ed. (1997), is a good overview. On Republican policies, see Richard Bensel, *The Political Economy of American Industrialization, 1877–1900* (2000); on tariff debates, Joanne Reitano, *The Tariff Question in the Gilded Age* (1994); on monetary policy, Walter T. K. Nugent, *The Money Question During Reconstruction* (1967). On foreign policy after the Civil War, see the relevant sections of Walter LaFeber, *The American Search for Opportunity* (1993). Thomas Bender explores U.S. nation building in *A Nation Among Nations* (2006).

On the West see Patricia Nelson Limerick's *The Legacy of Conquest* (1987), Richard White's *"It's Your Misfortune and None of My Own"* (1991), and Andrew Isenberg, *The Destruction of the Bison* (2000). On farming see Frieda Knobloch, *The Culture of Wilderness* (1996); on women, Susan Armitage and Elizabeth Jameson, eds., *The Women's West* (1987), and Sarah Barringer Gordon, *The Mormon Question* (2002). María Montoya explores Mexican displacement in *Translating Property* (2002). On the Indian wars see Robert Utley, *The Indian Frontier of the American West* (1984), and Mark David Spence, *Dispossessing the Wilderness* (1999). Assimilation policies are covered in Frederick Hoxie, *A Final Promise* (1984), and David Wallace Adams, *Education for Extinction* (1995). Good sites are **www.americanwest.com** and **www.pbs.org/nationalparks**.

## TEST YOUR KNOWLEDGE

To assess your command of the material in this chapter, see the Online Study Guide at **bedfordstmartins.com/henretta**.

For Web sites, images, and documents related to topics and places in this chapter, visit **bedfordstmartins.com/makehistory**.

## TIMELINE

| | |
|---|---|
| **1854** | United States "opens" Japan to trade |
| **1859** | Comstock silver lode discovered in Nevada |
| **1862** | Homestead Act |
| | Dakota Sioux uprising in Minnesota |
| **1864** | Sand Creek massacre of Cheyenne in Colorado |
| | Yosemite Valley reserved as public park |
| **1865** | Long Drive of Texas longhorns begins |
| **1866** | Sioux under Red Cloud succeed in closing Bozeman Trail in Montana |
| **1868** | Treaty confirms Sioux rights to Powder River hunting grounds |
| | Burlingame Treaty with China |
| **1869** | Transcontinental railroad completed |
| **1870** | Utah gives full voting rights to women |
| | Wyoming gives full voting rights to women |
| **1875** | John Wesley Powell publishes *Report on Arid Lands* |
| | Sioux ordered to vacate Powder River hunting grounds; war breaks out |
| **1876** | Battle of the Little Big Horn |
| **1877** | San Francisco anti-Chinese riots |
| | *Munn v. Illinois* Supreme Court decision |
| **1879** | Exoduster migration to Kansas |
| | United States placed fully on gold standard |
| **1886** | Dry cycle begins on the Great Plains |
| **1887** | Dawes Severalty Act |
| **1890** | Massacre of Indians at Wounded Knee, South Dakota |

# Documents

## The Declaration of Independence

### In Congress, July 4, 1776, The Unanimous Declaration of the Thirteen United States of America

When in the Course of human events, it becomes necessary for one people to dissolve the political bands which have connected them with another, and to assume among the Powers of the earth, the separate and equal station to which the Laws of Nature and of Nature's God entitle them, a decent respect to the opinions of mankind requires that they should declare the causes which impel them to the separation.

We hold these truths to be self-evident, that all men are created equal, that they are endowed by their Creator with certain unalienable rights, that among these are Life, Liberty, and the pursuit of Happiness. That to secure these rights, Governments are instituted among Men, deriving their just powers from the consent of the governed. That whenever any Form of Government becomes destructive of these ends, it is the Right of the People to alter or to abolish it, and to institute new Government, laying its foundation on such principles and organizing its powers in such form, as to them shall seem most likely to effect their Safety and Happiness. Prudence, indeed, will dictate that Governments long established should not be changed for light and transient causes; and accordingly all experience hath shown, that mankind are more disposed to suffer, while evils are sufferable, than to right themselves by abolishing the forms to which they are accustomed. But when a long train of abuses and usurpations, pursuing invariably the same Object evinces a design to reduce them under absolute Despotism, it is their right, it is their duty, to throw off such Government, and to provide new Guards for their future security.—Such has been the patient sufferance of these Colonies; and such is now the necessity which constrains them to alter their former Systems of Government. The history of the present King of Great Britain is a history of repeated injuries and usurpations, all having in direct object the establishment of an absolute Tyranny over these States. To prove this, let Facts be submitted to a candid world.

He has refused his Assent to Laws, the most wholesome and necessary for the public good.

He has forbidden his Governors to pass Laws of immediate and pressing importance, unless suspended in their operation till his Assent should be obtained; and, when so suspended, he has utterly neglected to attend to them.

He has refused to pass other Laws for the accommodation of large districts of people, unless those people would relinquish the right of Representation in the Legislature, a right inestimable to them and formidable to tyrants only.

He has called together legislative bodies at places unusual, uncomfortable, and distant from the depository of their public Records, for the sole purpose of fatiguing them into compliance with his measures.

He has dissolved Representative Houses repeatedly, for opposing with manly firmness his invasions on the rights of the people.

He has refused for a long time, after such dissolutions, to cause others to be elected; whereby the Legislative powers, incapable of Annihilation, have returned to the People at large for their exercise; the State remaining in the mean time exposed to all the dangers of invasion from without and convulsions within.

He has endeavoured to prevent the population of these States; for that purpose obstructing the Laws of Naturalization of Foreigners; refusing to pass others to encourage their migrations hither, and raising the conditions of new Appropriations of Lands.

He has obstructed the Administration of Justice, by refusing his Assent to Laws for establishing Judiciary powers.

He has made Judges dependent on his Will alone, for the tenure of their offices, and the amount and payment of their salaries.

He has erected a multitude of New Offices, and sent hither swarms of Officers to harass our People, and eat out their substance.

He has kept among us, in times of peace, Standing Armies without the Consent of our legislature.

He has combined with others to subject us to a jurisdiction foreign to our constitution, and unacknowledged by our laws; giving his Assent to their Acts of pretended Legislation:

For quartering large bodies of armed troops among us:

For protecting them, by a mock Trial, from Punishment for any Murders which they should commit on the Inhabitants of these States:

For cutting off our Trade with all parts of the world:

For imposing taxes on us without our Consent:

For depriving us, in many cases, of the benefits of Trial by jury:

For transporting us beyond Seas to be tried for pretended offences:

For abolishing the free System of English Laws in a neighbouring Province, establishing therein an Arbitrary government, and enlarging its Boundaries so as to render it at once an example and fit instrument for introducing the same absolute rule into these Colonies:

For taking away our Charters, abolishing our most valuable Laws, and altering fundamentally the Forms of our Governments:

For suspending our own Legislatures, and declaring themselves invested with Power to legislate for us in all cases whatsoever.

He has abdicated Government here, by declaring us out of his Protection and waging War against us.

He has plundered our seas, ravaged our Coasts, burnt our towns, and destroyed the lives of our people.

He is at this time transporting large armies of foreign mercenaries to compleat the works of death, desolation, and tyranny, already begun with circumstances of Cruelty & perfidy scarcely paralleled in the most barbarous ages, and totally unworthy the Head of a civilized nation.

He has constrained our fellow Citizens taken Captive on the high Seas to bear Arms against their Country, to become the executioners of their friends and Brethren, or to fall themselves by their Hands.

He has excited domestic insurrections amongst us, and has endeavoured to bring on the inhabitants of our frontiers, the merciless Indian Savages, whose known rule of warfare, is an undistinguished destruction of all ages, sexes, and conditions.

In every stage of these Oppressions We have Petitioned for Redress in the most humble terms: Our repeated Petitions have been answered only by repeated injury. A Prince, whose character is thus marked by every act which may define a Tyrant, is unfit to be the ruler of a free people.

Nor have We been wanting in attention to our British brethren. We have warned them from time to time of attempts by their legislature to extend an unwarrantable jurisdiction over us. We have reminded them of the circumstances of our emigration and settlement here. We have appealed to their native justice and magnanimity, and we have conjured them by the ties of our common kindred to disavow these usurpations, which would inevitably interrupt our connections and correspondence. They too have been deaf to the voice of justice and of consanguinity. We must, therefore, acquiesce in the necessity, which denounces our Separation, and hold them, as we hold the rest of mankind, Enemies in War, in Peace Friends.

We, therefore, the Representatives of the United States of America, in General Congress, Assembled, appealing to the Supreme Judge of the world for the rectitude of our intentions, do, in the Name, and by Authority of the good People of these Colonies, solemnly publish and declare, That these United Colonies are, and of Right ought to be FREE AND INDEPENDENT STATES; that they are Absolved from all Allegiance to the British Crown, and that all political connection between them and the State of Great Britain, is and ought to be totally dissolved; and that as Free and Independent States, they have full Power to levy War, conclude Peace, contract Alliances, establish Commerce, and to do all other Acts and Things which Independent States may of right do. And for the support of this Declaration, with a firm reliance on the Protection of Divine Providence, we mutually pledge to each other our Lives, our Fortunes, and our sacred Honor.

John Hancock

| | | | |
|---|---|---|---|
| Button Gwinnett | George Wythe | Geo. Taylor | Abra. Clark |
| Lyman Hall | Richard Henry Lee | James Wilson | Josiah Bartlett |
| Geo. Walton | Th. Jefferson | Geo. Ross | Wm. Whipple |
| Wm. Hooper | Benja. Harrison | Caesar Rodney | Matthew Thornton |
| Joseph Hewes | Thos. Nelson, Jr. | Geo. Read | Saml. Adams |
| John Penn | Francis Lightfoot | Thos. M'Kean | John Adams |
| Edward Rutledge | Lee | Wm. Floyd | Robt. Treat Paine |
| Thos. Heyward, Junr. | Carter Braxton | Phil. Livingston | Elbridge Gerry |
| Thomas Lynch, Junr. | Robt. Morris | Frans. Lewis | Step. Hopkins |
| Arthur Middleton | Benjamin Rush | Lewis Morris | William Ellery |
| Samuel Chase | Benja. Franklin | Richd. Stockton | Roger Sherman |
| Wm. Paca | John Morton | John Witherspoon | Sam'el Huntington |
| Thos. Stone | Geo. Clymer | Fras. Hopkinson | Wm. Williams |
| Charles Carroll of Carrollton | Jas. Smith | John Hart | Oliver Wolcott |

# Articles of Confederation and Perpetual Union

## Agreed to in Congress, November 15, 1777; Ratified March 1781

BETWEEN THE STATES OF NEW HAMPSHIRE, MASSACHUSETTS BAY, RHODE ISLAND AND PROVIDENCE PLANTATIONS, CONNECTICUT, NEW YORK, NEW JERSEY, PENNSYLVANIA, DELAWARE, MARYLAND, VIRGINIA, NORTH CAROLINA, SOUTH CAROLINA, GEORGIA.*

## Article 1

The stile of this confederacy shall be "The United States of America."

## Article 2

Each State retains its sovereignty, freedom and independence, and every power, jurisdiction, and right, which is not by this confederation expressly delegated to the United States, in Congress assembled.

## Article 3

The said states hereby severally enter into a firm league of friendship with each other for their common defence, the security of their liberties and their mutual and general welfare; binding themselves to assist each other against all force offered to, or attacks made upon them, or any of them, on account of religion, sovereignty, trade, or any other pretence whatever.

## Article 4

The better to secure and perpetuate mutual friendship and intercourse among the people of the different states in this union, the free inhabitants of each of these states, paupers, vagabonds, and fugitives from justice excepted, shall be entitled to all privileges and immunities of free citizens in the several states; and the people of each State shall have free ingress and regress to and from any other State, and shall enjoy therein all the privileges of trade and commerce, subject to the same duties, impositions, and restrictions, as the inhabitants thereof respectively; provided, that such restrictions shall not extend so far as to prevent the removal of property, imported into any State, to any other State of which the owner is an inhabitant; provided also, that no imposition, duties, or restriction, shall be laid by any State on the property of the United States, or either of them.

If any person guilty of, or charged with treason, felony, or other high misdemeanor in any State, shall flee from justice and be found in any of the United States, he shall, upon demand of the governor or executive power of the State from which he fled, be delivered up and removed to the State having jurisdiction of his offence.

Full faith and credit shall be given in each of these states to the records, acts, and judicial proceedings of the courts and magistrates of every other State.

## Article 5

For the more convenient management of the general interests of the United States, delegates shall be annually appointed, in such manner as the legislature of each State shall direct, to meet in Congress, on the 1st Monday in November in every year, with a power reserved to each State to recall its delegates, or any of them, at any time within the year, and to send others in their stead for the remainder of the year.

No State shall be represented in Congress by less than two, nor by more than seven members; and no person shall be capable of being a delegate for more than three years in any term of six years; nor shall any person, being a delegate, be capable of holding any office under the United States, for which he, or any other for his benefit, receives any salary, fees, or emolument of any kind.

Each State shall maintain its own delegates in a meeting of the states, and while they act as members of the committee of the states.

In determining questions in the United States, in Congress assembled, each State shall have one vote.

Freedom of speech and debate in Congress shall not be impeached or questioned in any court or place out of Congress: and the members of Congress shall be protected in their persons from arrests and imprisonments, during the time of their going to and from, and attendance on Congress, except for treason, felony, or breach of the peace.

## Article 6

No State, without the consent of the United States, in Congress assembled, shall send any embassy to, or receive any embassy from, or enter into any conference, agreement, alliance, or treaty with any king, prince, or state; nor shall any person, holding any office of profit or trust under the United States, or any of them, accept of any present, emolument, office or title, of any kind whatever, from any king, prince,

---

*This copy of the final draft of the Articles of Confederation is taken from the *Journals*, 9:907–25, November 15, 1777.

or foreign state; nor shall the United States, in Congress assembled, or any of them, grant any title of nobility.

No two or more states shall enter into any treaty, confederation, or alliance, whatever, between them, without the consent of the United States, in Congress assembled, specifying accurately the purposes for which the same is to be entered into, and how long it shall continue.

No state shall lay any imposts or duties which may interfere with any stipulations in treaties entered into by the United States, in Congress assembled, with any king, prince, or state, in pursuance of any treaties already proposed by Congress to the courts of France and Spain.

No vessels of war shall be kept up in time of peace by any State, except such number only as shall be deemed necessary by the United States, in Congress assembled, for the defence of such State or its trade; nor shall any body of forces be kept up by any State, in time of peace, except such number only as, in the judgment of the United States, in Congress assembled, shall be deemed requisite to garrison the forts necessary for the defence of such State; but every State shall always keep up a well regulated and disciplined militia, sufficiently armed and accoutred, and shall provide, and constantly have ready for use, in public stores, a due number of field pieces and tents, and a proper quantity of arms, ammunition and camp equipage.

No State shall engage in any war without the consent of the United States, in Congress assembled, unless such State be actually invaded by enemies, or shall have received certain advice of a resolution being formed by some nation of Indians to invade such State, and the danger is so imminent as not to admit of a delay till the United States, in Congress assembled, can be consulted; nor shall any State grant commissions to any ships or vessels of war, nor letters of marque or reprisal, except it be after a declaration of war by the United States, in Congress assembled, and then only against the kingdom or state, and the subjects thereof, against which war has been so declared, and under such regulations as shall be established by the United States, in Congress assembled, unless such State be infested by pirates, in which case vessels of war may be fitted out for that occasion, and kept so long as the danger shall continue, or until the United States, in Congress assembled, shall determine otherwise.

## Article 7

When land forces are raised by any State for the common defence, all officers of or under the rank of colonel, shall be appointed by the legislature of each State respectively, by whom such forces shall be raised, or in such manner as such State shall direct; and all vacancies shall be filled up by the State which first made the appointment.

## Article 8

All charges of war and all other expences, that shall be incurred for the common defence or general welfare, and allowed by the United States, in Congress assembled, shall be defrayed out of a common treasury, which shall be supplied by the several states, in proportion to the value of all land within each State, granted to or surveyed for any person, as such land and the buildings and improvements thereon shall be estimated according to such mode as the United States, in Congress assembled, shall, from time to time, direct and appoint.

The taxes for paying that proportion shall be laid and levied by the authority and direction of the legislatures of the several states, within the time agreed upon by the United States, in Congress assembled.

## Article 9

The United States, in Congress assembled, shall have the sole and exclusive right and power of determining on peace and war, except in the cases mentioned in the 6th article; of sending and receiving ambassadors; entering into treaties and alliances, provided that no treaty of commerce shall be made, whereby the legislative power of the respective states shall be restrained from imposing such imposts and duties on foreigners as their own people are subjected to, or from prohibiting the exportation or importation of any species of goods or commodities whatsoever; of establishing rules for deciding, in all cases, what captures on land or water shall be legal, and in what manner prizes, taken by land or naval forces in the service of the United States, shall be divided or appropriated; of granting letters of marque and reprisal in times of peace; appointing courts for the trial of piracies and felonies committed on the high seas, and establishing courts for receiving and determining, finally, appeals in all cases of captures; provided, that no member of Congress shall be appointed a judge of any of the said courts.

The United States, in Congress assembled, shall also be the last resort on appeal in all disputes and differences now subsisting, or that hereafter may arise between two or more states concerning boundary, jurisdiction or any other cause whatever; which authority shall always be exercised in the manner following: whenever the legislative or executive authority, or lawful agent of any State, in controversy with another, shall present a petition to Congress, stating the matter in question, and praying for a hearing, notice thereof shall be given, by order of Congress, to the legislative or executive authority of the other State in controversy, and a day assigned for the appearance of the parties by their lawful agents, who shall then be directed to appoint, by joint consent, commissioners or judges to constitute a court for hearing and determining the matter in question; but, if they cannot agree, Congress shall name three persons out of each of the United States, and from the list of such persons each party shall alternately strike out one, the petitioners beginning, until the number shall be reduced to thirteen; and from that number not less than seven, nor more than nine names, as Congress shall direct, shall, in the presence of Congress, be drawn out by lot; and the persons whose names shall be so drawn, or any five of them, shall be commissioners or judges to hear and finally determine the controversy, so always as a major part of the judges who shall hear the cause shall agree in the determination; and if either party shall neglect to attend at the day appointed, without shewing reasons which Congress shall judge sufficient, or, being present, shall refuse to strike, the Congress shall proceed to nominate three persons out of each State, and the secretary of Congress shall strike in behalf of such party absent or refusing; and the judgment and sentence of the court to be appointed, in the manner before prescribed, shall be final and conclusive; and if any of the parties shall refuse to submit to the authority of such court, or to appear or defend their claim or cause, the court shall nevertheless proceed to pronounce sentence or judgment, which shall, in like manner, be final and decisive, the judgment or sentence and other proceedings begin, in either case, transmitted to Congress, and lodged among the acts of Congress for the security of the parties concerned: provided, that every commissioner, before he sits in judgment, shall take an oath, to be administered by one of the judges of the supreme or superior court of the State where the cause shall be tried, "well and truly to hear and determine the matter in question, according to the best of his judgment, without favour, affection, or hope of reward:" provided, also, that no State shall be deprived of territory for the benefit of the United States.

All controversies concerning the private right of soil, claimed under different grants of two or more states, whose jurisdictions, as they may respect such lands and the states which passed such grants, are adjusted, the said grants, or either of them, being at the same time claimed to have originated antecedent to such settlement of jurisdiction, shall, on the petition of either party to the Congress of the United States, be finally determined, as near as may be, in the same manner as is before prescribed for deciding disputes respecting territorial jurisdiction between different states.

The United States, in Congress assembled, shall also have the sole and exclusive right and power of regulating the alloy and value of coin struck by their own authority, or by that of the respective states; fixing the standard of weights and measures throughout the United States; regulating the trade and managing all affairs with the Indians not mem-

bers of any of the states; provided that the legislative right of any State within its own limits be not infringed or violated; establishing and regulating post offices from one State to another throughout all the United States, and exacting such postage on the papers passing through the same as may be requisite to defray the expences of the said office; appointing all officers of the land forces in the service of the United States, excepting regimental officers; appointing all the officers of the naval forces, and commissioning all officers whatever in the service of the United States; making rules for the government and regulation of the said land and naval forces, and directing their operations.

The United States, in Congress assembled, shall have authority to appoint a committee to sit in the recess of Congress, to be denominated "a Committee of the States," and to consist of one delegate from each State, and to appoint such other committees and civil officers as may be necessary for managing the general affairs of the United States, under their direction; to appoint one of their number to preside; provided that no person be allowed to serve in the office of president more than one year in any term of three years; to ascertain the necessary sums of money to be raised for the service of the United States, and to appropriate and apply the same for defraying the public expences; to borrow money or emit bills on the credit of the United States, transmitting, every half year, to the respective states, an account of the sums of money so borrowed or emitted; to build and equip a navy; to agree upon the number of land forces, and to make requisitions from each State for its quota, in proportion to the number of white inhabitants in such State; which requisitions shall be binding; and thereupon, the legislature of each State shall appoint the regimental officers, raise the men, and cloathe, arm, and equip them in a soldier-like manner, at the expence of the United States; and the officers and men so cloathed, armed, and equipped, shall march to the place appointed and within the time agreed on by the United States, in Congress assembled; but if the United States, in Congress assembled, shall, on consideration of circumstances, judge proper that any State should not raise men, or should raise a smaller number than its quota, and that any other State should raise a greater number of men than the quota thereof, such extra number shall be raised, officered, cloathed, armed, and equipped in the same manner as the quota of such State, unless the legislature of such State shall judge that such extra number cannot be safely spared out of the same, in which case they shall raise, officer, cloathe, arm, and equip as many of such extra number as they judge can be safely spared. And the officers and men so cloathed, armed, and equipped, shall march to the place appointed and within the time agreed on by the United States, in Congress assembled.

The United States, in Congress assembled, shall never engage in a war, nor grant letters of marque and reprisal in time of peace, nor enter into any treaties or alliances, nor coin money, nor regulate the value thereof, nor ascertain the sums and expences necessary for the defence and welfare of the United States, or any of them: nor emit bills, nor borrow money on the credit of the United States, nor appropriate money, nor agree upon the number of vessels of war to be built or purchased, or the number of land or sea forces to be raised, nor appoint a commander in chief of the army or navy, unless nine states assent to the same; nor shall a question on any other point, except for adjourning from day to day, be determined, unless by the votes of a majority of the United States, in Congress assembled.

The Congress of the United States shall have power to adjourn to any time within the year, and to any place within the United States, so that no period of adjournment be for a longer duration than the space of six months, and shall publish the journal of their proceedings monthly, except such parts thereof, relating to treaties, alliances or military operations, as, in their judgment, require secrecy; and the yeas and nays of the delegates of each State on any question shall be entered on the journal, when it is desired by any delegate; and the delegates of a State, or any of them, at his, or their request, shall be furnished with a transcript of the said journal, except such parts as are above excepted, to lay before the legislatures of the several states.

## Article 10

The committee of the states, or any nine of them, shall be authorized to execute, in the recess of Congress, such of the powers of Congress as the United States, in Congress assembled, by the consent of nine states, shall, from time to time, think expedient to vest them with; provided, that no power be delegated to the said committee, for the exercise of which, by the articles of confederation, the voice of nine states, in the Congress of the United States assembled, is requisite.

## Article 11

Canada acceding to this confederation, and joining in the measures of the United States, shall be admitted into and entitled to all the advantages of this union; but no other colony shall be admitted into the same, unless such admission be agreed to by nine states.

# The Constitution of the United States of America

**Agreed to by Philadelphia Convention, September 17, 1787**
**Implemented March 4, 1789**

We the People of the United States, in Order to form a more perfect Union, establish Justice, insure domestic Tranquility, provide for the common defence, promote the general Welfare, and secure the Blessings of Liberty to ourselves and our Posterity, do ordain and establish this Constitution for the United States of America.

## Article I

**Section 1.** All legislative Powers herein granted shall be vested in a Congress of the United States, which shall consist of a Senate and a House of Representatives.

**Section 2.** The House of Representatives shall be composed of Members chosen every second Year by the People of the several States, and the Electors in each State shall have the Qualifications requisite for Electors of the most numerous Branch of the State Legislature.

No Person shall be a Representative who shall not have attained to the Age of twenty-five Years, and been seven Years a Citizen of the United States, and who shall not, when elected, be an Inhabitant of that State in which he shall be chosen.

Representatives and direct Taxes shall be apportioned among the several States which may be included within this Union, according to their respective Numbers, *which shall be determined by adding to the whole Number of free Persons, including those bound to Service for a Term of Years, and excluding Indians not taxed, three fifths of all other Persons.*\* The actual Enumeration shall be made within three Years after the first Meeting of the Congress of the United States, and within every subsequent Term of ten Years, in such Manner as they shall by Law direct. The Number of Representatives shall not exceed one for every thirty Thousand, but each State shall have at Least one Representative; and *until such enumeration shall be made, the State of New Hampshire shall be entitled to chuse three, Massachusetts eight, Rhode Island and Providence Plantations one, Connecticut five, New York six, New Jersey four, Pennsylvania eight, Delaware one, Maryland six, Virginia ten, North Carolina five, South Carolina five, and Georgia three.*

When vacancies happen in the Representation from any State, the Executive Authority thereof shall issue Writs of Election to fill such Vacancies.

The House of Representatives shall chuse their Speaker and other Officers; and shall have the sole Power of Impeachment.

**Section 3.** The Senate of the United States shall be composed of two Senators from each State, *chosen by the Legislature thereof,*† for six Years; and each Senator shall have one Vote.

*Immediately after they shall be assembled in Consequence of the first Election, they shall be divided as equally as may be into three Classes. The Seats of the Senators of the first Class shall be vacated at the Expiration of the second Year, of the second Class at the Expiration of the fourth Year, and of the third Class at the Expiration of the sixth Year, so that one-third may be chosen every second Year; and if Vacancies happen by Resignation, or otherwise, during the Recess of the Legislature of any State, the Executive thereof may make temporary Appointments until the next Meeting of the Legislature, which shall then fill such Vacancies.*‡

No person shall be a Senator who shall not have attained to the Age of thirty Years, and been nine Years a Citizen of the United States, and who shall not, when elected, be an Inhabitant of that State for which he shall be chosen.

The Vice President of the United States shall be President of the Senate, but shall have no Vote, unless they be equally divided.

The Senate shall chuse their other Officers, and also a President pro tempore, in the absence of the Vice President, or when he shall exercise the Office of President of the United States.

The Senate shall have the sole Power to try all Impeachments. When sitting for that Purpose, they shall be on Oath or Affirmation. When the President of the United States is tried, the Chief Justice shall preside: And no Person shall be convicted without the Concurrence of two-thirds of the Members present.

Judgment in Cases of Impeachment shall not extend further than to removal from Office, and disqualification to hold and enjoy any Office of honor, Trust or Profit under the United States: but the Party convicted shall nevertheless be liable and subject to Indictment, Trial, Judgment and Punishment, according to Law.

---

*Note:* The Constitution became effective March 4, 1789. Provisions in italics are no longer relevant or have been changed by constitutional amendment.
\*Changed by Section 2 of the Fourteenth Amendment.

---

†Changed by Section 1 of the Seventeenth Amendment.
‡Changed by Clause 2 of the Seventeenth Amendment.

**Section 4.**   The Times, Places and Manner of holding Elections for Senators and Representatives, shall be prescribed in each State by the Legislature thereof; but the Congress may at any time by Law make or alter such Regulations, except as to the Places of Chusing Senators.

The Congress shall assemble at least once in every Year, and such Meeting *shall be on the first Monday in December, unless they shall by Law appoint a different Day.**

**Section 5.**   Each House shall be the Judge of the Elections, Returns and Qualifications of its own Members, and a Majority of each shall constitute a Quorum to do Business; but a smaller number may adjourn from day to day, and may be authorized to compel the Attendance of absent Members, in such Manner, and under such Penalties, as each House may provide.

Each House may determine the Rules of its Proceedings, punish its Members for disorderly Behavior, and, with the Concurrence of two-thirds, expel a Member.

Each House shall keep a Journal of its Proceedings, and from time to time publish the same, excepting such Parts as may in their Judgment require Secrecy; and the Yeas and Nays of the Members of either House on any question shall, at the Desire of one-fifth of those Present, be entered on the Journal.

Neither House, during the Session of Congress, shall, without the Consent of the other, adjourn for more than three days, nor to any other Place than that in which the two Houses shall be sitting.

**Section 6.**   The Senators and Representatives shall receive a Compensation for their Services, to be ascertained by Law, and paid out of the Treasury of the United States. They shall in all Cases, except Treason, Felony and Breach of the Peace, be privileged from Arrest during their Attendance at the Session of their respective Houses, and in going to and returning from the same; and for any Speech or Debate in either House, they shall not be questioned in any other Place.

No Senator or Representative shall, during the Time for which he was elected, be appointed to any civil Office under the Authority of the United States, which shall have been created, or the Emoluments whereof shall have been increased, during such time; and no Person holding any Office under the United States, shall be a Member of either House during his Continuance in Office.

**Section 7.**   All Bills for raising Revenue shall originate in the House of Representatives; but the Senate may propose or concur with Amendments as on other Bills.

Every Bill which shall have passed the House of Representatives and the Senate, shall, before it becomes a Law, be presented to the President of the United States; If he approve he shall sign it, but if not he shall return it, with his Objections to that House in which it shall have originated, who shall enter the Objections at large on their Journal, and proceed to reconsider it. If after such Reconsideration two-thirds of that House shall agree to pass the Bill, it shall be sent, together with the Objections, to the other House, by which it shall likewise be reconsidered, and if approved by two-thirds of that House, it shall become a Law. But in all such Cases the Votes of both Houses shall be determined by Yeas and Nays, and the Names of the Persons voting for and against the Bill shall be entered on the Journal of each House respectively. If any Bill shall not be returned by the President within ten Days (Sundays excepted) after it shall have been presented to him, the Same shall be a Law, in like Manner as if he had signed it, unless the Congress by their Adjournment prevent its Return, in which Case it shall not be a Law.

Every Order, Resolution, or Vote to which the Concurrence of the Senate and the House of Representatives may be necessary (except on a question of Adjournment) shall be presented to the President of the United States; and before the Same shall take Effect, shall be approved by him, or being disapproved by him, shall be repassed by two-thirds of the Senate and House of Representatives, according to the Rules and Limitations prescribed in the Case of a Bill.

**Section 8.**   The Congress shall have Power To lay and collect Taxes, Duties, Imposts and Excises, to pay the Debts and provide for the common Defence and general Welfare of the United States; but all Duties, Imposts and Excises shall be uniform throughout the United States;

To borrow money on the credit of the United States;

To regulate Commerce with foreign Nations, and among the several States, and with the Indian Tribes;

To establish an uniform Rule of Naturalization, and uniform Laws on the subject of Bankruptcies throughout the United States;

To coin Money, regulate the Value thereof, and of foreign Coin, and fix the Standard of Weights and Measures;

To provide for the Punishment of counterfeiting the Securities and current Coin of the United States;

To establish Post Offices and post Roads;

To promote the Progress of Science and useful Arts, by securing for limited Times to Authors and Inventors the exclusive Right to their respective Writings and Discoveries;

To constitute Tribunals inferior to the supreme Court;

To define and punish Piracies and Felonies committed on the high Seas, and Offenses against the Law of Nations;

To declare War, grant Letters of Marque and Reprisal, and make Rules concerning Captures on Land and Water;

---

*Changed by Section 2 of the Twentieth Amendment.

To raise and support Armies, but no Appropriation of Money to that Use shall be for a longer Term than two Years;

To provide and maintain a Navy;

To make Rules for the Government and Regulation of the land and naval Forces;

To provide for calling forth the Militia to execute the Laws of the Union, suppress Insurrections and repel Invasions;

To provide for organizing, arming, and disciplining the Militia, and for governing such Part of them as may be employed in the Service of the United States, reserving to the States respectively, the Appointment of the Officers, and the Authority of training the Militia according to the discipline prescribed by Congress;

To exercise exclusive Legislation in all Cases whatsoever, over such District (not exceeding ten Miles square) as may, by Cession of particular States, and the acceptance of Congress, become the Seat of Government of the United States, and to exercise like Authority over all Places purchased by the Consent of the Legislature of the State in which the Same shall be, for the Erection of Forts, Magazines, Arsenals, dock-Yards, and other needful Buildings; — And

To make all Laws which shall be necessary and proper for carrying into Execution the foregoing Powers, and all other Powers vested by this Constitution in the Government of the United States, or in any Department or Officer thereof.

**Section 9.** The Migration or Importation of such Persons as any of the States now existing shall think proper to admit, shall not be prohibited by the Congress prior to the Year one thousand eight hundred and eight but a tax or duty may be imposed on such Importation, not exceeding ten dollars for each Person.

The privilege of the Writ of Habeas Corpus shall not be suspended, unless when in Cases of Rebellion or Invasion the public Safety may require it.

No Bill of Attainder or ex post facto Law shall be passed.

*No capitation, or other direct, Tax shall be laid, unless in Proportion to the Census or Enumeration herein before directed to be taken.*

No Tax or Duty shall be laid on Articles exported from any State.

No Preference shall be given by any Regulation of Commerce or Revenue to the Ports of one State over those of another: nor shall Vessels bound to, or from, one State, be obliged to enter, clear, or pay Duties in another.

No Money shall be drawn from the Treasury, but in Consequence of Appropriations made by law; and a regular Statement and Account of the Receipts and Expenditures of all public Money shall be published from time to time.

No Title of Nobility shall be granted by the United States: And no Person holding any Office of Profit or Trust under them, shall, without the Consent of the Congress, accept of any present, Emolument, Office, or Title, of any kind whatever, from any King, Prince, or foreign State.

**Section 10.** No State shall enter into any Treaty, Alliance, or Confederation; grant Letters of Marque and Reprisal; coin Money; emit Bills of Credit; make any Thing but gold and silver Coin a Tender in Payment of Debts; pass any Bill of Attainder, ex post facto Law, or Law impairing the Obligation of Contracts, or grant any Title of Nobility.

No State shall, without the Consent of the Congress, lay any Imposts or Duties on Imports or Exports, except what may be absolutely necessary for executing its inspection Laws: and the net Produce of all Duties and Imposts, laid by any State on Imports or Exports, shall be for the Use of the Treasury of the United States; and all such Laws shall be subject to the Revision and Control of the Congress.

No State shall, without the Consent of the Congress, lay any duty of Tonnage, keep Troops, or Ships of War in time of Peace, enter into any Agreement or Compact with another State, or with a foreign Power, or engage in War, unless actually invaded, or in such imminent Danger as will not admit of delay.

# Article II

**Section 1.** The executive Power shall be vested in a President of the United States of America. He shall hold his Office during the Term of four Years, and, together with the Vice President, chosen for the same Term, be elected, as follows:

Each State shall appoint, in such Manner as the Legislature thereof may direct, a Number of Electors, equal to the whole Number of Senators and Representatives to which the State may be entitled in the Congress; but no Senator or Representative, or Person holding an Office of Trust or Profit under the United States, shall be appointed an Elector.

*The Electors shall meet in their respective States, and vote by Ballot for two Persons, of whom one at least shall not be an Inhabitant of the same State with themselves. And they shall make a List of all the Persons voted for, and of the Number of Votes for each; which List they shall sign and certify, and transmit sealed to the Seat of the Government of the United States, directed to the President of the Senate. The President of the Senate shall, in the Presence of the Senate and House of Representatives, open all the Certificates, and the Votes shall then be counted. The Person having the greatest Number of Votes shall be the President, if such Number be a Majority of the whole Number of Electors appointed; and if there be more than one who have such Majority, and have an equal Number of Votes, then the House of Representatives shall immediately*

---

*Changed by the Sixteenth Amendment.

*chuse by Ballot one of them for President; and if no Person have a Majority, then from the five highest on the List the said House shall in like Manner chuse the President. But in chusing the President, the Votes shall be taken by States, the Representation from each State having one Vote; a quorum for this Purpose shall consist of a Member or Members from two thirds of the States, and a Majority of all the States shall be necessary to a Choice. In every Case, after the Choice of the President, the Person having the greatest Number of Votes of the Electors shall be the Vice President. But if there should remain two or more who have equal Votes, the Senate shall chuse from them by Ballot the Vice President.*\*

The Congress may determine the Time of chusing the Electors, and the Day on which they shall give their Votes; which Day shall be the same throughout the United States.

No Person except a natural born Citizen, or a Citizen of the United States, at the time of the Adoption of this Constitution, shall be eligible to the Office of President; neither shall any Person be eligible to that Office who shall not have attained to the Age of thirty five Years, and been fourteen Years a Resident within the United States.

In Case of the Removal of the President from Office, or of his Death, Resignation, or Inability to discharge the Powers and Duties of the said Office, the same shall devolve on the Vice President, *and the Congress may by Law provide for the Case of Removal, Death, Resignation, or Inability, both of the President and Vice President, declaring what Officer shall then act as President, and such Officer shall act accordingly, until the Disability be removed, or a President shall be elected.*†

The President shall, at stated Times, receive for his Services a Compensation, which shall neither be increased nor diminished during the Period for which he shall have been elected, and he shall not receive within that Period any other Emolument from the United States, or any of them.

Before he enter on the Execution of his Office, he shall take the following Oath or Affirmation:—"I do solemnly swear (or affirm) that I will faithfully execute the Office of President of the United States, and will to the best of my Ability, preserve, protect and defend the Constitution of the United States."

**Section 2.** The President shall be Commander in Chief of the Army and Navy of the United States, and of the Militia of the several States, when called into the actual Service of the United States; he may require the Opinion, in writing, of the principal Officer in each of the executive Departments,

upon any Subject relating to the Duties of their respective Offices, and he shall have Power to Grant Reprieves and Pardons for Offences against the United States, except in Cases of Impeachment.

He shall have Power, by and with the Advice and Consent of the Senate, to make Treaties, provided two thirds of the Senators present concur; and he shall nominate, and by and with the Advice and Consent of the Senate, shall appoint Ambassadors, other public Ministers and Consuls, Judges of the supreme Court, and all other Officers of the United States, whose Appointments are not herein otherwise provided for, and which shall be established by Law: but the Congress may by Law vest the Appointment of such inferior Officers, as they think proper, in the President alone, in the Courts of Law, or in the Heads of Departments.

The President shall have Power to fill up all Vacancies that may happen during the Recess of the Senate, by granting Commissions which shall expire at the End of their next Session.

**Section 3.** He shall from time to time give to the Congress Information of the State of the Union, and recommend to their Consideration such Measures as he shall judge necessary and expedient; he may, on extraordinary Occasions, convene both Houses, or either of them, and in Case of Disagreement between them, with Respect to the Time of Adjournment, he may adjourn them to such Time as he shall think proper; he shall receive Ambassadors and other public Ministers; he shall take Care that the Laws be faithfully executed, and shall Commission all the Officers of the United States.

**Section 4.** The President, Vice President and all civil Officers of the United States, shall be removed from Office on Impeachment for, and Conviction of, Treason, Bribery, or other high Crimes and Misdemeanors.

## Article III

**Section 1.** The judicial Power of the United States, shall be vested in one supreme Court, and in such inferior Courts as the Congress may from time to time ordain and establish. The Judges, both of the supreme and inferior Courts, shall hold their Offices during good Behaviour, and shall, at stated Times, receive for their Services a Compensation, which shall not be diminished during their Continuance in Office.

**Section 2.** The judicial Power shall extend to all Cases, in Law and Equity, arising under this Constitution, the Laws of the United States, and Treaties made, or which shall be made, under their Authority;—to all Cases affecting Ambas-

---

\*Superseded by the Twelfth Amendment.
†Modified by the Twenty-fifth Amendment.

sadors, other public Ministers and Consuls;—to all Cases of admiralty and maritime Jurisdiction;—to Controversies to which the United States shall be a Party;—to Controversies between two or more States;—*between a State and Citizens of another State;*\*—between Citizens of different States;—between Citizens of the same State claiming Lands under Grants of different States, and between a State, or the Citizens thereof, and foreign States, Citizens or Subjects.

In all Cases affecting Ambassadors, other public Ministers and Consuls, and those in which a State shall be Party, the supreme Court shall have original Jurisdiction. In all the other Cases before mentioned, the supreme Court shall have appellate Jurisdiction, both as to Law and Fact, with such Exceptions, and under such Regulations as the Congress shall make.

The trial of all Crimes, except in Cases of Impeachment, shall be by Jury; and such Trial shall be held in the State where said Crimes shall have been committed; but when not committed within any State, the Trial shall be at such Place or Places as the Congress may by Law have directed.

**Section 3.** Treason against the United States, shall consist only in levying War against them, or in adhering to their Enemies, giving them Aid and Comfort. No Person shall be convicted of Treason unless on the Testimony of two Witnesses to the same overt Act, or on Confession in open Court.

The Congress shall have Power to declare the Punishment of Treason, but no Attainder of Treason shall work Corruption of Blood, or Forefeiture except during the Life of the Person attainted.

## Article IV

**Section 1.** Full Faith and Credit shall be given in each State to the public Acts, Records, and judicial Proceedings of every other State. And the Congress may by general Laws prescribe the Manner in which such Acts, Records, and Proceedings shall be proved, and the Effect thereof.

**Section 2.** The Citizens of each State shall be entitled to all Privileges and Immunities of Citizens in the several States.

A Person charged in any State with Treason, Felony, or other Crime, who shall flee from Justice, and be found in another State, shall on demand of the executive Authority of the State from which he fled, be delivered up, to be removed to the State having Jurisdiction of the Crime.

*No Person held to Service or Labour in one State, under the Laws thereof, escaping into another, shall, in Consequence of* *any Law or Regulation therein, be discharged from such Service or Labour, but shall be delivered up on Claim of the Party to whom such Service or Labour may be due.*†

**Section 3.** New States may be admitted by the Congress into this Union; but no new State shall be formed or erected within the Jurisdiction of any other State; nor any State be formed by the Junction of two or more States, or parts of States, without the Consent of the Legislatures of the States concerned as well as of the Congress.

The Congress shall have Power to dispose of and make all needful Rules and Regulations respecting the Territory or other Property belonging to the United States; and nothing in this Constitution shall be so construed as to Prejudice any Claims of the United States, or of any particular State.

**Section 4.** The United States shall guarantee to every State in this Union a Republican Form of Government, and shall protect each of them against Invasion; and on Application of the Legislature, or of the Executive (when the Legislature cannot be convened) against domestic Violence.

## Article V

The Congress, whenever two-thirds of both Houses shall deem it necessary, shall propose Amendments to this Constitution, or, on the Application of the Legislatures of two-thirds of the several States, shall call a Convention for proposing Amendments, which, in either Case, shall be valid to all Intents and Purposes, as Part of this Constitution, when ratified by the Legislatures of three-fourths of the several States, or by Conventions in three-fourths thereof, as the one or the other Mode of Ratification may be proposed by the Congress; *Provided that no Amendment which may be made prior to the Year One thousand eight hundred and eight shall in any Manner affect the first and fourth Clauses in the Ninth Section of the first Article; and* that no State, without its Consent, shall be deprived of its equal Suffrage in the Senate.

## Article VI

All Debts contracted and Engagements entered into, before the Adoption of this Constitution, shall be as valid against the United States under this Constitution, as under the Confederation.

This Constitution, and the Laws of the United States which shall be made in Pursuance thereof; and all Treaties made, or which shall be made, under the Authority of the

---

\*Restricted by the Eleventh Amendment.

†Superseded by the Thirteenth Amendment.

United States, shall be the supreme Law of the Land; and the Judges in every State shall be bound thereby, any Thing in the Constitution or Laws of any State to the Contrary notwithstanding.

The Senators and Representatives before mentioned, and the Members of the several State Legislatures, and all executive and judicial Officers, both of the United States and of the several States, shall be bound by Oath or Affirmation, to support this Constitution; but no religious Test shall ever be required as a Qualification to any Office or public Trust under the United States.

## Article VII

The Ratification of the Conventions of nine States shall be sufficient for the Establishment of this Constitution between the States so ratifying the Same.

Done in Convention by the Unanimous Consent of the States present the Seventeenth Day of September in the Year of our Lord one thousand seven hundred and Eighty seven and of the Independence of the United States of America the Twelfth. In Witness whereof We have hereunto subscribed our Names.

Go. Washington
President and deputy from Virginia

*New Hampshire*
John Langdon
Nicholas Gilman

*Massachusetts*
Nathaniel Gorham
Rufus King

*Connecticut*
Wm. Saml. Johnson
Roger Sherman

*New York*
Alexander Hamilton

*New Jersey*
Wil. Livingston
David Brearley
Wm. Paterson
Jona. Dayton

*Pennsylvania*
B. Franklin
Thomas Mifflin
Robt.Morris
Geo. Clymer
Thos. FitzSimons
Jared Ingersoll
James Wilson
Gouv.Morris

*Delaware*
Geo. Read
Gunning Bedford jun
John Dickinson
Richard Bassett
Jaco. Broom

*Maryland*
James McHenry
Dan. of St. Thos. Jenifer
Danl. Carroll

*Virginia*
John Blair
James Madison, Jr.

*North Carolina*
Wm. Blount
Richd. Dobbs Spaight
Hu Williamson

*South Carolina*
J. Rutledge
Charles Cotesworth Pinckney
Pierce Butler

*Georgia*
William Few
Abr. Baldwin

# Amendments to the Constitution (Including the Six Unratified Amendments)

## Amendment I [1791]*

Congress shall make no law respecting an establishment of religion, or prohibiting the free exercise thereof; or abridging the freedom of speech, or of the press; or the right of the people peaceably to assemble, and to petition the Government for a redress of grievances.

## Amendment II [1791]

A well regulated Militia, being necessary to the security of a free State, the right of the people to keep and bear Arms shall not be infringed.

## Amendment III [1791]

No Soldier shall, in time of peace, be quartered in any house, without the consent of the Owner, nor in time of war, but in a manner to be prescribed by law.

## Amendment IV [1791]

The right of the people to be secure in their persons, houses, papers, and effects, against unreasonable searches and seizures, shall not be violated, and no Warrants shall issue, but upon probable cause, supported by Oath or affirmation, and particularly describing the place to be searched, and the persons or things to be seized.

## Amendment V [1791]

No person shall be held to answer for a capital or otherwise infamous crime, unless on a presentment or indictment of a Grand Jury, except in cases arising in the land or naval forces, or in the Militia, when in actual service in time of War or public danger; nor shall any person be subject for the same offence to be twice put in jeopardy of life or limb; nor shall be compelled in any criminal case to be a witness against himself, nor be deprived of life, liberty, or property, without due process of law; nor shall private property be taken for public use, without just compensation.

## Amendment VI [1791]

In all criminal prosecutions, the accused shall enjoy the right to a speedy and public trial, by an impartial jury of the State and district wherein the crime shall have been committed, which district shall have been previously ascertained by law, and to be informed of the nature and cause of the accusation; to be confronted with the witnesses against him; to have compulsory process for obtaining witnesses in his favor, and to have the Assistance of Counsel for his defence.

## Amendment VII [1791]

In suits at common law, where the value in controversy shall exceed twenty dollars, the right of trial by jury shall be preserved, and no fact tried by a jury, shall be otherwise reexamined in any Court of the United States, than according to the Rules of the common law.

## Amendment VIII [1791]

Excessive bail shall not be required, nor excessive fines imposed, nor cruel and unusual punishments inflicted.

## Amendment IX [1791]

The enumeration in the Constitution, of certain rights, shall not be construed to deny or disparage others retained by the people.

## Amendment X [1791]

The powers not delegated to the United States by the Constitution, nor prohibited by it to the States, are reserved to the States respectively, or to the people.

## Unratified Amendment

*Reapportionment Amendment (proposed by Congress September 25, 1789, along with the Bill of Rights)*

*After the first enumeration required by the first article of the Constitution, there shall be one Representative for every thirty thousand, until the number shall amount to one hundred, after which the proportion shall be so regulated by Congress, that there shall be not less than one hundred Representatives, nor less than one Representative for every forty thousand persons, until the number of Representatives shall amount to two hundred; after which the proportion shall be so regulated by Congress, that there shall not be less than two hundred*

---

*The dates in brackets indicate when the amendment was ratified.

*Representatives, nor more than one Representative for every fifty thousand persons.*

## Amendment XI [1798]

The Judicial power of the United States shall not be construed to extend to any suit in law or equity, commenced or prosecuted against one of the United States by Citizens of another State, or by Citizens or subjects of any foreign state.

## Amendment XII [1804]

The Electors shall meet in their respective States and vote by ballot for President and Vice-President, one of whom, at least, shall not be an inhabitant of the same State with themselves; they shall name in their ballots the person voted for as President, and in distinct ballots the person voted for as Vice-President, and they shall make distinct lists of all persons voted for as President, and of all persons voted for as Vice-President, and of the number of votes for each, which lists they shall sign and certify, and transmit sealed to the seat of government of the United States, directed to the President of the Senate;—the President of the Senate shall, in the presence of the Senate and House of Representatives, open all the certificates and the votes shall then be counted;—The person having the greatest number of votes for President, shall be the President, if such number be a majority of the whole number of Electors appointed; and if no person have such majority, then from the persons having the highest numbers not exceeding three on the list of those voted for as President, the House of Representatives shall choose immediately, by ballot, the President. But in choosing the President, the votes shall be taken by States, the representation from each State having one vote; a quorum for this purpose shall consist of a member or members from two-thirds of the States, and a majority of all the States shall be necessary to a choice. And if the House of Representatives shall not choose a President whenever the right of choice shall devolve upon them, before *the fourth day of March* next following, then the Vice-President shall act as President, as in the case of the death or other constitutional disability of the President.*—The person having the greatest number of votes as Vice-President, shall be the Vice-President, if such number be a majority of the whole number of Electors appointed; and if no person have a majority, then from the two highest numbers on the list, the Senate shall choose the Vice-President; a quorum for the purpose shall consist of two-thirds of the whole number of Senators, and a majority of the whole number shall be necessary to a choice.

But no person constitutionally ineligible to the office of President shall be eligible to that of Vice-President of the United States.

## Unratified Amendment

*Titles of Nobility Amendment (proposed by Congress May 1, 1810)*

*If any citizen of the United States shall accept, claim, receive or retain any title of nobility or honor or shall, without the consent of Congress, accept and retain any present, pension, office or emolument of any kind whatever, from any emperor, king, prince or foreign power, such person shall cease to be a citizen of the United States, and shall be incapable of holding any office of trust or profit under them, or either of them.*

## Unratified Amendment

*Corwin Amendment (proposed by Congress March 2, 1861)*

*No amendment shall be made to the Constitution which will authorize or give to Congress the power to abolish or interfere, within any State, with the domestic institutions thereof, including that of persons held to labor or service by the laws of said State.*

## Amendment XIII [1865]

**Section 1.** Neither slavery nor involuntary servitude, except as a punishment for crime whereof the party shall have been duly convicted, shall exist within the United States, or any place subject to their jurisdiction.

**Section 2.** Congress shall have power to enforce this article by appropriate legislation.

## Amendment XIV [1868]

**Section 1.** All persons born or naturalized in the United States, and subject to the jurisdiction thereof, are citizens of the United States and of the State wherein they reside. No State shall make or enforce any law which shall abridge the privileges or immunities of citizens of the United States; nor shall any State deprive any person of life, liberty, or property, without due process of law; nor deny to any person within its jurisdiction the equal protection of the laws.

**Section 2.** Representatives shall be apportioned among the several States according to their respective numbers, counting the whole number of persons in each State, ex-

---

*Superseded by Section 3 of the Twentieth Amendment.

cluding Indians not taxed. But when the right to vote at any election for the choice of electors for President and Vice-President of the United States, Representatives in Congress, the Executive and Judicial officers of a State, or the members of the Legislature thereof, is denied to any of the *male* inhabitants of such State, being *twenty-one* years of age and citizens of the United States, or in any way abridged, except for participation in rebellion, or other crime, the basis of representation therein shall be reduced in the proportion which the number of such *male* citizens shall bear to the whole number of *male* citizens *twenty-one* years of age in such State.

**Section 3.** No person shall be a Senator or Representative in Congress, or Elector of President and Vice-President, or hold any office, civil or military, under the United States, or under any State, who, having previously taken an oath, as a member of Congress, or as an officer of the United States, or as a member of any State legislature, or as an executive or judicial officer of any State, to support the Constitution of the United States, shall have engaged in insurrection or rebellion against the same, or given aid or comfort to the enemies thereof. Congress may, by a vote of two-thirds of each house, remove such disability.

**Section 4.** The validity of the public debt of the United States, authorized by law, including debts incurred for payment of pensions and bounties for services in suppressing insurrection or rebellion, shall not be questioned. But neither the United States nor any State shall assume or pay any debt or obligation incurred in aid of insurrection or rebellion against the United States, or any claim for the loss or emancipation of any slave; but all such debts, obligations, and claims shall be held illegal and void.

**Section 5.** The Congress shall have power to enforce, by appropriate legislation, the provisions of this article.

## Amendment XV [1870]

**Section 1.** The right of citizens of the United States to vote shall not be denied or abridged by the United States or by any State on account of race, color, or previous condition of servitude—

**Section 2.** The Congress shall have power to enforce this article by appropriate legislation.

## Amendment XVI [1913]

The Congress shall have power to lay and collect taxes on incomes, from whatever source derived, without apportionment among the several States, and without regard to any census or enumeration.

## Amendment XVII [1913]

**Section 1.** The Senate of the United States shall be composed of two Senators from each State, elected by the people thereof, for six years; and each Senator shall have one vote. The electors in each State shall have the qualifications requisite for electors of [voters for] the most numerous branch of the State legislatures.

**Section 2.** When vacancies happen in the representation of any State in the Senate, the executive authority of such State shall issue writs of election to fill such vacancies: Provided, that the Legislature of any State may empower the executive thereof to make temporary appointments until the people fill the vacancies by election as the Legislature may direct.

**Section 3.** *This amendment shall not be so construed as to affect the election or term of any Senator chosen before it becomes valid as part of the Constitution.*

## Amendment XVIII [1919; repealed 1933 by Amendment XXI]

**Section 1.** *After one year from the ratification of this article the manufacture, sale, or transportation of intoxicating liquors within, the importation thereof into, or the exportation thereof from the United States and all territory subject to the jurisdiction thereof, for beverage purposes, is hereby prohibited.*

**Section 2.** *The Congress and the several States shall have concurrent power to enforce this article by appropriate legislation.*

**Section 3.** *This article shall be inoperative unless it shall have been ratified as an amendment to the Constitution by the legislatures of the several States, as provided by the Constitution, within seven years from the date of the submission thereof to the States by the Congress.*

## Amendment XIX [1920]

**Section 1.** The right of citizens of the United States to vote shall not be denied or abridged by the United States or by any State on account of sex.

**Section 2.** Congress shall have the power to enforce this article by appropriate legislation.

## Unratified Amendment

*Child Labor Amendment*
*(proposed by Congress June 2, 1924)*

**Section 1.** *The Congress shall have power to limit, regulate, and prohibit the labor of persons under eighteen years of age.*

**Section 2.** *The power of the several States is unimpaired by this article except that the operation of State laws shall be suspended to the extent necessary to give effect to legislation enacted by Congress.*

## Amendment XX [1933]

**Section 1.** The terms of the President and Vice-President shall end at noon on the 20th day of January, and the terms of Senators and Representatives at noon on the 3rd day of January, of the years in which such terms would have ended if this article had not been ratified; and the terms of their successors shall then begin.

**Section 2.** The Congress shall assemble at least once in every year, and such meeting shall begin at noon on the 3rd day of January, unless they shall by law appoint a different day.

**Section 3.** If, at the time fixed for the beginning of the term of the President, the President-elect shall have died, the Vice-President-elect shall become President. If a President shall not have been chosen before the time fixed for the beginning of his term, or if the President-elect shall have failed to qualify, then the Vice-President-elect shall act as President until a President shall have qualified; and the Congress may by law provide for the case wherein neither a President-elect nor a Vice-President-elect shall have qualified, declaring who shall then act as President, or the manner in which one who is to act shall be selected, and such person shall act accordingly until a President or Vice-President shall have qualified.

**Section 4.** The Congress may by law provide for the case of the death of any of the persons from whom the House of Representatives may choose a President whenever the right of choice shall have devolved upon them, and for the case of the death of any of the persons from whom the Senate may choose a Vice-President whenever the right of choice shall have devolved upon them.

**Section 5.** Sections 1 and 2 shall take effect on the 15th day of October following the ratification of this article.

**Section 6.** This article shall be inoperative unless it shall have been ratified as an amendment to the Constitution by the Legislatures of three-fourths of the several States within seven years from the date of its submission.

## Amendment XXI [1933]

**Section 1.** The eighteenth article of amendment to the Constitution of the United States is hereby repealed.

**Section 2.** The transportation or importation into any State, Territory, or Possession of the United States for delivery or use therein of intoxicating liquors, in violation of the laws thereof, is hereby prohibited.

**Section 3.** This article shall be inoperative unless it shall have been ratified as an amendment to the Constitution by conventions in the several States, as provided in the Constitution, within seven years from the date of the submission thereof to the States by the Congress.

## Amendment XXII [1951]

**Section 1.** No person shall be elected to the office of the President more than twice, and no person who has held the office of President, or acted as President, for more than two years of a term to which some other person was elected President shall be elected to the office of President more than once. But this article shall not apply to any person holding the office of President when this Article was proposed by the Congress, and shall not prevent any person who may be holding the office of President, or acting as President, during the term within which this Article becomes operative from holding the office of President or acting as President during the remainder of such term.

**Section 2.** This article shall be inoperative unless it shall have been ratified as an amendment to the Constitution by the legislatures of three-fourths of the several States within seven years from the date of its submission to the States by the Congress.

## Amendment XXIII [1961]

**Section 1.** The District constituting the seat of Government of the United States shall appoint in such manner as the Congress may direct: A number of electors of President and Vice-President equal to the whole number of Senators and Representatives in Congress to which the District would be entitled if it were a State, but in no event more than the least populous State; they shall be in addition to those appointed by the States, but they shall be considered for the purposes of the election of President and Vice-President, to be electors appointed by a State; and they shall meet in the District and perform such duties as provided by the twelfth article of amendment.

**Section 2.** The Congress shall have the power to enforce this article by appropriate legislation.

## Amendment XXIV [1964]

**Section 1.** The right of citizens of the United States to vote in any primary or other election for President or Vice-President, for electors for President or Vice-President, or for Senator or Representative in Congress, shall not be denied or abridged by the United States or any State by reason of failure to pay any poll tax or other tax.

**Section 2.** The Congress shall have the power to enforce this article by appropriate legislation.

## Amendment XXV [1967]

**Section 1.** In case of the removal of the President from office or of his death or resignation, the Vice-President shall become President.

**Section 2.** Whenever there is a vacancy in the office of the Vice-President, the President shall nominate a Vice-President who shall take office upon confirmation by a majority vote of both Houses of Congress.

**Section 3.** Whenever the President transmits to the President pro tempore of the Senate and the Speaker of the House of Representatives his written declaration that he is unable to discharge the powers and duties of his office, and until he transmits to them a written declaration to the contrary, such powers and duties shall be discharged by the Vice-President as Acting President.

**Section 4.** Whenever the Vice-President and a majority of either the principal officers of the executive departments or of such other body as Congress may by law provide, transmit to the President pro tempore of the Senate and the Speaker of the House of Representatives their written declaration that the President is unable to discharge the powers and duties of his office, the Vice-President shall immediately assume the powers and duties of the office as Acting President.

Thereafter, when the President transmits to the President pro tempore of the Senate and the Speaker of the House of Representatives his written declaration that no inability exists, he shall resume the powers and duties of his office unless the Vice-President and a majority of either the principal officers of the executive department[s] or of such other body as Congress may by law provide, transmit within four days to the President pro tempore of the Senate and the Speaker of the House of Representatives their written declaration that the President is unable to discharge the powers and duties of his office. Thereupon Congress shall decide the issue, assembling within forty-eight hours for that purpose if not in session. If the Congress, within twenty-one days after receipt of the latter written declaration, or, if Congress is not in session, within twenty-one days after Congress is required to assemble, determines by two-thirds vote of both Houses that the President is unable to discharge the powers and duties of his office, the Vice-President shall continue to discharge the same as Acting President; otherwise, the President shall resume the powers and duties of his office.

## Amendment XXVI [1971]

**Section 1.** The right of citizens of the United States, who are eighteen years of age or older, to vote shall not be denied or abridged by the United States or by any State on account of age.

**Section 2.** The Congress shall have power to enforce this article by appropriate legislation.

## Unratified Amendment

*Equal Rights Amendment (proposed by Congress March 22, 1972; seven-year deadline for ratification extended to June 30, 1982)*

**Section 1.** *Equality of rights under the law shall not be denied or abridged by the United States or by any State on account of sex.*

**Section 2.** *The Congress shall have the power to enforce, by appropriate legislation, the provisions of this article.*

**Section 3.** *This amendment shall take effect two years after the date of ratification.*

## Unratified Amendment

*District of Columbia Statehood Amendment (proposed by Congress August 22, 1978)*

**Section 1.** *For purposes of representation in the Congress, election of the President and Vice President, and article V of this Constitution, the District constituting the seat of government of the United States shall be treated as though it were a State.*

**Section 2.** *The exercise of the rights and powers conferred under this article shall be by the people of the District constituting the seat of government, and as shall be provided by Congress.*

**Section 3.** *The twenty-third article of amendment to the Constitution of the United States is hereby repealed.*

**Section 4.** *This article shall be inoperative, unless it shall have been ratified as an amendment to the Constitution by the legislatures of three-fourths of the several states within seven years from the date of its submission.*

## Amendment XXVII [1992]

No law varying the compensation for the services of the Senators and Representatives, shall take effect, until an election of Representatives shall have intervened.

# Appendix

## The American Nation

### Admission of States into the Union

| State | Date of Admission | State | Date of Admission | State | Date of Admission |
|---|---|---|---|---|---|
| 1. Delaware | December 7, 1787 | 18. Louisiana | April 30, 1812 | 35. West Virginia | June 20, 1863 |
| 2. Pennsylvania | December 12, 1787 | 19. Indiana | December 11, 1816 | 36. Nevada | October 31, 1864 |
| 3. New Jersey | December 18, 1787 | 20. Mississippi | December 10, 1817 | 37. Nebraska | March 1, 1867 |
| 4. Georgia | January 2, 1788 | 21. Illinois | December 3, 1818 | 38. Colorado | August 1, 1876 |
| 5. Connecticut | January 9, 1788 | 22. Alabama | December 14, 1819 | 39. North Dakota | November 2, 1889 |
| 6. Massachusetts | February 6, 1788 | 23. Maine | March 15, 1820 | 40. South Dakota | November 2, 1889 |
| 7. Maryland | April 28, 1788 | 24. Missouri | August 10, 1821 | 41. Montana | November 8, 1889 |
| 8. South Carolina | May 23, 1788 | 25. Arkansas | June 15, 1836 | 42. Washington | November 11, 1889 |
| 9. New Hampshire | June 21, 1788 | 26. Michigan | January 26, 1837 | 43. Idaho | July 3, 1890 |
| 10. Virginia | June 25, 1788 | 27. Florida | March 3, 1845 | 44. Wyoming | July 10, 1890 |
| 11. New York | July 26, 1788 | 28. Texas | December 29, 1845 | 45. Utah | January 4, 1896 |
| 12. North Carolina | November 21, 1789 | 29. Iowa | December 28, 1846 | 46. Oklahoma | November 16, 1907 |
| 13. Rhode Island | May 29, 1790 | 30. Wisconsin | May 29, 1848 | 47. New Mexico | January 6, 1912 |
| 14. Vermont | March 4, 1791 | 31. California | September 9, 1850 | 48. Arizona | February 14, 1912 |
| 15. Kentucky | June 1, 1792 | 32. Minnesota | May 11, 1858 | 49. Alaska | January 3, 1959 |
| 16. Tennessee | June 1, 1796 | 33. Oregon | February 14, 1859 | 50. Hawaii | August 21, 1959 |
| 17. Ohio | March 1, 1803 | 34. Kansas | January 29, 1861 | | |

### Territorial Expansion

| Territory | Date Acquired | Square Miles | How Acquired |
|---|---|---|---|
| Original states and territories | 1783 | 888,685 | Treaty of Paris |
| Louisiana Purchase | 1803 | 827,192 | Purchased from France |
| Florida | 1819 | 72,003 | Adams-Onís Treaty |
| Texas | 1845 | 390,143 | Annexation of independent country |
| Oregon | 1846 | 285,580 | Oregon Boundary Treaty |
| Mexican cession | 1848 | 529,017 | Treaty of Guadalupe Hidalgo |
| Gadsden Purchase | 1853 | 29,640 | Purchased from Mexico |
| Midway Islands | 1867 | 2 | Annexation of uninhabited islands |
| Alaska | 1867 | 589,757 | Purchased from Russia |
| Hawaii | 1898 | 6,450 | Annexation of independent country |
| Wake Island | 1898 | 3 | Annexation of uninhabited island |
| Puerto Rico | 1899 | 3,435 | Treaty of Paris |
| Guam | 1899 | 212 | Treaty of Paris |
| The Philippines | 1899–1946 | 115,600 | Treaty of Paris; granted independence |

| Territory | Date Acquired | Square Miles | How Acquired |
|---|---|---|---|
| American Samoa | 1900 | 76 | Treaty with Germany and Great Britain |
| Panama Canal Zone | 1904–1978 | 553 | Hay–Bunau-Varilla Treaty |
| U.S. Virgin Islands | 1917 | 133 | Purchased from Denmark |
| Trust Territory of the Pacific Islands* | 1947–1986 | 717 | United Nations Trusteeship |

*A number of these islands have recently been granted independence: Federated States of Micronesia, 1990; Republic of the Marshall Islands, 1991; Republic of Palau, 1994. The Northern Mariana Islands is a commonwealth of the United States.

## Presidential Elections

| Year | Candidates | Parties | Percentage of Popular Vote* | Electoral Vote | Percentage of Voter Participation |
|---|---|---|---|---|---|
| 1789 | **George Washington** | No party designations | | 69 | |
| | John Adams† | | | 34 | |
| | Other candidates | | | 35 | |
| 1792 | **George Washington** | No party designations | | 132 | |
| | John Adams | | | 77 | |
| | George Clinton | | | 50 | |
| | Other candidates | | | 5 | |
| 1796 | **John Adams** | Federalist | | 71 | |
| | Thomas Jefferson | Democratic-Republican | | 68 | |
| | Thomas Pinckney | Federalist | | 59 | |
| | Aaron Burr | Democratic-Republican | | 30 | |
| | Other candidates | | | 48 | |
| 1800 | **Thomas Jefferson** | Democratic-Republican | | 73 | |
| | Aaron Burr | Democratic-Republican | | 73 | |
| | John Adams | Federalist | | 65 | |
| | Charles C. Pinckney | Federalist | | 64 | |
| | John Jay | Federalist | | 1 | |
| 1804 | **Thomas Jefferson** | Democratic-Republican | | 162 | |
| | Charles C. Pinckney | Federalist | | 14 | |
| 1808 | **James Madison** | Democratic-Republican | | 122 | |
| | Charles C. Pinckney | Federalist | | 47 | |
| | George Clinton | Democratic-Republican | | 6 | |
| 1812 | **James Madison** | Democratic-Republican | | 128 | |
| | DeWitt Clinton | Federalist | | 89 | |
| 1816 | **James Monroe** | Democratic-Republican | | 183 | |
| | Rufus King | Federalist | | 34 | |
| 1820 | **James Monroe** | Democratic-Republican | | 231 | |
| | John Quincy Adams | Independent Republican | | 1 | |
| 1824 | **John Quincy Adams** | Democratic-Republican | 30.5 | 84 | 26.9 |
| | Andrew Jackson | Democratic-Republican | 43.1 | 99 | |
| | Henry Clay | Democratic-Republican | 13.2 | 37 | |
| | William H. Crawford | Democratic-Republican | 13.1 | 41 | |
| 1828 | **Andrew Jackson** | Democratic | 56.0 | 178 | 57.6 |
| | John Quincy Adams | National Republican | 44.0 | 83 | |

*Prior to 1824, most presidential electors were chosen by state legislators rather than by popular vote. For elections after 1824, candidates receiving less than 1.0 percent of the popular vote have been omitted from this chart. Hence the popular vote does not total 100 percent for all elections.
†Before the Twelfth Amendment was passed in 1804, the Electoral College voted for two presidential candidates; the runner-up became vice president.

| Year | Candidates | Parties | Percentage of Popular Vote | Electoral Vote | Percentage of Voter Participation |
|------|-----------|---------|---------------------------|----------------|-----------------------------------|
| 1832 | **Andrew Jackson** | Democratic | 54.5 | 219 | 55.4 |
|      | Henry Clay | National Republican | 37.5 | 49 | |
|      | William Wirt | Anti-Masonic | 8.0 | 7 | |
|      | John Floyd | Democratic | ‡ | 11 | |
| 1836 | **Martin Van Buren** | Democratic | 50.9 | 170 | 57.8 |
|      | William H. Harrison | Whig | | 73 | |
|      | Hugh L. White | Whig | | 26 | |
|      | Daniel Webster | Whig | 49.1 | 14 | |
|      | W. P. Mangum | Whig | | 11 | |
| 1840 | **William H. Harrison** | Whig | 53.1 | 234 | 80.2 |
|      | Martin Van Buren | Democratic | 46.9 | 60 | |
| 1844 | **James K. Polk** | Democratic | 49.6 | 170 | 78.9 |
|      | Henry Clay | Whig | 48.1 | 105 | |
|      | James G. Birney | Liberty | 2.3 | | |
| 1848 | **Zachary Taylor** | Whig | 47.4 | 163 | 72.7 |
|      | Lewis Cass | Democratic | 42.5 | 127 | |
|      | Martin Van Buren | Free Soil | 10.1 | | |
| 1852 | **Franklin Pierce** | Democratic | 50.9 | 254 | 69.6 |
|      | Winfield Scott | Whig | 44.1 | 42 | |
|      | John P. Hale | Free Soil | 5.0 | | |
| 1856 | **James Buchanan** | Democratic | 45.3 | 174 | 78.9 |
|      | John C. Frémont | Republican | 33.1 | 114 | |
|      | Millard Fillmore | American | 21.6 | 8 | |
| 1860 | **Abraham Lincoln** | Republican | 39.8 | 180 | 81.2 |
|      | Stephen A. Douglas | Democratic | 29.5 | 12 | |
|      | John C. Breckinridge | Democratic | 18.1 | 72 | |
|      | John Bell | Constitutional Union | 12.6 | 39 | |
| 1864 | **Abraham Lincoln** | Republican | 55.0 | 212 | 73.8 |
|      | George B. McClellan | Democratic | 45.0 | 21 | |
| 1868 | **Ulysses S. Grant** | Republican | 52.7 | 214 | 78.1 |
|      | Horatio Seymour | Democratic | 47.3 | 80 | |
| 1872 | **Ulysses S. Grant** | Republican | 55.6 | 286 | 71.3 |
|      | Horace Greeley | Democratic | 43.9 | | |
| 1876 | **Rutherford B. Hayes** | Republican | 48.0 | 185 | 81.8 |
|      | Samuel J. Tilden | Democratic | 51.0 | 184 | |
| 1880 | **James A. Garfield** | Republican | 48.5 | 214 | 79.4 |
|      | Winfield S. Hancock | Democratic | 48.1 | 155 | |
|      | James B. Weaver | Greenback-Labor | 3.4 | | |
| 1884 | **Grover Cleveland** | Democratic | 48.5 | 219 | 77.5 |
|      | James G. Blaine | Republican | 48.2 | 182 | |
|      | Benjamin F. Butler | Greenback-Labor | 1.8 | | |
|      | John P. St. John | Prohibition | 1.5 | | |
| 1888 | **Benjamin Harrison** | Republican | 47.9 | 233 | 79.3 |
|      | Grover Cleveland | Democratic | 48.6 | 168 | |
|      | Clinton P. Fisk | Prohibition | 2.2 | | |
|      | Anson J. Streeter | Union Labor | 1.3 | | |
| 1892 | **Grover Cleveland** | Democratic | 46.1 | 277 | 74.7 |
|      | Benjamin Harrison | Republican | 43.0 | 145 | |
|      | James B. Weaver | People's | 8.5 | 22 | |
|      | John Bidwell | Prohibition | 2.2 | | |

‡Independent Democrat John Floyd received the 11 electoral votes of South Carolina; that state's presidential electors were still chosen by its legislature, not by popular vote.

| Year | Candidates | Parties | Percentage of Popular Vote | Electoral Vote | Percentage of Voter Participation |
|------|-----------|---------|----------------------------|----------------|-----------------------------------|
| 1896 | **William McKinley** | Republican | 51.1 | 271 | 79.3 |
|      | William J. Bryan | Democratic | 47.7 | 176 | |
| 1900 | **William McKinley** | Republican | 51.7 | 292 | 73.2 |
|      | William J. Bryan | Democratic; Populist | 45.5 | 155 | |
|      | John C. Wooley | Prohibition | 1.5 | | |
| 1904 | **Theodore Roosevelt** | Republican | 57.4 | 336 | 65.2 |
|      | Alton B. Parker | Democratic | 37.6 | 140 | |
|      | Eugene V. Debs | Socialist | 3.0 | | |
|      | Silas C. Swallow | Prohibition | 1.9 | | |
| 1908 | **William H. Taft** | Republican | 51.6 | 321 | 65.4 |
|      | William J. Bryan | Democratic | 43.1 | 162 | |
|      | Eugene V. Debs | Socialist | 2.8 | | |
|      | Eugene W. Chafin | Prohibition | 1.7 | | |
| 1912 | **Woodrow Wilson** | Democratic | 41.9 | 435 | 58.8 |
|      | Theodore Roosevelt | Progressive | 27.4 | 88 | |
|      | William H. Taft | Republican | 23.2 | 8 | |
|      | Eugene V. Debs | Socialist | 6.0 | | |
|      | Eugene W. Chafin | Prohibition | 1.4 | | |
| 1916 | **Woodrow Wilson** | Democratic | 49.4 | 277 | 61.6 |
|      | Charles E. Hughes | Republican | 46.2 | 254 | |
|      | A. L. Benson | Socialist | 3.2 | | |
|      | J. Frank Hanly | Prohibition | 1.2 | | |
| 1920 | **Warren G. Harding** | Republican | 60.4 | 404 | 49.2 |
|      | James M. Cox | Democratic | 34.2 | 127 | |
|      | Eugene V. Debs | Socialist | 3.4 | | |
|      | P. P. Christensen | Farmer-Labor | 1.0 | | |
| 1924 | **Calvin Coolidge** | Republican | 54.0 | 382 | 48.9 |
|      | John W. Davis | Democratic | 28.8 | 136 | |
|      | Robert M. La Follette | Progressive | 16.6 | 13 | |
| 1928 | **Herbert C. Hoover** | Republican | 58.2 | 444 | 56.9 |
|      | Alfred E. Smith | Democratic | 40.9 | 87 | |
| 1932 | **Franklin D. Roosevelt** | Democratic | 57.4 | 472 | 56.9 |
|      | Herbert C. Hoover | Republican | 39.7 | 59 | |
|      | Norman Thomas | Socialist | 2.2 | | |
| 1936 | **Franklin D. Roosevelt** | Democratic | 60.8 | 523 | 61.0 |
|      | Alfred M. Landon | Republican | 36.5 | 8 | |
|      | William Lemke | Union | 1.9 | | |
| 1940 | **Franklin D. Roosevelt** | Democratic | 54.8 | 449 | 62.5 |
|      | Wendell L. Willkie | Republican | 44.8 | 82 | |
| 1944 | **Franklin D. Roosevelt** | Democratic | 53.5 | 432 | 55.9 |
|      | Thomas E. Dewey | Republican | 46.0 | 99 | |
| 1948 | **Harry S Truman** | Democratic | 49.6 | 303 | 53.0 |
|      | Thomas E. Dewey | Republican | 45.1 | 189 | |
|      | J. Strom Thurmond | States' Rights | 2.4 | | |
|      | Henry Wallace | Progressive | 2.4 | | |
| 1952 | **Dwight D. Eisenhower** | Republican | 55.1 | 442 | 63.3 |
|      | Adlai E. Stevenson | Democratic | 44.4 | 89 | |
| 1956 | **Dwight D. Eisenhower** | Republican | 57.6 | 457 | 60.6 |
|      | Adlai E. Stevenson | Democratic | 42.1 | 73 | |

| Year | Candidates | Parties | Percentage of Popular Vote | Electoral Vote | Percentage of Voter Participation |
|------|-----------|---------|---------------------------|----------------|----------------------------------|
| 1960 | **John F. Kennedy** | Democratic | 49.7 | 303 | 62.8 |
|      | Richard M. Nixon | Republican | 49.5 | 219 | |
| 1964 | **Lyndon B. Johnson** | Democratic | 61.1 | 486 | 61.9 |
|      | Barry M. Goldwater | Republican | 38.5 | 52 | |
| 1968 | **Richard M. Nixon** | Republican | 43.4 | 301 | 60.8 |
|      | Hubert H. Humphrey | Democratic | 42.7 | 191 | |
|      | George C. Wallace | American Independent | 13.5 | 46 | |
| 1972 | **Richard M. Nixon** | Republican | 60.7 | 520 | 55.2 |
|      | George S. McGovern | Democratic | 37.5 | 17 | |
|      | John G. Schmitz | American | 1.4 | | |
| 1976 | **Jimmy Carter** | Democratic | 50.1 | 297 | 53.6 |
|      | Gerald R. Ford | Republican | 48.0 | 240 | |
| 1980 | **Ronald W. Reagan** | Republican | 50.7 | 489 | 52.6 |
|      | Jimmy Carter | Democratic | 41.0 | 49 | |
|      | John B. Anderson | Independent | 6.6 | 0 | |
|      | Ed Clark | Libertarian | 1.1 | | |
| 1984 | **Ronald W. Reagan** | Republican | 58.4 | 525 | 53.1 |
|      | Walter F. Mondale | Democratic | 41.6 | 13 | |
| 1988 | **George H. W. Bush** | Republican | 53.4 | 426 | 50.2 |
|      | Michael Dukakis | Democratic | 45.6 | 111** | |
| 1992 | **Bill Clinton** | Democratic | 43.7 | 370 | 55.2 |
|      | George H. W. Bush | Republican | 38.0 | 168 | |
|      | H. Ross Perot | Independent | 19.0 | 0 | |
| 1996 | **Bill Clinton** | Democratic | 49 | 379 | 49.1 |
|      | Robert J. Dole | Republican | 41 | 159 | |
|      | H. Ross Perot | Reform | 8 | 0 | |
| 2000 | **George W. Bush** | Republican | 47.8 | 271 | 51.3 |
|      | Albert Gore | Democratic | 48.4 | 267 | |
|      | Ralph Nader | Green | 2.7 | 0 | |
| 2004 | **George W. Bush** | Republican | 50.7 | 286 | 55.3 |
|      | John Kerry | Democratic | 48.3 | 252 | |
| 2008 | **Barack Obama** | Democratic | 52.9 | 365 | 56.8 |
|      | John McCain | Republican | 45.7 | 173 | |

**One Dukakis elector cast a vote for Lloyd Bentsen.

## Supreme Court Justices

| Name | Terms of Service | Appointed by | Name | Terms of Service | Appointed by |
|------|-----------------|--------------|------|-----------------|--------------|
| **John Jay,** * N.Y. | 1789–1795 | Washington | **Oliver Ellsworth**, Conn. | 1796–1800 | Washington |
| James Wilson, Pa. | 1789–1798 | Washington | Bushrod Washington, Va. | 1799–1829 | J. Adams |
| John Rutledge, S.C. | 1790–1791 | Washington | Alfred Moore, N.C. | 1800–1804 | J. Adams |
| William Cushing, Mass. | 1790–1810 | Washington | **John Marshall**, Va. | 1801–1835 | J. Adams |
| John Blair, Va. | 1790–1796 | Washington | William Johnson, S.C. | 1804–1834 | Jefferson |
| James Iredell, N.C. | 1790–1799 | Washington | Brockholst Livingston, N.Y. | 1807–1823 | Jefferson |
| Thomas Johnson, Md. | 1792–1793 | Washington | Thomas Todd, Ky. | 1807–1826 | Jefferson |
| William Paterson, N.J. | 1793–1806 | Washington | Gabriel Duvall, Md. | 1811–1835 | Madison |
| **John Rutledge**, S.C. | 1795 | Washington | Joseph Story, Mass. | 1812–1845 | Madison |
| Samuel Chase, Md. | 1796–1811 | Washington | Smith Thompson, N.Y. | 1823–1843 | Monroe |

| Name | Terms of Service | Appointed by | Name | Terms of Service | Appointed by |
|------|------------------|--------------|------|------------------|--------------|
| Robert Trimble, Ky. | 1826–1828 | J. Q. Adams | John H. Clarke, Ohio | 1916–1922 | Wilson |
| John McLean, Ohio | 1830–1861 | Jackson | **William H. Taft**, Conn. | 1921–1930 | Harding |
| Henry Baldwin, Pa. | 1830–1844 | Jackson | George Sutherland, Utah | 1922–1938 | Harding |
| James M. Wayne, Ga. | 1835–1867 | Jackson | Pierce Butler, Minn. | 1923–1939 | Harding |
| **Roger B. Taney**, Md. | 1836–1864 | Jackson | Edward T. Sanford, Tenn. | 1923–1930 | Harding |
| Philip P. Barbour, Va. | 1836–1841 | Jackson | Harlan F. Stone, N.Y. | 1925–1941 | Coolidge |
| John Cartron, Tenn. | 1837–1865 | Van Buren | **Charles E. Hughes**, N.Y. | 1930–1941 | Hoover |
| John McKinley, Ala. | 1838–1852 | Van Buren | Owen J. Roberts, Pa. | 1930–1945 | Hoover |
| Peter V. Daniel, Va. | 1842–1860 | Van Buren | Benjamin N. Cardozo, N.Y. | 1932–1938 | Hoover |
| Samuel Nelson, N.Y. | 1845–1872 | Tyler | Hugo L. Black, Ala. | 1937–1971 | F. Roosevelt |
| Levi Woodbury, N.H. | 1845–1851 | Polk | Stanley F. Reed, Ky. | 1938–1957 | F. Roosevelt |
| Robert C. Grier, Pa. | 1846–1870 | Polk | Felix Frankfurter, Mass. | 1939–1962 | F. Roosevelt |
| Benjamin R. Curtis, Mass. | 1851–1857 | Fillmore | William O. Douglas, Conn. | 1939–1975 | F. Roosevelt |
| John A. Campbell, Ala. | 1853–1861 | Pierce | Frank Murphy, Mich. | 1940–1949 | F. Roosevelt |
| Nathan Clifford, Me. | 1858–1881 | Buchanan | **Harlan F. Stone**, N.Y. | 1941–1946 | F. Roosevelt |
| Noah H. Swayne, Ohio | 1862–1881 | Lincoln | James R. Byrnes, S.C. | 1941–1942 | F. Roosevelt |
| Samuel F. Miller, Iowa | 1862–1890 | Lincoln | Robert H. Jackson, N.Y. | 1941–1954 | F. Roosevelt |
| David Davis, Ill. | 1862–1877 | Lincoln | Wiley B. Rutledge, Iowa | 1943–1949 | F. Roosevelt |
| Stephen J. Field, Cal. | 1863–1897 | Lincoln | Harold H. Burton, Ohio | 1945–1958 | Truman |
| **Salmon P. Chase**, Ohio | 1864–1873 | Lincoln | **Frederick M. Vinson**, Ky. | 1946–1953 | Truman |
| William Strong, Pa. | 1870–1880 | Grant | Tom C. Clark, Texas | 1949–1967 | Truman |
| Joseph P. Bradley, N.J. | 1870–1892 | Grant | Sherman Minton, Ind. | 1949–1956 | Truman |
| Ward Hunt, N.Y. | 1873–1882 | Grant | **Earl Warren**, Cal. | 1953–1969 | Eisenhower |
| **Morrison R. Waite**, Ohio | 1874–1888 | Grant | John Marshall Harlan, N.Y. | 1955–1971 | Eisenhower |
| John M. Harlan, Ky. | 1877–1911 | Hayes | William J. Brennan Jr., N.J. | 1956–1990 | Eisenhower |
| William B. Woods, Ga. | 1881–1887 | Hayes | Charles E. Whittaker, Mo. | 1957–1962 | Eisenhower |
| Stanley Matthews, Ohio | 1881–1889 | Garfield | Potter Stewart, Ohio | 1958–1981 | Eisenhower |
| Horace Gray, Mass. | 1882–1902 | Arthur | Bryon R. White, Colo. | 1962–1993 | Kennedy |
| Samuel Blatchford, N.Y. | 1882–1893 | Arthur | Arthur J. Goldberg, Ill. | 1962–1965 | Kennedy |
| Lucius Q. C. Lamar, Miss. | 1888–1893 | Cleveland | Abe Fortas, Tenn. | 1965–1969 | Johnson |
| **Melville W. Fuller**, Ill. | 1888–1910 | Cleveland | Thurgood Marshall, Md. | 1967–1991 | Johnson |
| David J. Brewer, Kan. | 1890–1910 | B. Harrison | **Warren E. Burger**, Minn. | 1969–1986 | Nixon |
| Henry B. Brown, Mich. | 1891–1906 | B. Harrison | Harry A. Blackmun, Minn. | 1970–1994 | Nixon |
| George Shiras Jr., Pa. | 1892–1903 | B. Harrison | Lewis F. Powell Jr., Va. | 1971–1987 | Nixon |
| Howell E. Jackson, Tenn. | 1893–1895 | B. Harrison | William H. Rehnquist, Ill. | 1971–1986 | Nixon |
| Edward D. White, La. | 1894–1910 | Cleveland | John Paul Stevens, Ill. | 1975–2010 | Ford |
| Rufus W. Peckham, N.Y. | 1896–1909 | Cleveland | Sandra Day O'Connor, Ariz. | 1981–2006 | Reagan |
| Joseph McKenna, Cal. | 1898–1925 | McKinley | **William H. Rehnquist**, Va. | 1986–2005 | Reagan |
| Oliver W. Holmes, Mass. | 1902–1932 | T. Roosevelt | Antonin Scalia, Va. | 1986– | Reagan |
| William R. Day, Ohio | 1903–1922 | T. Roosevelt | Anthony M. Kennedy, Cal. | 1988– | Reagan |
| William H. Moody, Mass. | 1906–1910 | T. Roosevelt | David H. Souter, N.H. | 1990–2009 | G. H. W. Bush |
| Horace H. Lurton, Tenn. | 1910–1914 | Taft | Clarence Thomas, Ga. | 1991– | G. H. W. Bush |
| Charles E. Hughes, N.Y. | 1910–1916 | Taft | Ruth Bader Ginsburg, N.Y. | 1993– | Clinton |
| **Edward D. White**, La. | 1910–1921 | Taft | Stephen G. Breyer, Mass. | 1994– | Clinton |
| Willis Van Devanter, Wy. | 1911–1937 | Taft | **John G. Roberts, Jr.**, Md. | 2005– | G. W. Bush |
| Joseph R. Lamar, Ga. | 1911–1916 | Taft | Samuel A. Alito Jr., N.J. | 2006– | G. W. Bush |
| Mahlon Pitney, N.J. | 1912–1922 | Taft | Sonia Sotomayor, N.Y. | 2009– | Obama |
| James C. McReynolds, Tenn. | 1914–1941 | Wilson | Elena Kagan, N.Y. | 2010– | Obama |
| Louis D. Brandeis, Mass. | 1916–1939 | Wilson | | | |

*Chief Justices are printed in bold type.

# The American People: a Demographic Survey

## A Demographic Profile of the American People

| Year | Life Expectancy at Birth - White | Life Expectancy at Birth - Black | Median Age at First Marriage - Men | Median Age at First Marriage - Women | Number of Children under 5 (per 1,000 Women Aged 20–44) | Percentage of Persons (age 16+) in Paid Workforce - Men | Percentage of Persons (age 16+) in Paid Workforce - Women | Percentage of Paid Workers Who Are Women |
|------|-------|-------|-----|-------|-------|------|------|------|
| 1820 | | | | | 1,295 | | 6.2 | 7.3 |
| 1830 | | | | | 1,145 | | 6.4 | 7.4 |
| 1840 | | | | | 1,085 | | 8.4 | 9.6 |
| 1850 | | | | | 923 | | 10.1 | 10.8 |
| 1860 | | | | | 929 | | 9.7 | 10.2 |
| 1870 | | | | | 839 | | 13.7 | 14.8 |
| 1880 | | | | | 822 | | 14.7 | 15.2 |
| 1890 | | | 26.1 | 22.0 | 716 | 84.3 | 18.2 | 17.0 |
| 1900 | 47.6 | 33.0 | 25.9 | 21.9 | 688 | 85.7 | 20.0 | 18.1 |
| 1910 | 50.3 | 35.6 | 25.1 | 21.6 | 643 | 85.1 | 24.8 | 20.0 |
| 1920 | 54.9 | 45.3 | 24.6 | 21.2 | 604 | 84.6 | 22.7 | 20.4 |
| 1930 | 61.4 | 48.1 | 24.3 | 21.3 | 511 | 82.1 | 23.6 | 21.9 |
| 1940 | 64.2 | 53.1 | 24.3 | 21.5 | 429 | 79.1 | 25.8 | 24.6 |
| 1950 | 69.1 | 60.8 | 22.8 | 20.3 | 589 | 81.6 | 29.9 | 27.8 |
| 1960 | 70.6 | 63.6 | 22.8 | 20.3 | 737 | 80.4 | 35.7 | 32.3 |
| 1970 | 71.7 | 65.3 | 22.5 | 20.6 | 530 | 79.7 | 41.4 | 38.0 |
| 1980 | 74.4 | 68.1 | 24.7 | 22.0 | 440 | 77.4 | 51.5 | 42.6 |
| 1990 | 76.1 | 69.1 | 26.1 | 23.9 | 377 | 76.4 | 57.4 | 45.2 |
| 2000 | 77.6 | 71.7 | 26.7 | 25.1 | 365 | 74.8 | 58.9 | 46.3 |
| 2010* | 78.9 | 73.8 | 27.7 | 26.0 | | 73.0 | 59.5 | 46.5 |

SOURCE: U.S. Bureau of the Census, *Historical Statistics of the United States, Colonial Times to 1970 (1975); Statistical Abstract of the United States, 2001; Statistical Abstract of the United States, 2010.*
*Or latest available data.

## Birth Rate, 1820–2010

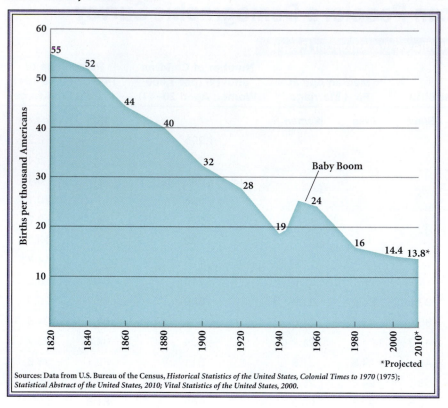

Sources: Data from U.S. Bureau of the Census, *Historical Statistics of the United States, Colonial Times to 1970* (1975); *Statistical Abstract of the United States, 2010; Vital Statistics of the United States, 2000.*

## Death Rate, 1900–2010

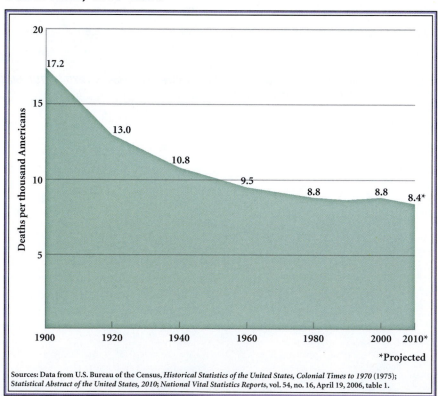

Sources: Data from U.S. Bureau of the Census, *Historical Statistics of the United States, Colonial Times to 1970* (1975); *Statistical Abstract of the United States, 2010; National Vital Statistics Reports,* vol. 54, no. 16, April 19, 2006, table 1.

## Life Expectancy (at Birth), 1900–2010

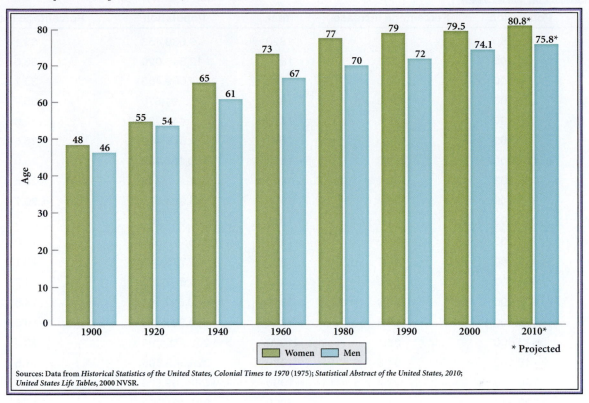

Sources: Data from *Historical Statistics of the United States, Colonial Times to 1970* (1975); *Statistical Abstract of the United States, 2010*; *United States Life Tables*, 2000 NVSR.

## The Aging of the U.S. Population, 1850–2010

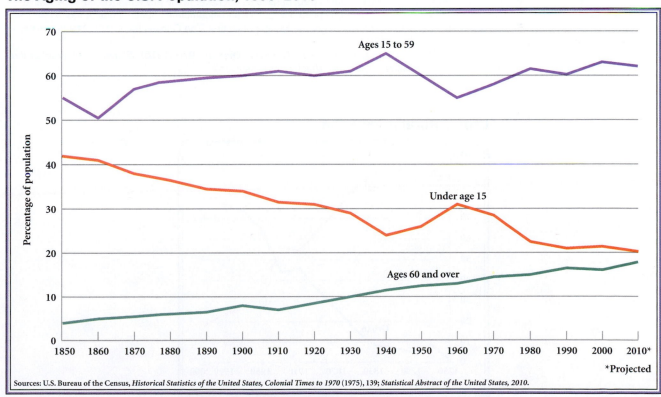

Sources: U.S. Bureau of the Census, *Historical Statistics of the United States, Colonial Times to 1970* (1975), 139; *Statistical Abstract of the United States, 2010*.

## Enumerated Population*

| Year | Population | Percentage Increase | Year | Population | Percentage Increase |
|---|---|---|---|---|---|
| 1610 | 350 | – | 1820 | 9,638,453 | 33.1 |
| 1620 | 2,300 | 557.1 | 1830 | 12,866,020 | 33.5 |
| 1630 | 4,600 | 100.0 | 1840 | 17,069,453 | 32.7 |
| 1640 | 26,600 | 478.3 | 1850 | 23,191,876 | 35.9 |
| 1650 | 50,400 | 90.8 | 1860 | 31,443,321 | 35.6 |
| 1660 | 75,100 | 49.0 | 1870 | 39,818,449 | 26.6 |
| 1670 | 111,900 | 49.0 | 1880 | 50,155,783 | 26.0 |
| 1680 | 151,500 | 35.4 | 1890 | 62,947,714 | 25.5 |
| 1690 | 210,400 | 38.9 | 1900 | 75,994,575 | 20.7 |
| 1700 | 250,900 | 19.2 | 1910 | 91,972,266 | 21.0 |
| 1710 | 331,700 | 32.2 | 1920 | 105,710,620 | 14.9 |
| 1720 | 466,200 | 40.5 | 1930 | 122,775,046 | 16.1 |
| 1730 | 629,400 | 35.0 | 1940 | 131,669,275 | 7.2 |
| 1740 | 905,600 | 43.9 | 1950 | 150,697,361 | 14.5 |
| 1750 | 1,170,800 | 29.3 | 1960 | 179,323,175 | 19.0 |
| 1760 | 1,593,600 | 36.1 | 1970 | 203,235,298 | 13.3 |
| 1770 | 2,148,100 | 34.8 | 1980 | 226,545,805 | 11.5 |
| 1780 | 2,780,400 | 29.4 | 1990 | 248,709,873 | 9.8 |
| 1790 | 3,929,214 | 41.3 | 2000 | 281,421,906 | 13.2 |
| 1800 | 5,308,483 | 35.1 | 2010 | 311,000,000 (proj.) | 10.5 |
| 1810 | 7,239,881 | 36.4 | | | |

*Note: These figures largely ignore the Native American population. Until 1890, census takers never made any effort to count the Native American people who lived outside their reserved political areas and compiled only casual and incomplete enumerations of those living within their jurisdictions. In 1890, the federal government attempted a full count of the Indian population: The Census found 125,719 Indians in 1890, compared with only 12,543 in 1870 and 33,985 in 1880.

SOURCES: U.S. Bureau of the Census, *Historical Statistics of the United States, Colonial Times to 1970* (1975); *Statistical Abstract of the United States, 2010*; U.S. Bureau of the Census, Population Finder, http://factfinder.census.gov.

## Urban/Rural Population

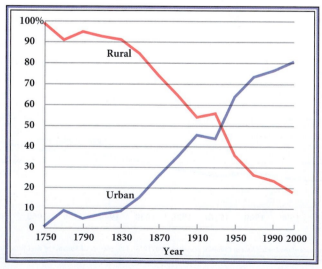

## The Ten Largest Cities by Population, 1700–2008

| | | City | Population | | | | City | Population |
|---|---|---|---|---|---|---|---|---|
| 1700 | 1. | Boston | 6,700 | | 1930 | 1. | New York | 6,930,446 |
| | 2. | New York | 4,937* | | | 2. | Chicago | 3,376,438 |
| | 3. | Philadelphia | 4,400† | | | 3. | Philadelphia | 1,950,961 |
| 1790 | 1. | Philadelphia | 42,520 | | | 4. | Detroit | 1,568,662 |
| | 2. | New York | 33,131 | | | 5. | Los Angeles | 1,238,048 |
| | 3. | Boston | 18,038 | | | 6. | Cleveland | 900,429 |
| | 4. | Charleston, S.C. | 16,359 | | | 7. | St. Louis | 821,960 |
| | 5. | Baltimore | 13,503 | | | 8. | Baltimore | 804,874 |
| | 6. | Salem, Mass. | 7,921 | | | 9. | Boston | 781,188 |
| | 7. | Newport, R.I. | 6,716 | | | 10. | Pittsburgh | 669,817 |
| | 8. | Providence, R.I. | 6,380 | | 1950 | 1. | New York | 7,891,957 |
| | 9. | Marblehead, Mass. | 5,661 | | | 2. | Chicago | 3,620,962 |
| | 10. | Portsmouth, N.H. | 4,720 | | | 3. | Philadelphia | 2,071,605 |
| 1830 | 1. | New York | 197,112 | | | 4. | Los Angeles | 1,970,358 |
| | 2. | Philadelphia | 161,410 | | | 5. | Detroit | 1,849,568 |
| | 3. | Baltimore | 80,620 | | | 6. | Baltimore | 949,708 |
| | 4. | Boston | 61,392 | | | 7. | Cleveland | 914,808 |
| | 5. | Charleston, S.C | 30,289 | | | 8. | St. Louis | 856,796 |
| | 6. | New Orleans | 29,737 | | | 9. | Washington, D.C. | 802,178 |
| | 7. | Cincinnati | 24,831 | | | 10. | Boston | 801,444 |
| | 8. | Albany, N.Y. | 24,209 | | 1970 | 1. | New York | 7,895,563 |
| | 9. | Brooklyn, N.Y. | 20,535 | | | 2. | Chicago | 3,369,357 |
| | 10. | Washington, D.C. | 18,826 | | | 3. | Los Angeles | 2,811,801 |
| 1850 | 1. | New York | 515,547 | | | 4. | Philadelphia | 1,949,996 |
| | 2. | Philadelphia | 340,045 | | | 5. | Detroit | 1,514,063 |
| | 3. | Baltimore | 169,054 | | | 6. | Houston | 1,233,535 |
| | 4. | Boston | 136,881 | | | 7. | Baltimore | 905,787 |
| | 5. | New Orleans | 116,375 | | | 8. | Dallas | 844,401 |
| | 6. | Cincinnati | 115,435 | | | 9. | Washington, D.C. | 756,668 |
| | 7. | Brooklyn, N.Y. | 96,838 | | | 10. | Cleveland | 750,879 |
| | 8. | St. Louis | 77,860 | | 1990 | 1. | New York | 7,322,564 |
| | 9. | Albany, N.Y. | 50,763 | | | 2. | Los Angeles | 3,485,398 |
| | 10. | Pittsburgh | 46,601 | | | 3. | Chicago | 2,783,726 |
| 1870 | 1. | New York | 942,292 | | | 4. | Houston | 1,630,553 |
| | 2. | Philadelphia | 674,022 | | | 5. | Philadelphia | 1,585,577 |
| | 3. | Brooklyn, N.Y. | 419,921‡ | | | 6. | San Diego | 1,110,549 |
| | 4. | St. Louis | 310,864 | | | 7. | Detroit | 1,027,974 |
| | 5. | Chicago | 298,977 | | | 8. | Dallas | 1,006,877 |
| | 6. | Baltimore | 267,354 | | | 9. | Phoenix | 983,403 |
| | 7. | Boston | 250,526 | | | 10. | San Antonio | 935,933 |
| | 8. | Cincinnati | 216,239 | | 2000 | 1. | New York | 8,008,278 |
| | 9. | New Orleans | 191,418 | | | 2. | Los Angeles | 3,694,820 |
| | 10. | San Francisco | 149,473 | | | 3. | Chicago | 2,896,016 |
| 1910 | 1. | New York | 4,766,883 | | | 4. | Houston | 1,953,631 |
| | 2. | Chicago | 2,185,283 | | | 5. | Philadelphia | 1,517,550 |
| | 3. | Philadelphia | 1,549,008 | | | 6. | Phoenix | 1,321,045 |
| | 4. | St. Louis | 687,029 | | | 7. | San Diego | 1,223,400 |
| | 5. | Boston | 670,585 | | | 8. | Dallas | 1,188,580 |
| | 6. | Cleveland | 560,663 | | | 9. | San Antonio | 1,144,646 |
| | 7. | Baltimore | 558,485 | | | 10. | Detroit | 951,270 |
| | 8. | Pittsburgh | 533,905 | | 2008 | 1. | New York | 8,364,000 |
| | 9. | Detroit | 465,766 | | (est.) | 2. | Los Angeles | 3,834,000 |
| | 10. | Buffalo | 423,715 | | | 3. | Chicago | 2,853,000 |

*Figure from a census taken in 1698.
†Philadelphia figures include suburbs.
‡Annexed to New York in 1898.

| | City | Population | | | City | Population |
|---|---|---|---|---|---|---|
| 4. | Houston | 2,242,000 | | 8. | Dallas | 1,280,000 |
| 5. | Phoenix | 1,568,000 | | 9. | San Diego | 1,279,000 |
| 6. | Philadelphia | 1,447,000 | | 10. | San Jose | 948,000 |
| 7. | San Antonio | 1,351,000 | | | | |

SOURCE: U.S. Census data.

## Percentage of Total Population Living in Metropolitan Areas, and in Their Central Cities and Suburbs

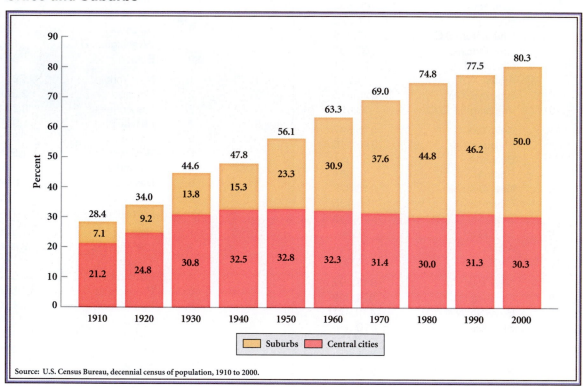

Source: U.S. Census Bureau, decennial census of population, 1910 to 2000.

## Immigration by Decade

| Year | Number | Immigrants during this Decade as a Percentage of Total Population | Year | Number | Immigrants during this Decade as a Percentage of Total Population |
|---|---|---|---|---|---|
| 1821–1830 | 151,824 | 1.6 | 1921–1930 | 4,107,209 | 3.9 |
| 1831–1840 | 599,125 | 4.6 | 1931–1940 | 528,431 | 0.4 |
| 1841–1850 | 1,713,251 | 10.0 | 1941–1950 | 1,035,039 | 0.7 |
| 1851–1860 | 2,598,214 | 11.2 | 1951–1960 | 2,515,479 | 1.6 |
| 1861–1870 | 2,314,824 | 7.4 | 1961–1970 | 3,321,677 | 1.8 |
| 1871–1880 | 2,812,191 | 7.1 | 1971–1980 | 4,493,000 | 2.2 |
| 1881–1890 | 5,246,613 | 10.5 | 1981–1990 | 7,338,000 | 3.0 |
| 1891–1900 | 3,687,546 | 5.8 | 1991–2000 | 9,095,083 | 3.7 |
| 1901–1910 | 8,795,386 | 11.6 | **Total** | **32,433,918** | |
| 1911–1920 | 5,735,811 | 6.2 | | | |
| **Total** | **33,654,785** | | 1821–2000 | | |
| | | | **GRAND TOTAL** | **66,088,703** | |

SOURCES: U.S. Bureau of the Census, *Historical Statistics of the United States, Colonial Times to 1970* (1975), part 1, 105–106; *Statistical Abstract of the United States, 2001.*

## Regional Origins

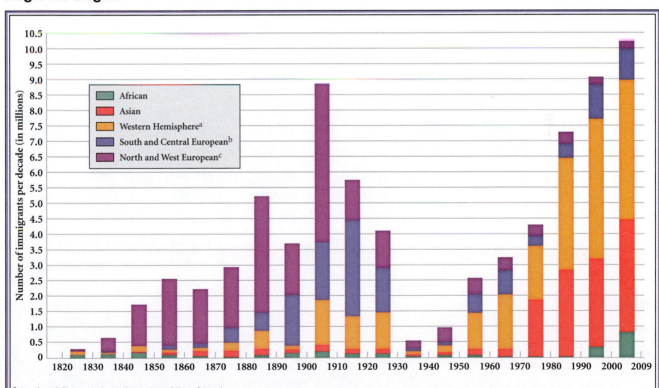

[a] Canada and all countries in South America and Central America.
[b] Italy, Spain, Portugal, Greece, Germany (Austria included, 1938–1945), Poland, former Czechoslovakia (since 1920), former Yugoslavia (since 1920), Hungary (since 1861), Austria (since 1861, except 1938–1945), former USSR (excludes Asian USSR between 1931 and 1963), Latvia, Estonia, Lithuania, Finland, Romania, Bulgaria, Turkey (in Europe), and other European countries not classified elsewhere.
[c] Great Britain, Ireland, Norway, Sweden, Denmark, Iceland, Netherlands, Belgium, Luxembourg, Switzerland, France.
Sources: Stephan Thernstrom, ed., *Harvard Encyclopedia of American Ethnic Groups* (1980), 480; U.S. Bureau of the Census, *Statistical Abstract of the United States, 1991;* U.S. Department of Homeland Security, *Yearbook of Immigration Statistics, 2009.*

## Race in the United States: 1790–2000

| Census year | Total population | White | Black (% Free/ Slave) | American Indian, Eskimo, and Aleut | Asian and Pacific Islander | Other Race | Hispanic Origin (of any race) |
|---|---|---|---|---|---|---|---|
| 1790 | 3,929,214 | 3,172,006 | 757,208 (7.9/92.1) | | | | |
| 1800 | 5,308,483 | 4,306,446 | 1,002,037 (10.8/89.2) | | | | |
| 1810 | 7,239,881 | 5,862,073 | 1,377,808 (13.5/86.5) | | | | |
| 1820 | 9,638,453 | 7,866,797 | 1,771,656 (13.2/86.8) | | | | |
| 1830 | 12,860,702 | 10,532,060 | 2,328,642 (13.7/86.3) | | | | |
| 1840 | 17,063,353 | 14,189,705 | 2,873,648 (13.4/86.6) | | | | |
| 1850 | 23,191,876 | 19,553,068 | 3,638,808 (11.9/88.1) | | | | |
| 1860 | 31,443,321 | 26,922,537 | 4,441,830 (11.0/89.0) | 44,021 | 34,933 | | |
| 1870 | 38,558,371 | 33,589,377 | 4,880,009 | 25,731 | 63,254 | | |
| 1880 | 50,155,783 | 43,402,970 | 6,580,793 | 66,407 | 105,613 | | |
| 1890* | 62,947,714 | 55,101,258 | 7,488,676 | 248,253 | 109,527 | | |
| 1900 | 75,994,575 | 66,809,196 | 8,833,994 | 237,196 | 114,189 | | |
| 1910 | 91,972,266 | 81,731,957 | 9,827,763 | 265,683 | 146,863 | | |
| 1920 | 105,710,620 | 94,820,915 | 10,463,131 | 244,437 | 182,137 | | |
| 1930 | 122,775,046 | 110,286,740 | 11,891,143 | 332,397 | 264,766 | | |
| 1940 | 131,669,275 | 118,214,870 | 12,865,518 | 333,969 | 254,918 | | 1,858,024 |
| 1950 | 150,697,361 | 134,942,028 | 15,042,286 | 343,410 | 321,033 | 48,604 | |
| 1960 | 179,323,175 | 158,831,732 | 18,871,831 | 551,669 | 980,337 | 87,606 | |
| 1970 | 203,211,926 | 177,748,975 | 22,580,289 | 827,255 | 1,538,721 | 516,686 | |
| 1980 | 226,545,805 | 188,371,622 | 26,495,025 | 1,420,400 | 3,500,439 | 6,758,319 | 14,608,673 |
| 1990 | 248,709,873 | 199,686,070 | 29,986,060 | 1,959,234 | 7,273,662 | 9,804,847 | 22,354,059 |
| 2000 | 281,421,906 | 211,460,626 | 34,658,190 | 2,475,956 | 10,641,833 | 15,359,073 | 35,305,818 |

**PERCENT**

| | | | | | | | |
|---|---|---|---|---|---|---|---|
| 1790 | | 80.7 | 19.3 | | | | |
| 1800 | | 81.1 | 18.9 | | | | |
| 1810 | | 81.0 | 19.0 | | | | |
| 1820 | | 81.6 | 18.4 | | | | |
| 1830 | | 81.9 | 18.1 | | | | |
| 1840 | | 83.2 | 16.8 | | | | |

| Census year | Total population | White | Black (% Free/ Slave) | American Indian, Eskimo, and Aleut | Asian and Pacific Islander | Other Race | Hispanic Origin (of any race) |
|---|---|---|---|---|---|---|---|
| 1850 | | 84.3 | 15.7 | | | | |
| 1860 | | 85.6 | 14.1 | 0.1 | 0.1 | | |
| 1870 | | 87.1 | 12.7 | 0.1 | 0.2 | | |
| 1880 | | 86.5 | 13.1 | 0.1 | 0.2 | | |
| 1890* | | 87.5 | 11.9 | 0.4 | 0.2 | | |
| 1900 | | 87.9 | 11.6 | 0.3 | 0.2 | | |
| 1910 | | 88.9 | 10.7 | 0.3 | 0.2 | | |
| 1920 | | 89.7 | 9.9 | 0.2 | 0.2 | | |
| 1930 | | 89.8 | 9.7 | 0.3 | 0.2 | | |
| 1940 | | 89.8 | 9.8 | 0.3 | 0.2 | | 1.4 |
| 1950 | | 89.5 | 10.0 | 0.2 | 0.2 | | |
| 1960 | | 88.6 | 10.5 | 0.3 | 0.5 | | |
| 1970 | | 87.5 | 11.1 | 0.4 | 0.8 | 0.3 | |
| 1980 | | 83.1 | 11.7 | 0.6 | 1.5 | 3.0 | 6.4 |
| 1990 | | 80.3 | 12.1 | 0.8 | 2.9 | 3.9 | 9.0 |
| 2000 | | 75.1 | 12.3 | 0.9 | 3.78 | 5.45 | 12.5 |

*Includes Indian Territory and Indian reservations.
SOURCE: U.S. Census Bureau

## The Labor Force (Thousands of Workers)

| Year | Agriculture | Mining | Manufacturing | Construction | Trade | Other | Total |
|------|-------------|--------|---------------|--------------|-------|-------|-------|
| 1810 | 1,950 | 11 | 75 | – | – | 294 | 2,330 |
| 1840 | 3,570 | 32 | 500 | 290 | 350 | 918 | 5,660 |
| 1850 | 4,520 | 102 | 1,200 | 410 | 530 | 1,488 | 8,250 |
| 1860 | 5,880 | 176 | 1,530 | 520 | 890 | 2,114 | 11,110 |
| 1870 | 6,790 | 180 | 2,470 | 780 | 1,310 | 1,400 | 12,930 |
| 1880 | 8,920 | 280 | 3,290 | 900 | 1,930 | 2,070 | 17,390 |
| 1890 | 9,960 | 440 | 4,390 | 1,510 | 2,960 | 4,060 | 23,320 |
| 1900 | 11,680 | 637 | 5,895 | 1,665 | 3,970 | 5,223 | 29,070 |
| 1910 | 11,770 | 1,068 | 8,332 | 1,949 | 5,320 | 9,041 | 37,480 |
| 1920 | 10,790 | 1,180 | 11,190 | 1,233 | 5,845 | 11,372 | 41,610 |
| 1930 | 10,560 | 1,009 | 9,884 | 1,988 | 8,122 | 17,267 | 48,830 |
| 1940 | 9,575 | 925 | 11,309 | 1,876 | 9,328 | 23,277 | 56,290 |
| 1950 | 7,870 | 901 | 15,648 | 3,029 | 12,152 | 25,870 | 65,470 |
| 1960 | 5,970 | 709 | 17,145 | 3,640 | 14,051 | 32,545 | 74,060 |
| 1970 | 3,463 | 516 | 20,746 | 4,818 | 15,008 | 34,127 | 78,678 |
| 1980 | 3,364 | 979 | 21,942 | 6,215 | 20,191 | 46,612 | 99,303 |
| 1990 | 3,223 | 724 | 21,346 | 7,764 | 24,622 | 60,849 | 118,793 |
| 2000 | 2,464 | 475 | 19,644 | 9,931 | 15,763 | 88,260 | 136,891 |
| 2008 | 2,168 | 819 | 15,904 | 10,974 | 16,533 | 98,964 | 145,362 |

SOURCES: U.S. Bureau of the Census, *Historical Statistics of the United States, Colonial Times to 1970* (1975), 139; *Statistical Abstract of the United States, 1998*, table 675; *Statistical Abstract of the United States, 2010*.

## Changing Labor Patterns

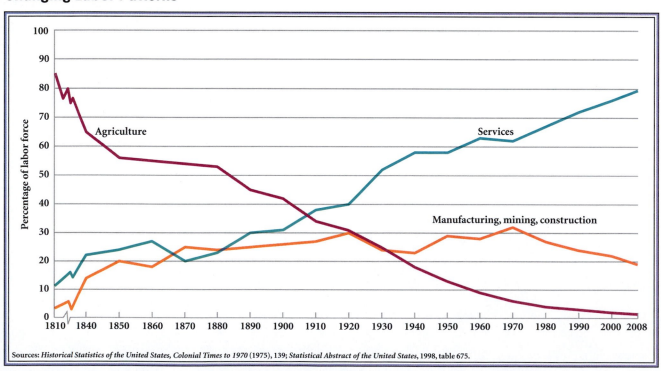

Sources: *Historical Statistics of the United States, Colonial Times to 1970* (1975), 139; *Statistical Abstract of the United States*, 1998, table 675.

**Real Gross Domestic Product per Capita, 1790–2010**

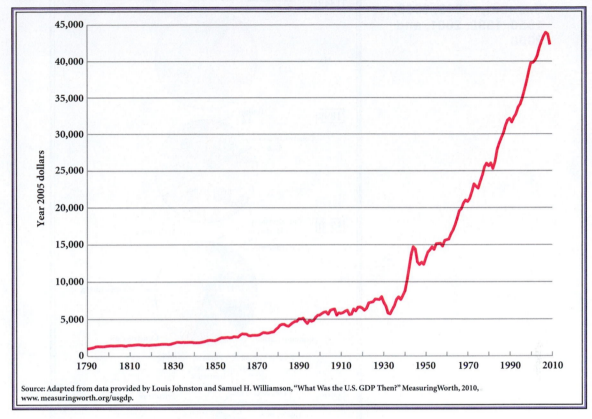

Source: Adapted from data provided by Louis Johnston and Samuel H. Williamson, "What Was the U.S. GDP Then?" MeasuringWorth, 2010, www.measuringworth.org/usgdp.

**Main Sectors of the U.S. Economy: 1849, 1899, 1950, 1990, 2001, and 2008**

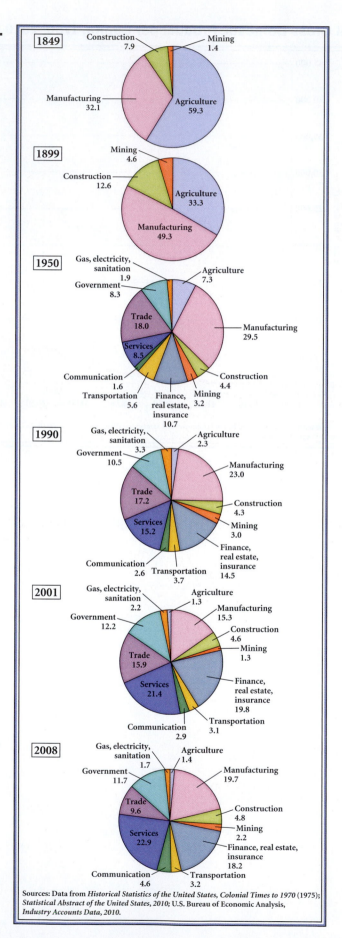

**1849**
- Construction 7.9
- Mining 1.4
- Agriculture 59.3
- Manufacturing 32.1

**1899**
- Mining 4.6
- Construction 12.6
- Agriculture 33.3
- Manufacturing 49.3

**1950**
- Gas, electricity, sanitation 1.9
- Government 8.3
- Agriculture 7.3
- Trade 18.0
- Manufacturing 29.5
- Services 8.5
- Communication 1.6
- Construction 4.4
- Transportation 5.6
- Finance, real estate, insurance 10.7
- Mining 3.2

**1990**
- Gas, electricity, sanitation 3.3
- Government 10.5
- Agriculture 2.3
- Trade 17.2
- Manufacturing 23.0
- Services 15.2
- Construction 4.3
- Mining 3.0
- Communication 2.6
- Transportation 3.7
- Finance, real estate, insurance 14.5

**2001**
- Gas, electricity, sanitation 2.2
- Government 12.2
- Agriculture 1.3
- Trade 15.9
- Manufacturing 15.3
- Services 21.4
- Construction 4.6
- Mining 1.3
- Communication 2.9
- Finance, real estate, insurance 19.8
- Transportation 3.1

**2008**
- Gas, electricity, sanitation 1.7
- Government 11.7
- Agriculture 1.4
- Trade 9.6
- Manufacturing 19.7
- Services 22.9
- Construction 4.8
- Mining 2.2
- Communication 4.6
- Finance, real estate, insurance 18.2
- Transportation 3.2

Sources: Data from *Historical Statistics of the United States, Colonial Times to 1970* (1975); *Statistical Abstract of the United States, 2010*; U.S. Bureau of Economic Analysis, *Industry Accounts Data, 2010*.

# Glossary

**American Renaissance** A burst of American literature during the 1840s, highlighted by the novels of Herman Melville and Nathaniel Hawthorne; the essays of Ralph Waldo Emerson, Henry David Thoreau, and Margaret Fuller; and the poetry of Walt Whitman. (p. 332)

**American System** The mercantilist system of national economic development advocated by Henry Clay and adopted by John Quincy Adams. It had three interrelated parts: a national bank to manage the nation's financial system; protective tariffs to provide revenue and encourage American industry; and a nationally funded network of roads, canals, and railroads. (p. 305)

**artisan republicanism** An ideology that celebrated small-scale producers, men and women who owned their own shops (or farms). It defined the ideal republican society as one constituted by, and dedicated to the welfare of, independent workers and citizens. (p. 280)

**assimilation** Efforts by U.S. government agents and Christian missionaries to persuade people of color to adopt white ways. Through assimilation policies, Native Americans, for example, were pressured to abandon their traditional religion, dress, and customs, and adopt Christianity, speak only English, accept U.S. laws concerning private property, and adapt their work and family life to white expectations. (p. 515)

**Benevolent Empire** A broad-ranging campaign of moral and institutional reforms inspired by evangelical Christian ideals and endorsed by upper-middle-class men and women in the 1820s and 1830s. Ministers who promoted benevolent reform insisted that people who had experienced saving grace should provide moral guidance and charity to the less fortunate. (p. 293)

**bills of exchange** Credit slips that British manufacturers, West Indian planters, and American merchants used in the eighteenth century in place of currency to settle transactions. (p. 94)

**Black Codes** Laws passed by southern states after the Civil War that denied ex-slaves the civil rights enjoyed by whites, intending to force blacks back to the plantations. (p. 464)

**blacklist** A list of people to be excluded from an activity or organization. In the nineteenth century, employers compiled lists of workers affiliated with unions and either fired them or refused to hire them. In the 1950s, governments and private businesses blacklisted alleged communists, denying them positions in government, motion pictures, and many industries and unions. (p. 281)

**business cycle** The periodic rise and fall of business activity characteristic of market-driven capitalist economies. To increase profits, producers increase output and eventually create a surplus (over-supply); the surplus then prompts a cutback in output, which produces an economic recession. The major periods of pre–World War II economic expansion — 1802–1818, 1824–1836, 1846–1856, 1865–1873, 1896–1914, 1922–1928 — were followed either by short financial panics or extended depressions (1837–1843, 1873–1896, and 1929–1939). In the postwar period, several short recessions — in 1945, 1949, 1953, 1958, 1961, and 1969 — were relatively minor exceptions to steady economic growth. After the steep downturns of 1974–1975 and 1980–1981, there was relatively sustained growth through the 1990s. In 2008, however, the United States experienced its deepest recession since the 1930s. (p. 239)

**capitalism** A system of economic production based on the private ownership of property and the contractual exchange for profit of goods, labor, and money (capital). Although some elements of capitalism existed in the United States before 1820, a full-scale capitalist economy — and society — emerged only with the Market Revolution (1820–1850). After the Civil War, American capitalism changed in character, as large corporations came to dominate sectors of the economy and state and federal governments increasingly sought to regulate business activity. See *Market Revolution*. (p. 237)

**carpetbaggers** A derisive name given by southerners to northerners who moved to the South during Reconstruction. (The word derived from the cheap suitcases, known as carpetbags, that held their belongings.) Former Confederates despised these northerners as transient exploiters. Carpetbaggers actually were a varied group that included Union veterans who had served in the South, reformers eager to help former slaves, and others looking for business opportunities. (p. 480)

**caste system** A form of social organization that divides a society along relatively rigid lines of status based primarily on birth. (p. 32)

**caucus** A meeting held by a political party to choose candidates, make policies, and enforce party discipline. (p. 305)

**chattel slavery** A system of bondage in which a slave has the legal status of property and so can be bought and sold like property. (p. 55)

**civic humanism** The belief that individuals owe a service to their community and its government. During the Renaissance, political theorists argued that selfless service to the polity was of critical importance in a self-governing republic. (p. 21)

**clan** A group of related families that share a real or legendary common ancestor. Most native peoples north of the Rio Grande organized their societies around clan groups; groups of clans that shared the same language and culture formed a people. (p. 14)

**classical liberalism** An ideology based on the economic principles of open markets and free competition propounded by Adam Smith and the political ideas of liberty and limited government advanced by John Locke. In the late twentieth century, many economic conservatives embraced the principles of classical liberalism and opposed the principles of social-welfare liberalism. See also *laissez-faire*. (p. 321)

**closed shop** A workplace in which a job seeker had to be a union member to gain employment. Nineteenth-century craft unions favored closed shops to keep out incompetent and lower-wage workers and to enhance their bargaining position with employers. For that reason, employers strongly opposed closed shops and sought laws to prohibit them. (p. 282)

**Columbian Exchange** The transfer in the sixteenth century of agricultural products and diseases from the Western Hemisphere to other continents, and those from other continents to the Western Hemisphere. (p. 31)

**common law** The centuries-old body of English legal customs and procedures that both protected the monarch's subjects against arbitrary acts of the government and resolved private disputes among those subjects. (p. 55)

**companionate marriage** A marriage based on equality and mutual respect—both republican values. Although husbands in these marriages retained significant legal power, they increasingly came to see their wives as loving partners rather than as inferiors or dependents. (p. 246)

**conscience Whigs** Whig politicians who opposed the Mexican War (1846–1848) on moral grounds. They argued that the purpose of the war was to expand and perpetuate slavery. They feared that the addition of more slave states would ensure the South's continuing control of the national government and undermine a society of yeomen farmers and "free labor" in the North. (p. 408)

**craft worker** An artisan or other worker who has a specific craft or skill—for example, a mason, a cabinetmaker, a printer, or a weaver. (p. 280)

**deism** The Enlightenment-influenced belief that the Christian God created the universe and then left it to run according to natural laws. (p. 116)

**desegregation** The legal requirement that people of all races have equal access to public facilities and services, including public schools, parks, water fountains, railroads, hotels, and restaurants. According to desegregation laws, African Americans in the South, for example, could not be forced to use separate facilities from whites. See also *integration*. (p. 483)

**division of labor** A system of manufacture that divides production into a series of distinct and repetitive tasks performed by machines or workers. The system took shape in the shoe industry between 1800 and 1830 and soon became the general practice. Although the division of labor improved productivity, it eroded workers' control and sense of achievement. (p. 274)

**domesticity** An ideology of marriage and family life, which called for men to practice self-discipline, temperance, and deference to female moral authority, while women refrained from paid labor in the workplace and devoted themselves to motherhood and family. Though domesticity stressed women's primary role in the home, it also sanctioned women's participation in religious missions and charitable efforts. Grounded in the ideals of republican motherhood and "separate spheres," domesticity was championed particularly by the elite and middle classes. See also *republican motherhood* and *separate spheres*. (p. 473)

**dower, dower right** A legal right originating in Europe and carried to the American colonies that provided a widow with the use of one-third of the family's land and goods during her lifetime. (p. 18)

**enclosure acts** Laws passed in sixteenth-century England that allowed landowners to fence in the open fields that surrounded many villages and use them for grazing sheep. These enclosures deprived peasants of land to cultivate and forced them to work as wage laborers or as wool spinners and weavers. (p. 37)

**encomiendas** Land grants in Spanish America given in the sixteenth century by the Spanish kings to privileged landholders (*encomenderos*). *Encomiendas* also gave the landholders legal control over native peoples who lived on or near their estates. (p. 31)

**established church** A church given privileged legal status by the government. Historically, established churches in Europe and America were supported by public taxes, and were often the only legally permitted religious institutions. (p. 258)

**ethnocultural politics** The practice of voting along ethnic, racial, and religious lines. Ethnocultural allegiances were a prominent feature of American political life in the mid-nineteenth and twentieth centuries. (p. 327)

**Exodusters** African Americans who left the Deep South in the late 1870s, in the wake of Reconstruction's collapse and the depression of 1873, and sought homesteads on the western frontier. The Exodusters sought better opportunities in states such as Kansas, but like many farmers, they confronted falling crop prices and a harsh Plains environment, which was difficult to farm. (p. 504)

**factory** A structure first built by manufacturers in the early nineteenth century to concentrate all aspects of production—and the machinery needed to increase output—in one location. (p. 274)

**Federalists** Supporters of the Constitution of 1787, which created a strong central government; their opponents, the Antifederalists, feared that a strong central government would corrupt the nation's newly won liberty. (p. 198)

**franchise** The right to vote. Between 1820 and 1860, most states revised their constitutions to extend the vote to all adult white males. In 1870, the Fifteenth Amendment gave the vote to black men; and in 1920, the Nineteenth Amendment extended the franchise to women. However, malapportionment of the state legislatures meant that some voters had more power than others did. (p. 304)

**freehold** Land owned in its entirety, without feudal dues or land-lord obligations. Freeholders have the legal right to improve, transfer, or sell their landed property. See *leasehold*. (p. 54)

**free market** A system of economic exchange in which prices of goods, labor, and capital are determined by supply and demand and no producer or consumer dominates the market. The term also refers to markets that are not subject to government regulation. (p. 195)

**free-soil movement** A political movement of the 1840s that opposed the expansion of slavery. Its members—mostly white yeomen farmers—believed that slavery benefited "aristocratic men." They wanted farm families to settle the western territories and install democratic republican values and institutions there. The short-lived Free-Soil Party (1848–1854) stood for "free soil, free labor, free men," which subsequently became the program of the Republican Party. (p. 408)

**gang-labor system** A system of work discipline used on southern cotton plantations in the mid-nineteenth century. White overseers or black drivers constantly supervised gangs of enslaved laborers to enforce work norms and achieve greater productivity. (p. 374)

**gentility** A refined style of living and elaborate manners that came to be highly prized among well-to-do English families after 1600. (p. 93)

**gentry** A class of wealthy English landholders who lacked the social privileges and titles of nobility. During the Price Revolution of the sixteenth century, the wealth and status of the gentry rose while that of the aristocracy fell. (p. 36)

**gold standard** Monetary system by which a country linked the amount of money circulating, at any given time, to the amount of gold held in its Treasury. Deliberate increases in the money supply, to encourage borrowing and stimulate economic activity, therefore depended not on federal policy decisions (as is the case today, through the Federal Reserve) but on increases in the national and global supply of gold. (p. 496)

**Great American Desert** The name given to the drought-stricken Great Plains by Euro-Americans in the early nineteenth century. Believing the region unfit for cultivation or agriculture, Congress designated the Great Plains as permanent Indian country in 1834. (p. 504)

**greenbacks** Paper money issued by the U.S. Treasury during the Civil War to finance the war effort. Greenbacks were legal tender in all public and private transactions. Because it was issued in large amounts and was not backed by gold or silver, the greenback dollar's value fell during the war from $1 to 40 cents. Unlike the Continental dollar issued during the Revolutionary War, which became virtually worthless, the greenback recovered its value as the Union government won the war and reduced its war-related debt. See *gold standard*. (p. 444)

**guild** An organization of skilled workers in medieval and early modern Europe that regulated the entry into, and the practice of, a trade. Guilds did not develop in colonial America because artisans generally were in short supply. (p. 21)

**habeas corpus** Latin for "you have the body," a legal writ forcing government authorities to justify their arrest and detention of an individual. Rooted in English common law, habeas corpus became a formal privilege in the U.S. Constitution (Article 1, Section 9), which also allows its suspension in cases of invasion or insurrection. During the Civil War, Lincoln suspended habeas corpus to stop protests against the draft and other anti-Union activities. The USA PATRIOT Act (2001) likewise suspended this privilege in cases of suspected terrorism. (p. 440)

**heresy** A religious doctrine inconsistent with the teachings of an established church. Some of the Crusades between 1096 and 1291 targeted groups of Christians whose beliefs the hierarchy of the Roman Catholic Church judged to be heretical. (p. 21)

**home rule** Self-government by a state within the federal system. After the Civil War, southern Democrats advocated for home rule by painting Reconstruction governments as illegitimate impositions. By 1876, northern Republicans, too, were inclined to accept this claim. (p. 487)

**homespun** Cloth spun and woven by American women and traditionally worn by poorer colonists. During the boycotts of British goods in the 1760s, wearing homespun clothes became a political act, and even wealthy Patriots began wearing them. Their work making homespun fabrics allowed women to contribute directly to the Patriot movement. (p. 152)

**ideology** A systematic philosophy or political theory that purports to explain the character of the social world or to prescribe a set of values or beliefs. (p. 21)

**impeachment** The first step in the constitutional process for removing the president from office, in which charges of wrongdoing (articles of impeachment) are voted on by the House of Representatives. If the articles pass in the House, the Senate then conducts a trial to determine whether the impeached president is guilty of the charges. (p. 468)

**indenture** A contract that required service for a specified period. In the seventeenth century, indentures brought thousands of workers to North America. In exchange for agreeing to work for four or five years without wages, the workers received passage across the Atlantic, room and board, and status as a free person at the end of the contract period. (p. 37)

**indulgence** A certificate granted by the Catholic Church that claimed to pardon a sinner from punishment in the afterlife. In his *Ninety-five Theses*, written in 1517, Martin Luther condemned the sale of indulgences, a common practice among Catholic clergy. (p. 32)

**Industrial Revolution** The great transformation in manufacturing goods that began in England about 1750 and spread eventually around the world. It consisted of three interrelated aspects: inanimate power (first from improved water wheels and then from steam engines), advances in machine technology, and disciplined labor working in factories. (p. 273)

**injunction** A court order that immediately requires or prohibits an activity, either temporarily or permanently. Especially between the 1830s and the 1930s, probusiness judges often issued injunctions to stop workers from picketing or striking. (p. 282)

**joint-stock corporation** A financial organization devised by English merchants around 1550 that facilitated the colonization of North America. In these companies, a number of investors pooled their capital and received shares of stock in the enterprise in proportion to their share of the total investment. (p. 58)

**King Cotton** A term used to describe the importance of raw cotton in the nineteenth-century economy. More specifically, the Confederate belief during the Civil War that their cotton was so important to the British and French economies that those governments would recognize the South as an independent nation and supply it with loans and arms. (p. 443)

**labor theory of value** The belief that human labor produces economic value. Adherents argued that the price of a product should be determined not by the market (supply and demand) but by the amount of work required to make it, and that most of the price should be paid to the person who produced it. The idea was advocated in the mid-nineteenth century by many farmers, independent craft workers, and trade unions. (p. 282)

**laissez-faire** French for "let do" or "leave alone." The principle that the less government does, the better, particularly in reference to the economy. This has been an influential philosophy in the United States. In the nineteenth century, Democrats tended to advocate laissez-faire against state-building Whigs and Republicans. In the twentieth century—especially from the New Deal onward—Republicans have become the main champions of laissez-faire. (p. 321)

**land bank** An institution, established by a colonial legislature, that printed paper money and lent it to farmers, taking a lien on their land to ensure repayment. (p. 99)

**leasehold, leaseholder** A piece of land rented out by means of a formal contract for a considerable period of time. The contract specified the obligations of the owner and the lessee. Some leaseholds ran for "three lives"—those of the lessee, his son or heir, and his grandson. See *freehold*. (p. 106)

**lien (crop lien)** A legal device enabling a creditor to take possession of the property of a borrower, including the right to have it sold in payment of the debt. During Reconstruction, furnishing merchants took such liens on cotton crops as collateral for supplies advanced to sharecroppers during the growing season. This system trapped farmers in a cycle of debt and made them vulnerable to exploitation by the furnishing merchant. (p. 476)

**machine tools** Cutting, boring, and drilling machines used to produce standardized metal parts that are then assembled into other machines such as textile looms and sewing machines. The rapid development of machine tools by American inventors in the early nineteenth century was a factor in speeding the spread of industrialization. (p. 279)

**Manifest Destiny** A term coined by columnist and editor John L. O'Sullivan in 1845 to describe the idea that Euro-Americans were fated by God to settle the entire North American continent. Manifest Destiny implied that the spread of American republican institutions and Protestant churches across the continent was part of God's plan for the world. In the late nineteenth century, the focus of the policy also included overseas expansion. (p. 398)

**manorial system** A quasi-feudal system of landholding. In the Hudson River Valley of New York, wealthy landlords leased farms to tenants, who paid rent and a quarter the value of all improvements (houses, barns, etc.) if they sold the lease; tenants also owed the landlord a number of days of personal service each year. (p. 74)

**manumission** From the Latin *manumittere*, "to release from the hand"; the legal act of relinquishing property rights in slaves, thereby allowing them their freedom. In 1782, the Virginia assembly passed an act allowing manumission, and within a decade, planters had freed 10,000 slaves. Worried that a large free black population would threaten the institution of slavery, the assembly repealed the law in 1792. (p. 252)

**Market Revolution** The dramatic increase between 1820 and 1850 in the exchange of goods and services in market transactions. The Market Revolution reflected the increased output of farms and factories, the entrepreneurial activities of traders and merchants, and the creation of a transportation network of roads, canals, and railroads. (p. 273)

**mass production** A system of factory production that often combines sophisticated machinery, a disciplined labor force, and assembly lines to turn out vast quantities of identical goods at low cost. In the nineteenth century, the textile and meatpacking industries pioneered mass production, which eventually became the standard mode for making consumer goods from cigarettes to automobiles, telephones, radios, televisions, and computers. (p. 274)

**matrilineal** Refers to a system of family organization in which social identity and property descend through the female line. Children are usually raised in their mother's household, and her brother (their uncle) plays a central role in their lives. (p. 15)

**mechanic** A nineteenth-century term used to refer to a skilled craftsman and inventor who built and improved machinery and machine tools for industry. Mechanics developed a professional identity and established institutes to spread their skills and knowledge. (p. 277)

**mercantilism** A system of political economy based on government regulation. Beginning in 1650, Britain enacted Navigation Acts that controlled colonial commerce and manufacturing for the enrichment of Britain. After 1790, the United States used tariffs and subsidies to bolster national wealth. Today, many Asian nations—such as Japan, China, and Korea—employ mercantilist policies for a similar purpose. (p. 36)

**mestizo** A person of mixed blood; specifically, the child of a European and a Native American. (p. 32)

**middle class**  In Europe, the class of traders and townspeople who were not part of either the aristocracy or the peasantry. The term was introduced in America in the early nineteenth century to describe both an economic group (of prosperous farmers, artisans, and traders) and a cultural outlook (of self-discipline, hard work, and social mobility). (p. 243)

**Middle Passage**  The brutal sea voyage from Africa to the Americas in the eighteenth and nineteenth centuries that took the lives of about 1.5 million enslaved Africans. (p. 84)

**Minutemen**  Colonial militiamen who stood ready to mobilize on short notice during the imperial crisis of the 1770s. These volunteers formed the core of the citizens' army that met British troops at Lexington and Concord in April 1775. (p. 163)

**national debt**  The financial obligations of the U.S. government for money borrowed from its citizens and foreign investors. Alexander Hamilton wanted wealthy Americans to invest in the national debt so that they would support the national government. In recent decades, similar thinking has led the United States to encourage individuals and institutions in crucial foreign nations—for example, Saudi Arabia, Japan, and China—to invest billions of dollars in the American national debt. (p. 206)

**nullification**  The constitutional argument that a state legislature or convention could void a law passed by Congress. The concept of nullification had its origins in the Kentucky and Virginia resolutions of 1798, which were drafted by Thomas Jefferson and James Madison, and was elaborated in John C. Calhoun's *South Carolina Exposition and Protest* (1828) and in the Ordinance of Nullification (1832). (p. 312)

**outwork**  A system of manufacturing, also known as *putting out*, used extensively in the English woolen industry in the sixteenth and seventeenth centuries. Merchants provided wool for landless peasants to spin and weave into cloth in their own homes; the merchants then sold the cloth in English and foreign markets. (p. 35)

**pagan**  A person whose spiritual beliefs center on the natural world. Pagans do not worship a supernatural God; instead, they pay homage to spirits and spiritual forces that they believe dwell in the natural world. (p. 19)

**patronage**  The power of elected officials to grant government jobs and favors to their supporters; also the jobs and favors themselves. Beginning around 1820, politicians systematically used—and abused—patronage to create and maintain strong party loyalties. After 1870, political reformers gradually introduced merit-based civil service systems in state and federal governments to reduce patronage. (p. 305)

**peasant**  The traditional term for a farmworker in Europe. Some peasants owned land, while others leased or rented small plots from landlords. In some regions, peasants lived in compact communities with strong collective institutions. (p. 17)

**peonage (debt peonage)**  Forced labor, under a pretext of debt. As cotton prices declined during the 1870s, and many sharecroppers fell into permanent debt, merchants often conspired with landowners to make this debt a pretext for the sharecropper's forced labor. (p. 477)

**personal-liberty laws**  Laws enacted in many northern states to protect free blacks and fugitive slaves from southern slave catchers. Early laws required a formal hearing before a local court. When the Supreme Court declared such provisions unconstitutional in *Prigg v. Pennsylvania* (1842), states enacted new laws prohibiting their officers from helping slave catchers. (p. 418)

**pocket veto**  A method by which the U.S. president can kill a piece of legislation without issuing a formal veto: The president "pockets" the bill by simply choosing not to sign it, and letting it expire after Congress adjourns. When congressional Republicans passed the Wade-Davis Bill in 1864, a harsher alternative to President Lincoln's restoration plan, Lincoln used a pocket veto to prevent the bill from being enacted. (p. 464)

**political machine**  Nineteenth-century term for highly organized groups operating within and intending to control political parties. Machines were regarded as antidemocratic by political reformers and were the target especially of Progressive-era leaders such as Robert La Follette. In municipal government, urban machines such as New York's Tammany Hall were often run by ethnic politicians; they won support from immigrant voters, who had few sources of aid in navigating the dangers of city life. Reformers instituted a merit-based civil service and primary elections to limit the power of political machines. (p. 305)

**poll tax**  A tax paid for the privilege of voting, used in the South beginning during Reconstruction to disenfranchise freed blacks. Nationally, the northern states used poll taxes to keep immigrants and others deemed unworthy from voting. (p. 469)

**polygamy**  The practice of marriage to multiple partners, most often, of one husband to multiple wives. Polygamy was customary among some Native American and African peoples; it was also practiced by many Mormons in the United States, particularly between 1840 and 1890. (p. 43)

**popular sovereignty**  The republican principle that ultimate power resides in the hands of the electorate. Popular sovereignty dictates that voters directly (or indirectly through their elected representatives) approve the constitutions and laws of the state and national governments. During the 1850s, the U.S. Congress used the principle of popular sovereignty in devising legislation giving the residents of a western territory the authority to allow or prohibit slavery there. (p. 167)

**praying towns**  Native American settlements in seventeenth-century New England supervised by a Puritan minister. Puritans used these settlements to encourage Indians to adopt Protestant Christianity and English culture. (p. 65)

**predestination**  The Protestant Christian belief that God chooses certain people for salvation before they are born. Sixteenth-century theologian John Calvin was the main proponent of this doctrine, which became a fundamental tenet of Puritan theology. (p. 33)

**Price Revolution**  The high rate of inflation in Europe in the mid-1500s and its consequences. American gold and silver, spent by Spain throughout Europe, doubled the money supply at a time when the population was also increasing. The abrupt rise in prices caused profound social changes—reducing the power of the aristocracy, leaving many peasant families on the brink of poverty, and encouraging substantial migration to America. (p. 36)

**primogeniture**  The practice of passing family land, by will or by custom, to the eldest son. Republic-minded Americans of the Revolutionary era felt this practice was unfair but did not prohibit it. However, most state legislatures eventually passed laws providing that if a father dies without a will, all his children must receive an equal portion of his estate. (p. 18)

**probate inventory**  An accounting of a person's property at the time of death, as recorded by court-appointed officials. Probate inventories list details of personal property, household items, and financial assets and debts, and tell historians a good deal about people's lives. (p. 96)

**proprietors**  Groups of settlers who received land grants from the General Courts of Massachusetts Bay and Connecticut, mostly between 1630 and 1720. The proprietors distributed the land among themselves, usually according to social status and family need. This system encouraged widespread ownership of land in New England. (p. 63)

**protective tariff**  An import duty designed to protect domestic products from cheaper foreign goods. A hot political issue throughout much of U.S. history, protective tariffs became particularly controversial in the 1830s and again between 1880 and 1914, when Whigs and Republicans (for protectionism) and Democrats (for free trade) centered their political campaigns on the issue. (p. 207)

**pueblos**  Multi-story and multi-room stone or mud-brick buildings built as residences by native peoples in the southwestern United States. (p. 12)

**Radical Whigs**  An eighteenth-century faction in the British Parliament that protested political corruption, the growing cost of the empire, and the influence on government of a wealthy class of financiers. (p. 97)

*reconquista*  The campaign by Spanish Catholics to drive North African Moors (Muslim Arabs) from the European mainland. After a centuries-long effort to recover their lands, the Spaniards defeated the Moors at Granada in 1492 and secured control of all of Spain. (p. 24)

**republic**  A state without a monarch or prince that is governed by representatives of the people. During the Renaissance, Italian moneyed elites ruled their city-states as republics. In 1776, Patriot leaders created republics with democratic features in the newly independent American states because they were suspicious of monarchical privilege, moneyed elites, and arbitrary executive power. (p. 21)

**republicanism**  A political ideology that repudiates hereditary rule by kings and princes and celebrates an elected, representative system of government and a virtuous, public-spirited citizenry. Historically, most republics limited active political participation to those with a significant amount of property. After 1800, the United States became a democratic republic with widespread participation by white adult men of all social classes; after 1920, women also became part of the electorate. (p. 183)

**republican motherhood**  The idea that the primary political role of American women was to instill a sense of patriotic duty and republican virtue in their children and mold them into exemplary republican citizens. (p. 246)

**revenue tariff**  A tax on imports levied to raise money for the government. See *protective tariff*. (p. 207)

**revival**  An outburst of religious enthusiasm, often prompted by the preaching of a charismatic Baptist or Methodist minister. The Great Awakening of the 1740s was significant, but it was the revival that swept across the United States between the 1790s and 1850s that imparted a deep religiosity to the culture. Subsequent revivals in the 1880s, 1890s, and late twentieth century helped maintain a strong evangelical Protestant culture in America. (p. 117)

**rotten boroughs**  Tiny electoral districts for Parliament whose voters were controlled by wealthy aristocrats or merchants who used the districts to gain entry to Parliament for themselves or their friends. In the 1760s, Radical Whig John Wilkes called for the elimination of rotten boroughs and greater representation for populous commercial and manufacturing areas. (p. 144)

**salutary neglect**  A term often used to describe British colonial policy during the reigns of George I (r. 1714–1727) and George II (r. 1727–1760). By relaxing their supervision of internal colonial affairs, royal bureaucrats inadvertently assisted the rise of self-government in North America. (p. 97)

**scalawags**  A pejorative term (in fact, an ancient Scots-Irish word for worthless animals) applied to southern whites who joined the Republicans during Reconstruction. Ex-Confederates used this term for ex-Whigs and yeomen farmers who had not supported the Confederacy and who believed that an alliance with the Republicans was the best way to attract northern capital and rebuild the South. (p. 480)

**secret ballot**  Before 1890, most Americans voted in public. That is, voters either announced their votes to a clerk or handed in ballots that had been printed by—and so were recognizable as the work of—a political party. Voting in private or in secret had first been used on a wide scale in Australia, and when the practice was adopted in the United States, it was known as the "Australian ballot." (p. 378)

**self-made man**  A nineteenth-century ideal; an ideology that celebrated men who rose to wealth or social prominence from humble origins through self-discipline, hard work, and temperate habits. (p. 292)

**sentimentalism**  A European cultural movement that emphasized emotions and a physical appreciation of God, nature, and people. Sentimentalism came to the United States in the late eighteenth century and was a factor in the shift to marriages based on love rather than on financial considerations. (p. 245)

**separate spheres** Term used by contemporaries and historians to describe the nineteenth-century view that men and women have different gender-defined characteristics and, consequently, that the sexes inhabit—and should inhabit—different social worlds. Men should dominate the public sphere of politics and economics, while women should manage the private sphere of home and family. In mid-nineteenth-century America, this cultural understanding was both sharply defined and hotly contested. (p. 354)

**severalty** Individual ownership of land. The Dawes Severalty Act of 1887 sought to end tribal ownership of land, and grant Indians deeds to individual property holdings; that is, severalty. Policymakers believed that individual landholdings, especially by male household heads, would contribute to Indian assimilation. (p. 516)

**sharecropping** The labor system by which freedmen agreed to exchange a portion of their harvested crops with the landowner for use of the land, a house, and tools. A compromise between freedmen and white landowners, this system developed in the cash-strapped South because the freedmen wanted to work their own land but lacked the money to buy it, while white landowners needed agricultural laborers but did not have money to pay wages. (p. 476)

**socialism** A theory of social and economic organization based on the common ownership or enjoyment of property and goods. Utopian socialists of the early nineteenth century envisioned small planned self-governing communities; later socialists campaigned for state ownership of railroads and large industries and an end to economic inequality. (p. 336)

**Sons of Liberty** Patriots—primarily middling merchants and artisans—who banded together to protest the Stamp Act and other imperial reforms of the 1760s. The group originated in Boston in 1765 but soon spread to all the colonies. (p. 148)

**spoils system** The widespread award of public jobs to political supporters after an electoral victory. In 1829, Andrew Jackson instituted the system on the national level, arguing that the rotation of officeholders was preferable to a permanent group of bureaucrats. The spoils system became a central, and corrupting, element in American political life. (p. 305)

**states' rights** An interpretation of the Constitution that exalts the sovereignty of the states and circumscribes the authority of the national government. Expressed first by Antifederalists in the debate over the Constitution, and then in the Virginia and Kentucky resolutions of 1798, the ideology of states' rights became especially important in the South. It informed white southerners' resistance to the high tariffs of the 1820s and 1830s, to legislation to limit the spread of slavery, and to attempts by the national government in the mid-twentieth century to end Jim Crow practices and, more generally, to extend its authority. (p. 211)

**suffrage** The right to vote. The classical republican ideology current in the United States before 1810 limited suffrage to men who held property and thus had "a stake in society." However, between 1810 and 1860, state constitutions extended the vote to virtually all adult white men and some free black men; subsequently, the Fifteenth (1870) and Nineteenth (1920) amendments to the U.S. Constitution granted the franchise respectively to black men and to women, making adult suffrage nearly universal. (p. 244)

**tariff** A tax on imports. *Tariffs for revenue* raise money to pay government expenses; *protective tariffs* also shield domestic products from foreign competition. See *revenue tariff* and *protective tariff*. (p. 207)

**temperance, temperance movement** A long-term reform movement that encouraged individuals and governments to limit the consumption of alcoholic beverages. Leading temperance groups include the American Temperance Society of the 1830s; the Washingtonian Association of the 1840s; the Women's Christian Temperance Union of the late nineteenth century; and Alcoholics Anonymous, which was founded in the 1930s. (p. 296)

**total war** A form of warfare, new to the nineteenth and twentieth centuries, that mobilized all of a society's resources—economic, political, and cultural—in support of the military effort. Governments fielded massive armies of conscripted civilians rather than small forces of professional soldiers, and attacked civilians and industries that supported the enemy's war efforts. Witness Sherman's march through Georgia in the Civil War; the massive Allied aerial bombing of Dresden and Hamburg and the U.S. air raids on Tokyo during World War II; and the bombing of North Vietnam during the Vietnam War. (p. 439)

**town meeting** A system of local government in New England in which all male heads of households meet regularly to elect selectmen; levy local taxes; and regulate markets, roads, and schools. (p. 63)

**transcendentalism** A nineteenth-century intellectual movement that posited the importance of an ideal world of mystical knowledge and harmony beyond the world of the senses. As articulated by Ralph Waldo Emerson and Henry David Thoreau, transcendentalism called for the critical examination of society and emphasized individuality, self-reliance, and nonconformity. (p. 332)

**trust** A legal entity, invented in the 1880s, which enabled a group of companies to combine and operate as a single unit. By doing so, they avoided competing with one another for customers, and were also able to raise market prices and gain near-monopoly power over a given market. To form a trust, each company agreed (sometimes under extreme pressure from a powerful competitor) to deposit stock with a central trustee and submit to the management of a central board of directors. In popular usage, *trust* came to mean any giant corporation that dominated a sector of the economy and wielded monopoly power. (p. 496)

**vice-admiralty court** A tribunal presided over by a judge, with no jury. The Sugar Act of 1764 required that offenders be tried in a vice-admiralty court rather than in a common-law tribunal, where a jury decided guilt or innocence. This provision of the act provoked protests from merchant-smugglers accustomed to acquittal by sympathetic colonial juries. (p. 146)

**virtual representation** A term coined by British politicians in the 1760s in arguing that the interests of the American colonists were adequately represented in Parliament by merchants trading with the colonies and by sugar planters living in England who owned estates in the West Indies. (p. 147)

**war of attrition** A military strategy of small-scale attacks used, usually by the weaker side, to sap the resources and morale of the stronger side. Examples include the attacks carried out by Patriot militias in the South during the War of Independence, and the guerrilla tactics of the Vietcong and North Vietnamese during the Vietnam War. (p. 181)

**Whigs, Whig party** An English political party that demanded a constitutional (rather than an absolutist) monarchy. The English Whigs rose to power following the Glorious Revolution of 1688 and governed Britain until the eve of the American Revolution. In 1834, an American political party headed by Henry Clay and Daniel Webster took the name *Whig* to protest the "monarchical" actions of Andrew Jackson, whom they called "King Andrew I." The American Whig party dissolved in the 1850s over the question of whether or not to extend slavery to the territories. See *Radical Whigs* and *conscience Whigs*. (pp. 77, 321)

**yeoman** In England between 1500 and 1800, a farmer who owned enough land to support his family in reasonable comfort. In America, Thomas Jefferson envisioned a nation of yeomen, that is, politically and financially independent farmers. (p. 36)

# Credits

## Chapter 1

Comparing American Voices: Friar Bernardino de Sahagún, *General History of New Spain*, trans., Arthur J. O. Anderson and Charles E. Dibble Copyright © 1975 Reprinted by permission of The University of Utah Press.

Voices from Abroad: John E. Worth, "Account of the Northern Conquest and Discovery of Hernando de Soto by Rodrigo Rangel" trans. by John E. Worth, in Lawrence A. Clayton et al. *The De Soto Chronicles: The Expedition of Hernando De Soto to North America in 1539–1543*, 2 vols. 1993 1:288–94. Copyright © 1993 Reprinted by permission of The University of Alabama Press.

## Chapter 2

Figure 2.2: From *The Chesapeake in the Seventeenth Century: Essays on Anglo-American Society* edited by Thad W. Tate and David L. Ammerman. Copyright © 1979 by the University of North Carolina Press. Used by permission of the publisher.

## Chapter 4

Comparing American Voices: Benjamin Franklin, "The Importance of a Virtuous Life" in *The Autobiography of Benjamin Franklin, with Related Documents,* Second Edition, ed. by Louis P. Masur (Boston, MA: Bedford/St. Martin's), pp. 73–74 and 93–94.

Voices from Abroad: From *Notebook of a Colonial Clergyman,* translated and edited by Theodore Tappert and John Doberstein. Copyright © 1958 Muhlenberg Press admin. Augsburg Fortress. Reproduced by permission.

## Chapter 6

Fig 6.1: Jackson T. Main, "Government by the People: The American Revolution and the Democratization of the Legislature." *William and Mary Quarterly*, ser. 3, Vol. 23. Copyright 1966 by Institute of Early American History and Culture. Reproduced with permission of Institute of Early American History and Culture.

## Chapter 7

Voices from Abroad: Reprinted from William Cobbett, *Peter Porcupine in America: Pamphlets on Republicanism and Revolution*, edited by David A. Wilson. Copyright © 1994 Cornell University. Used by permission of the publisher, Cornell University Press.

## Chapter 9

Voices from Abroad: Walter D. Kamphoefner, Wolfgang Helbich, and Ulrike Sommer, eds. *News from the Land of Freedom: German Immigrants Write Home*, trans. Susan Carter Vogel. 83–87. Copyright © 1991 Verlag C. H. Beck.

Figure 9.1: "Leading Branches of Manufacture" in Douglass North, *Growth and Welfare in the American Past*, Second Edition. Copyright © 1974. Reprinted with permission of the author.

Comparing American Voices: David B. Davis, excerpt from *Antebellum American Culture: An Interpretive Anthology,* pp. 395–98, 403–409. Pennsylvania State University Press. Copyright © 1987 David B. Davis. Reprinted by permission of the author.

## Chapter 11

Figure 11.2: Based on data from David M. Potter, *Division and Stresses of Reunion, 1845–1876*, Scott-Foresman History Series.

## Chapter 12

Comparing American Voices: Selections from "Mollie Dawson" from *Bullwhip Days: The Slaves Remember*, copyright © 1998 by James Mellon. Used by permission of Grove/Atlantic, Inc. Excerpt from *Plantation Life in the Florida Parishes of Louisiana 1836–1845 as Reflected in the Diary of Bennett H. Barrow.* Copyright © 1967 Columbia University Press. Reprinted with permission of the publisher.

Voices from Abroad: William Jeronimus, excerpts from *Travels by His Highness, Duke Bernhard of Saxe-Weimar-Eisenach, Through North America in the Years 1825 and 1826*, ed. by C. J. Jeronimus and translated by William Jeronimus. Copyright © 2001 University Press of America. Reprinted by permission.

Figure 12.1: From *Time on the Cross: The Economics of American Negro Slavery,* by Robert W. Fogel and Stanley L. Engerman. Copyright 1974 Little, Brown.

Figure 12.2: Based on data in Robert William Fogel and Stanley L. Engerman, *Time on the Cross: The Economics of American Negro Slavery* (Boston: Little, Brown, 1974), and Michael Tadman, *Speculators and Slaves: Masters, Traders, and Slaves in the Old South* (Madison: University of Wisconsin Press, 1996).

## Chapter 13

Comparing American Voices: Sean Wilentz, ed., *Major Problems in the Early Republic, 1787–1848* (Harcourt, Orlando: FL, 1991), and Victoria Bissell Brown and Timothy J. Shannon (eds.), *Going to the Source: The Bedford Reader in American History*, Second Edition (Boston: Bedford/St. Martin's), 2004.

## Chapter 14

Comparing American Voices: Minrose C. Gwin (ed.), *A Woman's Civil War* (Madison, WI: University of Wisconsin, 1992); and

Matthew Pace Andrews, *The Women of the South in War Times* (Baltimore: Norman Remington, 1924); and Rod Gragg, *The Illustrated Confederate Reader* (New York, NY: HarperCollins), 1989.

Voices from Abroad: Excerpts from Ernest Duvergier de Hauranne, "A Frenchman in Lincoln's America" translated by Ralph H. Bowen Copyright © 1974 R.R. Donnelly & Sons Company. Reprinted with permission.

## Chapter 15

Voices from Abroad: Allan Nevins (ed.) Excerpts from *America Through British Eyes*. Copyright © 1968 Peter Smith Publishers. Reprinted by permission.

## Chapter 16

Voices from Abroad: Excerpts from Oscar Handlin (ed.), *This Was America* (Cambridge, MA: Harvard University Press). Copyright © 1949 Reprinted by permission of the author.

## Additional Art Credits

"Voices from Abroad" images (left to right): *Yoichi Funabashi*: Claremont McKenna College. *Frances Trollope*: Miriam and Ira D. Wallach Division of Art, Prints and Photographs, The New York Public Library. Astor, Lenox and Foundations. *Ernestine Rose*: Schlesinger Library, Radcliffe Institute for Advanced Study, Harvard University. *José Martí*: The Granger Collection, New York.

"Comparing American Voices" images (left to right): *Thomas Paine*: Miriam and Ira D. Wallach Division of Art, Prints and Photographs, The New York Public Library. Astor, Lenox and Tilden Foundations. *Emma Hart Willard*: Miriam and Ira D. Wallach Division of Art, Prints and Photographs, The New York Public Library. Astor, Lenox and Tilden Foundations. *Franklin McCain*: © Corbis. All Rights Reserved. *Jesús Colón*: "Biographical Link from the Biographical Dictionary of Hispanic Literature in the United States"; Edited by Nicholas Kanellas; New York: Greenwood Press, 1989.

*Part 1 opener credits:* Page 2: Old State House, Boston: The Bostonian Society and Old State House Museum. Page 3: Dutch Farmstead painting: New-York State Historical Association; West Indies Sugar Mill: The Granger Collection.

Page 4: Sir William Berkeley: Bridgeman Art Library; Colonial village church procession: *J. Barber's History & Antiquities of N.E., N.Y. , N.J. & Pa.*/Picture Research Consultants & Archives; Colleges in Cambridge, MA, 1726: Massachusetts Historical Society.

*Part 2 opener credits:* Page 136: Pulling down the statue of George III: Library of Congress.

Page 137: Washington Addressing the Constitutional Convention: © Bettmann/Corbis; U.S. Bombardment of Tripoli, 1804: The Granger Collection.

Page 138: Bank of the United States, Philadelphia, 1800: Library Company of Philadelphia; York Pennsylvania Family, 1828: St. Louis Art Museum; *Benjamin Hawkins and the Creek Indians*: Greenville County Museum of Art.

*Part 3 opener credits:* Page 268: "Tippecanoe and Tyler Too" parade: Franklin D. Roosevelt Library.

Page 269: *Francis Cabot Lowell's mill in Waltham*: Courtesy Gore Place Society, Waltham, MA; *Auction in Chatham Street* by E. Didier: Museum of the City of New York.

Page 270: George Caleb Bingham, *Stump Speaking* (detail): Private Collection/The Bridgeman Art Library Ltd.; Camp Meeting at Eastham, MA, 1851: Library of Congress; "Am I Not a Woman and a Sister?": The Granger Collection, New York.

*Part 4 opener credits:* Page 392: Military expedition into the Black Hills: National Archives.

Page 393: Captured Sioux Indians in fenced enclosure on Minnesota River: Minnesota Historical Society; *Bombing of Fort Sumter* by Currier & Ives: Anne S. K. Brown Military Collection, Brown University Library.

Page 394: Freedmen Voting, 1871: The Granger Collection, New York; "Lightning Express, Flying Mail": Library of Congress. 1855 anti-immigrant cartoon: The Granger Collection, New York.

# Index

# About the Authors

**JAMES A. HENRETTA** is a professor emeritus at the University of Maryland, College Park. His publications include *"Salutary Neglect": Colonial Administration under the Duke of Newcastle* (1972); *The Evolution of American Society, 1700–1815: An Interdisciplinary Analysis* (1973); *Evolution and Revolution: American Society, 1600–1820* (1987); *The Origins of American Capitalism* (1991); and an edited volume, *Republicanism and Liberalism in America and the German States, 1750–1850* (2002). His most recent publication is a long article, "Charles Evans Hughes and the Strange Death of Liberal America" (*Law and History Review*, 2006), derived from his ongoing research on the liberal state in America: New York, 1820–1975.

**REBECCA EDWARDS** is a professor of history at Vassar College. Her research interests focus on the post–Civil War era and include electoral politics, environmental history, and the history of women and gender roles. She is the author of *Angels in the Machinery: Gender in American Party Politics from the Civil War to the Progressive Era* (1997) and *New Spirits: Americans in the "Gilded Age," 1865–1905* (second edition; 2010). She is currently working on a biography of women's rights advocate and People's Party orator Mary E. Lease.

**ROBERT O. SELF** is an associate professor of history at Brown University. His research focuses on urban history, the history of race and American political culture, post–1945 U.S. society and culture, and gender and sexuality in American politics. His first book, *American Babylon: Race and the Struggle for Postwar Oakland* (2003), won four professional prizes, including the James A. Rawley Prize from the Organization of American Historians (OAH). He is currently at work on a book about gender, sexuality, and political culture in the United States from 1964 to 2004.